Barclays Premier

Following the Fairways

THE 8TH HOLE AT DRUIDS GLEN GOLF CLUB Photograph courtesy of: **Druids Glen**

Editors: Nick Edmund, George Oldham

KENSINGTON WEST PRODUCTIONS

HEXHAM ENGLAND

www.golfcourseguide.com

Acknowledgements

Kensington West Productions Ltd
5 Cattle Market, Hexham,
Northumberland, NE46 1NJ
Tel (01434) 609933, Fax (01434) 600066/600422
e mail: info@kensingtonwest.co.uk
web site: www.kensingtonwest.co.uk

Championship Golf Editor
Nick Edmund

Contributing Editor
George Oldham

Assistant Editors
Mark Scandle, Kate McHugh

Production & Design
Diane Ridley

Cartography
Maps in Minutes

Origination
Pre-Press Limited Hong Kong

Printing
Liang Yu Printing Factory Limited,
Hong Kong

Front Cover
17th Hole, St. Andrews Old Course,
Courtesy of Baxter Prints

THE K CLUB *Photograph courtesy of:* **The K Club**

There have been all manner of hands that have guided the production of this, our updated, revised and expanded thirteenth edition of Following the Fairways.

The company acknowledges the kind and generous advice of many golf professionals, secretaries and enthusiasts from all parts of Great Britain and Ireland. It is only by constant updating that a guide of this type maintains its value.

In our endeavour to re-style the book, we have been kindly assisted by a number of tourist boards, golf courses and others. Although we have introduced photography into the book for the first time we are still pleased to include a section of fine art at the back of Following the Fairways. The colour work is all credited and we are most grateful to all our featured artists for giving us permission to use their work. We are especially grateful to Graeme Baxter, a renowned contemporary artist of the ancient game, for allowing us to use some of his work as illustrations most notably the front cover.

We greatly appreciate the assistance of the many people who helped us in selecting hotels, restaurants and pubs around the country, particularly those golf secretaries who so kindly gave so much time marking our card. We are confident that you will relish savouring some of our suggestions, but do please let us know if you come across a 19th hole that you can recommend. We are also grateful to the hoteliers who have helped us produce feature pages for the book.

I would like to thank Gary Player for penning our foreword. He is without question one of the greatest sportsmen, let alone golfers of all time and we are truly honoured. In recent years we have been privileged to have Arnold Palmer and Jack Nicklaus also pen forewords. When the great triumvirate stepped out together at Augusta earlier this year it sent a shiver down the spine - we are truly grateful for their kind assistance and wish them all well on and off the fairways.

I am also extremely grateful to Barclays Bank. By coincidence my company and I have both been customers of the bank for 15 years and we have made many friends along the way, none more so than our current manager Andrew Davidson - a great guy and a fine golfer (so he tells me)! I would also like to thank Jamie Cunningham and Ben Keogh of Professional Sports Partnerships for their advice and contributions.

Finally, I would like to thank Nick Edmund, author of the golf editorial, and George Oldham for their tremendous efforts in providing copy and I thank all those companies who have helped with the production for their accomplished work.

Julian West

Golf has been much of my life. It has taken me round the world and after many miles of travel the game has in return been generous to me.

I turned professional in 1953, joined the PGA Tour in 1957 and almost three decades later joined the Seniors Tour. In that time I have won 163 Championships including 9 majors.

But the game is not just about winning and money, it's about people and places and in the 12 million miles I've travelled (apparently more than any other sportsman in history) I've met many great people and enjoyed some wonderful golf courses.

I also enjoy designing them with over 100 courses throughout the world - golf as I say has been much of my life. Over the years, many of the world's golf courses have changed, some remain familiar but the world moves on apace.

So no matter what your form or fitness, no matter which golf course upon which you happen to play, I wish you well in the dawn of the new millennium on and off the fairways.

Gary Player

Gary Player's Major Championships and the Grand Slam.
Masters (1961, 1974, 1978), British Open (1959, 1968, 1974), PGA Championship (1962, 1972), US Open (1965).

Introduction

You are at Portsalon in a remote, hidden corner of County Donegal. The rather bulky golfing guide had promised that the journey was worth making. You walk slightly nervously, however, towards the 1st tee: the book had warned you not to hook your opening drive into Lough Swilley, and that water threatened again at the par three 2nd and this was followed by a vertigo-inducing tee shot and tough approach to the 3rd. But, yes, it had also told you that the accompanying views were overwhelming. To your left—between the golf course and the sea—is (officially) 'the second most beautiful beach in the world'. On your right side, and semi-circling round in front of you, are the Knockinalla Mountains which tumble into heather-clad foothills. It is such a stunning backdrop, how can you possibly concentrate? Moments later, 'Crack!' Straight down the middle. You are on your way—thankfully, following the fairways.

First published in 1986, Following the Fairways seeks to guide the golfer (and perhaps his or her non-golfing partner) on a leisurely journey around the golf courses of Great Britain and Ireland, suggesting some of the best 18 holes—links, parkland, clifftop and heathland, and recommending superior 19th holes—places to eat, drink and sleep along the way.

Following the Fairways can properly be described as a 'Where to play— where to stay' golf guide. Our intention over the years has been to try to establish it as the most informative, entertaining and authoritative book of its kind. We have also tried to make it different from all the others and if we have achieved this goal at the expense of it fitting into your glove compartment then we make no apologies! The book's content has changed considerably in the past decade but with so much happening on and off the fairways it has needed to. Moreover, the first edition was a purely British affair whereas something like a quarter of the book is now devoted to a celebration of golf in the Emerald Isle.

Apart from extending the book's scope to include golf in Ireland, the biggest impact on its content has been the 'golf course boom' of the late 1980's and early 1990's. Several of the 'Championship Courses' highlighted in this book (see below) were not in existence in 1986. We believe it is precisely because it explores the best of these new developments that Following the Fairways can claim to be the most up to date golf course guide.

So how does the book work? Beyond the introductory pages which include our 'British Golf Venue of the Year' and 'International Golf Venue of the Year' awards, the journey begins in Cornwall and ends in the West of Ireland. For easy reference the book is divided into 30 chapters or 'golfing areas', each with its own map. Each golf course within the area is included within a detailed directory section which we term 'Complete Golf'. For each club we list the telephone number, address and course yardages, together with approximate green fees and visitor policy. Some 2500 golf clubs are listed. Over 750 of the golf courses, as well as

perhaps three times as many nearby hotels, inns and restaurants are recommended in the golf area text, or 'Choice Golf'.

Many of the leading golf courses in Great Britain and Ireland are given special editorial attention. These featured courses comprise the aforementioned 'Championship Golf' and more than 130 such courses are now included. Among their number are all the famous courses of Great Britain and Ireland, including every one of the Open Championship venues plus the likes of Walton Heath, Gleneagles, Ballybunion, Sunningdale and Royal Dornoch. All details relating to these entries are carefully revised with each edition.

In addition to the 'greats', many lesser known but beautifully situated courses are also featured in Championship Golf—places

OLD HEAD GOLF LINKS *Photograph courtesy of:* **Old Head Golf Links**

we believe no holidaying golfer would want to miss, for instance: Machrihanish on the Mull of Kintyre, Connemara in Co Galway, St Enodoc in Cornwall, Castletown on the Isle of Man, Bamburgh Castle in Northumberland, Nefyn in North Wales, Rosapenna and Portsalon in Co Donegal and Tenby in South Wales. The 'new' courses are also well represented by the likes of Slaley Hall, Loch Lomond, Druids Glen, Old Head, Kingsbarns, Linden Hall, Skibo Castle, Celtic Manor, Carden Park, Powerscourt and The Warwickshire. Overall, we think it is a well balanced collection of the old and new, inland and seaside courses.

Before reading on, as editor I would like to thank everyone in Britain and Ireland who has assisted me over the years in my endeavours to produce the golf editorial. Special thanks are owing to George Oldham for his editorial assistance and, of course, to my wife, Teresa and our little sons George and Max for continuing to put up with my golfing wanderlust. Finally, I would like to thank Barclays for generously sponsoring this Millennium edition, Gary Player for providing the foreword, and wish you, the reader, good weather, good company and good fortune as you follow the fairways of Great Britain and Ireland.

Nick Edmund

Editor

*REDLIBBETS Photograph courtesy of: **Redlibbets Golf Club***

therefore his courses demonstrate an eclectic range of styles and influence. At Redlibbets near Sevenoaks for example, he has used the undulating parkland and oak wood setting to create a classic 20's 'Golden Age' traditional course, whilst at Willow Valley, high on the Yorkshire moors at Brighouse just off the M62, he has designed an extravagant American style course with breathtaking lakeside holes and large undulating greens which are as fine as any in the UK. Somewhere between the two (in fact two courses in one) is Wokefield Park near Reading. On the front nine, which enjoys a mature parkland setting of historic trees and limpid lakes, he has inserted a classic understated layout, whilst the back nine is more open ground, equally impressive but with lovely links-style holes threaded between acres of magnificent seed head grass.

Situated in a mature parkland setting (this time an historic deer park) and also by a relatively young architect, Simon Gidman, is the splendid Studley Wood course near Oxford. Here the mature trees and five new lakes provide challenging golf of the heroism or safety variety, all in a lovely landscape overlooked by a fine pavilion clubhouse.

Following in Nick Edmund's distinguished footsteps through 'Following the Fairways' I have been particularly impressed by four significant features. The first is the depth of the research which has characterised previous editions of 'Following the Fairways'. In de-constructing the 12th edition in order to put it together again in an up-dated form, I have marvelled, time and time again, at Nick's breadth of coverage and the quality of his writing about many of our much loved traditional courses. The second outstanding feature has been just how many new courses have come into play since last year's edition; over 100. The third is the user friendliness of the clubs towards the visiting golfer. Such a welcome is perhaps to be expected from the newer clubs who are in competition for visitor green fees and have to set out their stall accordingly. Less expected, but welcome nevertheless, is the increasing awareness among many private clubs that if they want a slice of this income they will have to become more customer orientated. Fourthly and lastly is the high quality of so many of the new courses which have immediately made the 'Choice Golf' section and which might next year, with increasing maturity, even reach 'Championship' status.

Staying with classic parkland venues, I can strongly recommend Donald Steele's Harleyford. Steele is perhaps the doyen of our senior golf architects, designer of literally dozens of classic courses such as Skibo and here at Harleyford his sensitive and restrained approach ideally suits this historic Thames-side setting.

Not all the architects of the courses new to 'Following the Fairways' are equally famous. Adrian Stiff, for example, is not particularly well known outside the South West where he has built a number of fine courses, including Dainton Park and Oake Manor. But if the Kendleshire is anything to go by this is not a situation which will last for very long. This splendid new course, just five minutes off the M4 near Bristol, with water on ten of the holes, is a delight and, as might be expected from a designer who was formerly a greenkeeper, beautifully maintained.

Part of my brief for this introduction was to highlight those new courses which have made the 'Choice Golf' section for the first time and which I have particularly enjoyed. Putting aside perhaps the finest of all, the Dukes Course at St Andrews (our featured British Venue of the Year), there is still an extraordinary long list; a fitting tribute to a number of very fine golf course architects involved in designing new courses and refurbishing some historic venues.

Starting with one of the youngest stars in the design firmament, mention must be made of three courses by Jonathan Gaunt. Jonathan's design philosophy is strictly of the 'observe the genius of the place' variety, and

*THE KENDLESHIRE Photograph courtesy of: **The Kendleshire and Phil Inglis***

THE OLD COURSE, ST ANDREWS Photograph courtesy of: **Scottish Tourist Board**

were content to rest on their historic laurels. The former has been transformed by the veteran architect Hamilton Strutt into a 27 hole clover leaf, each of the three loops having its own distinctive character. For a cliff-top location there is an unusual amount of water, including a lake with an island green in front of the impressive clubhouse, whilst the views across the Solent to the Needles are breathtaking.

Equally impressive are the sea views from the course at Falmouth where the distinguishing feature of the refurbishment policy has been not so much to modernise the design as to tighten it up and recapture the spirit of golf as it used to be played. The designer and owner of Falmouth, Bryan Patterson, well known as a distinguished golf coach, has strong views about traditional golfing virtues and it shows both on the course and in the comfortably refurbished clubhouse. Standing on the cliff top at Falmouth Golf Club with the sounds of the waves breaking far below and the songbirds above, the sun on one's face on a hot summer's day, gently cooled by a light breeze off the sea, it is hard to imagine a better spot to be, but every follower of the fairways has one of his or her favourites, their own best memories and a shared ambition to find that ultimate golf course.

Even less well known (new to me at least) is Frank Frayne who at Trethorne just outside Launceston has created a most picturesque course cleverly moulded through the hills and valleys of the Cornish landscape. Holiday golf does not get much better (or cheaper) than this.

There are so many more courses worthy of inclusion in this introduction, but space is limited to simply giving the reader a taste of what is to come in the Choice Golf section. However whilst we are in holiday mood, I would like to conclude with two South West cliff-top seaside courses to illustrate another feature of the current golf scene - the large number of well established courses (and clubhouses) which are being extensively refurbished to bring them up to the standards expected by today's more discerning customer. Both of our examples, Barton on Sea and Falmouth, recently celebrated their centenaries but neither

And this, of course, is what 'Following the Fairways' is all about; an invaluable guide to searching out the perfect place to play and also to stay. With over 2600 golf clubs listed, (and almost as many hotels and pubs), nearly 800 considered in greater detail in 'Choice Golf' sections and over 130 extensively described under 'Championship Golf' headings, we believe this to be as comprehensive a guide as you will find. Twelve previous editions have honed our artwork and layout which we believe to be incomparable, and in the latest edition we have also improved the indexing, the maps and cross referencing to make this the premier publication in it's field and the first point of reference for those readers who, like our editorial team, can think of no other pastime to compare with 'Following the Fairways'.

George Oldham

THE NINTH HOLE AT SANDMARTINS GOLF CLUB Photograph courtesy of: **Sandmartins**

Contents - Championship Golf

Contents

15th HOLE AT TEIGN VALLEY GOLF CLUB Photograph courtesy of: **Teign Valley**

STAPLEFORD PARK GOLF CLUB Photograph courtesy of: **Stapleford Park**

Contents

ST ANDREWS GOLF CLUB *Photograph courtesy of:* **Scottish Tourist Board**

Contents

FOTA ISLAND GOLF CLUB
Photograph courtesy of: Irish Tourist Board (Brian Lynch)

WATERFORD CASTLE GOLF CLUB *Photograph courtesy of: Waterford Castle*

Barclays Premier

Golf is a sport in which it is often necessary to enlist the skill and guidance of a professional if you wish to improve your standard and results. The guidance your Golfing Pro imparts starts from the premise that no two people's individual coaching needs are ever precisely the same.

It's much the same with Barclays Premier, a company which sets out to demonstrate true professionalism in everything we do. The exclusive financial planning service which our own professionals offer to busy and successful people is similarly designed to cater for each client's personal circumstances and priorities. Our experts' guidance is as individual as the growing numbers of highly demanding clients we serve.

As the working week grows longer and more exacting, spare time becomes more precious and the prospect of retirement ever more appealing. Our clients recognise that and, like millions of others, many look to golf as the panacea for their leisure hours.

To you - and to them - may I recommend this unique publication as the perfect companion to another year of enjoyment as you pursue your passion, Following the Fairways across the UK and Ireland.

John Church
Managing Director
Barclays Premier

SAUNTON FROM BEHIND THE SIXTEENTH GREEN *Photograph courtesy of:* **Saunton Golf Club**

Barclays Premier

Busy, successful professionals agree. As each year passes, the working week seems to get increasingly frenetic and more demanding. Spare time is even more precious because of it. And when retirement arrives, it's even sweeter. One way or another, managing one's own personal finances often gets put on the back burner.

For many of these people relishing retirement or juggling busy careers, Barclays Premier is already the solution. It's the bespoke service offered to selected customers who are looking for help and expert advice to ensure their funds work most effectively for them.

Distinctively, it's a service which works at their convenience. A service which has the reassuring support of one of the best-known and longest-established of Britain's high street banks.

Barclays Premier rewrites the definition of 'personal service'. It can best be described as a 'professional partnership'.

Dedicated Premier Account Managers are appointed to deal on a one-to-one basis with clients who appreciate the highest available standards of service, competence and professionalism and are prepared to pay a small annual fee to secure them.

Together with a supporting team of Account Executives, these Managers are responsible for just a small portfolio of clients. This means they can devote more time and attention to each individual and are able to establish a long-term relationship with every one.

The close relationship between the Premier Account Manager and the client is at the heart of this exclusive service.

Barclays Premier Managing Director, John Church, explains: "Our managers are encouraged to cultivate a close, enduring partnership with their clients, based on mutual trust and understanding. Continuity is an essential component. From the first, they develop a detailed knowledge of the client's financial needs, priorities and objectives - and of their business, domestic and financial circumstances."

Their select client portfolio gives each Premier Account Manager a high degree of flexibility when it comes to fixing the time and place of meetings. "They can almost always fit in with a client's schedule and arrange a meeting at their office, home or any other venue that the client nominates, either during or outside of office hours. It's that flexibility that appeals to the busy professionals with whom we deal."

One of the advantages first noticed by all new Premier clients is the ability to pick up the phone and speak direct to the Premier Account team on a dedicated line. If the Account Manager is out of the office when the call comes in, the support team is there to deal with the client's enquiry or request quickly and efficiently.

For Charlie Simpson, a re-insurance broker with Jardine Lloyd Thompson Group plc in the City, that is the single most important benefit. "If I have any problems I know they will be sorted fast just by picking up the phone and calling these guys. Financial advice is available when I ask for it. For instance, recently they set me up with the Barclayshare service so that I can deal through Barclays Stockbrokers."

There is, he says, a real comfort and convenience factor in the partnership. "Over the past three years I have got to know Nick Walden, my Premier Account Manager, and his team extremely well and they know me and my financial portfolio inside out. Nothing is ever too much trouble. They come to meetings when and where I want, which is important because my time is money. I trust them implicitly - it is very much a personal relationship that I value, and that I am prepared to pay for."

MOUNT JULIET *Photograph courtesy of:* **Mount Juliet Golf Club**

The Premier philosophy delivers very real benefits for clients. All recommendations, decisions and future action are tailored to the imperatives of the client's individual financial situation.

"It's all about sharing a common goal and working together to make the management of every single aspect of the client's financial affairs more efficient and more convenient," continues John Church. That could be arranging a mortgage, an introduction to stockbrokers, pension planning or asset management.

And as the name indicates, Premier offers a number of preferential benefits. It's clients are always among the first to hear about new Barclays services and products, some of which have features available exclusively to Premier.

Barclays Premier

When specialist advice and action is needed, Barclays Premier clients are offered a fast track to the relevant expertise and specialist funding within the Barclays global network. There's also exclusive access to the diverse range of Barclays financial products and services - pensions and savings, mortgages and loans, travellers cheques. Where a Premier client has specific investment needs, introductions are made to relevant specialists in Barclays Stockbrokers, Barclays Funds and Barclays Private Banking.

The service is characterised by a refreshing absence of bureaucracy and the direct contact and fast decision-making and solutions that follow from it.

As clients like Dr. David Sattelle discover, the personal contact, fast action and even faster decision-making offered by Barclays Premier gives a very useful edge when they need to move quickly.

A leading scientific researcher and consultant at Cambridge, David Sattelle secured a new role early in 2000 which meant a family move to Oxford. He and his wife had been Barclays Premier clients for several years: "So I already knew that at any time I could ring up and get ideas and guidance or that they would facilitate what I needed - and that this all happens at the drop of a hat."

So it proved with the house move. "Without the support of Chris Hoffman, our Barclays Premier Account Manager, we would have lost the house we are now living in," he says. "We were selling an older property and now looked for the equivalent in this more expensive area. We couldn't find it readily and when we did, the property had always gone in 24 hours. Because of the differential, we were forced to move up-market and needed a lot of help and actioning from Barclays Premier to arrange a larger mortgage and house insurance at very short notice."

It was even more complex. "Our own ideas on what would be appropriate changed once we got into the buying market. I had bigger responsibilities making even more demands on my time. My wife had started her own business in Cambridge just before I made my move, so needed a second start-up in Oxford while still managing the Cambridge operation. That meant extra funding, plus a reliable car to travel between the two cities. Basically, a lot of things came together at one time and we needed a financial manager who would understand our short term needs in the context of the bigger picture, in a way that freed us financially to make the most of our new challenges.

"Originally, we left another bank because we felt we were just getting computer banking and had lost any personal link with the bank manager or staff. Our personal circumstances weren't part of the equation. Now, with Barclays Premier, we get what was missing before. It is an excellent relationship."

Barclays Premier imposes no limits on the demands clients can make on their Account Manager. "When you have established such a close personal relationship over several years, you really want the best for your client and think nothing of making and receiving calls to them at all hours, when it's necessary," confirms Chris Hoffman, Dr. Sattelle's Premier Account Manager.

And looking to the future Managing Director, John Church, comments: "Throughout the year 2000 and beyond we plan to develop and improve our service still further to satisfy the fast expanding, increasingly sophisticated and ever more demanding affluent market in the UK. It promises to be an exciting time for Barclays Premier and all our clients."

For more information about Barclays Premier please telephone 0171 699 2288 or visit our web site www.premier.barclays.co.uk

OLD THORNS *Photograph courtesy of:* **Old Thorns Golf Club**

If golf writers have a fault, it's that they cannot resist compiling lists, you know the kind of thing; "The ten best par 3's in the U.K", "The ten most scenic holes in Europe", "The World's top ten courses"; we do it ourselves (see page 18). A regular feature in American golf magazines is The World's best Golf Resorts". Which is hardly surprising as the Americans practically invented the concept, and at Pinehurst, with its eight courses, they have the Grandaddy of them all and arguably the resort Mecca of the Universe.

Until now, that is; for with the development of its own Duke's Course, the Old Course Hotel at St Andrews must be a challenger, if not outright winner, of this particular Victor Ludorum. Consider the evidence: situated at the home of golf and enjoying the most evocative view in the game, the prospect over the Road Hole to the clubhouse of

the R&A and the backdrop of the historic town, the Old Course Hotel just has to have the world's best golf location. However a drawback has been that the hotel has had no special privileges to guarantee a round on the Old Course. It was this restriction which prompted its owners to create the new Duke's Course.

In addressing this, another problem facing the Old Course Hotel was that St Andrews had simply run out of suitable links land. However, this, it transpired, was a blessing in disguise, for just a couple of miles out of the town on elevated ground was a location that was simply made for golf–the former Craigtown Hospital site, which with 300 acres of surrounding woodland and farmland, provided an option to the seaside links golf, which it must be acknowledged is not every golfers preferred option, no matter how historic the venue. Bobby Jones might have famously said, "if I had to select one course on which to play the match of my life I should have selected the Old Course", but the contrary opinion of his counterpart Sam Snead, who won his solitary Open here in 1946, was that "down home we would plant cow beets on land like that". However, even "Slamming Sam" would have no trouble enjoying the Duke's Course which combines the best of traditional golf with modern agronomy techniques to provide perfect conditions for a great test of golf in a spectacular setting.

The key to the success of the Duke's Course probably lies in the appointment of Peter Thomson as its architect. Five times an Open winner, and well known for his espousal of traditional values, Thomson is schooled in the design philosophy of Alister Mackenzie who believed that every hole should be "enjoyable, tempting, free from irritation and torment and the humbug of lost balls". That Thomson should revere Mackenzie is hardly surprising, given that he grew up playing one of the architect's greatest courses, Royal Melbourne. That he should have produced a courses of such constant delight owes more to his keen intelligence and his deep knowledge of the game and its traditions.

A full description of the course is to be found on page 221, but the essence of the Duke's Course lies in the way in which Thomson has fashioned the ground to give a 'links' feel to what was previously forest and farmland. This is not a 'target golf' course, but one for strategic management of each hole and just as often bumping and running the ball through subtle swales around the greens, rather than playing a wedge. Pot bunkers abound to catch the less wary, but the course is fair, and the wide fairways make driving a pleasure. Mackenzies's edict on the "humbug of lost balls" has been thoroughly observed, but accurate positioning is *de regeur* if a good score is to be made.

Given its unique location, its five star excellence and now its fine new course, it is difficult to imagine a better U.K venue to celebrate the Millennium Open. The luxurious standards of this golf resort which would greet Sam Snead today are a world away from the austerity he found in post-war Britain. Asked then whether he had enjoyed St Andrews he observed; "Whenever you leave the U.S.A boy, you're just camping out". A latter day Churchill looking at this impressive resort hotel some fifty years on might be tempted to reply: "Some camping!"

Add the pleasure of walking through an undulating landscape of fine sward, sand and lakes all against a backdrop of brilliant yellow gorse, larch, birch and Scots pine and with stunning views across the town and St Andrews bay and you have a recipe for a near perfect golf venue. The clubhouse too plays its part in this; a well proportioned pavilion set high on the ridge, it enjoys memorable views to the Old Course and the hotel, from the well appointed bar and restaurant. The round over, a relaxed drink (or two) at the club and it only remains for the hotel guest to await the courtesy bus to the hotel and perhaps a swim and a sauna in the spa before enjoying an evening meal at the Road Hole Grill, the Old Course Hotel's award winning penthouse restaurant, with its incomparable panoramic views over the most hallowed turf in golf.

In the opening paragraph of our Introduction to 'Following the Fairways' we imagine a golfer wandering towards the 1st tee at Portsalon Golf Club in the remote north west corner of Donegal. Our 'bulky guide book' has sent him there to seek out one of the true hidden gems of Ireland, a classic old fashioned links course that is framed by hills and mountains and fringed by the Atlantic Ocean.

Now for something (and somewhere) completely different.

The purpose of our 'International Golf Venue of the Year' award is to highlight an outstanding must play – must stay golfing destination

– one that is situated overseas but is reasonably accessible from the UK. Of course, the golf at this location has to be first rate, but there must also be high quality on-site accommodation together with other compelling and preferably unique reasons for making more than a fleeting visit.

Since this is the year 2000 we think it important that our annual award is bestowed on somewhere very special, and we are confident that Les Bordes in northern France is precisely that.

At first it may seem a surprising choice. Many French golf courses are more widely known than Les Bordes, and yet it is located less than a 90 minute drive from Paris (via the A10 autoroute) and it has now been on the French golfing map for more than a dozen years. It may also seem a strange selection in that there is precious little to do at Les Bordes itself other than eat, sleep, drink and play golf. (Not that this will deter too many people!)

But there are reasons for Les Bordes' limited reputation; moreover, anyone who has a grasp of French geography, and who enjoys good architecture on and off the fairways, will better understand our rationale when they discover that Les Bordes nestles on the edge of the Loire Valley – close to several of France's greatest chateaux. Within striking distance of Les Bordes are the magnificent buildings at Chambord, Chenonceau, Amboise, Blois, Azay-le-Rideau and Cheverny. The club's precise location is 30 kilometres (18 miles) south west of Orleans at Saint-Laurent-Nouan.

Les Bordes' modest profile is a product of its history rather than its geography or its perceived quality. In the beginning – the course opened for play in 1987 – Les Bordes was essentially a golfing

playground for its two creators, Baron Marcel Bich – the inventor of Bic pens who owned the land – and Japanese entrepreneur Yoshiaki Sakurai and their friends. Although Les Bordes wasn't completely private, it was regarded as something of a secret retreat. Nowadays, whilst the aura of exclusivity has gone (the Baron died in 1994), Les Bordes retains its sanctuary-like ambience.

The sense of isolation begins the instant you turn into the estate, for the entrance drive journeys through a medieval forest. It is ancient hunting country, "a land of misty lakes and mature oaks that shut out the modern world", as Business Traveller magazine aptly described it. Aside from golfers, the domain's only residents are deer, wild boar and an array of birdlife: tranquillity reigns.

It was deep in this forest, then, that Baron Bich and his Japanese business partner determined to build their golf course. It was unlikely golfing terrain – not merely because the woodland was so dense, but because it is also very marshy in nature. It was a real challenge to build a championship standard golf course, never mind one that its discerning founders requested should be 'world class'. Fortunately, in Texan architect Robert van Hagge and his director of construction Jim Shirley, they found a team who were up to the task.

So is Les Bordes 'world class'? In a word, yes. It is probably the finest golf course in France. Indeed, according to the Peugeot European Golf Guide, Les Bordes ranks number two in Europe after Valderrama. An authoritative American publication, GOLF TRAVEL's Guide to the World's Greatest Golf Destinations, begins its review of Les Bordes by declaring, "Of the many golf courses we have played, Les Bordes is perhaps the most memorable."

It is a spectacular layout. In many ways it is a modern design, as evidenced by the fact that the course can be stretched beyond 7000 yards from the championship tees and water affects no fewer than 12 of the 18 holes (!) And yet Les Bordes also has the air of a century old golf course and is extremely 'natural looking'. The water hazards, for instance, appear as large (often interconnecting) ponds as opposed to Floridian style lakes, and they abound with wildlife.

Featuring large, boldly undulating greens and beautifully conditioned fairways, the site has few changes in elevation, thus the course twists and turns rather than tumbles; but above all it flows wonderfully from: green-to-tee-to-green.

There are no weak holes at Les Bordes with possibly the finest sequence occurring between the 4th, a stunning 'all or nothing' par three played over water, and the 7th, a dramatically curving par five. But the best hole of all is saved until last. "The 18th concludes a brilliant course in triumphant style" (to quote Golf World); a brave approach is required to carry some 70 yards of water to find a splendid stage-like green.

The accompanying golf facilities at Les Bordes reflect the standards of the golf course; the practice range is superb and the putting green – which is overlooked by an 18th century Rodin statue and is reputedly the largest in Europe – is equally impressive. What about the 19th hole? – this being France, it can be considered an integral part of the golf experience. At Les Bordes it really is a case of 'gourmet golf'. The food and, of course, the wines are excellent and the clubhouse itself oozes character. The interior is modelled on a traditional French hunting lodge with its wooden beamed ceilings, log fires and leather chairs.

The accommodation at Les Bordes is typically understated. It comprises a cluster of rustic farmhouse style cottages (with 40 bedrooms in total) that are situated to the left of the 18th fairway but largely hidden in amongst the trees. Spend a few nights here – after a few days on the golf course – and you'll know why Baron Bich and Mr Sakurai wanted to keep the place to themselves. And, yes, play Les Bordes, immerse yourself in the tranquillity, over-indulge at the 19th hole and go visit those nearby chateaux ... and discover why we chose Les Bordes as our 'International Golf Venue of the Year'.

Advanced warning: do not take these lists to heart!

After travelling the length and breadth of the British Isles the editor felt he should put down a few personal thoughts highlighting what he thought to be 'the best of Following the Fairways'. The selections are restricted to the courses which are featured in the Championship Golf section of Following the Fairways - some 130 courses. A handful of our classic courses are not featured (typically because they are very private) and this explains the absence of a few personal favourites such as The Addington, Rye, Swinley Forest and Royal Worlington. This said, the following have been carefully considered and if you feel there are some glaring omissions, the editor would be delighted to hear from you!

Links Courses

Most Scenic Holes:

Par 3's: — Royal Co Down (4th) / Old Head (16th)

Par 4's: — Turnberry (9th) / Royal Portrush (5th)

Par 5's: — Nefyn (12th) / Co Sligo (3rd)

Most Scenic Courses: — Waterville / Royal Co Down / Cruden Bay

Undiscovered Gems: — Montrose / Pennard / The Island

Most difficult/ Intimidating Holes:

Par 3's — Carnoustie (16th) / Royal Portrush (14th) / Waterville (17th)

Par 4's — St Andrews (17th) / Royal St George's (4th) / Tralee (12th)

Par 5's: — Royal Liverpool (16th) / Ballyliffin (13th) / Portmarnock (6th)

Inland Courses

Most Scenic Holes:

Par 3's: — Killarney (18th) / Loch Lomond (5th)

Par 4's: — Loch Lomond (18th) / Isle of Purbeck (5th)

Par 5's: — Roxburghe (14th) / St Mellion (12th)

Most Scenic Courses: — Loch Lomond / Killarney / Boat of Garten

Undiscovered Gems: — East Devon / Bamburgh Castle / Glasson

Most difficult/ Intimidating Holes:

Par 3's — West Sussex (6th) / Notts (13th) / Adare (16th)

Par 4's — The K Club (16th) / Royal Ashdown (17th) / Hanbury Manor (8th)

Par 5's: — Wentworth (17th) / Loch Lomond (6th) / Collingtree Park (18th)

OLD HEAD GOLF LINKS *Photograph courtesy of:* ***Old Head Golf Links***

Links Courses | *Inland Courses*

Most Characterful Holes:		*Most Characterful Holes:*	
Par 3's	Hunstanton (7th) Lahinch (6th)	*Par 3's*	Killarney (18th) St Mellion (11th)
Par 4's	North Berwick (13th) Portsalon (3rd)	*Par 4's*	Liphook (9th) Gleneagles (3rd)
Par 5's	Prestwick (3rd) Royal West Norfolk (8th)	*Par 5's*	Adare (18th) Lindrick (4th)
Most Characterful Courses:	Prestwick North Berwick Royal North Devon	*Most Characterful Courses:*	Gleneagles Royal Ashdown Forest Sunningdale
Most Interesting Fairways:	Machrihanish Ballyliffin Old Royal St George's	*Best Conditioned Fairways:*	Loch Lomond Carden Park Gleneagles
Most Interesting Greens:	Prestwick St Andrews Royal Dornoch	*Best Conditioned Greens:*	Walton Heath Loch Lomond Lindrick
Hazards: *Most Impressive Dunes*	Ballybunion Cruden Bay Hillside	*Hazards* *Most Impressive Heather:*	Walton Heath West Sussex Sunningdale
Most Severe Bunkers:	Royal St George's (4th) St Andrews (17th) Portmarnock Hotel (17th)	*Most Severe Bunkers:*	Ganton (14th) Walton Heath (16th) Woodhall Spa (12th)
Most Threatened By Ocean:	Machrihanish (1st) Old Head (4th) Ballybunion(11th)	*Most Threatened By Water:*	The K Club (16th) The Belfry (18th) Druids Glen (17th)
Most Spectacular Sequence *of Holes:*	Turnberry (4 - 11) Ballybunion (11 - 17) Cruden Bay (4 - 8)	*Most spectacular sequence* *of holes:*	St Mellion (10 - 12) Loch Lomond (16 - 18) Druids Glen (12 - 14)
Best bunkered courses:	Muirfield Royal Liverpool Carnoustie	*Best bunkered courses:*	Walton Heath Ganton Woodhall Spa
Most difficult courses:	Royal County Down Carnoustie Waterville	*Most difficult courses:*	St Mellion Woodhall Spa The 'K' Club
Most dramatic closing hole:	Old Head Royal Dublin	*Most dramatic closing hole:*	Adare Collingtree Park

WATERVILLE, CO. KERRY *Photograph courtesy of:* **Irish Tourist Board**

Links Courses   *Inland Courses*

Greatest Holes		**Greatest Holes:**	
Short Par 3's	Royal Troon (8th) Lahinch (11th) Ballybunion (8th)	**Short Par 3's**	Gleneagles (5th) Royal Ashdown (6th) Carlow (17th)
Medium Par 3's	Cruden Bay (4th) Royal Birkdale (12th) Western Gailes (7th)	**Medium Par 3's**	Moortown (10th) Druids Glen (12th) Stoke Poges (7th)
Long Par 3's	Royal County Down (4th) Ballybunion (15th) The Island (13th)	**Long Par 3's**	Killarney (18th) Notts (Hollinwell) (13th) The Berkshire (1st)
Short Par 4's	Portmarnock (14th) Machrihanish (8th) Royal Porthcawl (9th)	**Short Par 4's**	West Sussex (4th) Ganton (14th) Carden Park (6th)
Medium Par 4's	Prestwick (17th) Royal Lytham (18th) Southerness (12th)	**Medium Par 4's**	Woodhall Spa (11th) Chart Hills (4th) Sunningdale (6th)
Long Par 4's	St Andrews (17th) Ballybunion (11th) Turnberry (10th)	**Long Par 4's**	Gleneagles (13th) Slaley Hall (9th) Druids Glen (13th)
Short Par 5's	Royal Cinque Ports (16th) Carnoustie (6th) Silloth (13th)	**Short Par 5's**	Walton Heath (16th) East Devon (6th) Adare (18th)
Long Par 5's	St Andrews (14th) Muirfield (17th) Portmarnock (6th)	**Long Par 5's**	Chart Hills (1st) The K Club (7th) Alwoodley (8th)
Greatest Front 9	Royal Co Down Royal St Georges Royal Portrush	**Greatest Front 9**	Sunningdale (Old) Ganton Wentworth
Greatest Back 9	St Andrews Ballybunion Carnoustie	**Greatest Back 9**	Walton Heath Woodhall Spa Notts (Hollinwell)
Greatest Links Courses	St Andrews Royal Co Down Carnoustie	**Greatest Inland Courses**	Woodhall Spa Walton Heath Ganton
Best New Courses	Ballyliffin (Glashedy) Portmarnock Hotel Links	**Best New Courses**	Chart Hills Loch Lomond
Best Links Under 6400 yards	Cruden Bay Machrihanish	**Best Courses Under 6400 yards**	West Sussex The Berkshire

DRUIDS GLEN GOLF COURSE *Photograph courtesy of:* **Druids Glen**

1. (4) OUTSTANDING GOLF AND ACCOMMODATION

The Old Course Hotel, The Duke's Course, Fife
Sunlaws House, The Roxburghe, Roxburghshire
Portmarnock Hotel & Golf Links, Co Dublin
Carden Park, Cheshire

2. (5) ENGLISH INNS AND GOLF

The Inn at Whitewell and Royal Lytham
The Whipper-In, Oakham and Luffenham Heath
The Hoste Arms, Burnham and Royal Norfolk
The Worsley Arms, Worsley and Ganton
The Nobody Inn, Doddiscombleigh and Manor
House Hotel, Moretonhampstead

3. (4) GOLF AND BEACHES

Portsalon and Ballymastocker Bay, Co Donegal
Saunton and Saunton Sands, Devon
Royal Dornoch and Embo/Dornoch Bay, Highland
Tralee and 'Ryans Daughter' Beach, Co Kerry

4. (4) GOOD HOTELS NEAR GOOD GOLF - SCOTLAND

The Old Course Hotel and St Andrews (Fife)
Greywalls and Muirfield (Lothian)
Balbirnie House and Balbirnie (Fife)
Letham Grange, Colliston (Tayside)
Sunlaws House, The Roxburghe (Kelso)

5. (4) GOLF AND HISTORIC HOUSES (ACCOMMODATION)

Woburn and Woburn Abbey (Flitwick Manor)
Bamburgh Castle and Lindisfarne (Linden Hall)
Bowood and Bowood House (Queenwood Golf Lodge)
Murrayshall and Scone Palace (Murrayshall)

6. (3) GOLF AND SHOPPING (ACCOMMODATION)

York and Fulford (Mount Royale)
Bath and Castle Combe (The Manor House)
Edinburgh and Muirfield (Johnstounburn House)

7. (5) GOOD HOTELS NEAR GOOD GOLF - ENGLAND

Slaley Hall and Slaley Hall (Northumberland)
South Lodge and Mannings Heath (Sussex)
Horsted Place and East Sussex National (Sussex))
Forest of Arden (Warwickshire)
Hawkstone Park and Hawkstone Park (Shropshire)

8. (4) HOME FROM HOMES

Glin Castle, Co Limerick, Ireland (Ballybunion)
Dupplin Castle, Perthshire, Scotland (Blairgowrie)
Bardrochat, Ayrshire, Scotland (Turnberry)
Waterville House, Co Kerry, Ireland (Waterville)

9. (4) DORMY HOUSES

Burnham & Berrow, Somerset, England
Royal Porthcawl, Mid Glamorgan, Wales
Royal Lytham, Lancashire, England
Co Louth, Baltray, Ireland

10. (4) GOLF AND PUBS

Nefyn and The Ty Coch Inn, Gwynedd
Thurlestone and The Village Inn, Devon
Waterville and The Smugglers Inn, Co Kerry
Elie and The Ship Inn, Fife

11. (4) GOLF AND SEAFOOD

Old Head and Ahernes, Youghal
St Enodoc and The Seafood Restaurant, Padstow
Royal Portrush and Ramore, Portrush
Machrinanish and Lock 16 Restaurant, Crinan

12. (3) GOLF & CASTLES

Windsor Castle and Sunningdale
Harlech Castle and Royal St David's
Culzean Castle and Turnberry

13. (4) GOOD HOTELS NEAR GOOD GOLF - WALES

Marriott St Pierre Hotel and St Pierre (Gwent)
Penally Abbey and Tenby (Dyfed)
Celtic Manor and Celtic Manor (Gwent)
St Davids Hotel and Northop Country Park (Clwyd)

14. (5) FAMOUS HOTELS WITH GOLF COURSES

Turnberry, Ayrshire, Scotland
Gleneagles, Perthshire, Scotland
Kildare Hotel Golf & Country Club, Kildare,
Ireland
Mount Juliet, Kilkenny, Ireland
The Belfry, Warwickshire, England

15. (4) OLD AND NEW

Royal St Georges and Chart Hills (Kent)
Portmarnock Golf Club and Portmarnock Hotel
& Golf Links (Co. Dublin)
Dornoch and The Carnegie Golf Links (Highland)
Rolls of Monmouth and Celtic Manor (Wales)

16. (5) FISHING AND GOLF

The K Club, The River Liffey and The K Club
Gliffaes, The River Usk and Rolls of Monmouth
Kinnaird, The River Tay and Blairgowrie
Mount Falcon, The River Moy and Enniscrone
Sunlaws House, The River Teviot and The Roxburghe

17. (4) GOOD HOTELS NEAR GOOD GOLF - IRELAND

Adare Manor (Co Clare)
The Kildare Hotel & Country Club (Co Kildare)
Luttrellstown Castle (Co Dublin)
Mount Juliet (Co Kilkenny)

18. (4) GOLF COURSES AND RESTAURANTS

Royal Dublin and The Unicorn
St Andrews and The Peat Inn, Peat Inn
Gullane and La Potiniere, Gullane
Stoke Poges and the Fredricks, Maidenhead

It has to be the most self indulgent but satisfying round of all: eighteen of the best 19th holes. Presumably one wakes up at
The Old Course Hotel, St Andrews and dines at Fredericks at Maidenhead—five star pampering all the way.

Golf in Britain

SCOTTISH SUNSET Photograph courtesy of: **Scottish Tourist Board**

golfcourseguide.com

A complete online guide to golf courses in Great Britain and Ireland.

Where to play and where to stay.

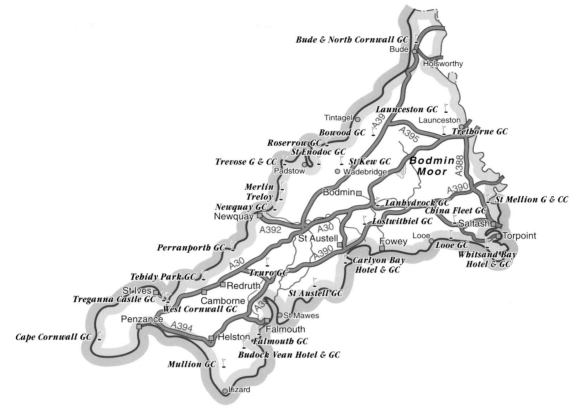

Cornwall Choice Golf

'Brandy for the Parson, Baccy for the Clerk'—Cornwall is the land of the smuggler's cove. It is also the land of King Arthur and the Knights of the Round Table—a land of legends. To cross the Tamar is to enter foreign soil: for centuries the Cornish Celts had more in common with the Welsh and the French Bretons than the ever-invading Anglo Saxons. Well, the Anglo-Saxons still invade but nowadays in a more peaceful manner. 'Grockles' they are called in Cornwall and they come in search of sun, sand and sea (not to mention a holiday home!) But there is also a fairly recent addition, a sub-species known as the 'golfing-grockle' who comes to Cornwall to seek out some of the finest golfing country in the Kingdom.

West of Plymouth

If one commences an imaginary tour by crossing the Tamar at Plymouth, **St Mellion Golf and Country Club** (01579) 351351 has surely to be the first port of call. It is one of the few places in Britain where one might bump into Jack Nicklaus. St Mellion has an onsite hotel and two fine courses, one of which was designed by the great man and is featured later in this chapter. Not far away in Saltash, a new course has recently opened called **China Fleet**, apparently the Navy (British—not Oriental) is the guiding force behind it.

Heading westwards **Looe** Golf Club is situated on high ground to the north of Looe, near Widegates. An 18 hole moorland course, it lies somewhat at the mercy of the elements and can get exceptionally windy. Not too far away at Portwinkle the **Whitsand Bay** Hotel (01503) 230276 is an ideal place to break a journey with its own gentle 18 hole golf course stretching out along the cliffs and looking down over Whitsand Bay.

The area around Looe abounds with good hotels and restaurants with seafood not surprisingly a speciality. Hannofoe Point (01503) 263273 and Fieldhead (01503) 262689 are friendly and serve fine

food. In Fowey, a restaurant to consider is Food For Thought (01726) 832221, a converted coastguard's cottage on the quayside, and the Fowey (01726) 832551 is a hotel worthy of note. Another hotel where the visitor can enjoy a little extra walking—on the cliffs as well as on the fairways is at Talland-by-Looe, the Talland Bay Hotel (01503) 272667. The Kitchen (01503) 272780 is an excellent restaurant in Polperro and in Golant, the Cormorant Hotel (01726) 833426 enjoys a glorious setting. Further inland the Old Rectory House (01579) 342617 at St Keyne offers good value.

Around St Austell

We'll now, if you'll pardon the expression, leave the Looe area and, still heading in a clockwise direction, set sail for St Austell where we find a twin attraction for golfers: the redoubtable **Carlyon Bay** and the **St Austell** Golf Club. The St Austell course is situated on the western edge of the town off the A390. Rather shorter than Carlyon Bay but with an ample spread of gorse and numerous bunkers, it possesses plenty of challenges and attractions of its own.

Carlyon Bay is surely one of Britain's best loved hotel courses. Not a Turnberry or a Gleneagles perhaps, but very pleasing with several challenging holes and views over a number of beaches—one of which I'm told is frequented by naturists! There are numerous facilities at the hotel and it is ideal for families.

St Austell is a pleasant place to spend a day or two and golfers may decide to stay at Carlyon Bay Hotel itself (01726) 812304: obviously very convenient but four star comfort as well. As a first rate alternative though, Boscundle Manor (01726) 813557 at Tregrehan is highly recommended—the food alone is worth a trip. Heading northwards to the **Lostwithiel** Golf and Country Club (01208) 873550, where fine golf and agreeable accommodation are the order of the day. Note also the 13th century Globe Inn (01208) 872501 while in Lostwithiel.

South of Falmouth

Falmouth—a glorious harbour and seagulls aplenty. More good golf awaits. Like St Austell, there are two sets of fairways on which to exercise the swing and burn off the extra holiday calories. Romantically located at the head of a wooded valley above the lovely Halford Passage. **Falmouth** Golf Club enjoys spectacular cliff top views over Falmouth Bay and has recently refurbished with the course tightened, extensive practice facilities provided and the clubhouse remodelled. Its designer-owner, Bryan Patterson, a distinguished golf coach, has strong views about traditional golfing values and it shows in every aspect of his club which is a joy to visit. **Budock Vean,** an attractive hotel course, has only nine holes but plenty of variety and is well kept.

For hotels, Budock Vean (01326) 250288 takes pride of place but others to note include the Royal Duchy (01326) 313042 and the Hotel St Michael's (01326) 312707. The opening words of The Wind in the Willows were written at the Greenbank (01326) 312440, clearly an inspiring place, while the Penmere Manor (01326) 211411 also has much to commend it. Two final thoughts for places to stay in this area are the Idle Rocks (01326) 270771 at St Mawes on the Roseland peninsula and the Meudon Hotel (01326) 250541 at Mawnan Smith.

Still heading along the south coast, the course at **Mullion** is one of the short but sweet brigade. Situated seven miles south of Helston, it can lay claim to being the most southerly on the British mainland. Nestling around the cliff edges overlooking some particularly inviting sands and with distant views towards St Michael's Mount, Mullion typifies the charm of Cornish holiday golf. With the spectacular scenery of the Lizard area, it's another good spot to spend a few days. In Mullion, or perhaps more precisely, Mullion Cove, Henscath House (01326) 240537 is perfect for the golf course.

The North Coast

Starting at mainland UK's most southern tip is the 18 hole **Cape Cornwall** Golf and Country Club at St Just. Further north, but in a far more sheltered spot, the **West Cornwall** Golf Club lies just beyond St Ives at Lelant. A beautiful and very natural old-fashioned type of links, it was laid out more than a hundred years ago by the then vicar of Lelant. Like St Enodoc, it is a genuine links course—sand dunes and plenty of sea breezes—and quite short. Jim Barnes, who won both the Open and US Open was born in Lelant village.

In St Ives, two hotels to note are the Tregenna Castle (01736) 795254 and the Garrack (01736) 796199—ideal for the nearby cliffs and beaches as well as the 18 hole par 59 **Treganna Castle** golf course. Slightly further afield at Carbis Bay, the aptly named Carbis Bay Hotel (01736) 795311 is particularly friendly and well recommended.

Passing numerous derelict tin and copper mines the inland course at **Tehidy Park** is soon reached. Located midway between Camborne and Portreath it presents a considerable contrast to the golf at Lelant. Here we are amidst pine trees, rhododendrons and bluebells. Getting back to the northern coast, **Perranporth** and **Newquay** look closer on the map than they are by road. Both are links type courses with outstanding sea views. Not far away at St Mawgan there is a 9 hole course, **Treloy**, and **Merlin**, an 18 hole course, has recently opened at Mawgan Porth.

Photograph courtesy of: **St Mellion Golf & Country Club**

In Newquay, where the crash of the Atlantic waves offers a surfers' paradise, there are several welcoming establishments. The Hotel Bristol (01637) 875181 is an ideal holiday base. A less expensive option is the Priory Lodge Hotel (01637) 874111. Connoisseurs of the public house might care to visit the Falcon at St Mawgan. Golfers at Tehidy may wish to note the Tregarthan Hotel (01209) 890399 at Mount Hawke—quite small but friendly and good value, and the Beach Dunes Hotel (01872) 572263 at Perranporth is very convenient for the Perranporth links.

Further along the coast lie two marvellous golfing challenges—**St Enodoc** at Rock and **Trevose** at Constantine Bay. Trevose is the longer course but much more open and it doesn't possess the massive sandhills that are the feature of St Enodocs links. Both courses are featured ahead. At a different level, but worth a visit whilst in this area are the two new courses at **Roserrow** and **St Kew**.

The most convenient places for the golfing gourmet to stay are, at Trevose, the splendid Treglos Hotel (01841) 520727 and for St Enodoc, try the Molesworth Arms (01208) 812055, a pleasant 16th century coaching inn near Wadebridge. An early start can also be made from Padstow, where Rick Stein's Seafood Restaurant (01841) 532700 has a great reputation—an ideal choice for gourmet golfers who may have overindulged the night before! The Castle Rock Hotel (01208) 880300 at Port Isaac can also be recommended. This delightful fishing village also houses the 17th century Port Gaverne Hotel and Green Door Cottages (01208) 880244—where tremendous food and a charming atmosphere await. Another gem is located in Polzeath—The Cornish Cottage Hotel (01208) 862213—a delightful establishment.

Our coastal tour ends appropriately at Bude—a pleasant and unassuming seaside resort with a very good golf links, **Bude** and **North Cornwall**, situated almost in the town centre and renowned for its rolling fairways and excellent greens. The town has an impressive array of hotels: the Burn Court Hotel (01288) 352872 is as comfortable as any and has the advantage of overlooking the golf course. One other popular spot for golfers in town is the Camelot (01288) 352361. In Morwenstow, a fine old pub the Bush is well worth visiting. The clifftop views are breathtaking.

Inland Golf

The golf course at Tehidy was mentioned on our coastal tour, but five other inland courses definitely merit attention: the first is **Truro**, a shortish parkland course close to the charming cathedral; then two fine courses at Launceston; **Launceston** Golf Club, a parkland course and **Trethorne**, a new course cleverly designed by Frank Fayne to exploit interesting terrain and with some very challenging holes; fourthly there is a highly rated new course near Camelford, called **Bowood**; and last but not least there is **Lanhydrock** near Bodmin which we explore in some detail ahead.

For stylish accommodation Truro golfers might wish to base themselves at the picturesque Trevispian-Vean Farm House (01872) 279514, and visitors to Bowood (which isn't far from Trevose) may opt for the comforts of the aforementioned Treglos, or the even closer Lanteglos Hotel (01840) 213551.

The White Hart coaching inn is an ideal base for exploring the countryside around Launceston, as is Penhallow Manor (01566) 86206. Lovers of angling as well as the fairways, should sample The Arundell Arms at Lifton (01566) 784666 a first class establishment in every way. However, the golf course itself at Launceston is where some of the best views can be enjoyed. Located on high ground, to the west stretches Bodmin Moor—bogs and mystery—and to the east, Dartmoor—more bogs and even more mystery.

Trevose

To some, mention of the north coast of Cornwall will invoke thoughts of golden sandy beaches and cool, inviting seas. For others, it may conjure up images of romantic coves, wild spectacular cliffs and incessant crashing waves. Either way, the place has a certain magic and after all it was here that King Arthur is said to have met Merlin. Such is the setting of the Trevose Golf and Country Club.

Located near the quaint little fishing port of Padstow, Trevose is an ideal spot for a golfing holiday—or any kind of holiday come to that, but those who haven't made space in the boot for the golf clubs are missing out on something rather special. The club has long boasted a splendid 18 hole championship course plus an adjacent nine hole short course. Now Trevose can entice the visiting golfer with a new 'full length' par 35 nine hole course which opened in 1993, thus making 36 holes in total.

From the championship tees (handicap certificate required) the 18 hole course measures 6608 yards (par 71, SSS 72). The forward tees reduce the length by about 170 yards, while the ladies play over 5713 yards, par 73. The course can properly be described as a golf links although the visitor need have no fears of having to carry Himalayan-like sandhills. The course is fairly flat and as a rule the rough is kept short. This should ensure that the golfer spends more time admiring the scenery than searching for his golf ball. A word about the views—they are indeed tremendous, particularly those across Booby's Bay which provide a dramatic backdrop to the 4th green.

The wind at Trevose can often play a decisive role and prevent low scoring. There are a great number of well-positioned bunkers and a stream meanders through much of the course. Among the best holes one might single out the par three 3rd, the above-mentioned 4th (a curving right to left dog-leg) the 7th and the 12th.

The clubhouse with its prime situation overlooking the course offers a whole range of first class facilities There is a large, comfortable bar and a dining room which can cater for over 100 people. For children, a separate games room is provided. Swimming, snooker and tennis are also all very much a part of the country club scene—and there is even a trendy boutique!

There is an unmistakably relaxed, holiday flavour about Trevose. The atmosphere is perhaps best epitomised by the story of four lady members involved in a foursomes game: apparently, when playing the short 16th they arrived at the green only to discover that they had been so busy chattering not one of them had remembered to tee off . . . so much for women drivers!

Trevose Golf & Country Club, Constantine Bay
Padstow, Cornwall PL25 8JB

Secretary	Patrick O'Shea (01841) 520208
Professional	Gary Alliss (01841) 520261
Green Fees	Championship £25-£36
	New Nine £18-£24
	Par Three £10
Restrictions	Proof of handicap for Championship

Directions
Four miles west of Padstow off the B3276.

St Mellion

I wonder what the golfing cynics would have said if a few years ago someone had suggested that Jack Nicklaus would one day be designing a championship course in Cornwall? 'Go tell it to the pixies', I should imagine. Well, in Cornwall myths, legends and fairy tales have a habit of turning out to be true.

St Mellion was the brainchild of farming brothers Martin and Hermon Bond. What made these charming people turn from profitable pig breeding and potato farming to golf course building remains something of a mystery. What is certain, however, is that their success has been nothing short of phenomenal.

The St Mellion story really has two parts to it. Act One commenced in the mid 1970s when the Bonds first decided to create a golf course. In short, their idea met with resounding success and a first class championship course was constructed. Within a few years, tournament golf came to Cornwall (TV cameras and all) for the first time. Ambition swelled and Act Two was conceived: 'Let's build the best course in Europe' (well, why not!) An additional two hundred acres of adjoining woodland was purchased from the Duchy of Cornwall and an approach was made to the great man himself, Jack Nicklaus. Negotiations followed and Nicklaus came over to inspect the new land. His initial thought was that the land was far too hilly and narrow—an impossible task. But of course, like the Bond brothers, Jack could never resist a challenge . . .

Plans were drawn up and at least on paper the object was a simple one, namely to build, in Jack's words, 'Potentially the world's greatest galleried golf course'. Let us just say that the construction team put in a few good hours! The end result is now ready for all the world to see. Some have described it as an 'Augusta in Cornwall'; others reckon it to be the toughest course in Britain. Perhaps the best idea is to go and judge for yourself—you'll be made most welcome.

While there is an understandable wish to play the Nicklaus Course, we shouldn't forget that there are two fine courses at St Mellion. When the Nicklaus course was being built, certain changes to the old championship course (now known as the 'Old Course') were necessary. However, it remains a worthy test of golf and is certainly a long way from your average 'holiday course'. Visitors are welcome to play either course, subject to making a booking with the **Advance Golf Reservations** on **tel: (01579) 352002 fax: (01579) 350537. Secretary** is **Roy Dransfield tel: (01579) 351351.** The club's full address is the **St Mellion Hotel, Golf & Country Club, St. Mellion, Saltash, Cornwall, PL12 6SD.** The green fees in 2000 are £45 per person per round on the Nicklaus Course, and £30 on the Old Course.

Although it nestles deep in the Cornish countryside, St Mellion is easily accessible from all directions. Travelling from afar most will come via Plymouth which is situated eight miles to the south east. Plymouth is linked to Exeter by the A38 and Exeter in turn to Bristol by the M5. On reaching Plymouth the A38 should be followed towards Liskeard and the turning for St Mellion is clearly signposted.

It is difficult to say which are the best holes on the Nicklaus Course. A few, however, do stand out and they exude the Nicklaus approach. The 3rd is an excellent hole—miss the fairway to the right and you can be facing a desperate uphill shot over a huge ravine to a heavily protected green. On the 5th, the drive is across a lake and thereafter the fairway sweeps around to the left towards the green which has a stream running in front of it. And so it goes on, but note especially the par three 11th and par five 12th which have been likened to Augusta's 12th and 13th.

However, for all the comparisons with Augusta and Jack's best courses in America, the golfer only has to lift his eyes and look around to be reminded where he is. The surrounding scenery is unmistakably Cornish: the rolling green fields, the babbling brook with its kingfisher and the gnarled trees that huddle around many of the greens and look as if they've endured a million English winters.

In May 1990, Benson and Hedges brought their prestigious International Open tournament to the Nicklaus Course and victory fittingly went to one of the world's leading players, Jose-Maria Olazabal. The Spaniard was succeeded as champion by Bernhard Langer and in 1994 the trophy was claimed by Seve Ballesteros—underlining the old adage that the greatest courses produce the greatest champions.

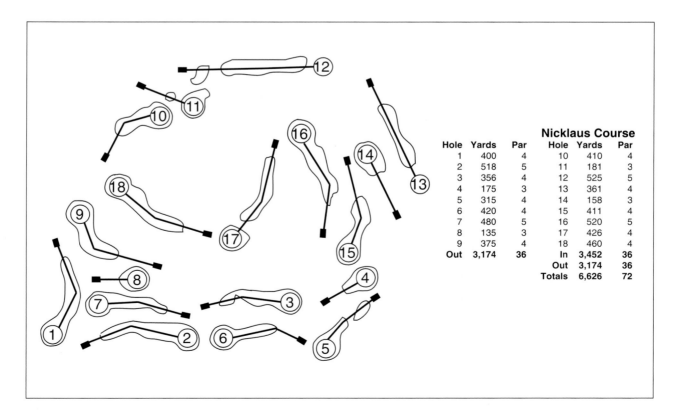

Nicklaus Course

Hole	Yards	Par	Hole	Yards	Par
1	400	4	10	410	4
2	518	5	11	181	3
3	356	4	12	525	5
4	175	3	13	361	4
5	315	4	14	158	3
6	420	4	15	411	4
7	480	5	16	520	5
8	135	3	17	426	4
9	375	4	18	460	4
Out	**3,174**	**36**	**In**	**3,452**	**36**
			Out	**3,174**	**36**
			Totals	**6,626**	**72**

St Mellion is an outstanding golf and country club situated in the Caradon District of South East Cornwall, just 10 miles from the historical city of Plymouth.

The golf at St Mellion is truly second to none with the Old Course and the Nicklaus Course, designed by the man himself, available for all guests to enjoy. The Old Course here offers an enjoyable and picturesque round to the club golfer and is in pleasant contrast to the challenge of the more demanding championship Nicklaus Course, home to the Benson and Hedges International Open between 1990-1995.

Guests can enjoy a full range of indoor and outdoor facilities: all weather tennis, squash, indoor 25metre training pool and leisure pool complex, steam room, sauna, spa pool and snooker. Guests can also take advantage of the fully equipped gymnasium, dance studio or relax in the on site Skin Care and Spa Centre. However, if you like to walk, the 450-acre estate offers some relaxing strolls along streams and lakes. There is much to explore in the surrounding Cornish countryside, with delightful villages and sandy beaches but a short distance away.

The St Mellion Hotel has everything to make a guest's stay enjoyable and comfortable and is located just a short stroll from the clubhouse. The bedrooms are attractively furnished with en-suite bathroom, colour television and tea/coffee making facilities.

Some visitors may prefer the comfort and luxury of the St Mellion fairway lodges, beautifully equipped and furnished with all the requirements for up to eight people. Fully equipped kitchens, en-suite bathrooms, colour television and video are standard and some lodges even have their own inbuilt sauna!

St Mellion has its own superb restaurant, Chimes, that offers a wide variety of International and West country cuisine as well as a diverse list of fine wines. Or, if you are after a lighter meal, the Gallery Brasserie serves everything from specialty coffees to traditional Cornish Cream Teas.

Whether you are a keen golfer, or just looking for a relaxing break, St Mellion will reward you with the holiday of a lifetime.

St Mellion Hotel Golf & Country Club
Nr Saltash, Cornwall PL12 65D
Tel (01579) 351351
Fax (01579) 350537
email stmellion@americangolf.uk.com
web site st-mellion.co.uk

St Enodoc

'It lay content
Two paces from the pin;
A steady putt and then it went
Oh, most securely in.
The very turf rejoiced to see
That quite unprecedented three.'

I suppose only Cornwall, and probably only St Enodoc come to that, could have inspired someone to write a poem about a birdie. Actually, it wasn't just 'someone', it was the Poet Laureate, Sir John Betjeman, who loved, and in later years lived beside this glorious West Country links. Everyone who visits St Enodoc, it seems, falls under a spell of some sorts. So why is it such a favourite and what are these charms?

Imagine a really classic links course:—huge sandhills, meandering, tumbling fairways, plenty of humps and hillocks, the odd awkward stance and blind shot perhaps but firm, fast greens and plenty of invigorating sea air. This is St Enodoc to a tee. Exhilarating, dramatic scenery? St Enodoc most definitely—situated on the northern coast of Cornwall and not too far from Padstow and Trevose, the views could hardly be mundane. The chance of a good score? Again yes—providing you stay on the fairways! St Enodoc, unlike all too many of today's courses won't put your length of drive on trial. It will, however, more than likely test every golf club in your bag. The holes are all very individual and bristle with old fashioned character. And then the accompanying atmosphere? Well, according to Sir John Betjeman even the turf finds time to rejoice in this splendidly relaxed environment. In short, St Enodoc is a sheer delight.

Doing his best to ensure that St Enodoc stays lost in this wonderful golfing time warp is the club's **Secretary, Mr L Guy**. He can be contacted by writing to the **St Enodoc Golf Club, Rock, Wadebridge, Cornwall, PL27 6LD**. Individual visitors are welcome throughout the week and, although it is likely to be difficult to arrange a tee time for the weekend, visitors are welcome after 2.30 pm on Saturdays. Bookings (at least four days in advance) should be made through the club's **Professional, Nick Williams, tel: (01208) 862402**. Golfing societies, or parties of ten or more will need to make arrangements with the Secretary's office on **(01208) 862200** or by **fax: (01208) 862976**. The clubhouse number is **(01208) 863216**.

Since 1982 there have been two 18 hole courses at St Enodoc. The main course is now named the **Church Course** and the newer (and considerably less testing) one is called the **Holywell Course**. To play on the Church Course visitors must possess a maximum handicap of 24 (28 for ladies). Green fees in 2000 for the Church Course are set at £35 a round midweek, £50 a day, with £40 per round and £55 per day payable at weekends. Fees for the Holywell Course are £15 per round, £25 per day. A round on both courses can be obtained for £40 during the week and £50 at weekends. Junior golfers (under 18) pay half rates and there are also various reductions available for those wishing to purchase weekly or fortnightly temporary memberships.

St Enodoc is much less remote and more easily reached than many people imagine. Coming by road the two towns to look for on the map are Bodmin and Wadebridge. The former is linked to Exeter by the A30 and to Plymouth by the A38. Wadebridge is 7 miles north of Bodmin. At Wadebridge the B3314 should be taken to St Minver and then a left turn should be taken at this village to Rock.

The Church Course takes its name from the tiny, half-sunken church which is situated near the far end of the links. Many years ago the church was barely visible after a violent storm practically covered it in sand. It is well worth inspecting and Sir John Betjeman is buried in the graveyard. The church almost comes into play on the celebrated 10th hole, the toughest par four on the 6243 yards, par 69 layout (the Holywell Course measures 4165 yards, par 62). As well as being the most difficult two shot hole on the course it is also one of the most memorable. The drive is downhill, but it must carry almost 200 yards to find a narrow, heavily contoured fairway; off to the left is a marshy area and a stream and to the right are steep sand dunes and uncompromising rough. The second shot to the green is almost as daunting as the tee shot!

Betjeman's birdie came at the 13th but the other hole that everyone talks about is the 6th. Here the golfer must confront the 'Himalayas', 'the highest sandhill, to the best of my belief, I have ever seen on a golf course' remarked the famous golf writer Bernard Darwin (another who was thoroughly enchanted by St Enodoc). With holes like the 6th it isn't difficult to see why St Enodoc is so often likened to Prestwick.

The area around Padstow is most fortunate in having both St Enodoc and Trevose so close at hand. Together they make a marvellous pair and offer two very different challenges. It is difficult to imagine anyone playing St Enodoc and not relishing a return visit . . . and who knows what an unexpected birdie might inspire!

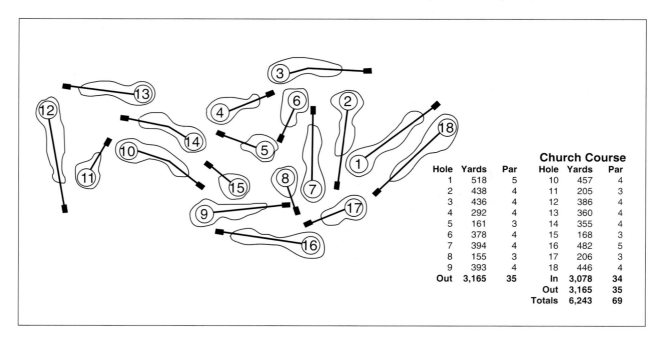

Hole	Yards	Par	Hole	Yards	Par
1	518	5	10	457	4
2	438	4	11	205	3
3	436	4	12	386	4
4	292	4	13	360	4
5	161	3	14	355	4
6	378	4	15	168	3
7	394	4	16	482	5
8	155	3	17	206	3
9	393	4	18	446	4
Out	**3,165**	**35**	**In**	**3,078**	**34**
			Out	**3,165**	**35**
			Totals	**6,243**	**69**

Church Course

Lanhydrock

Stand on the clubhouse verandah and drink in the view. Rolling hills and patchwork fields fill the horizon. Stretching out below, amidst a beautifully wooded valley is the golf course: lush undulating fairways, splashes of dazzling white sand and slick, subtly contoured greens—framed sometimes by water hazards and nearly always by a splendid mix of trees. It is wonderful countryside and classic golfing terrain.

Situated about one mile south of Bodmin off the B3268 via the A30/A38, Lanhydrock is one of Cornwall's most attractive golfing venues. A genuinely relaxed atmosphere prevails throughout the club and visitors are always made to feel extremely welcome. Significantly, there are no specific restrictions, although contacting the club in advance is strongly recommended. The **Manager**, **Graham Bond** can be contacted on **tel: (01208) 73600** and by **fax: (01208) 77325**, you can now also **e mail: postmaster@lanhydrock-golf.co.uk** or for further information visit their **web site: www.lanhydrock-golf.co.uk**

Green fees in 2000 were set for weekdays and weekends at £28 per round and £34 per day, juniors play for £16 per round and £22 per day. Lower rates applicable mid and low season.

If the vision from the verandah has most golfers drooling in anticipation, so the opening hole encapsulates the spirit of the challenge ahead. The 1st is a short par four, and with the tee shot being downhill to a generous landing area, few should have trouble finding the fairway. The difficulty, however, comes with the approach which must be hit over a small lake to an attractively sited green which, like several at Lanhydrock, slopes from back to front—towards the water's edge.

Four strong holes are followed by a relatively modest 5th but then comes the glorious 6th. Pity the golfer who does not relish a par three where the tee shot must be struck downhill across a lake to a target green. There may be many similarly styled holes in golf but few can have been as beautifully conceived. The hole occupies its own, almost hidden, corner of Lanhydrock. The backdrop to the green comprises a steep overgrown bank, a gently cascading stream and an impressive collection of tall trees. You reach the green via an understated wooden bridge, then putt out on golf's equivalent of an open-air stage.

The best sequence at Lanhydrock begins with the 10th. The very shape of this hole encourages a swashbuckling 'bite off as much as you dare' approach. From an elevated tee the fairway plunges across a valley and regains its height just as the hole dog-legs sharply away to the right. An ancient woodland known as Tregullan Moor envelops the 12th hole—for its entire length it is surrounded by a mass of gnarled, wizened old trees and prickly gorse. The 13th takes the golfer to the highest point on the course where the views are naturally the most spectacular . . . how often do you get the opportunity to contrast a strikingly modern clubhouse with an 18th century Cornish tin mine? !

The par five 18th can offer the chance of a closing birdie but only if the largest inland bunker in Cornwall is successfully avoided. This giant stretch of sand (Lanhydrock's version of 'Hell's Half Acre') occupies most of the land in between the 9th and 18th greens. Any hope of impressing those 'bewitched' folk on the verandah with a sneaky 'up and down' from the back of this monster? Certainly . . . in our dreams!

The course also features a 19th par 3 'fun/feature' hole with 'island' green surrounded almost entirely by water. Strategic use of this hole means that Lanhydrock hardly ever have to make use of temporary greens, being able to bring this hole into use when repair work is in hand.

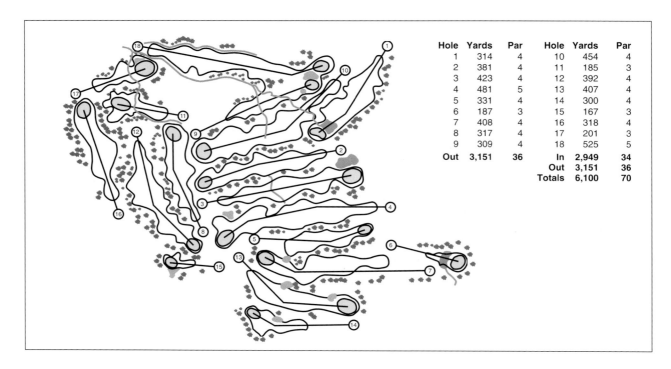

Hole	Yards	Par	Hole	Yards	Par
1	314	4	10	454	4
2	381	4	11	185	3
3	423	4	12	392	4
4	481	5	13	407	4
5	331	4	14	300	4
6	187	3	15	167	3
7	408	4	16	318	4
8	317	4	17	201	3
9	309	4	18	525	5
Out	**3,151**	**36**	**In**	**2,949**	**34**
			Out	**3,151**	**36**
			Totals	**6,100**	**70**

Key

*To avoid disappointment
it is advisable to telephone
in advance*

***Visitors welcome at most times*
**Visitors usually allowed on
weekdays only*
*Visitors not normally permitted
(Mon, Wed) No visitors
on specified days*

Approximate Green Fees
A   *£40 plus*
B   *£25 to £40*
C   *£20 to £30*
D   *£15 to £25*
E   *under £15*
F   *Green fees on application*

Restrictions
G Guests only
H–Handicap certificate required
H–(24) Handicap of 24 or less
L–Letter of introduction required
M–Visitor must be a member of
another recognised club

Bowood G.C.
(01840) 213017
Lanteglos, Camelford
(18) 6692 yards/***/B/H

Bude and North Cornwall G.C.
(01288) 352006
Burn View, Bude
(18) 6202 yards/**/B/H

Budock Vean Hotel & G.C.
(01326) 250288
Mawnan Smith, Falmouth
(9) 5153 yards/***/D/L/H

Cape Cornwall G.& C.C.
(01736) 788611
St Just, Penzance
(18) 5650 yards/**/D

Carlyon Bay Hotel G.C.
(01726) 814250
Carlyon Bay, St Austell
(18) 6463 yards/***/C

China Fleet C.C.
(01752) 848668
Saltash
(18) 6551 yards/***/F/H

Culdrose G.C.
(01326) 574121
Royal Naval Air Station, Culdrose
(18) 6432 yards/*/E/G

Falmouth G.C.
(01326) 314296
Swanpool Road, Falmouth
(18) 5680 yards/***/B/H

Holywell Bay G.C.
(01637) 830531
Holywell Bay, Newquay
(18) 2784 yards/***/E

Isle of Scilly G.C.
(01720) 422692
St Mary's, Isles of Scilly
(9) 6001 yards/***/D

Killiow Park G.C.
(01872) 70246
Kea,Truro,
(18) 3500 yards/**/D

Lanhydrock G.C.
(01208) 73600
Lostwithiel Road, Bodmin
(18) 6185 yards/***/F

Launceston G.C.
(01566) 773442
St. Stephens, Launceston
(18) 6407 yards/**/D/H/L

Looe G.C.
(01503) 240239
Widegates, Looe
(18) 5940 yards/***/F

Lostwithiel G.& C.C.
(01208) 873550
Lower Polscoe, Lostwithiel
(18) 6098 yards/**/D/H

Merlin G.C.
(01841) 540222
Mawgan Porth, Hewquay
(18) 5227 yards/***/E

Mullion G.C.
(01326) 241176
Cury, Helston
(18) 6022 yards/**/C/H

Newquay G.C.
(01637) 874354
Tower Road, Newquay
(18) 6140 yards/***/D/H

Perranporth G.C.
(01872) 572454
Budnick Hill, Perranporth
(18) 6286 yards/***/C/H

Porthpean G.C.
(01726) 64613
Porthpean, St Austell
(9) 3266 yards/***/E

Praa Sands G.C.
(01736) 763445
Germoe Crossroads, Penzance
(9) 4104 yards/***/D/H

Radnor G.C.
(01209) 211059
Treleigh, Redruth
(9) 1326 yards/***/E

Roserrow G. & C.C.
St Minver, Wadebridge
(01208) 863000
(18) 6507 yards/***/C

St Austell G.C.
(01726) 74756
Tregongeeves Lane, St Austell
(18) 6000 yards/***/F/M/H

St Enodoc G.C.
(01208) 862402
Rock, Wadebridge
(18) 6243 yards/***/B/H(24)
(18) 4165 yards/***/D

St Kew G.C.
(01208) 841500
St Kew Highway, Bodmin
(9) 2204 yards/***/E

St Mellion G.& C.C.
(01579) 352002
St Mellion, Saltash
(18) 6626 yards/**/A/H
(18) 5782 yards/**/B

Tehidy Park G.C.
(01209) 842208
Cambourne
(18) 6241 yards/***/B/H

Tregenna Castle Hotel G.C.
(01736) 797381
St Ives
(18) 3549 yards/***/F

Treloy G.C.
(01637) 878554
Treloy, Newquay
(9) 2143 yards/***/E

Trethorne G.C.
(01566) 86324
Kennards House, Launceston
(9) 3169 yards/***/E

Trevose G.& C.C.
(01841) 520208
Constantine Bay, Padstow
(18)6608 yards/***/F/H
(9) 3031 yards/***/F
(9) 1360 yards/***/F

Truro G.C.
(01872) 272640
Treliske, Truro
(18) 5347 yards/***/C/H

West Cornwall G.C.
(01736) 753401
Lelant, St Ives
(18) 5884 yards/***/B/H

Whitsand Bay Hotel G.C.
(01503) 230470
Portwrinkle, Torpoint
(18) 5800 yards/***/D/H/L

LANHYDROCK GOLF CLUB Photograph courtesy of: Lanhydrock Golf Club & David Cannon

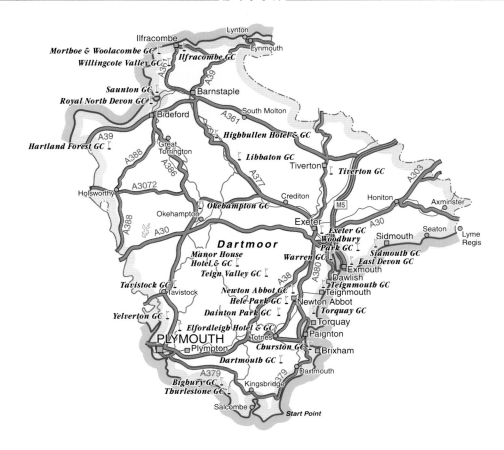

Devon Choice Golf

Glorious Devon they call it—beaches to the north, beaches to the south and Dartmoor in the middle. Amidst all the glory are over forty golf courses, the majority of which lie either directly on the coast or within a mile or so of it. The two most widely known are both in the north of the county: Royal North Devon (Westward Ho! as it is commonly known) and Saunton. The greater number of courses, however, are on the southern coast, or to put it another way, while North Devon may have the cream, most of the tees are to be found in the south.

Dartmoor

Firstly though, what about golf in the middle? The beautiful setting of the **Manor House** Hotel & Golf Course at Moretonhampstead is known to many. However, it is not the sole course within Dartmoor. **Okehampton** is another moorland type course and whilst not overly long, has a number of interesting holes and at Christow there is a particularly scenically spectacular new course set beside the River Teign and unsurprisingly called **Teign Valley**. Away from Dartmoor, but still fairly centrally located is the parkland course at **Tiverton**, easily reached from the M5 (junction 27).

With its many Tudor buildings, historic guildhall and impressive cathedral, Exeter makes an attractive county town. Golfwise, the city has an 18 hole course at Countess Wear, namely the **Exeter** Golf and Country Club, which has a very grand clubhouse and the course is renowned for its beautifully maintained greens, undoubtedly among the best in Devon. There are many outstanding places in which to spend a night or two when visiting this part of the world. Exeter is a likely base and here the Royal Clarence Hotel (01392) 319955 is extremely comfortable and enjoys a splendid position overlooking Cathedral Square. Also in the city, the St Olaves Court (01392) 217736 on South Street is a delightfully secluded inn with good

accommodation. One of the oldest and best known pubs in Exeter is the Ship on St Martins Lane—ideal unless you're over six feet tall!

On Dartmoor, the striking Manor House Hotel (01647) 440355 at Moretonhampstead is where many golfers will choose to hang up their spikes, but a number of splendid alternatives are at hand. Chagford offers the exceptional Gidleigh Park (01647) 432367 and the Mill End Hotel (01647) 432282. The former is lavish, the latter less so but thoroughly recommended. The White Hart in Moretonhampstead (01647) 440406 is a pleasant inn to note. In Lydford, Lydford House (01822) 820347 is comfortable, as is the Castle Inn (01822) 820242, while the Lodge Hill Farmhouse (01884) 252907 at Ashley is convenient for Tiverton. Whilst in the area, a visit to Huntsham may also be in order: Huntsham Court (01398) 361365 is a delight to those who enjoy the atmosphere of a relaxed country house. Lovers of classical music and fine food will feel particularly spoiled. After a game at Manor House, two popular pubs to note are the Nobody Inn (01647) 252394 at Doddiscombsleigh (excellent food and accommodation here as well) and the Ring of Bells in nearby historic North Bovey.

East of the Exe

On the east side of the River Exe and only half an hour's drive from Exeter are the courses at Sidmouth and Budleigh Salterton (**East Devon**). Both are on fairly high ground providing panoramic views out to sea. **Sidmouth** is perhaps more of a typical clifftop course with well wooded fairways and 'springy' turf, while East Devon is a cross between downland and heathland with much heather and gorse. East Devon's delights are detailed ahead. Convenient for both courses at Ottery St Mary is the charming 18th century country house hotel, Salston Manor Hotel (01404) 815581 which also offers inclusive golf packages for the highly acclaimed **Woodbury Park**.

*Photograph courtesy of: **The Manor House Hotel & Golf Course Moretonhampstead***

different game from Newton Abbot's course at Stover where abundant heather, woods and a meandering brook are likely to pose the most challenges. A word too, on the course at **Hele Park** which has greens reputedly second to none, and most strongly recommended is the new **Dainton Park** course at Ipplepen. This challenging course features good use of water and an excellent clubhouse. Speaking of challenges, mention must also be made of the **Dartmouth** Golf and Country Club at Blackawton, Totnes.

One of the most pleasant and convenient places to stay in this area is the Orestone Manor House (01803) 328098 in Maidencombe. In Torquay itself, there are numerous fine hotels. The most famous hotel is the Imperial (01803) 294301, which offers all manner of splendid facilities but charges for it! The Palace Hotel (01803) 200200 is less costly, but courtesy still prevails. Perhaps the best value to be found is at Homers Hotel (01803) 213456 with its first class restaurant. Another to note is The Osborne (01803) 213311—an excellent establishment.

If you are still seeking an ideal 19th hole, the Quayside Hotel (01803) 855751 in the popular resort of Brixham is charming and the town retains a much quieter atmosphere than its neighbour across the bay. In Dartmouth, one restaurant merits special comment: the Carved Angel (01803) 832465—a must for lovers of truly outstanding cuisine. Just outside Dartmouth, in Dittisham, Fingals at Old Coombe Manor (01803) 722398 is well worth the short trip and finally the Holne Chase Hotel (01364) 631471 in Ashburton—a glorious setting with a fine restaurant to match.

The South Coast

Heading further down the coast, the picturesque village of **Thurlestone** has one of the most popular courses in Devon. It is a superb clifftop course with several far-reaching views along the coast, on a fine day there are few better places to be. **Bigbury** lies a short distance from Thurlestone and although perhaps a little less testing it is also attractive and looks across to Burgh Island, a favourite (or hopefully an ex-favourite) haunt of smugglers. Both Thurlestone and Bigbury can be reached from Plymouth via the A379, or from the Torbay region via the A381. The Thurlestone Hotel (01548) 560382 is a perfect base not only for playing the two nearby courses, but also for exploring what is a delightful part of Devon. It also has its own very pleasant short 9 hole course. The Village Inn is a spendid pub for a post–round beverage or two. Buckland-Tout-Saints (01548) 853055 at Kingsbridge is also worthy of inclusion on any itinerary. For lovers of a good pub the Pilchard on Burgh Island is one of the best—but beware the tide coming in! For a less pricey resting hole, the Hope and Anchor in Hope Cove is most welcoming. Salcombe with its essentially sailing fraternity offers a worthy distraction for non golfers around Plymouth.

Golfers in Plymouth are never far from **St Mellion**, just over the border in Cornwall. Also close to the great seafaring city, the **Elfordleigh Hotel's** (01752) 336428 9 hole golf course at Plympton is very pleasant—and not as demanding as the Nicklaus course! Towards Dartmoor, **Yelverton** is certainly one not to be missed. Designed by Herbert Fowler, the architect of Walton Heath, Yelverton lies midway between Plymouth and Tavistock on the A386. It is a classic moorland course and very attractive, with much gorse and heather.

Tavistock is also not far from Plymouth. **Tavistock** Golf Club is perhaps not as attractive as Yelverton, but worth a visit all the same. For good places to stay, the Prince Hall Hotel is a small friendly

Woodbury has a very challenging 18 hole championship course designed by Hamilton Stutt plus a shorter 9 hole course and driving range. Note the spectacular par three 18th hole here—arguably the most dramatic closing hole in the south west.

To the west of the Exe estuary, the friendly **Warren** Golf Club at Dawlish offers the only true links golf in South Devon. Laid out on a narrow hook-shaped peninsula and covered in gorse with numerous natural bunkers this is Devon's answer to St Andrews—and if this sounds a little far-fetched just inspect the aerial photographs at the 19th! It is a much improved course with an interesting finishing hole that will have the wayward hitter threatening both the members in the clubhouse and/or quite possibly the passengers on a passing London to Penzance 125. A fairly near neighbour of the Warren is **Teignmouth** Golf Club. It may be near, but Teignmouth offers a totally different challenge, being situated some 900 feet above sea level on Haldon Moor. Teignmouth can become shrouded in fog during the winter, but when all is clear, it's a very pleasant course and most attractive too.

Those seeking a memorable 19th hole on their way to the south coast may have sped past Gittisham—a mistake, for Combe House (01404) 540400 provides great elegance and style. In Sidmouth, the Riviera (01395) 515201 is grand, and concessionary green fees can be arranged locally. Just east of Sidmouth, the charming Masons Arms (01297) 680300 at Branscombe is perfect for a relaxing dinner and a stopover if required. In Dawlish Warren, most convenient for the golf links is the Langstone Cliff Hotel (01626) 865155 (just roll down the hill and you're almost there). Not too far from the many courses of east Devon at Hawkchurch, near Axminster, the comfortable Fairwater Head Hotel (01297) 678349 is recommended. Just to the north west of Newton Abbot in Haytor lies the Bel Alp House Country Hotel (01364) 661217, an elegant country house offering genuine tranquillity. Another local favourite, worthy of its popularity, is the Rock Inn (01364) 661305. Just outside Teignmouth, Ness House (01626) 873480 is a small hotel offering good value breaks for golfers and also recommended is the Coombe Bank Hotel (01626) 772369 . Finally, Thomas Luny House (01626) 772976 a small Georgian town house of delightful character is ideal for a group of gourmet golfers.

The three handiest courses for those holidaying in the Torbay area are probably **Churston**, **Torquay** and **Newton Abbot**. The first two mentioned offer typical downland/clifftop type golf and a very hotel in country house style while the Moorland Links Hotel (01822) 852245 at Yelverton needs little explanation and for a place to celebrate one's birdie at the 18th the Who'd of Thought It at Milton Combe sounds highly appropriate—an excellent pub which serves good value lunches.

North Devon

From Plymouth, the north coast of Devon is about an hour and a quarter's drive—from Exeter, a little less. Unless there is some urgency, a leisurely drive is recommended for the scenery is truly spectacular. A few suggestions for breaking the journey include Milton Damerel, where the Woodford Bridge (01409) 261481 is a pleasant hotel with good facilities for the sporty. Hatherleigh offers the handsome George Hotel (01837) 810454 and Clawton near Holdsworthy the delightful Court Barn (01409) 271219. Then there is Winkleigh, where the Kings Arms is a popular pub. Just beyond Winkleigh, towards Barnstaple, there is a fine 18 hole course at **Libbaton** near Umberleigh—again definitely worth breaking the journey for.

North Devon can boast one of the oldest golf clubs in England, the **Royal North Devon** Club at Westward Ho! It can also claim to have seen the lowest known score for eighteen holes of golf. In 1936 the Woolacombe Bay professional recorded a 55 on his home course—29 out and 26 back, including a hole in one at the last! As this took place on the 1st January, one cannot help wondering quite what he did the night before! Unfortunately, this course closed long ago although there are 9 holes at **Morthoe & Woolacombe** and also at **Willingcott Valley**. Both provide good holiday golf as does the very popular 18 hole test at nearby **Ilfracombe**. Situated several hundred feet above sea level, this latter course offers many outstanding views of the North Devon coastline. The best hole is the par four 13th and there is an interesting selection of par three holes, one of which, the 4th, is played across a plunging ravine but measures a mere 80 yards. Whilst in the area, two notable hotels for golfing breaks in Ilfracombe are St Brannochs House Hotel (01271) 863873 and the Elmfield (01271) 863377 while yet another very recent addition to the county's golfing scene is the **Hartland Forest** Country Club near the famous 'sleepy village' of Clovelly.

Both Saunton and Westward Ho! deserve more than a fleeting visit and are featured ahead. Westward Ho! is a place for pilgrimage, but **Saunton** provides the more modern championship challenge.

There are two fine courses at Saunton, the East (the championship course) and the greatly improved West. Large sandhills dominate both courses, and when the wind blows . . .

Sleeping in the dunes is out of bounds so here are a few ideas for the 19th. Visitors to the North Devon area should consider Foxdown Manor (01237) 451325 at Horns Cross and the Anchorage Hotel (01271) 860655. Yeolden House (01237) 474400 in Bideford comes highly recommended, while in Saunton Sands, the hotel of the same name is first class and popular with golfers (01271) 890212. A noted nearby eating place is Otters Restaurant (01271) 813633 in Braunton. The Preston House Hotel (01271) 890472 is also close to Saunton's links and is again very highly regarded by golfers. At Fairy Cross, near Bideford, the Portledge Hotel (01237) 451262 is for the lover of peace and quiet. In Northam the Durrant House Hotel (01237) 472361 is great for recuperating after an excursion to Westward Ho!

More thoughts? Recommendations are many and various: in Westward Ho! Culloden House (01237) 479421 is small but friendly and there is also the popular Buckleigh Lodge guesthouse (01237) 475988. The small town of Umberleigh provides yet more worthy country house establishments in the shape of Northcote Manor (01769) 560501 and the **Highbullen Hotel** (01769) 540561. A marvellous golf course and other leisure pursuits make this particularly appealing. Woolacombe offers the superb Woolacombe Bay Hotel (01271) 870388 (more first rate activities here) and the award-winning Watersmeet Hotel (01271) 870333. Then there is Penhaven Country House (01237) 451388, a lovely old rectory transformed into a hotel at Parkham near Bideford and the elegant Halmpstone Manor (01271) 830321 at Bishop's Tawton near Barnstaple.

A good eating place in the area is Knoll House Hotel (01271) 882548 in Kentishbury. For those who prefer to cater for themselves in one of the many pretty cottages that abound in Devon, Country Holidays (01282) 445566 and Western Country Cottages (01626) 333678 are both worth contacting.

A final thought as we leave North Devon—should it actually happen and for some peculiar reason you do get stranded in the dunes at Saunton, the chances are you will wake up to a glorious sunrise. If this is the case, let's just hope the morning's golf is equally spectacular.

VIEW OF THE CLUB HOUSE FROM BEHIND 1ST GREEN, EAST COURSE, SAUNTON GOLF CLUB Photograph courtesy of: **Saunton Golf Club**

Saunton

At a time when John H Taylor and Horace Hutchinson were striding the windswept fairways on Northam Burrows, across the Taw Estuary on the Braunton Burrows, other men were busy trapping rabbits. It took more than thirty years for matters to be put right.

Saunton Golf Club was founded in 1897, some three decades after Westward Ho! Like many great clubs, Saunton's beginnings were rather modest. At first there were only nine holes and the original clubhouse was a room next to the Post Office. The course was extended to 18 holes before the First World War (and a new clubhouse acquired) but it wasn't until after the war that Saunton's reputation gained momentum. Chiefly responsible was golf architect Herbert Fowler, who having reshaped Westward Ho! performed a similar task at Saunton.

In 1932 the course was selected to stage the British Ladies Championship and this was followed by the English Amateur Championship of 1937. Unfortunately the links didn't fare too well during the Second World War as it was considered the perfect place for a battle school and concrete and barbed wire covered the fairways. Reconstruction didn't begin until 1951, C K Cotton this time directing matters. Once restored the course quickly re-established itself as one of Britain's leading championship links. In the early seventies a second 18 holes were added and today the two are known as the East (the former 'Old Course') and the West Course. More recently during Saunton's centenary year it hosted the EGU's Brabazon Trophy, which was won by David Park and the R & A's Boys Championship won by Sergio Garcia both of whom have now successfully moved in the professional ranks.

The **Secretary/Manager** at Saunton is **Trevor Reynolds tel: (01271) 812436 or fax: (01271) 814241 e mail: trevor@sauntongolf.co.uk web site: www.sauntongolf.co.uk**. The **Professional Albert Mackenzie** can be contacted on **tel: (01271) 812013**. Green fees for 2000 are week days £40 per round or £60 per day with a lunch voucher included, week ends £50 per round or £75 a day again with a lunch voucher included. The club address is **Saunton Golf Club, Saunton, Braunton, Devon EX33 1LG**. When travelling by car follow the A361 from Barnstaple and pick up the B3231.

At 6729 yards, par 71 (SSS 73) from the championship tees, the East Course is some 300 yards longer than the West (6403 yards par 71) and it could hardly be described as one of those that breaks you in gently—the first four holes all measure over 400 yards. There are several notable par fours early in the round, but perhaps the best are the 12th, the 14th with its ever-narrowing fairway, and the 16th which demands a tee shot over a vast sandhill with the second needing to be carried over a deep bunker in front of the green.

On more than one occasion I have read that if Saunton had a different geography it would be an Open Championship venue. Maybe I'm missing the point, but I've never fully appreciated the 'geography' argument. Surely North Devon is no more remote than certain parts of the east and west coasts of Scotland—especially now that a motorway runs as far as Exeter (one hour's drive away). Attendance figures? Such is the popularity of golf in modern times it seems most unlikely that the crowds wouldn't flock to the area, and as for accommodation North Devon abounds with places to stay. Come to think of it, what better place for a week's holiday in July?

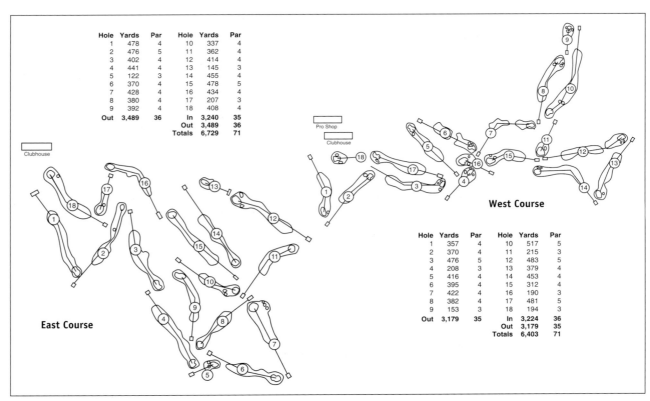

Hole	Yards	Par	Hole	Yards	Par
1	478	4	10	337	4
2	476	5	11	362	4
3	402	4	12	414	4
4	441	4	13	145	3
5	122	3	14	455	4
6	370	4	15	478	5
7	428	4	16	434	4
8	380	4	17	207	3
9	392	4	18	408	4
Out	**3,489**	**36**	**In**	**3,240**	**35**
			Out	**3,489**	**36**
			Totals	**6,729**	**71**

East Course

West Course

Hole	Yards	Par	Hole	Yards	Par
1	357	4	10	517	5
2	370	4	11	215	3
3	476	5	12	483	5
4	208	3	13	379	4
5	416	4	14	453	4
6	395	4	15	312	4
7	422	4	16	190	3
8	382	4	17	481	5
9	153	3	18	194	3
Out	**3,179**	**35**	**In**	**3,224**	**36**
			Out	**3,179**	**35**
			Totals	**6,403**	**71**

Preston House was built in 1895 as a summer home for the Christie family. Standing on the cliffs overlooking Bideford Bay towards Hartland point the views are stunning. Over a hundred years on, it still retains the character of a much loved home whilst offering its visitors an old world charm with some of the better trappings of the modern era.

The hotel itself has twelve rooms which are all en suite and individually designed with the comforts that you would expect from a country house hotel. A conservatory runs for the full length of south face of the house outside of which is a terrace. Both areas are ideal for enjoying the day's sunshine and watching the sun set in the evening. There is also a solar heated outdoor swimming pool to gently cool a warm day.

To start your day breakfast features home-made compote and marmalade along with smoked haddock, kippers and Cornish bacon and real sausages.

After a long day on the golf course you will return to the tranquillity of Preston House. Here you will find a well stocked bar and a comprehensive wine list at sensible prices. To replace a day's lost energies our menu features dishes such as marinated fillet of Cornish beef braised in red wine, a roasted best end of Welsh saltmarsh

Lamb or the best of the local fish. These, and a good selection of other dishes await to tempt you before trying a Cappuccino brulee, a wonderful sticky toffee pudding and local ice-cream or a selection of West Country cheeses. To round off a relaxing evening there is a wide range of liqueurs and brandies.

This part of North Devon is a haven for golfers of all abilities with many courses easily accessible. The twin delights of Saunton Golf Club are only minutes away, whilst a short drive will take players to Royal North Devon and, a little further to Burnham and Berrow. Also within easy reach are Ilfracombe, Willingcott Valley, Morthoe and Woolacombe, Highbullen and Hartland Forest. We are happy to make bookings on your behalf and can offer discounts at both Saunton and Royal North Devon.

The area surrounding Saunton offers the energetic superb walking, either on the costal footpath or on the miles of unspoilt beaches immediately beneath the hotel. Other activities including shooting, fishing, surfing, canoeing and sailing can also be arranged by the hotel.

Preston House enjoys a charm of years which have sadly passed and is the perfect place to stay for discerning golfers who are looking for quiet comfort.

PRESTON • HOUSE HOTEL

Preston House Hotel
Saunton
Braunton
North Devon
EX33 1LG
Tel: (01271) 890472
Fax: (01271) 890555
email: prestonhouse-saunton@zoom.co.uk
www.prestonhouse-hotel.co.uk

East Devon

Most clifftop courses are essentially downland or parkland in nature. Very often they are beautifully situated but the quality of the golf offered isn't quite out of the top drawer. East Devon at Budleigh Salterton is quite a rarity, for this is where heathland golf meets the sea. Laid out on cliffs some 250 to 400 feet above sea level, there are breathtaking views out to sea and along the South Devon coast in both directions. The views inland, mind you, are just as expansive, with the rolling Devon countryside presenting itself in all its glory.

But what is really special about East Devon is that the golf course takes full advantage of the location and the natural splendour of the terrain. East Devon is not as testing as somewhere like Walton Heath—it is not as long for a start—although at 6239 yards (par 70) it is not exactly short either, and the heather and gorse do not encroach to the point where they intimidate the golfer as on several of the south east's championship courses. However, variety and challenge present themselves at every hole. The layout is such that the course continually rises and falls, twists and turns. There are a couple of uphill drives and many dramatic downhill tee shots and there are some fine left and right dog-leg holes. Finally, there is the all year round quality of the putting surfaces—the best in Devon many players reckon—and for this the club must thank its excellent green keeper, who in turn must thank Mother Nature.

Probably the most outstanding sequence of holes at East Devon comes between the 6th and the 9th. What makes the par five 6th so spectacular is the choice facing the golfer after a good drive. The fairway narrows all the way to the green, out of bounds lurks to the right, thick woodland menaces to the left and if that isn't sufficiently fear-inducing, then twenty yards short of the green is a natural gulley full of humps and hillocks. The sensible shot is to lay up but the devil-may-care golfer will not be able to resist the challenge.

After a short walk through the woods, the magnificent back tee for the 7th is reached. The tree-lined fairway dog-legs sharply to the left 50 feet below and you can't see the green as you drive. The approach is slightly uphill and the amphitheatre-like green is protected by a mischievously placed deep bunker. The next hole is a tough par three measuring over 200 yards—miss the green to the right here and a par will be a major achievement. The 9th tumbles 450 yards downhill all the way and is perhaps the best of many exhilarating downhill holes at Budleigh. In 1934, a player actually drove to the edge of the green.

**East Devon Golf Club, North View Road
Budleigh Salterton, Devon EX9 6DQ**

Secretary	Mr R Burley (01395) 443370
	Fax (01395) 445547
Professional	Trevor Underwood (01395) 445195
Green Fees	WD£27/round; £35/day
	WE £35/round; £42/day
Restrictions	Proof of handicap required

Directions
The course is on the Exmouth side of Budleigh Salterton on the A376. Avoid driving through Exmouth by picking up the B3179 at Clyst St George. From the north use the A3025 Lyme Regis-Exeter road, exiting just north of Sidmouth.

1ST GREEN, WEST COURSE, SAUNTON GOLF COURSE Photograph courtesy of: **Saunton Golf Course**

Royal North Devon (Westward Ho!)

This is a club truly steeped in the history of the game. Westward Ho!, as it is commonly known, was the first English links course and being founded in 1864 the Royal North Devon Golf Club lays claim to being the oldest English club still playing over its original land. Furthermore it boasts the oldest Ladies Golf Club in the world, the Westward Ho! Ladies Golf Club, which was established in 1868. Originally designed by Tom Morris, and reconstructed by Herbert Fowler, the 18 holes are situated on Northam Burrows. The Burrows is a vast, exposed and relatively flat area of common land which stretches along the coast a couple of miles north of Bideford between Westward Ho! and Appledore.

Several of Britain's historic courses, particularly those in Scotland, have fascinating ties with common land and associated local rights which have existed since 'time immemorial', but whilst the inhabitants of St Andrews no longer use their hallowed turf for practising archery nor put their washing out to dry on the banks of the Swilcan Burn, the locals of Northam village still graze their sheep and horses on the Burrows.

There can surely be no other championship course in the world where you can have teed up on the first, taken a few steps backward to survey the drive ahead only to see a sheep wander up and peer inquisitively at your ball! One shouldn't get too alarmed though, the animals are well-versed in the etiquette of the game—they generally keep a respectful distance from the fairways and greens, they take care not to bleat when you putt and what's more they certainly won't contemplate stealing your golf ball as I'm told the crows do at Royal Aberdeen.

Seriously, golf at Westward Ho! is a rich experience and given the warm welcome visitors receive, definitely to be recommended. The **Secretary, Mr Bob Fowler**, can be contacted via **The Royal North Devon Golf Club, Golf Links Road, Westward Ho! Bideford, Devon EX39 1HD, tel: (01237) 473817.**

If you are considering a trip to the club you may find it advisable to telephone first in order to check if any tee reservations have been made. Fine weather can make the course particularly popular during the holiday season but it is now possible to pre-book a starting time. Societies are also welcomed and bookings can be arranged with the Secretary. In 2000 a green fee of £30 midweek (£36 at weekends) entitles the visitor to a single round with £36 midweek (£40 at weekends) payable for a full day's golf. The green fee for juniors is halved. The club's **Professional** is **Richard Herring**, who can be reached by telephone on **(01237) 477598.**

The course can be approached from both East and West via the A39, although travellers from the West may be able to avoid the busy town of Bideford by joining the B3236 near Abbotsham. Visitors travelling from the Dartmoor region should take the A386 road which runs from Okehampton to Bideford, whilst those coming from Exeter should follow the A377 to Barnstaple, thereafter joining the A39 as above.

From the championship tees the course measures 6653 yards, par 71 and is divided into two fairly equal halves. Westward Ho! has a traditional 'out and back' layout and there are some panoramic views across Bideford Bay, especially from the 6th tee where, on a clear day, the Isle of Lundy can be seen. In theory, the links receives a degree of protection from the elements from a large bank of shingle which separates the Burrows from the beach. I say 'in theory' for this is surely one of Britain's most windswept courses. However, the wind is not the only factor that can make scoring extremely difficult. There are numerous ditches and hidden pot bunkers, there is also the famous Cape bunker at the 4th (at least 100 yards wide) and then of course, there are the Great Sea Rushes. To the uninitiated a word of caution—these giant marshland reeds, unique to Westward Ho!, can literally impale golf balls, so do as the sheep do—stay clear!

Westward Ho! is not only known for its golf course, it has literary fame as well. The village was founded a year before the golf club and was named after Charles Kingsley's adventure novel about Elizabethan seafarers. A decade or so later Rudyard Kipling attended the local college and remembered his days there in Stalky and Co. Alas, there is no record to suggest that Mr Kipling was an exceedingly good golfer but while he was studying, a young boy from Northam was out on the course caddying for sixpence a round.

The boy was destined to become Open Champion on five occasions. John H Taylor learnt his game at Westward Ho! and his great affection for the club remained throughout his long life. In 1957 the club elected him their President.

In addition to a friendly atmosphere, the clubhouse offers some excellent catering. It also houses the club's museum. It is most interesting and contains a great variety of golfing memorabilia.

For the golfer who has confined himself to playing on gentle parkland fairways, sheltered from any wind by tall trees, a visit to Westward Ho! would probably create quite a shock to the system. But clearly, for those with even a moderate interest in the history of the game and, of course, who are not afraid of a stiff challenge, Westward Ho! is a golfing must.

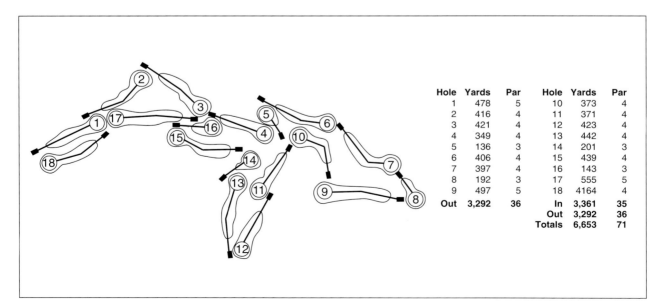

Hole	Yards	Par	Hole	Yards	Par
1	478	5	10	373	4
2	416	4	11	371	4
3	421	4	12	423	4
4	349	4	13	442	4
5	136	3	14	201	3
6	406	4	15	439	4
7	397	4	16	143	3
8	192	3	17	555	5
9	497	5	18	4164	4
Out	**3,292**	**36**	**In**	**3,361**	**35**
			Out	**3,292**	**36**
			Totals	**6,653**	**71**

Ashbury G.C.
(01837) 55453
Fowley Cross, Okehampton
(18) 5839 yards/***/D

Axe Cliff G.C.
(01297) 24371
Squires Lane, Axmouth,
(18) 5057 yards/***/C/H

Bigbury G.C.
(01548) 810207
Bigbury-on-Sea, Kingsbridge
(18) 6076 yards/***/C/H

Chulmleigh G.C.
(01769) 580519
Leigh Road, Chulmleigh
(18) 1450 yards/***/E

Churston G.C.
(01803) 842751
Churston, nr Brixham
(18) 6201 yards/***/B/H/M

Clovelly G.& C.C.
(01237) 431442
East Yagland, Wolsery, Bideford
(9) 5641 yards/***/D

Dainton Park G.C.
(01803) 813812
Totnes Road, Newton Abbot
(18) 6210 yards/***/D

Dartmouth G.& C.C.
(01803) 712650
Blackawton, Totnes
(18)7191 yards/***/B/H
(9) 2583 yards/***/D/H

Dinnaton G.C.
(01752) 892512
Ivybridge
(9) 4100 yards/***/D/H

Downes Crediton G.C.
(01363) 774464
Hookway, Crediton
(18) 5958 yards/***/C/H/M

Easewell Farm Holiday Park
(01271) 870225
Woolacombe
(9) 2426 yards/***/E

East Devon G.C.
(01395) 443370
North View Road, Budleigh Salterton
(18) 6239 yards/***/B/H

Elfordleigh Hotel G.& C.C.
(01752) 336428
Colebrook, Plympton, Plymouth
(9) 5664 yards/**/C

Exeter G. & C.C.
(01392) 874139
Countess Wear, Exeter
(18) 6000 yards/**/C

Fingle Glen G. & C.C.
(01647) 61817
Tedburn St Mary, Exeter
(9) 2466 yards/***/D

Hartland Forest G.C.
(01237) 431442
Woolsery, Bideford
(18) 6015 yards /***/F

Hele Park Golf Centre
(01626) 336060
Ashburton Road, Newton Abbot
(9) 2469 yards/***/E

Highbullen Hotel
(01769) 540561
Chittlehamolt
(9) 2210 yards/***/F

Holsworthy G.C.
(01409) 253177
Kilatree, Holsworthy
(18) 6062 yards/***/D

Honiton G.C.
(01404) 44422
Middlehills, Honiton
(18) 5940 yards/***/C/H/M

Hurdwick G.C.
(01822) 612746
Tavistock Hamlets, Tavistock
(18) 4861 yards/***/C

Ilfracombe G.C.
(01271) 862176
Hele Bay, Ilfracombe
(18) 5893 yards/***/D/H

Libbaton G.C.
(01769) 560269
High Bickington, Umberleigh
(18) 5812 yards/***/D

Manor House Hotel
(01647) 440998
Moretonhampstead
(18) 6016 yards/***/B/H

Morthoe & Woolacombe
(01271) 870225
Morthoe, Ilfracombe
(9) 4852 yards/***/E

Newton Abbot (Stover) G.C.
(01626) 352460
Bovey Road, Newton Abbot
(18) 5899 yards/***/C/H

Okehampton G.C.
(01837) 52113
off Tors Road, Okehampton
(18) 5300 yards/***/F/H

Padbrook Park G.C.
(01884) 38286
Cullompton
(9) 6108 yards/***/E

Royal North Devon G.C.
(01237) 473817
Golf Links Road, Westward Ho!
(18) 6653 yards/***/B/H

Saunton G.C.
(01271) 812436
Saunton, nr Braunton
(18) 6729 yards/***/A/H
(18) 6403 yards/***/A/H

Sidmouth G.C.
(01395) 516407
Peak Hill, Cotmaton Road,
(18) 5109 yards/***/D

Sparkwell G.C.
(01752) 837219
Blacklands, Sparkwell, Plymouth
(9) 5772 yards/***/E

Staddon Heights G.C.
(01752) 402475
Staddon Heights, Plymstock
(18) 5681 yards/***/D/H

Tavistock G.C.
(01822) 612344
Down Road, Tavistock
(18) 6250 yards/***/C

Teignmouth G.C.
(01626) 772894
Exeter Road, Teignmouth
(18) 6227 yards/***/C/H/M

Teign Valley Golf Club
(01647) 253026
Christow, nr Exeter
(18) 5900 yards/***/D

Thurlestone G.C.
(01548) 560405
Thurlestone, nr Kingsbridge
(18) 6340 yards/***/C/H/M

Tiverton G.C.
(01884) 252187
Post Hill, Tiverton
(18) 6236 yards/***/B/H/M

Torquay G.C.
(01803) 314591
Petitor Road, St Mary Church
(18) 6198 yards/***/C/H

Torrington G.C.
(01805) 622229
Weare Trees, Torrington
(9) 4419 yards/***/D

Warren G.C.
(01626) 862255
Dawlish Warren, Dawlish
(18) 5968 yards/***/C/H

Waterbridge G.C.
(01363) 85111
Down St Mary
(9) 3910 yards /***/E

Welbeck Manor G.C.
(01752) 837219
Sparkwell
(9) 2886 yards /***/E

Willincott Valley G.C.
(01271) 870173
Woolacombe
(9) 6012 yards /***/E

Woodbury Park G.C.
(01395) 233382
Woodbury Castle, Woodbury,
(18) 6707 yards/***/C

Wrangaton G.C.
(01364) 73229
Golf Links Road, Wrangaton
(18) 6040 yards/***/C/H

Yelverton G.C.
(01822) 852824
Golf Links Road, Yelverton
(18) 6363 yards/***/F/H/M

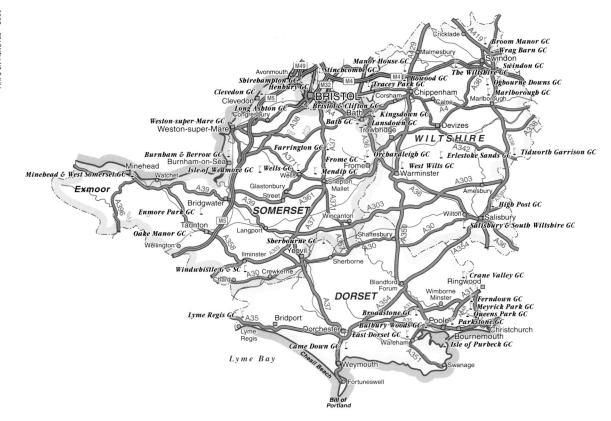

Somerset, Dorset & Wiltshire Choice Golf

From the wild beauty of Exmoor to the mystery of Stonehenge; the Quantocks and the Mendips; Lyme Regis and Bath; Avebury, Chesil Beach and Lulworth Cove. The West Country offers so much, no wonder those of us who do not live there are more than a little envious. The golf too can be equally spectacular. There may not be a Wentworth or a St George's here but the region offers a considerable variety and there is certainly no shortage of challenge. There is a true championship links at Burnham and Berrow and a magnificent heathland-cum-clifftop course at the Isle of Purbeck. Excellent downland golf can be enjoyed at Long Ashton and Bath while Bournemouth offers some majestic heathland and parkland type courses. We shall tee off in Somerset.

Coastal Somerset

Burnham and Berrow (featured ahead) is without doubt the finest course in the county and the place where John H Taylor wielded his famous mashie to great effect. The two holiday towns of **Minehead** and **Weston-Super-Mare** house the region's other two links courses. The **Minehead and West Somerset** Golf Club has more than a hundred years of history—it therefore remembers the quieter days in the years 'Before Butlins'. A fairly flat and windy course, it is situated on the eastern side of the town. Visitors are welcome, though during the peak season a quick telephone call to the club is advisable. The same can be said of Weston—a slightly longer, well maintained course, located just off the main A370 Bristol road.

After an arduous day's golf at Burnham, visitors can find more than adequate accommodation in the club's Dormy House. Some quite incredible steaks are served in the clubhouse: 'worth killing for!' according to one of my mashie wielding friends. Two recommended guesthouses to try in Burnham-on-Sea are the Warren Guest House (01278) 786726 and the Lulworth Guesthouse (01278) 784015, while further up the scale, between Burnham and Weston the Batch Farm

Country Hotel (01934) 750371 comes highly recommended. Weston has a number of hotels with the Grand Atlantic situated on the seafront (01934) 626543 the town's most vaunted hostelry. The Gascony (01643) 705939 and the Alcombe House Hotel (01643) 705130 are also suitable resting places, whilst slightly farther afield, try the Luttrell Arms (01643) 821555 in Dunster—a creeper–clad hotel of some historical note. Exmoor House (01643) 821268 is also an excellent port of call. Heading further north, **Clevedon** stares spectacularly out across the mouth of the Severn. Clevedon is a cliff top course rather than a links and is well worth visiting.

Bristol

By travelling inland from Clevedon towards Bristol along the B3128, two of the city's best courses are reached before the famous suspension bridge. **Long Ashton** is immediately off the B3128, while to find **Bristol and Clifton** a left turn should be taken along the B3129. There is probably little to choose between the two, both being particularly attractive examples of downland golf. **Henbury** Golf Club is closer to the centre of Bristol, about three miles to the north in the quiet suburb of Westbury-on-Trym. Henbury is a mature parkland course with an abundance of trees, making for some very attractive and challenging holes. One final club to recommend in Bristol is **Shirehampton**—always beautifully maintained.

Perhaps one of the most stylish hotel in Bristol is the aptly named Grand Hotel (0117) 929 1645 on Broad Street. Two recommended restaurants are Harveys (0117) 927 5034 and Restaurant Lettonie (01225) 446676 in Stoke Bishop. An excellent base towards the north of the city at Thornbury is the Tudor-style Thornbury Castle (01454) 281182.

Anyone travelling from Bath to Bristol is likely to pass within a few miles of the **Tracy Park** Golf and Country Club at Wick. If possible, a detour is recommended. Tracy Park is a newish course, built in the mid-seventies around a 400 year old mansion which acts as a rather impressive clubhouse. Although the course can get a little soggy in winter it offers a very good test of golf.

Bath and Wells

Everybody, they say, falls in love with Bath—the Romans did, the Georgians did and the Americans think it's cute. For visiting golfers, if the other half should come under the spell, the City has two attractive propositions: **Bath** Golf Club and **Lansdown** Golf Club. The former, commonly known as Sham Castle because of its situation adjacent to Bath's greatest fraud (there is a beautiful castle frontage but nothing else!) is laid out high above the city and provides tremendous views over the surrounding countryside. Lansdown occupies flatter ground adjacent to Bath racecourse.

Staying in Bath can be a sheer delight. The hotels in the city are among some of the finest in the country. Bath Spa (01225) 444424 and the Royal Crescent (01225) 823333 take pride of place but the Apsley House (01225) 336966, the Paradise House Hotel (01225) 317723 and the Priory (01225) 331922 can also be recommended with total confidence. The hotels themselves house excellent restaurants but other popular eating places in Bath include the Clos du Roy (01225) 444450 and the Hole in the Wall (01225) 425242. There is no shortage of guesthouses in and around Bath (the city does become incredibly busy in the summer—be warned!) while deeper in the countryside are a number of other outstanding establishments. Ston Easton Park (01761) 241631 boasts a considerable reputation as does Hunstrete House (01761) 490490. Another gem is the Homewood Park Hotel (01225) 723731 in Hinton Charterhouse. North of Bath the marvellously named Old Sodbury offers the charming Sodbury House Hotel (01454) 312847 and the Cross Hands Hotel (01454) 313000, and Dunkirk provides the Petty France Hotel (01454) 238361. Just outside Bath at Colerne is Lucknam Park (01225) 742777 a delightful early 18th century mansion converted into an hotel. Close by, near Corsham, is the stylish Rudloe Park Hotel (01225) 810555.

Travelling towards Wells, the **Mendip** Golf Club at Gurney Slade offers possibly the most spectacular vistas of any course in the south west. From its 4th fairway, almost 1000 feet above sea level, on a clear day it is possible to sight the Cotswolds and the Quantocks, the Welsh Mountains and the Purbeck Hills, Glastonbury Tor and Westbury's White Horse—need I go on? Mendip is an enjoyable course and very visitor-friendly. An agreeable pub to note in Gurney Slade

is the George Inn. There is also an unmissable new golf complex at Farrington Gurney. Designed by Peter Thomson, **Farrington** provides not only a challenging 18 hole course but also a 'state of the art' 9 hole executive' layout. The city of Wells is always worth inspecting. The cathedral is splendid and after a round on the **Wells** golf course a pleasant lunch can be enjoyed at Ritcher's (01749) 679085.

The Wiltshire Border

Travelling east, right on the border with Dorset, at Frome are two interesting new golf facilities, the attractive parkland course at the **Frome Golf Centre** and the splendid par 72 Brian Huggett designed course at **Orchardleigh**.

Along the M5

Just north of Bridgwater is the attractive new 18 hole parkland layout at the **Isle of Wedmore** Golf Club. More golf is found near Bridgwater at **Enmore Park**, located to the south of the town. The course enjoys a delightful setting and nestles around the foothills of the Quantocks. The White House Hotel (01984) 632306 at Williton is convenient for the golf club. Taunton's new course **Oake Manor** Golf Club is also well worth a visit with water hazards on ten holes.

In Taunton, the Castle (01823) 272671 is an outstanding place to stay and nearby The Mount Somerset in Lower Henlade (01823) 442500 is also a worthy suggestion. For the more energetically minded, the Cedar Falls Health Farm (01823) 433233 at Bishops Lydeard makes it all the easier to indulge elsewhere. In Yeovil, the Manor Hotel (01935) 423116 is very handy for Sherborne Golf Club over the border in Dorset.

Further south, and right on the Dorset border, is the magnificently titled **Windwhistle** Golf and Squash Club at Chard. The golf course is another laid out on high ground and offering extensive views. It's also close to the famous Cricket St Thomas Wildlife Park, where birdies and eagles abound.

North Dorset

The better golf courses in Dorset lie within a ten mile radius of the centre of Bournemouth. Having said that, **Sherborne** in the far north of the county is undoubtedly one of the prettiest inland courses to be found anywhere in Britain. In nearby Gillingham, you can stay at the Stock Hill House Hotel (01747) 823626 which comes with our highest recommendation and boasts an excellent restaurant to boot. Also, in Evershot, the Summer Lodge (01935) 83424 is a fine restaurant within a delightful country house hotel, and in Sturminster Newton stands Plumber Manor (01258) 472507 a gorgeous country house with most outstanding fare.

South West Dorset

Lyme Regis, famed for its fossils and more recently its French Lieutenant's Woman, has a fairly hilly 18 hole course which lies to the east of the town. The road between Lyme Regis and Weymouth provides dramatic views over Chesil Beach and passes through some of the most beautiful villages in England. The area north of Weymouth is Thomas Hardy country. Dorchester stands in the middle of it all and **Came Down** Golf Club is well worth noting when in these parts. Yalbury Cottage (01305) 262382 in Lower Bockhampton offers good accommodation and the countryside has remained gloriously unspoilt. In Lyme Regis, the Alexandra (01297) 442010 is a good bet.

MEYRICK PARK *Photograph courtesy of:* **Clubhaus**

En route to the minor golfing mecca of Bournemouth are the excellent two Martin Hawtree designed courses at the **East Dorset** complex near Wareham.

Around Bournemouth

The **Isle of Purbeck** and **Ferndown** are featured ahead but **Parkstone** and **Broadstone** also fall in the 'must be visited' category. They are beautiful heathland courses with much heather, gorse and pine trees and each is kept in immaculate condition. In addition to a game on one or more of these great courses, there are a handful of other easier to play courses around Bournemouth and Poole, including the **Bulbury Woods** Golf Club at Lytchett Matravers west of Poole and the newer **Crane Valley** course at Verwood, north of Ferndown. Bournemouth's public courses shouldn't be overlooked either: **Meyrick Park** is very good while **Queens Park** is often described as the finest public course in England.

The Bournemouth—Poole—Swanage area abounds with hotels and restaurants. Here are just a few suggestions: in Bournemouth, the Langtry Manor (01202) 553887, the Swallow Highcliff (01202) 557702, Royal Bath (01202) 555555 and the Hotel Collingwood (01202) 557575 are all good. In Poole, the Mansion House (01202) 685666 and its first class restaurant are recommended as is the outstanding Haven Hotel (01202) 707333. Swanage offers the Pines (01929) 425211 and Christchurch, Splinters Brasserie (01202) 483454. Ferndown golfers can look to the comfortable Dormy Hotel (01202) 872121 and Parkstone players can enjoy superb food at both Isabels (01202) 747885 and the Warehouse Brasserie on the quay (01202) 677238. People wishing to get away from the sea and sand, or the water hazards and bunkers should visit Tarrant Monkton and the popular Langton Arms (01258) 830225, where a converted stables makes for a really splendid little restaurant with some good value accommodation.

North Wiltshire

A decade ago there were only a dozen or so golf courses in Wiltshire, now there are over two dozen. Perhaps the two developments that have attracted most attention are the Dave Thomas designed championship course at **Bowood**, just off the A4 between Calne and Chippenham, and the dramatic layout at Castle Combe (now named the **Manor House** Golf Club) located to the north west of Chippenham, the handiwork of Peter Alliss and Clive Clark. Two very different courses, Bowood and the Manor House are both explored ahead. Recommended places to stay naturally include the Manor House (01249) 782206, situated within the 'prettiest village in England', while for Bowood any of the establishments mentioned

for Bath should prove convenient. There is also the outstanding Queenwood Golf Lodge (01249) 822228, an exclusive Georgian 5 star standard home which sits nestled in the heart of the course. Packages begin from £800 per night for upto 8 persons including unlimited golf, tea on arrival, a 3 course dinner and breakfast. Queenwood Lodge is locally known as the 'celebrity hideout'.

In Wooton Bassett, just west of Swindon, Alliss and Clark have constructed another course now called the **Wiltshire**, thus giving Swindon's golfers three courses close to the town. The two others are **Broome Manor** and **Wrag Barn**, both worth a visit. At **Ogbourne St George** is an undulating, downland type course, **Ogbourne Downs** (formerly the Swindon Club) designed by J H Taylor and very typical of the county's more established courses.

Swindon is one of the fastest growing towns in the British Isles. In Blunsdon the charming Blunsdon House (01793) 721701 offers extensive leisure facilities. The Robin Hood Inn at Ogbourne St George is very handy after a game at Swindon. **Marlborough** Golf Club is a near neighbour of Swindon Golf Club, being situated to the north west of the town on the Marlborough Downs. It offers similarly wide ranging views (and is similarly breezy!). The Castle and Ball (01672) 512201 in Marlborough is an ideal 19th—it offers good food in addition to reasonably priced accommodation. Also worth a visit is the Ivy House (01672) 515333. A pleasant drive westwards will take you to Lacock near Chippenham where the Sign of the Angel (01249) 730230 is a tremendous 15th century inn and, still further west, there is a reasonable golf course at **Kingsdown**.

South Wiltshire

Dropping down the county, the **West Wilts** Golf Club at Warminster, is very well established, the new 'pay and play' **Erlestoke Sands** course, south west of Devizes is popular and t'other side of Stonehenge, **Tidworth Garrison** is certainly one of Wiltshire's top courses. It lies on Salisbury Plain and is owned by the Army. (Note the excellent Antrobus Arms (01980) 623163 in nearby Amesbury). Salisbury offers two fine challenges, to the north, High Post and to the south west Salisbury and South Wilts. In the days before Bowood and the Manor House appeared on the county's ever-changing golf map **High Post** was generally considered to be the leading course in the county. It's another classic downland type. **Salisbury & South Wilts** golf course offers some splendid views of Salisbury's cathedral. One's best base near Salisbury is probably either the Rose and Crown Hotel (01722) 327908 at Harnham or Milford Hall (01722) 417411 in Castle Street.

BOWOOD GOLF CLUB *Photograph courtesy of:* ***Bowood Golf Club***

Burnham and Berrow

Iwonder how many people have travelled along the M5 between Bristol and Exeter and wondered what lay beyond the great Iron Age fort midway between Weston-super-Mare and Bridgwater that rises out of level ground, like something from out of 'Close Encounters'. Well, many golfers will know that a short distance behind the great hill lies one of England's finest links courses.

Burnham and Berrow appeared on the golfing map in 1891 and the first professional the club engaged was no lesser a man than John H Taylor. The great man was then in fact a lad of 19 although within three years he was to win the Open Championship at Sandwich—the first of his five victories. John Henry thought very highly of what, until quite recently, had been a 'wild rabbit infested waste of sandhills' for he said it was here, at Burnham, that he was 'given the splendid opportunity of developing my mashie play' (as the course) 'necessitated very accurate approach play.'

The present day visitor to the North Somerset club is most unlikely to confront a gathering of wild rabbits (at least of the animal variety) nor, one assumes, will he possess a mashie amongst his armoury. However, despite a number of alterations made over the years, the towering sandhills remain by far the course's most dominant feature.

Not surprisingly, Burnham and Berrow is a popular course and whatever the time of year visitors would be wise to telephone the club before setting off. **Mrs E L Sloman** is the **Secretary** and she can be contacted on **tel: (01278) 785760, fax: (01278) 795440.** The club's **Professional, Mark Crowther-Smith,** can be reached on **(01278) 784545.** Those interested in organising a society meeting are advised to write to the Secretary, the club's full address being, **Burnham and Berrow Golf Club, St Christopher's Way, Burnham-on-Sea, Somerset TA8 2PE.**

Green fees for 2000 are set at £38 for weekdays and £50 at weekends, fees being payable in the clubhouse. For juniors the fees are half the above rates. Furthermore, in addition to the 18 hole championship course there is also an adjacent 9 hole course situated alongside the sea. Whilst not quite up to the standard of the full championship course, at 3275 yards, par 36, it certainly represents a fine challenge and the green fee of £10 represents excellent value.

Approaching by car from both north and south the M5 is the most direct route, leaving at exit 22, then follow the B3140. The course is situated about a mile north of Burnham-on-Sea.

Right from the 1st hole the premium on accuracy becomes apparent. Anything short of a straight tee shot will leave a blind, not to mention very awkward second. At one time the layout of the course demanded the playing of several blind shots. However, today, accurate driving will largely eliminate such difficulties although on a number of holes the base of the flagstick will not be visible when playing the approach shot. As he or she stands on the 1st green, two features, in addition to the omnipresent sandhills, will strike the first time visitor. One is the condition of the greens which are quite superb; the other is the surrounding tangling rough—buckthorn it's called—avoid it like the plague! Burnham's 2nd is a good straight hole played from an elevated tee, whereas the 3rd, at least from the back, is one of those 'bite-off-as-much-as-you-dare' holes with the fairway dog-legging sharply to the left towards a sunken punchbowl green. From the 4th tee there is the first of several panoramic views of the Bristol Channel and distant Wales as the course moves nearer the sea. There are two strong par threes on the front nine, the 5th and the excellent 9th, which is one of the finest short holes to be found anywhere.

On reaching the turn anyone claiming to have mastered the large sandhills may well have to eat his words after playing the 10th, where a minor mountain must be carried from the tee and there is a severe drop away to the right—be warned! If the front nine is perhaps the more interesting of the halves, the second nine is probably the more testing. The 11th is a long par four and the 12th and 13th require very precise second shots. Both the short holes are exceptionally tricky and the 18th needs a couple of mighty big hits if it is to be reached in two.

Visitors should find the clubhouse atmosphere pleasantly informal. Catering is of a high standard and is offered daily between the hours of 11am and 6pm. Visitors might also wish to note the club's dormy house which can sleep eight.

Burnham and Berrow is a friendly club and well worth a visit. Clearly the message to all golfers who pass down the M5 oblivious to what goes on beyond the great hump is, quite simply, come on over!

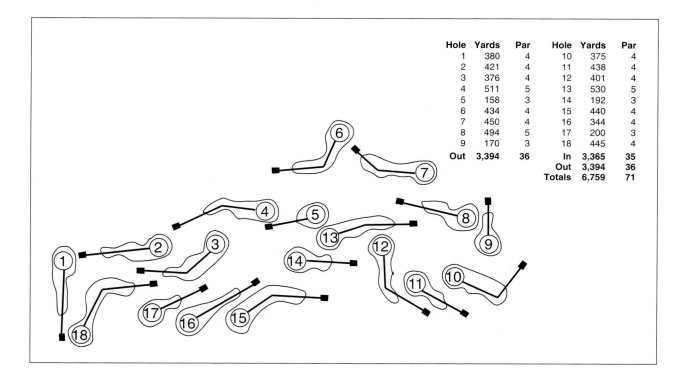

Hole	Yards	Par	Hole	Yards	Par
1	380	4	10	375	4
2	421	4	11	438	4
3	376	4	12	401	4
4	511	5	13	530	5
5	158	3	14	192	3
6	434	4	15	440	4
7	450	4	16	344	4
8	494	5	17	200	3
9	170	3	18	445	4
Out	**3,394**	**36**	**In**	**3,365**	**35**
			Out	**3,394**	**36**
			Totals	**6,759**	**71**

Bowood

The Golden Gate Bridge may lead you to San Francisco but the Golden Gates will lead you to Bowood. And Bowood is everything that California is not. Of all the great English country estates that in recent years have found the charms of the Royal and Ancient game impossible to resist, the development at Bowood seems destined to emerge as one of the best—best in terms of the quality and range of facilities and best in terms of the quality and condition of its 18 hole championship layout.

Notwithstanding the magnificently grand entrance to the Golf and Country Club—the above mentioned Golden Gates—there is nothing exclusive, or certainly no air of exclusivity, about Bowood. The atmosphere is extremely relaxed and informal and while there are golf club members at Bowood, visitors are actively encouraged seven days a week, with the exception of Saturday and Sunday mornings. The 19th hole facilities (the clubhouse is a beautifully restored 18th century farmhouse) include an extensive golf academy, incorporating three practice holes and a driving range.

Bowood is something of a rarity these days—a modern championship length golf course with a refreshingly unpretentious design. Architect Dave Thomas has not attempted to trade Wiltshire for Palm Springs, as one suspects many of his fellow designers might have tried to do. Lancelot 'Capability' Brown was the original architect of Bowood and surely he would have turned in his grave at any suggestion of deference to the American way! Water is a feature of the design but it doesn't lead the design, indeed it tends to frame rather than shape those holes where it is present. Each of the 18 holes certainly has an individual flavour and there is plenty of variety to accompany the subtlety of the challenge. Moreover there is a great feeling of space at Bowood—none of the holes encroaches on another and with the gentle mounding and graded rough there is considerable definition to each hole. There are some nice touches too, such as the additional putting green beside the 1st tee, and the huge double green shared by the 5th and 14th holes.

Subtlety aside for a moment, if there are two holes at Bowood that could be said to 'take your breath away' then they are the par four 8th and the par four 11th where on each a downhill tee shot must be perfectly positioned to open up a sharply dog-legging fairway. For my money, however, the real strength of Bowood is to be found in its outstanding quartet of par five holes, namely the 3rd, 4th, 10th and 15th, and in its superb closing hole, where a deft approach is required to find a well protected and well-contoured putting surface.

Bowood plays host to the European Challenge Tour Championship in 2000.

**Bowood Golf & Country Club,
Calne, Wiltshire SN11 9PQ
www.bowoodestate.co.uk**

| Head Professional | Max Taylor (01249) 822228
Fax (01249) 822218 |
|---|---|
| Green Fees | £34/18 holes; £40/27 holes;
£45/36 holes |
| Restrictions | No visitors before 1pm at weekends |

Directions
The course is 10 miles south of M4 junction 17 where the A4 meets the A432.

The Manor House (Castle Combe)

'Invest in land' Mark Twain advised, 'they're not building any more of it'. What value then, an area of dramatically rolling countryside bordering the beautiful Wiltshire village of Castle Combe? We are certainly talking about a very special place; it is the kind that if, some years ago, you were a golfer idly wandering across the land (daydreaming about your favourite pastime!) you would doubtless have sighed to yourself, 'my, what a marvellous setting this would make for a golf course!' Some daydreams can come true.

The Manor House Golf Club at Castle Combe opened in 1992, the 18 hole golf course that now winds its way through this spectacular piece of property was designed by Peter Alliss and Clive Clark. Not only does it make the most of the terrain (more of which later) but it genuinely 'accommodates' it. I choose this word because the golf course was never allowed to impose itself on the land and enormous care was taken at all stages of the development to preserve, and indeed encourage the natural flora and fauna and the abundant wildlife that inhabits the surrounding countryside.

At 6340 yards, par 73 from the back tees, Castle Combe is not a long course by the standards of many new 'high profile' layouts, but then added length is probably the last thing that this course needs. It opens with a relatively straightforward hole but the tempo immediately changes with the first of five really good par threes. Precision is vital at each of these short holes for the bad stroke is seriously punished. The 3rd is a classic par five, a genuine three shot hole where the terrain tumbles away from the tee in tiers to a far off island fairway; the second shot must somehow avoid a large tree, a stream and a small lake and then the approach is uphill to a green surrounded by sand. If the 3rd is the most memorable hole on the front nine, then the 7th, a beautifully curving, tree-lined par five is technically its equal.

The second nine at Castle Combe contains an even greater selection of hazards and outstanding holes. The sequence between the 11th (a stunning short hole where the tee shot must carry a little brook to find an angled green) and the par four 14th where there are two distinct options from the tee, is superb. Then comes the extraordinary finish with the vertigo-inducing par three 17th and intimidating par four 18th with its beautifully landscaped greenside lake.

The inhabitants of Castle Combe can not only claim that they reside in 'the prettiest village in England' but its golf club members can justifiably boast that they preside over 'the prettiest finish in England'.

**The Manor House Golf Club, Castle Combe,
Wiltshire SN14 7JW**

| Gen Manager | Susan Auld (01249) 783101
Fax (01249) 782992 |
|---|---|
| Green Fees | WD £37.50/round; £60/day
WE £50/round; £80/day |
| Restrictions | Proof of handicap required |

Directions
The club is directly off the B4039 between Chippenham and Bath, just beyond the village of Castle Combe.

Ferndown

Ask a group of golfers to give an example of a beautifully conditioned golf course and the chances are they'll cite the likes of Augusta National and Muirfield Village. There is little doubt that when it comes to perfectly manicured fairways and quick, ultra-true greens the American courses tend to be superior to their British counterparts. Ferndown, however, is a definite exception. Indeed the fairways and greens are often among the best kept in the whole of Britain. Someone clearly deserves a mighty large pat on the back!

There are in fact two courses at Ferndown, the **Old** and the **Presidents.** The Old Course was originally designed in 1912 by Harold Hilton, who was twice Open Champion before the turn of the century. The shorter Presidents Course, which has nine holes but eighteen tees, has a much more recent history being designed in 1969 by J Hamilton-Stutt and opened two years later.

The Old Course at Ferndown measures 6452 yards from the back tees, par and standard scratch both being 71. From the forward tees the length is reduced by a little over 200 yards. The layout is essentially one of two loops, an inner loop comprising holes one to eight and the outer containing the ninth to the eighteenth.

Ferndown's fairways are of the sandy, heathland type and are gently undulating throughout. The rough consists mainly of heather which together with the many pines and fir trees gives the course a most attractive appearance. There are a considerable number of dog-leg holes necessitating much thought from the tee. The toughest holes on the course are possibly the uphill 6th, which is normally played into the wind, the dog-leg 9th and the 11th—all fairly lengthy par fours from the back tees. One should also mention the 5th, an excellent par three where the rhododendrons provide a splash of colour in season, and the 16th, named 'Hilton's Hole' after its illustrious architect. At 5604 yards (par 70) the Presidents Course is less demanding in

terms of length but it too has its challenges and is set in equally beautiful surroundings.

Ferndown's clubhouse has a prime location, grandly surveying the course from its elevated position. On a clear day there are views across the course to the Isle of Wight.

In recent years the club has played host to many competitions and tournaments, such as the Women's English Amateur Championship in 1985 and the Hennessy Cognac Cup, a four man team competition, played over the Old Course in 1982 and 1984. The Ladies European Open visited the course in 1987, while in 1989 large crowds flocked to Ferndown to watch a most exciting Ladies British Open, won by leading American player Jane Geddes with an impressive four round total of 274.

Ferndown Golf Club, 119 Links Road, Ferndown, Wimborne, Dorset, BH22 8BU

Sec/Manager	Eddie Robertson (01202) 874602
Professional	Iain Parker (01202) 873825
Green Fees	WD £45/round/day
	WE £50/round or £60/day
	Presidents WD £18, WE £20
Restrictions	Prior arrangement; handicap certificate
	or letter

Directions
The club is 6 miles north of Bournemouth on the A31 exit at Trickett's Cross.

Isle of Purbeck

Most people are a little surprised when they learn that the Isle of Purbeck Golf Club was founded as long ago as 1892—a decade before Sunningdale and Walton Heath. They are probably even more surprised when they hear that Enid Blyton and her husband were once owners of the club. Originally only a 9 hole course, there are now 27 holes comprising the 18 hole **Purbeck** Course and an adjacent, shorter 9 hole course, the **Dene.** In 1966 a superb clubhouse was built using the local Purbeck stone and it was around this time that more and more people began to consider seriously the quality of the golf here as well as the sheer beauty of the club's setting. Today the club is owned and managed by the Robinson family.

Swanage has become a very popular holiday centre and keen golfers might consider the merits of a temporary membership of the club. There are reductions for joint membership and for those wishing to limit their golf to the Dene course. Visitors may also wish to note that the club stages a limited number of open competitions during the summer. Information concerning these can be obtained from the club's Managing Director, Mrs Robinson. Golfing societies are encouraged to come to the Isle of Purbeck and those organising should find the club very accommodating.

The south coast possesses a number of scenic courses, but one would be very pushed to find an equal to the magnificent views provided by the Isle of Purbeck. The view from the 5th on the Purbeck Course, 'Agglestone' is particularly outstanding as you tee off from the top of an ancient Saxon burial mound. The par three 11th, 'Island', with its backdrop of pines and two-tier green is also an exceptional hole.

For those who find the modern day monster courses somewhat tedious with the great emphasis they place on brute force (and ignorance?) the Purbeck Course should prove rather refreshing. From

the back tees it measures 6295 yards (par 70) whilst from the forward tees the course is reduced to 5986 yards (par 70). From the ladies' tees the course measures 5582 yards (par 73).

When in South Dorset many visitors like to take in a spot of fossil hunting. Lyme Regis and Charmouth are within easy reach, however golfers need not look beyond the four walls of the clubhouse—it is full of old fossils. Lest I be accused of insulting the members, I should quickly explain: when the clubhouse was built several fossilised dinosaur footprints and some massive ammonites were incorporated into the interior walls. It therefore follows—and golf historians please note—that to a limited extent the Isle of Purbeck could be said to possess the oldest clubhouse in the world!

The Isle of Purbeck Golf Club, Swanage, Dorset, BH19 3AB
web site: www.purbeckgolf.co.uk

Managing Director	Mrs Joan Robinson (01929) 450361
Professional	Ian Brake (01929) 450354
Green Fees	Purbeck WD £30/round, £40/day
	WE £35/round, £42.50/day
	Dene WD £13, WE £14 per day
Restrictions	Handicap certificates for Purbeck course

Directions
Take A351 to Corfe Castle, then B3351 towards Studland.

Key

SOMERSET

Bath G.C.
(01225) 463834
North Road, Bath.
(18) 6369 yards/***/B/H

Brean G.C.
(01278) 751570
Coast Road, Brean
(18) 5714 yards/**/F/H

Bristol and Clifton G.C.
(01275) 393474
Beggar Bush Lane, Failand
(18) 6294 yards/**/F/H

Burnham and Berrow G.C.
(01278) 785760
St Christophers Way,
Burnham-on-Sea
(18) 6668 yards/***/A/M
(9) 6332 yards/***/E

Cannington G.C.
(01278) 655050
Cannington, Bridgwater
(9) 2929 yards/***/D

Clevedon G.C.
(01275) 874057
Walton St Mary, Clevedon
(18) 6117 yards /**(Wed)/D

Enmore Park G.C.
(01278) 671481
Enmore, Bridgwater
(18) 6406 yards/***/C

Entry Hill G.C.
(01225) 834248
Entry Hill, Bath
(9) 4206 yards/***/E

Farrington G.C.
(01761) 241274
Marsh Lane, Farrington Gurney
(18) 6693 yards/B (9) 3022 yards /E

Filton G.C.
(0117) 969 4169
Golf Course Lane, Filton, Bristol
(18) 6264 yards/**/B

Fosseway C.C.
(01761) 412214
Charlton Lane, Midsomer Norton
(9) 4608 yards/***/D

Frome G.C.
(01373) 453410
Critchill Manor, Frome
(18) 4914 yards/***/E

Halstock G.C.
(01935) 891689
Common Lane, Halstock
(18) 4000 yards/***/E

Henbury G.C.
(0117) 950 0044
Henbury Hill, Westbury-on-Trym
(18) 6039 yards/**/B/H

Isle of Wedmore G.C.
(01934) 713649
Lineage, Wedmore
(18) 5850 yards/***/D

Kendleshire G.C.
(0117) 9567007
Henfield Road, Coalpit Heath, Bristol
(18) 6500 yards/D

Kingweston G.C.
(01458) 43921
Compton Dundon, Somerton
(9) 4516 yards/*/F

Knowle G.C.
(0117) 977 0660
Fairway, Brislington
(18) 6016 yards/**/B/H

Lansdown G.C.
(01225) 420242
Lansdown, Bath
(18) 6316 yards/***/B/H

Long Ashton G.C.
(01275) 392316
Long Ashton, Bristol
(18) 6077 yards/**/B/H/L

Long Sutton G.C.
(01458) 241017
Long Load, Langport
(18) 6367 yards/***/D

Mangotsfield G.C.
(0117) 956 5501
Carsons Road, Mangotsfield
(18) 5337 yards/***/E

Mendip G.C.
(01749) 840570
Gurney Slade, Bath
(18) 6033 yards/***/B/H

Mendip Spring G.C.
(01934) 852322
Honeyhall Lane, Congresbury
(18) 6328 yards/***/D
(9) 2287 yards/***/E

Minehead and West Somerset G.C.
(01643) 702057
Warren Road, Minehead
(18) 6228 yards/***/B

Oake Manor G.C.
(01823) 461993
Oake, Taunton
(18) 6109 yards/***/D

Orchardleigh G.C.
(01373) 454200
Frome
(18) 6810 yards/***/D

Puxton Park G.C.
(01934) 876942
Puxton, Weston-super-Mare
(18) 6600 yards/***/E

Saltford G.C.
(01225) 873513
Golf Club Lane, Saltford
(18) 6081 yards/***/B

Shirehampton Park G.C.
(0117) 982 2083
Park Hill, Shirehampton
(18) 5521 yards/**/C/H

Stockwood Vale G.C.
(0117) 986 6505
Keynsham. Bristol
(9) 2005 yards/***/E

Tall Pines G.C.
(01275) 472076
Downside, Backwell
(18) 5827 yards/***/D

Taunton and Pickeridge G.C.
(01823) 421537
Corfe, Taunton
(18) 5927 yards/***/F/H

Taunton Vale G.C.
(01823) 412220
Creech Heathfield, Taunton
(18) 6072 yards/***/D
(9) 2004 yards/***/E

Tickenham G.C.
(01275) 856626
Clevedon Road, Tickenham
(9) 2000 yards/***/E

Tracy Park G & C.C.
(0117) 937 2251
Bath Road, Wick, Bristol
(9) 6834 yards/***/B
(9) 6861 yards/***/B
(9) 6203 yards/***/B

Vivary Park G.C.
(01823) 333875
Taunton
(18) 4620 yards/***/E

Wells G.C.
(01749) 675005
East Horrington Road, Wells
(18) 6015 yards/***/D/H

Weston-super-Mare G.C.
(01934) 621360
Uphill Road North,
Weston-super-Mare
(18) 6251 yards/***/B/H

Wheathill G.C.
(01963) 240667
Wheathill, Somerset
(18) 5362 yards/***/E

Wincanton G.C.
(01963) 34606
Wincanton Racecourse
(9) 3333 yards/***/E

Windwhistle G. & C.C.
(01460) 30231
Cricket St Thomas, Chard
(18) 6500 yards/***/F

Woodspring G.C.
(01275) 394378
Yanley Lane, Long Ashton
(18) 6288 yards/***/B/H

Worlebury G.C.
(01934) 625789
Worlebury, Weston-super-Mare
(18) 5963 yards/***/B

Yeovil G.C.
(01935) 22965
Sherborne Road. Yeovil
(18) 6144 yards/***/B/H
(9) 4876 yards/***/D/H

DORSET

Ashley Wood G.C.
(01258) 452253
Wimborne Rd, Blandford Forum
(18) 6231 yards/***/C

Bridport & West Dorset G.C.
(01308) 421095
East Cliff, West Bay, Bridport
(18) 5246 yards/***/D

Broadstone G.C.
(01202) 692595
Wentworth Drive, Broadstone
(18) 6300 yards/**/A/H

Bulbury Woods G.C.
(01929) 459574
Lytchett Matravers, nr Poole
(18) 6020 yards/***/C

Came Down G.C.
(01305) 813494
Came Down, Dorchester
(18) 6244 yards/***/B/H

Canford School G.C.
(01202) 841254
Canford School, Wimborne
(9) 5918 yards/***/E/G

Chedington Court G.C.
(01935) 891413
Nr Beaminster, Dorset
(18) 6000 yards/***/D

Christchurch G.C.
(01202) 473817
Iford, Christchurch
(9) 4270 yards/***/E

Crane Valley G.C.
(01202) 814088
The Clubhouse, Verwood
(18) 6420 yards/***/C/H
(9) 2030 yards/***/E

Dorset Heights G.C.
(01258) 861386
Belchalwell, Blandford Forum
(18) 6500 yards/***/C

Dudsbury G.C.
(01202) 593499
Christchurch Road, Ferndown
(18) 6208 yards/***/F

East Dorset G.C.
(01929) 472244
Hyde, Wareham
(18) 6640 yards/***/C/H
(9) 2440 yards/***/D/H

Ferndown G.C.
(01202) 874602
Golf Links Road, Ferndown
(18) 6452 yards/***/A/H/L
(9) 5604 yards/***/C/H/L

Ferndown Forest G.C.
(01202) 876096
Forest Links Road, Ferndown
(9) 2810 yards/***/D

Halstock G.C.
(01935) 891689
Common Lane, Halstock
(18) 4351 yards/***/D

Highcliffe Castle G.C.
(01425) 272210
Lymington Road, Highcliffe-on-Sea
(18) 4686 yards/***/B/H/M

Iford Bridge G.C.
(01202) 888016
Barrack Road, Christchurch
(9) 2377 yards/***/F

Isle of Purbeck G.C.
(01929) 450354
Studland, Swanage
(18) 6295 yards/***/B/H
(9) 2022 yards/***/D

Knighton Heath G.C.
(01202) 572633
Francis Avenue, West Howe
(18) 5987 yards/**/F/H

Lyme Regis G.C.
(01297) 442963
Timber Hill, Lyme Regis
(18) 6220 yards/***/B/H

Lyons Gate G.C.
(01300) 345239
Lyons Gate, Dorchester
(9) 4200 yards/***/E

Moors Valley G.C.
(01425) 479776
Horton Road, Ringwood
(18) 6270 yards/***/E

Meyrick Park G.C.
(01202) 290862
Central Drive, Meyrick Park
(18) 5757 yards/***/E

Queen's Park G.C.
(01202) 396198
Queen's Park, Bournemouth
(18) 6072 yards/***/D

Parkstone G.C.
(01202) 707138
Links Road, Parkstone
(18) 6250 yards/**/A/H/M

Sherbourne G.C.
(01935) 812274
Higher Clatcombe, Sherbourne
(18) 5949 yards/***/B/H

Solent Meads Par Three G.C.
(01202) 420795
Hengisbury Head, Bournemouth
(18) 2325 yards/***/F

Sturminster Marshall G.C.
(01258) 858444
Moor Lane, Sturminster Marshall
(9) 4650 yards/***/E

Wareham G.C.
(01929) 554147
Sandford Road, Wareham
(18) 5603 yards/**/C/H

Weymouth G.C.
(01305) 773981
Links Road, Westham, Weymouth
(18) 6035 yards/***/B/H

WILTSHIRE

Bowood G. & C.C.
(01249) 822228
Derry Hill, Calne
(18) 7317 yards/***/B-A

Bradford-on-Avon G.C.
(01225) 868268
Trowbridge Road, Bradford-on-Avon
(9) 2297 yards/**/E

Brinkworth G.C.
(01666) 510277
Longman's Farm, Brinkworth
(18) 5900 yards/***/F

Bremhill Park G.C.
(01793) 782946
Shrivenham, Swindon
(18) 5880 yards/***/E

Broome Manor G.C.
(01793) 532403
Pipers Way, Swindon
(18) 6283 yards/***/E
(9) 2690 yards/***/E

Chippenham G.C.
(01249) 652040
Malmesbury Road, Chippenham
(18) 5540 yards/***/B/H/M

Cricklade Hotel G.C.
(01793) 750751
Common Hill, Cricklade
(9) 1830 yards/***/C

Cumberwell Park G.C.
(01225) 863322
Bradford-on-Avon
(18) 6807 yards/***/C

Erlestoke Sands G.C.
(01380) 831069
Erlestoke, Devizes
(18) 6649 yards/***/D

Hamptworth G. & C.C.
(01794) 390155
Hamptworth Road, Landford
(18) 6512 yards/**/C/H

High Post G.C.
(01722) 782219
Great Durnford, Salisbury
(18) 6297 yards/**/B/H

Highworth G.C.
(01793) 766014
Swindon Road, Highworth
(9) 3220 yards/***/E

Kingsdown G.C.
(01225) 743472
Kingsdown, Corsham
(18) 6445 yards/**/B

Manor House (Castle Combe) G. & C.C.
(01249) 782982
Castle Combe
(18) 6340 yards/***/A/H

Marlborough G.C.
(01672) 512147
The Common, Marlborough
(18) 6526 yards/***/B-A/H

North Wiltshire G.C.
(01380) 860627
Bishops Cannings, Devizes
(18) 6322 yards/**/C–A

Oaksey Park G.C.
(01666) 577995
Oaksey, Malmesbury
(9) 2900 yards/***/D

Ogbourne Downs G.C.
(01672) 841327
Ogbourne St George, Malborough
(18) 6226 yards/**/B/H

Rushmore Park
01725 516326
Tallard Royal, Shaftsbury
(18) 5580 yards/*** /E

Salisbury and South Wilts. G.C.
(01722) 742645
Netherhampton, Salisbury
(18) 6528 yards/***/B-A

RCMS Shrivenham
(01793) 785725
Shrivenham, Swindon
(12) 5547 yards/*/E/G

Shrivenham Park G.C.
(01793) 783853
Penny Hooks, Shrivenham
(18) 5989 yards/***/D

Thoulstone Park G.C.
(01373) 832825
Chapmanslade, Wesbury
(18) 6300 yards/***/D

Tidworth Garrison G.C.
(01980) 842301
Bulford Road, Tidworth
(18) 6101 yards/**/D

Upavon G.C.
(01980) 630787
Douglas Avenue, Swindon
(9) 5589 yards/**/D

West Wiltshire G.C.
(01985) 213133
Elm Hill, Warminster
(18) 5709 yards/**/B–A/H

Wiltshire G.C.
(01793) 849999
Wootton Bassett, Swindon
(18) 6496 yards/***/B - A/H

Wrag Barn G.C.
(01793) 861327
Shrivenham Road, Highworth
(18) 6548 yards/**/C

THE KENDLESHIRE GOLF CLUB *Photograph courtesy of:* **The Kendleshire Golf Club & Phil Inglis**

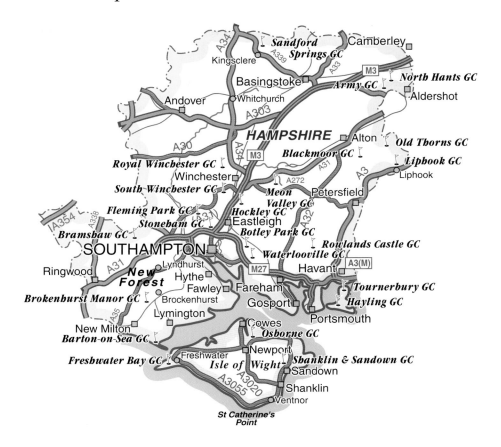

Even if the Isle of Wight and the Channel Islands were taken away from this region it would still score top marks, both for the quality of the golf and the quality of the accompanying scenery. With the New Forest to the south, the Downs to the north and Winchester Cathedral standing proudly in the middle, Hampshire is arguably the fairest of all English counties. And amongst all this finery stand the likes of Liphook, Old Thorns, North Hants, Blackmoor and Brokenhurst Manor—five of the country's leading inland courses.

The Northern Heathlands

Hampshire's traditional 'big three' of **Liphook**, **North Hants** and **Blackmoor** lie towards the east of the county close to the boundary with Surrey. Not surprisingly, they are staunch members of the heathland club—silver birch and pine, fir, heather and a dash of gorse. Liphook is possibly the pick of the three, though it's a close thing. Each measures between 6200 and 6300 yards and is maintained in superb condition. The **Army** Golf Club, just north of Aldershot is another fine and quite lengthy heathland type course with a reputation for separating the men from the boys, although it is perhaps not quite in the same league as the illustrious trio above. The final mention in this area goes to one of the county's newest recruits, the **Old Thorns** situated just south of Liphook. Both Liphook and Old Thorns are featured on a later page.

There's no shortage of comfortable hotels in the north of Hampshire and often quite hidden in the countryside are some delightful pubs and restaurants. Inns to ease the golfer's slumber include the Crown and Cushion in Minley and the Chequers in Well. Fleet bisects these two villages and the Lismoyne Hotel (01252) 628555 is ideally located. In Passfield, the Passfield Oak does good food and some popular real ales. In Liphook, as well as Old Thorns (01428) 724555,

the Links Hotel (01428) 723773 is very handy for the 9th and 10th tees on the Liphook course.

Basingstoke isn't Hampshire's most attractive town—too much London overspill—but a very good course nearby is the **Sandford Springs** Golf Club at Wolverton, built on the site of a former Roman shrine.

Around Winchester

Winchester golfers, like those at Liphook, are doubly fortunate having two first class courses at hand: **Royal Winchester** and **Hockley**. Both are well kept downland type courses. The attractive additions to the Winchester/South Hampshire area are the **Botley Park** Hotel and Country Club (01489) 780888 and the **South Winchester** Golf Club.

In Ampfield, south of Winchester, and Romsey, also south of the cathedral town, two ideal 19th hole establishments catch the eye. In the former, Potters Heron (02380) 266611 is comfortable and convenient for the A31 and the White Horse (01794) 512431 is a welcoming inn located in Romsey's marketplace. The Old Manor House (01794) 517357 is a restaurant to make a special diversion for.

In Winchester there are numerous restaurants, perhaps the best being the Old Chesil Rectory (01962) 851555. Also in Winchester, the Hotel du Vin and Bistro (01962) 841414 is not cheap but is particularly comfortable. North west of the city is Sparsholt, where one finds one of those exquisite English country house hotels, Lainston House (01962) 863588. People coming from, or returning to the west should note Middle Wallop—more specifically—Fifehead Manor (01264) 781565, a converted 16th century manor house with a good restaurant. Finally, I must point pub lovers in mid-Hampshire in the direction of Ovington where the Bush is tremendous fun.

Portsmouth

Returning to the fairways, and switching nearer to the south coast, the **Rowlands Castle** parkland course occupies a peaceful setting. The course can play fairly long, especially from the back markers. While we're on the subject of length, a hundred years ago the links at **Hayling Island** is said to have measured 7480 yards—so much for the modern-day monster courses! Today the course is less frightening but still quite a challenge in the wind and visitors are warmly received.

If another drink is needed then two fine pubs are at hand—the Old House at Home (superb name) in Havant and the Royal Oak in Langstone: both are ideally situated for Rowlands Castle. Another establishment to sample in this area is the notable Old House Hotel (01329) 833049 in Wickham and in Botley, Cobbett's (01489) 782068 is a fine French restaurant. Finally, back on Hayling Island, we recommend the Newtown House Hotel (01705) 466131 as ideal for all visitors to the area—with a new 9 hole course at **Tournerbury** nearby it provides a choice of golf.

Southampton and the New Forest

Stoneham, without doubt the pick of the courses in the Southampton area, is located just two miles north of the town. The venue of the first Dunlop British Masters tournament back in 1946, it is quite undulating with an ample sprinkling of gorse and heather and in spring some wonderful flowers.

Just outside of Portsmouth a fine 18 hole course to note is **Waterlooville**, although there are in fact a number of courses (including some very reasonable public courses, such as **Fleming Park** at Eastleigh) in and around Southampton and Portsmouth. Midway between Portsmouth and Southampton (M27 junction 7) is the **Meon Valley** Golf and Country Club. A parkland course, designed by J Hamilton Stutt, it too has an attractive setting which is not a million miles from the New Forest. For a night's rest the Meon Valley Hotel (01329) 833455 is the obvious selection, being both comfortable and highly convenient.

I'm afraid I know very little about William the Conqueror but I understand there are at least two things we should thank him for—one is the Domesday Book and the other is the New Forest—without doubt one of the most beautiful areas in Britain. There are two real golfing treats in the New Forest, one is **Bramshaw** Golf Club which is owned and run by the proprietors of the charming Bell Inn (02380) 812214—two 18 hole courses here, the Manor and the Forest courses—and the second is **Brokenhurst Manor**, a superb heathland course. Both venues are decidedly worth inspecting. A short distance from the New Forest, **Barton-on-Sea's** exposed clifftop course is also worth a visit if in the area. Recently extended to 27 varied holes, it provides some excellent challenges and some spectacular views across to the Isle of Wight and Christchurch Bay.

A few ideas for the 19th hole, and we make a start at Lyndhurst and the Parkhill House Hotel (02380) 282944—a pleasant spot with a good restaurant as well. Near Bramshaw at No Man's Land is Les Mirabelles (01794) 390205, offering good French food and views of forest ponies outside.

Two B's now, Beaulieu and Brockenhurst. In the former, the Montagu Arms (01590) 612324 and its fine restaurant is ideal to hang up one's clubs and in the latter a number of places should be considered; three definitely to include are Carey's Manor (01590) 623551, a great all rounder, Rhinefield House (01590) 622922, and Le Poussin (01590) 623063—a real beauty of a restaurant. Further south on the A337 we arrive at Lymington. In another good hotel setting stands the Passford House (01590) 682398 and for a stylish guesthouse, try Wheatsheaf House (01590) 679208. Among other things, the nearby South Lawn Hotel (01590) 643911 is convenient for ferries leaving for the Isle of Wight, while Limpets (01590)

BARTON-ON-SEA GOLF CLUB *Photograph courtesy of:* **Barton-on-Sea Golf Club**

675595, also in Lymington, has a tasty restaurant. Gordleton Mill (01590) 682219 is a real delight—aptly described as a restaurant with rooms, it is a classic of its type. In New Milton, we find the county's (quite probably the country's) finest country house hotel, Chewton Glen (01425) 275341.

Isle of Wight

There are no fewer than eight golf courses on the Isle of Wight. Of the two 18 hole courses, **Shanklin and Sandown** is the better (beautifully wooded with heather and gorse) and the other is **Freshwater Bay** (more of a downland/clifftop course.) Of the 9 holers, **Osborne** is the most scenic but a visit to any is appealing. All courses welcome visitors and green fees tend to compare favourably with those on the mainland. Note that in summer with the onset of holiday makers, the courses can be very busy and so a pre-match telephone call is strongly advised.

In Shanklin, the Cliff Tops (01983) 863262 stands out, though there are many good hotels on the island. Two pubs to visit in Shanklin include the Fisherman's Cottage—good food and a fine setting—and the Crab which provides more seafood in a high street position.

Elsewhere on the island, Cowes of course is busy and fun, especially during Cowes Week itself, but for our purposes Bonchurch beckons, where the Royal (01983) 852186 is a delightful restaurant with some rooms. There is also a tremendous selection of moderately priced establishments on the island. Suggestions include the Farringford Hotel (01983) 752500, The Albion (01983) 753631 at Freshwater, the Culver Lodge Hotel (01983) 403819 and the excellent St Catherine's Hotel (01983) 402392, both at Sandown.

The Channel Islands

If the Isle of Wight is good for golf, the Channel Islands are

even better. **La Moye**, **Royal Jersey** and **Royal Guernsey** are the three outstanding 18 hole courses, although it seems the German troops didn't share this opinion during the island's four year occupation—they demolished La Moye's clubhouse and dug up the fairways at Royal Guernsey. Both have long since recovered though and all three provide tremendous holiday golf. La Moye is featured ahead.

When it comes to hotels one is quite simply spoilt for choice. In Guernsey, St Peter's Port offers a whole handful of excellent establishments. The St Pierre Park (01481) 728282 is the most luxurious hotel, and for real character La Frégate Hotel (01481) 724624 is an 18th century manor house overlooking the harbour. The Old Government House (01481) 724921 is again beautifully stylish. For a good seafood restaurant try the Absolute End (01481) 723822 and for a cosy guest house, La Girouette (01481) 63269 near Perrelle Bay.

In Jersey, St Brelade's Bay offers the Atlantic Hotel (01534) 44101 (ideal for La Moye links). Other recommended hotels here are the Hotel L'Horizon (01534) 43101, and La Place Hotel (01534) 44261. St Helier boasts the aptly named Grand Hotel (01534) 22301—note especially the restaurant which is excellent—the less expensive Almorah Hotel (01534) 21648 and in St Peter, the Mermaid (01534) 41255. Perhaps the best restaurant on the island is to be found at St Saviour—Longueville Manor (01534) 25501 is an outstanding hotel as well. In Bouley Bay is the delightfully secluded Water's Edge Hotel (01534) 862777. However, the intrepid guesthouse brigade will find more than enough to please them at Millbrook House (01534) 33036 in St Helier and Bryn-y-Mor (01534) 20295 in St Aubin. Finally in Grouville Bay near the Royal Jersey Golf Club is La Hougue Grange, a charming country house and one of those treats where the words 'fore' and 'fare' can be combined so happily!

Liphook

Although it may sound more like a golfing nightmare than a golfing haven, Liphook is one of the most delightful inland courses in Southern England. The 18 holes straddle the Hampshire-Sussex boundary yet in character it 'belongs' to Berkshire or Surrey. Liphook is a classic heathland layout, indeed, many regard it as one of the classic heathland courses.

Liphook was designed in 1922, by Arthur Croome. Blessed with a wealth of magnificent pines and silver birches, the terrain is very sandy in nature—dazzling white in parts—and in September the heather turns a beautiful purple-pink. The beauty of Croome's creation is the way the course subtly blends into the landscape. There is enormous variety yet nothing appears contrived. Not withstanding the old A3 road which bisects the course, there is a very tranquil atmosphere, especially since the bypass was completed—Liphook exudes an air of 'Merry Old England'

At 6167 yards, par 69, Liphook is not overly long, but with relatively small greens and fairways bordered by thick heather, the wayward big hitter will be punished. The nature of the challenge is evident from the outset. The course begins, rather unusually, with a long par three. It is a fairly formidable opening hole with trees all along the left, heather in front of the green and a steep fall-away to the right.

The 2nd hole features a sloping fairway and an approach over a sandy track to an attractively sited green encircled by pines. Plenty of sand and heather frame the uphill par three 3rd and then comes a big two-shotter with a fairway running parallel with the 2nd.

Bold bunkering characterises the 5th and 6th. The short 7th and down and up 8th are threatened by a railway line to the right and the front nine concludes with an intriguing (some say infuriating) par four. The second shot to the ninth is played blind over a crest to a

green protected by humps and hillocks, a thoroughly old fashioned, almost links style hole.

You're encouraged to open your shoulders at the 10th, then asked to thread your drive between bunkers at the short 11th where a stand of pines provides a striking backcloth.

The 12th, 13th and 14th form a fine sequence amid the most picturesque part of the course. A wide fairway at the long, uphill 12th is deceptive in as much as the green is very small. The 13th 'Two Counties' has you teeing off in Sussex and holing out in Hampshire with a glorious approach across a valley to a plateau green. The 14th is a short par four that dog-legs right into another handsome green. The uphill 15th and downhill 16th are very much a pair, and finally, a heather strewn par three, and a rollercoasting par five guide you back to the clubhouse.

**Liphook Golf Club, Wheatsheaf Enclosure
Liphook, Hants GU30 7EH**

Secretary	Major J B Morgan (01428) 723785
Professional	Geoff Lee (01428) 723271
Green Fees	WD £33/round, £45/day
	WE £45/round, £55/day
Restrictions	No visitors Sun am or competition Sats
	Handicap certificates required
	Booking strongly recommended

Directions
One mile south west of Liphook off the B2070 Petersfield Road.

Old Thorns Hotel, Golf & Country Club

There are two reasons why we have selected Old Thorns as one of our featured courses in this edition of *Following the Fairways*. Firstly, it is because a visit to Old Thorns can fairly be described as a unique experience and the purpose of this book, after all, is to illustrate the wealth and variety of golfing challenges that these islands have to offer. The second, just as important, is that Old Thorns is both exceptionally attractive and visitor-friendly. Nature, with a little help from course designers Peter Alliss and Dave Thomas, is chiefly responsible for the beauty of the situation.

What about the unique experience? Old Thorns is where East meets West, not just on the golf course but at the 19th hole. Old Thorns is owned by a large Japanese publishing company, Kosaido who acquired the course and accompanying hotel only two years after its official opening in 1982. The Japanese inherited a very English set up. The centre piece of the clubhouse and hotel is a converted 150 year old tithe barn; a delightful building. The new owners have maintained, even enhanced, its traditional 'log fires in winter' ambience, but they have also added a Japanese Centre which includes a charming Japanese garden. The buildings have been extended generally to an extent that Old Thorns now boasts a splendid range of luxury facilities. The hotel has 32 well appointed rooms.

Just an hour's drive from London perhaps, but the capital can seem a world away when you arrive at the course. The surrounding countryside is some of Britain's finest; a great spread of oaks, beech trees, chestnuts and pines adorn the landscape and the golf course winds its way through the woods, gently rising and falling. Natural springs abound and much use has been made of them! Water hazards are numerous at Old Thorns; there are many streams and several times the golfer is asked to play over or across the edge of a small lake.

After holing out successfully on the tricky 18th green a stiff drink at the 19th may be in order—a glass of saki perhaps? A good meal may also be sought and some people reckon that this is where Old Thorns really comes into its own. There is a superb selection of European and Japanese cuisine in its very characterful restaurants. If you have never tried Japanese food before then the renowned Nippon Kan Restaurant and the Teppan Yaki tables are the perfect place for an introduction.

The **General Manager** at Old Thorns is **Ken Flockhart**, the **Professional** is **Alan Bott tel: (01428) 724555 fax: (01428) 725036**. For written correspondence contact **Old Thorns Hotel Golf & Country Club, Longmoor Road, Liphook, Hampshire, GU30 7PE** or visit **www.oldthorns.co.uk**. The green fees for 2000 are set at weekdays £35 per round, £40 per day, weekends £40 per round and £55 per day. It is advisable to book tee times with the professional.

Old Thorns is guaranteed to charm you from the moment you arrive to the time you leave.

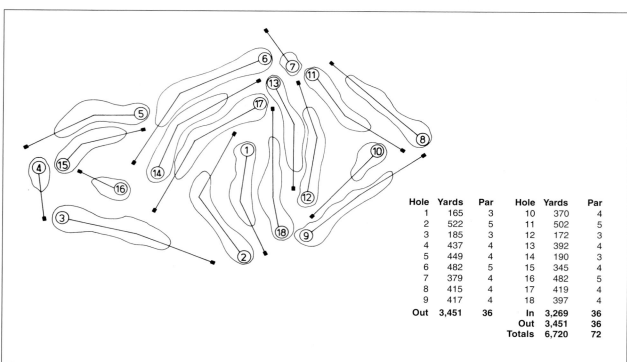

Hole	Yards	Par	Hole	Yards	Par
1	165	3	10	370	4
2	522	5	11	502	5
3	185	3	12	172	3
4	437	4	13	392	4
5	449	4	14	190	3
6	482	5	15	345	4
7	379	4	16	482	5
8	415	4	17	419	4
9	417	4	18	397	4
Out	**3,451**	**36**	**In**	**3,269**	**36**
			Out	**3,451**	**36**
			Totals	**6,720**	**72**

Old Thorns enjoys a wonderful location set in 400 acres of glorious Hampshire countryside. Easily accessible from the A3 London to Portsmouth route, Old Thorns is less than 30 minutes from the M25.

At Old Thorns, championship golf is combined with gracious living and warm hospitality. Originally a 17th century farmhouse, it offers facilities to rival any hotel in Southern England whilst retaining much of its original charm.

Each of the 32 bedrooms is comfortably furnished, with garden views and en-suite bath or shower, tea and coffee making facilities, satellite TV, radio and direct dial telephone.

Old Thorns offers a choice of dining experiences: fine dining in The Garden Room where fresh produce is combined to offer a menu of classical dishes. The award winning Nippon Kan, an authentic Japanese restaurant famed for its Teppan Yaki where the chefs prepare your meal in front of you. All day dining is available in Sands where light and exciting dishes are served in a relaxed and contemporary atmosphere.

Old Thorns is a renowned venue for business and corporate affairs and takes great pride in its reputation as the perfect setting for weddings.

The championship golf course was designed by Commander John Harris, one of Britain's best known golf course architects and completed by Peter Alliss and Dave Thomas. The rolling landscape makes idyllic golf terrain, peppered with mature trees, natural springs and several lakes, which add to the visual pleasure of playing. The course has been sympathetically designed for the less proficient player but still affords the better golfer a real challenge.

Additional facilities include a driving range, putting green and a well-stocked Pro Shop managed by resident PGA Professionals who also offer tuition. Buggies, trolleys, graphite clubs and shoes are all available for hire.

A range of golf day programmes, golf services and dining options mean that planning your next event couldn't be simpler.

For the non-golfer our leisure Club facilities include an indoor pool, sauna and steam room, fitness centre, outdoor tennis courts and a wide range of health and beauty treatments.

Old Thorns Hotel Golf & Country Club,
Griggs Green,
Liphook,
Hampshire,
GU30 7PE
Tel: (01428) 724555
Fax: (01428) 725036
web site: www.oldthorns.co.uk.

La Moye

England is part of the Channel Islands. Yes, England is part of the Channel Islands—at least this is what an islander will tell you. Apparently, the islands belonged to William, Duke of Normandy some time before he came over and added England to his territories.

So what of the golf in the 'mother country', the land where the great Harry Vardon was born? In short, there are three very fine courses: Royal Guernsey, Royal Jersey and La Moye. The first two certainly offer a marvellous day's golf but the general consensus is that La Moye sneaks it as the pick of an excellent trio. Its setting alone makes the course stand out, laid out as it is two hundred and fifty feet above St Ouen's Bay, Jersey's finest beach, on the south west tip of the island. From such a vantage point there are some tremendous views to be enjoyed from the course, particularly perhaps from the 13th where the four sister islands of Guernsey, Sark, Herm and Jetou can all be seen. Add to this a warm climate and of course, the quality of the championship links itself and you can see why people want to play golf here!

La Moye Golf Club was founded in 1902 by the then headmaster of the local school, one George Boomer. A course was mapped out but it didn't really take shape until James Braid added his skilful craftsmanship. Thereafter the course was left more or less untouched, so to speak, until 1977 when major alterations were made resulting in an improved and, when played from the back tees, much longer course.

The **Secretary** at La Moye is **Chris Greetham**, who can be contacted on **tel: (01534) 743401** or by writing to: **La Moye Golf Club, La Moye, Jersey, Channel Islands.** The club **Professional, Mike Deeley** can be reached on **(01534) 743130.**

In addition to being a superb championship course, La Moye doubles as a very popular holiday course in the best sense of the word. Visitors are always made most welcome. The only specific requirement is that they must be members of a recognised golf club. It isn't essential to book a tee time but during the summer months the course can become extremely busy. Making an early start is always a good idea.

The green fees for 2000 were set at £45 per round during the week and £50 at the weekend when only afternoon play is permitted.

As for finding the course, there really should be no problem. La Moye is only a mile or so from St Brelade and just five minutes by road from Jersey's airport. The island is such a size that it shouldn't take much more than half an hour to travel between La Moye and Royal Jersey in Grouville, though of course it depends on the traffic and on how much of Jersey you want to take in along the way.

From the championship tees, the course can be stretched to almost 6700 yards. The medal tees, however, are less exacting and the total yardage is 6416 yards, par 72—no pushover certainly, and there is often a very stiff wind. From the ladies tees the course measures 5903 yards, par 74. La Moye is a typical links type course—large sandhills, pot bunkers, the odd blind shot, gorse bushes and punishing rough (though it's not as punishing as at some). It really is full of variety with a number of dog-legs and plateau greens. Apart from the 13th and its enchanting views, many will probably remember the 17th hole best of all—a lengthy par four with the green dramatically set on the edge of the cliffs, rather like the famous 5th hole at Portrush.

The Jersey Seniors Open has established itself as a very popular event on the European Seniors Tour and the pros, inspired by the surroundings, have produced some very good scores—although La Moye has never been torn apart. Some well known names also won the Jersey Open when it used to be held here, including the Ryder Cup players Sandy Lyle, Tony Jacklin, Bernard Gallacher, Howard Clark, Ian Woosnam and Sam Torrance. So some of the best golfers in the world have played at La Moye.

All golfers, are sure to enjoy the club's excellent 19th. A spacious new clubhouse, it is one of a series for the club. The original burned down while the second was destroyed by German soldiers during the island's war-time occupation. Let's just wish the new one the best of British luck!

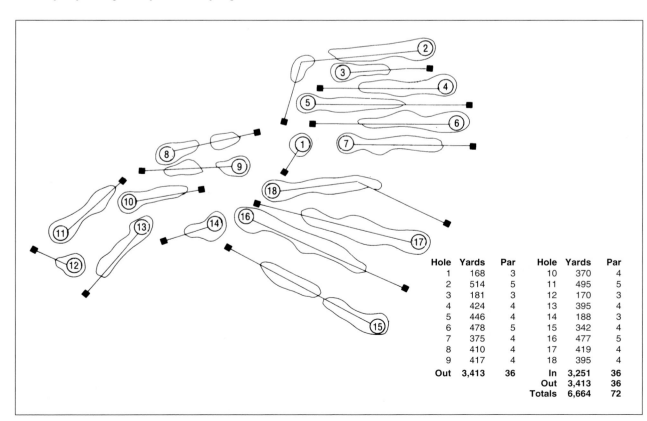

Hole	Yards	Par	Hole	Yards	Par
1	168	3	10	370	4
2	514	5	11	495	5
3	181	3	12	170	3
4	424	4	13	395	4
5	446	4	14	188	3
6	478	5	15	342	4
7	375	4	16	477	5
8	410	4	17	419	4
9	417	4	18	395	4
Out	**3,413**	**36**	**In**	**3,251**	**36**
			Out	**3,413**	**36**
			Totals	**6,664**	**72**

Key

To avoid disappointment
it is advisable to telephone
in advance

***Visitors welcome at most times
**Visitors usually allowed on
weekdays only
*Visitors not normally permitted
(Mon, Wed) No visitors
on specified days

Approximate Green Fees
A £40 plus
B £25 to £40
C £20 to £30
D £15 to £25
E under £15
F Green fees on application

Restrictions
G Guests only
H–Handicap certificate required
H–(24) Handicap of 24 or less
L–Letter of introduction required
M–Visitor must be a member of
another recognised club

HAMPSHIRE

Alresford G.C.
(01962) 733746
Cheriton Road, Alresford
(18) 5905 yards/**/C/H

Alton G.C.
(01420) 84774
Old Odiham Road, Alton
(9) 5744 yards/***/D/H

Ampfield Par Three G.C.
(01794) 368480
Winchester Road, Ampfield, Romsey
(18) 2478 yards/***/D/H

Andover G.C.
(01264) 323980
Winchester Road, Andover
(9) 5933/**/C

Army G.C.
(01252) 541104
Laffans Road, Aldershot
(18) 6579 yards/**/F/H

Barton-on-Sea G.C.
(01425) 615308
Marine Drive, Barton-on-Sea,
(18) 5737 yards/***/B/H

Basingstoke G.C.
(01256) 465990
Kempshott Park, Basingstoke
(18) 6350 yards/**/B/H/G

Bishopswood G.C.
(01734) 812200
Bishopswood Lane, Tadley
(9) 6474 yards/**(Mon,Wed)/D/M

Blackmoor G.C.
(01420) 472775
Golf Lane, Whitehill, Bordon
(18) 6232 yards/**/B/H

Blacknest G.C.
(01420) 22888
Frith End, Binstead
(9) 6726 yards/***/D

Botley Park Hotel & C.C.
(01489) 780888
Winchester Road, Boorley Green
(18) 6026 yards/***/C/H

Bramshaw G.C.
(01703) 813433
Brook, Lyndhurst
(18) 6257 yards/**/B/H
(18) 5774 yards/**/B/H

Brokenhurst Manor G.C.
(01590) 623332
Sway Road, Brockenhurst
(18) 6222 yards/***/B/H(24)

Burley G.C.
(01425) 402431
Cott Lane, Burley
(9) 3135 yards/***/D/H

Cams Hall G.C.
(01329) 827222
Cams Hill, Fareham
(18) 5890 yards/**/B/H
(9) 3059 yards/**/E/H

Chilworth G.C.
(01703) 740544
Main Road, Chilworth
(9) 2347 yards/***/E

Corhampton G.C.
(01489) 877279
Sheeps Pond Lane, Droxford
(18) 6088 yards/**/B/H

Dean Farm G.C.
(01420) 489478
Kingsley
(9) 1350 yards/***/F

Dibden G.C.
(01703) 843943
Dibden, Southampton
(18) 6206 yards/***/E
(9) 1520 yards/***/E

Dummer G.C.
(01256) 397888
Dummer, Basingstoke
(18) 6556 yards/**/C

Dunwood Manor G.C.
(01794) 340549
Shootash Hill, Romsey
(18) 5885 yards/**/B/H

Fleetlands G.C.
(01705) 544492
Fareham Road, Gosport
(9) 4852 yards/***/F/G

Fleming Park G.C.
(01703) 612797
Magpie Lane, Eastleigh
(18) 4436 yards/***/E

Furzeley G.C.
(01705) 231180
Furzeley, Denmead
(9) 1858 yards/***/E

Gosport and Stokes Bay G.C.
(01705) 527941
Off Fort Road, Haslar, Gosport
(9) 5966 yards/**/D

Great Salterns G.C.
(01705) 664549
Eastern Road, Portsmouth
(18) 5970 yards/***/E

OLD THORNS GOLF CLUB Photograph courtesy of: *Old Thorns Golf Club*

The Hampshire G.C.
(01264) 357555
Winchester Road, Goodworth
(18) 6318 yards/***/D
(9) 1050 yards/***/E

Hartley Wintney G.C.
(01252) 844214
London Road, Hartley Wintney
(9) 6096 yards/**/D

Hayling G.C.
(01705) 464446
Links Lane, Hayling Island
(18) 6489 yards/***/A/H/M/L

Hockley G.C.
(01962) 713165
Twyford, Winchester
(18) 6279 yards/**/F/G

Kingsley Par Three G.C.
(01420) 476118
Main Road, Kingsley, Bordon
(9) 1800 yards/***/E

Leckford and Longstock G.C.
(01264) 810320
Leckford, Stockbridge
(9) 3251 yards/*/F/G

Lee-on-the-Solent G.C.
(01705) 551170
Brune Lane, Lee-on-the-Solent
(18) 5959/**/B/H

Liphook G.C.
(01428) 723271
Wheatsheaf Enclosure, Liphook
(18) 6250 yards/**/A/H/L

Meon Valley G.& C.C.
(01329) 833455
Sandy Lane, Shedfield,
(18) 6519 yards/***/A
(9) 2885 yards/***/D

New Forest G.C.
(01703) 282752
Southampton Road, Lyndhurst
(18) 5742 yards/***/D

North Hants G.C.
(01252) 616443
Minley Road, Fleet
(18) 6257 yards/**/B/H/L

Old Thorns G.C.
(01428) 724555
Longmoor Road, Liphook
(18) 6533 yards/***/A

Otterbourne
(01962) 775225
Pales Lane, Otterbourne
(9) 1939 yards/***/E

Paultons G.C.
(01703) 813992
Ower, Romsey
(18) 6238 yards/***/D

Petersfield (New Course) G.C
(01730) 895165
Tankerdale Lane, Liss
(18) 6400 /***/B

Petersfield (Old Course) G.C
(01730) 267732
Sussex Road, Petersfield
(9) 3005 yards /***/E

Petersfield G.C.
(01730) 262386
Heath Road, Petersfield
(18) 5603 yards/**/C

Portsmouth G.C.
(01705) 372210
Crookhorn Road, Portsmouth
(18) 6139 yards/***/E

Romsey G.C.
(01703) 734637
Nursling , Southampton
(18) 5851 yards/**/B/H

Rowlands Castle G.C.
(01705) 412784
Links Lane, Rowlands Castle
(18)6627 yards/**/B/H

Royal Winchester G.C.
(01962) 852462
Sarum Road, Winchester
(18) 6218 yards/**/B/H/M

Sandford Springs G.C.
(01635) 297881
Wolverton, Basingstoke
(27) 6222 yards/**/B

Southampton G.C.
(01703) 768407
Golf Course Road, Bassett,
(18) 6218 yards/***/F
(9) 2391 yards/***/F

Southsea G.C.
(01705) 660945
The Mansion, Great Salterns
(18) 5900 yards/***/F

Southwick Park G.C.
(01705) 380131
Pinsley Drive, Southwick, Fareham
(18) 5972 yards/**/F

South Winchester G.C.
(01962) 877800
Pitt, Winchester
(18) 6697 yards/**/B/H/L

Southwood G.C.
(01252) 548700
Ively Road, Cove, Farnborough
(18) 5738 yards/***/D

Stoneham G.C.
(01703) 768151
Bassett Green Road, Bassett
(18) 6310 yards/**/B/H

Test Valley G.C.
(01256) 771737
Micheldever Road, Overton
(18) 6811 yards/***/C

Tournerbury G.C.
(01705) 462266
Tournerbury Road, Hayling Island
(9) 2956 yards/***/E

Tylney Park G.C.
(01256) 762079
Rotherwick, Basingstoke
(18) 6109 yards/**/B/H

Waterlooville G.C.
(01705) 263388
Cherry Tree Avenue, Cowplain
(18) 6647 yards/**/B/H

Wellow G.C
(01794) 323833
East Wellow
(3x9) 6295 yards /***/D

Weybrook Park G.C.
(01256) 20347
Aldermaston Road, Basingstoke
(18) 6100 yards/***/D

Worldham Park G.C.
(01420) 543151
Cahers Lane, Alton
(18) 5836 yards/***/D

ISLE OF WIGHT

Cowes G.C.
(01983) 292303
Crossfield Avenue, Cowes
(9) 5934 yards/***/D/H

Freshwater Bay G.C.
(01983) 752955
Afton Down, Freshwater Bay
(18) 5662 yards/***/C/H

Newport G.C.
(01983) 525076
St Georges Down, Newport
(9) 5704 yards/***/D/H

Osborne G.C.
(01983) 295421
Osborne House Estates,
East Cowes
(9) 6276 yards/**/D/H

Ryde G.C.
(01983) 614809
Binstead Road, Ryde
(9) 5287 yards/***/D/H

Shanklin & Sandown G.C.
(01983) 403217
The Fairway, Lake, Sandown
(18) 6000 yards/**/B/H/M

Ventnor G.C.
(01983) 853326
Steep Hill Down Road
(9) 5752 yards/***/F

CHANNEL ISLANDS

Alderney G.C.
(01481) 822835
Route des Carrieres, Alderney
(9) 2528 yards/***/D

La Grande Mare
(01481) 55313
Vason Bay, Guernsey
(18) 5026 yards/***/D

La Moye G.C.
(01534) 43401
La Moye, St Brelade, Jersey
(18) 6741 yards/***/A/H/L

Les Mielles G & C.C.
(01534) 482787
Val de la Mare, St Ouens
(18) 5610 yards/***/E/H

Royal Guernsey G.C.
(01481) 47022
L'Ancresse Vale, Guernsey
(18) 6206 yards/**/B/H

Royal Jersey G.C.
(01534) 854416
Grouville, Jersey
(18) 6059 yards/***(W/E pm)/A/H

St Clements G.C.
(01524) 821938
St Clements, Jersey
(9) 3972 yards/***(Sun pm)/D

St Pierre Park G.C.
(01481) 727039
Rohais, St Peter Port, Guernsey
(9) 2511 yards/***/D

BARTON-ON-SEA GOLF CLUB Photograph courtesy of: **Barton-on-Sea Golf Club**

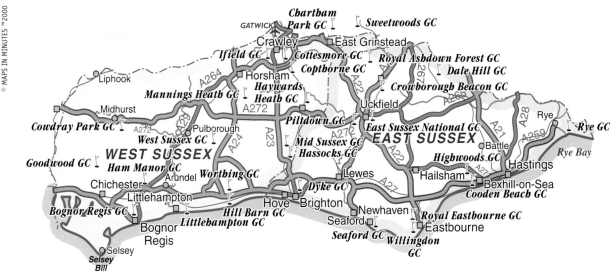

Sussex Choice Golf

Sussex, where the South Downs tumble gently towards spectacular chalk cliffs or as Tennyson wrote, 'green Sussex fading into blue'. Here is the county of downland and weald, of dramatic rollercoasting cliffs, the Seven Sisters and Beachy Head.

The situation in Sussex is superb. The golf is glorious as is the countryside all around, yet at no time can you claim to be isolated—except perhaps when you visit the gorse at Ashdown Forest. West Sussex is as charming an area as one could find—the golf course of the same name is delightful and reflects the quality of some splendid nearby country house hotels—while in Rye, the golfer must visit with a packed wallet in order to seduce a member in a local drinking haunt and thus secure that elusive thing—a round of golf at Rye. A more spectacular day could not be wished for.

Tempting as it is to think of Sussex as one region, there are of course two counties, East and West, and between them they possess over sixty courses, many of which are outstandingly good. Golfers in these parts can count themselves pretty fortunate!

Close to the Coast: West Sussex

On a selective tour of some of the better courses on or near the Sussex coast, there seems no more logical a place to commence than in the region's south west corner and **Goodwood**—glorious Goodwood to racegoers, though the golf course is in a similarly idyllic spot, nestling in the southern foothills of the South Downs. Some four miles north of Chichester on the A286 it is in fact located just below the racecourse and has a magnificent 18th century clubhouse.

In Goodwood itself, the **Marriott Goodwood Park Hotel** (01243) 775537 is an excellent place to stay and very convenient for the course, but the delights of Chichester are also close at hand. Here there are a variety of attractions including numerous antique shops and the excellent Festival Theatre (01243) 781312. The Dolphin and Anchor (01243) 790280 opposite the cathedral is most welcoming and a fine place for dinner is the Droveway (01243) 528832. A theatre of the open air variety can be found at Bosham, as can the pleasant Millstream Hotel (01243) 573234.

Staying in the south west of the region, **Bognor Regis** is worth a visit—a flattish but attractive parkland course with several testing par fours. Note the Royal Norfolk (01243) 826222 in town as well as the many hotels in and around Chichester. The course at **Littlehampton** lies about seven miles east of Bognor Regis off the A259. It is the nearest one gets to a true links course in West Sussex and is always

kept in first class condition. Further along the A259 at Angmering is the friendly club of **Ham Manor**. Like Bognor, it is a parkland course with an interesting layout of two distinct loops. It also boasts a beautiful clubhouse.

This corner of West Sussex is renowned for its tremendous hotels and after a day's golf there can be no better place to visit than Arundel where the Norfolk Arms (01903) 882101, a Georgian coaching inn has welcomed travellers for over two hundred years. Also to be found in Arundel are many pleasant guesthouses and inns, among them the Arden Hotel (01903) 882544, Bridge House and the Swan Hotel (01903) 882314. South of Arundel, lies Climping and the magnificent Bailiffscourt (01903) 723511, a 13th century replica offering superb comforts and an excellent restaurant. To the north of Arundel, Amberley Castle at Amberley (01798) 831992 is expensive but very good value, with a first class restaurant. Also the Boat House Restaurant (01798) 831059 has an excellent menu and is well worth a visit.

As a town Worthing is somewhat overshadowed by neighbouring Brighton (though apparently it inspired Oscar Wilde). Overshadowed or not, it has one of the leading clubs in Sussex. **Worthing** has two 18 hole courses, the Lower and the Upper. Both are exceptionally fine tests of golf. There is a reasonable public course too at Worthing, **Hill Barn**, while just north of Brighton are the new courses at **Hassocks** and **Mid Sussex**, picturesque courses at the foot of the South Downs. For a convenient 19th hole our recommendation in town is the Chatsworth Hotel (01903) 236103.

Close to the Coast: East Sussex

Moving into East Sussex and the town of Brighton, probably the best course in the area, and there are a number to choose from, is the **Dyke** Golf Club, located five miles north of the town centre. One of the more difficult courses in Sussex, it is on fairly high ground and provides some splendid views.

As arguably the most famous resort in Britain, it isn't surprising to find literally hundreds of hotels. Among the best are the Grand Hotel (01273) 321188 and Topps Hotel (01273) 729334. Brighton naturally has accommodation to suit everyone's taste and pockets and slightly less expensive are the Allendale Hotel (01273) 675436, the Croft Hotel and the Trouville Hotel (01273) 697384. A restaurant well worth a visit is Langans Bistro (01273) 606933.

A short distance along the A259 is Seaford. One of the older clubs in Sussex, the **Seaford** Golf Club at East Bletchington celebrated its centenary in 1987. A fair sprinkling of gorse and hawthorn is the feature of this outstanding downland course. The views too are quite spectacular being perched high above the town and overlooking the Channel. Also worth noting is the dormy house adjacent to the course.

As we continue to trek in an easterly direction, passing near to Beachy Head we arrive at Eastbourne where there are two fine courses—**Royal Eastbourne** and **Willingdon**. The former is situated very close to the town centre with the enviable address of Paradise Drive. Willingdon, north of the town off the A22, is quite a hilly course and very tough. Its interesting design has been likened to an oyster shell with the clubhouse as the pearl.

In the area around Bexhill, both **Cooden Beach** and **Highwoods** are well established courses. Hotels in the area are less plentiful than in Brighton but Eastbourne does offer the exceptionally fine Grand Hotel (01323) 412345, while in Battle, Netherfield Place (01424) 774455 is extremely elegant.

Before heading inland a quick word on **Rye**. It is unquestionably one of the greatest and most natural links courses in Britain—in many people's opinion the equal of Deal and Sandwich. However, visitors are normally permitted to play only if accompanied by a Member—hence the rather flippant remark in the second paragraph! Where might such a meeting take place then? In Rye itself, the Mermaid Inn (01797) 223065 is an historic establishment standing in a steep cobbled street, while for a cosy guest house, try the Old Vicarage (01797) 222119, Little Orchard House (01797) 223831 or the listed Jeakes House (01797) 222828. A charming inn nearby is the Hayes Arms (01797) 253142 in Northiam and the Flackley Ash in Peasmarsh is a fine country house style hotel (01797) 230651.

Further Inland: East Sussex

If the majority of the leading courses in Sussex are located either on the coast or within a few miles of it, perhaps the most attractive courses are to be found a few more miles inland. **Piltdown**, two miles to the west of Uckfield, is a good example. Piltdown is a natural heathland course with a beautiful setting and somewhat unusually, although it shares the curiosity with Royal Ashdown, it has no bunkers—though there are certainly enough natural hazards to set the golfer thinking.

Towards the north of East Sussex, **Dale Hill** is a much improved course with a stylish new hotel (01580) 200112 attached; moreover it has recently opened a second 18 holes designed by Ian Woosnam. Next comes a classic pair: **Royal Ashdown Forest** (see ahead) and **Crowborough Beacon**—two wonderfully scenic courses where the heather and gorse simply run riot. Crowborough's course is situated some 800 feet above sea level and on clear days the sea can be glimpsed from the clubhouse. Sir Arthur Conan Doyle would have taken in this view on many occasions for he lived adjacent to the course and was captain of the golf club in 1910. It really is the most beautiful of courses and has in the par three 6th one of the best short holes in Britain.

Although there may be closer places, the 16th century Middle House Hotel (01435) 872146 at Mayfield is recommended for a stay near Crowborough. For Royal Ashdown, several ideas here. For convenience the Ashdown Forest Hotel (01342) 824866 has its own fine course in addition to being adjacent to the royal club. In Forest Row the Chequers Hotel (01342) 824394 is popular, and the Brambletye Hotel (01342) 824144 and Roebuck Hotel (01342) 823811 both come highly recommended. Nearer East Grinstead is glorious Gravetye Manor (01342) 810567 a restaurant of excellence.

In Wych Cross, the Ashdown Park Hotel (01342) 824988 is well worth a visit—9 holes of golf and concessions at two good nearby courses, other leisure facilities are also good. East Grinstead also

boasts an excellent guesthouse in the shape of the Cranfield Lodge (01342) 321251, very close to the spendid new **Sweetwoods Park** 18 hole course just over the Kent border at Cowden and another newcomer, worth visiting **Chartham Park**, at Felcourt just in Surrey.

Further Inland: West Sussex

Crossing the boundary from East to West, moving from Uckfield to Cuckfield, **Haywards Heath** stands right in the middle of Sussex. A very good heathland course this, but the pride of West Sussex is undoubtedly Pulborough—the **West Sussex** Golf Club. Along with **Royal Ashdown**, **Mannings Heath** and **East Sussex National** it is featured on a later page.

Not too far from Pulborough, Brian Barnes has been the driving force behind the fine new development at West Chiltington and where the possibility for visitors of a weekend game is a definite bonus! Still in the West three more to note are in the north of the county, and very convenient for Gatwick, the **Ifield** Golf and Country Club, **Copthorne** and the **Cottesmore** (01293) 528256, which is also a luxurious country club in very attractive surroundings. Another popular course is found at **Cowdray Park**—very pleasant and ideal should you happen to play polo as well!

Places to stay? For Cowdray, the Spread Eagle (01730) 816911 at Midhurst—the hotel and restaurant are both excellent. Similar praise can be given to the Angel (01730) 812421—a decidedly fine hotel overlooking Cowdray Park. In Bepton, the Park House Hotel (01730) 812880 is also delightful.

For Pulborough, Little Thakeham (01903) 744416 at Storrington is outstanding, as is Horsted Place (01825) 750581, now linked with East Sussex National and offering excellent accommodation. The beautiful South Lodge Hotel (01403) 891711 at Lower Beeding is centrally situated for the above courses and is especially convenient for Mannings Heath.

In the course of our brief trip no doubt several splendid 19th hole establishments have been omitted, but such is life! In order to fit in more restaurants, please forgive this somewhat hasty appraisal of some of the best in both counties.

In Rusper, Ghyll Manor (01293) 871571 is first class and also provides a comfortable resting place. Returning to Alfriston, there is Moonrakers (01323) 870472—try a Hot Sussex Smokie! In Herstmonceux, the Sundial (01323) 832217 is French, whilst Jevington's Hungry Monk (01323) 482178 is outstanding. In Midhurst try Mida, in Pulborough plump for Stane Street Hollow (01798) 872819 and for a special occasion try the Old Forge (01903) 743402.

No trip to the heart of Sussex would be complete either without a visit to one of the many country houses, castles, pubs or inns. Here are a few more random thoughts for life beyond the 18th green: the White Horse Inn (01243) 535219 in Chilgrove has an excellent restaurant and the wine list is almost beyond compare, while the Shepherd and Dog in Fulking and the Lickfold Inn at Lickfold are also good.

Aside from the antiques of Chichester, Arundel (an excellent castle to see here) and Petworth, which offers the superb Petworth House, there is a summer of unsurpassed opera at Glyndebourne. In contrast, a totally flamboyant place to spend time is Brighton. The streets in the old town offer several bargains while the Grand Pavilion is as striking as ever.

Returning to the subject of castles, Bodiam in East Sussex is not too widely known, but nonetheless quite majestic. Any thoughts for the player who had trouble in the groping gorse at Ashdown? Well, Blackboys, the pub in the village of the same name is welcoming and resuscitating as is the Roebuck in Wych Cross (01342) 823811. Sussex, in short, is a true delight, both on and off the fairways.

Situated within the grounds of historical Goodwood House, ancestral home to the Dukes of Richmond, the Marriott Goodwood Park Hotel & Country Club is surrounded by 12,000 acres of Goodwood Park Estate. Sympathetically developed, the first class accommodation that distinguishes Marriott hotels provides 94 bedrooms including character and executive rooms.

The award-winning restaurant serves the best of modern English cuisine, and the Goodwood Sports Café Bar is available for more informal meals. The conference facilities can entertain from 2 to 150 delegates and for a uniquely sumptuous setting for a banquet or reception, the State Rooms of Goodwood House itself can be booked for functions linked to your conference.

The leisure facilities offered by the hotel include an indoor, ozone treated swimming pool, spa bath, sauna, steam room, aerobic studio, tennis courts and a fully equipped fitness gym. There is also health and beauty salons and a solarium.

The 18 hole golf course has for its backdrop beautiful Goodwood House. Clubs and buggies are available for hire and with a retail sports shop, practice ground and professional tuition the player's every need, both practical and aesthetic, is catered for.

Goodwood Racing Breaks are another popular feature of the hotel with the famous racecourse only one mile away and are offered on meetings throughout the season, May to September.

Guests wishing a more peaceful break will enjoy exploring the rolling Sussex Downs and a visit to Chichester is not to be missed with its harbour, cathedral and theatre. Arundel Castle is well worth a visit as is the town of Brighton.

Whether you are wanting to improve your golf handicap, visit the races, explore the sights of the South of England or simply unwind from the stress of everyday life, the thoughtful and helpful staff at Marriott Goodwood Park Hotel are waiting to welcome you.

Marriott
GOODWOOD PARK
HOTEL & COUNTRY CLUB
Goodwood
Chichester
West Sussex PO18 0QB
Tel: (01243) 775537
Fax: (01243) 520120

West Sussex (Pulborough)

*'Concentrate your mind on the match until
you are dormy. Then look at the surrounding
scenery and expatiate on its beauties.'*
(AJ Robertson)

In the opinion of many, West Sussex, or Pulborough as it is commonly known, is quite simply the most beautiful course in England. The setting is the South Downs and seclusion is total. Commander George Hillyard founded the club in 1930 having conceived the idea, so the story goes, as he looked out of his bathroom window one day while taking his morning shave! (His house, it should be explained, overlooked the present layout). The course was designed by Sir Guy Campbell and Major CK Hutchinson and opened for play in October 1930.

In a similar vein to Woodhall Spa in Lincolnshire, Pulborough has often been described as something of an oasis, the surrounding countryside being predominantly meadow and marshland with the course lying on sandy soil and heather running throughout. Heather naturally adds charm to any golf course but it is perhaps the magnificent spread of pines, oaks and silver birch trees that are most striking at Pulborough.

Colin Simpson is the present **Club Secretary**; he may be contacted via the **West Sussex Golf Club, Wiggonholt, Pulborough, West Sussex RH20 2EN tel: (01798) 872563** or by **fax: (01798) 872033** Visitors are welcome, but strictly by appointment only; the same applies to golfing societies. It should also be noted that three ball and four ball matches are not generally permitted—singles and foursomes being preferred. The only specific restrictions on times visitors can play are before 9.30am (throughout the week), on Fridays and at weekends. The green fees for 2000 are set at £45 for a single round or £55 for a day ticket. One final introduction: **Tim Packham** is the club's **Professional**, and he may be reached by telephone on **(01798) 872426.**

While Pulborough may enjoy a gloriously peaceful setting situated right in the heart of the Sussex countryside, it could hardly be described as remote and is easily accessible from all directions. The club's precise location is about two miles east of Pulborough just off the A283 road to Storrington. The A283 links Pulborough to the outskirts of Brighton on the south coast and to Milford (near Guildford) to the north. For those approaching from westerly directions the A272 from Winchester is likely to help—it joins the A283 at Petworth approximately five miles from Pulborough. Motoring from the London area the quickest route is probably to take the M23 towards Gatwick joining the A264 at Crawley and travelling through Horsham. The A264 merges into the A29 near Billingshurst which in turn joins with Pulborough.

One of the features of Pulborough is its conspicuous absence of a par five beyond the first hole—a hole which in any event becomes a four when played from the tees of the day. At 6221 yards, (SSS 70) the par of 68 is a difficult one to match. With none of the par fours being overly short there aren't any really obvious birdie opportunities. Perhaps the best known hole on the course is the par three 6th; measuring 224 yards it requires an exceptionally accurate tee shot across water to a small green that has an out-of-bounds and tall trees directly behind it. Henry Longhurst, a great admirer of Pulborough, very aptly said of the 6th, 'If ever there was an all or nothing hole, this is it.' Immediately after the potential disaster of the 6th, the 7th requires a long uphill drive to carry over some thick heather and scrub not to mention an enormous sand bunker. With holes of such a nature and quality as the 6th and 7th it isn't unrealistic to draw a comparison between this corner of Pulborough and Pine Valley in New Jersey. It is a brave comparison (and an enormous compliment) because the North American course is generally considered to be the finest and perhaps most naturally beautiful inland course in the world.

The 6th and 7th are not the only outstanding holes, mind you: the 4th, 5th and 8th are equally memorable while on the back nine perhaps the 10th, 13th, 16th and 17th are worthy of special praise (even expatiation!) As for its 19th, West Sussex has a very comfortable clubhouse offering full catering facilities including two bars. A jacket and tie should be worn in all public rooms.

Henry Longhurst is only one of a number of celebrated admirers of Pulborough and the late Bobby Locke, four times Open Champion, considered it his favourite English course. While no major professional tournament has been played over the course (again there is a parallel to be drawn with Pine Valley) the club has hosted several national amateur championships—both men's and ladies'.

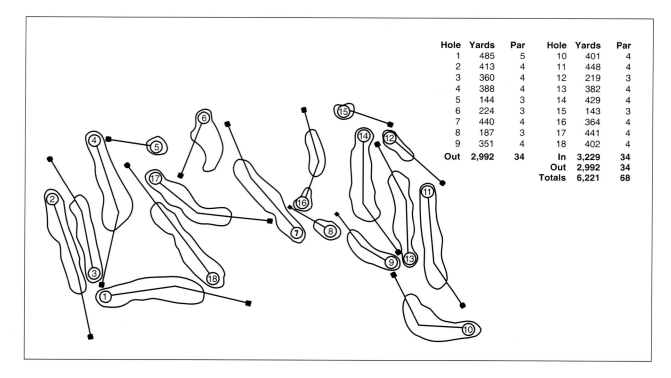

Hole	Yards	Par	Hole	Yards	Par
1	485	5	10	401	4
2	413	4	11	448	4
3	360	4	12	219	3
4	388	4	13	382	4
5	144	3	14	429	4
6	224	3	15	143	3
7	440	4	16	364	4
8	187	3	17	441	4
9	351	4	18	402	4
Out	**2,992**	**34**	**In**	**3,229**	**34**
			Out	**2,992**	**34**
			Totals	**6,221**	**68**

Mannings Heath

Mannings Heath is an extraordinary place. You stand on the terrace of what is possibly the finest 19th hole in England and you watch golfers descend into 'Sodom' and 'Gomorrah'. It is not quite what it seems. It is just that whoever named the opening holes on the **Waterfall Course** at Mannings Heath had a rather wry sense of humour (that or a wretched golf game). The perilous journey does not end at the 2nd as the next hole is called 'Gateway' and it leads immediately to 'Hell's Corner'. Presumably the gates of hell lie somewhere in between.

The visiting golfer shouldn't be alarmed. Mannings Heath is actually one of the most welcoming, as well as one of the most scenic courses in southern England. Nestling amidst beautiful countryside on the edge of the South Downs, the club was founded in 1905. For the best part of a century it has enjoyed a reputation as the 'hidden jewel of Sussex'. But Mannings Heath is unlikely to remain quite so hidden in the future. Two recent developments have ensured that.

The reference above to the 19th hole was not exaggerated. Mannings Heath may indeed possess the finest clubhouse in the country, and surely none is better appointed. The building in question is a beautifully restored manor house known as Fullers. Prior to the purchase of the golf club by its present owners in 1989 it was a private family residence. Today it has been tastefully converted into a clubhouse and is sumptuously furnished. Great comfort and great character combine to create a wonderfully relaxed golfing environment . . . the perfect 19th hole.

The other major development was the opening in 1996 of a second 18 holes, the **Kingfisher Course** designed by David Williams. Measuring 6217 yards, par 70, from the back markers and with full USGA greens and tees, the new course is maturing rapidly.

Visitors (individuals and groups) wishing to play either course can make arrangements by contacting **Lynn Barter** at the golf club on **tel: (01403) 248828** or **fax: (01403) 270974.** The club's full address is **Mannings Heath Golf Club, Fullers, Hammerpond Road, Horsham, West Sussex RH13 6PG.** Further information on Mannings Heath can be found at **www.exclusivehotels.co.uk** The 2000 green fees for both courses are set at £36 per round, £50 per day midweek, and £45 per round, £60 per day at weekends.

Mannings Heath is located two miles south of Horsham off the A281 Brighton Road. A further two miles beyond the golf club at Lower Beeding is South Lodge—a sister property and one of the finest country house hotels in southern England. Special golfing breaks in conjunction with the club are available throughout the week.

Measuring 6378 yards, par 73 from the back markers (5405 yards, par 73 from the ladies' tees) the Waterfall Course comprises an interesting mix of woodland, parkland and heathland holes. The terrain is naturally undulating throughout—as the opening drive and the final approach underline. Mature trees line the majority of the fairways and water, invariably in the form of a winding stream, affects no fewer than eleven holes.

The most memorable holes on the Waterfall course include all three of the short holes: the 5th, 'Punchbowl', the 10th, 'Waterfall' (both these holes have a superbly elevated tee and a tantalisingly small green) and the 14th, 'Blaster', which was no doubt christened by our friend from the opening paragraph. The most celebrated two-shotter is undoubtedly the 11th, 'Valley'. It is a superb natural golf hole and features a sunken fairway bordered for its entire length by a seemingly magnetic stream and a stage-like green surrounded by trees.

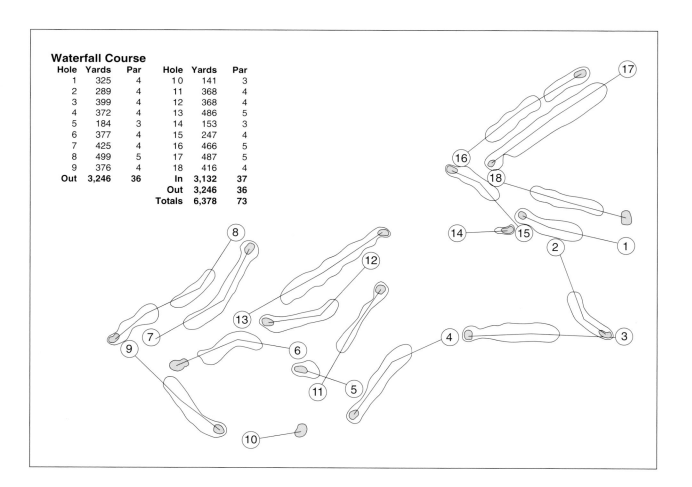

Waterfall Course

Hole	Yards	Par	Hole	Yards	Par
1	325	4	10	141	3
2	289	4	11	368	4
3	399	4	12	368	4
4	372	4	13	486	5
5	184	3	14	153	3
6	377	4	15	247	4
7	425	4	16	466	5
8	499	5	17	487	5
9	376	4	18	416	4
Out	**3,246**	**36**	**In**	**3,132**	**37**
			Out	**3,246**	**36**
			Totals	**6,378**	**73**

Royal Ashdown Forest

Although it is now less than an hour's drive from the frantic chaos of Greater London, Ashdown Forest is a place of great beauty, charm and tranquillity. And so it should be, for it was here, somewhere deep in this secluded forest of pine and silver birch, that the most famous of all 'Golden Bears', Winnie The Pooh pursued his never ending quest for honey. Such is the setting for one of Britain's most fortunate golf clubs.

In 1988 Royal Ashdown Forest celebrated its centenary. It was on Christmas Eve over a hundred years ago that the Reverend A T Scott teed up his ball and struck the very first shot. The course has changed little over the years, a fact which clearly speaks volumes for the original layout. The club acquired the title 'Royal' during Queen Victoria's reign and long before the turn of the century had established itself as one of the finest tests of golf in southern England.

Many great players have been associated with Royal Ashdown Forest over the years. The Cantelupe Club, the associate club connected to Royal Ashdown, included Abe Mitchell and Alf Padgham among its ranks and several noted amateurs have improved their technique on this most challenging course.

Casual visitors are welcomed at Royal Ashdown—rather more so, it must be said, than at some of the south east's leading courses. A recognised club handicap is, however, a requirement and it is normally advisable to telephone the club before finalising any plans. Not surprisingly the course is very popular in the summer months.

The club **Secretary, David Scrivens**, can be contacted via the **Royal Ashdown Forest Golf Club, Forest Row, East Sussex RH18 5LR tel: (01342) 822018**. Those wishing to organise a society meeting should write to Mr. Scrivens at the above address. Societies can normally be accommodated during the week, Tuesday being an exception. The green fees for 2000 are set at £42 per round or £50 per day for weekdays with £55 per round or per day payable at weekends and on bank holidays. Visitors should note that singles and foursomes are preferred. The club **Professional** is **Martyn Landsborough** who took over in 1990 from Alf Padgham's cousin, Hector, who had been the professional for over 40 years. Martyn can be reached on **tel: (01342) 822247.**

The club is located within Ashdown Forest, approximately 4 miles south of East Grinstead. Motoring from London and the north the A22 is by far the most direct route. This can be joined from the M25 at Junction 6. The A22 should be followed for some 4 miles beyond East Grinstead as far as Forest Row. There one should take the B2110 Hartfield road turning right after a quarter of a mile on to Chapel Lane where the club can be found. Approaching from the South the A22 can be joined from a number of roads north of Eastbourne.

The generally held view is that Royal Ashdown Forest is a particularly difficult course. On several holes a lengthy tee shot will be required in order to find the safety of the fairway. The ever-present stream and the considerable scattering of gorse and heather create a multitude of problems for the wayward golfer—and as if they were not enough, on several of the holes the fairway is exceptionally narrow and that beautiful forest will gratefully accept the result of a slice or a hook. The most celebrated hole at Royal Ashdown is probably the short 6th, the 'Island Hole' while the best of the par fours is probably the 17th with its exhilarating downhill approach.

Despite the variety of hazards, of all the country's leading courses Royal Ashdown Forest must surely be unique in not possessing a single bunker. Bernard Darwin is doubtless not the only golfer who failed to discover this fact until the conclusion of his game; as he put it, 'It is only at the end of a round that we realise with a pleasurable shock that there is not a single hideous rampart or so much as a pot bunker.' The club was prevented long ago by the Forestry Commission, or the then equivalent, from creating bunkers and their absence now forms part of the character and charm of the course. Furthermore, the undulating nature of the landscape produces some truly magnificent views over the forest and beyond.

The attractive clubhouse offers a very high standard of catering. A light lunch, such as a ploughman's, can be obtained whilst a full four course meal can also be arranged. During the months of November and December a full English breakfast is available—a welcome facility which many clubs would do well to copy. Golfers, like the forest's most famous inhabitant are hungry animals and some are more than quick to claim that the missed three footer is a result of a missed breakfast!

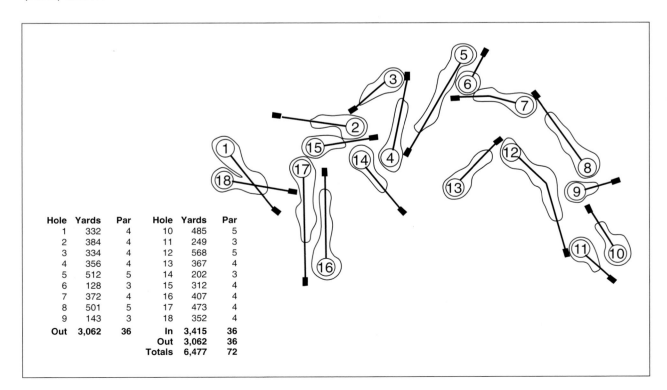

Hole	Yards	Par	Hole	Yards	Par
1	332	4	10	485	5
2	384	4	11	249	3
3	334	4	12	568	5
4	356	4	13	367	4
5	512	5	14	202	3
6	128	3	15	312	4
7	372	4	16	407	4
8	501	5	17	473	4
9	143	3	18	352	4
Out	**3,062**	**36**	**In**	**3,415**	**36**
			Out	**3,062**	**36**
			Totals	**6,477**	**72**

East Sussex National

Move over Sunningdale, Wentworth and Walton Heath! These three great championship venues, all situated in the magnificent heathland belt of Surrey and Berkshire, have had to make room for a newcomer from the heart of rural Sussex.

East Sussex National has two great golf courses, the East and West, which were officially opened for play as recently as April 1990. Both were designed by the American, Robert E Cupp, formerly Jack Nicklaus' senior designer. For the first time in Great Britain, bent grasses were used throughout from tee to green and the instant result was golf course conditioning of a type never witnessed before in this country.

Both courses measure in excess of 7000 yards from their championship tees and are similarly challenging but quite different in appearance. The East Course is the 'stadium' course and was specifically designed with a view to staging big events (the European Open has already been played over the course twice) hence the gentle 'gallery mounding' very evident around the 15th and 18th greens. The West Course is more intimate than the East. The landscape rises and falls quite sharply in parts. The surrounding woodland is more dense but because of the climbs there are many spectacular views over the South Downs.

East Sussex National was first conceived in the mid 1980s when a Canadian entrepreneur purchased Horsted Place, an elegant Victorian manor house which he immediately converted into one of Britain's leading country house hotels. Various parcels of adjoining land were also acquired which, when pieced together, totalled a massive 1100 acres of prime Sussex countryside. Construction began in May 1988 on the two 18 hole championship courses and, only 23 months later, both opened for play.

Aside from the golf courses, and of course Horsted Place, East Sussex National boasts superb golf practice facilities, including three full length academy holes. One of the best golf shops in the country, a striking 27,000 sq ft clubhouse, and a 10 bay driving range which houses the European Head Quarters of the David Leadbetter Academy.

Individuals, groups and corporate societies are welcome at East Sussex. Visitors will invariably play the East Course as the West is normally reserved for members. Bookings can be made by telephoning **Reservations** on **(01825) 880232/880231** or by **fax**: (01825) 880012. The visitors' green fees in 2000 are £40 for 18 holes, and £65 for 36 holes. Seasonal discounted rates are also available. The **Director of Golf** is **Phil Lewin** and all membership and corporate enquiries can be dealt with through the Sales Office on the above number. The address for written correspondence is **East Sussex National Golf Club, Little Horsted, Uckfield, East Sussex TN22 5ES**.

There are many outstanding holes on the **East Course** but perhaps the par fives are especially memorable. Three of the four, the 7th, 10th and 14th are as good a trio as one is likely to find on any inland course, anywhere. Of these, only the 10th is realistically reachable in two shots and then only after a brave downhill second is successfully hit over water—a hole not too dissimilar to the 15th at Augusta. There is also a great finish to the East Course, with the par four 17th being perhaps the best hole on either course.

Although the challenge isn't any greater on the **West Course**, in most people's minds it has the greater number of 'pretty' holes. In fact, 'provocatively spectacular' might be the description of some. Anyone wishing to put together a 'dream nine holes' could do worse than select the 1st, 2nd, 3rd, 9th, 10th, 12th, 13th, 14th and 18th on the East Sussex National West Course. This collection would provide two outstanding short holes, on both of which the tee shot must flirt with water; a pair of genuine par fives and five two-shot holes ranging from a drive and a short iron (the dog-leg 1st) to a truly intimidating stroke one hole (the monstrous 14th). And what a dramatic finale the 18th provides! In his course notes, architect Robert Cupp gives an interesting commentary on the closing holes of the West Course. Having metaphorically walked on to the back tee at the 18th he holds his breath and surveys the view ahead:

'The player has been restricted at fourteen, tempted at fifteen, devilled at sixteen and exhausted at seventeen. Now, he stands on the elevated tee, looking across a deep chasm to a fairway lined right and left by giant oaks, and a green guarded by huge bunkers and the clubhouse beyond. The word here is "test". The reaction in tournament conditions is clammy hands'.

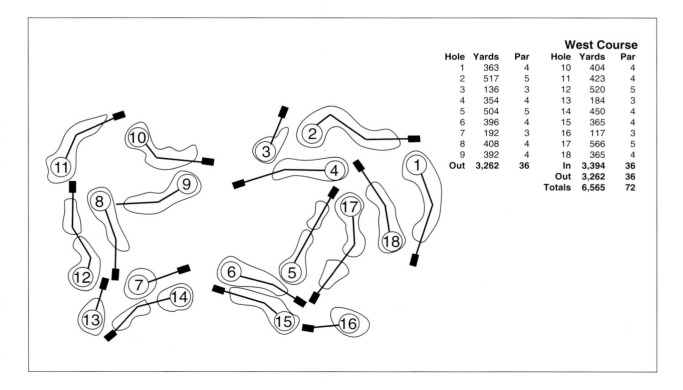

| | | | | **West Course** | |
Hole	Yards	Par	Hole	Yards	Par
1	363	4	10	404	4
2	517	5	11	423	4
3	136	3	12	520	5
4	354	4	13	184	3
5	504	5	14	450	4
6	396	4	15	365	4
7	192	3	16	117	3
8	408	4	17	566	5
9	392	4	18	365	4
Out	3,262	36	In	3,394	36
			Out	3,262	36
			Totals	6,565	72

WEST SUSSEX

Avisford Park Hotel & G.C.
(01243) 554611
Walberton, Arundel
(9) 3009 yards/***/D

Bognor Regis G.C.
(01243) 821929
Downview Road, Felpham,
(18) 6238 yards/**/B - A/H

Burgess Hill
(01444) 870615
Cuckfield Road, Burgess Hill
(9) 4433 yards/***/F

Chartham Park G.C.
(01342) 870340
Felcourt, East Grinstead
(18) 6688 yards/***/C

Chichester Golf Centre
(01243) 533833
Hoe Farm, Hunston
(18) 6174 yards/***/C
(18) 6461 yards/***/B

Copthorne G.C.
(01342) 712508
Borers Arms Road, Copthorne
(18) 6505 yards/**/B

Cottesmore G. & C.C.
(01293) 528256
Buchan Hill, Pease Pottage, Crawley
(18) 6280 yards/***/A
(18) 5489 yards/***/B

Cowdray Park G.C.
(01730) 813599
Petworth Road, Midhurst
(18) 6212 yards/**/B/H

Effingham Park G.C.
(01342) 716528
West Park Road, Copthorne
(9) 1749 yards/***/D

Foxbridge G.C
(01403) 753303
Foxbridge Lane, Plaistow
(9) 3015 yards/***/F/G

Gatwick Manor G.C.
(01293) 538587
Lowfield Heath, Crawley Heath
(9) 1246 yards/***/E

Goodwood G.C.
(01243) 774968
Goodwood, Chichester
(18) 6401 yards/***/B - A/H

Goodwood Park G. & C.C.
(01243) 775987
Goddwodd, Chichester
(18) 6530 yards/**/D/H

Ham Manor G.C.
(01903) 783732
Angmering, Littlehampton
(18) 6216 yards/***/F/H

Hassocks G.C.
(01273) 846990
London Road, Hassocks
(18) 5754 yards/***/D

Haywards Heath G.C.
(01444) 414457
High Beech Lane, Haywards Heath
(18) 6206 yards/***/B/H

Hill Barn G.C.
(01903) 237301
Hill Barn Lane, Worthing
(18) 6224 yards/***/D

Horsham Golf Park
(01403) 271525
Worthing Road, Horsham
(9) 2061 yards/***/E

Ifield G.& C.C.
(01293) 520222
Rusper Road, Ifield, Crawley
(18) 6314 yards/**/B/H

Littlehampton G.C.
(01903) 717170
Rope Walk, Littlehampton
(18) 6244 yards/**/B

Mannings Heath G.C.
(01403) 210228
Hammerpond Road, Mannings Heath
(18) 6378 yards/**/A/H
(18) 6217 yards/**/A/H

Osiers Farm G.C.
(01798) 344097
Osiers Farm, Petworth
(18) 6191 yards/***/E

Paxhill Park G.C.
(01444) 484467
Lindfield, Haywards Heath
(18) 6196 yards/**/D

Pease Pottage G.C.
(01293) 521706
Horsham Road, Pease Pottage,
(9) 3511 yards/***/E

Pyecombe G.C.
(01273) 845372
Pyecombe, Brighton
(18) 6234 yards/**/C

Selsey G.C.
(01243) 602203
Golf Links Lane, Selsey, Chichester
(9) 5834 yards/***/D

MARRIOTT GOODWOOD PARK HOTEL AND COUNTRY CLUB Photograph courtesy of: *Marriott Goodwood Park Hotel and Country Club*

Shillingtree G.C.
(01428) 653237
Chiddingfield, Godalming
(9) 2500 yards/***/D

Singing Hills G.C.
(01273) 835353
Albourne, Brighton
(9) 2826 yards/***/B/H
(9) 3253 yards/***/B/H
(9) 3348 yards/***/B/H

Slinfold Park G. & C.C.
(01403) 791154
Stane Street, Slinford, Horsham
(18) 6450 yards/***/B

Tilgate Forest G.C.
(01293) 530103
Titmus Drive, Crawley
(18) 6359 yards/***/D

West Chiltington G.C.
(01798) 813574
Broadford Bridge Road,
(18) 5969 yards/***/D

West Sussex G.C.
(01798) 872563
Hurston Lane, Pulborough
(18) 6221 yards/**/F/H/L

Worthing G.C.
(01903) 260801
Links Road, Worthing
(18) 6530 yards/***/F/H
(18) 5243 yards/***/F/H

EAST SUSSEX

Ashdown Forest Hotel G.C.
(01342) 824866
Chapel Lane, Forest Row
(18) 5510 yards/***/F

Beauport Park G.C.
(01424) 852977
St Leonards-on-Sea
(18) 6033 yards/***/F

Brighton and Hove G.C.
(01273) 556482
Dyke Road, Brighton
(9) 5722 yards/***/C

Cooden Beach G.C.
(01424) 842040
Cooden Sea Road, Cooden
(18) 6470 yards/***/B - A/H

Crowborough Beacon G.C.
(01892) 661511
Beacon Road, Crowborough
(18) 6279 yards/**/B/H/L

Dale Hill G.C.
(01580) 200112
Ticehurst, Wadhurst
(18) 6150 yards/***/B - A/H

Dewlands Manor G.C.
(01892) 852266
Cottage Hill, Rotherfield
(9) 3186 yards/***/B

Dyke G.C.
(01273) 857296
Dyke Road, Brighton
(18) 6611 yards/***(Sun)/B - A

MANNINGS HEATH GOLF CLUB *Photograph courtesy of:* **Mannings Heath Golf Club**

Eastbourne Downs G.C.
(01323) 720827
East Dean Road, Eastbourne
(18) 6635 yards/***/D

Eastbourne Golfing Park
(01323) 520400
Lottbridge Drove, Eastbourne
(9) 5046 yards/***/D

East Brighton G.C.
(01273) 604838
Roedean Road, Brighton
(18) 6436 yards/***/H

East Sussex National G.C.
(01825) 880232
Little Horsted, Uckfield
(18) 7154 yards /*/A
(18) 7138 yards/***/A

Hastings G.C.
(01424) 852977
Battle Road, St Leonards-on-Sea
(18) 6248 yards/***/F

Highwoods G.C.
(01424) 212625
Ellerslie Lane, Bexhill-on-Sea
(18)6218 yards/***/B/H

Hollingbury G.C.
(01273) 500086
Ditchling Road, Brighton
(18) 6415 yards/***/D

Holtye G.C.
(01342) 850635
Holtye, Edenbridge
(9) 5325 yards/***/C

Horam Park G.C.
(014353) 813477
Chiddingly Road, Horam,
(9) 5864 yards/***/D

Lewes G.C.
(01273) 473245
Chapel Hill, Lewes
(18) 6218 yards/**/C

Mid Sussex G.C.
(01273) 846547
Spatham Lane, Ditchling
(18) 6227 yards/**/C

Nevill G.C.
(01892) 525818
Benhall Mill Road,
Tunbridge Wells
(18) 6336 yards/**/A/H

Peacehaven G.C.
(01273) 512571
Brighton Road, Newhaven
(9) 5235 yards/***/D

Piltdown G.C.
(01825) 722033
Piltdown, Uckfield
(18) 6070 yards/**/B/H/L

Royal Ashdown Forest G.C.
(01342) 822018
Chapel Lane, Forest Row
(18) 6477 yards/**/B - A/H
(18) 5586 yards/**/B - A/H

Royal Eastbourne G.C.
(01323) 729738
Paradise Drive, Eastbourne
(18) 6109 yards/***/B
(9) 2147 yards/***/E

Rye G.C.
(01797) 225241
Camber, Rye
(18) 6301 yards/***/G
(9) 6625 yards/***/G

Seaford G.C.
(01323) 892442
East Blatchington, Seaford
(18) 6233 yards/**/F

Seaford Head G.C.
(01323) 894843
Southdown Road,
Seaford
(18) 5812 yards/***/D

Sedlescombe G.C.
(01424) 870898
Kent Street,
Sedlescombe
(18) 6218 yards/**/F/H

Sweetwoods Park G.C.
(01342) 850729
Cowden,
Edenbridge
(18) 6400 yards/***/D

Waterhall G.C.
(01273) 508658
Devil's Dyke Road,
Brighton
(18) 5775 yards/***/D

Wellshurst G.& C.C
(01435) 813636
North Street,
Hellingly
(18) 5717 yards/***/C - B

West Hove G.C.
(01273) 419738
Church Farm, Hangleton, Hove
(18) 6201 yards/***/F

Willingdon G.C.
(01323) 410981
Southdown Road, Eastbourne
(18) 6049 yards/**/H

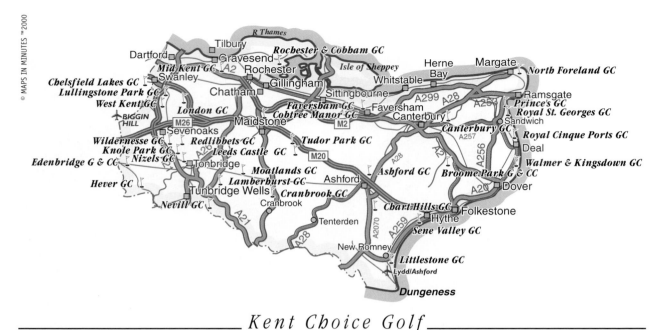

_____ *Kent Choice Golf* _____

From the mysterious and desolate lands of Romney Marsh to the famous White Cliffs of Dover; from the rich orchards of the Garden of England to the outskirts of Greater London; from the windswept links of Sandwich and Deal to the secluded parks of Belmont and Knole—a county of great contrasts.

Kent's reputation as one of the country's greatest golfing counties has been built around a three mile stretch of links land lying midway between St Margaret's Bay and Pegwell Bay. Within this short distance lie three Open Championship courses: **Prince's** (1932), **Royal Cinque Ports** (1909 and 1920) and **Royal St George's**. Kent has a few other fine links courses but the golfer who sticks hard to the coast will be missing out on some of the most enjoyable inland golf southern England has to offer.

Off the M25

In common with each of the counties that border Greater London, many of Kent's courses are gradually finding themselves more in London than in Kent. When the Blackheath golfers left their famous Common and set up base at Eltham they were doubtless surrounded by the green fields of Kent. Even Charles Darwin's village of Orpington is now feeling the pinch but the new course **Chelsfield Lakes** at Orpington is worth exploring, and happily the **West Kent** Golf Club near Bromley and nearby **Lullingstone Park** provide pleasant retreats.

Enough grousing! The ancient town of Sevenoaks is categorically in Kent and a very fortunate place too with **Wildernesse** Golf Club to the north and **Knole Park** to the south. The former is rated one of the finest inland courses in the county. With narrow fairways and quite thickly wooded, it is also one of the toughest. Knole Park is especially scenic and is one of several Kentish courses that enjoy stately surroundings, being laid out in the handsome deer park of Lord Sackville. To add to these riches a lovely new course, **Redlibbets**, designed by Jonathan Gaunt, a classic 20's 'Golden Age' traditional course set in a landscape of undulating parkland and Oak woods.

In the south west of the county, Tunbridge Wells is a very pretty, if congested, old town. **Nevill** Golf Club is just over the border in Sussex and there are 36 holes at the **Edenbridge** Golf and Country Club, but the most exciting developments in this area are the **Hever** Golf Club which is located adjacent to the famous castle and the Anglo-Japanese creation at **Moatlands** at Brenchley. The visitor to

this part of Kent should also note **Nizels** Golf Club - a fine course and a rustic clubhouse to delight even the most disillusioned golfer.

Hever Golf & Country Club
Hever, Kent TN8 7NP
Tel: (01732) 700771
Fax: (01732) 700775

Set among the hills that straddle the counties of Kent, Sussex and Surrey in its own 250 acres, Hever Golf and Country Club is the ideal venue for golfing breaks, corporate golf days, society visits and (if local) membership.

The luxury hotel suites have been designed with the history of Hever in mind and is just yards from the first tee. Along with the golf course and hotel you'll find a fully equipped fitness studio, spa and a full range of beauty and relaxation treatments available. Within easy reach of London and set in such beautiful surroundings a finer venue is hard to find.

For a stopover in Sevenoaks, the Royal Oak Hotel (01732) 451109 is comfortable, as is the Bull Hotel (01732) 789800 in nearby Wrotham Heath. A fine restaurant close at hand is the outstanding Thackeray's House (01892) 511921, in Tunbridge Wells. If you require a place to stay in Tunbridge Wells, the Royal Wells Inn (01892) 511188 is particularly good value with a fine restaurant, and for a second place try the Spa Hotel (01892) 520331. Finally in the south western corner of the county there is an outstanding pub—great for lunches—at Speldhurst, namely the 13th century George and Dragon.

North Kent

To the north of the county, both **Mid Kent's** downland course at Gravesend and **Rochester and Cobham Park** are handy for those travelling along the A2 although Rochester and Cobham is currently under alteration due to the Channel rail link. Further along this road is the attractive town of Faversham and south of the town off the A251 is Belmont Park, the estate of Lord Harris and the home of **Faversham** Golf Club. Here golf is played in the most tranquil of settings and can be particularly delightful in autumn when the fairways abound with countless strolling pheasants.

Beyond the 18th green a few ideas emerge for a 19th hole. In Shorne, the Inn On The Lake (01474) 823333 is a fairly modern place to stay.

18TH GREEN AND HOLE, REDLIBBETS GOLF CLUB Photograph courtesy of: **Redlibbets Golf Club**

An alternative for pub lovers is the Dickensian Leather Bottle (01474) 814327 in Cobham which also has comfortable bedrooms. More expensive accommodation is located near Ash Green in the alarmingly named village of Fawkham where the Brands Hatch Place (01474) 872239 offers tremendous comfort and a good restaurant. Two pubs in the area are the Golden Eagle in Burham and the particularly pleasant and aptly named Little Gem in Aylesford. Close to Ash Green and Brands Hatch, golfers might wish to note the new **London** Golf Club, a 36 hole multi-million pound venture including a Jack Nicklaus - designed championship course. It should be emphasised, however, that this is a very private club and visitors can only play the Nicklaus (Heritage Course) as guests of a member. Back towards Faversham, there is the extremely popular Reads (01795) 535344.

Leaving Faversham, famous pheasants and all, we must make a pilgrimage. The **Canterbury** Golf Club, situated to the east of the beautiful cathedral city along the A27 is well worth a visit. Surprisingly undulating, it is a first class parkland course—one of the best in the county. South of Canterbury (via A2 and A260) at Barham is the **Broome Park** Golf and Country Club, set in the grounds of yet another famous country house—this time a beautiful 300 year old mansion, the former home of Lord Kitchener. It too is a very pleasant parkland course and quite lengthy. Whether it's the proliferation of nearby golf courses (Sandwich and Deal are just 15 miles away) or the cathedral, or even the glorious Kent countryside that attracts most, Canterbury deserves more than a short visit. Perhaps the leading hotel which also houses a commendable restaurant is the County (01227) 766266. The House of Agnes Hotel (01227) 472185 can also be recommended, and just outside the city, Howfield Manor (01227)

738294 at Chartham Hatch is a charming small country house hotel with a good restaurant. Ersham Lodge (01227) 463174 and Magnolia House (01227) 765121 also receive many favourable reports. The aforementioned glorious countryside is riddled with village pubs: two of note are the Duck Inn at Petts Bottom and the White Horse at Chilham Castle.

Mid Kent

Maidstone may not have the appeal of Canterbury but to the south east of this busy commuter town is one of England's most attractive 'pay and play' golf courses, **Leeds Castle**. The castle itself was described by Lord Conway as the most beautiful in the world and the setting really is quite idyllic. There are nine very individual holes and as it's a public course (like Lullingstone Park, mentioned above, and **Cobtree Manor Park** on the Chatham Road) there are no general restrictions on times of play (although it can naturally get very busy). Another fairly recent golfing addition to the area is **Tudor Park** near Bearsted. Like Broome Park it is part of a country club. The golf course was designed by Donald Steel and is especially popular with golfing societies. The Tudor Park Hotel (01622) 734334 is predictably convenient.

The golf course at **Ashford** is pretty much in the middle of the county, and is strongly worth inspecting. Ashford is a heathland type course, which in itself is fairly unique to Kent and where visitors are always made to feel welcome. We're now in the heart of the Kent Downs and a variety of fine establishments beckon. Eastwell Manor (01233) 219955 takes pride of place; elegant and relaxing with a splendid restaurant—in fact outstanding in every way. In Wye, the

Wife of Bath (01233) 812540 is a tremendous restaurant. An ideal tavern is the Compasses at Side Street and for an inn with good value accommodation the Chequers Inn (01233) 770217 at Smarden is recommended.

Back to the fairways and a word for **Cranbrook**, a very pleasant and greatly improved parkland course. This was the scene of Bing Crosby's last round in England. Apparently he was close to purchasing the course before his untimely death in Spain. Also in Cranbrook is one of Kent's most popular hotels, the Kennel Holt Hotel (01580) 712032—excellent for dinner and equally convenient for **Lamberhurst** Golf Club.

The final inland course demanding inspection is to be found at Biddenden, the outstanding Nick Faldo-Steve Smyers designed **Chart Hills** which opened for play in late 1993. We view the course on a later page.

Around the Coast

Switching from the countryside of Kent we now visit the coast. **Littlestone** is the first port of call, and the contrast is a stark one. Situated on the edge of the flatlands of Romney Marsh, it enjoys a very remote setting. Littlestone is a splendid links and an Open Championship qualifying course, which doesn't deserve to be overshadowed by Kent's more illustrious trio further along the coast. Littlestone's best holes are saved for near the end of the round—the par four 16th and par three 17th typify all that's best about links golf. Not too far from Littlestone is the town of Hythe where the Hythe Imperial (01303) 267441 is a fine base, as there are 9 holes in the 'back garden'! There is also a good course at **Sene Valley** with terrific views over Romney Bay.

North of Sandwich is the **North Foreland** Club at Broadstairs which, like Littlestone, is also an Open qualifying course, although its 27

holes are more strictly clifftop than links in nature. The Castlemere (01843) 861566 in Broadstairs is another fine place to stay, as is the intimate Rothsay Hotel. To the south of Deal is **Walmer and Kingsdown**, a course providing far reaching views. Perhaps not surprisingly, where there is one great golf links there is often another nearby: Troon, Turnberry and Prestwick in Ayrshire; Birkdale, Hillside and Formby in Lancashire. Kent's famous three, **Royal St George's**, **Royal Cinque Ports** and **Prince's** are all featured ahead.

Despite the great quality of golf on offer there aren't too many places along the famous three mile stretch where one can put the feet up (or the golf clubs for that matter). Anyway, in Sandwich the Bell Hotel (01304) 613388 is very comfortable and convenient: its quayside setting is also handy for the Fisherman's Wharf Restaurant (01304) 613636. St Crispin's Inn (01304) 612081 is a charming alternative. Two pubs to note in Sandwich are the King's Arms (01304) 617330 and the Fleur-de-Lis (01304) 611131. In Deal, Sutherland House (01304) 362853 is a popular golfing haunt.

Others to note include the Royal Hotel (01304) 375555, the Kings Head (01304) 368194 and the popular Dunkerleys (01304) 375016 which comes highly recommended. St Margaret's Bay, located on National Trust land is worth a look and the Cliffe Tavern (01304) 852749 nearby is a good place to wet one's whistle and stay if you wish. The Guildford House Hotel (01304) 375015 located on Beach Street in Deal, where there is a wider choice of accommodation is another ideal 19th hole if you're playing the famous courses nearby.

As a final tip it might be a good idea to take the car on a short drive to Westcliffe, where Wallett's Court (01304) 852424 is supremely welcoming (despite its name!) As we conclude our trip another thought emerges . . . Hardelot, Le Touquet . . . Why, we could nip down to Lydd where an aeroplane can whisk us off to Le Touquet quicker than we can drive back to London.

PRINCE'S GOLF CLUB *Photograph courtesy of:* **Prince's Golf Club**

Royal Cinque Ports

In the year 55 BC Julius Caesar landed on the coast near Deal. In 1920, an American invader by the name of Walter Hagen came to Deal to play in his first Open Championship. Both came, both saw, but neither conquered. In fact, both returned whence they came, tails firmly between legs—small wonder Deal is often considered the toughest of England's championship links!

The Royal Cinque Ports golf club was founded in February 1892 by Major General J M Graham whilst at lunch in Deal's Black Horse Hotel. The 18 hole course was opened in 1895 and has required very few alterations during its distinguished history.

Very often it is Mother Nature who provides the greatest challenge at Deal. Strong winds billowing in from the sea, capable of changing direction several times during a round, can turn what appear to be modest holes into monsters. The course measures 6407 yards from the medal tees (par 70) with the championship tees extending the course to some 6787 yards (par 72). From the ladies' tees the course measures 5686 yards, (par 74).

The outward nine is generally considered the easier half—Michael Bonallack turned in 31 during his record amateur score of 65 (a record which has stood for more than a third of a century). Certainly the back nine is longer and Deal is renowned for its tough finish, the classic par five 16th perhaps being the most difficult (and best) hole on the course. The fairways are humpy and hillocky and well bunkered, and many of the greens stand on natural plateaux. On a clear day there are some magnificent views across the course towards the English Channel and to the distant white cliffs beyond Pegwell Bay.

Two Open Championships have been held at Deal, in 1909 and in 1920. The 1909 championship was won by the Englishman John H

Taylor, his fourth victory in the event. The 1920 Open has already been referred to—the luckless Hagen in fact finished fifty third in a field of fifty four. Also entitled to feel somewhat peeved that year was Abe Mitchell who allowed George Duncan to come from thirteen strokes behind to snatch victory. Plans to stage a third championship at Deal in 1949 had to be abandoned when extensive flooding led to a temporary closure of the course.

It would not be fair, either to the Romans or Mr Hagen, to leave Deal without recording that both did eventually achieve their ambitions. The Romans returned a century later and conquered the Brits, and as for 'Sir Walter', he didn't have to wait quite so long, for in 1922 he won the first of four Open Championships, none of which though, alas, was at Deal.

	Royal Cinque Ports Golf Club, Golf Road, Deal, Kent CT14 6RF	
Secretary	Colin Hammond (01304) 374007	
Professional	Andrew Reynolds (01304) 374170	
Green Fees	£60/day; £10 reduction after 1 pm Twilight green fee £25 Mon, Tues, Thurs after 5 pm May - September	
Restrictions	Handicap required (max 20)	

Directions
Take the M20 from London to Dover. There pick up the A258 to Deal. The course is a mile north of the town.

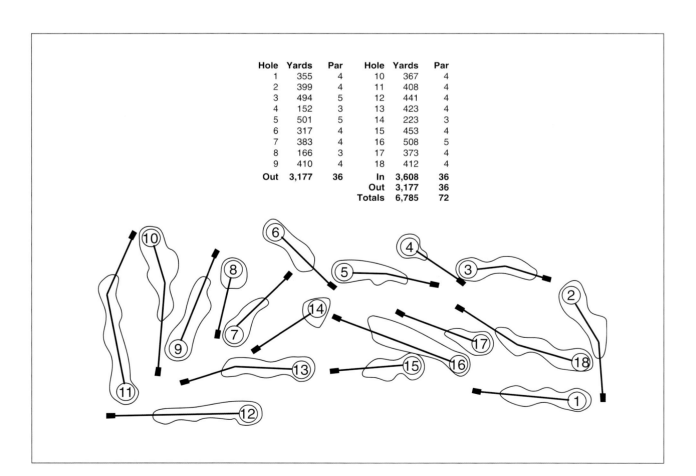

Hole	Yards	Par	Hole	Yards	Par
1	355	4	10	367	4
2	399	4	11	408	4
3	494	5	12	441	4
4	152	3	13	423	4
5	501	5	14	223	3
6	317	4	15	453	4
7	383	4	16	508	5
8	166	3	17	373	4
9	410	4	18	412	4
Out	**3,177**	**36**	**In**	**3,608**	**36**
			Out	**3,177**	**36**
			Totals	**6,785**	**72**

Royal St George's

Royal St George's was founded in 1887, rather ironically by two Scottish gentlemen, Dr Laidlaw Purves and Henry Lamb, after what can only be described as a rather eccentric venture. Like all good Scotsmen they had been bitten by the bug; however, both were presently living in Victorian London which meant that their golf was more or less confined to the various commons, where the game was played alongside every conceivable activity imaginable. To them golf was meant to be played on a links by the sea. Hence the pair found themselves at Bournemouth setting off in an easterly direction looking for a suitable site. Having reached the eastern shore of Kent, so the story goes, they had drawn the proverbial blank (one presumes that they experienced one of those infamous Victorian pea-soupers the day they passed through Rye). With patience no doubt wearing thin, suddenly 'land ahoy!' Doctor Purves sights a vast stretch of duneland at Sandwich. The theory is that he 'spied the land with a golfer's eye' from the tower of St Clement's Church. Quite what he was doing at the top of the tower is irrelevant—St George's had been located. Within seven short years the Open Championship had 'come south' and St George's was the first English venue.

More than one hundred years on **Gerald Watts** is the **Secretary** at St George's and he can be contacted by telephone on **(01304) 613090** or by fax on (01304) 611245. All written communication should be directed to him at **The Royal St George's Golf Club, Sandwich, Kent CT13 9PB**. As a general guide visitors are welcome between Mondays and Fridays. Gentlemen must possess a handicap of no more than 18 and ladies no more than 15 and introductions are required. There are no ladies tees and other points to note are that the 1st tee is reserved daily for members until 9.45am and between 1.00pm and 2.15pm; however, the 10th tee is usually free in the early mornings. St George's is essentially a singles and foursomes club and three ball and four ball matches are only permissible with the agreement of the Secretary.

The green fees for 2000 were set at £65 per round, £90 per day. During the months of December, January and February the £65 fee is applicable for a full day's golf. In 2000 an extended period of play has been introduced to include November when a dy's golf can be enjoyed for £65. Should there be a wish to hire golf clubs, a limited supply are for hire through the **Professional, Andrew Brooks, (01304) 615236**. Finally, the services of a caddie can be booked via the **Caddiemaster** on **(01304) 617380**.

Please excuse the awful pun but finding Sandwich should be a 'piece of cake.' The town is linked with Canterbury to the west by the A257, a distance of approximately 15 miles, and with Deal, 6 miles south east of Sandwich, by the A258. Motoring from London, the most direct route is to head for Canterbury using a combination of the A2 and M2 and thereafter following the A257 as above. For those coming from the south coast Ashford is the place to head for: Ashford is joined to Canterbury by the A28. Sandwich can also be reached by train.

Since its first Open in 1894, won by John H Taylor, the Championship has been held at Sandwich on twelve further occasions, most recently in 1993 when Australian Greg Norman won his second Championship after an epic final day's play. The Open Championship return to the club in 2003. The visitor will not have to tackle the course from the Open Championship tees (6930 yards) but he'll still have to confront the many dunes, the great undulations and the awkward stances that St George's is so renowned for.

It is difficult to say which is the best or most famous hole at Sandwich. The chief candidates are probably the 4th, which features the 'tallest and deepest bunker in the United Kingdom', and the short 6th, the fabled 'Maiden'. It is more than likely, however, that the par five 14th, 'Suez', will shortly be competing with these for it was, in 1998, redesigned and may well now witness even more dramas than it has done in the past. The 17th and 18th provide an exacting finish.

Having done battle with the elements the golfer will find the clubhouse welcoming. Excellent lunches are served daily and both breakfasts and dinners can be obtained with prior arrangement. A jacket and tie must be worn in all public rooms.

Although the 1993 Championship seems destined to be remembered as St George's greatest Open, when Nick Faldo and Payne Stewart set the course record at 63, there have been many other famous happenings: Walter Hagen won the Championship in 1922 and promptly handed his winnings straight to his caddie; Henry Cotton's opening 67-65 in the 1934 Championship (a record that stood until Nick Faldo scored 66-64 at Muirfield in 1992) and then the Harry Bradshaw broken bottle episode of 1949. After 32 years the Open returned to St George's in 1981, when American Bill Rogers won, and again four years later when Sandy Lyle became the first British winner for sixteen years. The Amateur Championship was played here for the twelfth time in 1997.

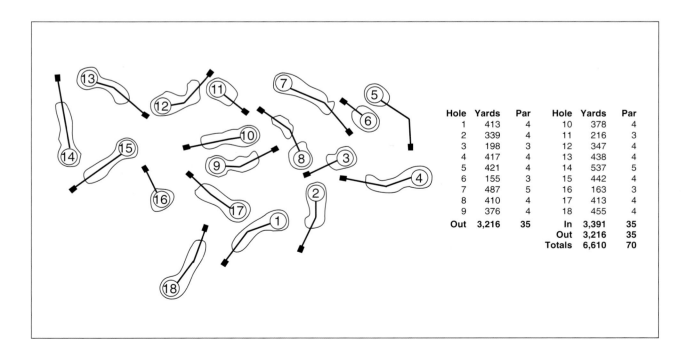

Hole	Yards	Par	Hole	Yards	Par
1	413	4	10	378	4
2	339	4	11	216	3
3	198	3	12	347	4
4	417	4	13	438	4
5	421	4	14	537	5
6	155	3	15	442	4
7	487	5	16	163	3
8	410	4	17	413	4
9	376	4	18	455	4
Out	**3,216**	**35**	**In**	**3,391**	**35**
			Out	**3,216**	**35**
			Totals	**6,610**	**70**

Chart Hills

You and I might visit Ballybunion or Royal Dornoch on a golfing pilgrimage. Our mouths water at the prospect of tackling the great sandbelt courses of Melbourne. And we would do anything to play golf at Pine Valley in New Jersey, widely acknowledged as the finest inland course in the world. For us, the stuff of dreams—for Nick Faldo, a day at the office.

It is not that Faldo is a killjoy—quite the contrary, he has as much fun playing the great courses as anyone—it's just that nowadays whenever he makes a special visit to a famous golfing shrine he is thinking 'design'. Beyond the 18th green, and after his family, golf course design has become his major interest. Moreover, when his extraordinary resolve and desire to be recognised as one of the all-time greats has been satisfied (when he is confident people will tell their grandchildren 'I saw Faldo play') golf course design will take over full time. The comparison with Jack Nicklaus is striking, and since it was a vision of Nicklaus playing at Augusta back in 1971 that ignited the golfing flame, it is also rather neat.

Chart Hills was the first course Nick Faldo designed in Europe (he has subsequently created, among others, Sporting Club Berlin which in 1997 was rated 'Best New Course in Continental Europe' by *Golf World* magazine. At Chart Hills Faldo teamed up with one of America's most talented golf course architects, Steve Smyers.

Imagine a setting in the heart of the Kent countryside, where ancient oak trees stand proud. Imagine a golf course that has clusters of fairway bunkers reminiscent of those at Royal Melbourne; where the fairways comprise a variety of sweeping tree-lined dog-legs and island sanctuaries; where holes twist and tumble downhill in an almost links-like fashion towards huge contoured greens, and where entry to the putting surfaces is protected by winding creeks and steep revetted pot bunkers similar to Carnoustie and Muirfield. This is Chart Hills.

But one shouldn't gain the impression that Chart Hills is merely a melting pot for design theories. There has been no crude imitation, rather it is the flavour of these great courses that has been incorporated and it has been done very subtly. Indeed, the golf course doesn't so much occupy the land as seemingly melt into it. A very natural look has been achieved and, young though it is, Chart Hills is developing its own special character and charm. It is a unique course; it has the hallmarks of a great course and, importantly (at

least for the purposes of Following the Fairways !) it is a great course that visitors can play.

The club recommends that all those seeking to play should telephone in advance of arrival. The **Head Professional**, **Danny French** and his staff can be contacted on **(01580) 292148 fax (01580) 292233**. Handicap certificates are not required. **Roger Hyder** is the **General Manager** at Chart Hills. The summer green fees in 2000 are £55 per round midweek and £65 on Sundays although a number of special packages are also available.

The 19th hole at Chart Hills has something of an American country club atmosphere, being luxurious but not overly formal. This North American ambience starts to recede the instant you stand on the 1st tee. Not only are you staring across at the green fields of Kent but below is an extraordinary opening hole, a par five of almost 600 yards that includes elements of nearly all the design influences described earlier: a Mackenzie-like spread of fairway bunkers must be confronted with the drive; to the left of the fairway the rough is savage and there is a creek off to the right but the tee shot is perhaps not quite so intimidating as it appears for the landing area is quite generous. The hole then dog-legs sharply to the right, sweeping down towards the green as the fairway narrows and becomes heavily contoured—a genuine links feel have been created. Just short of the green there is another nest of traps and guarding the front right entrance are two fairly cavernous pot bunkers. The green itself is very large and full of wicked borrows—a five at this hole is a good start !

And so the challenge continues, with dramatic holes being followed by more subtle ones and constant changes in direction and elevation. Among the outstanding holes at Chart Hills are the short 3rd (with its 'Redan' fortress-style green), the 4th (a hole that would grace Royal Melbourne), the 8th (shades of Augusta's 14th?), the 9th (a hint of Pine Valley?) and on the back nine, perhaps the finest sequence of all, the 12th, 13th and 14th.

According to Smyers, a great golf course should excite, thrill and sometimes frighten. Applying this test literally, the golfer walking off the 18th green at Chart Hills is likely to be emotionally disturbed. As for Faldo, he is on record as saying that his twin ambitions in course design are to create the best inland course in Great Britain and the best links course—Nick never was one to set himself modest goals ! Play Chart Hills, though, and you may reckon him halfway there already.

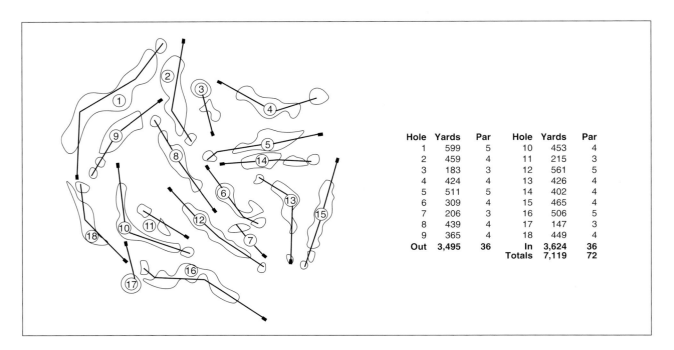

Hole	Yards	Par	Hole	Yards	Par
1	599	5	10	453	4
2	459	4	11	215	3
3	183	3	12	561	5
4	424	4	13	426	4
5	511	5	14	402	4
6	309	4	15	465	4
7	206	3	16	506	5
8	439	4	17	147	3
9	365	4	18	449	4
Out	3,495	36	In	3,624	36
			Totals	7,119	72

Prince's

One of the highlights of the magnificent 1993 Open Championship at Royal St George's was the delightful speech made at the prize presentation by the legendary American golfer, Gene Sarazen. For many years the late Sarazen, performed the traditional honour of hitting the first tee shot at the US Masters tournament and it was always a moving occasion. Sarazen was one of golf's greatest characters and certainly one of the finest players ever to have graced the sport. One of only four golfers in history (Nicklaus, Hogan and Player the others) to have won all four of golf's grand slam events. And Sarazen's link with Prince's? It was the scene of his one British Open victory in 1932 which, no thanks to Adolf Hitler, was Prince's one and only Open Championship.

Sarazen's total score of 283 was then a record for the Open Championship but today's golfer cannot properly walk in Sarazen's footsteps for the 18 hole links was dismembered during the last War. For a time it looked as if the military might retain the land, but in 1950 Sir Guy Campbell and John Morrison were invited to restore the links. Remarkably, given the heavily scarred landscape, seventeen of the pre-war greens could still be used. Campbell and Morrison decided, however, that they could best utilise the available land by creating three loops of nine and this is what greets the present day visitor to Prince's.

I'm not sure that 'greets' is actually the right terminology. Prince's may have lost its Open Championship status, but it has not lost its teeth. The three nines, the Dunes, Himalayas and Shore are each tremendously testing and, being a relatively exposed links, the golfer is at the mercy of the elements.

The Prince's links are beginning a new phase in their development. Under the guidance of Ronan Rafferty and his partner, golf architect Martin Gillett, the Shore and Dunes courses will be modified so that Prince's continues to provide a tough challenge to the modern tournament player whilst at the same time presenting amateur players with a fair test of golf.

The golf club however, most definitely 'greets' the visitor. This must be one of southern England's most welcoming clubs and, subject to availability, visitors with handicaps can generally play at all times. The most recent development at Prince's has been the building of a new clubhouse. Opened by Peter Alliss in 1985 it provides stunning panoramic views over the course. It's restaurant can cater for up to 200 diners, whilst the famous 'Tee-Bar' provides an opportunity for a brief 'pick-me-up'. For those wishing to extend their stay their Bell Hotel (01304) 613388 in Sandwich is a splendid old golfing hotel, it offers excellent cuisine and lavishes old fashioned hospitality upon its guests.

General Manager Bill Howie can be contacted at **Prince's Golf Club, Sandwich Bay, Sandwich, Kent CT13 9QB**, for bookings call **Ali McGuirk, Golf Events Co-ordinator tel: (01304) 611118.** The **Professional** at Prince's is **Derek Barbour (01304) 613797.** For further information you can also visit Prince's web site: **www.princes-leisure.co.uk** For 2000, the cost of a weekday round is £30 low season, £45 high season or £36/£55 per day, Saturdays £35/£55 per round or £30/£55 per day, packages range from £35 - £70.

Golfers playing 36 holes will play two eighteens from the following three combinations: **Dunes/Himalayas** 6506 yards, par 71; **Himalayas/Shore** 6510 yards, par 72 and **Shore/Dunes** 6690 yards, par 72. Each course is of a similarly high standard with a plethora of plateaued greens, ridges, humps and hollows but not too many bunkers. There are few, if any, weak holes at Prince's, but if one were to single out a balanced 'nine of the best' from the 27 then I might venture a combination of the 2nd, 7th and 8th from the Himalayas; the 3rd, 6th and 9th from the Shore and the 3rd, 4th and 6th from the Dunes.

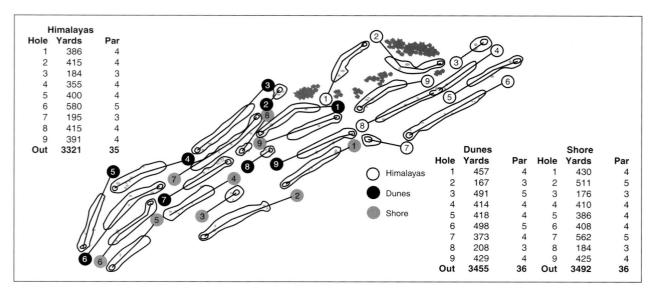

Himalayas		
Hole	Yards	Par
1	386	4
2	415	4
3	184	3
4	355	4
5	400	4
6	580	5
7	195	3
8	415	4
9	391	4
Out	**3321**	**35**

	Dunes			Shore	
Hole	Yards	Par	Hole	Yards	Par
1	457	4	1	430	4
2	167	3	2	511	5
3	491	5	3	176	3
4	414	4	4	410	4
5	418	4	5	386	4
6	498	5	6	408	4
7	373	4	7	562	5
8	208	3	8	184	3
9	429	4	9	425	4
Out	**3455**	**36**	**Out**	**3492**	**36**

○ Himalayas
● Dunes
● Shore

Aquarius G.C.
(0181) 693 1626
Marmora Road, Honor Oak
(9) 5246 yards/**/F/M

Ashford G.C.
(01233) 622655
Sandyhurst Lane, Ashford
(18) 6246 yards/***/B/H

Austin Lodge G.C.
(01322) 863000
nr Eynsford Station
(18) 6600 yards/***/C

Barnehurst G.C.
(01322) 523746
Mayplace Road, East Barnehurst
(9) 5448 yards/*/E

Bearsted G.C.
(01622) 738198
Ware Street, Bearsted,Maidstone
(18) 6278 yards/**/B/L/M

Birchwood Park G.C.
(01322) 662554
Birchwood Road, Wilmington
(18) 6364 yards/***/C

Boughton G.C.
(01227) 752277
Brickfield Lane, Boughton
(18) 6452 yards/***/C

Broke Hill G.C.
(01959) 533810
Sevenoaks Road, Halstead
(18) 6454 yards/***/C

Bromley G.C.
(0181) 462 7014
Magpie Hall Lane, Bromley
(9) 5538 yards/***/F

Broome Park G.& C.C.
(01227) 831701
Barham, Canterbury
(18) 6610 yards/**/B/H

Canterbury G.C.
(01227) 453532
Scotland Hills, Canterbury
(18) 6249 yards/**/B/H

Chart Hills G.C.
(01580) 292222
Weeks Lane, Biddenden
(18) 7086 yards/***/A/H

Chelsfield Lakes Golf Centre
(01689) 896266
Court Road, Orpington
(18) 6077 yards/***/D

Cherry Lodge G.C.
(01959) 572250
Jail Lane, Biggin Hill
(18) 6652 yards/**/B

Chestfield G.C.
(01227) 794411
103 Chestfield Road, Whitstable
(18) 6181 yards/**/B/H

Chigwell G.C.
(0181) 500 2059
High Road, Chigwell
(18) 6279 yards/**/A/H

Chislehurst G.C.
(0181) 467 3055
Camden Place, Chislehurst
(18) 5128 yards/***/B/H

Cobtree Manor G.C.
(01622) 753276
Maidstone
(18) 5716 yards/***/E

Corinthian G.C.
(01474) 707559
Gay Dawn Farm, Fawkham
(9) 6045 yards/**/D

Cranbrook G.C.
(01580) 712833
Benenden Road, Cranbook
(18) 6351 yards/**/C

Cray Valley G.C.
(01689) 831927
Sandy Lane, St Pauls Cray
(18) 5624 yards/***/D

Darenth Valley G.C.
(01959) 522944
Station Road, Shoreham
(18) 6356 yards/***/D

Dartford G.C.
(01322) 223616
Dartford Heath
(18) 5914 yards/**/B/L/M

Deangate Ridge G.C.
(01634) 251180
Hoo, Rochester
(18) 6300 yards/***/B

Edenbridge G.& C.C.
(01732) 867381
Crouch House Road, Edenbridge
(18) 6646 yards/**/C
(18) 5671 yards/**/C

Eltham Warren G.C.
(0181) 850 1166
Bexley Road, Eltham
(9) 5840 yards/***/B

Etchinghill G.C
(01303) 862280
Canterbury Road, Etchinghill.
(18) 6147 yards/***/D

Faversham G.C.
(01795) 890251
Belmont Park, Faversham
(18) 6030 yards/**/C

Gillingham G.C.
(01634) 853017
Woodlands Road, Gillingham
(18) 5911 yards/**/D

Hawkhurst G.C.
(01580) 752396
High Street, Hawkhurst, Cranbrook
(9) 5774 yards/**/D

Herne Bay G.C.
(01227) 373964
Eddington, Herne Bay
(18) 5466 yards/***/D/H

Hever G.C.
(01732) 700771
Hever
(18) 7002 yards/***/A/H

Hewitts G.C.
(01689) 896266
Court Road, Orpington
(18) 6077 yards/***/D

High Elms G.C.
(01689) 858175
High Elms Road, Downe
(18) 6210 yards/***/F

Holtye G.C.
(01342) 850635
Holtye Common, Cowden,
(9) 5289 yards/**/F

CHELSFIELD LAKES GOLF CENTRE *Photograph courtesy of:* **Clubhaus**

12TH IN FOREGROUND, 16TH IN BACKGROUND, CHART HILLS GOLF CLUB Photograph courtesy of: *Chart Hills Golf Club*

Sittingbourne & Milton Regis G.C.
(01795) 842261
Wormdale, Newington,
(18) 6272 yards/**/D/H/L

Sundridge Park G.C.
(0181) 460 1822
Garden Road, Bromley
(18) 6490 yards/**/A/H
(18) 6007 yards/**/A/H

Sweetwoods Park G.C.
(01342) 850729
Cowden, Edenbridge
(18) 6400 yards/***/D

Tenterden G.C.
(01580) 763987
Woodchurch Road, Tenterden
(18) 6030 yards/**/D

Tudor Park G.& C.C.
(01622) 734334
Ashford Road, Bearsted
(18) 6000 yards/***/B/H

Upchurch River Valley G.C.
(01634) 360626
Upchurch, Sittingbourne
(18) 6160 yards/***/E

Walmer & Kingsdown G.C.
(01304) 373256
The Leas, Kingsdown, Deal
(18) 6160 yards/***/C/H

Weald of Kent G.C.
(01622) 890866
Maidstone Road, Headcorn
(18) 6169 yards/***/D

Westgate & Birchington G.C.
(01843) 831115
Canterbury Road,
Westgate-on-Sea
(18) 4926 yards/**/D/H/L

West Kent G.C.
(01689) 851323
West Hill, Downe, Orpington
(18) 6392 yards/**/F/H/L

West Malling G.C.
(01732) 844785
London Road, Addington,
Maidstone
(18) 6142 yards/**/B
(18) 6240 yards/**/B

Whitstable & Seasalter G.C.
(01227) 272020
Collingwood Road, Whitstable
(9) 5276 yards/**/C

Wildernesse G.C.
(01732) 761199
Seal, Sevenoaks, Maidstone
(18) 6478 yards/**/B/H/L

Woodlands Manor G.C.
(01959) 523805
Tinkerpot Lane, Sevenoaks
(18) 5858 yards/**/F/H

Wrotham Heath
(01732) 884800
Seven Mile Lane, Comp, Sevenoaks
(9) 5959 yards/**/C/H

Hythe Imperial G.C.
(01303) 267441
Princes Parade, Hythe
(9) 5560 yards/**/B

Knole Park G.C.
(01732) 452150
Seal Hollow Road, Sevenoaks
(18) 6249 yards/**/B/H

Lamberhurst G.C.
(01892) 890241
Church Road, Lamberhurst
(18) 6232 yards/**/B

Leeds Castle
(01622) 880467
Maidstone
(9) 2880 yards/***/F

Littlestone G.C.
(01797) 363355
St Andrews Road, Littlestone
(18) 6460 yards/**/B/H

London G.C.
(01474) 879899
Stansted Lane, Ash Green
(18) 7208 yards/*/F/M
(18) 7005 yards/*/F/M

Lullingstone Park G.C.
(01959) 533793
Park Gate, Chelsfield, Orpington
(18) 6779 yards/***/F
(9) 2445 yards/***/E

Lydd G.C.
(01797) 320808
Romney Road, Lydd
(18) 6517 yards/**/D

Mid Kent G.C.
(01474) 568035
Singlewell Road, Gravesend
(18) 6206 yards/**/F/H

Moatlands G.C.
(01892) 724400
Watermans Lane, Brenchley
(18) 6460 yards/***/A/H

Nizels G.C.
(01732) 833138
Nizels Lane, Hildenborough
(18) 6279 yards/***/A

North Foreland G.C.
(01843) 862140
Convent Road, Broadstairs
(18) 6382 yards/**/B/H

Oastpark G.C.
(01634) 242818
Malling Road, Snodland
(18) 6200 yards/***/E

Parkwood G.C.
(01959) 577744
Chestnut Avenue, Westerham
(18) 6835 yards/**/C

Poult Wood G.C.
(01732) 364039
Higham Lane, Tonbridge
(18) 5569 yards/***/E

Princes G.C.
(01304) 611118
Sandwich Bay, Sandwich
(9) 3321 yards***/A/H
(9) 3492 yards***/A/H
(9) 3455 yards***/A/H

Redlibbets G.C.
(01474) 872278
Ash, Sevenoaks
(18) 6619 yards/***/B

The Ridge G.C.
(01622) 844382
Chartway Street, East Sutton
(18) 6254 yards/***/B/H

Rochester & Cobham Park G.C.
(01474) 823411
Park Dale, by Rochester
(18) 6467 yards/**/B/H

Romney Warren G.C.
(01797) 362231
St Andrews Road, Littlestone
(18) 5126 yards/***/E

Royal Cinque Ports G.C.
(01304) 374007
Sandwich
(18) 6744 yards/**/F/H

Royal St Georges G.C.
(01304) 613090
Sandwich Bay Road, Sandwich
(18) 6857 yards/**/A/H

Ruxley Park G.C.
(01689) 871490
Sandy Lane, St Pauls Cray,
(18) 6027 yards/***/D

St Augustines G.C.
(01843) 590333
Cottingham Road, Cliffsend,
Ramsgate
(18) 5197 yards/***/C/H

Sene Valley G.C.
(01303) 268513
Sene, Folkestone
(18) 6320 yards/***/B/H

Sheerness G.C.
(01795) 662585
Power Station Road, Sheerness
(18) 6460 yards/**/D/H

Shortlands G.C.
(0181) 460 2471
Shortlands, Bromley
(9) 5261 yards/F/G

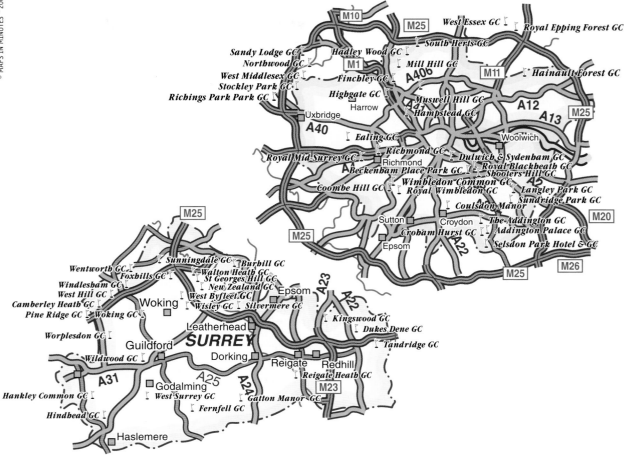

Capital Golf

Records suggest that golf was first played in England in 1608: the venue was Blackheath in London but the participants were Scottish not English. James I (James VI of Scotland) and his courtiers are generally credited with bringing the game south of the border. The exact date that the English caught the bug is unclear. Certainly in the 18th century it was still pretty much an alien pastime—in his first English dictionary compiled in 1755 Dr Samuel Johnson described golf as 'a game played with a ball and a club or bat'.

Historic Golf

During its formative years golf in London was largely confined to the public commons such as those at Blackheath, Clapham, Chingford and Tooting Bec, the golfers having to share their rather crudely laid out courses with 'nurse-maids, dogs, horses and stubborn old ladies and gentlemen'.

Not surprisingly when the first golf clubs started to form the tendency was to retreat from the public stage. The **Royal Blackheath** Golf Club, fittingly enough the first English club to be founded (it dates from 1787) eventually moved from the Heath and now plays on a private course at Eltham. Golf is no longer played (or at least shouldn't be!) on the commons at Clapham and Tooting Bec. However, golf does survive on those at **Wimbledon** and Chingford, the latter being the home of **Royal Epping Forest** and where golfers are still required to wear red clothing in order that they can be distinguished from other users of the common.

The Northern Suburbs

The majority of London clubs are for obvious reasons set in deepest suburbia and with many it is often far from clear as to whether they fall within Greater London or not. In anyone's book **Muswell Hill** is in London, which for present purposes is just as well because it's an excellent course. Measuring close to 6500 yards and quite undulating, it represents a fairly stiff test from the back tees. Other good 18 hole courses to the north of London include **Finchley** (with its elegant Victorian clubhouse), **Mill Hill** (which has something of a heathland feel to it) and **Highgate** (which is particularly pretty), while **Hampstead** has an enjoyable nine holes.

A cluster of fine courses lie a little further to the north west of the capital. Near neighbours of one another are **Northwood** and **Sandy Lodge**. The latter could be said to be sandy by name, sandy by nature—a heathland course but it can play more like a golf links at times. Anyway, it's certainly an exceptionally fine course and hosts many top class events. Northwood is in parts parkland, in parts heathland with a very good back nine. A mention also for **West Middlesex**, one of West London's better parkland courses.

On the other side of the M1 one finds **South Herts** and **Hadley Wood**. South Herts is somewhat tucked away in Totteridge but well worth finding. The club can boast having both Harry Vardon and Dai Rees among its past professionals. Hadley Wood, near Barnet is a very beautiful course designed by Alister Mackenzie with lovely tree-lined fairways. The clubhouse is very elegant too. Over towards Essex, Royal Epping Forest has been mentioned. Also within Epping Forest itself,

West Essex is a very fine parkland course and there are two first rate public courses at **Hainault Forest**.

A 19th Hole

Before looking at a golf in the south of the metropolis a word on some of London's better hotels. Finding real value in the capital isn't easy—local knowledge helps and it may be a case of rub of the green. The following appraisal is dedicated to the American and Japanese visitor—and to any of us who have a generous expense account!

In Park Lane, the Inn on the Park (020) 7499 0888 is quite excellent and its restaurant, the Four Seasons is outstanding. Luxury of the highest order is also offered in the Dorchester (020) 7629 8888 as it proudly overlooks Hyde Park (alas no golf). The Grill Room and the Terrace are both restaurants of distinction. The international class of the Ritz (020) 7493 8181 is obvious—one can quite simply sniff the style. Nearby, Browns (020) 7493 6020 is contrastingly English and justifiably proud of it. A few more? Well, how about the Savoy (020) 7836 4343. Note the delightful settings of its restaurants the Grill Room and the River Restaurant. Guests here have temporary membership of Wentworth —a major plus for lovers of first class fairways. Another member of the Savoy group is Claridges (020) 7629 8860—traditional to a tee but still extremely popular.

For people not wishing to stay in Central London these hotels may be of some help: in Hadley Wood the West Lodge Park (020) 8440 8311 is a superb 19th century mansion—very convenient for the many courses of South Hertfordshire. A galleried hall is one of the features of the Grym's Dyke Hotel (020) 8954 4227. The former home of W S Gilbert, this hotel is located in Harrow Weald—ideal for playing at Moor Park. Slightly further north of town, but still only twenty miles from Central London, the five star comforts of Hanbury Manor near Ware (01920) 487722 take some beating (18 great holes of golf too) while south of the capital golfers in Croydon will also find Selsdon Park Hotel (020) 8657 8811 very comfortable and convenient.

If some of the above are slightly out of the price range of the majority of ordinary mortals then it goes without saying that London provides a veritable feast of accommodation at vastly varying rates. Two recommended establishments combining comfort and value are Aston Court (020) 7602 9954 in West Kensington and in NW4 the Peacehaven Hotel (020) 8202 9758.

The South and West

Those looking for a game in south west London might consider looking in the Wimbledon area where there are several courses. **Royal Wimbledon** is just about the best in London but golfers may find it easier to arrange a game (during the week at any rate) on the nearby course at **Wimbledon Common**. **Coombe Hill** is another of the capital's most prestigious clubs—its well manicured fairways are just about visible from Royal Wimbledon. A little further out at Richmond, games can be enjoyed at **Royal Mid Surrey** (two courses here, an Outer and an Inner and a superb clubhouse which doubles as a museum to some of the great names of golf—a must for lovers of the game's history or a good lunch!) and at **Richmond** Golf Club with its superb Georgian clubhouse. There is also a public course at Richmond. A quick mention must be made here of Cannizaro House (020) 8879 1464, a truly delightful hotel on Wimbledon Common. It is perfect for the London and Surrey golfer, and also an ideal spot for the many shops to be found in Wimbledon Village. In Richmond, the Petersham (020) 8940 7471 is an excellent hotel with a good restaurant (good restaurants abound in Richmond). Due west of London, **Ealing** offers a reasonable test and there are again a number of public courses in the vicinity. Further west still, almost opposite each other on either side of the M25 and only a few minutes from Heathrow are two very interesting new courses; **Stockley Park** and **Ritchings Park**. The former, sited on what was once the largest rubbish tip in Europe, is now a typically challenging and highly contoured Robert Trent Jones Snr layout—a real exotic. The latter,

just over the border in Bucks, has by way of contrast, been carefully integrated into an 18th century park by British architect, David Williams.

South of London the Croydon area is yet another that is thick with clubs. Although it may be difficult to arrange a game on, **Addington** is generally considered the best; it is a lovely heathland course covered in heather, pines and silver birch and has in the par three 13th one of golf's toughest and most beautiful short holes. **Addington Palace** is also well thought of, as indeed is **Croham Hurst**. To make up a four, especially if one requires a base, **Selsdon Park** must be the selection—a pleasant parkland course set around the Selsdon escarpment. Seldson Park is very popular with societies. Not far from Croydon, the course at **Coulsdon Court** has a welcoming reputation and an extraordinary selection of trees. Two of the better courses towards the south east of London are **Langley Park** (at Beckenham)—heavily wooded with a particularly good series of holes towards the end of the round including an attractive par three finishing hole—and **Sundridge Park**, where indeed there are two good courses, an East and a West.

The South East Suberbs

Elsewhere in the south east there is a popular public course at **Beckenham Place Park** and there are interesting layouts at **Shooters Hill** and **Dulwich and Sydenham**, but the final mention goes to **Royal Blackheath**. The club has a great sense of history and the course is full of character. Early in the round one may confront the famous 'Hamlet Cigar bunker' while its 18th isn't so much difficult as unusual, requiring a pitch over a hedge to the green. In some ways it's unfortunate that the club ever had to leave its famous common—Blackheath village is charming—but then the author of this tome may just be a little biased!

Surrey

When Providence distributed land best suited for building golf courses it wasn't done in the most democratic of spirits. Take for instance the quite ridiculous amount of majestic links land to be found along the coast of Lancashire—it's enough to make every good Yorkshireman weep. And then there's Surrey, blessed with acre upon acre of perfect inland golfing terrain—what a contrast to poor Essex!

It is probably safe to suggest that **Walton Heath**, **Sunningdale** and **Wentworth** are the county's three leading clubs, and each is detailed separately in this chapter. Walton and Wentworth are only two of Surrey's famous 'W Club'—there's also **Worplesdon** and **Woking**, **West Hill**, **West Surrey**, **West Byfleet** and to this list we can now add **Wildwood**, **Windlesham** and **Wisley**—three of the country's newest and (in the case of Wisley) most exclusive developments.

Located close to the A32 to the west of Woking, Worplesdon, West Hill and Woking Golf Clubs lie practically next door to one another. Indeed it might be possible to devise a few dramatic cross-course holes—though in view of the value of some of the adjacent properties that would have to be driven over it's perhaps not such a good idea! West Hill is generally considered to be the most difficult of the three, the fairways at times being frighteningly narrow; Worplesdon is probably the most widely known (largely due to its famous annual foursomes event), while Woking, founded a century ago, possesses the most distinctive architecture and perhaps the greatest charm. Whatever their particular merits, all three are magnificent examples of natural heathland and heather courses.

Marginally closer to the capital and still very much in the heart of the stockbroker-belt is a second outstanding trio of courses centred around Weybridge: **St George's Hill**, **New Zealand** and **West Byfleet**. Once again, these are heathland type courses where golf is played amidst heavily wooded surroundings, the combination of pines, silver birch, purple heather and, at St George's Hill and New Zealand especially, a magnificent spread of rhododendrons, making for particularly attractive settings. St George's Hill is one of the more undulating courses in Surrey and calls for several spectacular shots—indeed, many people rate it on a par with Wentworth and Walton Heath.

Golf in Surrey isn't of course all heathland and heather. **Tandridge** is one of the best downland courses in Southern England while just a short drive from Weybridge is the delightful parkland course at **Burhill**, situated some two miles south of Walton-on-Thames. Burhill's clubhouse is a particularly grand affair—at one time it was the home of the Dowager Duchess of Wellington. Much less grand, but to some of equal interest, is the Dick Turpin cottage sited on the course and reputed to have been used by the infamous highwayman (not a golfer so far as we know). Also worth noting is a nearby public course, **Silvermere**, located midway between Byfleet and Cobham where it may be easier to arrange a game—at least in theory, as it does get very busy—and where green fees are naturally lower.

Some thoughts for the 19th hole are required. Surrey is a rich county—in more ways than one. Quality golf comes in abundance, so too do first class country houses, pubs, hotels and restaurants. Here are a few suggestions. The Burford Bridge (01306) 884561 and the Thatched House (020) 8642 3131 are good choices for those visiting Walton Heath. The nearby Partners Brasserie (020) 8644 7743 is a worthy suggestion for a winning foursome. Chez Max (020) 8399 2365 in Surbiton is another for a celebratory feast of note. Another convenient hotel for Walton Heath is the Heathside Hotel (01737) 353355 in Burgh Heath. After a day's golf on any of the courses in the Woking area the Wheatsheaf Hotel (01483) 773047 is a good spot to collect one's thoughts. Another relaxing hotel is the Oatlands Park Hotel (01932) 847242—centrally located and extremely pleasant. The Cricketers (01932) 862105 on Downside Common, Cobham is a sporting little pub. Two fine restaurants are Casa Romana (01932) 843470) in Weybridge, and in Reigate, La Barbe (01737) 241966. Finally, two of the county's (and the country's) finest country house hotels are in this area, again convenient for Wentworth—Pennyhill Park (01276) 471774 near Bagshot and Great Fosters (01784) 433822 near Egham—and also in Egham one can stay at the Jacobean style Savill Hotel (01784) 434355 which is ideal for trips to Wentworth and Sunningdale.

Generally speaking, golf in the Home Counties and golf in America have precious little in common. However, the **Foxhills** Club at Ottershaw (off the A320) can make a genuine claim to have married the two successfully. A Jacobean style manor house run on American country club lines including an outstanding range of leisure facilities, it has two championship length heathland type courses and 16 rooms to accommodate golfers in some style (01932) 872050. Not surprisingly, Foxhills is a very popular haunt for golfing societies. Another fairly newish set up in this area is the **Fernfell** Golf and Country Club at Cranleigh just south of Guildford—a worthy thought for the itinerant golfer. A hotel of considerable charm is the historic Angel (01483) 564555—well worth considering.

The country club scene may not of course appeal to all types and excellent golf in an extremely sedate atmosphere can be enjoyed at **Gatton Manor** situated in Ockley near Dorking. The course has a very scenic layout running through woods and alongside lakes. One doesn't have to look too far for a good night's rest—the manor house is now a very relaxing hotel (01306) 627555 with golf obviously very much on the menu. Note also the Punch Bowl in nearby Oakwood Hill—an excellent country pub.

Heading towards Walton Heath, if a game cannot be arranged over one of its famous courses then there is golf of a similar (if less challenging) nature at **Reigate Heath** and not too far away at **Kingswood** there is a fine parkland course. **Duke's Dene** is also well worth a trip - located in the delightful Halliloo Valley it is a real pleasure to play.

The rich heathland seam runs the breadth of the county and over to the west, practically straddling the three counties of Surrey, Berkshire and Hampshire, lies the superb **Camberley Heath**. There is also a first rate public course in Camberley, **Pine Ridge**, which opened in 1992. Down in the south-west corner of Surrey there is yet another outstanding trio of clubs: **Hindhead**, **West Surrey** and **Hankley Common**. Hankley Common was for many years a favourite of the late South African Bobby Locke, who once owned a house adjacent to the course. Hankley Common is widely known for its spectacular 18th hole—one of the greatest closing holes in golf. A vast gulley which seems to possess magnetic powers looms in front of the green—nine out of ten first timers fail to reach the putting surface.

The south-west corner of Surrey is particularly scenic. The hustle and bustle of London seems a world away—and of course in a way it is. In Bramley, the Bramley Grange Hotel (01483) 893434 is an ideal base from which to explore the countryside. Close to the Sussex borders lies Haslemere and another fine hotel, a timbered farmhouse on this occasion, the Lythe Hill Hotel (01428) 651251 where bedrooms in the original house have great character. People who have still not found a restaurant to visit must surely do so here for Fleur de Sel (01428) 651462 offers some simply splendid dishes and a most delightful atmosphere.

DUKE'S DENE GOLF CLUB *Photograph courtesy of:* **Clubhaus**

Sunningdale

On seeing the spectacularly beautiful 18th hole at Killarney during one of his visits to Ireland, the late Henry Longhurst declared, 'What a lovely place to die'. Now whilst one rarely wishes to dwell on the subject of meeting our maker, golfers have been known to indulge in a considerable amount of speculation as to the type of course they might find on the arrival of such an occasion. There is a story of one heated discussion which involved, quite by chance, an Englishman, a Scotsman and an American. The latter argued with great conviction that a large number of the holes would, 'as sure as hell,' resemble Augusta, whilst the Scotsman vehemently insisted that even the most minute deviation from the Old Course at St Andrews would constitute an act of heresy; as for the Englishman, he naturally had no doubts whatsoever that he could stroll through the Pearly Gates and meet a second Sunningdale.

Well, perhaps the heavenly blend is a mixture of all three, but in any event, the gentleman in charge of the terrestrial Sunningdale is the Secretary, **Stewart Zuill**. Mr. Zuill may be contacted on **(01344) 621681**. **Keith Maxwell** is the club's resident **Professional** and he can be reached on **(01344) 620128**.

In common with neighbouring The Berkshire, Sunningdale has two eighteen hole courses, the **Old**, designed in 1900 by Willie Park, and the **New** which was constructed by Harry Colt in 1922. Both are splendid, and many would say the leading examples of the famous Berkshire/Surrey heathland type course. The holes wind their way through glorious forests of conifer and pine with heather and bracken bordering each fairway. All around there are splashes of silver sand.

With its great reputation and close proximity to the capital, Sunningdale is not surprisingly very popular. Unless accompanied by a member, visitors are restricted to playing between Mondays and Thursdays and must make prior arrangement with the Secretary. A letter of introduction is also required. All written communications should be addressed to Mr. Zuill at **The Sunningdale Golf Club, Ridgemount Road, Sunningdale, Berkshire SL5 9RR**. In 2000 the green fees are set at £110 for a round on the Old Course and £78 for the New Course, while a combined ticket at £135 entitles the visitor to a round over both courses. Sets of clubs can be hired from the professional shop should the need arise. Those keen to organise a society meeting are also advised to approach Mr. Zuill via the above address.

Sunningdale is situated just off the A30, about 28 miles west of London. Motoring from the south and west the M3 (leaving at junction 3) and the M4 (junction 10) may be of assistance, while from the north both the A332 and the A330 pass through nearby Ascot. The club's precise location is some 300 yards from Sunningdale railway station.

When golfers talk of Sunningdale, invariably it is the Old Course they have in mind, this despite the fact that a large number of people consider the New to be its equal. The former has acquired such pre-eminence largely as a result of the many major professional and amateur tournaments that have been staged there. However the Old Course is perhaps best known for a single round of golf played by the legendary Bobby Jones. In qualifying for the 1926 Open Championship, which he in fact went on to win, the great man put together what has often been described as the finest 18 holes of golf ever seen. Jones' record 66, a remarkable achievement in the 1920s, comprised twelve fours and six threes—33 for the front nine and 33 for the back nine. More amazingly Jones played only 33 shots from tee to green and took 33 putts—as Bernard Darwin put it, 'incredible and indecent'.

In more recent years Sunningdale has hosted numerous prestigious events including the European Open. In 1987 the Walker Cup was played at Sunningdale; in 1997 the Weetabix British Open was staged on the Old Course, and in April 2000 the inaugural Seve Ballesteros Trophy.

At 6581 yards (par 72) the Old Course is slightly shorter than the New (6617 yards, par 70). The respective distances from the Ladies' tees are 5825 yards and 5840 yards (both being par 74). It seems somehow wrong to single out individual holes, each course possessing its own wealth of variety and charm. The views from the 5th and 10th tees on the Old Course are, however, particularly outstanding and the 18th also provides a spectacular closing hole as it gently dog-legs towards the green and the giant spreading oak tree, very much the symbol of Sunningdale.

Sunningdale's glorious setting has been described as both 'heavenly' and 'hauntingly beautiful'. Certainly the golfer privileged to stroll up the final fairway on a summer's evening as the sun begins its leisurely dip, can be forgiven if he amends the words of Henry Longhurst and declares 'What a lovely place to be alive!'

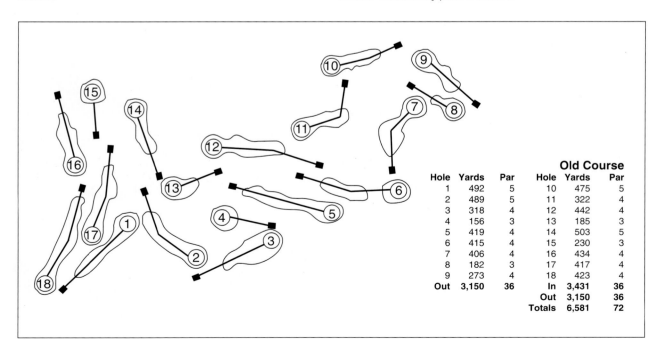

Hole	Yards	Par		Hole	Yards	Par
			Old Course			
1	492	5		10	475	5
2	489	5		11	322	4
3	318	4		12	442	4
4	156	3		13	185	3
5	419	4		14	503	5
6	415	4		15	230	3
7	406	4		16	434	4
8	182	3		17	417	4
9	273	4		18	423	4
Out	**3,150**	**36**		**In**	**3,431**	**36**
				Out	**3,150**	**36**
				Totals	**6,581**	**72**

Gatton Manor Hotel, Golf & Country Club is set in 250 acres of parkland in the heart of the beautiful Surrey countryside and boasts a well established 18 hole, par 72 championship length golf course of 6653 yards. The whole course has immense character incorporating the natural waters of the River Arun. It has the advantage of three starting points at the first, fourth and tenth and veers over undulating ground through the peace and tranquillity of woods, with fourteen scenic water holes.

The enjoyable and interesting course is designed to challenge every golfer and has arguably the best finishing hole in the south. Firstly you are faced with a tee shot over water to the sloping fairway. Your second shot has to carry a stream some 50 yards from the middle of the green. The green itself is bunkered from left to right and is enclosed round the back with an interesting selection of fir trees.

Golf is certainly not all that Gatton Manor has to offer. The golfer, in his leisure moments, or indeed the non-golfer, can enjoy the benefits of the purpose-built gymnasium and health club which houses all the latest equipment, saunas, jacuzzi and solarium. Take a leisurely walk around the estate, and see many of the specimen trees and shrubs from the magnificent hybrid rhododendrons to the exotic magnolias and vast tulip tree. The estate also teems with wildlife and the keen observer can see such birds as kingfisher, greenfinch and yellowhammer, whilst animals such as otter, and roe deer are to be seen in their natural habitat. Other outdoor activities available include tennis, bowls and coarse fishing. Alternatively guests can relax in the oak-beamed Golf Bar.

The attractive manor was built in 1728 and has been tastefully decorated to a high standard providing eighteen hotel rooms, all of which have en suite facilities. Adjoining the manor house is the delightful two-tiered dining room, residents' lounge, and private conference suites.

Whatever your reason for visiting Gatton Manor, you will not be disappointed. Ideally situated between London and the south coast, and within 15 miles of Gatwick airport and the M25 (exit 9), you will find Gatton Manor nestling off a quiet country lane to the west of the picturesque village of Ockley on the A29.

Gatton Manor Hotel, Golf & Country Club
Standon Lane
Ockley, nr Dorking
Surrey, RH5 5PQ
Tel: (01306) 627555
Fax: (01306) 627713
Pro Shop: (01306) 627557
E mail: gattonmanor@enterprise.net

Walton Heath

Gavrilo Princip may have pulled the trigger that ignited the Great War but our history books tell us that tension in Europe had sometime earlier reached boiling point. In their palaces in St Petersburg and Berlin the Czar and the Kaiser pondered the strength of their armies. Meanwhile the great statesmen of Britain were engaged in battles of a different nature. . .

All square as they reach the 18th green on the Old Course at Walton Heath, Churchill turns to Lloyd-George and says, 'Now then, I will putt you for the Premiership'.

Herbert Fowler once said, 'God builds golf links and the less man meddles the better for all concerned'. Herbert Fowler designed Walton Heath. However, before the opening of the Old Course in May 1904, at least a little meddling was called for. The glorious heathland through which the emerald fairways were cut was once covered, or nearly covered in thick heather, in parts as much as two feet thick (the members will tell you it still is!) While many of Britain's leading clubs took several years to establish their reputations, that of Walton Heath was assured months before the first stroke was even played—in January 1904 James Braid agreed to become Walton's first professional. Braid initially signed a seven year contract and his performances in the next seven Open Championships were: 2nd, 1st, 1st, 5th, 1st, 2nd and 1st, after which he became the first ever golfer to win five Opens. Hardly surprisingly his contract was extended and so indeed began an association with the club that was to last for nearly fifty years.

In the years immediately before the first world war Walton Heath members included no fewer than 24 MPs (including Winston Churchill and Lloyd-George) and 21 members of the House of Lords. Another famous Walton golfer was W G Grace (it was once cruelly suggested that he compiled as many hundreds on the Heath as he did at the Oval). After the war a more royal flavour dominated, with the Prince of Wales becoming an Honorary Member in 1921 and Captain in 1935.

Time to leap forward to the present and introduce the club's **Secretary, Nick Lomas.** He may be contacted at **The Walton Heath Golf Club, Tadworth, Surrey KT20 7TP, tel: (01737) 812380.** Subject to prior arrangement with the Secretary, golfers are welcome to visit Walton Heath between Mondays and Fridays. Proof of both club membership and an official handicap is required. The green fees for 2000 are set at £74 for a full day's golf, with a reduced rate of £62 available to those teeing off after 11.30am. The hire of golf

clubs can be arranged through the club's popular **Professional, Ken MacPherson, (01737) 812152.**

Located south of London, motoring to the club is assisted greatly by the M25. Those approaching on this motorway should leave at junction 8 turning north on to the A217. The A217 should be followed for approximately 2 miles after which a left turn should be taken on to the B2032. The golf club is situated a mile or so along this road. Travelling from further afield, the M25 is linked to the M23 to the South, the M20 to the East and to the North and West by the M3, M4 and M1.

There are two great courses at Walton Heath, the **Old** and the **New** (the latter first appearing as nine holes in 1907 but later extended to the full 18). Lying adjacent to one another, each possesses the same classical heathland characteristics: sandy subsoil, heather, bracken, gorse, pines and silver birch. The finishing three holes on the Old are thought by many (including no lesser a judge than Tom Weiskopf) to be the finest on any course. The classic 16th is a very mild dog-leg to a raised green which slopes from left to right, with the right side of the green guarded by an extremely cavernous bunker. The par three 17th has sand traps practically encircling the green, creating a near island effect and the 18th requires a testing second to carry an enormous cross bunker.

Over the years Walton Heath has played host to many important tournaments. The major amateur championships have included the English Amateur and both the Ladies English Amateur and the Ladies British Open Amateur Championships. Among the professional events, twenty-two of the PGA Matchplay Championships were staged at Walton Heath and in recent years The Ryder Cup of 1981 as well as five European Open Championships.

Walton Heath has a fine clubhouse with an excellent restaurant and lounge. Lunches are served between 12.00 pm and 2.30pm.

Understandably wherever you turn in the clubhouse you are likely to see a reminder of the long association with James Braid. One small note sent to him from the Prince of Wales conveys a message all golfers can appreciate. It relates how the Prince came to the 18th requiring a four for a 79. After explaining how his second finished just through the green he tells how, 'with the chance of breaking 80, I couldn't stand the nerve-strain and fluffed the chip and took two putts . . .' How the mighty fall!

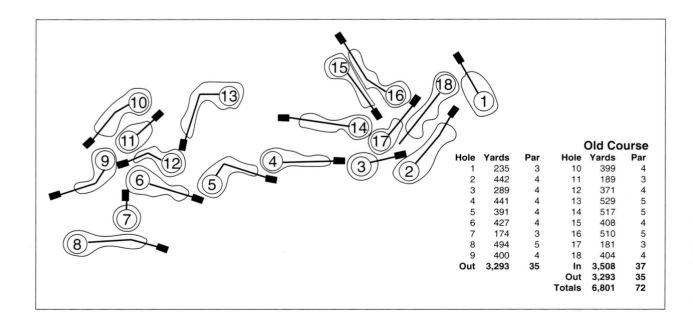

Hole	Yards	Par		Hole	Yards	Par
1	235	3		10	399	4
2	442	4		11	189	3
3	289	4		12	371	4
4	441	4		13	529	5
5	391	4		14	517	5
6	427	4		15	408	4
7	174	3		16	510	5
8	494	5		17	181	3
9	400	4		18	404	4
Out	**3,293**	**35**		**In**	**3,508**	**37**
				Out	**3,293**	**35**
				Totals	**6,801**	**72**

Old Course

Wentworth

*I*t is autumn. A reddish gold leaf scurries across the 18th green. The huge gallery is silent. Fully 50 yards away to the right of the fairway, close to the trees and in the rough is the young Severiano Ballesteros. He is one hole down to the legendary Arnold Palmer and he needs a miracle. The blade flashes and the ball flies towards the green. It pitches, it rolls and it drops . . . the eagle has landed.

A stunningly beautiful place, Wentworth is set in the heart of the famous Surrey Heath. The name first appeared on the golfing map in the mid 1920s when Harry Colt, perhaps the greatest of all British golf architects, was commissioned to design two 18 hole courses. The East Course was the first to open in 1924, with the West Course following two years later. A third 18 hole championship course, the Edinburgh, designed by John Jacobs in collaboration with Gary Player and the club's former professional, Bernard Gallacher was officially opened in 1990.

Before the War, it was the **East** Course that captured the limelight by staging the club's first important events, in 1926 an unofficial match between British and American teams and in 1932 the inaugural Curtis Cup. In the period since 1945, the longer **West** Course has taken most of the glory with the Ryder Cup in 1953, the Canada Cup—a forerunner of the World Cup—three years later, and each year since 1964 the World Matchplay Championship. Through the televising of the latter and the annual Volvo PGA Championship, the West has become arguably England's best known golf course. Every 'armchair golfer' is very familiar with the first two holes and the final six or seven on what is known affectionately (and respectfully!) as the 'Burma Road' course. The West certainly has a formidable opening and an exciting finish but arguably the two most picturesque holes on the course are rarely captured on camera—the sweeping downhill par five 4th and the 8th, a classic two-shotter where the approach is played across an attractive pond.

The owners of the club, Wentworth Group Holdings, have invested substantially in the courses and the facilities during the past decade and under Chairman, Elliott Bernerd, and Chief Executive, Willy Bauer, standards now match the best golf and country clubs in the world. Following the completion of the Edinburgh, a computerised irrigation system was installed on the West, a new Halfway House built serving the East and West, another on the Edinburgh, and the outdoor heated

swimming pool has been refurbished. A new tennis and health club has been opened in 1998, providing exceptional sporting facilities and superior service to encourage members to combine fitness with relaxation.

In October 1993 a major redevelopment of the clubhouse was completed. The golfing facilities are now all under one roof including the pro shop, the caddymaster, bagstore and visitors' locker rooms. The new club lounge plus dining room combining brasserie style and formal dining, Burma Bar, private meeting rooms and gabled ballroom offer plenty of flexibility for social and business entertainment.

The summer green fees for 2000 are set, per round, at £190 for the West Course with the East and Edinburgh courses at £100 and £125 respectively. Club, buggy and trolley hire and caddies may be booked in advance while special packages are available for groups of 20 or more.

Wentworth is located directly off the A30 between Bagshot and Egham, and may be approached via the M25 junction 13 or M4 through Bracknell or Windsor and Ascot. Heathrow Airport is only 15 minutes away.

Managing Director and **General Manager**, **Julian Small** and his staff ensure that all visitors feel welcome. It is advisable to pre-book a starting time and, unless accompanied by a Wentworth member, visitors are restricted to weekdays. A handicap certificate is required and the club's handicap limits are 24 (ladies 32) for the West Course and 28 (ladies 45) for the East and Edinburgh courses.

Enquiries should be addressed to: **Wentworth Club, Wentworth Drive, Virginia Water, Surrey GU25 4LS tel: (01344) 842201, fax (01344) 842804.**

It is spring. The PGA Championship is reaching a nailbiting climax as the two players walk down the first fairway in the sudden death play off. A decade has passed and the now legendary Ballesteros hasn't won for some time. He desperately needs a victory. The blade flashes and a 5 iron is struck 220 yards towards the green. It lands, skips, rolls and finishes two feet from the pin . . . El Gran Senor is back!

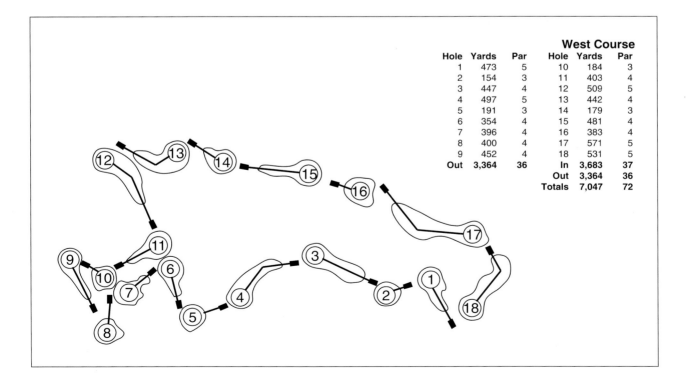

West Course

Hole	Yards	Par	Hole	Yards	Par
1	473	5	10	184	3
2	154	3	11	403	4
3	447	4	12	509	5
4	497	5	13	442	4
5	191	3	14	179	3
6	354	4	15	481	4
7	396	4	16	383	4
8	400	4	17	571	5
9	452	4	18	531	5
Out	**3,364**	**36**	**In**	**3,683**	**37**
			Out	**3,364**	**36**
			Totals	**7,047**	**72**

Key

To avoid disappointment
it is advisable to telephone
in advance

***Visitors welcome at most times
**Visitors usually allowed on
weekdays only
*Visitors not normally permitted
(Mon, Wed) No visitors
on specified days

Approximate Green Fees
A £40 plus
B £25 to £40
C £20 to £30
D £15 to £25
E under £15
F Green fees on application

Restrictions
G Guests only
H–Handicap certificate required
H–(24) Handicap of 24 or less
L–Letter of introduction required
M–Visitor must be a member of
another recognised club

**GREATER LONDON
(including Middlesex)**

Airlinks G.C.
(0181) 561 1418
Southall Lane, Hounslow
(18) 6002 yards/***/D

Arkley G.C.
(0181) 449 0394
Rowley Green Road, Barnet
(9) 6045 yards/**/C/H

Ashford Manor G.C.
(01784) 257687
Fordbridge Road, Ashford
(18) 6343 yards/***/B/H/M

Beckenham Place Park G.C.
(0181) 650 2292
Beckenham Hill Road, Beckenham
(18) 5722 yards/***/E

Bexleyheath G.C.
(0181) 303 6951
Mount Road, Bexleyheath
(9) 5239 yards/**/D

Brent Valley G.C.
(0181) 567 1287
Church Road, Hanwell
(18) 5426 yards/***/F

Bush Hill Park G.C.
(0181) 360 5738
Bush Hill, Winchmore Hill
(18) 5809 yards/**/B/L

C & L Country Club
(0181) 845 5662
West End Road, Northolt
(9) 4440 yards/***/E

Chingford G.C.
(0181) 529 2107
Station Road, Chingford
(18) 6336 yards/***/F

Chislehurst G.C.
(0181) 467 2782
Camden Park Road, Chislehurst
(18) 5128 yards/**/C/H

Crews Hill G.C.
(0181) 363 0787
Cattlegate Road, Crews Hill, Enfield
(18) 6230 yards/**/F/H/M

Dulwich and Sydenham Hill G.C.
(0181) 693 3961
Grange Lane, College Road,
(18) 6610 yards/**/B/H(22)/L

Dyrham Park C.C.
(0181) 440 3361
Galley Lane, Barnet
(18) 6369 yards/***/F/G

Ealing G.C.
(0181) 997 0937
Perivale Lane, Greenford
(18) 6216 yards/**/B/H

Elstree G.C.
(0181) 953 6115
Watling Street, Elstree
(18) 6100 yards/***/F

Eltham Warren G.C.
(0181) 850 1166
Bexley Road, Eltham
(9) 5840 yards/**/B/H/M

Enfield G.C.
(0181) 363 3970
Old Park Road South, Enfield
(18) 6137 yards/**/B/H/M

Finchley G.C.
(0181) 346 2436
Nether Court, Frith Lane, Mill Hill
(18) 6411 yards/***/A

Fulwell G.C.
(0181) 977 7732
Wellington Road, Hampton Hill
(18) 6544 yards/**/A/L

Gryms Dyke G.C.
(0181) 428 4539
Oxhey Lane, Hatch End, Pinner
(18) 5600 yards/**/B/H

Hadley Wood G.C.
(0181) 449 4486
Beech Hill, Barnet
(18) 6473 yards/**/A/H/M

Hampstead G.C.
(0181) 455 0203
Winnington Road, Hampstead
(9) 5812 yards/***/B/H

Harrow School G.C
(0181) 869 1253
High Street, Harrow-on-the-Hill
(9) 3690 yards/*/G

Hartsbourne G.& C.C.
(0181) 950 1133
Hartsbourne Avenue, Bushey Heath
(18) 6305 yards/*/F/G/M
(9) 5432 yards/*/F/G/M

Haste Hill G.C.
(01923) 825224
The Drive, Northwood
(18) 5794 yards/***/F

Heathpark
(01895) 444232
Stockley Road, West Drayton
(9) 2032 yards/***/F

Hendon G.C.
(0181) 346 6023
Devonshire Rd, Mill Hill
(18) 6266 yards/**/B/M

Highgate G.C.
(0181) 340 1906
Denewood Road, Highgate
(18) 5982 yards/**(Wed)/B/H

Hillingdon G.C.
(01895) 233956
18 Dorset Way, Hillingdon
(9) 5459 yards/**(Thu)/C/H/M

The Holiday Inn
(01895) 444232
Stockley Road, West Drayton
(9) 3800 yards/***/E

Horsendon Hill G.C.
(0181) 902 4555
Woodland Rise, Greenford
(9) 3236 yards/***/E

Hounslow Heath G.C.
(0181) 570 5271
Staines Road, Hounslow
(18) 5901 yards/**/E

Ilford G.C.
(0181) 554 2930
Wanstead Park Road, Ilford
(18) 5251 yards/**/D

Langley Park G.C.
(0181) 650 2090
Barnfield Wood Road, Beckenham
(18) 6488 yards/**/A/H

Lee Valley G.C.
(0181) 803 3611
Picketts Lock Lane, Edmonton
(18) 4902 yards/***/D

The London Golf Centre
(0181) 841 6162
Ruislip Road, Northolt
(9) 5838 yards/***/E

London Scottish G.C.
(0181) 789 0135
Windmill Enclosure, Wimbledon Common
(18) 5436 yards/**/F/H

Magpie Hall Lane G.C.
(0181) 462 7014
Magpie Hall Lane, Bromley
(9) 2745 yards/***/F

Mill Hill G.C.
(0181) 959 2339
Barnet Way, Mill Hill
(18) 6309 yards/***/B/H

Muswell Hill G.C.
(0181) 888 2044
Rhodes Avenue, Wood Green
(18) 6474 yards/**/B/H(24)

North Middlesex G.C.
(0181) 445 1732
Friern Barnet Lane, Whetstone
(18) 5625 yards/***/B/H

Northwood G.C.
(01923) 821384
Rickmansworth Road, Northwood
(18) 6553 yards/**/B/H

Perivale Park G.C.
(0181) 575 7116
Argyle Road, Greenford
(9) 5267 yards/***/E

Pinner Hill G.C.
(0181) 866 0963
Southview Road, Pinner Hill
(18) 6293 yards/**/F/H

Roehampton G.C.
(0181) 876 1621
Roehampton Lane, London
(18) 6046 yards/**/F/L

Royal Blackheath G.C.
(0181) 850 1795
Court Road, Eltham
(18) 6214 yards/**/A/H/L

Royal Wimbledon G.C.
(0181) 946 2125
Camp Road, Wimbledon
(18) 6300 yards/**/A/H(18)/L

Ruislip G.C.
(01895) 638835
Ickenham Road, Ruislip
(18) 5703 yards/***/D

Sandy Lodge G.C.
(01923) 825429
Sandy Lodge Lane, Northwood
(18) 6340 yards/***/F/H/M

Shooters Hill G.C.
(0181) 854 6368
Eaglesfield Road, Shooters Hill
(18) 5736 yards/**/B/H/M

Shortlands G.C.
(0181) 460 2471
Meadow Road, Shortlands, Bromley
(9) 5261 yards/*/D/G

Sidcup G.C.
(0181) 300 2150
Hurst Road, Sidcup
(9) 5722 yards/**/D/H/L

South Herts G.C.
(0181) 445 2035
Links Drive, Totteridge
(18) 6470 yards/**/F/H(24)/L

Springfield Park G.C.
(0181) 871 2468
Burntwood Lane, Wandsworth
(9) 4451 yards/**/E

Stanmore G.C.
(0181) 954 2599
Gordon Avenue, Stanmore
(18) 5881 yards/**/E-C/H

Stockley Park G.C.
(0181) 813 5700
Stockley Park, Uxbridge
(18) 6548 yards/***/A

Strawberry Hill G.C.
(0181) 894 1246
Wellesley Road, Twickenham
(9) 2381 yards/**/C

Sudbury G.C.
(0181) 902 3713
Bridgewater Road, Wembley
(18) 6282 yards/**/F/H/M

Sunbury G.C.
(01932) 772898
Sunbury
(9) 3105 yards/***/D

Sundridge Park G.C.
(0181) 460 0278
Garden Road, Bromley
(18) 6467 yards/**/A/H
(18) 6007 yards/**/A/H

Trent Park G.C.
(0181) 366 7432
Bramley Road, Southgate
(18) 6008 yards/***/D

Twickenham Park G.C.
(0181) 783 1698
Staines Road, Twickenham
(9) 6014 yards/***/E

Uxbridge G.C.
(01895) 272457
The Drive, Harefield Place, Uxbridge
(18) 5753 yards/***/D

Wanstead G.C.
(0181) 989 0604
Overton Drive, Wanstead
(18) 6262 yards/**(Wed,Thu)/B/H

West Middlesex G.C.
(0181) 574 3450
Greenford Road, Southall
(18) 6242 yards/**/C

Whitewebbs G.C.
(0181) 363 2951
Beggars Hollow, Clay Hill, Enfield
(18) 5863 yards/***/D

Wimbledon Common G.C.
(0181) 946 0294
Camp Road, Wimbledon Common
(18) 5438 yards/**/C

Wimbledon Park G.C.
(0181) 946 1250
Home Park Road, Wimbledon
(18) 5465 yards/**/B/H/L/M

Wyke Green G.C.
(0181) 560 8777
Syon Lane, Isleworth
(18) 6242 yards/**/A/H

SURREY

Addington G.C.
(0181) 777 1055
Shirley Church Road, Croydon
(18) 6242 yards/**/F/H/L

Addington Court G.C.
(0181) 657 0281
Featherbed Lane, Addington
(18) 5577 yards/***/D
(18) 5513 yards/***/D
(9) 1812 yards/***/E

Addington Palace G.C.
(0181) 654 3061
Gravel Hill, Addington
(18) 6410 yards/**/B/H/G

American Golf at Sunbury
(01932) 771414
Charlton Lane, Shepperton
(9) 6210 yards /***/ F

Ashford Manor G.C
(01784) 257687
Fordbridge Road, Ashford
(18) 6352 yards /**/C/H

Banstead Downs G.C.
(0181) 642 2284
Burdon Lane, Belmont
(18) 6169 yards/**/B/H

Barrow Hills G.C.
(01344) 635770
Longcross, Chertsey
(18) 3090 yards/**/F/G

Betchworth Park G.C.
(01306) 882052
Reigate Road, Dorking
(18) 6266 yards/**(Tue,Wed)/A

Blacknest G.C
(01420) 22888
Binsted, Farnham
(18) 5858 yards /***/D

Bletchingley G.C.
(01883) 744666
Church Lane, Bletchingley
(18) 6504 yards/**/B

Bowenhurst G.C.
(01252) 851695
Mill Lane, Crondham, Surrey
(9) 2007 yards/***/D

Bramley G.C.
(01483) 892696
Bramley, Guildford
(18) 5990 yards/**/B

Broadwater Park G.C.
(01483) 429955
Guildford Road, Farncombe
(9) 1323 yards/***/E

Burhill G.C.
(01932) 227345
Walton-on-Thames
(18) 6224 yards/**/F/H/L

Camberley Heath G.C.
(01276) 23258
Golf Drive, Camberley
(18) 6337 yards/**/A/H

Chessington Golf Centre
(0181) 391 0948
Garrison Lane, Chessington
(9) 1400 yards/***/E

Chiddingfold G.C.
(01428) 685888
Petsworth Road, Chiddingfold
(18) 5500 yards/***/C

Chipstead G.C.
(01737) 555881
How Lane, Coulsdon
(18) 5454 yards/**/B

Chobham G.C.
(01276) 855584
Chobham Road, Chobham
(18) 6000 yards/*/F/G/H

Clandon Regis G.C.
(01483) 224888
Epsom Road, West Clandon
(18) 6412 yards/**/B/H

Coombe Hill G.C.
(0181) 942 2284
Golf Club Drive, Kingston
(18) 6303 yards/**/A/H/L

Coombe Wood G.C.
(0181) 942 0388
George Road, Kingston Hill
(18) 5210 yards/**/F/H

Coulsdon Manor G.C.
(0181) 668 0414
Coulsdon Court Road, Coulsdon
(18) 6037 yards/***/D

Croham Hurst G.C.
(0181) 657 5581
Croham Road, South Croydon
(18) 6286 yards/**/A/H/L

Cuddington G.C.
(0181) 393 0952
Banstead Road, Banstead
(18) 6394 yards/**/A/H/L

Dorking G.C.
(01306) 886917
Chart Park, Dorking
(9) 5120 yards/**/D

Drift G.C.
(01483) 284641
The Drift, East Horsley
(18) 6425 yards/**/B

Duke's Dene G.C.
(01883) 653501
Woldingham
(18) 6390 yards/***/B

Dunsfold Aerodrome G.C.
(01483) 265472
Dunsfold Aerodrome, Godalming
(9) 6090 yards/*/E/G

Effingham G.C.
(01372) 452203
Guildford Road, Effingham
(18) 6488 yards/**/A/H/G(weekends)

Epsom G.C.
(01372) 721666
Longdown Lane South, Epsom
(18) 5701 yards/**/C

Farleigh Court G.C.
(0188362) 7711 & 7733
Old Farleigh Road, Farleigh
(18) 6414 yards /***/B
(9) 6562 yards /E

Farnham G.C.
(01252) 782109
The Sands, Farnham
(18) 6325 yards/**/B/H/M

Fernfell G.& C.C.
(01483) 268855
Barhatch Lane, Cranleigh
(18) 5599 yards/**/B

Foxhills G.C.
(01932) 872050
Stonehill Road, Ottershaw
(18) 6680 yards/**/A
(18) 6547 yards/**/A
(9) 1300 yards/**/A

Gatton Manor G.& C.C.
(01306) 627555
Ockley, Dorking
(18) 6902 yards/***/C

Goal Farm Par Three.
(01483) 473205
Gole Road, Pirbright
(9) 1283 yards/***/E

Guildford G.C.
(01483) 63941
High Path Road, Merrow
(18) 6090 yards/**/B

Hankley Common G.C.
(01252) 792493
Tilford Road, Tilford, Farnham
(18) 6418 yards/**/A/H/L

Hindhead G.C.
(01428) 604614
Churt Road, Hindhead
(18) 6373 yards/***/A/H

Hoebridge G.C.
(01483) 722611
Old Woking Road, Old Woking
(18) 6536 yards/***/D
(18) 2298 yards/***/E
(9) 2294 yards/***/E

Home Park G.C.
(0181) 977 2423
Hampton Wick, Kingston
(18) 6610/***/C

Horton Park C.C.
(0181) 393 8400
Hook Road, Ewell
(18) 5208 yards/***/D

Hurtmore G.C.
(01483) 426492
Hurtmore Road, Hurtmore
(18) 5444 yards/***/D

Kingswood G.C.
(01737) 832188
Sandy Lane, Kingswood
(18) 6880 yards/***/A/H

Laleham G.C.
(01932) 564211
Laleham Reach, Chertsey
(18) 6203 yards/**/C

Leatherhead G.C.
(01372) 843966
Kingston Road, Leatherhead
(18) 6157 yards/***/A

Limpsfield Chart G.C.
(01883) 723405
Westerham Road,Limpsfield
(9) 5718 yards/**(Thu)/C/H

Lingfield Park G.C.
(01342) 834602
Racecourse Road, Lingfield
(18) 6500 yards/**/B

Malden G.C.
(0181) 942 0654
Traps Lane, New Malden
(18) 6295 yards/**/F/H

Milford G.C.
(01483) 419200
Station Lane, Milford
(18) 6224 yards/**/B/H

Mitcham G.C.
(0181) 648 1508
Carshalton Road, Mitcham Junction
(18) 5935 yards/**/D/H(18)

Moore Place G.C.
(01372) 463533
Portsmouth Road, Esher
(9) 4186 yards/***/E

New Zealand G.C.
(01932) 345049
Woodham Lane, Addlestone
(18) 6012 yards/*/A

North Downs G.C.
(01883) 653298
Northdown Road, Caterham
(18) 5843 yards/**/B/H

Oak Park G.C.
(01252) 850880
Crondall, nr Farnham
(18) 6437 yards/***/C

Oak Sports Centre
(0181) 643 8363
Woodmansterne Road, Carshalton
(18) 6033 yards/***/D
(9) 1590 yards/***/E

Pachesham Golf Centre
(01372) 843453
Oaklawn Road, Leatherhead
(9) 1752 yards/***/E

Pennyhill Park G.C
(01276) 471774
London Road, Bagshot
(9) 2095 yards /***/F

Pine Ridge G.C.
(01276) 20770
Old Bisley Road, Frimley
(18) 6458 yards/***/D

Purley Downs G.C.
(0181) 657 8347
Purley Downs Road, Purley
(18) 6212 yards/**/A/H/M/L

Puttenham G.C.
(01483) 810498
Heath Road, Puttenham, Guildford
(18) 6204/**/C/H

Pyrford G.C.
(01483) 723555
Warren Lane, Pyrford
(18) 6201 yards/**/A/H

RAC Country Club
(01372) 276311
Woodcote Park, Epsom
(18) 6709 yards/*/F
(18) 5598 yards/*/F

Redhill G.C.
(01737) 770204
Canada Avenue, Redhill
(9) 1901 yards/***/E

Redhill and Reigate G.C.
(01737) 244433
Pendleton Road, Redhill
(18) 5238 yards/***/D

Reigate Heath G.C.
(01737) 226793
Reigate Heath, Reigate
(9) 5658 yards/**/F

Reigate Hill G.C.
(01737) 645577
Gatten Bottom, Reigate
(18) 6175 yards/**/C

Richmond G.C.
(0181) 940 1463
Sudbrook Park, Richmond
(18) 5977 yards/**/A/H

Richmond Park G.C.
(0181) 876 3205
Roehampton Gate, Richmond Park
(18) 5940 yards/***/F
(18) 5969 yards/***/F

Roker Park G.C.
(01483) 236677
Holly Lane, Guildford
(9) 3037 yards/***/E

Royal Mid Surrey G.C.
(0181) 940 1894
Old Deer Park, Richmond
(18) 5544 yards/***/A/H/M
(18) 6343 yards/***/A/H/M

Rusper G.C.
(01293) 871871
Rusper Road, Newdigate
(9) 6069 yards/**/F

St Georges Hill G.C.
(01932) 847758
St. Georges Hill, Weybridge
(18) 6600 yards/**/A/H/L
(9) 3000 yards/**/A/H/L

Sandown Golf Centre
(01372) 463340
More Lane, Esher
(9) 5656 yards/***/D
(9) 1193 yards/***/E

Selsdon Park Hotel G.C.
(0181) 657 8811
Addington Road, Sanderstead
(18) 6402 yards/***/B/H

Shillinglee Park G.C.
(01428) 653237
Chiddingfold, Godalming
(9) 2500 yards/***/D

Shirley Park G.C.
(0181) 654 1143
Addiscombe Road, Croydon
(18) 6210 yards/**/B/H

Silvermere G.C.
(01932) 867275
Redhill Road, Cobham
(18) 6333 yards/***/C

Sunningdale G.C.
(01344) 21681
Ridgemount Road, Sunningdale
(18) 6586 yards/**/A/H/L
(18) 6676 yards/**/A/H/L

Sunningdale Ladies G.C.
(01344) 20507
Cross Road, Sunningdale
(18) 3622 yards/***/B

Surbiton G.C.
(0181) 398 3101
Woodstock Lane, Chessington
(18) 6211 yards/**/A/H

Sutton Green
(01483) 766898
New Lane, Sutton Green
(18) 6305 yards/***/F

Tandridge G.C.
(01883) 712273
Oxted
(18) 6250 yards/**(Tue,Fri)/A/H

Thames Ditton and Esher G.C.
(0181) 398 1551
Portsmouth Road, Esher
(9) 5190 yards/***/D

Tyrrells Wood G.C.
(01372) 376025
Tyrrells Wood, Leatherhead
(18) 6234 yards/**/A/H/L

Walton Heath G.C.
(01737) 812380
Tadworth
(18) 6801 yards/**/A/H/L
(18) 6609 yards/**/A/H/L

Wentworth G.C.
(01344) 842201
Wentworth Drive, Virginia Water
(18) 6945 yards/**/A/H
(18) 6176 yards/**/A/H
(18) 7006 yards/**/A/H

West Byfleet G.C.
(01932) 345230
Sheerwater Road, West Byfleet
(18) 6211 yards/**/B

West Hill G.C.
(01483) 474365
Bagshot Road, Brookwood
(18) 6368 yards/**/A/H

West Surrey G.C.
(01483) 421275
Enton Green, Godalming
(18) 6300 yards/**/A/H

Wildwood G.C.
(01403) 753255
Horsham Road, Afold
(18) 6650 yards/***/A/H

Windlemere G.C.
(01276) 858727
Windlesham Road, West End, Woking
(9) 5346 yards/***/D

Windlesham G.C.
(01276) 452220
Grove End, Bagshot
(18) 6515 yards/A/H

Wisley G.C.
(01483) 211022
Ripley, Woking
(9) 3355 yards/*/A
(9) 3473 yards/*/A
(9) 3385 yards/*/A

Woking G.C.
(01483) 760053
Pond Road, Hook Heath, Woking
(18) 6322 yards/**/A/H/M/L

Woodcote Park G.C.
(0181) 668 2788
Meadow Hill, Bridle Way, Coulsdon
(18) 6669 yards/**/B/H

Worplesdon G.C.
(01483) 472277
Heath House Road, Woking
(18) 6440 yards/**/A/H/L

WINDLESHAM GOLF CLUB *Photograph courtesy of:* **Windlesham Golf Club**

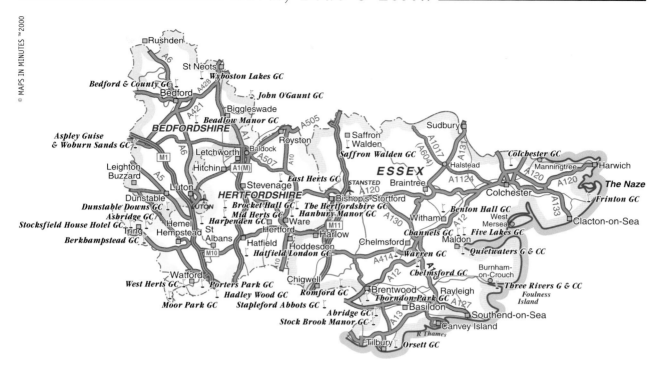

© MAPS IN MINUTES ™2000

Herts, Beds & Essex Choice Golf

Unfortunately, for all too many, the first and often lasting impression of a place can be determined by the great blue ribbons that now stretch the length and breadth of the country—Britain's ever expanding motorway network. The M1 (not to mention the M25) cuts through the heart of Hertfordshire and slices off the left ear of Bedfordshire. Between London and Luton it is a fearsome animal at the best of times and passing beyond these two counties one often draws a sigh of relief. The greater expanse of Essex fares a little better, escaping with a few nasty scratches, but in all three counties the deeper realms are not as often explored as they might be, except, needless to say, by those who live there.

The golfing breed is a little more fortunate than most. In every county in Britain he, and she, can visit golf courses that are tucked away in the most secluded and tranquil of settings and even in the 'there's an open space—lets build on it' 90s, Hertfordshire, Bedfordshire and Essex are not exceptions to the rule.

Hertfordshire
A glance at the map tells you that **Ashridge** in Hertfordshire isn't all that great a distance from London and the M1 but it occupies a particularly peaceful spot and the approach road which runs near **Berkhamsted** Golf Club passes through some glorious countryside—the kind that once covered much of this part of the world. Both are delightful heathland/parkland courses. Berkhamsted is best known for its conspicuous absence of bunkers though, like Royal Ashdown Forest in Sussex, it has more than enough natural hazards to test the courage of any golfer. Ashridge is perhaps most famed for its long association with Henry Cotton, for many years the club's professional. There are many fine par fours at Ashridge, the 9th and 14th being two of the best. The approach to the latter bears an uncanny resemblance to the 17th at St Andrews—the mischievously positioned bunker front left and the road behind the green—though it's not quite as frightening! Both courses are decidedly worth a visit.

There is certainly no shortage of golf courses in Hertfordshire and several new layouts have recently opened including the **The Hertfordshire** at Broxbourne and the **Stock's Country House Hotel**

(01442) 851341, situated at Aldbury, near Tring—quite close to Ashridge. In the upper realms of the county, **Harpenden**, convenient for those motoring along the M1. A short distance away at Wheathampstead is the **Mid Herts** Golf Club, while on the other side of the country's most famous blue ribbon lies **East Herts** near Buntingford. In the heart of Hertfordshire stands the exclusive and impressive **Brocket Hall** Golf Club near Welwyn. The greater concentration of courses, however, perhaps not surprisingly, is in the area just north of London. **Moor Park**, featured a few pages on, is the most widely known, though nearby **Porters Park** (in the quiet of Radlett) and **West Herts** (on the edge of Watford, yet similarly peaceful) also strongly merit attention.

West Herts was once more commonly known as Cassiobury Park after its location. Bernard Darwin in his famous 'Golf Courses of the British Isles' sang its praises highly: 'Of all the race of park courses, it would scarcely be possible in point of sheer beauty, to beat Cassiobury Park near Watford.' One other course to note in Hertfordshire is the first class public course at Essendon, confusingly called the **Hatfield London Country Club**.

It is possible to view the county's best courses from a London base. This isn't to say, however, that a number of excellent establishments can't be found beyond the city limits. In Thundridge, near Ware, **Hanbury Manor** (01920) 487722 is a five star country house hotel which can boast, among many things, a golf course first laid by Harry Vardon in the 1920s and recently completely redesigned by Jack Nicklaus Jr. The course is explored on a separate page in this chapter. In **Hadley Wood**, where there is a well established 18 hole course, the West Lodge Park is an elegant mansion house (020) 8440 8311, while Boreham Wood carries a restaurant to note—Signor Battis.

The best bet if you are playing Moor Park and looking for nearby quality accommodation is the Grym's Dyke hotel (020) 8954 4227 in Harrow Weald. St Albans and Harpenden, where the traffic races through, are both littered with good pubs off the busy high streets. St Albans offers its superb cathedral and the delightful St Michael's Manor (01727) 864444 which lies in its shadow. Sopwell House

(01727) 864477 offers excellent leisure facilities amidst its elegant Georgian frame. Harpenden's House (01582) 449955 is a little pricey but extremely well thought of. An idea for East Herts—the Redcoats Farmhouse (01438) 729500 at Little Wymondley is very cosy.

For golfers seeking genuine excellence—a true pinnacle perhaps—the Briggens House Hotel (01279) 829955 and its elegant restaurant at Ware should serve admirably. Briggens House has its own 9 hole golf course and is only 6 miles away from Hanbury Manor.

North Bedfordshire
Arguably the two leading clubs in Bedfordshire are **John O'Gaunt** at Sandy and **Beadlow Manor** near Shefford; both have more than one course. The former is more established: its two courses, the championship John O'Gaunt course and the shorter Carthegena are curiously very different in character, the John O'Gaunt being a very pretty parkland type, the Carthegena a heathland course. Visitors to both John O'Gaunt and Beadlow Manor can expect first class facilities and a friendly welcome and for the latter the Beadlow Manor Hotel (01525) 860800 is naturally very convenient.

Elsewhere in the north of the county, **Aspley Guise and Woburn Sands** (the more famous Woburn Golf and Country Club lies over the border in Buckinghamshire) is another that provides far-reaching views and a word also for the **Bedford and County** Golf Club. Just north of the county town off the A6, near St Neots in Cambridgeshire but just within Bedfordshire, **Wyboston Lakes** is a pleasant pay and play course.

In Woburn some excellent hotels and restaurants can be found in addition to the delightful stately home and game reserve. The Paris House (01525) 290692 is an outstanding restaurant while the Bedford Arms (01525) 290441 is a welcoming Georgian coaching inn. The Black Horse is a notable pub to visit and the Bell Inn (01525) 290280 is thoroughly recommended for its atmosphere and value. Outside the town, Moore Place (01908) 282000 in Aspley Guise is extremely relaxing and in Flitwick, the 17th century Flitwick Manor (01525) 712242 and its restaurant are tremendous. En route to the county town the Rose & Crown (01525) 280245 in Ridgmont serves a good pint and bar snacks. In Bedford itself we could call upon the services of the Moat House group—the Bedford Moat House (01234) 799988 or the less expensive Clarenden House Hotel. For grander accommodation, the Woodlands Manor (01234) 363281 in Clapham offers a delightful hotel with a quality restaurant.

South Bedfordshire
Finally in the south of the county is one of its better courses, **Dunstable Downs**, laid out on high ground and offering remarkably extensive views—both Surrey to the south and Warwickshire to the north west can be sighted. It is a classic downland type course.

In nearby Berkhamsted, La Fiorentina (01442) 863003 is an excellent restaurant offering fine Italian food and a knowledgeable golfing host (The town is actually in Herts, but as well as being convenient for Ashridge, it is ideal for the courses of South Bedfordshire). In Whipsnade, the zoo is excellent while the downs nearby are a good place to get rid of some energy. In Dunstable the Old Palace Lodge (01582) 662201 is well worth an overnight visit. Pendley Manor (01442) 891891 is also a quality establishment.

Essex: around the M25
Not much of Essex could be described as 'natural golfing country' yet of all England's counties this is the one that witnessed perhaps the biggest explosion in golf course site applications during the late 1980s. Strange, isn't it? Two of the top courses in the county are **Thorndon Park** (two miles south of Brentwood) and **Orsett** (two miles east of Grays and in the wonderfully named area of Mucking and Fobbing). Neither is a great distance from the M25 and both can be reached via the A128. Thorndon Park, as its name suggests, is a parkland type course situated in a former deer park belonging to

Thorndon Hall—a quite stunning mansion. Orsett is much more of the heathland variety with sandy subsoil.

In a similar vein to neighbouring Hertfordshire, a number of the county's better courses have been gradually swallowed up by Greater London—the fine parkland course at **Abridge** with its splendidly luxurious clubhouse being one of them, now lying the wrong side of the M25. **Romford** is one that holds its Essex identity. A well bunkered and fairly flat course, Romford was the home of James Braid before he moved to Walton Heath. Just beyond the M25 the new Martin Gillett-designed course at Billericay, **Stock Brook Manor**, has a growing reputation.

Around Colchester and Chelmsford
Still further afield, both **Colchester** (the oldest town in England) and **Saffron Walden** have courses set in very pretty surroundings and for lovers of seaside golf there is a pleasant (though windy!) course at **Frinton-on-Sea**. One of the county's newest attractions is the **Five Lakes** Golf and Country Club (01621) 868888 at Tolleshunt D'Arcy, not far from Maldon, where there are 36 holes. This large complex offers an abundance of leisure facilities as well as good golf. Finally, for those visiting Chelmsford, both the **Chelmsford** Golf Club, to the south of the town and the **Channels** Golf Club to the north with its superb Elizabethan clubhouse can be recommended, as can the nearby **Warren** Golf Club at Woodham Walter (a very interesting collection of short holes here) and **The Three Rivers** Golf and Country Club in Purleigh (two courses here).

Benton Hall with 27 holes or **Stapleford Abbots** with 45 holes are also well worth ear marking for a good days golf. Essex is blessed with many outstanding hotels and restaurants. Dedham presents an ideal starting point. Here we find the superb La Talbooth (01206) 323150. This is a monument to good food, an ideal place to celebrate a special round of golf. Close by, the Maison Talbooth (01206) 322367 offers stylish accommodation. This delightful village with its views of the Stour also offers the Dedham Vale Hotel (01206) 322273 and its first class restaurant. All are also convenient for the nearby Suffolk courses. Resisting the temptation to venture further up the Stour and discover the delights of Constable country we arrive at the coast and Harwich—heading directly for the Pier (01255) 241212, where, as you may suspect, the seafood is the speciality of the house—some accommodation here as well.

More thoughts and in Arkesden a thatched pub, the Axe & Compasses provides good food and a cheerful hostelry. Saffron Walden offers the Saffron Hotel (01799) 522676 and the charming Newhouse Farm. In the quiet village of Little Walden lies The Crown—good bar food. Another Essex hotel handy for a motorway, the M11 this time, is the Green Man (01279) 442521 in Old Harlow; situated opposite the village green, the hotel totally belies the proximity of the nearby autoroute. Another Green Man (01992) 522255 is also recommended on this occasion at Toot Hill—good food here in the bar and main restaurant. Not particularly close to the county's best golf courses, but well worth a trip is the Whitehall Hotel (01279) 850603 in Broxted where the restaurant is excellent.

Finally we visit Great Dunmow, close to Stansted Airport and where the legendary Flitch trials take place. The Saracens Head Hotel (01371) 873901 in town is smallish but pleasant. If you are rushing home and cannot spend a night in the area then dinner at the Starr (01371) 874321 may still be a possibility—it's an outstanding restaurant and now has some rooms. Incidentally, for those unfamiliar with the Flitch trials, the basic idea is to test (by some rather interesting methods) the suitability of man and woman. Not apparently a necessity for selecting one's golf partner. . .but it's a thought!

Moor Park

I don't suppose many would dispute that the R&A clubhouse at St Andrews is the best known 'nineteenth' in the world. However, for the title of 'most magnificent' or 'most grand' it is doubtful whether Moor Park can have many serious rivals. The Moor Park Mansion dates from the 13th century. In its illustrious history it has been the home of earls, dukes, cardinals, archbishops and even a Queen—Catherine of Aragon living there in the 16th century. During the last war the mansion was requisitioned, becoming first the headquarters of the Territorial Army, then of the ATS and later of the American 2nd Airborne Corps and it was from within Moor Park that preparations were made for the ill-fated invasion of Arnhem in 1944.

Golf first came to Moor Park in 1923, Lord Ebury founding the golf club just four years after the estate had been purchased by Lord Leverhulme. Leading architect Harry Colt was called in to design three golf courses, two of which, the **High** and the **West** courses, remain with the club, the third now being a public course (Rickmansworth) although it is in fact maintained by the Moor Park club.

The major championships staged at Moor Park are all played over the High Course. Measuring 6713 yards (par 72, SSS 72) it is some 900 yards longer than the West Course, though this at 5815 yards (par 69, SSS 68) is certainly no pushover. The High Course begins with a fairly straightforward, slightly uphill 1st but the 2nd which dog-legs to the right is one of the toughest 'fours' of the round. Towards the middle of the front nine a sliced tee shot will send a ball into some particularly pleasant properties whose gardens border the fairways (attempting to retrieve your ball is not recommended!) The back nine contains three excellent short holes including the 12th where the attractive two-tiered green is surrounded by willows and is surely one of the best par threes in the country.

Within two years of the club being founded, Moor Park played host to the 1925 PGA Matchplay Championship, won by Archie Compston.

Since then, several memorable professional tournaments and pro-ams have been played here. However, perhaps the best known game of golf at Moor Park took place back in 1928. A 72 hole challenge match was played between the American Walter Hagen, the leading professional of the day, and the aforementioned Archie Compston, one of Britain's finest players. With only one hole of the final round completed the match was all over, Hagen having been defeated 18 up with 17 to play—the greatest margin of victory ever recorded in a matchplay event.

Moor Park Golf Club,
Rickmansworth, Herts WD3 1QN
www.moorparkgolf.co.uk

Secretary	Tel: (01923) 773146
	Fax: (01923) 777109
Professional	Lawrence Farmer
Green Fees	£60/day (one round over both courses)
Restrictions	Weekdays only

Directions
Leave the M25 at junction 17 or 18. The course is off the A404 Northwood to Rickmansworth Road and about three-quarters of a mile from Moor Park station.

Hanbury Manor

There can be few golfing venues in Europe where 'Old' meets and marries 'New' as successfully and interestingly as it appears to have done at Hanbury Manor in Hertfordshire.

The 'Old' is the manor itself, which since the late 19th century has been dominated by a striking Jacobean style mansion and its wonderful grounds which, since 1918, have included a 9 hole parkland golf course. The 'New' is the recent conversion of the estate into the Hanbury Manor Golf and Country Club including restoration and transformation of the mansion into an extremely elegant five star country house hotel and the complete redesign of the golf course into an 18 hole championship length American-style golf course.

The original Hanbury Manor course was designed by Englishman Harry Vardon. Vardon was the greatest of the 'Great Triumvirate' of Vardon, Braid and Taylor who dominated golf between 1894 and 1914. The architect of the new Hanbury course is American Jack Nicklaus II, eldest son (or chief cub) of the 'Golden Bear', the greatest of the big three of Nicklaus, Palmer and Player who dominated golf from the late 1950s until the mid 1970s.

So how new, how good and how American is the course at Hanbury Manor? The official opening took place in the summer of 1991. Jack Jr was naturally present and so too were Tony Jacklin and Dave Stockton who played a friendly match billed as 'The Ryder Cup Captains' Challenge' and which, like the real thing, was won by Stockton. Both Stockton and Jacklin were very complimentary of both the condition of the course and its design. Stockton was also quoted as saying that it was, 'by far the best course I've played outside of the United States'. A shade rash, you might think—especially given that it was uttered by someone who played in several Open Championships—but Hanbury Manor undoubtedly is first class and, while the superior conditioning of the course (it may be the best maintained course in Great Britain) and the extravagant use of water hazards give the course a very American feel, the surrounding countryside is unmistakably rural England.

Hanbury Manor is located approximately 25 miles north of London, directly off the A10, just north of the Ware turn off. It is important to note that *golf is restricted to hotel residents, club members and their guests*. The residential green fees in 2000 are £75 weekdays and weekends. The hotel offers a number of 'packaged residential golf breaks' and those interested should telephone the hotel on **(01920) 487722** for details. The **Director of Golf**, **Marc Newey** and the **Head Professional**, **Peter Blaze** can also be contacted via the above number. Written correspondence should be addressed to **Hanbury Manor Golf and Country Club, Ware, Hertfordshire SG12 0SD**.

Only the very brave (or rash?) should attempt to tackle Hanbury Manor from the championship tees—at 7016 yards it is monstrously long and many of the par fours are beyond the reach of most mortals. From the medal tees, 6622 yards (par 72) is much more realistic, while the forward tees and ladies' tees reduce the course to 6057 yards and 5285 yards (par 72) respectively. As well as the mix of an American-type course in a very English setting, Hanbury Manor offers two very different challenges within an 18 hole round. The two nines are laid out on opposite sides of the mansion; the first nine has a much newer feel as here the Nicklaus team had to shape virgin golfing terrain (essentially farmland prior to its development) whereas on the back nine they built over the existing mature parkland of the Vardon layout. The degree of challenge, however, is comparable and both nines contain a number of dramatic and beautifully sculpted holes.

The threat of water looms as early as the twisting, downhill 2nd, one of two outstanding par fives on the front nine. The green at this hole has been raised and built at such an angle with fronting traps that even the biggest hitters are unlikely to attempt the water carry with their second shot. A small lake also features on the par three 6th and the very difficult par four 8th, but many people regard the 7th and 9th as even better holes.

On the back nine both the 10th and 15th fairways are bordered by a splendid variety of mature trees and the 13th and 17th call for dramatic do-or-die shots over water. Respite comes at the 18th, for though there is yet more water to be carried from the tee, it is not a big carry—besides, the opulent comforts of Hanbury's 5 star Marriott Hotel are now within sight.

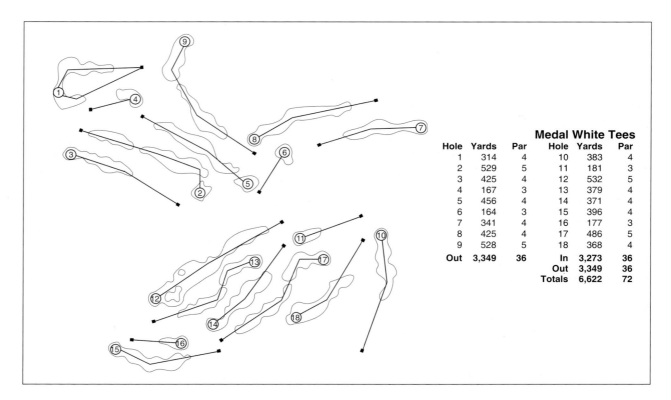

		Medal White Tees			
Hole	Yards	Par	Hole	Yards	Par
1	314	4	10	383	4
2	529	5	11	181	3
3	425	4	12	532	5
4	167	3	13	379	4
5	456	4	14	371	4
6	164	3	15	396	4
7	341	4	16	177	3
8	425	4	17	486	5
9	528	5	18	368	4
Out	**3,349**	**36**	**In**	**3,273**	**36**
			Out	**3,349**	**36**
			Totals	**6,622**	**72**

The Marriott Hanbury Manor Hotel & Country Club, awarded a much sought after 5 star rating by the AA, is a country house experience to be savoured. A lovingly restored mansion with 96 bedrooms and 10 conference suites, turn of the century charm blends with every modern comfort and service that is always friendly and courteous.

The beautiful 200 acre estate provides a vast array of amenities, including a championship golf course, tennis, snooker and a fully equipped health club. The elegantly appointed bedrooms spoil the most discerning traveller, whilst fine dining is available in two enticingly different restaurants, the gourmet Zodiac Restaurant and the less formal Vardon's. The perfect place to relax or to combine business with pleasure, Hanbury Manor is easily accessible, only 25 miles north of London.

One of many highlights of a stay at Hanbury Manor will undoubtedly be the magnificent 18 hole golf course, created out of rolling Hertfordshire countryside by Jack Nicklaus II, of Nicklaus Design. The course measures a testing 7016 yards from the championship tees, with a number of strategically placed bunkers and several picturesque water hazards providing a series of challenges for all levels of players. Marriott Hanbury Manor has hosted the PGA European Tour English Open for three consecutive years 1997-1999, with Lee Westwood and Darren Clarke among the winners.

The contrasting nature of the Downfield nine, beautifully sculpted out of existing meadowland and an old quarry site, and the inward half - set in breathtaking parkland with mature trees provides a remarkable variety of panoramic scenery that makes for a whole series of spectacular memories. The careful design and conditioning of the course makes Hanbury Manor one of the most beautifully manicured layouts anywhere in Britain.

In the walled garden is a herb bed where chefs come daily to select leaves to flavour dishes, while fruits are plucked from the orchard and inside the Peach House and Vine conservatory. Elements within the garden that have been restorated include a secret garden built by prisoners of war and a rose garden designed by Robert Glendinning. A woodland path leads to the arboretum, where you can view several magnificent California Redwoods, some over 200 years old.

Whether toning up or winding down, Hanbury provides the perfect environment for relaxing after a game on the championship standard golf course. Indoors or out, the variety of freely accessible leisure activities are numerous, making Hanbury Manor a genuine resort property. The centrepiece of the magnificently equipped leisure facilities is undoubtedly the 17m x 7m swimming pool where a warm welcome is tendered to all aquaphiles under a stunning Romanesque canopy. Steam rooms, Swedish sauna, and a jacuzzi are offered as wonderful wet alternatives and vie with the Hanbury Beauty Studio and sumptuous gymnasium for guests' attention.

Hanbury Manor has set out to offer guests a level of facilities and service that redefine traditional standards. Whether as a hotel guest, or as a member of the golf and leisure sections, Hanbury Manor is quite simply an experience not to be missed.

Marriott Hanbury Manor Hotel & Country Club
Ware
Hertfordshire
SG12 0SD
Tel: (01920) 487722
Fax: (01920) 487692

The Melbourne Course is a golfing gem inspired by the beautiful rolling landscape surrounding the Hall, designed by Peter Allis and Clive Clark at the beginning of the last decade. They have utilised the land to provide one of the most beautiful parkland courses in the country.

After avoiding the River Lea, which runs the length of the par 4 first hole, you are confronted by the Broadwater which separates the second tee from the green. This has become a veritable graveyard for golf balls and the first place our diver investigates when reclaiming lake balls. The fourth hole provides the next challenge, as your second shot of around 200 yards is predominately over water to a well protected green. A four on this hole is a real bonus and considered a Birdie by most. The par 3 sixth is a hole where accuracy is at a premium due to the severely contoured putting surface, if your tee shot finishes above the hole a three putt is a real possibility. The greens on the course can be exceptionally fast in the summer months and give everyone a succession of short swinging putts, which if missed will provide you with another putt of equal length on the other side of the hole.

The front nine finishes with the short downhill nine, which provides a lovely view of the Auberge du Lac restaurant and the river from the tee.

The par 5 10th gives longer hitters the opportunity of a Birdie as the prevailing wind is normally following. Although if successful your joy soon turns to apprehension when you are confronted by the par 4 11th, which is almost the same length as the 10th but played into the wind. The members consider this a par 5.

The twelfth and thirteenth are heavily bunkered, but if you can avoid the traps they are relatively straightforward. You now have the woodlands on your left for the next few holes before you are confronted by the 16th. A 422 yard par 4 which requires your second shot to carry the broadwater before reaching a green which is split into three segments, so a second shot onto the green doesn't guarantee a par as some putts can be in excess of 40 yards.

The finishing hole provides the golfer with the most magnificent view of the Hall while walking down the fairway to the ferry which transports you to the last green, a unique and very pleasant way to finish your round. This course is a must if you are privileged enough to be invited by a member.

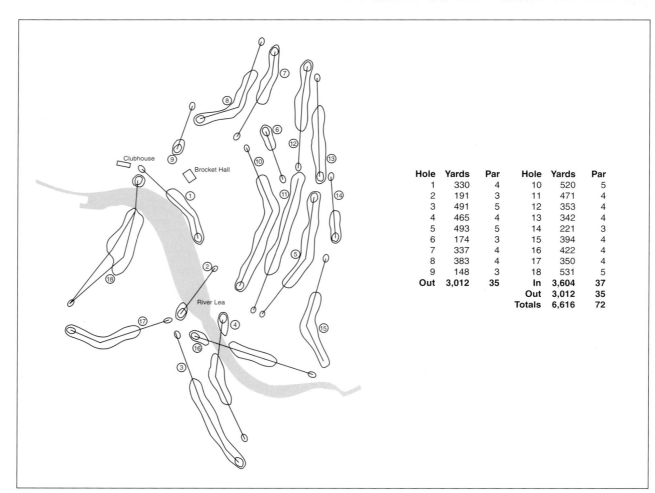

Hole	Yards	Par	Hole	Yards	Par
1	330	4	10	520	5
2	191	3	11	471	4
3	491	5	12	353	4
4	465	4	13	342	4
5	493	5	14	221	3
6	174	3	15	394	4
7	337	4	16	422	4
8	383	4	17	350	4
9	148	3	18	531	5
Out	**3,012**	**35**	**In**	**3,604**	**37**
			Out	**3,012**	**35**
			Totals	**6,616**	**72**

Brocket Hall has one of the most intriguing histories of any of Britain's famous stately homes. The grade 1 listed building constructed in 1760 by Sir Matthew Lamb, to the design of the renowned architect, James Paine, and stands on the site of many of its predecessors, the very first Brocket Hall having been built in 1239. Sir Matthew's son went on to become the first Lord Melbourne, largely through the efforts of his wife, then mistress of the flamboyant Prince Regent. The prince later became George IV and was a frequent visitor to Brocket Hall.

Lady Caroline Lamb, although the wife of the second Lord Melbourne, was rather better known for her stormy and passionate relationship with the poet Lord Byron. Melbourne himself became Prime Minister and formed a friendship with Queen Victoria who often visited the Hall and who came to regard Melbourne as her mentor. On the death of Melbourne in 1848 the Hall passed to his sister who married Lord Palmerston, who went on to become Prime Minister and died in extremely unusual circumstances at the Hall.

Set in a 543 acre country estate of exceptional beauty in Hertfordshire and located within an easily accessible 22 miles of London, Brocket Hall provides spectacular golf from courses named after the two Prime Ministers who helped both shaped the Hall and the country. Located in the grounds of the estate Melbourne Lodge dates back to the 17th Century. Overlooking the beautiful waters of the Broadwater, the 9th green of the Melbourne course and the Hall itself, Melbourne Lodge boasts 16 additional luxurious bedrooms with en-suite facilities.

Brocket Hall itself offers first class conference and banqueting facilities hosting events up to 1,000 people. The accommodation includes 30 elegant and exquisitely furnished bedrooms and suites with panoramic views of the estate.

For the golfing enthusiast Brocket Hall has a great deal to offer; 36 holes of championship golf; a 6 hole par 3 executive course; plus a groundbreaking golfing academy. The original Melbourne course is a

Peter Alliss and Clive Clarke design. At 6, 584 yards in length, the par 72 provides a rigorous, yet enjoyable test of golf. Set within the 18th century parkland surrounding the Hall it follows the natural contours and undulations of the Estate.

The Melbourne course has recently been joined by the new par 73 championship Palmerston course. Designed by the renowned architect Donald Steel, the new course is a challenging contrast to the Melbourne as it wends its way through beautiful mature woodland, rather than the picturesque parkland of the older course. The first hole drives past rare Hornbeam trees, and Scotch pine, Corsican pine and mature beech, some over 300 years old, characterise this delightful course.

Brocket Hall attracts professional and pro-am tournaments and club and corporate golf days. Professional Keith Wood and his team administer the impressive Brocket Hall Golf Academy which offers an affordable entry platform to the world of golf for players of any age or ability.

The Golf Academy incorporates an executive golf course, a driving range, an expansive putting area and a short game area. Here golfers can make use of two pitching areas surrounded by a variety of bunkers and hollows, and an expansive three-tier putting green offers flat, undulating and contoured conditions.

The extensive members' facilities are situated in the Watershyppes Clubhouse, a beautifully restored 18th century building providing a restaurant bar and lounge, billiard room, banqueting hall, meeting rooms and guest rooms.

At the end of a fulfilling day in these stunning surroundings, the perfect place to relax and reflect is the highly acclaimed restaurant Auberge du Lac. Situated on the banks of the River Broadwater, the former 17th century hunting lodge has been transformed into a restaurant which has earned an enviable reputation.

Brocket Hall
Welwyn Hertfordshire
AL8 7XG
Tel: (01707) 390055 Fax: (01707) 390052
e mail: golf@brocket-hall.co.uk
web site: www.brocket-hall.co.uk

HERTFORDSHIRE

Aldenham G.& C.C.
(01923) 853929
Church Lane, Aldenham
(18) 6500 yards/***/B

Aldwickbury Park
(0181) 449 0394
Piggotshill, Wheathamstead
(18) 6333 yards/**/C

Arkley G.C.
(0181) 449 0394
Rowley Green Road, Barnet
(9) 6045 yards/**/D

Ashridge G.C.
(01442) 842244
Little Gaddesden, Berkhamsted
(18) 6547 yards/**/F

Barkway Park G.C.
(01763) 849070
Nuthamstead Road, Royston
(18) 6997 yards/***/D

Batchwood Hall G.C.
(01727) 833349
Batchwood Drive, St Albans
(18) 6487 yards/**/E

Berkhamsted G.C.
(01442) 865832
The Common, Berkhamsted
(18) 6605 yards/***/B - A/H

Bishops Stortford G.C.
(01279) 654715
Dunmow Road, Bishops Stortford
(18) 6440 yards/**/C

Boxmoor G.C.
(01442) 259439
Box Lane, Hemel Hempstead
(9) 4854 yards/**/D

Brickendon Grange G.C.
(01992) 511258
Brickendon, Hertford
(18) 6315 yards/**/F/H

Briggens House Hotel
(01279) 793742
Briggens Park, Stanstead Abbots
(9) 5825 yards/***/F

Brocket Hall G.C.
(01707) 390055
Welwyn
(18) 6584 yards/*/A/G/H

Brookmans Park G.C.
(01707) 652487
Golf Club Road, Hatfield
(18) 6459 yards/**/B/H

Bushey G. & C.C.
(0181) 950 2283
High Street, Bushey
(9) 3000 yards/**/E

Bushey Hall G.C.
(01923) 222253
Bushey Hall Drive, Bushey
(18) 6099 yards/**/E

Chadwell Springs G.C.
(01920) 463647
Hertford Road, Ware
(9) 3021 yards/**/C

Chesfield Downs G.C.
(01462) 482929
Jacks Hill, Graveley
(18) 6630 yards/***/D

Cheshunt G.C.
(01992) 24009
Park Lane, Cheshunt
(18) 6608 yards/***/E

Chorleywood G.C.
(01923) 282009
Common Road, Chorleywood
(9) 2838 yards/**/D

Danesbury Park G.C.
(01438) 840100
Codicote Road, Welwyn
(9) 4150 yards/***/F/G

Dyrham Park C.C.
(0181) 440 3361
Galley Lane, Barnet
(18) 6369 yards/***/F/G

East Herts G.C.
(01920) 821923
Hamels Park, Buntingford
(18) 6455 yards/**(Wed)/F/H

Elstree G.C.
(0181) 953 6115
Watling Street, Elstree
(18) 6166 yards/***/F

Great Hadham G.C.
(01279) 843558
Great Hadham Road, Much Hadham
(18) 6854 yards/**/C

Hadley Wood G.C.
(0181) 449 4328
Beech Hill, Hadley Wood
(18) 6457 yards/**/F/H

Marriott Hanbury Manor Hotel & G.C.
(01920) 487722
Thundridge, Ware
(18) 7016 yards/*/F/G/H/M

Harpenden G.C.
(01582) 712580
Hammonds End, Harpenden
(18) 6381 yards/**/B

Harpenden Common G.C.
(01582) 712856
East Common, Harpenden
(18) 5664 yards/**/B

Hartsbourne G & C.C.
(0181) 950 1133
Hartsbourne Avenue, Bushey Heath
(18) 6305 yards/*/F/G/M
(9) 5432 yards/*/F/G/M

Hatfield London C.C.
(01707) 642624
Bedwell Park, Essendon
(18) 6854/***/C

The Hertfordshire G.C.
(01992) 466666
White Stubbs Lane, Broxbourne
(18) 6400 yards/***/C/H

Kingsway Golf Centre
(01763) 262727
Cambridge Road, Melbourn, Royston
(9) 2500 yards/***/E

Knebworth G.C.
(01438) 814681
Deards End Lane, Knebworth
(18) 6492 yards/**/B/H

Letchworth G.C.
(01462) 683203
Letchworth Lane, Letchworth
(18) 6181 yards/**/B

Little Hay G.C.
(01442) 833798
Box Lane, Hemel Hempstead
(18) 6610 yards/***/E

Manor of Groves G.& C.C.
(01279) 722333
High Wych, Sawbridgeworth
(18) 6250 yards/***/D

Mid Herts G.C.
(01582) 832242
Gustard Wood, Wheathampstead
(18) 6060 yards/**/F/H

Mill Green G.C.
(01707) 276900
Mill Green, Welwyn Garden
(18) 6713 yards/**/F/H
(18) 5823 yards/**/F/H

Moor Park G.C.
(01923) 773146
Moor Park Mansion, Rickmansworth
(18) 6713 yards/**/B/H
(18) 5823 yards/**/B/H

Much Hadham
(01279) 843253
Little Hadham Road, Much Hadham
(18) 6516 yards/***/E

Old Fold Manor G.C.
(0181) 440 9185
Hadley Green, Barnet
(18) 6471 yards/**/B/H

Oxhey Park G.C.
(01923) 248312
Prestwick Road, South Oxhey
(9) 1637 yards/***/E

Panshanger G.C.
(01707) 338507
Herns Lane, Welwyn Garden City
(18) 7178 yards/***/F

Porters Park G.C.
(01923) 854127
Shenley Hill, Radlett
(18) 6313 yards/**/A/H

Potters Bar G.C.
(01707) 652020
Darkes Lane, Potters Bar
(18) 6279 yards/**/C/H

Redbourn G.C.
(01582) 793493
Kinsbourne Green Lane, Rickmansworth
(18) 6407 yards/**/D
(9) 1361 yards/**/E

Rickmansworth G.C.
(01923) 775278
Moor Lane, Rickmansworth
(18) 4493 yards/***/E

Royston G.C.
(01763) 242696
Baldock Road, Royston
(18) 6032 yards/**/C

Sandy Lodge G.C.
(01923) 825429
Sandy Lodge Lane, Northwood
(18) 6340 yards/***/F/H/M

Shendish Manor G.C.
(01442) 232220
Aspley, Hemel Hempstead
(9) 6076 yards/**/C/H

South Herts G.C.
(0181) 445 2035
Links Drive, Totteridge
(18) 6470 yards/**/F/H/L

Stevenage G.C.
(01438) 880322
Aston Lane, Stevenage
(18) 6451 yards/***/E

Stocks Hotel & C.C.
(01442) 851341
Stocks Road, Aldbury
(18) 7016 yards/***/A/H

Verulam G.C.
(01727) 853327
London Road, St Albans
(18) 6457 yards/**/B/H

Welwyn Garden City G.C.
(01707) 325243
High Oaks Road, Welwyn
(18) 6100 yards/**/F/H

West Herts G.C.
(01923) 224264
Cassiobury Park, Watford
(18) 6488 yards/**/C/H

Whipsnade Park G.C.
(01442) 842330
Studham Lane, Dagnall
(18) 6812 yards/**/B

Whitehill G.C.
(01920) 438495
Dane End, Ware
(18) 6636 yards/***/D/H

BEDFORDSHIRE

Aspley Guise and Woburn Sands G.C.
(01908) 582264
West Hill, Aspley Guise
(18) 6135 yards/**/B/H

Aylesbury Vale G.C.
(01525) 240196
Wing, Leighton Buzzard
(18) 6622 yards/***/D/H

Beadlow Manor Hotel G. & C.C.
(01525) 860800
Beadlow, Shefford
(18) 6238 yards/***/D/H
(9) 6042 yards/***/D/H

Bedford and County G.C.
(01234) 352617
Green Lane, Clapham
(18) 6347 yards/**/B/H

Bedfordshire G.C.
(01234) 53241
Bromham Road, Biddenham
(18)6185 yards/**/F

Chalgrave Manor G.C.
(01525) 876556
Dunstable Road, Chalgrove
(18) 6382 yards/***/D

Colmworth G.C.
(01234) 266636
New Road, Colmworth
(18) 6420 yards/***/D

Colworth G.C.
(01234) 781781
Unilever Research, Sharnbrook
(9)2500 yards/***/F/G`

Dunstable Downs G.C.
(01582) 604472
Whipsnade Road, Dunstable
(18) 6255 yards/**/F/H

Griffin G.C.
(01582) 415573
Chaul End Road, Caddington
(18) 6161 yards/**/D

Henlow G.C.
(01462) 851515
Henlow Camp, Henlow
(9) 5618 yards/*/E/G

John O'Gaunt G.C.
(01767) 260360
Sutton Park, Sandy
(18) 6513 yards/***/A/H
(18) 5869 yards/***/A/H

Leighton Buzzard G.C.
(01525) 373811
Plantation Road, Leighton Buzzard
(18) 6101 yards/**/C/H

Lyshott Heath
(01525) 840252
Millbrook Village, Millbrook
(18) 7100 yards (Thur)/D

Millbrook G.C.
(01525) 840252
Millbrook, Ampthill
(18) 6530 yards/**(Thu)/B

Mount Pleasant G.C.
(01462) 850999
Station Road, Lower Stondon
(9)6172 yards/***/D

Mowsbury G.C.
(01234) 216374
Kimbolton Road, Bedford
(18) 6514 yards/***/E

Pavenham Park G.C.
(01234) 822202
Pavenham, Bedford
(18) 6353 yards/**/D

South Beds G.C.
(01582) 591500
Warden Hill Road, Luton
(18) 6332 yards/**/C
(9) 4954 yards/**/E

Stockwood Park G.C.
(01582) 413704
London Road, Luton
(18) 6049 yards/***/E

Tilsworth G.C.
(01525) 210721
Dunstable Road, Tilsworth
(18) 5303 yards/***/E

Wyboston Lakes G.C.
(01480) 212501
Wyboston Lakes, Wyboston
(18) 5721 yards/***/D

ESSEX

Abridge G.& C.C.
(01708) 688396
Epping Lane, Stapleford Tawney
(18) 6703 yards/**/A/H

Ballards Gore G.& C.C.
(01702) 258917
Gore Road, Canewdon
(18) 7062 yards/**/C

Basildon G.C.
(01268) 533297
Clay Hill Lane, Basildon
(18) 6153 yards/***/D

Belfairs Park G.C.
(01702) 525345
Eastwood Road North, Leigh-on-Sea
(18) 5802 yards/***/D

Belhus Park G.C.
(01708) 854260
Belhus Park, South Ockendon
(18) 5188 yards/***/E

Bentley G. & C.C.
(01277) 373179
Ongar Road, Brentwood
(18) 6709 yards/**/B/H

Benton Hall G.C.
(01376) 502454
Wickham Hill, Witham
(18) 6520 yards/***/D

Birch Grove G.C.
(01206) 734276
Layer Road, Colchester
(9) 4108 yards/***/D

Boyce Hill G.C.
(01268) 793625
Vicarage Hill, Benfleet
(18) 5882 yards/**/B

Braintree G.C.
(01376) 346079
Kings Lane, Braintree
(18) 6161 yards/***/B/H

Braxted Park Estate G.C.
(01621) 892305
Maldon
(9) 1980 yards/**/E

Bunsay Downs G.C.
(01245) 412648
Little Baddow Road, Woodham Walter
(9) 2913 yards/***/F

Burnham-on-Crouch G.C.
(01621) 782282
Ferry Road, Burnham-on-Crouch
(18) 6056 yards/**/C

Burstead G.C.
(01277) 631171
Tythe Common Road, Little Burstead
(18) 6150 yards/**/C/H

Canons Brook G.C.
(01279) 421482
Elizabeth Way, Harlow
(18) 6728 yards/**/B

Castle Point G.C.
(01268) 698909
Somnes Avenue, Canvey Island
(18) 5627 yards/***/E

Channels G.C.
(01245) 440005
Little Waltham, Chelmsford
(18) 6272 yards/**/B
(18) 4779 yards/**/B

Chelmsford G.C.
(01245) 256483
Widford Road, Chelmsford
(18) 5944 yards/**/A - B/G

Chigwell G.C.
(0181) 500 2059
High Road, Chigwell
(18) 6279 yards/**/A/H

Clacton-on-Sea G.C.
(01255) 421919
West Road, Clacton-on-Sea
(18) 6244 yards/***/B/H

Colchester G.C.
(01206) 853396
Braiswick, Colchester
(18) 6319 yards/**/B

Colchester & Lexden Golf Centre
(01206) 843333
Bakers Lane, Colchester
(18) 5500 yards /***/D

Colne Valley G.C.
(01787) 224343
Station Road, Earls Colne
(18) 6272 yards/***/F

Crondon Park G.C.
(01277) 841115
Stock Road, Stock
(18) 6585/**/C

Earls Colne G.C.
(01787) 224466
Earls Colne, Colchester
(18) 6585 yards/**/D

Epping Forest G & C.C.
(0181) 500 2549
Abridge Road, Chigwell
(18) 6048 yards/*/G/F

Essex G.C.
(01272) 601701
Eastern Avenue, Southend-on-Sea
(18) 6237 yards/***/D

Essex G & CC
(01787) 224466
Earls Colne
(18) 6800 yards/D
(9) 2190 yards /*** /D

Fairlop Waters G.C.
(0181) 500 9911
Barkingside, Ilford
(18) 6288 yards/***/E

Five Lakes Hotel Golf & C.C.
(01621) 868888
Tolleshunt Knights, nr Maldon
(18) 6250 yards/***/C/H
(18) 6765 yards/***/A/H

Forrester Park G.C.
(01621) 891406
Beckingham Road, Great Totham
(18) 6073 yards/**/C

Frinton G.C.
(01255) 674618
Esplanade, Frinton-on-Sea
(18) 6259 yards/**/B/H
(9) 2508 yards/***/E

Gosfield Lake G.C.
(01787) 474747
Gosfield, Halstead
(18) 6707 yards/**/C/H
(9) 4180 yards/***/E

Hainault Forest G.C.
(0181) 500 0385
Chigwell Row, Hainault Forest
(18) 5754 yards/***/F
(18) 6600 yards/***/F

Hanover G.& C.C.
(01702) 272377
Hullbridge Road, Rayleigh
(18) 6669 yards/**/B/H
(18) 3700 yards/***/D

Hartswood G.C.
(01277) 218850
King George's Playing Fields, Brentwood
(18) 6238 yards/***/F

Harwich and Dovercourt G.C.
(01255) 503616
Station Road, Parkeston
(9) 2950 yards/***/F

Havering G.C.
(01708) 741429
Lower Bedfords Road, Romford
(18) 5237 yards/***/D

Ilford G.C.
(0181) 554 2930
Wanstead Park Road, Ilford
(18) 5251 yards/***/D

Langdon Hills G.C.
(01268) 548444
Lower Dunton Road, Bulphan
(18) 6485 yards/***/D/H

Loughton G.C.
(0181) 502 2923
Clays Lane, Debden Green
(9) 4735 yards/***/E

Maldon G.C.
(01621) 853212
Beeleigh, Langford, Maldon
(9) 6197 yards/**/C/H

Maylands G.& C.C.
(01708) 373080
Harold Park, Romford
(18) 6351 yards/**/B/L

North Weald G.C.
(01992) 522118
North Weald Bassett, Epping
(18) 6239 yards/**/C/H

Nazeing G.C.
(01992) 893915
Middle Street, Nazeing
(18) 6598 yards/***/B/H

Orsett G.C.
(01375) 891352
Brentwood Road, Orsett
(18) 6614 yards/**/A/H

Pipps Hill G.C.
(01268) 523456
Cranes Farm Road, Basildon
(9) 2829 yards/***/F

Risebridge G.C.
(01708) 741429
Lower Bedfords Road, Romford
(18) 6280 yards/***/E

Rochford Hundred G.C.
(01702) 544302
Hall Road, Rochford
(18) 6255 yards/**/F/H

Romford G.C.
(01708) 740986
Heath Drive, Gidea Park, Romford
(18) 6395 yards/**/B

Royal Epping Forest G.C.
(0181) 529 2195
Station Road, Chingford
(18) 6220 yards/***/D

Saffron Walden G.C.
(01799) 522786
Windmill Hill, Saffron Walden
(18) 6608 yards/**/A/H

St Cleres G.C.
(01268) 591798
St Cleres Hall, Stanford le Hope
(18) ***/D/H

Stapleford Abbots G.C.
(01708) 381108
Tysea Hill, Stapleford Abbots
(18) 6487 yards/**/C - A/H
(18) 5965 yards/**/C - A/H
(9) 1140 yards/**/C - A/H

Stock Brook Manor G.C.
(01277) 653616
Queens Park Avenue, Billericay
(18) 6725 yards/***/B/H
(9) 2977 yards/***/B/H

Stoke-by-Nayland G.C.
(01206) 262836
Keepers Lane, Leavenheath
(18) 6516 yards/**/B/H/M
(18) 6544 yards/**/B/H/M

Theydon Bois G.C.
(01992) 813054
Theydon Road, Epping
(18) 5480 yards/**/B/H

Thorndon Park G.C.
(01277) 810345
Ingrave, Brentwood
(18) 6481 yards/**/B/L

Thorpe Hall G.C.
(01702) 582205
Thorpe Hall Avenue, Thorpe Bay
(18) 6286 yards/**/B/H

Three Rivers G.& C.C.
(01621) 828631
Stow Road, Purleigh
(18) 6609 yards/***/C/H
(9) 1071 yards/***/C/H

Toot Hill G.C.
(01277) 365747
Toot Hill, Ongar
(18) 6013 yards/**/B/H

Top Meadow G.C.
(01708) 852239
Fen Lane, North Ockendon
(18)5500 yards/**/D
(9)1633 yards/**/D

Towerlands G.C.
(01376) 326802
Panfield Road, Braintree
(9) 2703 yards/**/E

Upminster G.C.
(01708) 222788
Hall Lane, Upminster
(18) 5926 yards/***/D/M

Wanstead G.C.
(0181) 989 3938
Wanstead, London
(18) 6262 yards/**/B/H

Warley Park G.C.
(01277) 224891
Magpie Lane, Little Warley
(27)(3 x 9)/**/B/H

Warren G.C.
(01245) 223258
Woodham Walter, Maldon
(18) 6211 yards/**/B - A/H

Weald Park G.C.
(01277) 375101
South Weald, Brentwood
(18) 6308 yards/***/B/H

West Essex G.C.
(0181) 529 7558
Sewardstonebury, Chingford
(18) 6289 yards/**/B/H

Woodford G.C.
(0181) 504 3330
Sunset Avenue, Woodford Green
(9) 5806 yards/**/C

BROCKET HALL GOLF CLUB *Photograph courtesy of:* **Brocket Hall Golf Club**

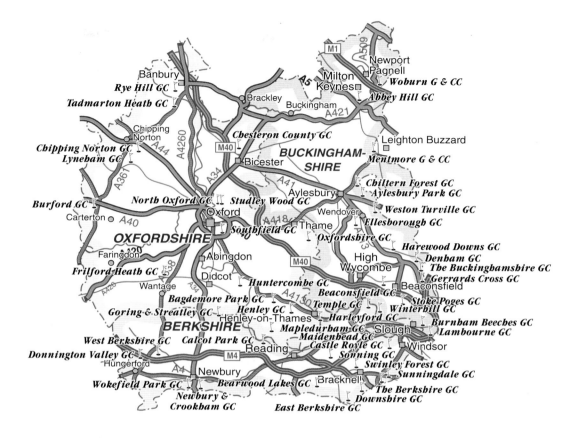

© MAPS IN MINUTES ™ 2000

Berks, Bucks & Oxon Choice Golf

Berkshire, Buckinghamshire and Oxfordshire—three very English counties. The region extends from the edge of the Chilterns to the edge of the Cotswolds and occupies a very prosperous part of southern Britain.

Berkshire: East

Berkshire—or should one say 'Royal Berkshire'—is often described as being cigar-shaped. Now whilst this may not say much for the talents of cigar-makers it does serve as a rough description in as much as the county is peculiarly long and thin. When it comes to surveying the county's twenty or so golf courses it is tempting to adopt another cigar analogy in that one end could be said to glow rather more brightly than the other.

To the east of the county there is a famous heathland belt and it is here that the twin pearls of **Sunningdale** and **The Berkshire** are to be found. Both clubs possess two 18 hole courses which for sheer enjoyment can stand comparison with anything golf has to offer. Sunningdale is better known than the Berkshire but it is difficult to imagine a more delightful setting than the tranquil, tree-lined fairways of the Red and the Blue Courses at the Berkshire—and so close to London too. Sunningdale is featured in our Surrey section; the Berkshire is described in this chapter. **Swinley Forest** is the other outstanding heathland course in the area, a veritable paradis terrestre indeed although individual visitors are normally only permitted to play as guests of members.

Still in heather and pine country is the very attractive **East Berkshire** course at Crowthorne. Also in close proximity is the highly acclaimed—but private—**Bearwood Lakes** golf club near Wokingham, and the popular **Downshire** public course where the green fees are naturally less expensive.

Windsor is where many visiting the area will choose to spend a night or two. Pride of place must go to Oakley Court (01753) 609988. Its comfortable rooms are complemented by splendid grounds and a delightful dining room, the Oak Leaf. Melrose House (01753) 865328 meanwhile, will delight those for whom money is far from no object! In the Ascot area there are a number of good establishments. The Thatched Tavern (01344) 620874 is a pleasant place to have lunch or dinner while the Berystede Hotel (0870) 400 8111 is an outstanding place to stay. In Sunninghill, near Ascot, the Royal Berkshire (01344) 623322 is perhaps the crème de la crème and admirably reflects the quality of the nearby courses. However, a night spent in Ascot does not have to be extravagantly expensive; for affordable comfort, try the Highclere Hotel (01344) 625220. A good local pub is the Winkfield in Winkfield Row—a fine atmosphere and a charming restaurant. This area of Berkshire, of course, borders Surrey and we shouldn't forget its many delights. One tip is Pennyhill Park (01276) 471774 in Bagshot—a superb hotel and very convenient (not to mention appropriate) for the likes of Sunningdale. What Sunningdale is to golf so Cliveden (01628) 668561 is to hotels—excellence of the highest order.

Time for some more golf and **Temple's** fine course can be glimpsed from the main A23 Maidenhead to Henley Road. It has an interesting layout with many fine trees and lush fairways. Designed by Willie Park early this century, it was for a number of years the home of Henry Cotton. The course is always maintained in first class condition. The golf course at **Winter Hill** is on fairly high ground—apparently its name derives from the particularly chilling winds that sweep across in winter (I have no explanation for nearby Crazies Hill!) From the course there are some spectacular views over the Thames—definitely worth a visit. So for that matter is classy **Sonning**, situated further towards Reading. There is a reasonable course in (or on the outskirts of) **Maidenhead** and just beyond the boating villages of **Goring and Streatly** lies the fairly tough Goring and Streatly course. With the delights of Windsor Castle and Legoland close at hand **Castle Royle Golf and Country Club** is an ideal spot for those with non-golfers at hand. It's beautifully maintained and a good challenge.

In Maidenhead, Fredrick's Hotel (01628) 635934 has a considerable reputation for comfort and warm hospitality—its dining room is also highly acclaimed—while in nearby Bray the Waterside Inn (01628) 620691 is an outstanding restaurant. The Boulters Lock Hotel (01628) 621291 on Boulters Island is a delightful place to stay. North of here in Hurley one finds yet another gem, Ye Olde Bell (01628) 825881, a very popular Norman inn.

Meandering further down the Thames, recommended hotels must include the Great House at Sonning (0118) 9692277 with its charming Elizabethan courtyard and also in Sonning, the French Horn (0118) 969 2204 is a super restaurant. In Streatly, the Swan Diplomat (01491) 878800 has a splendid riverside setting. In need of a pub? A visit to the Bell at Aldworth should do the trick. Another nearby local is the Crown and Horns at East Ilsley. Two locations with good hotel and restaurant combinations are at Pangbourne, the Copper Inn (0118) 984 2244 and Yattendon, the Royal Oak (01635) 201325. The Beetle and Wedge (01491) 651381 rejoices in a glorious Thameside setting and offers fare of the highest order—some bedrooms are also available.

Berkshire: West

On the western edge of Reading **Calcot Park** golf course poses many interesting challenges. It can boast Guinness Book of Records fame too in that one sterling fellow sprinted round the course in a motorised cart in just over 24 minutes—a more leisurely round is suggested! A recommended 19th hole around Reading is the Rennaisance Hotel (0118) 958 6222. To the north west of Reading is the increasingly popular **Mapledurham** course and visiting golfers will find suitable accommodation at the Holiday Inn (0118) 925 9988.

Newbury is of course better known for its racing than its golf, but the **Newbury and Crookham** Golf Club close to Greenham Common is one of the oldest clubs in Southern England and is strongly recommended. The course is hilly and well-wooded, though not overly long. Meanwhile, at nearby Donnington there is excellent accommodation and cuisine to be enjoyed (not forgetting golf) at the **Donnington Valley Hotel and Golf Course** (01635) 551199.

Before leaving Berkshire it is worth noting two of the county's more recent additions, **West Berkshire**, situated just south of the village of Chaddleworth, it is a splendid downland course, but not exactly one for the weak-kneed—it stretches to around the 7000 yard mark with one par five measuring well over 600 yards. Perhaps even more impressive is **Wokefield Park** the setting for an historic mansion now a conference centre and a challenging new course designed by Jonathan Gaunt to provide nine holes of parkland golf and a back nine of links style holes, all threaded between acres of seedhead rough—not to be missed

Buckinghamshire: North

Moving into Buckinghamshire, **Woburn** (featured ahead) stands rather alone in the far north of the county. For a brief thought on where to stay, stylish Flitwick Manor (01525) 712242 is a favourite with golfers and deservedly so. In Woburn Park, the Paris House (01525) 290692 is a highly recommended restaurant, Moore Place (01908) 282000 in nearby Aspley Guise and the Bedford Arms (01525) 290441 in Woburn village also come highly recommended. In Milton Keynes, overlooking the **Abbey Hill** public golf course, is the suitably named Quality Friendly Hotel (01908) 561666 while the Red Lion Country Hotel (01908) 583117 is likely to please.

Heading down the county, the **Mentmore** Golf and Country Club boasts 36 holes of wonderfully manicured golf beneath the watchful gaze of Mentmore Towers, the former residence of the Rothschild family. **Ellesborough's** golf course is yet another with rather stately surroundings, being located on part of the property of Chequers. Quite a hilly course and well worth inspecting, not least because there are some commanding views across the Bucking-hamshire countryside. Elsewhere in the centre of the county, there is a fairly lengthy parkland course at **Weston Turville**, south of Aylesbury. And just north of Aylesbury lies **Aylesbury Park**, a new course in a delightful setting.

Ideas for a 19th hole in these parts include in Ivinghoe, the Kings Head (01296) 668388, which has a splendid restaurant in a 17th century inn, and two 'Bells', the Bell (01296) 89835 in Aylesbury's market place and the Bell (01296) 630252 in Aston Clinton (note the superb wine list here). A couple of good pubs to savour are the Rising Sun at Little Hampden and the Fox at Dunsmore.

Buckinghamshire: South

It is in southern Buckinghamshire that most of the county's better courses are to be found. **Stoke Poges** has staged many leading amateur and professional events—not at all surprisingly, this being one of the finest parkland courses in England. It also now offers some very stylish accommodation, we explore Stoke Poges on a later page. **Denham** Golf Club is a close neighbour of Stoke Poges lying some three miles north of Uxbridge, and as an old club handbook will tell you 'half an hours drive from Marble Arch'. (Add an extra 60 minutes nowadays if you're attempting the journey during rush hour). It is worth making the escape though for Denham enjoys a beautiful setting, deeply secluded amidst some glorious countryside. It is a very good golf course and the clubhouse is a most unusual building having been built around a 16th century tithe barn.

In equally beautiful surroundings are the **Burnham Beeches** Golf Club, four miles west of Slough and the **Lambourne** course at Burnham. Others to note in southern Buckinghamshire are **Beaconsfield**, **Harewood Downs** (at Chalfont St Giles), **Gerrards Cross** and at Denham Court the **Buckinghamshire** Golf Club designed by John Jacobs. And note that we now have The Berkshire, The Oxfordshire and The Buckinghamshire !

There are a number of very comfortable hotels in the south Buckinghamshire area. They include the Bellhouse Hotel (01753) 887211 just outside Beaconsfield, the Burnham Beeches Hotel (01628) 429955, a former hunting lodge—ideal for the golf course, the Compleat Angler Hotel (01628) 484444 at Marlow Bridge and Danesfield House (01628) 891010 just outside Marlow. This impressive hotel is particularly convenient for Donald Steel's sensitively designed parkland course at the **Harleyford** club. Two good pubs are the Kings Arms in Amersham and the Lions at Bledlow.

Oxfordshire: South

We start at **Huntercombe**, a charming golf club with an interesting history. In the early years of the century three rather old Daimler motor cars were used to ferry members to and from the local station and later a thirty seater bus was acquired for the same purpose. The course itself has passed through various owners—first a property company, then an insurance company (the Norwich Union) and later Viscount Nuffield before finally becoming a members' club in 1963. On the edge of the Chilterns at some 700 feet above sea level are some marvellous views across the Oxford Plain. The course itself is fairly flat and kept in first class condition. Nearby in Henley there are two courses worth inspecting, the more established **Henley** Golf Club and **Badgemore Park**, a course that has settled down quickly.

A suitable 19th hole? The Red Lion in Henley (01491) 572161 is commendable. In Nettlebed, the White Hart (01491) 641245 is a pleasing inn with some good value bedrooms (handy for Huntercombe) and North Stoke offers the excellent Springs Hotel

(01491) 836687 which has a first class restaurant and its own golf course .

So to the best golf in the county and, just as The Berkshire has a Red and Blue, so **Frilford Heath** has a Red, a Blue and a Green. Frilford Heath is featured later in this chapter. Good food and drink can be found in nearby Fyfield at the White Hart. A short trip to Abingdon can be recommended, where the Upper Reaches Hotel (0870) 400 8101 is most welcoming. Those golfers who have missed a crucial short putt on the 18th should consider the aptly named Dog House (01865) 390830 in Frilford Heath. We also hear good news about the recently opened Merry Miller at Cothill.

Around Oxford

If there is a club that may one day challenge Fril ford as the county's best it is the new **Oxfordshire** Golf Club at Thame, close to the M40. It is a fairly private club but if the chance of a game materialises don't pass it by! Either side of Oxford both **Studley Wood** and **Southfield** are certainly worth a game. The former designed by Simon Gidman in a former deer park provides exhilarating golf whilst the latter, always challenging, is the home of University golf.

The Randolph (0870) 400 8200 is the best known of the Oxford hotels, but the part 17th century Old Parsonage (01865) 310210 will delight those who enjoy the smaller hotel—its a classic—and for first class restaurants, the Cherwell Boathouse (01865) 552746 is certainly among the best. Oxford, naturally, is more than a little used to visitors of all tastes and for reasonably priced accommodation try the

Courtfield Hotel (01865) 242991. Outside in Cumnor, the Bear and Ragged Staff serves good food while a little further afield in Stanton Harcourt, the Harcourt Arms (01865) 310630 has a tremendous atmosphere, a good restaurant and accommodation. Another fine restaurant and hotel near Oxford and within striking distance of Frilford is the Plough at Clanfield (01367) 810222. A final recommendation for the true golfing/culinary connoisseur is Le Manoir Aux Quat' Saisons (01844) 278881 in Great Milton—possibly the country's finest restaurant and a splendid hotel as well.

Oxfordshire: West and North

Back on the fairways (suitably fed one hopes!) and beyond the Oxford area there is a flattish parkland course near Bicester, the **Chesterton** Golf Club and a much improved course at **Burford**. Inching up towards the Cotswolds there are pleasant courses at **Lyneham** and **Chipping Norton** but the best in the north of the county, although it may be a little more difficult to arrange a game upon, is clearly **Tadmarton Heath**. At less than 6000 yards in length, it is fairly short by modern standards but the narrow fairways and a great spread of gorse can make it a very difficult test. It also has a wonderfully remote setting. Right beside Tadmarton is the new course at **Rye Hill**, which is worth a visit. Not far away, the village of Deddington provides an admirable place to rest the heather-clad spikes, more specifically, the Holcombe Hotel (and restaurant) (01869) 338274. Burford offers the Lamb (01993) 823155, a truly charming Cotswold inn. A final thought, the Feathers at Woodstock (01993) 812291 is an extremely fine hotel well situated for Blenheim Palace.

The Berkshire

The horse racing, golf playing residents of Ascot must number among the luckiest folk in England for right on their doorsteps lie the cream of each sport. They have of course, three golfing pearls close at hand, Sunningdale, Wentworth and The Berkshire—the youngest of the illustrious trio.

The two 18 hole courses of The Berkshire, the **Red** and the **Blue**, were designed in 1928 by Herbert Fowler—a master golf architect whose other great works include Walton Heath and Saunton. They occupy some 400 acres of Crown Land over which Queen Anne's carriage used to pass en route to the hunting in Swinley Forest.

Today, both courses give the appearance of having been hewn out of a dense forest, rather in the way that the Duke and Duchess courses were created at Woburn. This, in fact, was not the case, as much clearing of the ancient forest occurred during the First World War when the land was used for military purposes, and most of the present thick woodland is of comparatively recent origin.

The Berkshire is often described as being primarily a 'members' club', this largely through the conspicuous absence of any big-time professional golf tournament. Perhaps the club does not wish to have its tranquillity stirred or its rough trampled over by hordes of excited spectators, but this does not imply that the club closes its doors to the outside world or makes visitors unwelcome. Indeed, The Berkshire is a busy and popular club with a great number of societies, most of which choose to return year after year.

The two courses are of fairly similar length—the Red slightly longer, measuring 6369 yards to the Blue's 6260 yards, although the latter's par is one fewer at 71. The Red course is perhaps the better known of the two, to some extent due to its comprising an unusual six par threes, six par fours and six par fives. In any event, most people agree

that there is little to choose between the two, both in terms of beauty and degree of difficulty.

The Berkshire is especially famed for its glorious tree-lined fairways. There is a splendid mix of mature pines, chestnuts and silver birch and both courses are kept in the most superb condition. Much of the rough consists of heather, ensuring that the wayward hitter is heavily punished.

The club may have avoided professional tournaments, but it does play host to a number of important amateur events. The Berkshire Trophy is one of the annual highlights on the amateur calendar and before turning professional Messrs Faldo and Lyle were both winners.

The Berkshire Golf Club, Swinley Road Ascot, Berkshire SL5 8AY	
Secretary	Major P D Clarke (01344) 621496
Professional	Paul Anderson (01344) 622351
Green Fees	£60/round; £80/day
Restrictions	No visitors at weekends

Directions
The club lies just off the A332 between Ascot and Bagshot. The A332 can be joined from Windsor to the north and Guildford to the south, while driving from Reading, leave the M4 at junction 10 and follow the A329 to Ascot.

Woburn

A magnificent stately home housing one of the finest art collections in the world, the largest wildlife safari park in Europe and two (indeed, soon to be three) of the finest inland golf courses in Britain—it's quite a place Woburn!

The stately home is of course Woburn Abbey which since the reign of Henry VIII has been the home of the Dukes of Bedford, while the wildlife park and the golf courses lie within the grounds of the great estate.

In a game that prides itself on its antiquity the Woburn Golf and Country Club might be described as a remarkably precocious youngster. It was founded as recently as 1976 and its original two courses, aptly named the Duke's and Duchess, were not opened until 1977 and 1979 respectively. In such a short period of time Woburn has acquired an enviable reputation.

In charge of all golfing matters at Woburn is **Eddie Bullock** the **Managing Director** and he may be contacted on **(01908) 370756.** The **Professional** is **Luther Blacklock**, who can be reached on **(01908) 626606.** The club fax number is **(01908) 378436.**

Visitors, societies and company days are all welcome from Monday to Friday at Woburn, although prior booking is essential. In addition, visitors must be members of recognised golf clubs and be able to provide proof of handicap. All written enquiries should be addressed to the **Managing Director, Woburn Golf and Country Club, Bow Brickhill, Milton Keynes, MK17 9LJ.** The green fees for 2000 were set at £125 per person per day for parties of nine and above, and £100 for parties of less than nine. This fee is inclusive of golf and lunch while dinner can also be arranged if there are 24 people or more.

Having booked a game, travelling to Woburn ought not to present too many problems. The club is located approximately 45 miles from London and 73 miles from Birmingham and is well served by major roads. Both the M1 (junction 13) and the A5 pass close by. For those using British Rail, Bletchley Station, some four miles away has good connections from both London and Birmingham. Luton and Heathrow Airports are also within fairly easy reach. The town of Woburn and the Abbey are both actually within the county of

Bedfordshire while the Golf and Country Club lies a short distance over the boundary in Buckinghamshire; presumably the lions amble from county to county.

Thirty years ago if someone had suggested that a championship course (never mind three) could have been built on the Woburn Estate, the famous lions would probably not have been the only ones to roar. The present site was then a dense forest, with giant trees and bracken restricting vision beyond a few yards. Golf architect Charles Lawrie of Cotton Pennink was called in and plans were drawn up. The bulldozers soon arrived and from amidst the pines and the chestnuts great avenues were carved. The fairways flourished on the sandy subsoil and within two years of opening, the **Duke's Course** was considered fit to stage a major professional tournament. It proved a popular decision and a succession of sponsors decided to follow suit. Following its opening, the **Duchess Course** matured with equal rapidity and Woburn soon possessed two precious gems. In June 2000 Woburn will unveil its third 18 hole layout the **Marquess Course.**

The tournaments held at Woburn have included numerous British Masters Championships, The Ford Ladies Classic and the Weetabix Women's British Open. The British Masters winners have included such great names as Trevino, McNulty, Ballesteros, Lyle and Faldo. During the 1992 event, won in such thrilling style by Christy O'Connor Jr, Bernhard Langer was quoted as saying of the Duke's Course, 'It is as good a golf course as we play all year'.

From the back markers the Duke's Course stretches to 6940 yards (72), while the Duchess measures 6651 yards (72). The corresponding distances for the ladies are 6060 yards (75) and 5831 yards (74). The best hole at Woburn? Not easy when there are 36 fine holes to choose from, but many people single out the picturesque short 3rd on the Duke's Course. For my money, however, the 13th is one of the best par fours in the country.

As one might expect from a modern golf and country club the facilities at Woburn are excellent. The newly rebuilt clubhouse offers a full complement of catering, though dinners must be pre-arranged. For the sporty types there is tennis and an open-air heated swimming pool. The majority of golfers, however, will probably head for one of the two bars . . . and toast the Duke, the Duchess and the Marquess.

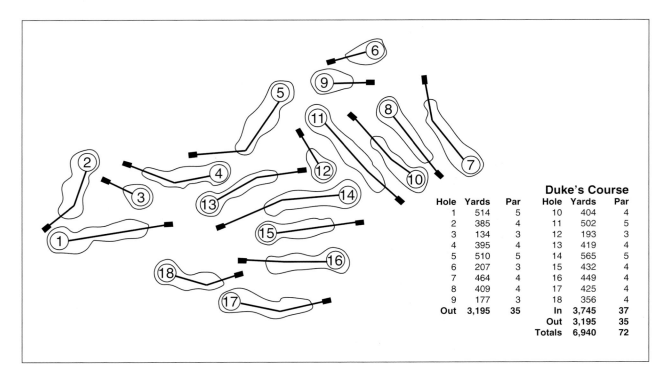

Duke's Course					
Hole	Yards	Par	Hole	Yards	Par
1	514	5	10	404	4
2	385	4	11	502	5
3	134	3	12	193	3
4	395	4	13	419	4
5	510	5	14	565	5
6	207	3	15	432	4
7	464	4	16	449	4
8	409	4	17	425	4
9	177	3	18	356	4
Out	3,195	35	In	3,745	37
			Out	3,195	35
			Totals	6,940	72

Danesfield House is set in the heart of Buckinghamshire and stands in 65 acres of beautiful English and Italian styled gardens which overlook the river Thames and Chiltern Hills. There has been a manor house on the site since 1638 but the current house, the grandest of all, was built in 1899 and opened as a luxury hotel in 1991.

In all, there are 87 individually furnished bedrooms in the main house all of which have satellite TV, minibar, 24 hour room service, two telephone lines (one to accommodate a personal fax or laptop computer), trouser press and hairdryer. Many bedrooms have the original fireplaces and balconies overlooking the Thames. There is also a range of suites, some with jacuzzis and four poster beds

The hotel offers a choice of two restaurants, the Oak Room and the less formal Orangery Mediterranean Brasserie. Both offer fine food in elegant surroundings. The Danesfield Spa is scheduled to open late 2000.

Danesfield House is within easy reach of many of England's finest golf courses. The newly opened Harleyford Golf Club is right on the doorstep whilst slightly further afield we find such gems as Stoke Poges, Mentmore, Sunningdale, Woburn and Donnington Valley. For the non-golfer there is plenty at hand; Ascot and Newbury races, boating on the Thames, tennis, croquet, clay pigeon shooting, hot air ballooning and historic sites such as Windsor Castle and Blenheim Palace close by.

Danesfield House offers superb private function facilities with a range of prestigious dining suites all luxuriously decorated and restored to their former glory, suites can accommodate up to 100 guests and the excellent conference facilities up to 80 delegates.

Finding Danesfield House is no problem, situated as it is on the banks of the Thames between Marlow and Henley, approximately 45 minutes by car from central London and just half an hour from Heathrow. The hotel boasts a Thames mooring and clients can be transported to the hotel via restored steam launches. The hotel is also directly accessible via the M4 from Heathrow or even by air, by helicopter! But whatever your means of travel Danesfield House offers a luxurious retreat from the world outside.

Danesfield House
Henley Road
Marlow on Thames
Buckinghamshire SL7 2EY
Tel: (01628) 891010
Fax: (01628) 890408

Stoke Poges

How does it go? 'The first thing we do, let's kill all the lawyers.' Never utter this Shakespearean line at Stoke Poges. Not only will it insult some of the members but it will likely stir the former Lord of the Manor. Sir Edward Coke, the first Lord Chief Justice of England (and the judge who put paid to Guy Fawkes) once owned the estate on which Stoke Poges Golf Club now stands and his presence is still greatly felt, for his towering monument can be seen from many parts of the course.

While no one disputes that the best golf in the Home Counties is to be found south west of London, especially in the celebrated heathland belt of Surrey and Berkshire, to continually visit the heather and gorse can get a little frustrating at times. For this reason alone there is good cause for investigating Stoke Poges, near Slough in southern Buckinghamshire, but there are many better reasons for doing so. Stoke Poges is arguably the finest 'established' parkland course in England; it is certainly one of the loveliest and its palatial mansion clubhouse is one of the most historic and attractive that any travelling golfer is likely to come across.

Writing in 1910, just a year after golf first came to Stoke Poges, Bernard Darwin gave his opinion on the merits of the site. 'It is a beautiful spot, and there is very good golf to be played here; the club is an interesting one, moreover, as being one of the first and most ambitious attempts in England at what is called in America, a Country Club, there are plenty of things to do at Stoke besides playing golf. We may get very hot at lawn tennis or keep comparatively cool at bowls or croquet, or, coolest of all, we may sit on the terrace or in the garden and give ourselves wholly and solely to loafing'. Well, the good news is it's still a marvellously relaxing place!

Seriously, much has happened at Stoke Poges in recent years—both on and off the fairways. A decade ago there was a 'frayed at the edges' air to the club—the course was good but a little tired looking while the mansion was, quite literally starting to crumble. Since coming under new ownership in 1993, substantial investment in the facilities has transformed Stoke Poges. The mansion has been restored to its former glory, with 21 first floor en suite bedrooms, while back on the fairways the golf course has been sympathetically upgraded, with the addition of a further nine holes re-establishing the original 27 hole layout.

The club's **Director of Golf, Mr D. Woodward** may be contacted by telephone on **(01753) 717171** and by fax on **(01753) 717181.** The club's address is **Stoke Poges Golf Club, North Drive, Park Road, Stoke Poges, Bucks SL2 4PG** or visit **www.stokeparkclub.com** Visitors are welcome between Mondays and Fridays and at weekends. Societies are also very welcome and they can make weekday bookings by telephoning the above number. All players must possess a handicap. Stoke Poges' **professional shop** can be reached on **(01753) 717172.**

The green fees for 2000 are weekdays £110 per round, £180 per day and £180 per round at weekends. A reduced rate of £40 is payable after 5pm. Junior golfers under the age of 14 and accompanied by an adult pay £30 per round.

Travellers from London should head towards Stoke Poges using either the M4 (junction 6) or the A40 (leaving at Gerrards Cross). Approaching from the south and west the M3 (junction 3) and the M4 (junction 6) are likely to prove helpful. The course is 8 miles from Heathrow.

Harry Colt was the architect of Stoke Poges. Perhaps the greatest of all golf course designers, at Stoke Poges Colt made magnificent use of a very wooded landscape. Some of the short holes he created here are among the most seductive in England. The 7th is the most talked about. It is not an especially long par three but the tee shot must be measured to perfection for the narrow green has been built at an angle and is fronted by a brook, surrounded by trees and has a devilishly positioned bunker at the back of the 'safest' side of the green. There are also at least half a dozen very good two-shot holes, and here one might single out the 4th, 6th, 8th, 12th, 17th and 18th.

The 19th hole at Stoke Poges is the spectacular mansion referred to in the second paragraph 'A dazzling vision of white stone' was Darwin's description. It was built in 1795 by one of the Penn family of Pennsylvania fame and was assaulted by Odd Job after his evil master, Goldfinger, had been caught cheating by James Bond. What a pity Lord Coke didn't catch him!

Stoke Poges now has 27 holes, the course plan and the yardage card below shows only part of the course now available to play. However, as with the first 18 they will inspire all those who love to follow the fairways.

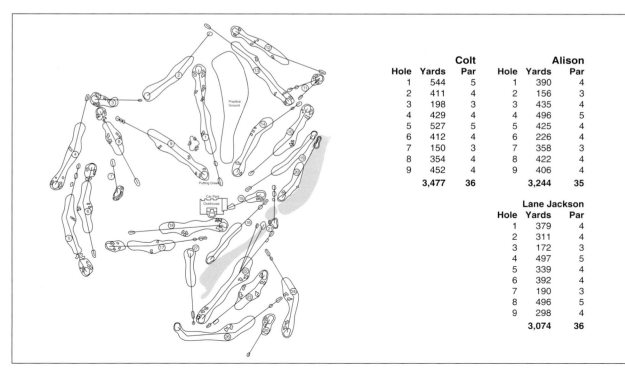

		Colt			**Alison**	
Hole	Yards	Par	Hole	Yards	Par
1	544	5	1	390	4
2	411	4	2	156	3
3	198	3	3	435	4
4	429	4	4	496	5
5	527	5	5	425	4
6	412	4	6	226	4
7	150	3	7	358	3
8	354	4	8	422	4
9	452	4	9	406	4
	3,477	**36**		**3,244**	**35**

	Lane Jackson	
Hole	Yards	Par
1	379	4
2	311	4
3	172	3
4	497	5
5	339	4
6	392	4
7	190	3
8	496	5
9	298	4
	3,074	**36**

Mention the name Stoke Poges to a group of Americans and it will probably bring a smile to their faces. How frightfully English-sounding, one will remark. A place called Stoke Poges must have an amazing history, another will say. And of course, it has.

Golf came to Stoke Poges early in the 20th century. In his seminal book The Golf Courses of the British Isles, published in 1910, Bernard Darwin gave an extremely favourable description of the golf course and its extraordinary clubhouse - the Stoke Park mansion. He described the latter as: A dazzling vision of white stone, and added: It is a beautiful spot, and there is very good golf to be played here; the club is an interesting one, moreover, as being one of the first and most ambitious attempts in England at what is called in America, a Country Club.

The golf course was laid out in 1908 by the distinguished course architect, Harry Colt. Stoke Poges was one of his early designs and, he was still to produce his most famous works amid the heathlands of Surrey and Berkshire, and yet to revise the great links courses of Muirfield and Royal Portrush.

The 1960's saw the filming at Stoke Poges of James Bond's epic encounter with Goldfinger. Bond, if you recall the story, caught his opponent cheating and claimed the match. Goldfinger's assistant and caddie, Oddjob, responded by vandalising the mansion - decapitating a sculpture with his bowler hat. In 1990 the entire estate was acquired by an ambitious English family, determined to restore Stoke Poges to its former glory. In fact, their plans went well beyond restoration - an immense task in itself - for they aimed to transform Stoke Poges from a rather sleepy golf club into the most stylish club in the country, a place where first-rate golf would be accompanied by unrivalled off-course facilities. Work on the golf course has been continuous and today Stoke Poges has arguably the truest and quickest greens of any inland course in Britain. The bunkers all appear beautifully sculpted, and

since 1997 the fairways have benefited from a new state-of-the-art irrigation system.

Anyone visiting Stoke Poges for the first time in five or six years is certain to be very pleasantly surprised by the enhanced condition of the golf course. That same person is likely to be amazed and astonished when he or she approaches the 19th hole. Under the watchful but admiring eye of English Heritage, the Grade I Listed Stoke Park mansion has been brought back to life - and more than that, its sparkle has returned. The building once again dazzles from within and without. Beautiful paintings, vast tapestries and glittering chandeliers greet you as you enter the building, while outside, and all around, fountains have sprouted and statues mushroomed amid emerald lawns and gleaming terraces. It is a wondrous sight and, for golfers, it is a wonderful clubhouse. Stoke Poges has become a haven for the gourmet golfer (or the golfing gourmet, possibly?). In addition to a splendid, relaxing Orangery, there is a first-class formal restaurant and, newly opened this year, a chic, art deco inspired Brasserie - one that has already been awarded two AA red rosettes.

The extent and pace of change at Stoke Poges borders on the bewildering. In addition to the opening of a superb Brasserie, the Club unveiled 20 luxury bedrooms occupying the entire top two tiers of the mansion. The quality of the furnishings within each of these rooms is again exceptional. Also, in 1999 Stoke Poges became a 27-hole golf club with the opening of a new nine holes, designed by Donald Steel. The course enjoys magnificent views of the far side of the mansion and the championship 18 as it weaves its way around the now-resurrected Capability Brown lakes on the edge of the estate.

Stoke Poges is undoubtedly one of British golf's success stories of the 1990's. Renovated, restored and transformed, it now has a genuine claim to the unofficial title of most stylish golf club in Great Britain.

Stoke Park Club
Park Road Stoke Poges
Bucks SL2 4PG
Tel: (01753) 717171
Fax: (01753) 717181
email: info@stokeparkclub.com
web site: stokeparkclub.com

Frilford Heath

In 1910, just two years after the golf club was founded, Bernard Darwin described Frilford Heath as, 'A wonderful oasis in a desert of mud. The sand is so near the turf,' he enthused, 'that out of pure exuberance it breaks out here and there in little eruptions'.

The sand must be the only thing that has ever erupted at Frilford Heath. Peaceable and peaceful, this is one of England's most pleasant and understated golfing retreats. It is possibly also one of England's most underrated venues. In Darwin's day there was only one 18 hole course, but today the club has 54 holes—a third course having been built and opened for play in July 1994. They are quite marvellous tests of golf but although the club has hosted a number of important championships, its reputation is still not as widespread or as great as it merits. Moreover the condition and quality of the courses seem to be continually improving. It is always pleasing to see the construction of new tees and the careful planting of indigenous trees but at Frilford additional gorse and heather have also been introduced, and a lot of thought has clearly gone into the many subtle alterations. When added to the fact that the greens at Frilford have never been better and the rough really is rough (so rare these days) there is certainly much to admire.

Visitors wishing to inspect any or all of the courses, the **Red**, **Green** and **Blue** as they are known, should make arrangements with the club's **Secretary**, **Mr S Styles** preferably by telephoning in advance on **(01865) 390864**. Handicap certificates are required. The **Professional** at Frilford is **Derek Craik**, **(01865) 390887** and the club's full address is **Frilford Heath Golf Club, Abingdon, Oxford OX13 5NW**. The green fees in 2000 are set at £45 Monday to Friday with £60 payable at weekends and on bank holidays. After 5pm fees are reduced to £29.

The clubhouse has been recently refurbished and extended and can now seat 120 visitors in the dining room. In addition the new 10 million gallon reservoir should be adequate for all Frilford's watering needs even in the driest of summers.

The club is located three miles west of Abingdon off the A338 Oxford to Wantage road (an old Roman Road). It is only a few minutes from the A420, the A415 and the A34, the latter linking Oxford to the M4.

The **Red Course** (6843 yards, par 73 from the back markers) opening holes have been modified to accommodate several holes of the new Blue Course. Arguably the best sequence on the Red comes between the 5th and the 9th. The 5th is a difficult par four with a fiendish cross bunker that often comes into play as the prevailing wind is against. If the wind is blowing then the par five 6th is reachable in two, although its green, like most at Frilford, is heavily contoured. The 7th is a difficult par four—the key here being a long and accurate drive, and the stroke one 8th has a hog's back shaped fairway, making it a veritable 'beast' of a hole. Beauty follows beast though in the form of the par three 9th where the tee shot is struck over a picturesque pond. On the back nine the golfer confronts a two-tiered green on the short 11th and a saucer-shaped green on the 13th. Two other notable holes are the 12th, with its backdrop of magnificent trees and the 16th, where a new back tee has turned the hole into a very good dog-leg.

The **Green Course** (6006 yards, par 69) begins more impressively than the Red with a heavily wooded, sweeping par five followed by a most attractive par three. The 2nd is in fact one of two outstanding short holes on the front nine, the other being the 6th. The dog-leg 12th is perhaps the most memorable of the two-shot holes on this course—the drive here is over a natural lake, and there is a trio of lengthy par fours starting at the 14th, but in the right conditions the 18th is just about driveable—thus affording the perfect opportunity to show off in front of the clubhouse!

As mentioned, the **Blue Course** opened in July 1994 is maturing rapidly. Like the Red, it is of championship length, stretching to 6728 yards, par 72. The Blue Course can properly be described as a 'modern design' for in amongst the more traditional natural hazards the architect has incorporated a number of water hazards. Moreover, the bunkers are invariably large, quite shallow and strategically positioned. However, unlike many 'modern designs', Frilford's Blue Course distributes challenge and charm in equal proportion. Apparently, some members already regard it as Frilford's best 18—and that is some compliment.

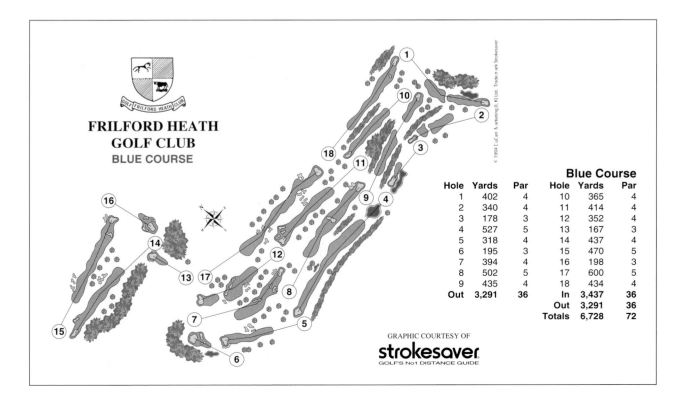

FRILFORD HEATH GOLF CLUB
BLUE COURSE

Blue Course

Hole	Yards	Par	Hole	Yards	Par
1	402	4	10	365	4
2	340	4	11	414	4
3	178	3	12	352	4
4	527	5	13	167	3
5	318	4	14	437	4
6	195	3	15	470	5
7	394	4	16	198	3
8	502	5	17	600	5
9	435	4	18	434	4
Out	3,291	36	In	3,437	36
			Out	3,291	36
			Totals	6,728	72

GRAPHIC COURTESY OF

strokesaver
GOLF'S No1 DISTANCE GUIDE

Key

*To avoid disappointment
it is advisable to telephone
in advance*

***Visitors welcome at most times
**Visitors usually allowed on
weekdays only
*Visitors not normally permitted
(Mon, Wed) No visitors
on specified days

Approximate Green Fees
A £40 plus
B £25 to £40
C £20 to £30
D £15 to £25
E under £15
F Green fees on application

Restrictions
G Guests only
H–Handicap certificate required
H–(24) Handicap of 24 or less
L–Letter of introduction required
M–Visitor must be a member of
another recognised club

BERKSHIRE

Bearwood G.C.
(0118) 976 0060
Mole Road, Sindlesham
(9) 5624 yards/**/E/H

Bearwood Lakes G.C.
(0118) 979 7900
Wokingham
(18) 6805 yards/*/B/G

The Berkshire G.C.
(01344) 621495
Swinley Road, Ascot
(18) 6369 yards/**/A/L
(18) 6260 yards/**/A/L

Bird Hills G.C.
(01628) 7710307
Drift Road, Hawthorn Hill
(18) 6212 yards/***/D

Blue Mountain Golf Centre
(01344) 300200
Wood Lane, Binfield
(18) 6097 yards/***/D

Calcot Park G.C.
(0118) 942 7124
Bath Road, Calcot, Reading
(18) 6283 yards/**/F

Castle Royal G.C.
(01628) 829252
Knowl Hill, Reading
(18) 6700 yards/***

Datchet G.C.
(01753) 543887
Buccleuch Road, Datchet
(9) 5978 yards/**/C/E(WE)

Donnington Grove G.C.
(01635) 581000
Donnington, Newbury
(18) 7050 yards/**8/B

Donnington Valley G.C.
(01635) 32488
Old Oxford Road, Donnington
(18) 4002 yards/***/F

Downshire G.C.
(01344) 302030
Easthampstead Park, Wokingham
(18) 6382 yards/***/E

East Berkshire G.C.
(01344) 772041
Ravenswood Avenue, Crowthorne
(18) 6345 yards/**/A/H

Goring & Streatley G.C.
(01491) 873229
Rectory Road, Streatley
(18) 6255 yards/**/B

Hennerton G.C.
(01734) 401000
Crazies Hill Road, Wargrave
(9) 2730 yards/***/D

Hurst G.C.
(0118) 934 4355
Sandford Lane, Hurst, Wokingham
(9) 3013 yards/***/E

Lambourne G.C.
(01628) 666755
Dropmore Road, Burnham
(18) 6771 yards/***/A/H

Lavender Park G.C.
(01344) 890940
Swinley Road, Ascot
(9) 1104 yards/***/F

Maidenhead G.C.
(01628) 24693
Shoppenhangers Road, Maidenhead
(18) 6360 yards/**/B/H

Mapledurham G.C.
(0118) 946 3353
Chazey Heath, Mapledurham
(18) 5625 yards/***/D

Mill Ride G.C.
(01344) 886777
Mill Ride, North Ascot
(18) 6690 yards/***/A/H

Newbury & Crookham G.C.
(01635) 40035
Burys Bank Road, Greenham
(18) 5880 yards/**/B/M

Pincents Manor G.C.
(01734) 323511
Pincents Lane, Calcot
(9) 4882 yards/***/E

Reading G.C.
(0118) 947 2909
Kidmore End Road, Emmer Green
(18) 6212 yards/**(not Friday)/B

Royal Ascot G.C.
(01344) 25175
Winkfield Road, Ascot
(18) 5716 yards/**/F/G

Sand Martins G.C.
(01734) 792711
Finchampstead Road, Wokingham
(18) 6297 yards/**/B

Sonning G.C.
(0118) 969 3332
Duffield Road, Sonning
(18) 6366 yards/**/F/H

Swinley Forest G.C.
(01344) 20197
Coronation Road, South Ascot
(18)6011 yards/*/A/G/H

Temple G.C.
(01628) 824248
Henley Road, Hurley, Maidenhead
(18) 6206 yards/**/A/H

West Berkshire G.C.
(01488) 638574
Chaddleworth, Newbury
(18) 7053 yards/**/C

Winter Hill G.C.
(01628) 527613
Grange Lane, Cookham, Maidenhead
(18) 6408 yards/**/B/H

BUCKINGHAMSHIRE

Abbey Hill G.C.
(01908) 563845
Two Mile Ash, Stony Stratford
(18) 6193 yards/***/F

Aylesbury Golf Centre
(01296) 393644
Hulcott Lane, Bierton
(9) 5488 yards/***/E

Aylesbury Park G.C.
(01296) 399196
Oxford Road, Aylesbury
(18) 6146 yards/***/D

Aylesbury Vale G.C.
(01525) 240196
Stewkley Road, Wing
(18) 6612 yards/***/E

Beaconsfield G.C.
(01494) 676545
Seer Green, Beaconsfield
(18) 6487 yards/**/A/H

Buckingham G.C.
(01280) 815566
Tingewick Road, Buckingham
(18) 6082 yards/**/B/M

Buckinghamshire G.C.
(01895) 835777
Denham Court, Denham
(18) 6880 yards/**(not Friday)/A/L

Burnham Beeches G.C.
(01628) 661448
Green Lane, Burnham
(18) 6463 yards/**/A/H/L

Chalfont Park G.C.
(01494) 876293
Three Households, Chalfont St Giles
(9) 3000 yards/***/E

Chartridge Park G.C.
(01494) 791772
Chartridge, Chesham
(18) 5721 yards/***/B

Chesham and Ley Hill G.C.
(01494) 784541
Ley Hill, Chesham
(9) 5240 yards/**/F

Chiltern Forest G.C.
(01296) 630899
Aston Hill, Halton, Aylesbury
(18) 6038 yards/**/B

Denham G.C.
(01895) 832022
Tilehouse Lane, Denham
(18) 6451 yards/**(Fri)/A/H/L

Ellesborough G.C.
(01296) 622114
Butlers Cross, Aylesbury
(18) 6271 yards/**/F/H/L

Farnham Park G.C.
(01753) 647065
Park Road, Stoke Poges
(18) 6172 yards/***/E

Flackwell Heath G.C.
(01628) 520027
Treadaway Road, Flackwell Heath
(18) 6207 yards/**/B/H

Gerrards Cross G.C.
(01753) 883263
Chalfont Park, Gerrards Cross
(18) 6295 yards/**/A/H

Harewood Downs G.C.
(01494) 762184
Cokes Lane, Chalfont St Giles
(18) 5958 yards/**/B/H

Harleyford G.C.
(01628) 487878
Henley Road, Harlow
(18) 6604 yards/***/A/H

Hazelmere G.&C.C.
(01494) 714722
Penn Road, High Wycombe
(18) 6039 yards/***/B

Iver G.C.
(01753) 655615
Hollow Hill Lane, Iver
(9) 6214 yards/***/E

Ivinghoe G.C.
(01296) 668696
Wellcroft, Ivinghoe
(9) 4508 yards/***/E

Lambourne G.C.
(01628) 666755
Dropmore Road, Burnham
(18) 6746 yards/***/A/H/L

Little Chalfont G.C.
(01494) 764877
Lodge Lane, Little Chalfont
(9) 5852 yards/***/D

Mentmore G.&C.C.
(01296) 662020
Mentmore, Leighton Buzzard
(18) 6777 yards/**/B/H

Princes Risborough G.C.
(01844) 346989
Lee Road, Saunderton Lee
(9) 5017 yards/***/D

Richings Park G.C.
(01753) 655352
North Park, Iver
(18) 6200 yards/**/B

Silverstone G.C.
(01280) 850005
Silverstone Road, Stowe
(18) 6164 yards/***/D

Stoke Poges G.C.
(01753) 717171
Stoke Park, Park Road, Stoke Poges
(18) 6654 yards/**/A/H/L

Stowe G.C.
(01280) 813650
Stowe, Buckingham
(9) 4573 yards/**/F/G

Thorney Park G.C.
(01895) 422095
Thorney Mill Lane, Iver
(9) 3000 yards/**/E

Three Locks G.C.
(01525) 270470
Great Brickhill, Milton Keynes
(9) 6654 yards/***/E

Wavendon Golf Centre
(01908) 281811
Wavendon, Milton Keynes
(18) 5800 yards/***/E

Weston Turville G.C.
(01296) 24084
New Road, Weston Turville
(18) 6782 yards/***/D

Wexham Park G.C.
(01753) 663271
Wexham Street, Slough
(18) 5390 yards/***/D
(9) 2383 yards/***/E
(9) 2585 yards/***/E

Whiteleaf G.C.
(018444) 274058
Whiteleaf, Aylesbury
(9) 5391 yards/**/C/H

Windmill Hill G.C.
(01908) 378623
Tattenhoe Lane, Bletchley
(18) 6773 yards/***/E

Woburn G. & C.C.
(01908) 370756
Bow Brickhill, Milton Keynes
(18) 6940 yards/**/F/H
(18) 6641 yards/**/F/H

Wycombe Heights G.C.
(01494) 816686
Rayners Avenue, Loudwater
(18) 6300 yards/***/D

OXFORDSHIRE

Aspect Park G.C.
(01491) 578306
Remenham Hill, Henley on Thames
(18) 6369 yards/**/C/H

Badgemore Park G.C.
(01491) 573667
Badgemore Park, Henley on Thames
(18) 6112 yards/***/B/H

Banbury G.C.
(01285) 810449
Aynho Road, Adderbury
(18) 6333 yards/***/E

Brailes G.C.
(01608) 685633
Sutton Lane, Brailes
(18) 6270 yards/**/C/M

Burford G.C.
(01993) 822149
Burford
(18) 6405 yards/**/B/H

Carswell C.C.
(01367) 870422
Carswell, Faringdon
(18) 6133 yards/***/D

Cherwell Edge G.C.
(01295) 711591
Chacombe, Banbury
(18) 5925 yards/***/E

Chesterton G.C.
(01869) 241204
Chesterton, Bicester
(18) 6224 yards/***/D/H

Chipping Norton G.C.
(01608) 642383
Southcombe, Chipping Norton
(18) 6283 yards/**/C

Drayton Park G.C.
(01235) 550607
Steventon Road, Drayton
(18) 6500 yards/***/D

Frilford Heath G.C.
(01865) 390864
Frilford Heath, Abingdon
(18) 6728 yards/***/A/H
(18) 6395yards/***/A/H
(18) 6006 yards/***/A/H

Hadden Hill G.C.
(01235) 510410
Wallingford Road, Didcot
(18) 6563 yards/***/D

Henley G.C.
(01491) 573304
Harpsden, Henley on Thames
(18) 6330 yards/**/A/H

Huntercombe G.C.
(01491) 641207
Nuffield, Henley on Thames
(18) 6301 yards/**/A/H

Lyneham G.C.
(01993) 831841
Lyneham, Chipping Norton
(18) 6669 yards/***/D

North Oxford G.C.
(01865) 554415
Banbury Road, Oxford
(18) 5805 yards/***/B/H

The Oxfordshire G.C.
(01844) 278300
Rycote Lane, Milton Common, Thame
(18) 7187 yards/***/F/M/L

RAF Benson G.C.
(01491) 837766
Royal Air Force, Bensen
(9) 4395 yards/***/G

Rye Hill G.C.
(01295) 721818
Boon Farm, Milcombe
(18) 6569 yards/***/E

Southfield G.C.
(01865) 242158
Hill Top Road, Oxford
(18) 6230 yards/**/B/H

Shrivenham Park
(01793) 783853
Penny Hooks, Shrivenham
(18) 5713 yards/***/D

Tadmarton Heath G.C.
(01608) 737278
Wiggington, Banbury
(18) 5917 yards/**/B/H

Waterstock G.C.
(01844) 338093
Oxford Road, Cowley
(18) 6482 yards/***/D

Witney G.C.
(01993) 779000
Downs Road, Witney
(18) 6460 yards/***/D

THE 7TH, STOKE POGES GOLF CLUB *Photograph courtesy of:* **Stoke Poges Golf Club**

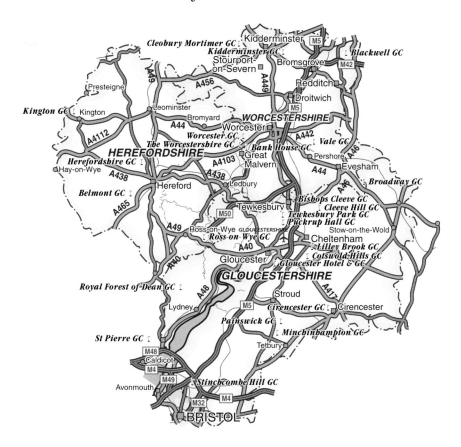

Ahush descends as you ponder your first swing in old Worcestershire. Apple and cherry trees are in blossom and in the distance a herd of white faced Herefords appraise your stance. You're fortunate, for several hundred years ago the air in these parts was thick with the clatter of sword against sword but now there is peace. Crack! Straight down the fairway—the echo resounds and then dies—you're on your way.

Herefordshire, Worcestershire and Gloucestershire—what a lovely trio! Bordering the principality, the region is arguably the most tranquil in England. It is an area of rich pastures and cider orchards, of small market towns and sleepy villages rather than crowded cities, and encompasses the Cotswolds and the Malverns, the beautiful Wye Valley and the splendid Vale of Evesham. Truly a green and pleasant land!

Gloucestershire

Heading into Gloucestershire, I trust that when Doctor Foster went to Gloucester he wasn't a well travelled golfer. Up until the last few years, the county had very few courses and Gloucester itself didn't possess one at all until 1976. However, the recent explosion of new golf developments has transformed the situation and the golf can now be said to match up to the undeniable quality of its scenery and hostelries.

Starting at **Broadway Golf Club**, located the course being a mile and a half or so from 'the loveliest village in England'. True to form there are some marvellous views from the golf course looking out across the Vale of Evesham. It really is a beautiful part of the world and those wishing to do some exploring will find several superb hotels, any of which will make an ideal base. The Lygon Arms (01386) 852255 in Broadway with its outstanding frontage probably takes pride of place but for excellent value the Collin House Hotel (01386) 858354 takes some beating. Both have fine restaurants. Our final recommendation in this area is Buckland

Manor (01386) 852626, an hotel with an exceptional restaurant.

Around Cheltenham

Heading south, the county's two best known courses are probably **Cotswold Hills** and **Lilley Brook**, located to the north and south of Cheltenham respectively. Both offer commanding views of the Gloucestershire countryside, especially perhaps Lilley Brook, one of southern England's most undulating courses. Each is well worth a visit and the beautiful Regency manor of the Cheltenham Park Hotel (01242) 222021 is only minutes from both.

Cleeve Hill is Cheltenham's third 18 hole course. Situated on high ground to the north of the town it can get rather cold in winter. One wag said that he enjoyed Lilley Brook in the summer as half of him was mountain goat, and Cleeve Hill in the winter because the other half of him was eskimo!

The Cheltenham area has many fine hotels, but perhaps the best known is the Queens Hotel (0870) 400 8107. On The Park (01242) 518898 is a popular and excellent alternative. A good hotel in the surrounding hills is the splendid Greenway (01242) 862352 in Shurdington, which offers a first class menu and beautiful grounds. In Cleeve Hill, the Malvern View Hotel (01242) 672017 is well thought of, a little further north in Bishops Cleeve, Cleeveway House (01242) 672585 has rooms and an outstanding restaurant.

South Gloucestershire

Outside Cheltenham, **Minchinhampton** has perhaps the biggest golfing reputation. A club of great character, it celebrated its centenary in 1989. There are three very varied courses here, including the acclaimed Old course. In the south of the county, **Stinchcombe Hill** is also well thought of. A first class place to stay nearby is Burleigh

Court (01453) 883804, while to the north the Amberley Inn (01453) 872565 in Amberley, with its fine views over Woodchester Valley has considerable charm. For a good pub visit **Painswick** for the Royal Oak—a short golf course here too.

The 18 hole course at **Cirencester** is probably the nearest one gets to golf in the Cotswolds. Cirencester is certainly pleasant but to most of us the real Cotswolds are the many wonderfully named villages—Bourton-on-the-Water, Stow-on-the-Wold, Upper Slaughter and Lower Slaughter.

Around Gloucester

Gloucester's newest course lies within the grounds of the **Jarvis Gloucester Hotel & Country Club** (01452) 525653 at Robinswood Hill. A luxurious country club, there are in fact 27 holes here plus numerous leisure facilities. The 18 hole course enjoys a pleasant setting and has matured very rapidly. The same can be said of **Tewkesbury Park** Hotel's golf course (01684) 295405 which is laid out on the site of the famous Roses battle of 1471. Both hotels are comfortable and their courses are open to residents and non-residents alike. However, for a special occasion, we can recommend a stay at **Puckrup Hall** (01684) 296200, an elegant Regency house set in 40 acres of parkland with an adjacent 18 hole golf course. At Upton St Leonards, near Gloucester, Hatton Court (01452) 617412 is most relaxing.

Close to the Border

The Forest of Dean is our next port of call—another beauty spot and some good golf too at the **Royal Forest of Dean** Golf Club in Coleford. In Coleford itself, there is the lovely 16th century Poolway House (01594) 833937. A notable inn nearby is the Speech House (01594) 822607. Staying a few days in the area is recommended—the countryside is splendid and just eight miles away, over the border in Wales, lies Chepstow and the delights of **St Pierre**.

Herefordshire

Herefordshire and Worcestershire have at last officially regained their separate identities—but one doubts they ever lost them. Golf courses aren't exactly plentiful, but those there are tend to be very scenic, often hidden away deep in the glorious countryside. To the north west of Hereford, **Kington** and **Herefordshire** are typical examples and both warmly welcome visitors. Kington is closer to Wales and is reputedly the highest course in either country—a place where poor golf can always be blamed on the rarified atmosphere. South of Hereford is another attractive course, **The Belmont Lodge and Golf Course** (01432) 352666, a newer course but one that has already gained a good reputation.

Hereford is a natural base when golfing in the area and there are a number of good hotels. The Graftonbury Hotel (01432) 268826 is a charming garden hotel with easy access to Belmont Golf Club. The Green Dragon Hotel (01432) 272506 is particularly comfortable—note the many four poster beds—and in nearby Much Birch, the Pilgrim Hotel (01981) 540742 is a splendid former rectory. The Hopbine Hotel (01432) 268722 offers reasonably priced accommodation near to Hereford city centre. A short drive to Weobley reveals the Red Lion (01544) 318419, a 14th century inn in the centre of a delightful village—very handy for Herefordshire Golf Club. Ye Olde Salutation Inn (01544) 318443 is a delightful hostelry with excellent food. Near the same golf course is a good pub, the Bell at Tillington, while for Belmont, the Butchers Arms is recommended (some accommodation here too). Kington has a first class restaurant, Penrhos Court (01544) 230720—some quaint bedrooms here too. It also boasts the Oxford Arms (01544) 230322, a 16th century coaching inn near the golf course. Visitors to this pleasant area should also consider the excellent Allt-yr-Ynys Hotel (01873) 890307 in Walterstone—an ideal retreat.

Ross-on-Wye is a renowned beauty spot and the town's golf course reflects the reputation. Set in the heart of the Wye Valley and surrounded by a blaze of colour, it's hard to believe that the M50 is under a mile away (junction 4). If staying in the area, the Pengethley Manor Hotel (01989) 730211 is most charming and Peterstow Country House boasts

an award-winning restaurant. Alternatively, try the New Inn (01989) 730274 in St Owens Cross where you are sure of a warm welcome.

Worcestershire

Worcester is an attractive city with a beautiful cathedral overlooking the famous county cricket ground. A mile from the town centre, off the A4103, is the **Worcester** Golf and Country Club. The oldest course in the county, and possibly the finest is the appropriately named **Worcestershire** Golf Club, two miles south of Great Malvern. The course has extensive views of the Malverns, the Severn Valley and the Cotswolds. Elsewhere in the county, the **Vale** Golf and Country Club near Pershore boasts 27 testing holes and a driving range. A newer development is the **Bank House** in Bransford. The hotel here offers good leisure facilities and is ideal for a weekend away (01886) 833551. The final recommendations in Worcestershire are **Kidderminster**, the highly regarded and beautifully maintained **Blackwell** Golf Club near Bromsgrove and the relatively new **Cleobury Mortimer**.

Near Worcester, the Elms Hotel (01299) 896666 at Abberley is an outstanding country house hotel while Malvern Wells offers the delightful Cottage in the Wood hotel (01684) 575859 and an excellent restaurant, the Croque-en-Bouche (01684) 565612. Worcester itself contains the stylish Fownes Hotel (01905) 613151 and the moderately priced Giffard Hotel (01905) 726262. Browns restaurant (01905) 26263 is also well worth a visit. Great Malvern provides a charming 19th century coaching inn, the Foley Arms (01684) 573397. A highly recommended hotel in Redditch is the Old Rectory (01527) 523000, and a final suggestion is to visit Tenbury Wells where the Cadmore Lodge (01584) 810044 is an ideal setting with its own 9 hole course.

The Cottage in the Wood Hotel
Holywell Road, Malvern Wells,
Worcestershire WR14 4LG
Tel: (01684) 575859 Fax: (01684) 560662

The Cottage in the Wood Hotel and Restaurant, perched high on the Malvern Hills, enjoys one of the finest views in Britain.

There are twenty bedrooms, all of different sizes and decor, some with four posters, all en suite and most with spectacular views. The hotel's restaurant is well known and highly regarded (2 AA Rosettes) with an extensive and lovingly compiled wine list, a finalist in the last two years AA wine award contest.

For the sightseer, Worcester, Hereford and Gloucester are nearby and the Cotswolds and the Welsh Marches are within easy reach. Sportsmen are equally well catered for with some fine racecourses, including Cheltenham, and with special arrangements for guests at the Worcestershire golf course lying immediately beneath the hotel.

Key

GLOUCESTERSHIRE

Brickhampton Court G.C.
(01452) 859444
Chltenham Road, Churchdown
(18) 6449 yards/C
(9) 1859 yards/***/E

Broadway G.C.
(01386) 853683
Willersley Hill, Broadway
(18) 6216 yards/**/B/H

Chipping Sodbury G.C.
(01454) 319042
Chipping Sodbury, Bristol
(18) 6912 yards/***/B
(9) 6194 yards/***/E

Cirencester G.C.
(01285) 652465
Cheltenham Road, Bagendon
(18) 6021 yards/***/B/H

Cleeve Hill G.C.
(01242) 672592
Cleeve Hill, Nr Prestbury
(18) 6444 yards/**/F

Cotswold Edge G.C.
(01453) 844167
Upper Rushmire, Wotton-under-Edge
(18) 6170 yards/**/C/H

Cotswold Hills G.C.
(01242) 522421
Ullenwood, Cheltenham
(18) 6716 yards/***/B/H/L

Forest of Dean G.C.
(01594) 832583
Lords Hill, Coleford
(18) 5682 yards/***/D

Forest Hills G.C.
(01594) 810620
Mile End Road, Coleford
(18) 5988 yards/***/D

Gloucester Hotel G.& C.C.
(01452) 525653
Matson Lane, Robinswood Hill
(18) 6135 yards/***/C/H

Lilley Brook G.C.
(01204) 526785
Cirencester Road, Charlton Kings
(18) 6226 yards/**/B/H/L

Lydney G.C.
(01594) 841561
Lakeside Avenue, Lydney
(9) 5382 yards/**/D

Minchinhampton G.C.
(01453) 833866
Minchinhampton, Stroud
(18) 6295 yards/**/D/H
(18) 6244 yards/**/B/H
(18) 6270 yards/**/B/H

Naunton Downs G.C.
(01451) 850090
Naunton, Cheltenham
(18) 6174 yards/***/C

Painswick G.C.
(01452) 812180
Painswick, Stroud
(18) 4780 yards/**/D

Puckrup Hall Hotel & G.C.
(01684) 296200
Tewkesbury
(18) 6431 yards/**/B/H

Rodway G.C.
(01452) 384222
Highnam
(18) 5860 yards/***/E

Sherdons G.C.
(01684) 274782
Manor Farm, Tredington
(9) 2654 yards/***/E

Stinchcombe Hill G.C.
(01453) 542015
Stinchcombe Hill, Dursley
(18) 5734 yards/**/C/H

Streamleaze G.C.
(01453) 843128
Bradley, Wotton-under-Edge
(9) 4582 yards/***/E

Tewkesbury Park Hotel G.C.
(01684) 295405
Lincoln Green Lane, Tewkesbury
(18) 6533 yards/**/B/H

Thornbury G.C.
(01454) 281144
Bristol Road, Thornbury
(18) 6154 yards/***/D
(18) 2195 yards/***/D

West Country G.C.
(01275) 856626
Clevedon Road, Tickenham
(9) 2000 yards/***/D

Westonbirt G.C.
(01666) 880242
Westonbirt, Tetbury
(9) 4504 yards/**/F

Woodlands G. & C.C.
(01454) 618121
Woodlands Lane, Almondsbury
(18) 5550 yards/***/D

HEREFORD & WORCESTER

Abbey Park G.& C.C.
(01527) 63918
Dagnell End Road, Redditch
(18) 6411 yards/**/D

Bank House Hotel & C.C.
(01886) 833551
Bransford, Worcester
(18) 6101 yards/***/B

Belmont Lodge G.C.
(01432) 352666
Belmont House, Belmont
(18) 6480 yards/***/F

Blackwell G.C.
(0121) 445 1781
Blackwell, Bromsgrove
(18) 6202 yards/**/A/H

Bromsgrove G.C.
(01527) 575886
Stratford Road, Bromsgrove
(9) 3159 yards/***/E

Burghill Valley G.C.
(01432) 760456
Tillington Road, Burghill
(18) 6239 yards/***/D
(9) 3075 yards/***/E

Cadmore Lodge G.C.
(01584) 810018
Berrington Green, Tenbury Wells
(9) 5130 yards/***/E

Churchill and Blakedown G.C.
(01562) 700018
Churchill Lane, Blakedown
(9) 6472 yards/**/D

Cleobury Mortimer
(01299) 271112
Wyre Common, nr. Kidderminster
(18) 6438 yards/***/C/H

Droitwich G.& C.C.
(01905) 770129
Ford Lane, Droitwich
(18) 6040 yards/**/B/H

Evesham G.C.
(01386) 860395
Cray Combe Links, Fladbury
(9) 6415 yards/**/C/H

Fulford Heath G.C.
(01564) 824758
Tanners Green Lane, Wythall
(18) 6216 yards/**/B/H

Gay Hill G.C.
0121 474 6001
Alcester Road, Hollywood
(18) 6532 yards/**/F

Gaudet Luce G.C.
(01905) 796375
Middle Lane, Hadzor
(18) 5887 yards/***/F

Habberley G.C.
(01562) 745756
Habberley, Kidderminster
(9) 5400 yards/**/D

Hereford Municipal G.C.
(01432) 278178
Holmer Road, Hereford
(9) 3060 yards/***/E

Herefordshire G.C.
(01432) 830219
Ravens Causeway, Wormsley
(18) 6100 yards/***/D

Kidderminster G.C.
(01562) 822303
Russell Road, Kidderminster
(18) 6405 yards/**/B/H

King's Norton G.C.
(01564) 826789
Brockhill Lane, Weatheroak
(27) 7060 yards/**/B

Kington G.C.
(01544) 230340
Bradnor Hill, Kington,
(18) 5840 yards/**/D

Leominster G.C.
(01568) 612863
Ford Bridge, Leominster
(9) 6100 yards/***/C/H

Little Lakes G.& C.C.
(01299) 266385
Lye Head, Bewdley
(9) 6247 yards/**/D

Ombersley G.C.
(01905) 620747
Bishops Wood Road, Ombersley
(18) 6139 yards/***/E

Perdiswell Municipal G.C.
(01905) 754668
Bilford Road, Worcester
(9) 6004 yards/***/E

Pitcheroak G.C.
(01527) 541054
Plymouth Road, Redditch
(9) 4584 yards/***/F

Redditch G.C.
(01527) 543309
Green Lane, Callow Hill
(18) 6671 yards/**/B

Ross-on-Wye G.C.
(01989) 720267
Gorsley, Ross-on-Wye
(18) 6500 yards/**/B/M

Sapey G.C.
(01886) 853288
Whitley Road, Upper Sapey
(18) 5900 yards/***/C

South Herefordshire G.C.
(01989) 740612
Hartleton, Upton Bishop
(18) 6672 yards/***/C

Tolladine G.C.
(01905) 21074
Tolladine Road, Worcester
(9) 5134 yards/**/D/H

The Vale G.& C.C.
(01386) 462781
Hill Furze Road, Bishampton
(18) 7041 yards/***/B
(9) 2960 yards/***/E

Wharton Park G.C.
(01299) 405222
Longbank, Bewdley
(18) 6600 yards/***/C

Worcester G. & C.C.
(01905) 422555
Boughton Park, Worcester
(18) 6154 yards/**/B/H

Worcestershire G.C.
(01684) 575992
Wood Farm, Malvern Wells
(18) 6449 yards/***/B/H

Wyre Forest G.C.
(01299) 822682
Zortech Avenue, Kidderminster
(18) 5790 yards/***/E

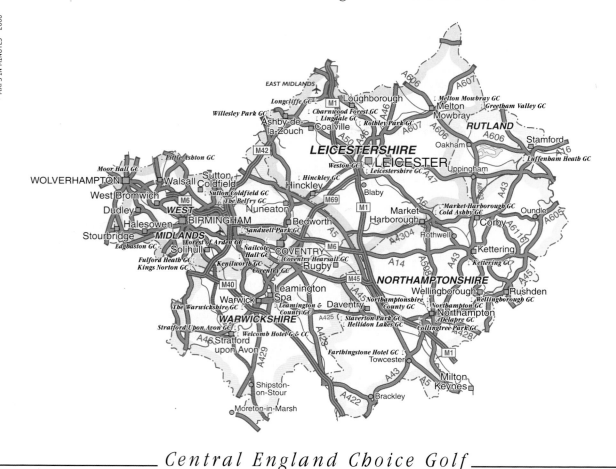

© MAPS IN MINUTES ™ 2000

EAST MIDLANDS

Longcliffe GC · M1 · Loughborough · Melton Mowbray GC · Greetham Valley GC
Willesley Park GC · Charnwood Forest GC · Melton Mowbray · A607
Ashby-de-la-Zouch · Lingdale GC · Rothley Park GC · A607 · A606 · RUTLAND
Coalville · Oakham · A606 · Stamford · A16
M42 · LEICESTERSHIRE · LEICESTER · Luffenham Heath GC
Little Ashton GC · Weston GC · Leicestershire GC · A47 · Uppingham
Moor Hall GC · Sutton Coldfield · Hinckley GC · Blaby
WOLVERHAMPTON · Walsall · Sutton Coldfield GC · Hinckley · A6
West Bromwich · The Belfry GC · M69 · Market Harborough GC
Dudley · M6 · WEST · Nuneaton · M1 · Market Harborough · Cold Ashby GC · Oundle
Halesowen · BIRMINGHAM · Bedworth · A5 · Rothwell · A605
Stourbridge · MIDLANDS · Sandwell Park GC · A4304 · Kettering GC · A6116
Edgbaston GC · Forest of Arden GC · A14 · A43
Solihull · Nailcote Hall GC · COVENTRY · Kettering
Fulford Heath GC · Coventry Hearsall GC · A4508 · Kettering GC
Kings Norton GC · Kenilworth GC · Coventry GC · Rugby · NORTHAMPTONSHIRE
M40 · Wellingborough · Rushden
Leamington Spa · M45 · Northamptonshire County GC · Wellingborough GC
Warwick · Leamington & County GC · Daventry · Northampton GC · Northampton
The Warwickshire GC · WARWICKSHIRE · A425 · Staverton Park GC · Delapre GC · Collingtree Park GC
Stratford Upon Avon GC · Welcomb Hotel G & CC · Hellidon Lakes GC · A428
A46 · Stratford upon Avon · A429 · Farthingstone Hotel GC · M1
Shipston-on-Stour · A422 · Towcester · A43 · Milton Keynes · A5
Moreton-in-Marsh · Brackley

Birmingham

Golfers in the City of London have often been known to get frustrated at having to travel many a mile for a decent game of golf. In 1919 one obviously disgusted individual teed up at Piccadilly Circus and proceeded to play along the Strand, through Fleet Street and Ludgate Hill firing his last shot at the Royal Exchange. Such behaviour is unknown in Birmingham—as far as I'm aware, the Bull Ring and the NEC have never been peppered with golf balls. This I suspect may be because the needs of its golfing citizens have been properly attended to.

Within easy access of the town centre lie the likes of **The Belfry** and **Little Aston** to the north, **Fulford Heath**, **Copt Heath** and **Kings Norton** to the south, and **Sandwell Park** and **Edgbaston** somewhere in the middle. Golfers north of Birmingham are indeed particularly fortunate for, in addition to The Belfry and Little Aston, there is also **Sutton Coldfield** and **Moor Hall**. All provide extremely pleasant retreats from the noise and confusion of England's second largest city. One need hardly add that there are also a number of public courses dotted around the outskirts of Birmingham.

Despite its relative youth, The Belfry (featured ahead) has become the area's best known golfing attraction thanks largely to the thrilling Ryder Cup encounters staged there. However, Little Aston has long been regarded as one of Britain's finest inland courses and has hosted numerous major events—both amateur and professional.

Looking in and around Birmingham for places to stay a few obvious thoughts emerge. The Belfry Hotel (01675) 470301 is most luxurious and ideal for its own two courses (as well as the plethora of golf courses in the Sutton Coldfield area). It offers practically every activity under the sun. As an alternative, and very close

to The Belfry is the elegant Moxhull Hall (0121) 329 2056 which provides a more intimate atmosphere. Moor Hall (0121) 3083751 also provides a most comfortable and convenient 19th hole—an attractive mansion this. Still in Sutton Coldfield, Penns Hall (0121) 351 3111 enjoys a peaceful lakeside setting, while a short distance away in Aldridge is another alternative, the Fairlawns Hotel (01922) 455122. A 9 hole par 3 course will add further to the attractions of a stay at the delightful New Hall (0121) 378 2442—one of the country's finest hotels—not the cheapest but thoroughly recommended. For an inexpensive hotel in the Sutton Coldfield area, we recommend the Standbridge Hotel (0121) 354 3007.

Solihull to the south of Birmingham is also surrounded by good golf. The Jarvis International (0121) 7112121 is a modernised coaching inn and a very comfortable place to stay. Another suburb, Edgbaston, provides the restaurant The Baytree (0121) 4556697. Two popular pubs to visit are the Bear at Berkswell and the White Lion in Hampton-in-Arden.

More centrally in Birmingham, the Hyatt Regency (0121) 6431234 is a first rate hotel

Coventry

Like Birmingham, the city of Coventry has now been relieved of its West Midlands label and warrants its own mention. **Coventry** Golf Club enjoys a peaceful setting at Finham Park, two miles south of the city on the A444. The course is good enough to have staged the British Seniors Championship. To the north west of Coventry at Meriden, the **Forest of Arden Golf** and Country Club (featured on a later page) offers a marvellous day's golf—36 holes to savour with outstanding leisure facilities at the Country Club Hotel (01676) 522335.

MARRIOTT FOREST OF ARDEN HOTEL & COUNTRY CLUB
Photograph courtesy of: **Marriott Forest of Arden Hotel & Country Club**

The major tourist attraction in Coventry is undoubtedly the spectacular cathedral. A fine piece of modern architecture sadly not reflected in the city's hotels—but then Coventry is no different from most. The Britannia Hotel (024) 7663 3733 near the cathedral is perhaps the best in the city. The Hearsall Lodge Hotel (024) 7667 4543 offers more modest accommodation but is perfectly comfortable and very convenient for **Coventry Hearsall** Golf Club, just south of the city off the A46. Another recommendation is **Nailcote Hall** (024) 7646 6174, west of Coventry in Berkswell, offering a 9 hole golf course, good leisure facilities and a pleasant atmosphere.

Warwickshire

Birmingham and Coventry removed, Warwickshire has been left with only a handful of courses. The county's two most popular towns are unquestionably Stratford and Warwick. Until recently Warwick had only a 9 hole course located inside its racetrack, but now, not far away from Warwick at Leek Wooton (close to junction 15 of the M40) is **The Warwickshire** where 36 holes of championship golf await (see ahead). Shakespeare-spotters who've sneaked the clubs into the boot will also be well rewarded. There are two fine 18 hole courses in Stratford, **Stratford** Golf Club and the **Welcombe Hotel** Golf Course.

The Welcombe Hotel (01789) 295252 is a beautiful mansion with comfortable rooms and a good restaurant, definitely one for lovers of good golf and fine hotels. But there are many outstanding alternatives for those spending a night or two in the Stratford area. Pride of place must go to Billesley Manor (01789) 279955 to the west of the town.

Of the countless guest houses and B&Bs in the vicinity, two that are frequently acclaimed are Moonraker House (01789) 299346 and Oxtalls Farmhouse (01789) 205277. For pubs, a short drive towards Oxhill is recommended where the Peacock and the Royal Oak (in Whatcote village) will provide excellent sustenance. Those of you choosing to play the excellent fairways of The Warwickshire and who enjoy a first class hotel, should note the elegant Ettington Park (01789) 450123—first class.

Warwick has a famous castle, and a good restaurant to note nearby is Randolphs. **Kenilworth** also has a castle (and a pretty reasonable golf course too). Here the Clarendon House (01926) 857668 is a good place to stay and a restaurant to savour is the Restaurant Bosquet (01926) 852463.

Lastly we visit Leamington Spa. It may not have the attractions of a Stratford or a Warwick but it does have a very fine golf course.

Leamington and County is a hilly parkland course to the south of Leamington.

After an enjoyable round at Leamington, the Lansdowne (01926) 450505 is a smallish well priced hotel in town. Crandon House a comfortable farmhouse in the vicinity, but if one is looking to spoil oneself then we recommend a trip to Bishops Tachbrook and Mallory Court (01926) 330214, where superb rooms and a terrific restaurant await.

North Leicestershire

The best course in Leicestershire, **Luffenham Heath**, lies over to the far east of the county, very close to the border with Lincolnshire. It is without question one of the most attractive heathland courses in England and, being in a conservation area, a haven for numerous species of wildlife. It isn't the longest of courses but then, thankfully, golf isn't always a question of how far you can belt the ball! A visit here is strongly recommended and there is no shortage of 19th holes nearby.

The splendid Rutland countryside reveals many outstanding establishments. Hambleton Hall (01572) 756991 overlooks Rutland Water and is quite tremendous and very convenient for the new course at Greetham, **Greetham Valley**. If you cannot spend the night here the restaurant is equally superb. The Whipper Inn Hotel (01572) 756971 in Oakham's market square is also most enjoyable—a fine inn with good beers, snacks and some comfortable accommodation too.

Note that this is Ruddles country and some excellent country pubs lie in wait. The King's Arms in Wing is a good example and there's a nearby maze in which to lose the children before a round of golf or a pint of County. Barnsdale Lodge (01572) 724678 is also well worth considering.

Rothley Park Golf Club, adjacent to the 13th century Rothley Court (0116) 2374141, a hotel of merit, is one of Leicestershire's most picturesque parkland courses and is within easy access of Leicester, lying some seven miles to the north west of the city, off the A6. Leicester is well served by golf courses and there are no fewer than three 18 hole municipal courses within four miles of the centre of Leicester, **Western Park** perhaps being the best of these. **Leicestershire** Golf Club, just two miles from the city centre along the A6 is one of the top courses in the county—try to avoid the ubiquitous stream that runs through it.

Leicester may not be the country's most attractive city but it does have its good points. The Haymarket theatre offers a variety of productions while the art gallery includes works by English sporting artists and, if you have business in town, the Jarvis Grand Hotel (0116) 2555599 may prove the best selection.

Looking further afield, in the north of the county the ancient town of Melton Mowbray has a fine 18 hole course sited on high ground to the north east of the town and Loughborough possesses a heathland type course, **Longcliffe**, which is heavily wooded with a wealth of bluebells, not to mention a particularly testing front nine. A game here is always a challenge.

The village of Woodhouse Eaves lies on the eastern edge of the Forest with two extremely pleasant courses at hand, Lingdale and Charnwood Forest. Though less than two miles apart they offer quite different challenges. **Lingdale** has a parkland setting with a trout stream flowing through it, while **Charnwood Forest** is a heathland type course—9 holes, no bunkers but several outcrops of granite around which one must navigate. The commendable Quorn Country Hotel (01509) 415050 is the 19th to shortlist.

East Leicestershire

Hinckley is linked to the centre of Leicester by the A47. Hinckley's golf course is fairly new, built over the original 9 hole Burbage Common layout. Several lakes and much gorse have to be confronted making this potentially the toughest in the county. **Willesley Park** at Ashby-de-la-Zouch provides a parkland-heathland mix with good greens and well worth a visit.

South Leicestershire

In the south of the county, **Market Harborough's** course offers extensive views across the surrounding countryside.

Some ideas for life beyond the 18th fairway. If a pork pie and a piece of Stilton is what you're after then Melton Mowbray is an answer to your prayers—try the George (01664) 562112—a charming inn with comfortable rooms.

In the Loughborough area the Kings Head (01509) 233222 is popular. Lovers of true style and comfort and no little love of leisure pursuits should shortlist Stapleford Park (01572) 787522—one of the best. Finally, the Crown in Old Dalby is another good pub—ideal for sampling the various local specialities.

Northamptonshire

The much admired **Northamptonshire County** course is situated five miles north of Northampton at Church Brampton, and is often referred to locally as Church Brampton. Famed for its many testing par fours, it is a splendid heather and gorse type with a fair few undulations in its 6500 yards. Rather like Liphook in Hampshire a railway line bisects the course. In the past it has staged the British Youths' Championship.

Though not as good as Church Brampton, **Northampton** Golf Club can also be recommended, as most certainly can **Collingtree Park**, Johnny Miller's spectacularly designed course (see feature page).

One final mention for visitors to the county town is the **Delapre** Golf Complex where a game should be easily arranged.

For a night in Northampton, the Moat House Hotel (01604) 739988 is very modern but comfortable and handy for the town centre, while the Quality Hotel (01604) 739955 is a mansion with modern additions. For value and friendly service, Garenden Park Hotel (01509) 236557 should not disappoint.

North of Northampton

To the north there is a reasonable course at **Kettering** and not far away there is a better course at **Wellingborough**, two miles east of the town. Quite hilly and set around the former Horrowden Hall, it has several lakes and a mass of mature trees. and is certainly one of the best courses in the county.

The **Hellidon Lakes** Hotel and Country Club (01327) 262550 offers some fine golf, while good leisure facilities and accommodation make this doubly worthy of attention. **Cold Ashby** (near the site of the famous Battle of Naseby of 1645) with its superb views across the Northamptonshire uplands is also worth a visit.

Pleasant countryside surrounds the towns of Wellingborough and Kettering. Perhaps the best bet for accommodation near the former is the Hind (01933) 222827.

South of Northampton

In the south of the county other courses to note include **Staverton Park** at Daventry, and the popular **Farthingstone Hotel Golf and Leisure Centre** near Towcester. Recommedned in this area are The Crossroads (01327) 340354 at Weedon and the Saracens Head (01327) 350414 at Towcester, although The Farthingstone Hotel (01327) 3612911 must be a good bet here.

COLLINGTREE PARK GOLF CLUB *Photograph courtesy of:* **Collingtree Park Golf Club**

Being something of a racing man "I've gotta horse", are words that almost always fill my heart with gloom. You're trapped you see . . . if you don't have a bet you feel dramatically foolish if the nag in question wins but more often than not the wretched beast will not deliver the goods. In golf however, my experiences are altogether different. Perched in sunny Menorca, of all places, after a decent 18 holes (lovely island, limited golf) I struck up some conversation as one does and we discussed the merits of various golf courses. "What's good and new?" I enquired of my newly found friend, who seemed to know his stuff. "The Warwickshire" he proclaimed - "It's stunning".

This little natter took place several years ago and since then the Warwickshire has been praised by many and is a worthy newcomer to our list of championship golf courses. Today the course is the UK flagship of the expanding Clubhaus Group and it offers golfers 36 exciting holes on four separate loops, respectively titled the **North**, **South**, **East** and **West** courses.

The courses are situated amidst 465 acres of rolling mature parkland. Avenues of trees and various water hazards provide daunting obstacles but delightful scenery. They were designed by Karl Litten (of The Emirates course, Dubai fame), and it is fair to say that golfers of all standards will be put to the test.

Despite the relative youth of these courses (The Warwickshire opened in the summer of 1993), this is definitely the type of venue that people will delight in playing. The acreage and the setting allows length and variety on all four loops. The toughest combination is the West/North and the 7th on the North is particularly memorable. On the East the 3rd is a wonderful golf hole and those who enjoy water hazards will find the par five 7th on the South course particularly appealing.

Golfers seeking a somewhat less daunting challenge will enjoy the nine hole par three course and driving range. While all visitors to the Warwickshire will surely savour the club's 19th hole for it is one of the best and most welcoming in the country.

If you're looking for a challenging round or two as well as a reason to be cheerful you should head for the middle of England where you will find the answer to your prayers. The Warwickshire might not be winning any races but it's a real favourite in any golfing company.

The Warwickshire, Leek Wootton, Warwick
Warwickshire CV35 7QT
web site: www.clubhaus.com

Gen Manager	Mark Warne (01926) 409409
Professional	Danny Peck
Green Fees	WD/WE £45 per round
Restrictions	Handicap certificate required

Directions
Two miles off junction 15 on the M40, just off the A46 to Coventry near Kenilworth

---

THE WARWICKSHIRE _Photograph courtesy of:_ **Clubhaus**

The Belfry

To adopt lawyers' jargon, it is 'beyond any reasonable doubt' that the game of golf was invented in Scotland. A handful of golfing pioneers brought the game south and today, with the exception of a few notable areas in the north, where to live is to play golf, the sport is almost as popular south of the border.

One cannot help wondering quite what those early pioneers would have made of The Belfry project . . . 'American-style target gowff? . . . and what d'ya mean artificial burns with manmade mounds and lakes!' . . . 'More than 7000 yards did ya say?'. . .'Too many whiskies m'friend, you must be oot o'your wee mind!'

The 'Belfry project' involved not only a plan to build a championship course on American lines where in due course the Ryder Cup could be staged, but also the siting of a new headquarters for the PGA. Peter Alliss and Dave Thomas were given the task of creating the showpiece, and a very great task it was, for the land they were given was flat, uninteresting and comprised one small lake, a stream and numerous acres of potato fields.

Well, the boys didn't hang about. Earth mountains were moved, the potatoes disappeared and hundreds of trees were planted. The end result in fact produced two 18 hole courses, opened in June 1977. The feature course was named the **Brabazon**, after Lord Brabazon, a former President of the PGA, and the shorter, easier course, the **Derby**.

June 1977—the month when Hubert Green survived a death threat to win the US Open and a month before Nicklaus and Watson fought out the 'Duel in the Sun' at Turnberry. So much has happened since then and to cite the history of The Belfry since its creation is almost to chart the rise of European golf—they are of course indelibly linked.

Of all Europe's successes around the world the 1985 Ryder Cup triumph at The Belfry will perhaps be remembered best of all. It was, after all, the first time the Americans had been defeated in nearly 30 years, and no other single event has been more responsible for generating the golf boom that has swept right across the continent.

So successfully staged were the matches in 1989 (a tie) and 1993 (a US victory) that The Belfry has been awarded the match for a fourth time in 2001.

To prepare for the Ryder Cup, the Brabazon course has undergone extensive remodelling at a cost of some £2.4 million. Another major development has been the construction of a third course at The Belfry. The **PGA National** course opened for play in the spring of 1997 and was designed by Dave Thomas.

A key feature of The Belfry is that it is not a club—all three courses open their doors to the general public at all times, all the year round. However, golfers should note that a handicap of 24 or better (32 for ladies) is required to play the Brabazon and PGA National courses. The green fees in 2000 are £90 per round on the Brabazon, £60 per round on the PGA National and £30 per round on the Derby.

The **Golf Manager**, **Robert Maxfield** and his staff can be contacted on **(01675) 470301**. Special residential packages are available and persons wishing to make reservations should contact the **Sales Office** on **(01675) 470033**, fax: **(01675) 470256**, or write to: **The Belfry, Wishaw, N Warks B76 9PR.**

In addition to being a four star hotel with a full complement of facilities, The Belfry has twenty one meeting and conference rooms, eight public bars and five restaurants open to the general public, as well as a fully equipped leisure centre and a nightclub in the hotel grounds. If after a meal and a few drinks you're still not satisfied with your golf there's a final opportunity to put things right on the impressive floodlit covered driving range.

Situated close to the country's industrial heart, there is surely no golfing complex in Britain better served by communication networks. The Belfry is one mile from the M42 (junction 9), five miles from the M6 (junction 4), nine miles from Birmingham city centre and less than ten minutes from Birmingham International Airport and the NEC railway station. The exact position of the golf club is at the apex of the A446 and A4091.

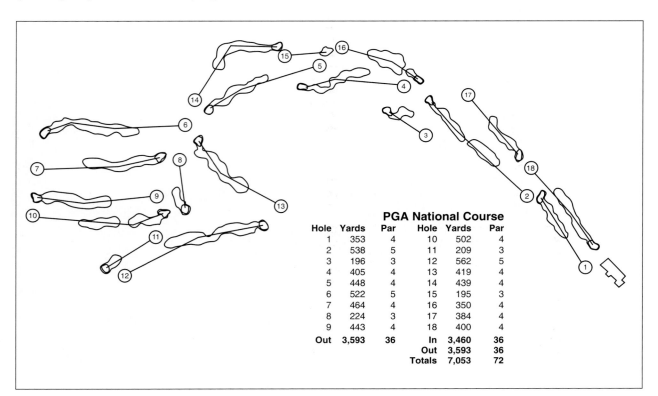

PGA National Course

Hole	Yards	Par	Hole	Yards	Par
1	353	4	10	502	4
2	538	5	11	209	3
3	196	3	12	562	5
4	405	4	13	419	4
5	448	4	14	439	4
6	522	5	15	195	3
7	464	4	16	350	4
8	224	3	17	384	4
9	443	4	18	400	4
Out	**3,593**	**36**	**In**	**3,460**	**36**
			Out	**3,593**	**36**
			Totals	**7,053**	**72**

Reputedly the oldest moated manor house in England, New Hall is now a country house hotel of unrivalled style and presence. Personally run by Ian and Caroline Parkes it has been awarded 4 Red Stars by the AA, 3 AA Rosettes for food and was the AA Inspectors' Hotel of the Year for England in 1993/94. Among other accolades it also holds the highest RAC award, the Blue Ribbon for seven years.

Guests dine in the 16th century oak-panelled restaurant, where the award-winning chef creates superb cuisine which is unmistakeably English but exhibits flair and imagination. The comprehensive wine list, selected personally by Ian Parkes, contains the best of the old world but also features some superb newcomers.

Part of the restaurant lends itself to semi-private dining, while the Oak Room provides private dining for up to eight people. Boardroom facilities are also available in the Garden Room, the Sir Alfred Owen Room and the Chadwick Room, while the Great Chamber provides an inspiring setting for meetings of up to 40 people.

Set in twenty six acres of private garden and surrounded by a lily-filled moat, the hotel provides extensive leisure facilities—a croquet lawn, archery, putting, an all-weather tennis court and its own 9 hole par 3 golf course. Keen golfers will be delighted by New Hall's close proximity to The Belfry's championship course. The hotel can arrange golf here for its guests as well as at Moor Hall and Little Aston. Other championship courses in the immediate vicinity include Forest of Arden, Copt Heath and Fulford Heath. Truly a golfer's paradise.

New Hall is seven miles from the centre of Birmingham. Warwick, Coventry, Lichfield and Stratford upon Avon are all within easy reach. A veritable haven for the golfer and non-golfer alike.

New Hall
Walmley Road
Royal Sutton Coldfield
B76 1QX
Tel: 0121 378 2442
Fax: 0121 378 4637
e mail: new.hall@thistle.co.uk
web site: http://www.slh.com/newhallc/

Collingtree Park

In recent years we have grown accustomed to watching Australian Greg Norman tear golf courses apart: 62s at Doral and Glen Abbey; 63s at St Andrews, Augusta and Turnberry and 64s at Troon and St George's. A tournament isn't over, they say, whilst Greg Norman is within seven shots of the leader. In the 1970s the man with a similar reputation for shooting extraordinary, par shattering rounds was American Johnny Miller. Twice in as many weeks in 1975 he returned a score of 61. That year he won the first three tournaments he entered in America, all by very large margins and he finished one shot away from catching Jack Nicklaus in the Masters after closing rounds of 65 and 66. In 1973, he stormed through the field with a final round of 63 to win the US Open; the score still stands as the lowest ever to win a major. In 1974 he won eight tournaments on the US Tour and in 1976 charged around a dry and dusty Royal Birkdale in a course record equalling 66 on the final day of the Open to win by six strokes. He was a dashing champion whose hobby (like Norman's) was driving superfast cars. Johnny Miller is also the man who designed Collingtree Park.

Opened in May 1990, it is Miller's first course in Europe. Without question, he has produced a dramatic golf course which, in time, may be considered one of the finest of its type in England. It is certainly one of the most challenging with 11 acres of lakes to be negotiated and more than 72,000 imported trees and shrubs in a layout that can be stretched to close on 7000 yards.

Collingtree Park is much more than an exciting new golf course. In addition to Miller's creation, there is a golf academy which includes three full length practice holes, a 16 bay floodlit driving range and an indoor video teaching room and computerised custom fitting centre. All golf enquiries should be made to the **Joint Club Professionals**, **Geoff Pook**, **Henry Bareham** and their staff who may be contacted on **(01604) 700000** or by **fax: (01604) 702600**. The **General Manager** is **Jim Laidler**. The address for written correspondence is **Collingtree Park Golf Course, Windingbrook Lane, Northampton NN4 0XN**.

For individual visitors and groups of fewer than twelve players bookings can be made up to one week in advance. Handicaps are required and green fees for 2000 are set at £17.50 per round during the week

and £23 at the weekend. Details of corporate day packages and tuition courses can be obtained by telephoning the above number.

Travelling to Collingtree Park should be fairly straightforward. Very centrally located in the heart of England, it is just on the outskirts of Northampton, one of Britain's fastest growing towns and very close to the M1. Junction 15 is the exit to use, immediately picking up the A508 road to Northampton. This road should be followed for about half a mile and Collingtree Park's entrance is the second turning on the left. The golf course is sixty-five miles from London, thirty-five miles from Birmingham and about twenty miles from Milton Keynes.

When Johnny Miller first viewed the site in 1986 it is doubtful that he could have thought it the most natural setting for a golf course he had ever seen. Part meadowland, part wasteland, it required a massive amount of work. With the support of Jack Nicklaus' technical services team it certainly received it. Work commenced in 1987 with the movement of over 350,000 cubic metres of earth. A positive drainage system with sixteen miles of underground piping was installed and then the course was landscaped. Work still continues and minor alterations have recently been made on the 1st, 5th, 11th, 12th and 15th holes.

'I designed the course along American lines, but not without respect for the English countryside. I wanted Collingtree to combine the best of both English and American course ideas' said Miller. At 6777 yards from the medal tees and 5146 yards from the ladies' tees it is a formidable challenge. There isn't a bad hole at Collingtree Park but on the front nine the par three 5th across the edge of a lake and the 9th—one of those par fives that can be reached with two good shots but where disaster awaits the failed attempt—are especially memorable and on the much more difficult back nine there is the spectacular finishing hole, perhaps the most dramatic in Great Britain. The 18th measures 602 yards from the back tees and the third shot (you won't be going for this one in two) must be played to an island green—Florida comes to Northamptonshire! It is Miller's masterstroke and you can guarantee that almost all conversation at the 19th hole will centre around 'how did you fare at the last?' And I dare say there will be one or two tall stories.

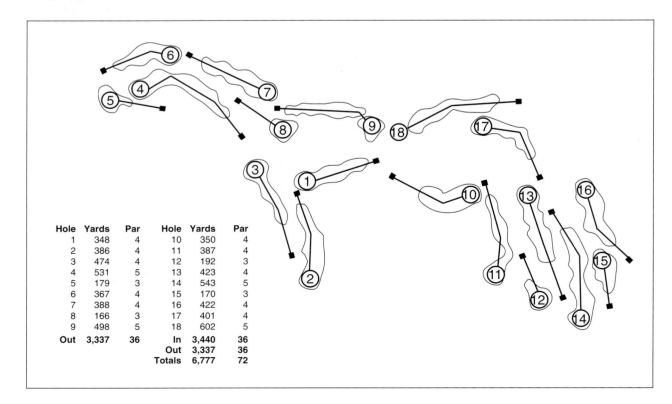

Hole	Yards	Par	Hole	Yards	Par
1	348	4	10	350	4
2	386	4	11	387	4
3	474	4	12	192	3
4	531	5	13	423	4
5	179	3	14	543	5
6	367	4	15	170	3
7	388	4	16	422	4
8	166	3	17	401	4
9	498	5	18	602	5
Out	**3,337**	**36**	**In**	**3,440**	**36**
			Out	3,337	36
			Totals	6,777	72

Forest of Arden

If 'Forest of Arden' has always had something of an enchanting ring to it, it is only over relatively recent times that the images conjured up would have a golfing theme. The resort, which has now firmly established itself as one of the UK's premier business, leisure and golfing destinations, has somehow managed to retain something of the countrified, unspoiled atmosphere sadly lacking from many of the modern all-purpose resorts. In actual fact, it is difficult to think of many inland venues with such a happy combination of new and old, where modern course design blends quite so harmoniously with ancient oak trees and grazing deer.

If the above sounds a little too much like the marketing blurb so favoured in glossy hotel brochures, then rest assured that this is one much-hyped golfing destination where reality will invariably meet expectation. Forget for a moment the conference delegates, aqua-aerobics or any other of Forest of Arden's manifold delights. If your poison is exhilarating golf on a course coaxed out of a classic English landscape, then look no further than the Arden course, host to the 1998 One-2-One British Masters.

To the probable chagrin of its nevertheless fortunate members, Forest of Arden welcomes all authentic golfers, with starting times bookable through the **Golf Shop (01676) 526113.** Individual and group lessons can be booked through **Kim Thomas** and his team of professionals on **(0958) 632170.** The full address is **c/o David MacLaren, Director of Golf, Marriott Forest of Arden Hotel and Country Club, Maxstoke Lane, Meriden, Warwickshire, CV7 7HR.**

Guests are advised to contact the hotel regarding prices and any seasonal offers. A range of residential packages are available, with golf included on the **Arden** course and its less celebrated sister the **Aylesford.** 2000 green fees for visitors are: Arden course £50 weekdays, £60 weekends; Aylesford course: £25 weedays and £30 weekends.

To find Forest of Arden, take junction 6 from the M42 and follow the A45 towards Coventry. After about a mile, turn left into Shepherds Lane by the Little Chef restaurant. You will find the hotel some one and a half miles on the left. Birmingham International Airport is only four miles away, with the world renowned National Exhibition Centre even closer.

Although it is the back nine on the Arden which is likely to have you reaching into the golf bag for camera and additional balls, the front nine does not fail to provide a stern and scenic challenge. A relatively benign opening quickly gives way to a succession of testing holes, with tortuous short holes interspersed with par fives which could leave even Tiger Woods struggling for breath. It is, however, at the 8th and 9th holes that the course really starts to bare its teeth. Both rely on water to define their challenge, with shot selection at the 8th meaning the difference between a birdie opportunity and a watery grave. The 9th is one of the favourite holes of no less celebrated a judge than Colin Montgomerie, who ranks the second shot, usually hit with a long iron at best, as one of the toughest anywhere.

The back nine derives much of its character from the ancient oaks and massive expanses of bracken which make even the most miserable scores a more bearable experience. It is, however, the herds of roaming deer that will provide perhaps the most vivid memories and the hotel's management is to be commended on its live-and-let-live approach to the estate's varied wildlife. Holes that particularly stand out from the generally scenic ambience include the 12th, 17th and 18th. The first two are both par fives, with yet more water all too ready to turn a birdie into bogey. The final hole on the Arden course also requires an airborne approach but at over two hundred yards, golfers are likely to be more confident of the culinary delights that lie beyond the green. Like its sister resort at St Pierre which also closes with a gigantic par three, the 18th is in many ways a fitting climax to a course that merits the tag of championship.

Although considerably less spectacular than the Arden, the shorter Aylesford course will nevertheless provide good golfing in a pleasant environment.

If your supply of golf balls has been extinguished by the Arden's water and wildlife hazards, fear not, for the resort offers a wealth of alternative attractions. With 215 bedrooms, a fully equipped leisure club, two restaurants, the celebrated Packington trout lakes and even a teaching academy for learning golf, the resort makes a great venue for golfing widows or widowers.

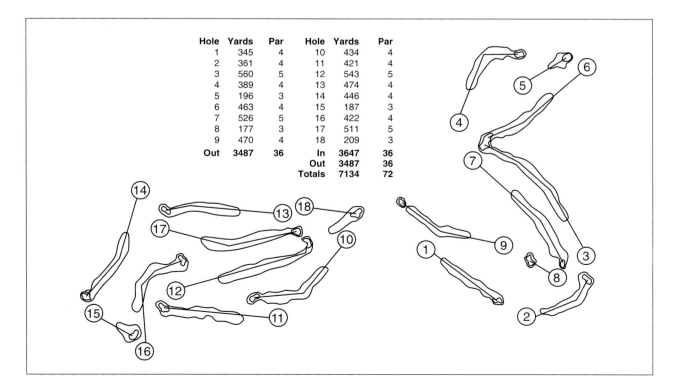

Hole	Yards	Par	Hole	Yards	Par
1	345	4	10	434	4
2	361	4	11	421	4
3	560	5	12	543	5
4	389	4	13	474	4
5	196	3	14	446	4
6	463	4	15	187	3
7	526	5	16	422	4
8	177	3	17	511	5
9	470	4	18	209	3
Out	**3487**	**36**	**In**	**3647**	**36**
			Out	**3487**	**36**
			Totals	**7134**	**72**

NORTHAMPTONSHIRE

Brampton Heath G.C.
(01604) 843939
Sandy Lane, Church Brampton
(18) 6054 yards/***/D

Cherwell Edge G.C.
(01295) 711591
Chacombe, Banbury
(18) 5925 yards/***/E

Cold Ashby G.C.
(01604) 740548
Stanford Road, Cold Ashby
(27) 6308 yards/**/D

Collingtree Park G.C.
(01604) 700000
Windingbrook Lane, Northampton
(18) 6821 yards/***/B/H

Corby G.C.
(01526) 260756
Stamford Road, Weldon
(18) 6677 yards/***/F

Daventry and District G.C.
(01327) 702829
Norton Road, Daventry
(9) 5812 yards/**/E

Delapre G.C.
(01604) 763957
Eagle Drive, Northampton
(18) 6356 yards/***/D
(9) 2146 yards/***/E

Elton Furze G.C.
(01832) 280189
Haden, Peterborough
(18) 6291/*/B

Embankment G.C.
(01933) 228465
The Embankment, Wellingborough
(9) 3374 yards/***/E

Farthingstone Hotel G.C.
(01327) 361291
Farthingstone, Towcester
(18) 6248 yards/***/C-B

Hellidon Lakes Hotel & C.C.
(01327) 62550
Hellidon, Daventry
(18) 6691 yards/***/C/H

Kettering G.C.
(01536) 511104
Headlands, Kettering
(18) 6036 yards/**/C/H

Kingsthorpe G.C.
(01604) 710610
Kingsley Road, Northampton
(18) 6006 yards/**/B/H

Northampton G.C.
(01604) 845155
Kettering Road, Northampton
(18) 6534 yards/**/C/H

Northamptonshire County G.C.
(01604) 843025
Sandy Lane, Church Brampton
(18) 6503 yards/***/A/H

Oundle G.C.
(01832) 273267
Benefield Road, Oundle
(18) 5900 yards/**/F

Overstone Park G.C.
(01604) 671471
Willow Lane, Little Billing
(18) 6260 yards/***/D

Priors Hall G.C.
(01536) 260756
Stamford Road, Weldon
(18) 6677 yards/***/E

Rushden and District G.C.
(01933) 312581
Kimbolton Road, Chelveston
(10) 6335 yards/**/C

Staverton Park G.C.
(01327) 705911
Staverton, Daventry
(18) 6634 yards/**/C/H

Wellingborough G.C.
(01933) 677234
Horrowden Hall, Great Horrowden
(18) 6620 yards/**/B/H

West Park G.& C.C.
(01327) 858092
Whittlebury, Towcester
(36) 4 x 9 7000 yards/***/B/H

LEICESTERSHIRE

Beedles Lake G.C.
(0116) 260 6759
Broome Lane, East Goscote
(18) 6412 yards/***/E

Birstall G.C.
(0116) 267 4450
Station Road, Birstall
(18) 6222 yards/***/B/H/G/L

Blaby G.C.
(0116) 278 4804
Lutterworth Road, Blaby
(9) 2600 yards/***/E

Breedon Priory G.C.
(01332) 863081
Wilson, Derby
(18) 5700 yards/**/D

Charnwood Forest G.C.
(01509) 890259
Breakback Lane, Woodhouse Eaves
(9) 5960 yards/**/C/H

Cosby G.C.
(0116) 286 4759
Chapel Lane, Cosby
(18) 6418 yards/**/B/H

Enderby G.C.
(0116) 284 9388
Mill Lane, Enderby
(9) 4356 yards/***/E

Forest Hill G.C.
(01455) 824800
Markfield Lane, Botcheston
(18) 6039 yards/***/F

Glen Gorse G.C.
(0116) 271 4159
Glen Road, Oadby
(18) 6603 yards/**/B/H

Greetham Valley G.C.
(01780) 460444
Greetham, Oakham
(18) 6656 yards/***/C

Hinckley G.C.
(01455) 615124
Leicester Road, Hinckley
(18) 6517 yards/**(Tue)/B/H

Humberstone Heights G.C.
(0116) 276 1905
Gipsy Lane, Leicester
(18) 6444 yards/***/E

Kibworth G.C.
(0116) 279 2301
Weir Road, Kibworth Beauchamp
(18) 6282 yards/**/C

Kilworth Springs G.C.
(01858) 575082
South Kilworth Road, Lutterworth
(18) 6718 yards/***/C

Kirby Muxloe G.C.
(0116) 239 3107
Station Road, Kirby Muxloe
(18) 6303 yards/**/B/H

Langton Park G. & C.C.
(01858) 545374
Langton Hall, Leicester
(18) 6965 yards/***/B-A/H/L
(9) 3362 yards/***/D

Leicestershire G.C.
(0116) 273 8825
Evington Lane, Leicester
(18) 6330 yards/***/B/H

Leicestershire Forest G.C
(01455) 824800
Markfield Lane, Botcheston
(18) 6111 yards/***/D

Lingdale G.C.
(01509) 890703
Joe Moores Lane, Woodhouse Eaves
(18) 6545 yards/***/C

Longcliffe G.C.
(01509) 239129
Snell's Nook Lane, Nanpantan
(18) 6551 yards/**/B/H

Luffenham Heath G.C.
(01780) 720205
Ketton, Stamford
(18) 6254 yards/***/A/H

Lutterworth G.C.
(01455) 552532
Rugby Road, Lutterworth
(18) 5570 yards/**/C/H

Market Harborough G.C.
(01858) 463684
Oxendon Road, Market Harborough
(18) 6027 yards/**/C/H

Melton Mowbray G.C.
(01664) 62118
Waltham Road, Thorpe Arnold
(18) 6222 yards/**/C/H

Oadby G.C.
(0116) 270 9052
Leicester Road, Oadby
(18) 6228 yards/***/D

Park Hill G.C.
(01509) 815454
Park Hill, Seagrave
(9) 6800 yards/***/C/H

RAF Cottesmore G.C.
(01572) 812241
Oakham, Leicester
(9) 5622 yards/*/E/G

RAF North Luffenham G.C.
(01780) 720041
North Luffenham, Oakham
(9) 6006 yards/***/F

Rothley Park G.C.
(0116) 230 2809
Westfield Lane, Rothley
(18) 6487 yards/**(Tues)/B/H/M

Rutland County G.C.
(01780) 460239
Great Casterton, Stamford
(18) 6189 yards/***/C/H

Scraptoft G.C.
(0116) 241 8863
Beeby Road, Scraptoft
(18) 6166 yards/**/B/H

Ullesthorpe Court Hotel
(01455) 209023
Frolesworth Road, Ullesthorpe
(18) 6650 yards/**/D

Western Park G.C.
(0116) 287 2339
Scudamore Road, Braunstone Frith
(18) 6532 yards/***/E

Whetstone G.C.
(0116) 286 1424
Cambridge Road, Cosby
(18) 5795 yards/**/D/H

Willesley Park G.C.
(01530) 414596
Tamworth Road, Ashby-de-la-Zouch
(18) 6304 yards/***/B/H/M

BIRMINGHAM & COVENTRY

Aston Wood G.C.
(0121) 353 0363
Blake Street, Sutton Coldfield
(18) 6480 yards/**B/H

Blackwell G.C.
(0121) 445 1994
Blackwell, nr Bromsgrove
(18) 6202 yards/**/B/H

Bloxwich G.C.
(01922) 476593
Stafford Road, Bloxwich
(18) 6286 yards/**/F/H

Boldmere G.C.
(0121) 354 3379
Monmouth Drive, Sutton Coldfield
(18) 4463 yards/***/E

Brandhall G.C.
(0121) 552 2195
Heron Road, Oldbury, Warley
(18) 5813 yards/***/D

Bromsgrove Golf Centre
(01527) 570505
Stratford Road, Bromsgrove
(9) 3159 yards/**/E

Calderfields G.C.
(01922) 640540
Aldridge Road, Walsall
(18) 6636 yards/***/D

City of Coventry G.C.
(Brandon Wood)
(01203) 543141
Brandon Lane, Brandon, Coventry
(18) 6610 yards/***/F

Cocks Moor Woods G.C.
(0121) 444 3584
Alcester Road South, Kings Heath
(18) 5742 yards/***/F

Copt Heath G.C.
(01564) 772650
Warwick Road, Knowle, Solihull
(18) 6504 yards/**/A/H/M

Coventry G.C.
(01203) 414152
Finham Park, Coventry
(18) 6613 yards/**/A/H

Coventry Hearsall G.C.
(01203) 713470
Beechwood Avenue, Coventry
(18) 5983 yards/**/C/H

Dartmouth G.C.
(0121) 588 2131
Vale Street, West Bromwich
(9) 6060 yards/**/D

Druids Heath G.C.
(01922) 55595
Stonnal Road, Aldridge
(18) 6914 yards/**/B/H

Dudley G.C.
(01384) 233877
Turners Hill, Rowley Regis, Warley
(18) 5715 yards/**/D

Edgbaston G.C. .
(0121) 454 1736
Church Road, Edgbaston
(18) 6118 yards/***/A/H

Enville G.C.
(01384) 872551
Highgate Common, Enville
(18) 6556 yards/**/B-A/H
(18) 6217 yards/**/B-A/H

Forest of Arden G.& C.C.
(01676) 522335
Maxstoke Road, Meriden
(18) 7100 yards/**/F/H
(18) 6525 yards/**/F/H

Gay Hill G.C.
(0121) 430 6523
Alcester Road, Hollywood,
(18) 6522 yards/**/B/H

GPT (Grange G.C.).
(01203) 451465
Copsewood, Coventry
(9) 6002 yards/**/D/H

Great Barr G.C.
(0121) 358 4376
Chapel Lane, Great Barr,
Birmingham
(18) 6546 yards/**/B/H/L

Hagley G.C.
(01562) 883701
Wassell Grove, Hagley, Stourbridge
(18) 6353 yards/**/B/H

Halesowen G.C.
(0121) 550 1041
The Leasowes, Halesowen
(18) 5754 yards/**/C

Handsworth G.C.
(0121) 554 3387
Sunningdale Close, Handsworth
(18) 6312 yards/**/C/H

Harborne G.C.
(0121) 427 1728
Tennal Road, Birmingham
(18) 6240 yards/**/A/H

Harborne Church Farm G.C.
(0121) 427 1204
Vicarage Road, Harborne
(9) 4914 yards/***/E

Hatchford Brook G.C.
(0121) 743 9821
Coventry Road, Sheldon
(18) 6164 yards/***/E

Hilltop G.C.
(0121) 554 4463
Park Lane, Handsworth
(18) 6114 yards/***/E

Himley Hall G.C.
(01902) 895207
Himley Hall Park, Dudley
(9) 3145 yards/**/E

Kings Norton G.C.
(01564) 826789
Brockhill Lane, Weatheroak
(18) 7057 yards/**/B/H
(9) 3300 yards/**/B/H

Ladbrook Park G.C.
(01564) 742264
Tanworth-in-Arden, Solihull
(18) 6427 yards/**/B-A/H

Lickey Hills G.C.
(0121) 453 3159
Rose Hill, Rednal
(18) 6010 yards/***/E

Little Aston G.C.
(0121) 353 2942
Streetly, Sutton Coldfield
(18) 6724 yards/**/F

Maxstoke Park G.C.
(01675) 464915
Castle Lane, Coleshill
(18) 6437 yards/**/A

Moor Hall G.C.
(0121) 308 6130
Four Oaks, Sutton Coldfield
(18) 6249 yards/**/B-A/H

Moseley G.C.
(0121) 444 2115
Springfield Road, Kings Heath
(18) 6285 yards/***/A/H/L

North Warwickshire G.C.
(01676) 22259
Hampton Lane, Meriden
(9) 3186 yards/**(not Thurs)/C

North Worcestershire G.C.
(0121) 475 1047
Frankley Beeches Road, Northfield
(18) 5959 yards/**/B/H

Olton G.C.
(0121) 705 1083
Mirfield Road, Solihull
(18) 6229 yards/**(Weds)/B/H

Oxley Park G.C.
(01902) 20506
Bushbury, Wolverhampton
(18) 6168 yards/***/C

Patshull Park Hotel G. & C.C.
(01902) 700100
Pattingham, Wolverhampton
(18) 6412 yards/***/B-A

***COLLINGTREE PARK GOLF CLUB** Photograph courtesy of:* **Collingtree Park Golf Club**

Penn G.C.
(01902) 341142
Penn Common, Wolverhampton
(18) 6465 yards/**/C

Perton Park G.C.
(01902) 380103
Wrottesley Park Road, Perton
(18) 7007 yards/***/E

Pype Hayes G.C.
(0121) 351 1014
Eachelhurst Road, Walmley
(18) 5811 yards/***/E

Robin Hood G.C.
(0121) 706 0061
St Bernards Road, Solihull
(18) 6635 yards/**/B-A/H

Sandwell Park G.C.
(0121) 553 4637
Birmingham Road, West Bromwich
(18) 6470 yards/**/A/H

Sedgley Golf Centre
(01902) 880503
Sandyfields Road, Sedgley
(9) 3150 yards/***/E

Shirley G.C.
(0121) 744 6001
Stratford Road, Solihull
(18) 6510 yards/**/B-A/H

South Staffordshire G.C.
(01902) 751065
Tettenhall, Wolverhampton
(18) 6513 yards/**(Tues)/B/H
Sphinx G.C.
(01203) 451361
Sphinx Drive, Coventry
(9) 4104 yards/***/E

Stonebirdge G.C.
(01676) 522442
Somers Road, Meriden
(18) 6240 yards/***/D

Stourbridge G.C.
(01384) 395566
Worcester Lane, Pedmore
(18) 6178 yards/**/C/H

Sutton Coldfield G.C.
(0121) 353 9633
Thornhill Road, Streetly
(18) 6541 yards/***/A/H

Swindon G.C.
(01902) 897031
Bridgnorth Road, Swindon
(18) 6042 yards/**/C
(9) 1135 yards/**/C

Tidbury Green G.C.
(01564) 824466
Tilehouse Lane, Shirley
(9) 2473 yards/***/E

Walmley G.C.
(0121) 377 7272
Brooks Road, Wylde Green
(18) 6537 yards/**/B

Walsall G.C.
(01922) 613512
The Broadway, Walsall
(18) 6243 yards/**/A/H

Wergs G.C.
(01902) 742225
Keepers Lane, Tettenhall
(18) 6949 yards/***/D

Widney Manor G.C.
(0121) 711 3646
Saintbury Drive, Solihull
(18) 4709 yards/***/E

Windmill Village Hotel & G.C.
(01203) 407241
Birmingham Road, Coventry
(18) 5200 yards/***/D

WARWICKSHIRE

Ansty Golf Centre
(01203) 621341
Brinklow Road, Ansty
(18) 5823 yards/***/E

Atherstone G.C.
(01827) 713110
The Outwoods, Atherstone
(18) 6239 yards/**/C/H
(18) 6006 yards/**/C/H

The Belfry G.C.
(01675) 470301
Lichfield Road, Wishaw
(18) 7177 yards/***/A/H
(18) 6186 yards/***/B/H

Bidford Grange G.C.
(01789) 490319
Bidford Grange, Bidford-on-Avon
(18) 7233 yards/***/D

Brailes G.C.
(01608) 685336
Sutton Lane, Lower Brailes
(18) 6270 yardfs/**/F

Crocketts Manor G.& C.C.
(01564) 793715
Henley-in-Arden
(18) 6933 yards/***/B/H

Henley G & CC
(01564) 793715
Birmingham Road, Henley-in-Arden
(18) 6933 yards/D

Ingon Manor G.C.
(01789) 731857
Ingon Lane, Snitterfield
(18) 6554 yards/***/C/H

Kenilworth G.C.
(01926)854296
Crew Lane, Kenilworth
(18) 6413 yards/***/B-A/H

Lea Marston Hotel & Leisure Complex
(01675) 470707
Haunch Lane, Lea Marston
(9) 1027 yards/***/F

Leamington & County G.C.
(01926) 425961
Whitnash, Leamington Spa
(18) 6425 yards/***/B-A/H

Newbold Comyn G.C.
(01926) 421157
Newbold Terrace, Leamington Spa
(18) 6315 yards/***/E

Nuneaton G.C.
(01203) 347810
Golf Drive, Whitestone
(18) 6412 yards/**/C/H

Oakridge G.C.
(01676) 541389
Arley Lane, Ansley Village
(18) 6242 yards/**/F

Purley Chase G.C.
(01203) 393118
Ridge Lane, Nuneaton
(18) 6604 yards/**/D/H

Rugby G.C.
(01788) 542306
Clifton Road, Rugby
(18) 5457 yards/**/F

Stoneleigh Deer Park G.C.
(01203) 639991
The Old Deer Park, Stoneleigh
(18)6083 yards/**/D
(9) 1251 yards/**/E

Stratford Oaks G.C.
(01789) 731571
Bearley Road, Snitterfield
(18) 6100 yards/***/D

Stratford-upon-Avon G.C.
(01789) 205749
Tiddington Road, Stratford
(18) 6309 yards/***/F/H

Warley G.C.
(0121) 429 2440
Lightswood Hill, Warley
(9) 2606 yards/***/F

Warwick G.C.
(01926) 494396
The Racecourse, Warwick
(9) 2682 yards/***(not racedays)/E

The Warwickshire G.C.
(01926) 409409
Leek Wootton, Warwick
(18) 7178 yards/***/A
(18) 7154 yards/***/A

Welcombe Hotel G.C.
(01789) 295292
Warwick Road, Stratford
(18) 6217 yards/**/A/H

Whitefields Hotel & Golf Complex
(01788) 521800
Coventry Road, Thurlaston
(18) 6433 yards/***/D/H

HENLEY GOLF & COUNTRY CLUB Photograph courtesy of: **Henley Golf & Country Club**

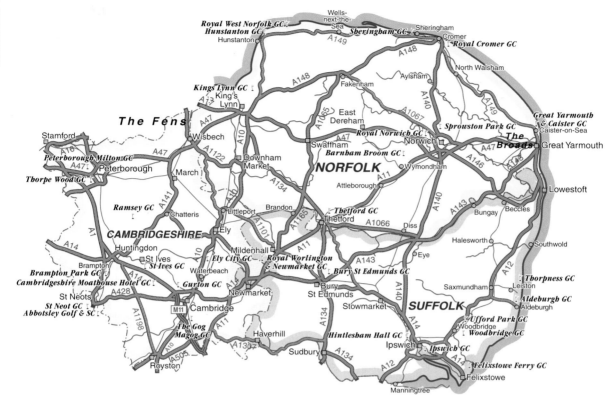

© MAPS IN MINUTES ™ 2000

East Anglia Choice Golf

The counties of East Anglia, which for our purposes comprise Norfolk, Suffolk and Cambridgeshire, stretch from Constable Country in the south, through the Fens and the Broads to the tip of the Wash. For golfers this means it stretches from Felixstowe Ferry, through Thetford to Hunstanton. There are numerous other combinations capable of whetting the golfing appetite, for East Anglia is one of the game's richest regions. Certainly for quality and variety it has few equals. It is also a corner of Britain where golf has long been a popular pastime.

Norfolk

It is doubtful whether any county in England can surpass Norfolk's great range of outstanding courses. In short it offers the golfer a bit of everything. There are the magnificent links courses at **Hunstanton** and **Brancaster**, some terrifically scenic golf along the cliffs at **Sheringham** and **Cromer** and a number of superb inland courses of which **Thetford**, **Barnham Broom** and **Kings Lynn** are prime examples.

The North Coast

However, the title of 'Oldest Club' in Norfolk goes to **Great Yarmouth and Caister**, founded in 1882. A fine seaside links, it is located to the north of Great Yarmouth close to the old Roman town of Caister-on-Sea and near to the start of the A149 coastal road. Punters may wish to note that the golf course is actually situated inside part of Great Yarmouth racecourse. Anyone who does think of combining the two might look to Gorleston on Sea for a night's rest at the Cliff Hotel (01493) 662179 or in Yarmouth itself we recommend the Imperial Hotel (01493) 851113, which is a family run hotel, and the Carlton (01493) 855234.

Cromer, some twenty five miles north along the M49 is apparently famed for its crabs - the town, not the golf course I hasten to add - and also for its 150 year old lighthouse. The latter is a feature of **Royal Cromer's** attractive clifftop course. The 14th, the 'Lighthouse Hole', was played by Tony Jacklin during his '18 holes at 18 different courses helicopter round'. Several elevated tees and a generous spread of gorse make for a very interesting game.

Sheringham is only five miles further along the coast and is Norfolk's other great clifftop course. Founded some three years after Cromer in 1891 it is perhaps less exacting than its neighbour but certainly no less scenic. The view from the 5th hole is particularly stunning looking out across the rugged north Norfolk coastline.

A glorious day's golf (followed perhaps by some early evening bird watching - don't forget the binoculars) and time to relax. Well, in Sheringham, Southlands (01263) 822679 and the Beaumaris (01263) 822370 are handy, and inexpensive, whilst in nearby Weybourne the Maltings Hotel (01263) 588731 is a perfect base. On the road towards Brancaster (still the A149) the Blakeney area offers a glorious coastline and two beautifully situated hotels, the Manor (01263) 740376 and the Blakeney (01263) 740797.

And so on to **Royal West Norfolk** and **Hunstanton**, an outstanding pair to put it mildly. We feature both courses, or both links to be precise, later in this section. Once again, there's no shortage of places in which to relax and reflect on the day's golf. In Old Hunstanton, Le Strange Arms (01485) 534411 on Golfhouse Road, is highly thought of, as is the Fieldsend Guesthouse (01485) 532593 on Homefields Road. The village of Thornham lies between Hunstanton and Brancaster and here one might consider the popular Lifeboat Inn (01485) 512236. To the south east of

Brancaster the Old Rectory (01328) 820597 at Great Snoring is the perfect place for a particularly long rest and a little nearer at Brancaster Staithe, the Jolly Sailors (01485) 210314 is a good pub with an accompanying restaurant.

Further accommodation can be found at Titchwell, the Titchwell Manor (01485) 210221-a good value and thoroughly agreeable establishment. For two seafood restaurants we recommend the Moorings in Wells and Fishes (01328) 738588 in Burnham Market. We would also recommend the aptly named Hoste Arms (01328) 738777 a spendid 17th century inn with excellent food and accommodation.

Kings Lynn is our next port of call, and another very good golf course. Although the **Kings Lynn** Golf Club was founded back in 1923, it has played at Castle Rising to the north of the town since 1975. An Alliss/Thomas creation, it's very heavily wooded and quite a demanding test of golf. Returning to the town itself suggestions for an overnight stay might include the Dukes Head Hotel (01553) 774996 and Russet House (01553) 773098. Meanwhile at Knights Hill village, the Knights Hill Hotel (01553) 675566 has excellent leisure facilities and great character. A short journey to Grimston and one finds a real gem in Congham Hall (01485) 600250, an elegant and very well run Georgian manor house hotel.

Around Norwich

The golfing visitor to Norwich, one of England's more attractive county towns, should have little difficulty in finding a game. **Sprowston Park** is a welcoming club on the edge of the city while for a fine combination of the old and the new try **Royal Norwich** and **Barnham Broom**. Both clubs have excellent parkland courses. Barnham Broom is part of an hotel and country club complex (01603) 759393 and has two courses with numerous accompanying leisure facilities.

If Norwich is to be the base though, then the Maids Head Hotel (01603) 209955 is most comfortable. Slightly less imposing, but no less comfortable, are the Grange Hotel (01603) 434734 and the Marlborough House Hotel (01603) 628005. Among many good restaurants are Adlard's (01603) 633522 (an outstanding establishment) Marcos (01603) 624044, the Brasted's (01508) 491112 and Greens Seafood (01603) 623733. Our final thought is Sprowston Manor (01603) 410871, good leisure facilities and in close proximity to the public course that lies adjacent to the hotel.

Last but not least, we must visit **Thetford**, right in the very heart of East Anglia and close to the Norfolk- Suffolk boundary. Thetford is surely one of England's most beautiful inland courses. Set amid glorious oaks, pines and silver birch trees it is also a great haven for wildlife (rather like Luffenham Heath in Leicestershire). Golden pheasant abound and one can also sight red deer and even, so I'm told, Chinese Water Deer (whatever they may be!) The green fee here is always money well spent. The second place to invest the cash is at the Bell Hotel (01842) 754455 in Thetford-a jolly good place to rest the spikes.

Suffolk

Of the twenty or so golf clubs in Suffolk, about half were founded in the 19th century and the **Felixstowe Ferry** Golf Club which dates from 1880 is the fifth oldest club in England Given its antiquity, and the fact that it was here that the 'father of golf writers' Bernard Darwin began to play his golf, Felixstowe Ferry is as good a place as any to begin our brief golfing tour of Suffolk.

The course lies about a mile to the north east of Felixstowe and is a classic test of traditional links golf. This part of Suffolk is fairly remote and at times it could easily be imagined that one was playing one of the better Scottish links courses. The greens are first class and the wind is often a major factor. Those looking to spend some time in this area (the courses at Ipswich and Woodbridge are only a short drive away) should note the Marlborough Hotel (01394) 285621 in Felixstowe. Lovers of fish and chips should note the splendid Felixstowe Ferry fish and chip restaurant on the beach- the finest for miles around!

The A45 links Felixstowe with Suffolk's largest town. The **Ipswich** Golf Club at Purdis Heath, three miles east of Ipswich, was designed by James Braid and is a fine heath and course. Always well maintained, the fairways wind their way between two large ponds and are bordered by heather and an attractive assortment of hardwood trees and silver birch. **Woodbridge** offers a similar type of challenge. Like the Ipswich course it's beautifully mature but is much more undulating. The golf club is located two miles east of Woodbridge along the B1084 Orford road.

The Ipswich-Woodbridge area is blessed with some outstanding places to stay and the seafood served in these parts is some of the best in Britain. In Woodbridge, Seckford Hall (01394) 385678 is superb while Melton Grange (01394) 384147 also appeals. A recent addition to the 'where to stay, where to play' map is provided by the new **Ufford Park** Hotel (01394) 383555 at Ufford, near Woodbridge. Here 18 holes of golf and numerous leisure facilities are offered in a pleasant country club setting. In Ipswich the Marlborough Hotel (01473) 257677 is both comfortable and good value and to the west of the town at Hintlesham is the 16th century **Hintlesham Hall** (01473) 652 334, where a glorious country house with an excellent restaurant and golf course await - gourmet golf itself! Other hotel suggestions in the Ipswich area would include the good value Bentley Tower Hotel (01473) 212142.

Hintlesham Hall

Hintlesham, Suffolk IP8 3NS
Tel: (01473) 652268 Fax: (01473) 652463
e mail: reservations@hintlesham-hall.co.uk

Hintlesham Hall, originally built in the 1570s, with a stunning Georgian facade offers the best in country house elegance and charm. Gracious living, good food and wine, attentive service and tranquil relaxation greet every guest to the hotel.

The Hall is set in over 170 acres of rolling Suffolk countryside, some of which is devoted to a beautiful 18 hole championship golf course, and has 33 luxurious bedrooms and suites of differing shapes and sizes, some with four-poster beds.

Head Chef, Alan Ford, believes good food starts with good produce. French truffles, Scottish salmon, Cornish scallops and Suffolk lobsters are just some of the enticements of the menu which changes seasonally. There is also an award winning 300 bin wine list which ranges the world from France to Australia.

A little further up the Suffolk coast lie two delightful holiday courses: **Thorpeness** and **Aldeburgh**. Although close to the sea both are again heather and gorse types. The town of Aldeburgh is of course famed for its annual music festival and Benjamin Britten once lived next to the club's 14th fairway. Thorpeness, yet another James Braid creation, is about two miles north of Aldeburgh and is especially scenic. One hole that everyone remembers is the par three 7th, played across an attractive pond. On the 18th an unusual water tower (the 'House in the Clouds') and a restored windmill provide a unique background.

Thorpeness Golf Club has its own Golf Hotel (01728) 452176 which is naturally very convenient, and in Aldeburgh there are a number of alternatives, many of which specialise in golfing breaks. Ideas here include the Wentworth (01728) 452312, the White Lion (01728) 452720 and the Uplands Hotel (01728) 452420. Also worth a visit is the White Horse Hotel (01728) 830694 in nearby Leiston. A final thought before moving inland is the Crown (01502) 722275 at Southwold-some pleasant rooms and some very good beer!

Over to the west of Suffolk the two courses that stand out are the parkland layout at **Bury St Edmunds** and the near-legendary **Royal Worlington**. Royal Worlington and Newmarket, to give its full title, is located two miles from Mildenhall, midway between Cambridge and Bury St Edmunds. A marvellous inland course with an almost links feel, it was once described as the finest 9 hole course in the world.

For a night's stopover, Bury St Edmunds offers a first rate hotel in the Angel (01284) 753926 while to the south of the town the Countrymen (01787) 312356 at Long Melford is an extremely welcoming abode. Chimneys (01787) 379806 is a first rate restaurant to look out for as is the popular Swan (01787) 247477 at Lavenham. Finally the Bedford Lodge Hotel (01638) 663175 at Newmarket is renowned for its hospitality.

Cambridgeshire

Having ventured west it is time to inspect the land of the fens and the courses of Cambridgeshire. Not exactly a county renowned for its golf, the courses tend, as one might expect, to be rather flat. One

great exception though is the **Gog Magog** Golf Club situated to the south east of Cambridge which offers a tremendously enjoyable test of golf. The club takes its name from the ridge of low hills on which it lies. Apparently taking a line due east from here the next range of hills one comes across is the Ural Mountains! Among many fine holes, the par four 16th stands out and is surely one of the best (and toughest!) two-shot holes in the country.

A second good course, though not in the same league as Gog Magog, close to the famous University city belongs to the **Cambridgeshire Moat House** Hotel (01954) 249988. It is a particularly challenging course when played from the back tees with a lake and several ditches providing the challenges. Just north of Cambridge, **Girton** Golf Club is also worth inspecting.

Cambridge with its magnificent colleges is a marvellous place to spend a day or two and the Moat House is just one of many fine hotels. Of the others the Garden House Hotel (01223) 259988 perhaps takes pride of place and is particularly welcoming. It also possesses a first class restaurant. Another good eating place in town is the Marguerite (01223) 315232. Among the less expensive hotels, both Bon Accord House (01223) 411188 and the Lensfield Hotel (01223) 355017 are recommended as is Dykelands Guest House (01223) 244300. Orton Hall Hotel (01733) 391111 near Peterborough is one of the finest in Cambridgeshire. Some notable hostelries in the county include the Plough and Fleece at Horningsea, the Three Horse Shoes at Madingley and the Green Man at Grantchester.

Other golf courses in Cambridgeshire which can be recommended include **Ramsey**, **St Ives** and **St Neots**. To the east of St Neots is the **Abbotsley** Golf Hotel (01480) 474000, and situated in the grounds is the course of the same name-one for the shortlist. In Huntingdon the Old Bridge (01480) 434700 is thoroughly recommended and is conveniently located from the testing course at **Brampton Park**. A duo to note just outside of bustling Peterborough are **Peterborough Milton** and the public course, **Thorpe Wood**. Finally, in Ely there is the attractive **Ely City** course which provides some excellent views of the stunning 12th century cathedral and where, rather interestingly, the course record is held by one Lee Trevino.

HINTLESHAM HALL GOLF CLUB *Photograph courtesy of:* **Hintlesham Hall Golf Club**

Royal West Norfolk (Brancaster)

Excluding those which have staged an Open Championship, there are perhaps two courses in Britain that exude a sense of tradition, history and character above all others. One is Westward Ho! and the other is Brancaster or, to give them their correct titles, Royal North Devon and Royal West Norfolk.

Apart from their rather geographical names, they have much in common: both enjoy a wondrously remote setting yet are still fairly close to a superb championship links (Saunton and Hunstanton); both have a unique hazard (Devon's sea rushes and Norfolk's tidal marshes) and both are particularly friendly clubs, emphasising that tradition need not accompany aloofness.

Brancaster is something of a golfers' Camelot. Having reached the attractive little village there is every possibility that a high tide will have flooded the road that leads to the course. Indeed, many choose to leave their car in the village and walk the remainder of the journey. (Don't worry, it's not that far!) The golf course lies in a range of sandhills between marshland and sea. There is a story that the course was laid out on the suggestion of the Prince of Wales (later King Edward VII) having conceived the idea while out shooting on the land. Certainly it was he who bestowed patronage upon the club immediately on its foundation in 1891. The Royal flavour has continued and there have been no fewer than four Royal Captains, most recently the Duke of Kent in 1981.

The **Secretary** at Brancaster is **Major Nigel Carrington Smith** and he can be contacted on **(01485) 210087**. The club's full address is **The Royal West Norfolk Golf Club, Brancaster, Nr Kings Lynn, Norfolk, PE31 8AX**. Individual visitors and societies are both welcome at Brancaster although all visiting parties must make prior arrangements with the Secretary—an introduction is preferred. Due to increased demand, no visitors are received at any time, unless playing with a member, during the last week in July and until the end of the first week in September.

In 2000, the green fee is £43 during the week and £53 at weekends and on bank holidays. The preferred days for golfing societies are Mondays, Wednesdays and Fridays. The **Professional** at Brancaster, **Simon Rayner**, can be contacted on **(01485) 210616**.

Travelling to the course can be a lengthy journey. Brancaster is approximately eight miles from Hunstanton and twenty-five miles from Kings Lynn, to the south and south west respectively, and about

thirty miles from Cromer to the east. Linking each to the other is the A149.

Like our friend Westward Ho!, Brancaster has the traditional out and back links layout. A quick glance at the scorecard tells us that one nine is considerably shorter than the other, the outward half measuring 3369 yards to the inward's 3059 yards. However, as at every good seaside course, wind direction is all important and on many occasions the back nine can play, or at least seem much longer. In total, the 6428 yards, par 71 represents a considerable test of golf. From the ladies' tees the course measures 5927 yards, par 75.

As well as the tidal marshes which come into play around the 8th and 9th, Brancaster is famed for its great wooden sleepered bunkers. Many are cross bunkers, which, as Sir Peter Allen observed, 'can be alarming to play over and frightening to play out of'. The course has received very few alterations over the years although two greens were lost to the sea in 1939 and 1940. There is no gentle beginning; the first three holes all measure over 400 yards and the great cross bunkers can come into play as early as the 3rd hole, one of the most difficult on the course. The bunker is fifty yards short of the green, which itself sits on a plateau. The 4th is a short par three but is deceptively tricky, especially into the wind. The 8th and 9th have been mentioned and the marshes must be carried twice on the 8th and from the tee on the dog-legged 9th which has a cross bunker in front of the green. The 11th and 12th are played deep amid the dunes but the 14th is perhaps the most difficult hole, with the 18th close behind—a hole with sleepered bunkers both to the front and back of the green.

The clubhouse, which is only a year younger than the course, is decidedly comfortable and is separated from the sea only by a sea wall. This famous last line of defence had to be repaired in 1991 after high seas wreaked havoc in 1990. The clubhouse also has a lovely verandah from which there are some glorious views. The setting really is something special and nobody described it better than the late Tom Scott.

'It has a quiet and restful beauty, and when you leave the clubhouse and drive across the marsh to the main road in the dusk of a summer evening, look back for a minute and perhaps you will be rewarded, as I have frequently been, with a view of the red sun setting over the sea with a golden glow. You will see too, the long shadows cast by the great sandhills, and you will hear the call of the many birds across the marshes, a sound to my mind typical of Norfolk.'

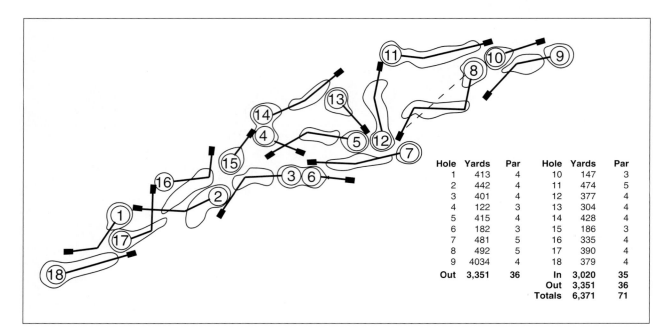

Hole	Yards	Par		Hole	Yards	Par
1	413	4		10	147	3
2	442	4		11	474	5
3	401	4		12	377	4
4	122	3		13	304	4
5	415	4		14	428	4
6	182	3		15	186	3
7	481	5		16	335	4
8	492	5		17	390	4
9	4034	4		18	379	4
Out	**3,351**	**36**		**In**	**3,020**	**35**
				Out	**3,351**	**36**
				Totals	**6,371**	**71**

Hunstanton

Imagine you are standing on the tee of a particularly difficult par three hole. It is a difficult hole on a still day—188 yards long and with six deep bunkers encircling the green—but it is particularly tough on this day because the wind is dead against. You select a one iron and hit the perfect shot; so perfect that it lands a few feet from the flag and rolls into the hole. Marvellous, but what a pity this is only a practice round! A day later, in the tournament itself, you reach the 16th but this time the wind is with you. You choose a six iron and incredibly you repeat the trick—in it goes for a second hole in one. Much celebration follows at the 19th. The next day (the second of the tournament) the wind is once more at your back as you walk onto the tee of what is now your favourite hole. If a six iron was good enough yesterday, it must be good enough today you reckon. Your calculations are entirely accurate and your well struck shot never really looks like missing. Three aces in three days at the same hole! Are you a liar, a dreamer . . . or Robert Taylor?

Taylor performed this remarkable feat in the summer of 1974 on the 16th at Hunstanton. Nobody has ever matched his extraordinary achievement and probably never will.

Founded over a hundred years ago, Hunstanton Golf Club celebrated its centenary in 1991. Although it is situated on the east coast of England the course actually faces north west and looks over the Wash towards Lincolnshire. Hunstanton has the kind of geography that causes its members to lose sleep over talk of global warming. It is a very good golf course—in the opinion of many, the east coast's finest 18 hole challenge between Sandwich and Muirfield, a distance of about 400 miles. It is a boast regularly expressed by Hunstanton's members that a player from Brancaster happens to be within earshot. But theirs is a valid claim, for Hunstanton is a truly classic links course. Like Brancaster, the course runs out and back although not rigidly so, rather it meanders away from the clubhouse, reaches the 8th green and meanders its way home. The outward holes have the River Hun for company—normally it is off to the right and the inward ones are closer to the shore. At first glance, the links looks very flat, and indeed there aren't any major climbs, up or down, but the course has more than its fair share of subtle undulations and there are a number of elevated tees and plateau greens, some of which offer extensive views of both sea and country.

It isn't the views though that are likely to be best remembered after a round at Hunstanton—it is the greens and bunkers. The putting surfaces are as quick (and usually as well prepared) as any in Britain—including the Open Championship courses. As for the

bunkers, they are numerous, strategically (and sometimes sadistically) placed and often quite deep. Avoid the bunkers and putt well and you'll probably score well here!

The club is very happy to receive visitors on weekdays and occasionally at weekends. All must be members of golf clubs and have current handicaps. It is worth noting that the 1st tee is reserved on weekdays before 9.30am, but in any event it is a good idea to contact the club a few days prior to any visit. The **Secretary** at Hunstanton, **Mr Malcolm Whybrow** can be approached by writing to **The Hunstanton Golf Club, Old Hunstanton, Norfolk PE36 6JQ.** Mr Whybrow can also be contacted by telephone on **(01485) 532811.** **Mr John Carter** is the club's **Professional** and he can be reached on **(01485) 532751.**

The green fees for 2000 are £50 per day during the week and, when available, £60 per day at weekends. Junior golfers pay half the above rates. Play is in two ball format only ie. singles and foursomes.

From the championship tees, Hunstanton measures 6735 yards, par 72 (SSS 72); while from the medal tees it is reduced by some 400 yards to 6333 yards, and for ladies the course measures 5973 yards, par 75. We have already referred to the ingenious and severe bunkering and the four par three holes emphasise this: the 4th is only 172 yards in length but has eight bunkers; the 7th is a similar length and has only one trap, but what a trap! The tee shot is an exhilarating one over a gully to a plateau green. Anything short is almost certain to plummet into a deep, yawning bunker that almost runs the entire width of the entrance—a low runner is not the desired shot here. The 14th requires a blind tee shot of 200 yards plus and again eight bunkers are waiting to greet the player who fails to find the putting surface.

The par four holes at Hunstanton offer a range of challenges. The 3rd, for instance, demands a very long approach shot if the prevailing wind is up to its tricks. By contrast, the 6th is a modest length hole but a deft touch is required to pitch onto the plateau green and the 17th and 18th provide a very strong finish. However, the best hole on the course is generally considered to be the 11th, which runs parallel to the shore. A high tee gives a spectacular view of both the hole and the surrounding countryside. At 439 yards it needs two perfectly hit shots along an ever narrowing valley-fairway to reach the green.

Numerous major amateur events have been staged at Hunstanton over the years, including the 1990 British Boys Amateur Championship, won by Michael Welch and the 1995 English Amateur Championship won by Mark Foster.

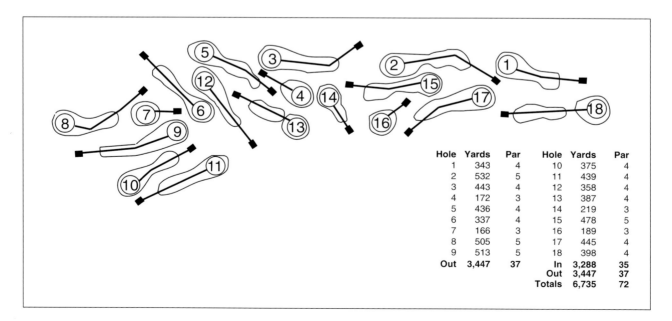

Hole	Yards	Par	Hole	Yards	Par
1	343	4	10	375	4
2	532	5	11	439	4
3	443	4	12	358	4
4	172	3	13	387	4
5	436	4	14	219	3
6	337	4	15	478	5
7	166	3	16	189	3
8	505	5	17	445	4
9	513	5	18	398	4
Out	**3,447**	**37**	**In**	**3,288**	**35**
			Out	**3,447**	**37**
			Totals	**6,735**	**72**

Key

*To avoid disappointment
it is advisable to telephone
in advance*

***Visitors welcome at most times**
**Visitors usually allowed on
weekdays only*
*Visitors not normally permitted
(Mon, Wed) No visitors
on specified days*

Approximate Green Fees
A   £40 plus
B   £25 to £40
C   £20 to £30
D   £15 to £25
E   under £15
F   Green fees on application

Restrictions
G   Guests only
H–Handicap certificate required
H–(24) Handicap of 24 or less
L–Letter of introduction required
M–Visitor must be a member of
another recognised club

CAMBRIDGESHIRE

Abbotsley G.C.
(01480) 474000
Eynesbury Hardwicke, St Neots
(18) 6150 yards/***/C

Bourn G.C.
(01954) 718057
Toft Road, Bourn
(18) 6275 yards/**/C

Brampton Park G.C.
(01480) 434700
Buckden Road, Brampton
(18) 6403 yards/***/B

Cambridge G.C.
(01954) 789388
Station Road, Longstanton
(9) 3464 yards/***/D

Cambridge Meridian
(01233) 264700
Comberton Road, Toft
(18) 6277 yards/***/C

Cambridgeshire Moat House Hotel G.C.
(01954) 780555
Bar Hill
(18) 6734 yards/***/C/L/M

Elton Furze G.C.
(01733) 280189
Bullock Road, Haddon
(18) 6291 yards/*/B

Ely City G.C.
(01353) 662751
Cambridge Road, Ely
(18) 6686 yards/**/B

Girton G.C.
(01223) 276169
Dodford Lane, Girton
(18) 6085 yards/**/C

Gog Magog G.C.
(01223) 247626
Shelford Bottom
(18) 6386 yards/**/B/H/L
(9) 5833 yards/**/B/H/L

Hemingford Abbots G.C.
(01480) 495000
New Farm Lodge, Cambridge Road
(9) 5468 yards/**/F

Heydon Grange G. & C.C.
(01763) 208988
Heydon, Royston
(18) 6512/***/C
(9) 3249/***/C

Lakeside Lodge G.C.
(01487) 740540
Fen Road, Pidley
(18) 6600 yards/***/E

Malton G.C.
(01763) 262200
Meldreth, Royston
(18) 6708 yards/***/D

March G.C.
(01354) 652364
Frogs Abbey, Grange Road, March
(9) 6200 yards/**/D/H

Old Nene G.& C.C.
(01487) 813519
Muchwood Lane, Bodsey, Ramsey
(9) 5524 yards/***/E

Orton Meadows G.C.
(01733) 237478
Ham Lane, Peterborough
(18) 5800 yards/***/E

Peterborough Milton G.C.
(01733) 380489
Milton Ferry, Peterborough
(18) 6431 yards/**/A/H

Ramsey G.C.
(01487) 812600
Abbey Terrace, Ramsey,
(18) 6136 yards/**/C/H

St Ives G.C.
(01480) 468392
Westwood Road, St Ives
(9) 6052 yards/**/C/H

St Neots G.C.
(01480) 472363
Crosshall Road, St Neots
(18) 6027 yards/**/B/H

Thorney Golf Centre
(01733) 270570
English Drove, Thorney, Peterborough
(18) 6104 yards/***/E

Thorpe Wood G.C.
(01733) 267701
Thorpe Wood, Peterborough
(18) 7076 yards/***/D

SUFFOLK

Aldeburgh G.C.
(01728) 452890
Saxmundham Road, Aldeburgh
(18)6330 yards/***/F/H
(9) 2114 yards/***/F/H

Brett Vale G.C.
(01473) 310718
Noakes Road, Raydon
(18) 5808 yards/***/C

Bungay and Waveney Valley G.C.
(01986) 892337
Outney Common, Bungay
(18)6063 yards/**/C/H

Bury St Edmunds G.C.
(01284) 755979
Tut Hill, Bury St Edmunds
(18) 6615 yards/**/B/H
(9) 4644 yards/**/D/H

Cretingham G.C.
(01728) 685275
Cretingham, Woodridge
(9) 2260 yards/***/E

Diss G.C.
(01379) 642847
Stutson Road, Diss
(18) 6238 yards/**/C

Felixstowe Ferry G.C.
(01394) 286834
Ferry Road, Felixstowe
(18) 6324 yards/***/C/H

Flempton G.C.
(01284) 728291
Flempton, Bury St Edmunds
(9) 6240 yards/**/C/H

Fynn Valley G.C.
(01473) 785463
Witnesham, Ipswich
(18) 5700 yards/***/D

Halesworth G.C.
(01986) 875567
Bramfield, Halesworth
(18) 6580 yards/H/D
(9) 3059 yards/E

Haverhill G.C.
(01440) 61951
Coupals Road, Haverhill
(9) 5707 yards/***/D

Hintlesham Hall G.C.
(01473) 652761
Hintlesham, Ipswich
(18) 6630 yards/***/B

Ipswich G.C.
(01473) 728941
Purdis Heath, Bucklesham Road
(18) 6405 yards/**/A/H(18)
(9) 1950 yards/***/E

Links G.C.
(01638) 663000
Cambridge Road, Newmarket
(18) 6424 yards/***/B/H

Newton Green G.C.
(01787) 377217
Newton Green, Sudbury
(18) 5488 yards/**/D/H

Rookery Park G.C.
(01502) 560380
Beccles Road, Carlton Coleville
(18) 6649 yards/**/C/H

Royal Worlington and Newmarket G.C.
(01638) 712216
Worlington, Bury St Edmunds
(9) 3105 yards/**/B/H

Rushmere G.C.
(01473) 725648
Rushmere Heath, Ipswich
(18) 6287 yards/***/C/H

Seckford G.C.
(01394) 388000
Seckford Hall Road, Woodbridge
(18) 5088 yards/***/D

Southwold G.C.
(01502) 723248
The Common, Southwold
(9) 6001 yards/***/D

St Helena G.C.
(01986) 875567
Bramfield Road, Halesworth
(18) 6580 yards/***/C/H
(9) 3059 yards/***/E/H

Stoke-by-Nayland G.C.
(01206) 262836
Keepers Lane, Colchester
(18) 6544 yards/***/B/H
(18) 6516 yards/***/B/H

Stowmarket G.C.
(01449) 736473
Lower Road, Onehouse, Stowmarket
(18) 6101 yards/***/B-A/H

Suffolk G. & C.C.
(01284) 706777
St Johns Hill, Bury St Edmunds
(18) 6212 yards/**/C

Thorpeness Golf Hotel
(01728) 452176
Thorpeness, Leiston
(18) 6241 yards/***/B

Ufford Park Hotel & G.C,
(01394) 383836
Yarmouth Road, Ufford,Woodbridge
(18) 6335 yards/***/D

Waldringfield Heath G.C.
(01473) 736768
Newbourne Road, Waldringfield
(18) 6153 yards/**/C

Woodbridge G.C.
(01394) 382038
Bromeswell Heath, Woodbridge
(18) 6314 yards/**/B/H
(9) 2243 yards/**/B/H

Wood Valley G.C.
(01502) 712244
The Common, Beccles
(9) 2781 yards/**/D

NORFOLK

Barnham Broom G.C.
(01603) 759393
Barnham Broom, Norwich
(18) 6603 yards/**/B/H
(18) 6470 yards/**/B/H

Bawburgh G.C.
(01603) 746390
Long Lane, Bawburgh, Norwich
(18) 6066 yards/***/D

Caldecott Hall Golf & Leisure
(01493) 488488
Beccles Road, Great Yarmouth
(18) 6318 yards/**/E

Costessey Park G.C.
(01603) 746333
Costessey Park, Costessey
(18) 6104 yards/**/C

Dereham G.C.
(01362) 695900
Quebec Road, Dereham
(9) 6225 yards/**/C/H

Dunham G.C.
(01328) 701718
Little Dunham, Kings Lynn
(9) 2132 yards/***/D

Dunston Hall G.C.
(01508) 470444
Ipswich Road, Dunston
(9) 6408 yards/***/D

Eagles G.C.
(01553) 827147
School Road, Kings Lynn
(9) 2142 yards/***/E

Eaton G.C.
(01603) 451686
Newmarket Road, Norwich
(18) 6135 yards/**/B

Fakenham G.C.
(01328) 863534
The Racecourse, Fakenham
(9) 5879 yards/**/D

Feltwell G.C.
(01842) 827644
Thor Avenue, Feltwell, Thetford
(9) 6260 yards/**/D

Gorleston G.C.
(01493) 662103
Warren Road, Gorleston
(18) 6400 yards/***/C/H

Great Yarmouth and Caister G.C.
(01493) 728699
Beach House, Caister-on-Sea
(18) 6284 yards/**/B

Hunstanton G.C.
(01485) 532811
Golf Course Road, Old Hunstanton
(18) 6735 yards/***/A/H

Kings Lynn G.C.
(01553) 631654
Castle Rising, Kings Lynn
(18) 6646 yards/**/A/H

Links Country Park Hotel G.C.
(01263) 838383
West Runton, Cromer
(9) 4814 yards/***/C

Mattishall G.C.
(01362) 850464
South Green, Mattishall, Dereham
(9) 6218 yards/***/E

Middleton Hall G. & C.C.
(01553) 841800
Middleton, Kings Lynn
(9) 5570 yards/**/D

Mundesley G.C.
(01263) 720095
Links Road, Mundesley
(9) 5410 yards/***/C

RAF Marham G.C.
(01760) 337261
RAF Marham, Kings Lynn
(9) 5244 yards/**/E

Reymerston G.C.
(01362) 850297
Hingham Road, Reymerston
(18) 6603 yards/**/B

Richmond Park G.C.
(01953) 881803
Saham Road, Watton
(18) 6300 yards/***/C

Royal Cromer G.C.
(01263) 512884
Overstrand Road, Cromer
(18) 6508 yards/***/B/H

Royal Norwich G.C.
(01603) 429928
Drayton High Road, Hellesdon
(18) 6603 yards/**/B/H

Royal West Norfolk G.C.
(01485) 210087
Brancaster, Kings Lynn
(18) 6428 yards/**/A/G/H

Royston Park G.C.
(01366) 382133
Denver, Downham Market
(9) 6292 yards/**/B/G/H

Sheringham G.C.
(01263) 823488
Weybourne Road, Sheringham
(18) 6464 yards/**/B/H

Sprowston Park G.C.
(01603) 410657
Wroxham Road, Sprowston
(18) 5985 yards/***/D/H

Swaffham G.C.
(01760) 721611
Cley Road, Swaffham
(9) 6252 yards/**/C

Thetford G.C.
(01842) 752169
Brandon Road, Thetford
(18) 6879 yards/***/B/H

Wensum Valley G.C.
(01603) 261012
Beech Avenue, Taverham
(18) 6000 yards/**/D
(18) 4862 yards/**/D

Weston Park G.C.
(01603) 872363
Weston Longville, Norwich
(9) 3132 yards/**/C/H

SWYNFORD PADDOCKS HOTEL & RESTAURANT *Photograph courtesy of:* **Swynford Paddocks Hotel & Restaurant**

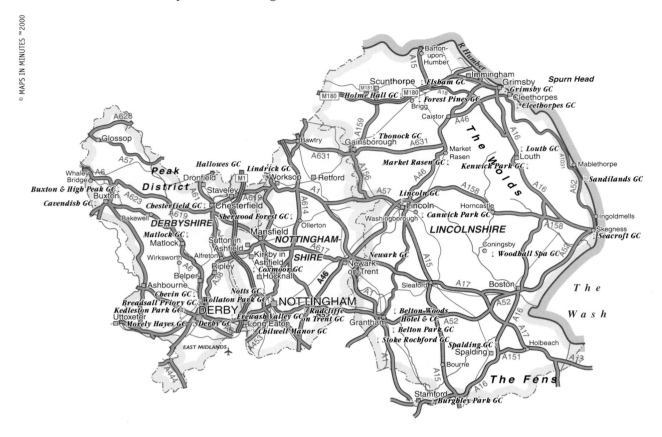

Derby, Nottinghamshire & Lincolnshire Choice Golf

Derbyshire

Not wishing to be unkind, but Derby the town isn't one of Earth's more inspiring places but Derbyshire the county is a different matter altogether. The Peak District is without question one of the most scenic regions in England and commencing only a short distance north of Derby, it covers the greater part of the county. The Pennine Way of course starts in Derbyshire.

Around Derby

As well as being the beginning of all things beautiful, the area just north of Derby is where three of the county's leading golf courses are to be found: Kedleston Park, Breadsall Priory and Chevin. Located approximately four miles from Derby off the A111 (and well signposted) **Kedleston Park** golf course occupies a beautiful situation and is generally rated as the finest course in Derbyshire. Quite lengthy from the back tees, it has a variety of challenging holes. Eyeing the course from across a lake is the impressive Kedleston Hall, historic home of Lord Scarsdale. Lying east of Kedleston is **Morley Hayes**—a challenge to all golfers with some good par 4s.

I'm not sure what the 13th century monks would have made of Breadsall Priory Golf and Country Club, three miles north east of Derby at Morley, but for heathens of the 20th century it provides an ideal setting for one of the most enjoyable games in the Midlands. Golfwise, **Breadsall Priory** has only been on the map since 1976 but the undulating parkland course with its imported Cumberland turf greens has matured rapidly and the second 18 holes admirably complement the plush leisure centre.

Chevin lies slightly further north off the A6 at Duffield. It has an interesting layout; the first ten holes are a steady climb towards a spectacular vantage point after which holes 11 to 18 gently bring you

down to earth (or at least to Duffield!) Another course to recommend in the south of the county and over towards Nottingham is the wooded layout at **Erewash Valley**, noted for its two quarry holes.

If Derby is the chosen resting place then the the Midland Hotel (01332) 345894 is a comfortable hotel and reasonably priced. La Gondola (01332) 332895 is also good. In Belper, Makeney Hall (01332) 842999 is a splendid country house hotel—a perfect place to celebrate one's closing birdie at Chevin. Breadsall Priory (01332) 832235 itself of course offers a most satisfying 19th hole and is ideal for an action packed or more leisurely weekend away. Finally, Kedleston Country House (01332) 559202 is well placed for the excellent 18 holes of Kedleston Park.

The Peak District

Moving up country, the picturesque town of **Matlock** has a fairly short but pleasant course situated north of the town off the Chesterfield road and **Chesterfield's** course at Walton is also well worth a visit. There are also two public courses close to the town centre. A recommendation for a memorable night is Riber Hall (01629) 582795 near Matlock—a first rate restaurant and hotel—and in Matlock itself the New Bath Hotel (01629) 583275 is well worth a visit.

The town of Buxton lies in the heart of the Peak District and is many people's idea of the perfect town. This may have something to do with the fact that some of the finest pubs in England are located round about, but it also helps that there are two excellent golf courses either side of the town—**Buxton and High Peak** and **Cavendish**. Of similar length it is difficult to say which is the better, but in any event both warmly welcome visitors at green fees that should leave a few pennies for celebrating nearby. After a day on the fairways (not to mention an evening in a Buxton pub) a suitable hotel is required. The

Old Hall Hotel (01298) 22841 is a historic hotel just one mile from the Cavendish course. There is also the Lee Wood Hotel (01298) 23002 which overlooks the cricket ground. Having done my bit for the Buxton tourist board another suggestion for this delightful area can be found in Hassop. Hassop Hall (01629) 640488 is a splendid establishment whilst the nearby Riverside Country House Hotel (01629) 814275 offers good food and comfortable rooms.

Other good locals include the Old Bulls Head, Little Hucklow; in Hathersage, the George; and in Beeley, the Devonshire Arms which is near to Chatsworth, and no trip to the area would be complete without visiting this incredible stately home, perhaps England's finest. A similar comment could be made about Fischer's at Baslow Hall (01246) 583259—an excellent restaurant with rooms to match the finest 18 holes in the country.

Nottinghamshire

Moving into Nottinghamshire, the famous **Notts** Golf Club at Hollinwell is featured separately on a later page; however, in addition to this rather splendid 'Nottingham gorse affair' those visiting the county town should strongly consider the merits of **Wollaton Park**, an attractive course set amidst the deer park of a stately home and surprisingly close to the centre of Nottingham. The city's two 18 hole municipal courses are also fairly good. Slightly further afield but well worth noting are the parkland courses at **Chilwell Manor** (A6005) and **Radcliffe on Trent** (A52 east of the town).

Nottingham has no shortage of comfortable modern hotels and the Forte Crest (0870) 4009061 and the Royal (0115) 9369988 are first rate and centrally located. To the north of the city at Arnold, Bestwood Lodge (0115) 9203011 is less stylish but good value. To the south, lovers of the country house scene will delight in Langar Hall (01949) 860559 at Langar (seems to have a golfing ring to it, don't you think?) The best known pub in town is probably the Olde Trip to Jerusalem—said to be the oldest in England. Mansfield is only about 15 minutes drive from Hollinwell, here we find a pleasant guesthouse Tichfield House (01623) 810356.

Two of the county's finest courses lie fairly close to one another near the centre of Nottinghamshire, **Coxmoor** and **Sherwood Forest**. The former is a moorland type course situated just south of Mansfield at Sutton in Ashfield. The Sherwood Forest course is more of a heathland type—well wooded (as one might expect given its name) with much tangling heather. Measuring over 6700 yards it is quite a test too.

Over towards the border with Lincolnshire is the attractive town of Newark with its 12th century castle and cobbled market square. **Newark** Golf Club lies four miles east of the town off the A17. Reasonably flat and quite secluded, the golf is a little less testing than at some of the county's bigger clubs. An attractive place to stay is the Old Rectory, north of Newark in Kirkton. Also in town the Old Kings Arms is a fine pub (01636) 703416.

Before inspecting Lincolnshire, a brief word on **Lindrick**. Although its postal address is in Nottinghamshire the majority of the course lies in South Yorkshire. In any event, it is featured in our Yorkshire chapter. If a night's rest is required 'this side' of the border, then Ye Olde Bell Hotel at Barnby Moor (01777) 705121 is a pleasant coaching inn and the Angel in Blyth is a friendly pub with some accommodation also.

Lincolnshire

Lincolnshire is a large county—bigger now that Humberside has disintegrated and Grimsby, Scunthorpe and Cleethorpes are all back in the fold. So now, by my reckoning there are over forty worthwhile golf courses in the county. **Woodhall Spa** is of course head and shoulders above the rest but although the county as a whole is unlikely to be the venue for many golfing holidays there are certainly a handful of courses well worth a visit.

Lincoln and the South

Lincoln really is an attractive city—a beautiful cathedral, a castle and a wealth of history. The White Hart (01522) 526222 is a noted hotel and there are several fine restaurants. including The Jew's House (01522) 524851, a fascinating building with first rate food. Excellent food and a great pub can be found in the Wig and Mitre (01522) 535190. The award winning D'Isney Place Hotel (01552) 538881 will lure many and disappoint none. Outside the city in Branston, the Moor Lodge Hotel (01522) 791366 is good value. The best golf to be found in **Lincoln** is at Torksey just to the north west of the city. It's a fairly sandy, heathland type course with a lovely selection of trees. **Canwick Park**, on the opposite side of Lincoln is a shorter parkland course, but challenging in its own way.

Woodhall Spa is featured ahead. For those fortunate enough to be able to spend a few days playing its two courses, here are some suggestions. The appropriately named Golf Hotel (01526) 353535 is a popular and convenient place in which to stay, but the Abbey Lodge (01526) 352538, Duns (01526) 352969 and Petwood House (01526) 352411 are also recommended. The Edwardian Dower House (01526) 352588 is also very pleasant. Lincoln of course may be a base and for those not minding a bit of a drive or, alternatively, The George (01780) 755171 at Stamford is quite excellent—a charming atmosphere with a very fine restaurant. Stamford in fact is a delightful town: Burghley is found here, an outstandingly attractive Elizabethan house, whilst **Burghley Park** Golf Club is noted for its greens and its links with Mark James.

The south of the county comprises much rich agricultural land but not too much in the way of golf. **Stoke Rochford** however is a popular parkland course and **Spalding** is worth inspecting particularly at the time of year when the famous bulbs have flourished. An 18 hole course here, and in the south west there is the very established **Belton Park** course and the much newer **De Vere Belton Woods Hotel & Country Club** (01476) 593200 which enjoys a peaceful setting outside Grantham. The hotel itself is very large but is well thought of and it has two 18 hole courses, the Lancaster and Wellington, and as there is a lot of water to be negotiated a few Barnes Wallis type shots may be called for!

North Lincolnshire

Three courses of note towards the north of the county are at **Gainsborough**, **Market Rasen** and Louth. All are very welcoming. Gainsborough is owned by the Ping company and has a classic parkland layout (Thonock), and a great new links style layout (Karston Lakes); Market Rasen is a very good woodland type course while **Louth** has an attractive setting in a local beauty spot, the Hubbards Hills. A second course near Louth, **Kenwick Park**, recently opened and already promises to be one of the region's top courses. The Limes Country House Hotel (01673) 842357 is ideal for Market Rasen, and in Louth, the Priory (01507) 602930 offers a comfortable stop-over. (There are some fine pubs in Louth too—note the Wheatsheaf). The Kenwick Park Hotel (01507) 608806 is handy for the fairways of the same name.

Around Scunthorpe

A real beauty of a course is to be found in Broughton, **Forest Pines**, a real gem. **Elsham** is well thought of (an old haunt of Tony Jacklin's this) and, slightly nearer to Scunthorpe, **Holme Hall** at Bottesford is a championship length parkland course.

The Lincolnshire Coast

Finally over to the Lincolnshire coast, both **Grimsby** and **Cleethorpes** are also worth a game. Both towns are full of character (characters as well) and if you do play at Grimsby don't miss out on the local fish and chips—they're reckoned to be the best in Britain! In Cleethorpes, the Kingsway (01472) 601122 is a seafront hotel to note.

Skegness is a famous resort—perhaps not everyone's cup of tea, but a game here is certainly recommended for those who like their links golf. **Seacroft** is the place: flattish, windy and plenty of sand dunes—a most underrated course. Further up the coast, a less severe challenge is offered at **Sandilands** where the Grange and Links Hotel (01507) 441334 is adjacent to the course.

Woodhall Spa - The Hotchkin Course

Between them, Sunningdale and Walton Heath have seventy two holes, each with an Old and a New course. Many may disagree but if a composite eighteen were created, taking the best eighteen holes from the four courses I still don't think we would see a better (or more challenging) course than the round offered at Woodhall Spa—and I certainly don't view Sunningdale and Walton Heath as anything less than outstanding.

Woodhall Spa Golf Club was founded in 1905. The course itself was originally laid out by Harry Vardon, although substantial alterations were made firstly by Harry Colt and later by Colonel Hotchkin. A great deal has been happening of late. The club became the National Golf Centre of the English Golf Union in 1995. Since then they have built a second course, the Bracken Course, which opened for play in June 1998 and has been rated in the top ten new course developments in the UK by Golf World. The original course, renamed the Hotchkin Course, was recently ranked 29th best course in the world by the US publication Golf Magazine of America and top inland course in England.

As one of the country's greatest (and most beautiful) heathland layouts, Woodhall Spa is extremely popular. Visitors (both individuals and societies) looking for a game must make prior arrangements with the **Booking Office tel: (01526) 352511**, or by **fax: (01526) 351817**, or in writing to **The National Golf Centre, Woodhall Spa, Lincs, LN10 6PU.**

The green fees at Woodhall Spa for 2000 are £50 per round or £90 per day. Reduced rates are available to English Golf Union members (£35 per round, £60 per day) but an EGU card or a letter of introduction providing proof of such membership must be produced.

Glancing at the map, Woodhall Spa looks fairly close to Lincoln. By road the distance is, in fact, at least twenty miles. Those approaching from the cathedral city should take the B1188 towards Sleaford, taking a left fork onto the B1189 towards the village of Martin. At Martin the B1191 road should be picked up and followed to Woodhall Spa, the club being directly off this road. Those travelling from further north will probably need to use a combination of motorways before joining the A15, which links Lincoln to the M180 (junction 4). Those motoring from the south may have to do even more map-reading! The A1 is likely to be a good starting point. It should be left just north of Colsterworth and the B6403 then taken towards Ancaster and RAF Cranwell, joining the A15 just beyond the RAF base. A right fork should be taken towards the hamlet of Ashby de la Launde on the B1191 which takes us to Martin and then to Woodhall Spa.

Often described as the ultimate golfing oasis, Woodhall Spa has all the classic heathland characteristics—sandy subsoil, heather running riot and glorious tree-lined fairways.

The Hotchin course measures a lengthy 6921 yards, par 73 from the championship tees, 6501 yards, par 71 from the men's tees and 5731 yards, par 73 from the ladies' tees. It is arguably most renowned for its vast cavernous bunkers and while it is almost impossible to select individual holes, perhaps those that particularly stand out are the 3rd, and a strong sequence towards the middle of the round, between the 9th and the 14th. The 11th is quite possibly the finest par four in the country and certainly one of the prettiest. A plaque beside the 12th tee records how in March 1982 two members halved the hole in one.

Another feature of Woodhall Spa is the remarkable variety of wildlife which the golfer is likely to come across (especially the more wayward hitter!) One hawkish, but obviously dedicated, individual claimed after hitting a rather poor drive to the 18th that he was 'distracted by the merry gathering of partridges and pheasants to the right of the tee and by the squirrel who was chasing a magpie across the fairway.'

The members are fortunate in having a wonderfully intimate clubhouse. The atmosphere is both friendly and informal and there's an almost Colonial feel about the place—a Raffles in Lincolnshire perhaps? A full complement of catering is offered throughout the week with a variety of very reasonably priced meals.

This is a golf club of excellence. It is sometimes grosly misleading to make comparisons particularly at the top level but make no mistake the golf to be enjoyed at Woodhall Spa as well as the various other facilities are outstanding.

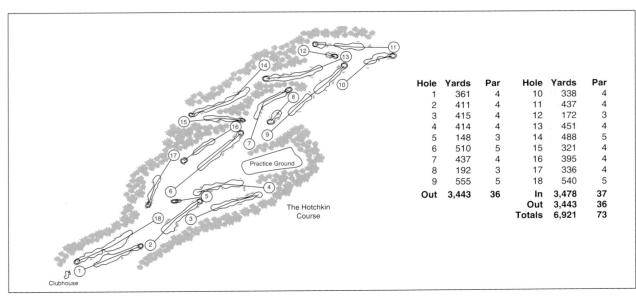

Hole	Yards	Par		Hole	Yards	Par
1	361	4		10	338	4
2	411	4		11	437	4
3	415	4		12	172	3
4	414	4		13	451	4
5	148	3		14	488	5
6	510	5		15	321	4
7	437	4		16	395	4
8	192	3		17	336	4
9	555	5		18	540	5
Out	**3,443**	**36**		**In**	**3,478**	**37**
				Out	**3,443**	**36**
				Totals	**6,921**	**73**

The Hotchkin Course

Clubhouse

Notts (Hollinwell)

The Notts Golf Club was founded in 1887, although the club's first home was, in fact, nearer to Nottingham itself at Bulwell Forest. Apparently the proposed move from Bulwell to Hollinwell which occurred around the turn of the century initially met with considerable opposition. Undeterred, the radicals invited Willie Park Jr to design the new course and by the time John H Taylor had added some finishing touches, not a squeak of discontent was to be heard. Messrs. Park and Taylor had presented the members with a masterpiece.

The gentleman presently looking after the interests of the Notts golfers is the **Secretary, Mr Stuart Goldie.** Visitors seeking a game are advised to contact him some time in advance of intended play. Mr Goldie can be contacted by telephone on **(01623) 753225** while the address for written correspondence is **The Notts Golf Club, Hollinwell, Derby Road, Kirkby-in-Ashfield, Nottinghamshire, NG17 7QR.**

As a general guide, visitors can play between Mondays and Fridays although it should be noted that Friday is often busy, it being Ladies' Day. The first tee is reserved for members between 12.00pm and 1.00pm on Mondays and Tuesdays, and on Wednesdays and Thursdays between 12.00pm and 2.00pm or 11.30am and 1.30pm during the winter months. Societies are welcome with Mondays and Tuesdays being the favoured days. In 2000 the green fees are £45 per round or £65 per day. Another thing visitors might wish to note is the club's popular driving range.

Since the club's move to Hollinwell in 1900 it has had, somewhat remarkably, only five professionals. Brian Waites, probably our best known 'club pro', retired recently after 29 years service. Brian made history in 1983 by becoming the oldest British player to make his debut in the Ryder Cup. Now a very successful member of the Seniors Tour, Waites has played for the Rest Of The World Seniors against the American Seniors in the United States. His successor, **Alasdair Thomas** is already well-known to local golfers having served eight years at the club as Brian's senior assistant. He and his staff may be contacted on **(01623) 753087.**

The course is located to the north west of Notting-ham on the A611. Approaching from either the North or South of England, the M1 is very convenient. The motorway should be left at junction 27 at which point the A608 should be followed until it joins the A611. The club is then two miles away and is signposted off to the right.

From the championship tees, the course is something of a minor monster stretching to a shade over 7000 yards (7030 yards, par 72). Even from the forward tees, it represents a formidable test at 6619 yards. The ladies' course measures 5882 yards, par 75. If Hollinwell is a monster, then it's a pretty one (if there can be such a creature!) with a wealth of heather and gorse lining the fairways, together with some superb oaks and silver birch trees; certainly a splendid setting in which to enjoy a day's golf.

Similar to Woodhall Spa, the 1st at Hollinwell is relatively straight-forward and has been described as 'ideal for the early morning top!'—something to be avoided on the lengthy 2nd, a hole famed for the huge rock which guards the back of the green known as Robin Hood's Chair. Another notable hole on the front nine is the 8th, perhaps not so intimidating from the forward tee, but from the medal tee it requires a very straight and solid drive to carry an attractive lake. Half hidden by trees to the right of the tee is the 'holy well' from which the name Hollinwell derives. Whether its waters will give you divine inspiration to tackle the back nine is debatable but it's worth a look. Actually, a prayer or two, or at least a little luck may be required when the downhill 13th is confronted. One of only three short holes, although short is hardly apt, it was once called 'an absolute terror', having 'trouble everywhere'. The 15th is another very challenging hole and the round ends with a stiff par four which, if achieved, will certainly earn you a drink at the club's comfortable 19th.

Championship golf regularly visits Hollinwell. Both Sandy Lyle and Nick Faldo have triumphed here, Lyle winning the 1975 English Open Stroke Play Championship (an event which returned to Hollinwell in 1992) as a precocious seventeen year old, and Faldo the European Tournament Players Championship of 1982. Arguably the most celebrated event was the 1970 John Player Classic when Christy O'Connor pocketed a cheque for £25,000, at the time a world record first prize—no doubt a few Irish eyes were smiling.

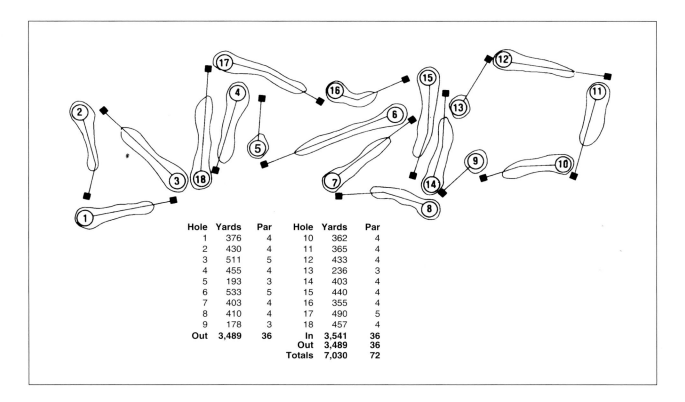

Hole	Yards	Par	Hole	Yards	Par
1	376	4	10	362	4
2	430	4	11	365	4
3	511	5	12	433	4
4	455	4	13	236	3
5	193	3	14	403	4
6	533	5	15	440	4
7	403	4	16	355	4
8	410	4	17	490	5
9	178	3	18	457	4
Out	**3,489**	**36**	**In**	**3,541**	**36**
			Out	**3,489**	**36**
			Totals	**7,030**	**72**

DERBYSHIRE

Alfreton G.C.
(01773) 832070
Wingfield Road, Oakerthorpe
(9) 5074 yards/**/D

Allestree Park G.C.
(01332) 550616
Allestree Hall, Derbyshire
(18) 5749 yards/***/E

Ashbourne G.C.
(01335) 342078
Clifton, Ashbourne
(9) 5359 yards/***/D

Bakewell G.C.
(01629) 812307
Station Road, Bakewell
(9) 5240 yards/**/D

Blue Circle G.C.
(01433) 620317
Cement Works, Hope
(9) 5350 yards/*/B-A/G

Bondhay G. & C.C.
(01909) 723608
Bondhay Lane, Whitwell
(18) 6785 yards/**/C ˜

Breadsall Priory G.& C.C.
(01332) 832235
Moor Road, Morley
(18) 6201 yards/***/B/H
(18) 6028 yards/***/B/H

Burton-on-Trent G.C.
(01283) 544551
Ashby Road East, Burton-On-Trent
(18) 6555 yards/***/B/H/L

Buxton & High Peak G.C.
(01298) 23453
Town End, Buxton
(18) 5954 yards/***/B

Carsington Water
(01629) 85650
Carsington, Wirksworth
(9) 6000 yards/***/F

Cavendish G.C.
(01298) 23494
Gadley Lane, Buxton
(18) 5833 yards/***/B/H

Chapel-en-le-Frith G.C.
(01298) 812118
Manchester Road, Stockport
(18) 6119 yards/***/B

Chesterfield G.C.
(01246) 279256
Walton, Chesterfield
(18) 6326 yards/**/B/H

Chesterfield Municipal G.C.
(01246) 273887
Crow Lane, Chesterfield
(9) 6013 yards/***/E

Chevin G.C.
(01332) 841864
Golf Lane, Duffield
(18) 6057 yards/**/B

Derby G.C.
(01332) 766323
Sinfin, Derby
(18) 6153 yards/***/F

Erewash Valley G.C.
(0115) 932 4667
Stanton-by-Dale, Ilkeston
(18) 6492 yards/**/B/H

Glossop & District G.C.
(01457) 865247
Sheffield Road, Glossop
(18) 5800 yards/***/C

Grassmoor Golf Centre
(01246) 856044
North Wingfield Road, Grassmoor
(18) 5800 yards/***/E

Hallowes G.C.
(01246) 413734
Hallowes Lane, Dronfield
(18) 6342 yards/**/F

Horsley Lodge G.C.
(01332) 780838
Smalley Mill Road, Horsley
(18) 6434 yards/***/C/H

Ilkeston G.C.
(0115) 930 4550
West End Drive, Ilkeston
(9) 4116 yards/***/E

Kedleston Park G.C.
(01332) 840035
Kedleston, Quarndon, Derby
(18) 6600 yards/***/B/H

Matlock G.C.
(01629) 582191
Chesterfield Road, Matlock
(18) 5800 yards/**/B

Maywood G.C.
(0115) 939 2306
Rushy Lane, Risely
(18) 6424 yards/**/C

Mickleover G.C.
(01332) 518662
Uttoxeter Road, Mickleover
(18) 5708 yards/***/B/H

Morley Hayes G.C.
(01332) 780480
Main Road, Morley
(18) 6800 yards/***/C

New Mills G.C.
(01663) 743485
Shaw Marsh, New Mills
(9) 5633 yards/***/F/G

Ormonde Fields G.& C.C.
(01773) 570043
Nottingham Road, Codnor, Ripley
(18) 6000 yards/***/F

Pastures G.C.
(01332) 521074
Pastures Hospital, Mickleover
(9) 5005 yards/*/F

Renishaw Park G.C.
(01246) 432044 or 435484
Mill Lane, Renishaw
(18) 6262 yards/(Thu, Sat, Sun)/F

Shirland G.& C.C.
(01773) 834935
Lower Delves, Shirland
(18) 6072 yards/**/C

Sickleholme G.C.
(01433) 651306
Saltergate Lane, Bamford
(18) 6064 yards/***(Wed am)/B

Sinfin G.C.
(01332) 766462
Wilmore Road, Sinfin
(18) 6163 yards/***/E

Stanedge G.C.
(01246) 566156
Walton Hay Farm, Chesterfield
(9) 4867 yards/**(pm)/C

Tapton Park G.C.
(01246) 273887
Murray House, Tapton
(18) 6010 yards/***/F

NOTTINGHAMSHIRE

Beeston Fields G.C.
(0115) 925 7062
Beeston, Nottingham
(18) 6400 yards/***/B/H

Bramcote Hills G.C.
(0115) 928 1880
Thoresby Road, Bramcote
(18) 1500 yards/***/E

Bulwell Forest G.C.
(0115) 977 0576
Hucknall Road, Bulwell
(18) 5746 yards/***/E

Chilwell Manor G.C.
(0115) 925 8958
Meadow Lane, Chilwell
(18) 6379 yards/**/C/H
(18) 5438 yards/**/C/H

College Pines G.C.
(01909) 501431
College Drive, Worksop
(18) 6663 yards/***/D

Cotgrave Place G.& C.C.
(0115) 933 3344
Stragglethorpe, Radcliffe on Trent
(27) 6560 yards/***/C

Coxmoor G.C.
(01623) 557359
Coxmoor Road, Sutton-in-Ashfield
(18) 6501 yards/**/B/H

Edwalton Municipal G.C.
(0115) 923 4775
Wellin Lane, Edwalton
(9)3360 yards/***/E

Kilton Forest G.C.
(01909) 472488
Blyth Road, Worksop
(18) 6600 yards/***(Sun)/E

Leen Valley G.C.
(0115) 9642037
Wigwarm Lane, Hucknall
(18) 6233 yards/***/E

Lindrick G.C.
(01909) 475282
Lindrick Common, Worksop
(18) 6606 yards/***(winter)/A/H

Mansfield Woodhouse G.C.
(01623) 23521
Leeming Lane, Mansfield Woodhouse
(9) 2446 yards/***/E

Mapperley G.C.
(0115) 926 5611
Mapperley, Nottingham
(18) 6224 yards/***/D/H

Newark G.C.
(01636) 626241
Coddington, Newark
(18) 6421 yards/***/B/H

Nottingham City G.C.
(0115) 927 6916
Bulwell, Nottingham
(18) 6218 yards/**/E

Notts G.C.
(01623) 753225
Hollinwell, Kirkby-in-Ashfield
(18) 7020 yards/**/F/H

Oakmere Park G.C.
(0115) 965 3545
Oaks Lane, Oxton
(18) 6617 yards/***/D
(9) 3495 yards/***/E

Radcliffe-on-Trent G.C.
(0115) 933 3000
Cropwell Road, Radcliffe-on-Trent
(18) 6381 yards/***/B/H

Ramsdale Golf Centre
(0115) 965 5600
Oxton Road, Calverton
(18) 6546 yards/***/D

Retford G.C.
(01777) 703733
Ordsall, Retford
(9) 6301 yards/**/C

Ruddington Grange G.C.
(0115) 921 1951
Wilford Road, Ruddington
(18) 6500 yards/**/D/H

Rufford Park G.C.
(01623) 825253
Rufford Lane, Newark
(18) 5953 yards/***/D
(9) 868 yards/***/E

Rushcliffe G.C.
(01509) 852959
Stocking Lane, East Leake
(18) 6090 yards/***/B

Serlby Park G.C.
(01777) 818268
Serlby
(9) 5325 yards/*/F/G

Sherwood Forest G.C.
(01623) 26689
Eakring Road, Mansfield
(18) 6714 yards/**/F/H

Southwell G.C.
(01636) 816501
Southwell Racecourse, Rolleston
(9) 5500 yards/***/D

Springwater G.C.
(0115) 965 4946
Moor Lane, Calverton
(9) 3203 yards/***/D

Stanton on the Wolds G.C.
(0115) 937 4885
Stanton Lane, Keyworth
(18) 6437 yards/**/B/H

Trent Lock Golf Centre
(0115) 9464398
Lock Lane, Sawley
(18) 6211/***/E

Wollaton Park G.C.
(0115) 978 7574
Wollaton Park, Nottingham
(18) 6494 yards/***/F

Worksop G.C.
(01909) 477731
Windmill Lane, Worksop
(18) 6651 yards/**/C

LINCOLNSHIRE

Ashby Decoy
(01724) 866561
Burringham Road, Scunthorpe
(18) 6281 yards/*(Sun, Tue)/D

Belton Park G.C.
(01476) 567399
Belton Lane, Grantham
(9) 6412 yards/**/B/H
(9) 6109 yards/**/B/H
(9) 5857 yards/**/B/H

Belton Woods Hotel & C.C.
(01476) 593200
(18) 7021 yards/***/B/H
(18) 6875 yards/***/B/H
(9) 1184 yards/***/B/H

Blankney G.C.
(01526) 320263
Blankney, Lincoln
(18) 6402 yards/***/C/H

Boston G.C.
(01205) 350589
Horncastle Road, Boston
(18) 6483 yards/***/C/H

Burghley Park G.C.
(01780) 762100
St Martins, Stamford
(18) 6236 yards/**/C/H/L

Canwick Park G.C.
(01522) 522166
Washingborough Road, Lincoln
(18) 6257 yards/**/D

Carholme G.C.
(01522) 523725
Carholme Road, Lincoln
(18) 6114 yards/**/F

Cleethorpes G.C.
(01472) 812059
Kings Road, Cleethorpes
(18) 6015 yards/***/C

Elsham G.C.
(01652) 680291
Barton Road, Elsham
(18) 6411 yards/**/C/H

Forest Pines G.C.
(01652) 650756
Brigg, Lincs
(18) 6882 yards/***/A

Gainsborough G.C.
(01427) 613088
Thonock, Gainsborough
(18) 6620 yards/**/B/H

Gedney Hill G.C.
(01406) 330922
West Drove, Gedney Hill
(18) 5450 yards/**/E

Grimsby G.C.
(01472) 342630
Littlecoates Road, Grimsby
(18) 6058 yards/***/C/H

Holme Hall G.C.
(01724) 862078
Bottesford Road, Scunthorpe
(18) 6475 yards/**/C/H

Horncastle G.C.
(01507) 526800
West Ashby, Horncastle
(18) 5782 yards/***/D

Immingham G.C.
(01469) 575298
Immingham, Grimsby
(18) 6161 yards/**/D

Kenwick Park G.C.
(01507) 607161
Kenwick Hall, Louth
(18) 6815 yards/***/B/L

Kingsway G.C.
(01724) 840945
Kingsway, Scunthorpe
(9) 1915 yards/***/E

Kirton Holme G.C.
(01205) 290669
Holme Road, Kirton Holme
(9) 2884 yards/***/E

Lincoln G.C.
(01427) 718721
Torksey, Lincoln
(18) 6438 yards/**/C/H

Louth G.C.
(01507) 602554
Crowtree Lane, Louth
(18) 6477 yards/***/C

Manor G.C.
(01472) 873468
Laleby Manor, Grimsby
(9) 3127 yards/***/E

Market Rasen G.C.
(01673) 842319
Legsby Road, Market Rasen
(18) 6043 yards/**/C/H/L

Millfield G.C.
(01427) 718255
Laughterton, Lincoln
(18) 5583 yards/***/E
(18) 4300 yards/***/E

Normanby Hall G.C.
(01724) 720226
Normanby Park, Scunthorpe
(18) 6548 yards/***/D

North Shore G.C.
(01754) 763298
North Shore Road, Skegness
(18) 6134 yards/***/F/H

RAF Waddington G.C.
(01552) 720271
Waddington, Lincoln
(18) 5223 yards/***/F

Sandilands G.C.
(01507) 441432
Sea Lane, Sandilands
(18) 5995 yards/***/D

Scunthorpe G.C.
(01724) 866561
Burringham Road, Scunthorpe
(18) 6281 yards/**/C/H/M

Seacroft G.C.
(01754) 763020
Drummond Road, Seacroft
(18) 6501 yards/***/B/H

Sleaford G.C.
(01529) 488273
Willoughby Road, South Rauceby
(18) 6443 yards/**/B/H

South Kyme G.C.
(01526) 861113
Skinners Lane, South Kyme
(18) 6597 yards/***/D

Spalding G.C.
(01775) 680234
Surfleet, Spalding
(18) 6478 yards/***/F/H

Stoke Rochford G.C.
(01476) 530275
Great North Road, Grantham
(18) 6251 yards/***/B-A/H

Sudbrook Moor G.C.
(01400) 250796
Charity Lane, Grantham
(9) 4566 yards/***/E

Sutton Bridge G.C.
(01406) 350323
New Road, Sutton Bridge, Spalding
(9) 5804 yards/**/C/H

Tetny G.C.
(01472) 211644 or 811344
Station Road, Cleethorpes
(18) 6100 yards/***/D

Toft Hotel & G.C.
(01778) 590614
Toft, Courne
(18) 6486 yards/***/D

Woodhall Spa G.C.
(01526) 352511
The Broadway, Woodhall Spa
(18) 6921 yards/***/A/H(20)
(18) 7000 yards/***/B-A

Woodthorpe Hall G.C.
(01507) 450294
Woodthorpe, Alford
(18) 5222 yards/***/E

FOREST PINES GOLF CLUB *Photograph courtesy of:* **Forest Pines Golf Club**

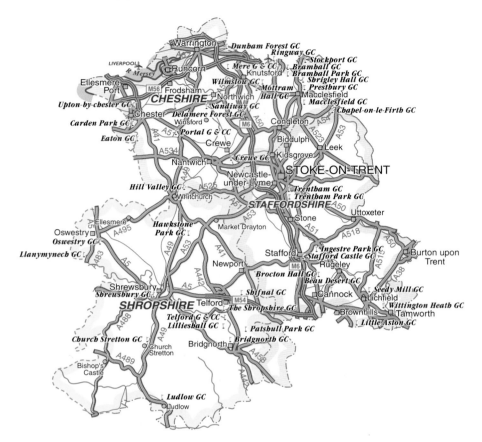

© MAPS IN MINUTES ™ 2000

Staffs, Shropshire & Cheshire Choice Golf

Staffordshire, Shropshire and Cheshire: three essentially rural counties. Staffordshire shares a boundary with the Midlands and Cheshire has two rather ill defined borders with the industrial areas around Manchester and Liverpool. As for Shropshire, it enjoys a splendid peace, broken only perhaps by the mooing of cows and the cries of Fore! from the county's many lush fairways.

Each of the three has a great deal to offer the visiting golfer: in Staffordshire, Beau Desert and Whittington Heath are two of the best (and prettiest) courses in the Midlands; Cheshire offers Carden Park, Tytherington, Mere, Portal and some heathland gems (we have described Hoylake and the Wirral courses in the 'Lancashire' section) while Shropshire, in addition to possessing the likes of Hawkstone Park and Patshull Park can boast at having produced two US Masters champions—both Sandy Lyle and Ian Woosnam who were bred if not born in the county.

South Staffordshire

Making a start in the south of the county, **Whittington Heath** and **Beau Desert** have already been mentioned. The former, located near Lichfield off the A51 was known until recently as Whittington Barracks. As its new name implies, it is a heathland type course with fine views towards the three spires of Lichfield Cathedral—quite possibly the county's toughest challenge. Beau Desert Golf Club near Hazel Slade occupies an unlikely setting in the middle of Cannock Chase. Surrounded by fir trees and spruces it also lives up to its name and is quite a haven both for golfers and for wildlife.

After a relaxing day on the golf course, some thoughts for a suitable 19th hole are in order. In Lichfield the Little Barrow Hotel (01543) 414500 is a comfortable hotel for a night's stay and Thrales (01543) 255091 is a particularly good restaurant. The George Hotel

(01543) 414822, an old coaching inn, is also recommended. (Note also the new 18 hole pay-and-play course in Lichfield, the charmingly named **Seedy Mill**.) After a round at Beau Desert, Rugeley may be the place to head for. Here the Cedar Tree Hotel (01889) 584241 is welcoming but if a restaurant is sought then nearby Armitage offers the Old Farmhouse (01543) 490353. On the other side of Lichfield, in Tamworth, the Castle Hotel (01827) 57181 is recommended.

Stafford

Stafford, the county town, is pretty much in the middle of things. Once again a pair of 18 hole courses to note here: to the south of Stafford is **Brocton Hall** and to the north east, set in the grounds of the former home of the Earl of Shrewsbury is **Ingestre Park**. Both offer a very relaxing game. There is also an enjoyable 9 holer at **Stafford Castle**. If a bed is needed then the De Vere Tillington Hall (01785) 253531 in Stafford is pleasant and, although a bit of a drive away, Rolleston on Dove offers the engaging Brookhouse Hotel (01283) 814188, a splendidly converted William and Mary building. Those who prefer Georgian architecture may care to consider Dovecliffe Hall (01283) 531818, a delightful restaurant with rooms.

Stoke

From the heart of Cannock Chase to the heart of the Potteries, there are a number of courses in and around Stoke-on-Trent. **Trentham** and **Trentham Park**, near neighbours to the south of the city, are both well worth a visit. Each is well wooded and there are many delightful views. In Stoke, the North Stafford (01782) 744477, the Stakis (01782) 202361 and the Moat House (01782) 609988 are all large but comfortable hotels, while at Basford, Haydon House (01782) 711311 is more intimate but equally good and worthy of note. However, as the recommended courses are south of the town Stone may be the most convenient place to spend a night. The Stone House (01785)

815531 is particularly comfortable. East of Stoke, the Old Beams (01538) 308254 in Waterhouses is an excellent restaurant with some delightful bedrooms, while in nearby Cauldon the Yew Tree is a superb hostelry. Non golfers and golfers alike will delight in the Wedgwood Visitors Centre which is well worth a visit.

Central Shropshire

Moving into Shropshire, many will wish to head straight for **Hawkstone Park** (01939) 200611 and its fine hotel. Hawkstone is featured ahead but Shropshire has a lot more than Hawkstone Park on the menu. **Patshull Park** (01902) 700100 makes a marvellous starter, especially considering its closeness to the Midlands—an ideal retreat in fact. As at Hawkstone, golf is played amid very peaceful and picturesque surroundings and overnight accommodation is immediately at hand. The delightful setting of Patshull Park owes much to the fact that the land was originally landscaped by 'Capability' Brown.

Shrewsbury is a pleasant county town with many charming half-timbered buildings. **Shrewsbury** Golf Club is situated about five miles from the town centre off the A49. It is an interesting course with a railway track running through the middle. The Prince Rupert Hotel (01743) 499955 in Shrewsbury is good value for an overnight stay and the oak beams and sloping floors add to the character. Fieldside Hotel (01743) 353143 has no pretensions to grandeur but is extremely comfortable.

The largest town in Shropshire is Telford. It's a strange mixture of the old and the new: a modern centre yet surrounded by a considerable amount of history—Brunel's famous Ironbridge is here. The popular **Telford Hotel** Golf and Country Club (01952) 429977is situated near to the Ironbridge Gorge, high above it in fact, and is easily accessible from the M54 (junction 4 or 5). Full leisure facilities are offered at the hotel, whilst here don't miss **The Shropshire**, Barton Hawtree's fine 27 hole layout at Muxton. Further south of Telford,

towards Bridgnorth, **Lilleshall Hall** offers a very pleasant round with two nicely contrasting nines. The Hundred House Hotel (01952) 730353 is a charming Georgian inn with a first rate restaurant—an excellent choice.

To the east of Telford, **Shifnal** Golf Club is set in a glorious park and an old manor house serves as an impressive clubhouse. The Park House Hotel (01952) 460128 in Shifnal is an excellent place for a stopover and the hotel's restaurant, the Idsall Rooms is particularly good.

Southern Shropshire

Travelling a little further down the A49 into southern Shropshire, **Church Stretton**, set amidst the Long Mynd Hills is well worth a visit. Not the longest course in Britain but one that offers quite outstanding views. Mynd House (01694) 722212 is an exceptionally welcoming establishment to head for but the Belvedere Guest House (01694) 722232 can also be recommended and those needing to quench their thirst might note the Royal Oak in Cardington (some accommodation also).

To the east, **Bridgnorth** is one of the oldest and longest courses in the county (note the distinguished Haywain Restaurant (01746) 780404 at Hampton Loade) and in the far south is historic **Ludlow**. It's now a fairly quiet market town but in former times was the capital of the West Marches. The golf course takes you around the town's racecourse—or is it vice versa?—Anyway, it's an interesting challenge and if a round of golf is being combined with a weekend's racing, the Feathers (01584) 875261 in Ludlow provides an ideal place in which to relax—note the outstanding Jacobean facade. In Brimfield, near Ludlow, you might stop at the Roebuck (01584) 711230—the adjoining restaurant, Poppies (01584) 711230 is outstanding. Not too great a distance from Ludlow is Hopton Wafers where the Crown offers some first rate cooking and a fine drop of ale. A final thought, consider Dinham Hall (01584) 876464 a superb hotel.

CARDEN PARK GOLF CLUB *Photograph courtesy of:* **Carden Park**

West and North Shropshire

Heading west and north of Shrewsbury three courses are recommended. **Oswestry** is one clearly to seek out—if only because this is where Ian Woosnam relaxes. Note the popular Wynnstay Hotel (01691) 655261 in town. Close to the Welsh border, **Llanymynech** (Woosie's first course) lies on high ground and is very scenic. On the 4th hole you stand on the tee in Wales and drive into England (always good for the ego). After a game here, a visit to the Bradford Arms (01691) 830582 in Llanymynech is essential as it boasts a particularly fine restaurant. Still high in the hills another 'Llany', not Wadkins but Blodwel: Llanyblodwel is where excellent refreshment can be found—the Horseshoe, with its spectacular setting. The third recommendation, **Hill Valley** near Whitchurch, brings us down to earth. We may get wet as well with water affecting many holes on this fairly new American-style course. As well as the water there are many other challenges and it's well worth inspecting. Terrick Hall Hotel (01948) 663031 is practically adjacent to the course and in Whitchurch itself there is Dearnford Hall (01948) 662319, another fine hotel.

Around Chester

Starting our tour of Cheshire in the far west, Chester the county town demands inspection—a fascinating Roman city with all manner of attractions. Two of the best places to swing a club are at Upton, namely the delightful **Upton-by-Chester** Golf Club and at **Eaton**, a parkland course to the south of the city. Just 15 minutes drive from Chester is the hugely impressive **Carden Park** (01829) 73100. The hotel offers first class facilities and is thoroughly recommended; we feature it's two championship golf courses on a later page.

If staying in Chester, the best hotel is the Chester Grosvenor (01244) 324024 (note the superb restaurant). Hoole Hall Hotel (01244) 350011 on the Warrington Road is less grand but is good. An interesting alternative though is the Blossoms Hotel (01244) 323186. Crabwall Manor (01244) 851666 is also outstanding in every way.

South east of Chester near Tarporley much has been happening. The **Portal** Golf and Country Club comprises 45 holes and, along with Hawkstone Park and Carden Park is explored separately in this chapter. Strongly recommended for golfers visiting Portal are the Wild Boar at Beeston (01829) 260305 a 17th century part-timbered house and the Swan Hotel in Tarporley (01829) 733838.

Cheshire: The Sand Belt

Cheshire could be described as the 'Surrey of the North'. In many parts it's decidedly affluent, with a great band of commuter towns lining its northern fringes. There's also a sand belt where heathland golf is found—no Sunningdale here perhaps but **Delamere Forest** and **Sandiway** would certainly be at home in either Surrey or Berkshire. Delamere is particularly good. A creation of Herbert Fowler, who also designed Walton Heath and The Berkshire, it's a marvellous heather and gorse type course—some superb trees also. The words 'temporary green' do not exist at Delamere Forest (something winter golfers might wish to bear in mind) nor apparently does the word 'par'—the old fashioned term 'bogey' being preferred as a more realistic yardstick of a hole's difficulty—at least for the non-pro.

There are a number of first class places in which to stay in the area but pride of place must go to Rookery Hall (01270) 610016 in Worleston near Nantwich. Part Georgian, part Victorian, it's a wonderful hotel with a restaurant to match. Nearer to Sandiway in Hartford, Hartford Hall (01606) 75711 is very pleasant, and in Sandiway itself Nunsmere Hall (01606) 889100 is very convenient and comfortable. In Acton Bridge the Rheingold Riverside Inn (01606) 852310 offers some really stylish food. Finally, a handy pub for Delamere is the Ring of Bells at Overton.

Mere is certainly one of the leading courses in Cheshire. Although fairly close to Sandiway and Delamere, Mere is a classic parkland course, and a beautiful one too with a testing closing stretch including the spectacular par five 18th, where a new green has been built on the edge of a small lake. After eagling the 18th at Mere the perfect place for celebration is in Lower Peeover at the Bells of Peeover (01565) 722269 (pronounced 'Peever' I'm assured). Cottons Hotel (01565) 650333 has a good local reputation and is also well placed.

South Manchester

Towards the north of the region, **Ringway** Golf Club is a good parkland challenge, but our final visit takes us to the end of a very leafy lane in Altrincham—the impressive **Dunham Forest Golf and Country Club**. Only two miles from the M56 (junction 7) and not all that far from the whirl of Manchester it nonetheless delights in an incredibly tranquil setting. The beautifully mature tree-lined fairways are a sheer delight to play on and if you cannot enjoy your golf here, well, let's just say you've got problems! The Quality Hotel (0161) 928 7121 is a suitably relaxed establishment in which to ponder on your game.

The Wilmslow Area

Heading east, the area around Wilmslow is fairly thick with clubs. **Wilmslow** itself and **Prestbury** have two of the better courses. For many years the former was the venue of the Greater Manchester Open. Both are extremely well kept. The popular Stanneylands Hotel (01625) 525225 at Wilmslow is convenient for both courses although again there are many fine hotels nearby to choose from, one strong recommendation being **Mottram Hall** (01625) 828135 at Mottram St Andrews—quite magnificent. The hotel now boasts a challenging 18 hole course, designed in fine style by Dave Thomas.

Stockport and Points South

Stockport provides a dramatic contrast to rural Cheshire—not the prettiest of places perhaps but full of character. Offerton is where **Stockport** Golf Club is found. It's a good test and well worth visiting; so for that matter are the two courses at Bramhall, **Bramhall** and **Bramhall Park**. **Macclesfield's** course offers some extensive views and between Macclesfield and Prestbury is the fairly new, but highly acclaimed **Tytherington** Club. **Shrigley Hall** (01625) 575757 in Pott Shrigley, again near to both Prestbury and Macclesfield, has another newish golf course in a wonderful setting with views over the Cheshire Plain. Well situated for these courses is the Alderley Edge Hotel (01625) 583033 which offers some excellent food as well as first class accommodation. Over to the far east of Cheshire, close to the Derbyshire border and the splendid Peak District is **Chapel-en-le-Frith**. A really friendly club, this and some enjoyable golf too.

HAWKSTONE PARK 1ST FAIRWAY *Photograph courtesy of:* **Hawkstone Park**

Carden Park

As you meander along the entrance drive and see the herd of deer grazing on the estate you will be struck by the wonderful views of the surrounding Cheshire countryside. Then as you look out across the lake on the 17th hole of the Nicklaus course you will get views of a truly outstanding 19th hole—the luxurious Carden Park Hotel.

Carden Park, a 750 acre estate that dates back to the 17th century, is situated in the heart of Cheshire. Having recently undergone a major transformation this is surely destined to become one of Europe's leading golf resorts.

With the help and guidance of Jack Nicklaus and Golden Bear International, a comprehensive range of quality golf facilities has been created. This includes two 18 hole courses—the **Cheshire** Course and the new **Nicklaus** Course, designed by Jack and his son Steve. There is also the par 3 **Azalea** Course, a magnificent clubhouse and Europe's first Jack Nicklaus Residential Golf School.

The 6850 yards, par 72 Cheshire Course, which opened in 1993, is a stern but fair test of golf from the back tees and has played host to several championships, including the Cheshire and North Wales Open.

In 1996, in consultation with Nicklaus Design, the layout was revised. Well bunkered and heavily wooded, the Cheshire course is remarkably scenic and, being quite undulating, provides commanding views - Cheshire at its finest with the Welsh hills providing an attractive backdrop. The best sequence of holes on the front nine may be the 3rd to the 5th, the most dramatic vista is from the 9th tee, while the most interesting run of holes on the back nine begins at the 12th.

However, the jewel in the crown at Carden is the 7070 yards, par 72 Nicklaus Course, the first co-design between Jack and his son Steve. Of all Jack's creations in Europe, this in undoubtedly one of his finest. It is also one of his most understated in that the mounding is very subtle and the bunkering is more of a traditional style. There are many outstanding holes, including the 5th, 6th and 7th on the front nine, and, on the back nine, the 15th, 17th and 18th.

In addition to this, the Jack Nicklaus Residential Golf School caters for the needs of golfers at all skill levels. The philosophy, developed by Jack and his personal coach Jim Flick, is simply to help golfers play to their full potential, consistently, so that they can derive a lot more pleasure on the golf course. Courses at the school range from one to three days, and most include tuition and time for playing golf each day.

Adjacent to the first tees of the Nicklaus and Cheshire courses is the spacious two-storey clubhouse, which provides a range of excellent facilities. The ground floor supplies well appointed locker rooms with adjoining relaxation areas and an extensive golf shop. On the first floor you will find the club bar and lounge, dining room and private suites, all with verandas offering stunning views over the golf courses.

The luxurious hotel with its superb selection of 192 bedrooms and suites provides an excellent complement to the golf. There are a number of places to eat and the visitor can also enjoy a superbly equipped health spa and a host of other leisure activities. The estate even boasts its own vineyard!

Whatever your reason for visiting Carden Park, be it business or pleasure, you will quickly realise that you have arrived at a very special place.

De Vere Carden Park Hotel, Golf Resort & Spa, Carden, Broxton, Nr Chester CH3 9D
www.cardenpark.co.uk

Executive Head Professional
David Llewelyn (01829) 731600

Green Fees	£40 per round, Cheshire Course
	£60 per round, Nicklaus Course
Restrictions	Must have a current handicap certificate. Non metal spikes only.

Directions
Junction 20 off the M6 towards Chester, then turn off on to the A41. Follow the A41 till you reach the Broxton roundabout, head towards Wrexham and after 2 miles you will find Carden Park on your left.

Portal

Americans who are apt to drool at English country houses, their grounds and gardens, should head for Tarporley in Cheshire; and English golfers who believe that the only good courses being built nowadays are 'American style' designs should go with them. Portal Hall in Tarporley is the kind of dwelling that would grace the front cover of Country Life magazine: the house is splendid and the gardens resplendent. Adjacent to Portal Hall is the Portal Golf and Country Club and possibly the finest new golf course in the north of England.

Many of the courses constructed in Britain during the last decade tend to be either very average (due usually to the poor quality of the site or terrain) or very American— and, as somebody once remarked, there's nothing wrong with American golf courses . . . in America! The reality is that Britain doesn't have America's climate and unless there is a vast amount of money behind a project to build such a course then achieving and maintaining the standard of conditioning required is unlikely to happen. (Interestingly, how many attempts to build a Scottish style golf links in North America have succeeded?) Portal is different and very special.

Like many golf clubs, it owes its existence to the dream and ambition of one man. John Lilley was the guiding force behind the creation of Portal and while he lived to see its opening (June 1991) he is no longer with us to enjoy its success. Portal is his gift to golf. The present owners, under the enthusiastic direction of Chairman, Michael Taylor are determined to enhance this legacy. The club has recently acquired and now manages the former Oaklands Golf and Country Club which is situated just half a mile away. Thus Portal now comprises the original 18 hole Portal Course, now called the **Portal Championship** course and the former Oaklands course which has been renamed **Portal Premier**. A further nine hole course, the **Arderne**, is located close to the Portal Championship layout, so providing the complex with a total of 45 holes.

A large indoor golf academy beside the Arderne course offers driving bays, chipping lanes, contoured putting greens and a unique practice bunker facility, along with the latest computerised teaching equipment. The Championship course also has an outdoor driving range and a new all-weather synthetic putting green. Plans are in hand to add a 50-bedroom facility and a leisure centre.

Individual visitors and corporate and society visitors who wish to play at the Portal Championship Course and Portal Premier, can make bookings by contacting the **Director of Golf**, **David Wills** on **(01829) 733933** or **fax (01829) 733928**. The green fees in 2000 are £45 per round (7 days a week) for the Portal Championship course with £30 per round on weekdays and £35 at weekends on the Portal Premier course.

Portal Championship Course was designed by British architect Donald Steel. Steel considers it to be one of his best and he is justifiably very proud of his work. As you may have gathered from the preceding comments, he has not tried to fashion an American-style course amidst this very natural and very English parkland setting. There are no Nicklaus-style mounds at Portal, and Steel has no Trent Jones-like obsession with long water carries. There are, however, plenty of sweeping elevational changes—some are dramatic as at the 4th, 16th and 17th and some more subtle, as at the 2nd, 3rd, and 6ththere is also a huge variety of mature trees, as well as lakes and ponds, but they are not designed to terrify. Indeed the purpose behind their placement is as much visual as strategic.

The visual pleasure aspect is of course where Portal gains a significant advantage over most new designs. There are many strong and challenging holes—the course measures well over 7000 yards from the championship tees but it is the stunning beauty of two in particular, the par three 14th and par five 3rd that are likely to leave the most lasting impression after a visit to Portal. Stand on the stage-like green at the short 14th and you feel surrounded by cascading ponds, stately trees and rhododendron bushes—golf landscaping at its best. Stand on the tee at the long 3rd with its rockery banks of heather and shock of flowers and your mind may wander from golf to horticulture. Dangerous, as there are 600 yards of fairway and hazards to negotiate!

The 19th hole is the final treat at Portal—the clubhouse is an extraordinary circular building; its unusual design apparently reflects the turrets of nearby Beeston and Peckforton castles. In character with the whole set-up the facilities inside are first class and the atmosphere is relaxed and informal.

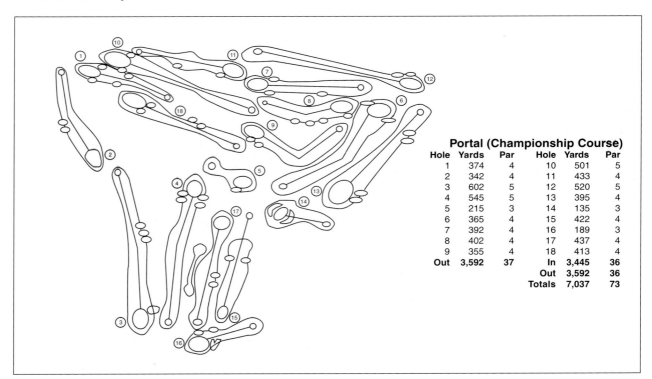

Portal (Championship Course)

Hole	Yards	Par	Hole	Yards	Par
1	374	4	10	501	5
2	342	4	11	433	4
3	602	5	12	520	5
4	545	5	13	395	4
5	215	3	14	135	3
6	365	4	15	422	4
7	392	4	16	189	3
8	402	4	17	437	4
9	355	4	18	413	4
Out	**3,592**	**37**	**In**	**3,445**	**36**
			Out	**3,592**	**36**
			Totals	**7,037**	**73**

The Donald Steel Championship Course, acclaimed as "Golf Course of the Year" by Following the Fairways (1995) is now established as one of Northern Europe's finest courses. Steel has worked on many projects, both in this country and overseas, but he regards the layout at Portal as perhaps his most accomplished work.

Portal exudes quality; a strikingly modern, yet very elegant clubhouse and a truly first rate golf course set in the scenic heartland of Cheshire with breathtaking panoramic views. The Championship course offers 18 holes from prairie-like open fairways to elegant wooded greens. In addition there is the 9 hole Arderne Course (a test for the most skilful) the largest indoor golf academy in the UK, with golf shows, clinics and video facilities, an outdoor driving range and an extensive all-weather putting green.

The course is superbly landscaped and presented with countless flower beds, banks of heather and rockeries around trees and greens. The lakes and ponds are not merely water hazards - they are works of art with a special feature being the dramatic cascading waterfall and rock garden forming the backdrop of the 18th hole.

There are many strong and challenging holes. The course measures over 7000 yards from the Championship tees but it is the stunning beauty of two in particular—the par three 14th and par five 3rd—that are likely to leave the most lasting impression after a visit to Portal.

The 19th hole is the final treat. The clubhouse is an extraordinary circular building, its unusual design reflecting the turrets of nearby Beeston and Peckforton castles. The facilities are excellent and the atmosphere relaxed and informal. The clubhouse offers well appointed bar and dining areas with private visitors and banqueting rooms available providing first class catering and hospitality for both small and large groups.

Portal has, over the years, established a reputation for having the highest standard of presentation and service in the North West of England. A team of experienced professionals and staff can organise your day from start to finish involving pre-match planning, various game formats, reception, tournaments controllers, starter and the provision of unique prizes and trophies. Other features include catering before, during (via on course catering or halfway house) and after play, a large fleet of buggies, spacious wood-panelled locker rooms with private facilities and cars and golf clubs are available on request.

As a corporate, society or individual visitor to Portal, you will enjoy a day to remember in an ideal atmosphere in which to develop friendships, positive relationships and create business potential. In fact, Portal exudes more than quality and character - it has style. Golf in this country has waited a long time for a club and course like Portal.

Portal Golf & Country Club
Cobblers Cross Lane
Tarporley
Cheshire CW6 0DJ
Tel: (01829) 733933
Fax: (01829) 733928

Hawkstone Park

What is a man to do when his two daughters, his pride and joy, tell him that they wish to leave home? Well, such was the dilemma facing a certain Sir William Gray in 1921. His solution you might think was an admirable one— he promised to build them a golf course. For two young ladies much bitten by the bug it proved irresistible—clearly bribery of the highest calibre. In 1921 the ingenious Sir William owned Hawkstone Park, and the golf course, the subject of this tale, grew from an original nine holes to the present day Hawkstone Course.

Today probably every golfer from Land's End to John O'Groats has heard of Hawkstone Park—not because of the 'golfing Grays', but thanks to one Sandy Lyle, Open Champion of 1985 and US Masters Champion of 1988. Sandy's association with Hawkstone Park has been life-long. Whilst there is probably no truth in the rumour that he was born adjacent to the first tee he certainly grew up nearby. For many years his father Alex served as club professional and in every sense it was here that Sandy learnt his game.

Hawkstone Park is, of course, much more than the birthplace of Sandy Lyle. Today there are two 18 hole courses, the well established **Hawkstone** and the newer **Windmill** Course (built in the main over the former Weston Course which was completely redesigned and extended). Both are set in the beautiful grounds of the Hawkstone Park Hotel. A 6 hole academy course completes the picture.

The hotel itself is certainly a grand affair. In a guide book of 1824 it was described as 'more like the seat of a nobleman than an hotel' and the grounds are not only exceptionally beautiful—exotic plants and flowers abound—but are also steeped in history and legend. The hotel runs the golf courses and other than an early morning tee reservation for residents there are no general restrictions on visitors, but starting times must be pre-booked. This can be done by telephoning the **Golf Centre** on **(01939) 200611, fax: (01939) 200311.** Green fees in 2000 vary with the season. For winter months the rates are £16 midweek and £22 at weekends. The equivalent summer rates are £30 and £38. Those wishing to play 27 or 36 holes will be charged £45 during the week and £53 at weekends. In summer there is a special twilight rate after 5.00 pm of £15 on weekdays

and £19 at weekends. Parties of twelve or more are deemed to be golfing societies, subject again to making prior arrangements. They are equally welcome and written applications may be made in writing to Golf Reservations at **The Golf Centre, Hawkstone Park Hotel, Weston-under-Redcastle, Nr Shrewsbury SY4 5UY.**

It has been said that one of the reasons for Hawkstone Park enjoying such a delightfully peaceful setting is that it is 'miles from anywhere'—not strictly true: it is only seven miles south of Whitchurch, or if you prefer, twelve miles north of Shrewsbury, and is easily accessible. The A49 is the best route when approaching from either of these towns. Shrewsbury itself is linked to the West Midlands by way of the M54 and the A5, while those motoring from the north will find the M6 of assistance.

I mentioned that all 18 holes of the Windmill course were in play by April 1995—in fact, a great deal has been happening of late at Hawkstone Park. The aforementioned 'Golf Centre' is itself a new building and serves as a very modern three-tiered clubhouse, one where traditional 19th hole facilities are supplemented by a teaching academy run by the **Head Professional**, **Paul Wesselingh**.

Brian Huggett is the architect responsible for completely reshaping the old Weston Course and while that was a fairly modest affair, the Windmill Course measures some 6476 yards and features a series of dramatic holes where the golfer must confront do-or-die shots over and alongside water. It provides a great contrast and complement to the celebrated challenges of the Hawkstone Course. A recent visit in February when a day of beauty was stolen from May's calendar found both courses in amazing condition for the time of year.

The hotel and golf course complex provides comprehensive facilities for golf meetings at a corporate or local level. A wide range of good value golfing breaks is offered throughout the year and many golfers regularly travel great distances to sample the delights of this Shropshire golfing paradise. It's all come a long way since the days of Sir William Gray and his golf-mad daughters, but one suspects that they would approve.

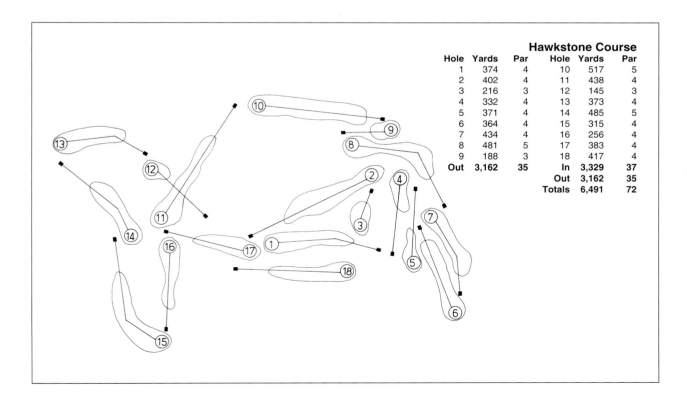

Hawkstone Course

Hole	Yards	Par	Hole	Yards	Par
1	374	4	10	517	5
2	402	4	11	438	4
3	216	3	12	145	3
4	332	4	13	373	4
5	371	4	14	485	5
6	364	4	15	315	4
7	434	4	16	256	4
8	481	5	17	383	4
9	188	3	18	417	4
Out	**3,162**	**35**	**In**	**3,329**	**37**
			Out	**3,162**	**35**
			Totals	**6,491**	**72**

Key

_To avoid disappointment
it is advisable to telephone
in advance_

***Visitors welcome at most times
**Visitors usually allowed on
weekdays only
*Visitors not normally permitted
(Mon, Wed) No visitors
on specified days_

Approximate Green Fees

A _£40 plus_
B _£25 to £40_
C _£20 to £30_
D _£15 to £25_
E _under £15_
F _Green fees on application_

Restrictions

G –_Guests only_
H –_Handicap certificate required_
H–(24) _Handicap of 24 or less_
L –_Letter of introduction required_
M –_Visitor must be a member of
another recognised club_

STAFFORDSHIRE

Alsager G.& C.C.
(01270) 875700
Andley Road, Stoke-on-Trent
(18) 6206 yards/**/C/M

Barlaston G.C.
(01782) 372795
Meaford Road, Barlaston, Stone
(18) 5800 yards/**/C

Beau Desert G.C.
(01543) 422626
Hazelslade, Hednesford, Cannock
(18) 6300 yards/***/A/H

Branston G. & C.C.
(01283) 512211
Burton Road, Branston
(18) 6541 yards/**/C

Brocton Hall G.C.
(01785) 661901
Brocton
(18) 6095 yards/***/B/H/L

Burslem G.C.
(01782) 837006
Wood Farm, High Lane, Tunstall
(9) 5354 yards/**/D

Burton upon Trent G.C.
(01283) 568708
Ashby Road East, Burton-upon-Trent
(18) 6555 yards/***/B/H/L/M

Cannock Park G.C.
(01543) 578850
Stafford Road, Cannock
(18) 4559 yards/***/E

The Craythorne G.C.
(01283) 564329
Craythorne Road, Stretton
(18) 5230 yards/***/D/H

Drayton Park G.C.
(01827) 251139
Drayton Park, Tamworth
(18) 6414 yards/**/B/H

Enville G.C.
(01384) 872074
Highgate Common, Kinver
(18) 6217 yards/**/B/H

Golden Hill G.C.
(01782) 234200
Golden Hill, Stoke-on-Trent
(18) 5957 yards/***/E

Greenway Hall G.C.
(01782) 503158
Stockton Brook, Stoke-on-Trent
(18) 5676 yards/**/E

Himley Hall G.C.
(01902) 895207
School Road, Himley
(9) 3125 yards/**/F

Ingestre Park G.C.
(01889) 270845
Ingestre, Stafford
(18) 6334 yards/**/B/H

Izaak Walton G.C.
(01785) 760900
Cold Norton, Stone
(18) 6281 yards/***/D/H

Lakeside G.C.
(01889) 575667
Rugeley Power Station, Rugeley
(18) 5534 yards/*/F/G

Leek G.C.
(01538) 384779
Cheddleton Road, Leek
(18) 6240 yards/**/B/H

Manor Kingstone G.C.
(01889) 563234
Leese Hill, Kingstone, Uttoxeter
(9) 3523 yards/***/D

Meadow Vale G.C.
(01785) 760900
Cold Norton, Stone
(18) 6500 yards/***/C

Newcastle Municipal G.C.
(01782) 627596
Keele Road, Newcastle-under-Lyme
(18) 6256 yards/***/E

Newcastle-under-Lyme G.C.
(01782) 616583
Whitmore Road
(18) 6427 yards/**/B/H

Parkhall G.C.
(01782) 599584
Holme Road, Weston Coyney
(18) 2335 yards/***/E

St Thomas's Priory
(01534) 491116
Armitage, Lichfield
(18) 6637 yards/*/G

Seedy Mill G.C.
(01543) 417333
Elmshurst, Lichfield
(18) 6247 yards/***/F/H

Stafford Castle G.C.
(01785) 223521
Newport Road, Stafford
(9) 6347 yards/**/D

Stone G.C.
(01785) 813103
Filley Brooks, Stone
(9) 6299 yards/**/C

Tamworth G.C.
(01827) 53850
Eagle Drive, Tamworth
(18) 6695 yards/***/F

Trentham G.C.
(01782) 658309
Barlaston Road, Trentham
(18) 6644 yards/**/B/H

Trentham Park G.C.
(01782) 658800
Trentham Park, Trentham
(18) 6403 yards/***/B/H

Uttoxeter G.C.
(01889) 564884
Wood Lane, Uttoxeter
(18) 5468 yards/***/D

Westwood G.C.
(01538) 398385
Newcastle Road, Wallbridge, Leek
(18) 6156 yards/**/C

Whiston Hall G.C.
(01538) 266260
Whiston Cheadle
(18) 5724 yards/***/D

Whittington Heath G.C.
(01543) 432212
Tamworth Road, Lichfield
(18) 6457 yards/**/A/H

Wolstanton G.C.
(01782) 622413
Dimsdale Old Hall, Hassam Parade
(18) 5807 yards/**/C/H

SHROPSHIRE

Arscott G.C.
(01743) 860114
Arscott, Pontesbury
(18) 6035 yards/**/C

Bridgnorth G.C.
(01746) 763315
Stanley Lane, Bridgnorth
(18) 6668 yards/***/C

Chesterton Valley G.C.
(01476) 783682
Worfield, Bridgnorth
(9) 3392 yards/***/E

Church Stretton G.C.
(01694) 722281
Trevor Hill, Church Stretton
(18) 5008 yards/**/D/H

Cleobury Mortimer G.C.
(01299) 271112
Wyre Common, Cleobury Mortimer
(9) 2942 yards/***/D
(9) 3271 yards/***/D
(9) 3167 yards/***/D

Hawkstone Park Hotel G.C.
(01939) 200611
Weston-under-Redcastle
(18) 6465 yards/***/B/H
(18) 6655 yards/***/B/H

Hill Valley G.& C.C.
(01948) 663584
Terrick Road, Whitchurch
(18) 6517 yards/***/C
(18) 5285 yards/***/E

Lilleshall Hall G.C.
(01952) 604104
Lilleshall, Newport
(18) 5906 yards/**/C/H

Llanymynech G.C.
(01691) 830542
Pant, Oswestry
(18) 6114 yards/**/D/H

Ludlow G.C.
(01584) 77285
Bromfield, Ludlow
(18) 6239 yards/***/C/H

Market Drayton G.C.
(01630) 652266
Sutton, Market Drayton
(18) 6214 yards/**/C

Meole Brace G.C.
(01743) 364050
Meole Brace, Shrewsbury
(12) 5830 yards/***/F

Mile End G.C.
(01691) 671246
Mile End, Oswestry
(9) 6136 yards/***/D

Oswestry G.C.
(01691) 610448
Aston Park, Oswestry
(18) 6046 yards/***/C/H/M

Patshull Park Hotel & G.C.
(01902) 700100
Nr Wolverhampton
(18) 6400 yards/***/B/H

Severn Meadows G.C.
(01746) 862212
Highley, Bridgnorth
(9) 2520 yards/***/E

Shifnal G.C.
(01952) 460467
Decker Hill, Shifnal
(18) 6422 yards/**/C/H/L

Shrewsbury G.C.
(01743) 872976
Condover, Shrewsbury
(18) 6212 yards/***/C/H

The Shropshire G.C.
(01952) 677866
Muxton Grange, Telford
(9) 3286 yards/***/D
(9) 3303 yards/***/D
(9) 3334 yards/***/D

Telford Moat House G.& C.C.
(01952) 429977
Great Hay, Telford
(18) 6766 yards/***/B/H

Welsh Border G.C.
(01734) 884247
Middletown, Welshpool
(9) 3250 yards/***/F

Worfield G.C.
(01746) 716541
Worfield, Bridgnorth
(18) 6801 yards/***/C

Wrekin G.C.
(01952) 244032
Ercall Woods, Wellington, Telford
(18) 5657 yards/**/C

CHESHIRE

Alder Root G.C.
(01925) 291919
Alder Root Lane, Winwick
(9) 5564 yards/***/C

Alderley Edge G.C.
(01565) 872385
Brook Lane, Alderley Edge
(9) 5839 yards/***/C/H/G

Alvaston Hall G.C.
(01270) 624341
Middlewich Road, Nantwich
(9) 1806 yards/***/E

Astbury G.C.
(01260) 272772
Peel Lane, Astbury, Congleton
(18) 6277 yards/**/B/H/G

Birchwood G.C.
(01925) 818819
Kelvin Close, Risley, Warrington
(18) 6808 yards/**/C/H

Carden Park G.C.
(01829) 731199
Carden, Tilston, Chester
(18) 6828 yards/***/B/H
(18) 7070yards/***/B/H

Chapel-en-le-Frith G.C
(01298) 812118
Manchester Road, Stockport
(18) 6119 yards/***/B

Cheadle G.C.
(0161) 4282160
Shiers Drive, Cheadle
(9) 5006 yards/(*** D/H-L

Chester G.C.
(01244) 677760
Curzon Park North, Chester
(18) 6487 yards/***/B/H

Congleton G.C.
(01260) 273540
Biddulph Road, Congleton
(18) 5103 yards/***/D

Crewe G.C.
(01270) 584099
Fields Road, Haslington, Crewe
(18) 6259 yards/**/B/H

Davenport G.C.
(01625) 876951
Middlewood Road, Higher Poynton
(18) 6066 yards/**/B/H

Delamere Forest G.C.
(01606) 883800
Station Road, Delamere, Northwich
(18) 6305 yards/**/B

Disley G.C
(01663) 762071
Stanley Hall Lane, Stockport
(18) 6051 yards/***/B

Eaton G.C.
(01244) 335885
Guy Lane, Waverton
(18) 6446 yards/***/F/H

Ellesmere Port G.C.
(0151) 339 7689
Chester Road, Hooton
(18) 6432 yards/***/E

Frodsham G.C.
(01928) 732159
Simons Lane, Frodsham
(18) 6289 yards/**/B

Helsby G.C.
(01928) 722021
Towers Lane, Helsby, Warrington
(18) 6229 yards/**/B/H

Heyrose G.C.
(01565) 733664
Budworth Road, Knutsford
(18) 6449 yards/***/C

Knights Grange G.C.
(01606) 557406
Grange Lane, Winsford
(9) 6210 yards/***/E

Knutsford G.C.
(01565) 633355
Mereheath Lane, Knutsford
(9) 6288 yards/**/C

Leigh G.C.
(01925) 763130
Kenyon Hall, Culcheth
(18) 6861 yards/***/B/H

Lymm G.C.
(01925) 755020
Whitbarrow Road, Lymm
(18) 6304 yards/**/C/H

Macclesfield G.C.
(01625) 423227
The Hollins, Macclesfield
(18) 5625 yards/**/C/H

Malkins Bank G.C.
(01270) 583509
Betchton Road, Sandbach
(18) 6071 yards/***/E

Mere G.& C.C.
(01565) 830155
Chester Road, Mere, Knutsford
(18) 6817 yards/**(Wed,Fri)/A/H/L

Mersey Valley G.C.
(0151) 424 6060
Warrington Road, Widnes
(18) 6400 yards/**/C

Mottram Hall Hotel & G.C.
(01625) 828135
Mottram St Andrews
(18) 7006 yards/***/A/H

New Mills G.C.
(01663) 743485
Shaw Marsh, New Mills, Stockport
(9) 5707 yards/**/F

Onneley G.C.
(01782)750577
Onneley, Crewe
(9) 5584 yards/**/C

The Portal G & C..C.
(01829) 733933
Cobbler's Cross Lane, Tarporley
(18) 7037 yards/***/A/H
(9) 3250 yards/***/C

Portal Premier G.C
(01829) 733884
Forest Road, Tarporley
(18) 6508 yards/***/A

Poulton Park G.C.
(01925) 812034
Cinnamon Brow, Warrington
(9) 5512 yards/**/C

Prestbury G.C.
(01625) 829388
Macclesfield Road, Prestbury
(18) 6359 yards/**/B/H/L

Pryors Hayes G.C.
(01829) 740140
Willingdon Drove, Oscroft
(18) 5923 yards/***/C

Queens Park G.C.
(01270) 628352
Queens Park Gardens, Crewe
(9) 5370 yards/***/E

Reaseheath College G.C.
(01270) 625131
Reaseheath, Nantwich
(9) 3334 yards/***/E/G

Runcorn G.C.
(01928) 574214
Clifton Road, Runcorn
(18) 6035 yards/**/C/H

Sandbach G.C.
(01270) 762117
Middlewich Road, Sandbach
(9) 5614 yards/**/C/H

Sandiway G.C.
(01606) 883247
Chester Road, Sandiway, Northwich
(18) 6435 yards/***/A/H/L

Shrigley Hall G.C.
(01625) 575757
Shrigley Park, Pott Shrigley
(18) 6305 yards/***/B

St Michael's Jubilee G.C.
(0151) 424 6230
Dundark Road, Widnes
(18) 5612 yards/***/F/L

Styal G.C.
(01625) 531359
Station Road, Styal
(18) 6301 yards/***/D

Tytherington G.C.
(01625) 434562
Tytherington, nr Macclesfield
(18) 6737 yards/***/B-A/H

Upton-by-Chester G.C.
(01244) 381183
Upton Lane, Upton-by-Chester
(18) 5875 yards/***/B/H

Vicars Cross G.C.
(01244) 335174
Tarvin Road, Littleton
(18) 6234 yards/**/C

Walton Hall G.C.
(01925) 266775
Warrington Road, Higher Walton
(18) 6843 yards/***/E

Warrington G.C.
(01925) 261775
Appleton, Warrington
(18) 6305 yards/***/F/H

Widnes G.C.
(0151) 424 2440
Highfield Road, Widnes
(18) 5719 yards/**/B/H

Wilmslow G.C.
(01565) 872148
Mobberley, Knutsford
(18) 6607 yards/**/A/H

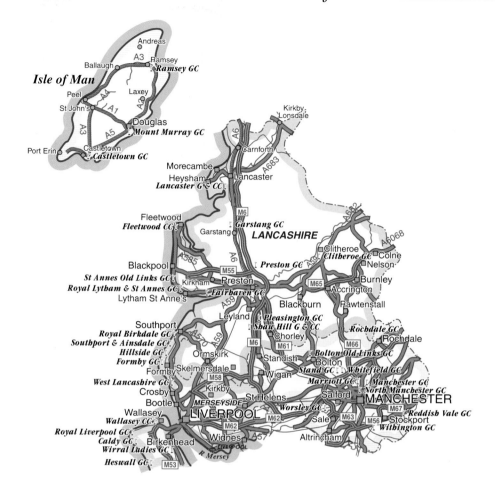

Lancashire & The Isle of Man Choice Golf

Caddies are not allowed on the greens when wearing clogs'—recorded in the minutes of a Lancashire golf club, 1894.

The Lancashire Coast

I don't suppose they appreciate it in the slightest but the many horses that race across the sands near Southport early each morning (and the donkeys that do their best to race across the same sands) are performing within a few yards of one of the greatest stretches of golfing country in the world. On the Lancashire coast between Liverpool and Blackpool lies a magnificent collection of natural golfing links. Being more specific, between Hoylake on the Wirral Peninsula and **Lytham St Annes** (a distance of less than 40 miles) are to be found the likes of **Royal Liverpool**, **Wallasey**, **West Lancashire**, **Formby**, **Southport and Ainsdale**, **Royal Birkdale**, **Hillside**, **Royal Lytham**, **Fairhaven** and **St Annes Old Links**. A truly formidable list. Hoylake, Birkdale and Lytham have, of course, each staged the Open Championship on a number of occasions, while the Amateur Championship has been played at both Hillside and Formby, and Southport and Ainsdale has twice hosted the Ryder Cup. When the wind hammers across from the Irish Sea any of the links mentioned can become treacherously difficult and the famous Lancashire sandhills rarely provide shelter from the elements. Hoylake, Birkdale, Hillside, Formby and Lytham are each featured on later pages but a visit to any of the above will certainly not meet with disappointment (though it may result in a little damaged pride!)

Having done battle with the elements, and perhaps after visiting the treacherous Gumbley's bunker at S & A or the heather and pines at Formby, a drink will be in order. A good meal and a comfy bed for the night may also be required. Here are some suggestions. The Woolton Redbourne Hotel (0151) 421 1500 is extremely comfortable and particularly convenient for Royal Birkdale. In Southport, the Scarisbrick Hotel (01704) 543000, the Prince of Wales (01704) 536688 and the Royal Clifton (01704) 533771 are probably the pick of the hotels but there are numerous others. The Metropole Hotel (01704) 536836 and the Bold Hotel (01704) 532578 are also good and amongst the less expensive options the Ambassador Hotel (01704) 543998 should not disappoint. In Formby, the Tree Tops (01704) 572430 is an ideal base.

Lytham St Annes is another golfer's paradise. It's a pleasant town and hotels to note in the area are the Chadwick (01253) 720061 on the seafront, the Clifton Arms Hotel (01253) 739898 at Lytham, the Dormy House at the course itself and the New Glendower Hotel (01253) 640069. The Dalmeny Hotel (01253) 712236 has a host of leisure facilities and a good restaurant. C'est La Vie is an ideal watering hole while Sunray Hotel (01253) 351937 and Strathmore (01253) 725478 also have good reputations. **Fleetwood** to the north, is a pleasant seaside links. The North Euston Hotel (01253) 876525 is an inexpensive base here.

Blackpool, famed for its 'golden mile', its great tower and impressive funfair is more of a paradise for children than golfers, but then if golf is being sneaked in on the family holiday it may be the best choice for a stay. On the North Promenade is one of the town's best hotels the Imperial (01253) 623971. Comfort here is guaranteed but there are numerous, slightly cheaper alternatives and pot luck may be the order of the day. The Fairmont (01253) 351050 and the Surrey House Hotel (01253) 51743 fall into the less glamorous category but offer pleasant accommodation and on Shaftesbury Avenue you can find the Brebyns Hotel (01253) 354263, noted for its good food. To the east, at Little Singleton there is a listed historic house and excellent hotel in the Mains Hall (01253) 885130. A restaurant in Blackpool to note is September Brasserie (01253) 623282.

It may be that some business in Liverpool has to be dealt with before one can put on one's plus fours and stride out onto the fairways. If you are staying in the Liver city the Atlantic Tower (0151) 227 4444 is a good bet. The city has a reputation for splendid Indian and Chinese food but two European establishments are our recommendations: on the one hand Ristorante Del Secolo (0151) 236 4004 and on the other Bar Italia (0151) 236 3375. The nearest of the great links courses is West Lancashire, although Formby—note also the **Formby Ladies'** club here—and the Southport courses are also within easy reach. The A565 is the road to take out of Liverpool.

For the purposes of this piece Liverpool and Manchester have been included in Lancashire, a county to which they both once belonged (and still do in spirit). As the whole of what was once Merseyside has been included—it's here that Royal Birkdale and Royal Liverpool are now situated—parts of former Cheshire are also included. Confused? Let's visit the Wirral. For such a relatively small area the peninsula is fairly thick with golf clubs. In addition to the famous links at Hoylake, **Wallasey** offers another tremendous seaside test amid some impressive sand dunes while **Heswall** offers a quite outstanding parkland challenge. Situated alongside the River Dee off the A540, it's a medium length course, beautifully maintained with views towards the distant Welsh hills. A mention for **Caldy** which is a parkland-cum-

clifftop course, and for the **Wirral Ladies'** Golf Club near Birkenhead. If an hotel is sought on the Wirral then the splendidly named Bowler Hat Hotel (0151) 652 4931 at Birkenhead is most comfortable.

Inland Golf in Lancashire

Looking to play more centrally in Lancashire, the **Shaw Hill** Golf and Country Club (012572) 69221 is most definitely one to note if travelling along the M6. Located just north of Chorley at the appropriately named Whittle-le-Woods it enjoys a very peaceful setting, despite its proximity to the motorway, and is a particular favourite of golfing societies. Visitors are welcome throughout the week, and there is some high quality accommodation immediately beyond the 18th green.

On the other side of the M6, **Pleasington** Golf Club enjoys similarly secluded and picturesque surroundings. The course is situated three miles west of Blackburn along the A59 and is undoubtedly one of the best parkland courses in the north of England. You're bound to build up a good appetite here—in which case head for Northcote Manor (01254) 240555—a restaurant par excellence with some rooms as well. Still moving 'up' the country, **Preston** has a pleasantly undulating course, just north of the town. It too can easily be reached from the M6 (junction 32). The Broughton Park (01772) 864087 is a large hotel with good leisure facilities.

Another of the better inland courses in the county is **Clitheroe** Golf Club, situated on the edge of the Forest of Bowland. The course lies approximately two miles south of the town with views across to Pendle Hill.

Lancashire wouldn't be complete without mentioning its county town. There are a number of clubs at hand, perhaps the best being

MARRIOTT MANCHESTER HOTEL & COUNTRY CLUB *Photograph courtesy of:* **Marriott Manchester Hotel & Country Club**

the **Lancaster** Golf and Country Club located three miles south of the city on the A588 at Stodday. An attractive parkland course, it is laid out close to the River Lune estuary (and can be breezy!).

A few more ideas for the 19th hole now follow. The city of Lancaster lies west of some majestic moorland scenery. The M6 carves its way through and near to junction 34 the Posthouse Hotel (01524) 65999 is ideal for travellers. Recommended alternatives include Edenbreck House (01524) 32464 and Lancaster House (01524) 844822. A little further north in Heaton with Oxcliffe a pub with a splendid riverside setting is the Golden Ball—well worth a visit when in these parts. In Morecambe the Strathmore (01524) 421234 is welcoming and a good spot for the marvellous seaside golf to be enjoyed at Morecambe where the views will make you feel glad to be alive. Closer to the M6, **Garstang** Country Hotel & Golf Club (01995) 600950 is a newly built hotel which stands next to a fine course and is well worth a visit.

THE CASTLETOWN GOLF LINKS *Photograph courtesy of:* **Castletown Golf Links Hotel**

At Whitewell, amid the delightful Forest of Bowland lies the Inn at Whitewell (01200) 448222 which offers excellent bar snacks, a first rate restaurant and some charming bedrooms. If you are looking for a self-catering holiday in the region, we recommend you contact either Red Rose Cottage Holidays (01200) 420101 or Country Holidays (01282) 445533. More thoughts for celebrating after a day at Preston or Clitheroe? In Hurst Green, the Shireburn Arms Hotel (01254) 826518 is well worth a visit. Not only can you enjoy the splendid Ribblesdale countryside but also some tremendous cuisine. An alternative eating establishment, a restaurant on this occasion, is Tiffany at Great Harwood, where the fish is particularly good. In Clitheroe itself, the Swan and Royal Hotel (01200) 423130 is convenient and nearby in Slaidburn is the Parrock Head Farm Hotel (01200) 446614. In Preston, the Gibbon Bridge (01995) 61456 offers excellent facilities. Finally, a recommendation for the first class Mytton Fold Farm Hotel (01254) 240662 which now boasts its own course at Langho, near Blackburn.

Manchester and Surrounds

And so to Manchester. The city itself is famed the world over for the liberal amount of rain that falls. Mancunians will tell you that this is pure poppycock (or something like that). Of course, the only time that rain can be guaranteed these days is during the five days of an Old Trafford test match. If you do happen to get caught in the rain, be it on the streets or the fairways, here are a few superior shelters. You ought to be able to find a room in the Britannia Hotel (0161) 228 2288 for there are 365 (one for every day of the year?) Alternatives include the Jarvis Piccadilly (0161) 236 8414, and the Portland Thistle (0161) 228 3400.

Outside the city there are many attractive options. To the north in Egerton, the Egerton House (01204) 307171 is good value as is the Last Drop Village Hotel (01204) 591131—well appointed and well run. Another thought is the Bramhall Moat House (0161) 439 8116—ideal for the many courses in northern Cheshire. Near to Manchester Airport one finds Etrop Grange (0161) 499 0500—comfortable and convenient. Altrincham has a trio to consider: the Cresta Court (0161) 927 7272 is modern but well equipped; the Bowdon (0161) 928 7121 is Victorian and comfortable; while a former coaching inn, the George and Dragon (0161) 928 9933 has most charm. Some of the very best restaurants in the Manchester area include: the Market Restaurant (0161) 834 3743 and the excellent Royal Orchid (0161) 236 5183.

It is probably a fair assessment to say that for golf courses, Manchester, rather like London, gets top marks for quantity but is a little shaky on the quality score. Certainly it compares unfavourably with Liverpool and Leeds—which is a shame because historically Manchester was the scene of some of the earliest golf outside Scotland. The Old Manchester Club was founded back in 1818. Its current status is 'temporarily without a course'—one can only hope that its members have found somewhere else to play—**North Manchester** perhaps? A worthy ddition can be found at the **Marriott Manchester Hotel and Country Club** where the new course is a fine challenge to any golfer. Only four miles from the city centre this is one of the best in the county. A close neighbour of North Manchester is the excellent **Manchester** Golf Club. Elsewhere around Manchester, **Stand**, **Whitefield** and **Worsley** (Eccles) are fine courses, while to the north **Rochdale** is well worth travelling to. There is a cluster of courses close to the River Mersey in the Didsbury/Sale area. The best is perhaps **Withington**, and there are about ten public courses in and around the city centre. Over towards Stockport, there is a very enjoyable Alistair Mackenzie course at **Reddish Vale** and the area around Bolton again boasts a number of courses of which **Bolton Old Links** is probably the finest. It is a tough and interesting moorland course at which visitors are always made welcome. As for the title 'Links' it may sound a bit quaint—but there again, what are we to make of Wigan Pier?

The Isle of Man

There are seven 18 hole courses on the island, with the links courses at **Castletown**, **Ramsey** and **Mount Murray** being particularly good. With fairly modest green fees and numerous relaxing places to stay the island would appear to be an ideal place for a golf holiday—ask Nigel Mansell who brought Greg Norman here! In Castletown, a restaurant to note; Rosa's Place (01624) 822940, whilst the Castletown Golf Links Hotel (01624) 822201 is very comfortable. Castletown golf course is featured ahead. Further up the east coast is the Mount Murray Hotel and Country Club, which opened in 1994 and provides a stern challenge to any golfer

At the other end of the island, Ramsey offers the large Grand Island Hotel (01624) 812455 and the Harbour Bistro (01624) 814182, an informal and friendly restaurant. Finally there are, of course, many places to stay in Douglas and here we can recommend the Palace Hotel (01624) 662662 and the Sefton (01624) 626011.

Royal Birkdale

Back in 1889 your average JP was possibly not the most popular man in town. However, in a certain Mr J C Barrett, Birkdale possessed a man of rare insight and one clearly cognisant of the finer things in life. Mr Barrett was a golfer. On the 30th July 1889, he invited eight fellow addicts to his home and together they resolved to form a golf club. One can imagine their enthusiasm as they formulated their plans, perhaps over a brandy and cigars, I know not, but very quickly a clubhouse was secured—a single room in a private residence at a four shilling per week rental! Land (at £5 per year rental) was acquired and soon a nine hole course was laid out. It all sounds rather unsophisticated, but compared with today's problems of first finding a suitable site and then obtaining planning permission, I suppose it was relatively straightforward.

Although no one could question its present day status as one of the country's leading championship courses, historically Birkdale set off rather like the proverbial tortoise. Forced eviction in 1897 led to the club's rerooting in its present position where a full eighteen holes were immediately available. During the 1930s a striking art deco style clubhouse was built and John H Taylor and Fred Hawtree were commissioned to redesign the course. As one would expect, they made a splendid job of it and it was now only a question of time (and the small matter of a world war) that prevented Birkdale from staging an Open Championship. Since the war our golfing tortoise has left many of the hares behind. No fewer than eight Open Championships have now been held at Birkdale (the last in 1998) in addition to two Ryder Cups and numerous other major events.

Golfers wishing to play at Birkdale must belong to a recognised golf club and produce a current handicap certificate. Visitors should make prior arrangements with the **Secretary, Mike Gilyeat**. This applies to individual visitors as well as those hoping to organise a society game. Mr Crewe can be contacted at **The Royal Birkdale Golf Club, Waterloo Road, Birkdale, Southport, Merseyside PR8 2LX tel: (01704) 567920** and **fax: (01704) 562327**. Golf clubs may be hired from the **Professional, Richard Bradbeer, (01704) 568857** and it may also be possible to obtain the services of a caddy. Individual visitors may play from Monday to Friday and on a Sunday morning, green fees in 2000 are £98 per round or £125 per day and £125 per round on Sundays.

The club is situated approximately two miles from the centre of Southport close to the main A565 road. From the North this road can be reached via the A59, leaving the M6 at Preston and from the South via the M62 and M57 or alternatively, as when travelling from Manchester and the East, by taking the A580 and then following the A570 into Southport.

Whilst the course possesses many of the towering sandhills so familiar with good links golf, the holes tend to wind their way between and beneath the dunes along fairly flat valleys. From the fairways the awkward stance and blind shot are the product of poor golf, not poor fortune.

With its par fives the back nine is probably the easier half—at least to the longer hitter—although with the buckthorn infested rough and narrow strategically bunkered fairways the wild long hitter will be severely penalised. A journey into the rough on the 16th, however, is recommended although only to visit Arnold Palmer's plaque—placed in memory of the great man's miraculous 6 iron shot when he somehow contrived to find the green after driving deep into the undergrowth. The two finest holes at Birkdale are thought by many to be the 6th, a very demanding left to right dog-leg and the 12th, a classic par three where the green nestles in the sand dunes.

Birkdale may have a relatively short history as an Open course, but her list of champions is impressive: Peter Thomson (twice), Arnold Palmer, Lee Trevino, Johnny Miller, Tom Watson—who claimed his fifth title in nine years when winning in 1983—Ian Baker-Finch, who set alight the 1991 championship with a brilliant front nine of 29 on the final day, and the memorable victory by Mark O'Meara in 1998 following his win at Augusta in the Masters in April.

The course has indeed thrown up more than its fair share of drama. Perhaps most notably in 1969 when Jack Nicklaus, ever the sportsman, conceded Tony Jacklin's very missable putt on the 18th green, so tying the Ryder Cup. In the 1961 Palmer's Open, an almighty gale threatened to blow the tented village far out into the sea. In stark contrast was the 1976 Open when fire engines were close at hand as Birkdale (and all of Britain come to that) suffered in the drought.

That 1976 championship saw the mercurial Miller at his brilliant best as he shook off first the challenge of Nicklaus and then of an inexperienced and unknown 19 year old who had a name no one at the time could pronounce . . . Severiano Ballesteros.

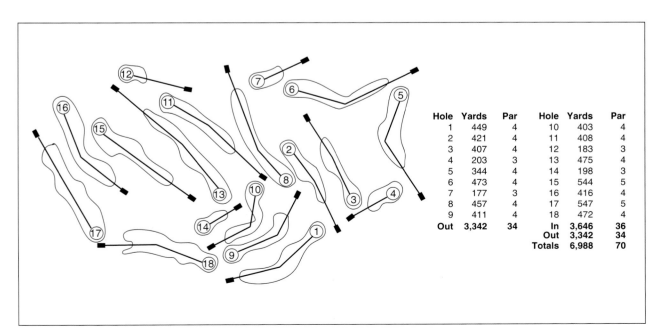

Hole	Yards	Par	Hole	Yards	Par
1	449	4	10	403	4
2	421	4	11	408	4
3	407	4	12	183	3
4	203	3	13	475	4
5	344	4	14	198	3
6	473	4	15	544	5
7	177	3	16	416	4
8	457	4	17	547	5
9	411	4	18	472	4
Out	**3,342**	**34**	**In**	**3,646**	**36**
			Out	**3,342**	**34**
			Totals	**6,988**	**70**

Royal Lytham & St Annes

There goes a hundred thousand bucks . . .' the immortal words of Al Watrous after having witnessed the most magnificently outrageous stroke in golfing history. Imagine yourself in his shoes, striding down the 17th fairway, sharing the lead in the Open Championship. You have played two strokes and are safely on the edge of the green, your partner (and effectively your opponent) has driven wildly into the rough and has found a small bunker. He faces a terrifying shot over sandhills, scrub and goodness knows what else—a blind shot of fully 170 yards. Seconds later the impossible happens and his ball is lying a few yards from the hole, well inside your second. Minutes later you walk from the green having taken five to your opponent's four. The occasion was the 1926 Open Championship at Royal Lytham and the opponent, the incomparable Bobby Jones.

Few golf clubs in the world can have enjoyed such a rich and colourful history. There have been nine Open Championships, four Seniors' British Opens and many other major events.

Presently in charge of all administrative matters at Royal Lytham is the club's **Secretary, Mr L Goodwin**, who may be contacted on **tel: (01253) 724206** and by **fax: (01253) 780946. Eddie Birchenough** is the club's **Professional** and he may be reached on **(01253) 720094.** Visitors wishing to tread the famous fairways are asked to provide a letter of introduction, but subject to this requirement they are welcome between Mondays and Thursdays. Thursdays are specifically reserved as visitors' days, but restrictions apply at weekends. Advance booking is essential, preferably two to three weeks in advance. Those wishing to write to the club should address correspondence to the **Assistant Secretary, Royal Lytham and St Annes Golf Club, Links Gate, Lytham St Annes, Lancashire FY8 3LQ.**

The green fees at Lytham in 2000 are £90 for a single round inclusive of lunch and a 'golfers welcome pack'. Dormy house facilities are available at the 19th hole (telephone the club for details) and Royal Lytham's clubhouse is a marvellous Victorian building. Golfers can enjoy the excellent catering service which is offered throughout the day.

Motoring to the course is assisted greatly by the M6 and the M61. Both northbound and southbound travellers should leave the M6 at junction 32 to pick up the M55. The M55 runs out of steam at junction 4 but a left turn will take you to Lytham St Annes. The M61 links the Greater Manchester area to the outskirts of Preston. From Preston, the A583 should be followed, joining the A584 which also runs to Lytham St Annes. The course is situated only a mile from the centre of the town close to St Annes railway station.

The railway line is, in fact, a major feature of the opening holes at Lytham, forming a continuous boundary to the right. From the medal tees the course measures 6685 yards par 71 (SSS 74) with the ladies playing over 5814 yards par 75 (SSS 75). Rather unusually, Lytham opens with a par three, which at over 200 yards is quite a testing opener, although the real threat of the railway looms on the 2nd and 3rd. The two-shot 8th is many people's favourite hole and among the short holes perhaps the 12th stands out. Normally played into a prevailing wind, it calls for a searching tee shot towards a raised and heavily guarded green. The back nine is invariably the more difficult of the two halves, although the determining factor at Lytham (as on most links courses) will nearly always be the wind. The 17th has been mentioned and a plaque marks the spot from where the Jones miracle recovery shot was played. As for the superbly bunkered 18th, it of course invokes so many Open Championship memories: Tony Jacklin's arrow straight drive en route to winning the 1969 Championship; Gary Player putting left handed from up against the clubhouse wall in 1974; Seve Ballesteros storming to victory in 1979 and again in 1988; and the most recent Championship in 1996 when Tom Lehman became the first American to win at Lytham since Jones. The Open returns to Lytham in 2001.

The 1988 championship will always be remembered for the fantastic duel between Ballesteros and Nick Price. Price led by two shots going into the final round. He produced an almost flawless 69 yet lost by two. 'A round that happens once every 25 or 50 years' was Seve's description of his scintillating 65. Perhaps Nick Price alone can understand how Al Watrous felt.

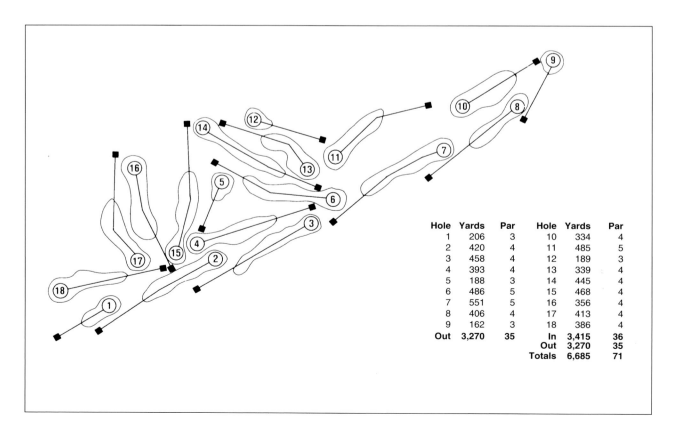

Hole	Yards	Par	Hole	Yards	Par
1	206	3	10	334	4
2	420	4	11	485	5
3	458	4	12	189	3
4	393	4	13	339	4
5	188	3	14	445	4
6	486	5	15	468	4
7	551	5	16	356	4
8	406	4	17	413	4
9	162	3	18	386	4
Out	**3,270**	**35**	**In**	**3,415**	**36**
			Out	**3,270**	**35**
			Totals	**6,685**	**71**

Royal Liverpool (Hoylake)

The Royal Hotel at Hoylake (alas no longer with us) played a starring role in the early history of the Royal Liverpool Golf Club. In 1869 a meeting was held there which led to the famous club's formation. Perhaps of greater significance that day, with no disrespect whatsoever to those founding members, was the presence in the hotel of a seven year old boy. John Ball, whose father was the hotel proprietor, grew to become not only Hoylake's favourite son, but also the finest amateur golfer Britain has ever produced.

In the early days, golf at Hoylake must have been at times a trifle frustrating, for the club shared the links with a racecourse and hoofprints on the fairways were a fairly common hazard. However, by 1876 the horses (doubtless equally frustrated) had found elsewhere to gallop and the golf course quickly developed into England's premier championship test. The 1869 birthdate in fact makes Hoylake England's second oldest links course—just four years younger than Westward Ho! in Devon.

Ten Open Championships and seventeen Amateur Championships later, visitors are welcome to play at Hoylake, subject to proof of handicap or letter of introduction from their home club. Green Fee rates for 2000 are: £65 per round/£90 per day on weekdays and £100 per round on weekends, only after 2.30pm. The tee is reserved for members until 9.30am and between 1.00pm and 2.00pm.

On weekdays, individual bookings must be made through the **Secretary, Group Captain Christopher Moore, tel: 0151 632 3101** or by **fax: 0151 632 6737**, who will also authorise limited weekend bookings. Organisers should address written applications to: **The Secretary, Royal Liverpool Golf Club, Meols Drive, Hoylake, Wirral, Merseyside CH47 4AL.** You may also contact the club by **e mail: sec@rlgc.u-net.com** or at **http://www.royal-liverpool.golf.com.**

John Heggarty is the club's **Professional.** Through him, lessons can be booked, clubs hired, and caddies obtained. Mr Heggarty can be reached on **tel: (0151) 632 5868.**

Hoylake is located at the tip of the Wirral peninsula, approximately ten miles west of Liverpool and fifteen miles north of Chester. The north west of England is particularly well served by motorway connections and finding the course shouldn't be a

problem. Approaching from either the north or south the M6 is likely to be of assistance; it passes midway between Manchester and Liverpool and should be left at junction 19A. Thereafter the M56 can be followed towards Chester joining the M53 at junction 15. The M53 will then take you to the far end of the Wirral where the A553 Hoylake road should be picked up. (In a nutshell: M6—M56—M53—A553).

The course occupies fairly flat ground and is very exposed to the elements. It is most unusual for the wind not to blow. (You have been warned!) It was his mastery of the wind, a skill acquired playing at Hoylake that enabled John Ball to win many of his record eight Amateur Championships. His victories were achieved between 1888 and 1912. Ball's great rival during those years, both remarkably, and ironically, was a fellow Hoylake man, Harold Hilton. Hilton himself won four Amateur Championships. In addition both Hilton and Ball won the Open Championship, Ball in 1890 and Hilton twice, in 1892 and 1897. The great Bobby Jones is the only other amateur golfer to have won the Open title.

Even on those very rare occasions when all is calm, Hoylake is still an exceptionally difficult test. From the medal tees the course measures 6848 yards, par 72, and it can play every inch of its length. If the most interesting and classic links type sequence of holes occurs between the 8th and the 13th, the end of the round provides a real 'sting in the tail'. Rather like Carnoustie, Hoylake is renowned for its exacting final stretch. It contains two par fives and three par fours, any of which is capable of wrecking a potentially good score. The long 16th in particular can be cruelly punishing with its out of bounds to the right of the fairway.

The ten Opens held at Hoylake produced ten different champions and among them some of the game's greatest names: Harold Hilton, John H Taylor, Walter Hagen and Bobby Jones. The latter's victory in 1930 was the second leg of the historic grand slam.

The sole reason for the course being presently 'off the Open rota' (the last staging was in 1967 when Roberto de Vicenzo won) is that the course cannot accommodate the vast crowds that the event now attracts. Unfortunately, it is the same enthusiastic public who suffer most, for there are many who maintain that Hoylake remains the

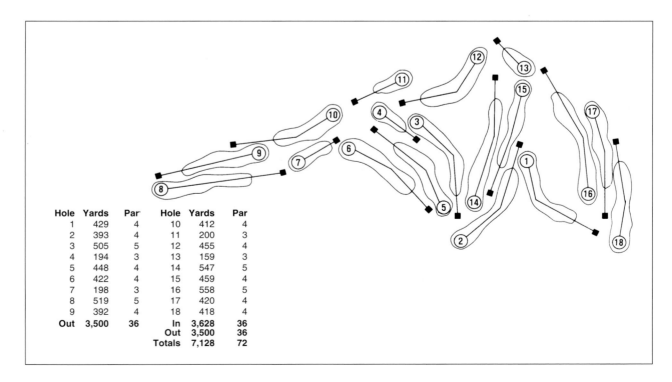

Hole	Yards	Par	Hole	Yards	Par
1	429	4	10	412	4
2	393	4	11	200	3
3	505	5	12	455	4
4	194	3	13	159	3
5	448	4	14	547	5
6	422	4	15	459	4
7	198	3	16	558	5
8	519	5	17	420	4
9	392	4	18	418	4
Out	**3,500**	**36**	**In**	**3,628**	**36**
			Out	**3,500**	**36**
			Totals	**7,128**	**72**

Hillside

If Royal Birkdale is the finest golf links in England (and most commentators seem to think it is) then Hillside must surely be number two. Why so? Well, firstly, they occupy the very same magnificent golfing country being laid out literally side by side amid a vast stretch of sandhills near Southport and, secondly, when analysing the quality of the individual golf holes people find it very difficult to separate the two courses. Perhaps it is only Birkdale's Open Championship history which accords it precedence. And why hasn't Hillside staged the 'Big One'? Presumably it's because it is only since 1967, when Hillside's back nine holes were completely reshaped, that it has deserved to be ranked alongside its more illustrious neighbour. The front nine at Hillside has long been highly regarded, but the newer second nine is really outstanding and indeed very spectacular—a bit like Ballybunion minus the Atlantic Ocean.

Since 1967 Hillside has hosted a number of important championships. In the late 1970s both the British Ladies Championship and the Amateur Championship were held here and in 1982 came the European Tour's prestigious PGA Championship. A great course and a great event produced a great winner when Tony Jacklin defeated the up-and-coming Bernhard Langer in a thrilling playoff.

From the back tees Hillside measures a daunting 6850 yards, par 72. The first two holes, however, are fairly straightforward—provided you don't hook on to the railway line! The 3rd is a really first class dog-leg hole where the approach must be played over a brook to a green that is well protected by deep traps. Stray to the right with your second shot and you'll land in a pond. Stray to the right at the next, the short 4th, and your ball will be greeted by one of three bunkers that are just as devilish as those on the 3rd. The 5th is a real teaser. It is a par five that can be reached with two good blows, and you can see everything from the tee by virtue of a gap in the dunes fifty yards short of the green. The problem is that a

seemingly magnetic sleepered bunker has been placed in the gap. Three of the next four holes are difficult dog-leg par fours. The 7th is the breather—a lovely par three played downhill towards a generous green backed by some magnificent tall pines.

The second nine commences with another outstanding short hole. The 10th measures only 147 yards but it's a much tougher green to hit than most and is ringed by a series of alarmingly cavernous bunkers—yes, Hillside is inundated with them! Of the remaining holes only the 12th and the 15th could be described as anything less than superb, with the two par fives, the 11th and 17th which both weave a path through a wonderful dune-lined valley, being possibly the best holes of the entire round.

Hillside Golf Club, Hastings Road, Hillside, Southport, Merseyside, PR8 2LU	
Sec/Manager	John Graham (01704) 567169
Professional	Brian Seddon (01704) 568360
Green Fees	WD £45/round, £60/day
	Sunday pm £60/round
Restrictions	No visitors on Saturdays; limited Sunday golf, handicap certificates.

Formby

According to the traditionalist, as opposed to the pure pleasure-seeker, there is only one genuine form of golf and that is the sort played on a links. To this person golf might be just as enjoyable (and probably a darn sight easier when the wind blows!) on an inland course but it is not quite the real thing: Sunningdale, Gleneagles, Wentworth—all wonderful places but . . . By contrast, from the pure pleasure-seeker's point of view these courses may be more attractive, not because the challenge is less intimidating but because many of the best links courses tend to be fairly bleak places where the golfer is exposed. Trees are either very rare or non-existent. Often the layout of the course is a tiresome 'straight out and straight back'.

Formby is a very special place, for it is here that the traditionalist and the pure pleasure-seeker can play a round of golf together and not fall out. Formby is a links—no question about it—firm, fast seaside greens, natural sandy bunkers and some fairly prodigious sandhills. But Formby is also blessed with a plethora of pine trees which add great beauty to the scene and often considerable shelter. Many of Formby's holes weave their way a good bit below the level of the surrounding dunes, creating a feeling of privacy, or at least occasional intimacy, so rare on a links course. And Formby certainly doesn't stretch 'out and back'—in fact, the bird's eye view of the links reveals eleven distinct changes of direction.

Included among most people's favourite holes at Formby are the par five 3rd and the par three 5th; the 7th with its raised green and avenue of pines and the genuinely glorious 12th. Formby's celebrated 4-3-5-4 finish calls for some very precise shot making and at the end of the round there is every chance that the golfer will have used every club in his bag. In total the course measures 6993 yards, par 72.

Although the Open Championship has never visited Formby the club regularly hosts important amateur events. Just a week after the Open

was played at Royal Birkdale in 1991, the English Amateur was being staged 'down the road' at Formby.

In the piece on Royal Birkdale, featured elsewhere in this chapter, we mentioned how in the Open of 1976 a raw and hitherto unknown 19 year old burst on to the scene finishing joint runner up to Johnny Miller. Arguably the high point of Ballesteros' career came in 1984 when he overcame Tom Watson to win his second Open title at St Andrews. Later that same summer, Formby, celebrating its centenary, hosted the Amateur Championship and another teenage Spaniard wrote his name into the history books—Jose-Maria Olazabal who produced some sensational golf to defeat a future British Ryder Cup star, Colin Montgomerie. Perhaps the Spanish Armada should have tried landing in Lancashire all those centuries ago.

Formby Golf Club, Golf Road, Formby, Liverpool, L37 1LQ www.formbygolfclub.co.uk	
Sec/Manager	K.R. Wilcox (01704) 872164
Professional	Gary Butler (01704) 873090
	Fax (01704) 833028
Green Fees	WD £60 in Summer
	Winter rates on application
Restrictions	Limited golf is available at weekends
	Handicap certificates are required.
Directions	
Formby lies 12 miles north of Liverpool and 4 miles south of Southport on the A565.	

Castletown

Was the Isle of Man ever part of the mainland? If so, which mainland? Situated almost exactly midway between Great Britain and Ireland and roughly equidistant, as the seagull flies, from England, Scotland, Northern Ireland and the Republic, it looks as if Providence deliberately positioned it in mid-ocean so that no-one could claim it as theirs.

The Irish theory, however, has much appeal. One of the Emerald Isle's greatest heroes, Finn McCool—a legend in his own lifetime, and the Giant who started to build the famous Causeway—was really responsible for its location. One day, Finn got out of bed on the wrong side and started to have one of those days. Finn's personality problem was his temper—the only thing about him that was short. This particular day he completely lost his rag and Finn McCool became Finn Not-so-Cool. He grabbed the largest rock he could find and hurled it 50 miles into the sea. Today, that huge rock is known as the Isle of Man.

Enough about the geography and history of the island. What of the golf? Put Castletown aside for a second and it is pretty fair, add Castletown to the equation and it is pretty excellent. What really makes Castletown is its extraordinary location on the island. Like St Andrews the course is laid out on a fairly thin strip of land but unlike St Andrews it is surrounded by water on three sides, the golf links being laid out on a very unusual, triangular peninsula. This is the Langness Peninsula, more commonly known as Fort Island, situated right on the south eastern tip of the Isle of Man only a few minutes from the island's airport at Ronaldsway.

The extraordinary location produces some amazing seascapes and is more or less perfect links terrain, the architect who designed Castletown was given a mighty head start by Mother Nature. Fortunately for you and me they didn't give the task to any old architect either. The original layout was prepared by 'Old' Tom Morris—he of course was the chap who reckoned that Machrihanish was 'designed by The Almighty for playing golf'. What must he have thought of this site? (Interestingly, there is more than a hint of Machrihanish about some of the holes at Castletown). After the last war Castletown was reshaped and this time another celebrated architect was brought in to oversee the project—Mackenzie Ross, the man who converted Turnberry from a battle station into the majestic links it now is.

Unless one is fortunate enough to be a member of Castletown Golf Club, by far the easiest way of inspecting Ross's masterpiece is to stay overnight at the adjacent Castletown Golf Links Hotel. The hotel actually owns the golf course and booking a game is much easier for hotel guests. Residents have priority over visitors and pay reduced green fees. Non residents can only book tee times one month in advance. This is not to say that they are unwelcome at short notice, it is just that it may be a case of pot luck. Bookings may be made through the **Hotel Golf Secretary, Tony Karran tel: (01624) 825435** or by **fax: (01624) 824633**. Visitors who do not have a tee reservation should contact the club's **Professional, Murray Crowe (01624) 822211**. The green fees for 2000 are £25 per day for hotel residents. Visitors pay £28.50 per day between Monday and Thursday and £33 at all other times.

Because of the hotel, its adjoining links and its course architect, Castletown has been called the 'Poor Man's Turnberry'. This is actually intended as a compliment.

Certainly, there is nothing poor about the hotel or its golf course— the quality of both is excellent. In fact many people believe the golf at Castletown is just as enjoyable (if a little less testing) and scenically as enchanting as the famous Ailsa Course. From its championship tees the links can be stretched to 6711 yards, par 72. The corresponding lengths from the medal and forward tees are 6534 yards and 6093 yards respectively.

Among the best holes on the course are two fine par threes, the 8th and the 13th, the sharply dog-legging 4th and a truly spectacular pair, the 5th and the 17th. The former carries a famous name, 'The Road Hole.' There are no railway sheds to drive over here but terror does lurk all the way down the right side of the fairway—a sliced drive will either end up on tarmac, the beach or the sea. Take the road away and from the back tee the 5th is almost a mirror image of the 1st at Machrihanish—it is of a similar length too at 422 yards. There are no bunkers around the green but then getting there is problematical enough.

The 17th is called 'The Gully' and again a brave long drive is needed if the direct route to the green is taken. The carry is nearly 200 yards over a deep chasm, and rocks and frothy water await the mishit shot. You stand on the 17th tee at Castletown with the knowledge that your drive could finish up in England, Scotland, Ireland or even Wales. As the great Nigel would say, only the best drivers stay on the Isle of Man.

Hole	Yards	Par	Hole	Yards	Par
1	253	4	10	355	4
2	391	4	11	443	4
3	557	5	12	503	5
4	377	4	13	139	3
5	422	4	14	394	4
6	384	4	15	373	4
7	567	5	16	186	3
8	164	3	17	417	4
9	389	4	18	417	4
Out	**3,484**	**37**	**In**	**3,227**	**35**
			Out	**3,484**	**37**
			Totals	**6,711**	**72**

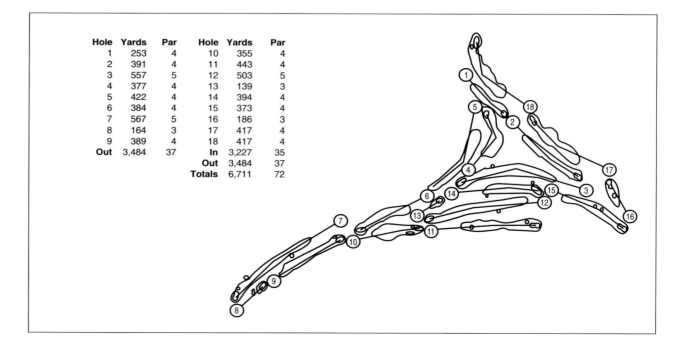

MANCHESTER AREA

Acre Gate G.C.
(0161) 748 1226
Pennybridge Lane, Flixton
(18) 4395 yards/***/E

Altrincham G.C.
(0161) 928 0761
Stockport Road, Timperley
(18) 6162 yards/***/D

Ashton-in-Makerfield G.C.
(01942) 727267
Garswood Park, Ashton-in-Makerfield
(18) 6250 yards/**(Wed)/C/G

Ashton-on-Mersey G.C.
(0161) 976 4390
Church Lane, Sale
(9) 3076 yards/**(Tues)/C/H

Ashton-under-Lyne G.C.
(0161) 330 1537
Gorsey Way, Ashton-under-Lyne
(18) 6209 yards/**/G

Avro G.C.
(01942) 870757
Old Hall Lane, Woodford
(9) 5735 yards/*/F/G

Blackley G.C.
(0161) 643 2980
Victoria Avenue East, Blackley
(18) 6237 yards/**(Thurs)/C

Bolton G.C.
(01204) 843067
Chorley Old Road, Bolton
(18) 6215 yards/***/B

Bolton Old Links
(01204) 840050
Links Road, Bolton
(18) 6406 yards/***/A

Bolton Open Golf
(01204) 309778
Longsight Lane, Harwood
(9)/**/E

Brackley G.C.
(0161) 790 6076
Bullows Road, Little Hulton
(9) 6006 yards/***/E

Bramhall G.C.
(0161) 439 4057
Ladythorn Road, Bramhall
(18) 6293 yards/***(Thurs)/B/M

Bramhall Park G.C.
(0161) 485 3119
Manor Road, Bramhall
(18) 6214 yards/***/B-A/L

Breightmet G.C.
(01204) 827381
Red Bridge, Ainsworth, Bolton
(9) 6416 yards/**/C

Brookdale G.C.
(0161) 681 4534
Woodhouses, Failsworth
(18) 6040 yards/***/C/H

Bury G.C.
(0161) 766 4897
Unsworth Hall, Blackford Bridge
(18) 5961 yards/**/C/H

Castle Hawk G.C.
(01706) 40841
Heywood Road, Castleton,
(18) 5398 yards/***/E
(9) 3158 yards/***/E

Cheadle G.C.
(0161) 428 2160
Shiers Drive, Cheadle
(9) 5006 yards/***(Tues/Sat)C/H/L

Chorlton-cum-Hardy G.C.
(0161) 881 5830
Barlow Hall Road, Chorlton
(18) 6003 yards/***/C/H

Crompton & Royton G.C.
(0161) 624 0986
Highbarn, Royton, Oldham
(18) 6222 yards/**(Tues/Wed)/B/H

Davyhulme Park G.C.
(0161) 748 2260
Gleneagles Road, Davyhulme
(18) 6237 yards/**(Wed)/B/H/L

Deane G.C.
(01204) 861944
Broadford Road, Deane, Bolton
(18) 5583 yards/**/C/H/M

Denton G.C.
(0161) 336 3218
Manchester Road, Denton
(18) 6290 yards/**/B/H

Didsbury G.C.
(0161) 998 9278
Ford Lane, Northenden
(18) 6273 yards/**/C/H

Disley G.C.
(01663) 762071
Stanley Hall Lane, Digby
(18) 6015 yards/***/B

Dukinfield G.C.
(0161) 338 2340
Lyne Edge, Ashton-under-Lyne
(18) 5585 yards/**/D

Dunham Forest G.& C.C.
(0161) 928 2605
Oldfield Lane, Altrincham
(18) 6636 yards/**/B/H

Dunscar G.C.
(01204) 598228
Longworth Lane, Bromley Cross
(18) 6085 yards/**/B/H

Ellesmere G.C.
(0161) 799 0554
Old Clough Lane, Worsley
(18) 5957 yards/***/C/H/M

Fairfield Golf & Sailing Club
(0161) 370 1641
Booth Road, Audenshaw
(18) 5654 yards/**/D

Flixton G.C.
(0161) 748 2116
Church Road, Flixton
(9) 6410 yards/**/D

Gathurst G.C.
(01257) 252861
Miles Lane, Shevington, Wigan
(9) 6308 yards/**(Wed)/C

Gatley G.C.
(0161) 437 2091
Styal Road, Heald Green, Gatley
(9) 5934 yards/**(Tues)/C

Great Lever & Farnworth G.C.
(01204) 656137
Lever Edge Lane, Bolton
(18) 5859 yards/**/C/H

Greenmount G.C.
(01204) 883712
Greenmount, Bury
(9) 4920 yards/**(Tues)/D/H

Haigh Hall G.C.
(01942) 833337
Haigh Country Park, Haigh, Wigan
(18) 6423 yards/***/E

Hale G.C.
(0161) 980 4225
Rappax Road, Hale
(9) 5780 yards/**(Thurs)/C

Harwood G.C.
(01204) 522878
Roading Brook Road, Bolton
(9) 5993 yards/**/D

Hazel Grove G.C.
(0161) 483 3978
Buxton Road, Stockport
(18) 6310 yards/***/B/H

Heaton Moor G.C.
(0161) 432 2134
Heaton Mersey, Stockport
(18) 5876 yards/***(Tues)/B-A

Heaton Park G.C.
(0161) 798 0295
Heaton Park, Prestwich
(18) 5849 yards/***/E

Hindley Hall G.C.
(01942) 255131
Hall Lane, Hindley, Wigan
(18) 5904 yards/**(Wed)/B/H/L

Horwich G.C.
(01204) 696980
Victoria Road, Horwich, Bolton
(9) 5404 yards/*/F/G

Houldsworth G.C.
(0161) 442 9611
Reddish, Stockport
(18) 6078 yards/**/C

Lowes Park G.C.
(0161) 764 1231
Hill Top, Bury
(9) 6043 yards/**(Wed)/C/M

Manchester G.C.
(0161) 643 2718
Rochdale Road, Middleton
(18) 6464 yards/**/B/H

Manor G.C.
(01204) 705651
Moss Lane, Kearsley
(18) 5000 yards/**/E

Marple G.C.
(0161) 427 2311
Hawk Green, Marple
(18) 5700 yards/***(Thurs)/B/H

Mellor & Townscliffe G.C.
(0161) 427 2208
Tarden, Gibb Lane, Mellor
(18) 5925 yards/**/B

North Manchester G.C.
(0161) 643 9033
Manchester Old Road, Middleton
(18) 6527 yards/***/C

Northenden G.C.
(0161) 998 4738
Palatine Road, Northenden
(18) 6469 yards/***/B/H

Oldham G.C.
(0161) 624 4986
Lees New Road, Oldham
(18) 5045 yards/***/F

Pennington G.C.
(01942) 876444
St Helens Road, Leigh
(9) 2919 yards/***/F

Pike Folds G.C.
(0161) 740 1136
Victoria Avenue, Blackley
(9) 5789 yards/**/D

Prestwich G.C.
(0161) 773 2544
Hilton Lane, Prestwich
(18) 4712 yards/**/C/H

Reddish Vale G.C.
(0161) 480 2359
Southcliffe Road, Reddish
(18)6086 yards/**/C/H

Regent Park G.C.
(01204) 844170
Chorley New Road, Bolton
(18) 6069 yards/***/E

Ringway G.C.
(0161) 904 9609
Hale Barns, Altrincham
(18) 6494 yards/***/B-A/H

Romiley G.C.
(0161) 430 2392
Goosehouse Green, Romiley
(18) 6421 yards/***/B

Saddleworth G.C.
(01457) 873653
Mountain Ash, Uppermill
(18) 5976 yards/***/B/H

Sale G.C.
(0161) 973 1638
Sale Lodge, Golf Road, Sale
(18) 6346 yards/***/B/H/M

Stamford G.C.
(01457) 832126
Huddersfield Road, Stalybridge
(18) 5701 yards/**/F

Stand G.C.
(0161) 766 3197
Ashbourne Grove, Whitefield
(18) 6425 yards/***/B/H

Standish Court G.C.
(01257) 425777
Rectory Lane, Standish
(18) 5625 yards/***/D

Stockport G.C.
(0161) 427 8369
Offerton Road, Offerton, Stockport
(18) 6326 yards/***/A/M

Swinton Park G.C.
(0161) 794 0861
East Lancashire Road, Swinton
(18) 6712 yards/**/F/H

Turton G.C.
(01204) 852235
Wood End Farm, Bromley Cross
(18) 5894 yards/**(Wed)/D

Walmersley G.C.
(0161) 764 1429
Garretts Close, Walmersley, Bury
(9) 3057 yards/**(Tues)/C

Werneth G.C.
(0161) 624 1190
Green Lane, Garden Suburb, Oldham
(18) 5363 yards/**/D

Werneth Low G.C.
(0161) 368 2503
Werneth Low Road, Hyde
(9) 5734 yards/**/C

Westhoughton G.C.
(01942) 811085
Westhoughton, Bolton
(9) 5834 yards/**/D

Whitefield G.C.
(0161) 766 2904
Higher Lane, Whitefield
(18) 6045 yards/***/B/H/L
(18) 5755 yards/***/B/H/L

Whittaker G.C.
(01706) 378310
Whittaker Lane, Littleborough
(9) 5576 yards/***(Sun)/D

William Wroe G.C.
(0161) 748 8680
Pennybridge Lane, Flixton
(18) 4395 yards/***/E

Withington G.C.
(0161) 445 9544
Palatine Road, West Didsbury
(18) 6411 yards/***(Thurs)/B/H

Worsley G.C.
(0161) 789 4202
Stableford Avenue, Monton, Eccles
(18) 6217 yards/***/B/H/L

LANCASHIRE

Accrington & District G.C.
(01254) 381614
West End, Oswaldtwistle
(18) 5954 yards/***/D

Ashton & Lea G.C.
(01772) 735282
Tudor Avenue, Lea, Preston
(18) 6289 yards/***/C

Bacup G.C.
(01706) 873170
Maden Road,Bacup
(9) 5652 yards/***(Tues)/D

Baxenden & District G.C.
(01254) 234555
Top o' th' Meadow, Baxenden
(9) 5740 yards/**/D

Beacon Park G.C.
(01695) 622700
Beacon Hill, Dalton, Up Holland, Wigan
(18) 5996 yards/***/F

Bentham G.C.
(01524) 261018
Robin Lane, Bentham
(9) 5760 yards/***/D

Blackburn G.C.
(01254) 51122
Beardwood Brow, Blackburn
(18) 6147 yards/**(Tues)/C/H

Blackpool North Shore G.C.
(01253) 351017
Devonshire Road, Blackpool
(18) 6442 yards/***(Thurs/Sat)/B/H

Blackpool Park G.C.
(01253) 397916
North Park Drive, Blackpool
(18) 6192 yards/***/E

Burnley G.C.
(01282) 421045
Glen View, Burnley
(18) 5899 yards/***/C/H

Charnock Richard G.C.
(01257) 470707
Prestoon Road, Chasrnock Richard
(18) 6234 yards/D

Chorley G.C.
(01257) 480263
Hall o' th' Hill, Heath Charnock, Chorley
(18) 6295 yards/**/C/H/L

Clitheroe G.C.
(01200) 422292
Whalley Road, Pendleton
(18) 6326 yards/***/B/H

Colne G.C.
(01282) 863391
Law Farm, Skipton Old Road
(9) 5961 yards/***/D

Darwen G.C.
(01254) 701287
Winter Hill, Darwen
(18) 5752 yards/***(Sat)/D

Dean Wood G.C.
(01695) 622219
Lafford Lane, Up Holland, Skelmersdale
(18) 6137 yards/**/B

Duxbury Park G.C.
(01257) 265380
Duxbury Hall Road, Chorley
(18) 6390 yards/***/E

Fairhaven G.C.
(01253) 736741
Lytham Hall Park, Ansdell, Lytham
(18) 6883 yards/***/B/H

Fishwick Hall G.C.
(01772) 798300
Glenluce Drive, Farringdon Park, Preston
(18) 6092 yards/**/B

Fleetwood G.C.
(01253) 873661
Princes Way, Fleetwood
(18) 6723 yards/***/B/H

Garstang Country Hotel & G.C.
(01995) 600100
Garstang Road, Bowgreave
(18) 6050 yards/***/E

Ghyll G.C.
(01282) 842466
Ghyll Brow, Barnoldswick
(9) 5422 yards/***(Sun)/D

Great Harwood G.C.
(01254) 884391
Whalley Road, Harwood Bar
(9) 6413 yards/***/D

Green Haworth G.C.
(01254) 237580
Green Haworth, Accrington
(9) 5556 yards/***/D

Herons Reach G.C.
(01253) 838866
East Park Drive, Blackpool
(18) 6416 yards/***/B/H

Heysham G.C.
(01524) 851011
Trumacar Park, Middleton Road, Heysham
(18) 6258 yards/***/C/H

Hurlston Hall G.C.
(01704) 840400
Hurlston Lane, Scarisbrick
(18) 6700 yards/**/C/H

Ingol Golf and Squash Club
(01772) 734556
Tanterton Hall Rd, Ingol
(18) 5868 yards/***/C

Knott End G.C.
(01253) 810576
Knott End on Sea
(18) 5789 yards/**/C/H

Lancaster G.& C.C.
(01524) 751247
Ashton Hall, Ashton-with-Stodday
(18) 6282 yards/**/B/H

Lansil G.C.
(01524) 39269
Caton Road, Lancaster
(9) 5608 yards/***/D/H

Leyland G.C.
(01772) 436457
Wigan Road, Leyland
(18) 6123 yards/**/C

Lobden G.C.
(01706) 343228
Whitworth, Rochdale
(9) 5750 yards/***/D/H

Longridge G.C.
(01772) 783291
Fell Barn, Jeffrey Hill, Longridge
(18) 5800 yards/***/C

Lytham Green Drive G.C.
(01253) 737390
Ballam Road, Lytham
(18) 6175 yards/**/B-A/H

Marland G.C.
(01706) 49801
Springfield Park, Rochdale
(18) 5237 yards/***/E

Marsden Park G.C.
(01282) 614094
Townhouse Road, Nelson
(18) 5806 yards/***/F

Morecambe G.C.
(01524) 418050
Bare, Morecambe
(18) 5766 yards/***/B/H

Mytton Fold G.C.
(01254) 240662
Langho, Blackburn
(18) 6217 yards/***/D

Nelson G.C.
(01282) 614583
Kings Causeway, Brierfield, Nelson
(18) 5967 yards/**(Thurs/Sat)/C/H

Ormskirk G.C.
(01695) 572227
Cranes Lane, Lathom, Ormskirk
(18) 6358 yards/***(Sat)/B/H/L

Penwortham G.C.
(01772) 744630
Blundell Lane, Penwortham
(18) 5915 yards/**(Tues)/B

Pleasington G.C.
(01254) 202177
Pleasington, Blackburn
(18) 6417 yards/**(Tues)/B/H

Poulton-le-Fylde G.C.
(01253) 892444
Breck Road, Poulton-le-Fylde
(9) 2979 yards/***/E

Preston G.C.
(01772) 700011
Fulwood Hall Lane, Fulwood, Preston
(18) 6233 yards/**/B/H

Rishton G.C.
(01254) 884442
Eachill Links, Blackburn
(9) 6094 yards/**/D

Rochdale G.C.
(01706) 43818
Edenfield Road, Bagslate, Rochdale
(18) 6002 yards/***/B

Rossendale G.C.
(01706) 213056
Ewood Lane, Haslingden
(18) 6267 yards/***(Sat)/B

Royal Lytham & St Annes G.C.
(01253) 724206
St Annes on Sea, Lytham
(18) 6685 yards/**/A/H/L

St Annes Old Links G.C.
(01253) 723597
Highbury Road, Lytham St Annes
(18) 6616 yards/**(Tues)/B-A/H

Shaw Hill G.& C.C.
(01257) 269221
Whittle-le-Woods, Chorley
(18) 6467 yards/***/A/H

Silverdale G.C.
(01524) 701300
Red Bridge Lane, Silverdale, Carnforth
(9) 5417 yards/***/D

Springfield Park G.C.
(01706) 56401
Springfield Park, Bolton Road, Rochdale
(18) 5209 yards/***/E

Stonyhurst Park G.C.
(01254) 826478
Hurst Green, Blackburn
(9) 5529 yards/**/D

Towneley G.C.
(01282) 451636
Todmorden Road, Burnley
(18) 5862 yards/***/E

Tunshill G.C.
(01706) 342095
Kiln Lane, Milnrow
(9) 5812 yards/**(Tues pm)/F

Whalley G.C.
(01254) 822236
Portfield Lane, Whalley, Blackburn
(9) 6258 yards/***/C

Wigan G.C.
(01257) 421360
Arley Hall, Haigh, Wigan
(9) 6058 yards/***(Tues/Sat)/B

Wilpshire G.C.
(01254) 248260
Whalley Road, Wilpshire, Blackburn
(18) 5911 yards/***/B/H

LIVERPOOL AREA

Allerton Park G.C.
(0151) 428 1048
Allerton, Liverpool
(18) 5494 yards/***/E
(9) 1845 yards/***/E

Arrowe Park G.C.
(0151) 677 1527
Arrowe Park, Woodchurch, Birkenhead
(18) 6377 yards/***/E

Bidston G.C.
(0151) 638 8685
Bidston Link Road, Wallasey
(18) 6207 yards/**/D

Blundells Hill G.C.
(01744) 24892
Blundells Lane, Rainhill
(18) 6347 yards/***/B

Bootle G.C.
(0151) 928 6196
Dunnings Bridge Road, Bootle
(18) 6362 yards/***/F

Bowring G.C.
(0151) 489 1901
Bowring Park, Roby Road, Huyton
(9) 5592 yards/***/F

Brackenwood G.C.
(0151) 608 3093
Bracken Lane, Bebington
(18) 6285 yards/***/F

Bromborough G.C.
(0151) 334 2155
Raby Hall Road, Bromborough
(18) 6650 yards/**/B

Caldy G.C.
(0151) 625 5660
Links Hey Road, Caldy, Wirral
(18) 6675 yards/**/F

Childwall G.C.
(0151) 487 0654
Naylors Road, Gateacre
(18) 6425 yards/**(Tues)/B/H

Dudley Golf Club
(0151) 428 7490
Allerton Park, Allerton
(18) 5494 yards/**/E

Eastham Lodge G.C.
(0151) 327 3003
Ferry Road, Eastham, Wirral
(15) 5813 yards/**/C/H

Formby G.C.
(01704) 872164
Golf Road, Formby
(18) 6695 yards/**(Wed/Sun))/A/H/L

Formby Ladies G.C.
(01704) 873493
Golf Road, Formby
(18) 5374 yards/***(Thurs)/B-A/H

Grand National G.C.
(0151) 523 5157
Melling Road, Aintree
(18) 6624 yards/**/E

Grange Park G.C.
(01744) 26318
Prescot Road, St Helens
(18) 6429 yards/**/B/L

Haydock Park G.C.
(01925) 228525
Golbourne Park, Newton-le-Willows
(18) 6043 yards/**(not Tues)/B/M

Hesketh G.C.
(01704) 536897
Cockle Dicks Lane, Southport
(18) 6478 yards/**/B-A/H

Heswall G.C.
(0151) 342 1237
Cottage Lane, Gayton, Heswall
(18) 6472 yards/***/A/H

Hillside G.C.
(01704) 567169
Hastings Road, Hillside, Southport
(18) 6850 yards/**/A/H/M

Hoylake Municipal G.C.
(0151) 632 2956
Carr Lane, Hoylake
(18) 6330 yards/***/E

Huyton and Prescot G.C.
(0151) 489 3948
Hurst Park, Huyton Lane, Huyton
(18) 5738 yards/**/F/L

Kirkby (Liverpool Municipal) G.C.
(0151) 546 7031
Ingoe Lane, Kirkby
(18) 6571 yards/***/F/H

Leasowe G.C.
(0151) 677 5852
Leasowe Road, Moreton, Wirral
(18) 6204 yards/***/C/H

Lee Park G.C.
(0151) 487 3882
Childwall Valley Road, Gateacre
(18) 6024 yards/***/F/L

Park G.C.
(01704) 530133
Park Road, Southport
(18) 6200 yards/**/F

Prenton G.C.
0151 608 1053
Golf Links Road, Prenton, Birkenhead
(18) 6411 yards/***/B/H

Royal Birkdale G.C.
(01704) 569903
Waterloo Road, Birkdale, Southport
(18) 6988 yards/**/A/H/L

Royal Liverpool G.C.
0151 632 3101
Meols Drive, Hoylake, Wirral
(18) 7128 yards/**/A/H/L

Sherdley Park Municipal G.C.
(01744) 813149
Sherdley Road, St Helens
(18) 5941 yards/***/E

Southport & Ainsdale G.C.
(01704) 578000
Bradshaws Lane, Ainsdale, Southport
(18) 6612 yards/**/A/H/M

Southport G.C.
(01704) 535286
Park Road West, Southport
(18) 6400 yards/***/F

Southport Old Links G.C.
(01704) 28207
Moss Lane, Southport
(9) 6486 yards/**(Wed)/C/H

Wallasey G.C.
0151 691 1024
Bayswater Road, Wallasey
(18) 6607 yards/**/B/H/M

Warren G.C.
0151 639 5730
Grove Road, Wallasey
(9) 5914/***/F

West Derby G.C.
0151 254 1034
Yew Tree Lane, Liverpool
(18) 6333 yards/**/B

West Lancashire G.C.
0151 924 1076
Hall Road West, Blundellsands, Crosby
(18) 6756 yards/***/B-A/H

Wirral Ladies G.C.
0151 652 1255
Bidston Road, Oxton, Birkenhead
(18) 4966 yards(ladies)***/F/H/L
(18) 5170 yards/(men)***F/H/L

ISLE OF MAN

Castletown G.C.
(01624) 822201
Fort Island, Derbyhaven
(18) 6711 yards/***/C

Douglas G.C.
(01624) 675952
Douglas
(18) 6080 yards/***/F

King Edward Bay G.& C.C.
(01624) 672709
Groudle Road, Onchan
(18) 5457 yards/***/D

Mount Murray G & C.C.
(01624) 661111
Santon
(18) 6709 yards/***/E-D/H

Peel G.C.
(01624) 844232
Rheast Lane, Peel
(18) 5914 yards/**/D/H

Port St Mary G.C.
(01624) 497387
Kallow Road, Port St Mary
(9) 2711 yards/***/F

Pulrose G.C.
(01624) 661558
Pulrose Road, Douglas
(18) 6080 yards/***/F

Ramsey G.C.
(01624) 812244
Brookfield, Ramsey
(18) 6019 yards/**/D/H

Rowany G.C.
(01624) 834108
Rowany Drive, Port Erin
(18) 5840 yards/***/D/H

Map labels (Yorkshire golf courses):

© MAPS IN MINUTES ™ 2000

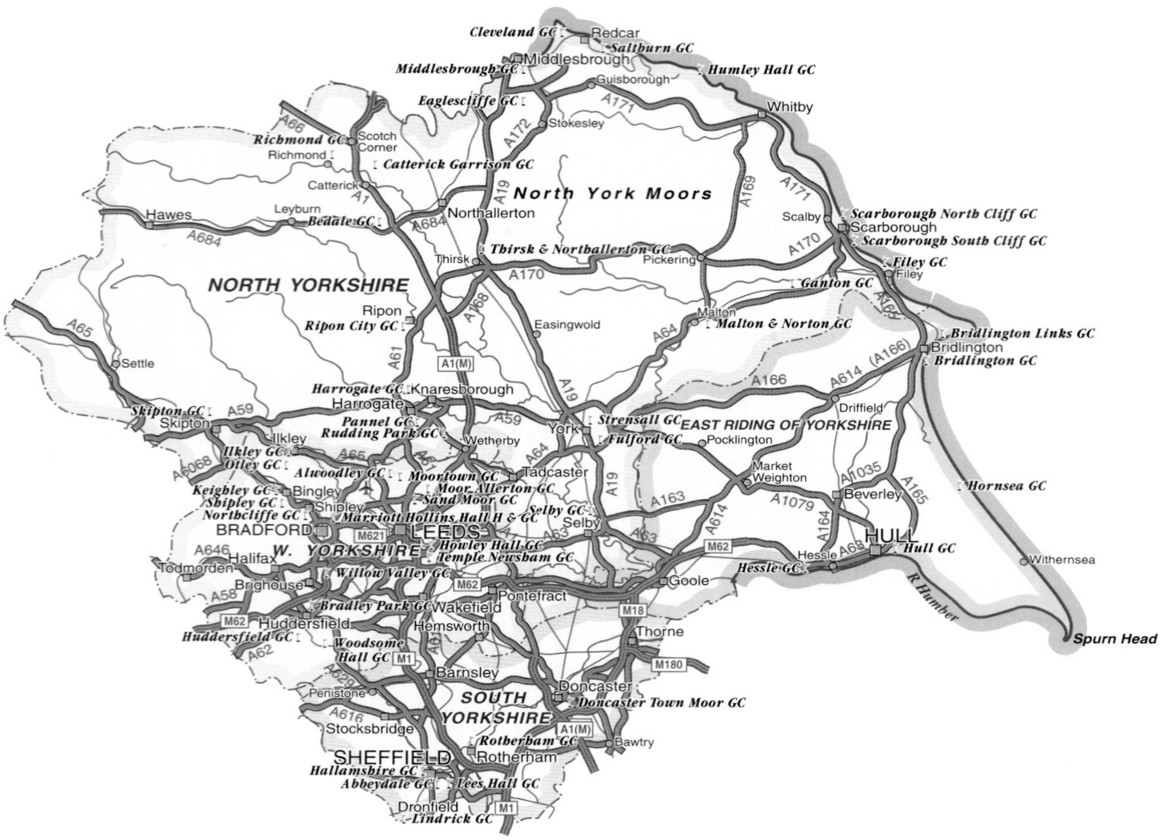

Cleveland GC · Redcar · Saltburn GC · Middlesbrough · Middlesbrough GC · Humley Hall GC · Guisborough · Whitby · Eaglescliffe GC · Stokesley · A171 · A172 · A169 · A171 · Richmond GC · Scotch Corner · Catterick Garrison GC · Richmond · Catterick · A1 · Leyburn · Northallerton · North York Moors · Scalby · Scarborough North Cliff GC · Scarborough · Scarborough South Cliff GC · Hawes · A684 · Bedale GC · A684 · Thirsk · Thirsk & Northallerton GC · Pickering · Filey GC · Filey · Ganton GC · A170 · NORTH YORKSHIRE · A65 · Ripon · A168 · A19 · Easingwold · Malton · Malton & Norton GC · A64 · Bridlington Links GC · Bridlington · Bridlington GC · Settle · A61 · A1(M) · A166 · A614 (A166) · Driffield · Harrogate GC · Knaresborough · A59 · EAST RIDING OF YORKSHIRE · Hornsea GC · Skipton GC · Skipton · A59 · Pannel GC · Rudding Park GC · Wetherby · York · Strensall GC · Fulford GC · Pocklington · Market Weighton · Ilkley GC · Otley GC · A65 · A64 · A1035 · A165 · Keighley GC · Bingley · Alwoodley GC · Moortown GC · Tadcaster · A19 · A163 · A1079 · Beverley · Shipley GC · Shipley · Moor Allerton GC · Sand Moor GC · Selby GC · A164 · HULL · Northcliffe GC · Marriott Hollins Hall H & GC · Selby · Hull GC · BRADFORD · M621 · LEEDS · A63 · Withernsea · A646 · Halifax · Howley Hall GC · Temple Newsam GC · M62 · Hessle · Hessle GC · R. Humber · Todmorden · W. YORKSHIRE · Brighouse · Willow Valley GC · M62 · Pontefract · Goole · Spurn Head · M62 · Huddersfield · Bradley Park GC · Wakefield · M18 · Huddersfield GC · Hemsworth · Thorne · A62 · Woodsome Hall GC · M62 · Barnsley · M180 · Penistone · SOUTH YORKSHIRE · Doncaster · A616 · Stocksbridge · A1(M) · Doncaster Town Moor GC · Bawtry · SHEFFIELD · Rotherham GC · Hallamshire GC · Rotherham · Abbeydale GC · Lees Hall GC · Dronfield · M1 · Lindrick GC

Yorkshire Choice Golf

While many consider the delights of Yorkshire to be exclusive to its northernmost area this is totally wrong. The small villages that nestle amid the southern Pennines or the Dales are delightful and the river Wharfe carves its way through south Yorkshire revealing extraordinary beauty along its trail. From the haunting howls of Haworth and the Bronte country to the jovial singing in a pub on Ilkley Moor, there is a rich tradition. Yorkshire folk are a proud breed—better reserve your best golf for the 18th fairway.

South Yorkshire

Perhaps the pick of the courses in the Sheffield area are the moorland course at **Hallamshire**, three miles west of the city off the A57, **Abbeydale**, a fine wooded parkland test to the south west and **Lees Hall**, a mix of parkland and meadowland, located south of the town centre and occupying a lofty situation with marvellous views over the city.

Having saved your best golf for the 18th fairway a few thoughts now emerge for the 19th. A pleasant hotel in this city of nudity is the well run Staindrop Lodge (0114) 284 6727, while the Forte Posthouse (0114) 267 0067 is particularly convenient for the Hallamshire course. Sheffield also offers the comfortable Charnwood Hotel (0114) 2589411. The city has many good Asian restaurants, one of the best being Nirmal's (0114) 2724054; whilst for French food enthusiasts we suggest the Neptune (0114) 2796677. Finally, we ought to recommend a good pub (the area is naturally riddled with them) but try the Fat Cat in downtown Sheffield—a great establishment.

Before noting some of the other courses in South Yorkshire, a brief word on **Lindrick** (featured separately). According to the postman it properly belongs in Nottinghamshire although the club's administrative ties are with Yorkshire and a great number of members live in the Sheffield area. Anyway, whichever side of the fence it's on it is quite superb! The same can be said of the Old Vicarage (0114) 2475814—a classic restaurant.

Rotherham's excellent course is located at Thrybergh Park, two miles north of the town on the A630 and is well worth inspecting. Crossing the A1 we arrive at Doncaster. The **Doncaster Town Moor Golf Club** is situated very close to the famous racetrack. Like Rotherham, it's a parkland type course though not as testing. In Doncaster, the Danum Swallow (01302) 342261 and the Grand St Leger (01302) 364111 are two recommended establishments. In the countryside surrounding the busy railway town, Cadeby provides the cosy Cadeby Inn, while in Hatfield Woodhouse the Green Tree offers a warm welcome and some good snacks. The Crown at Bawtry (01302) 710341 is a pleasant high street inn. Those seeking more creature comforts should try Hellaby Hall (01709) 702701 which is very handy for the M18 and well worth a visit.

Around Leeds

West Yorkshire has a greater number of golf courses. Quantity is certainly matched by quality with the area just to the north of Leeds being particularly outstanding. Within a short distance of one another are **Alwoodley** and **Moortown** (both are featured ahead), **Sand Moor** and **Moor Allerton**, all of which are of championship standard.

Whilst Alwoodley, Moortown and Sand Moor are predominantly heathland and moorland in character, Moor Allerton, where there are 27 holes, is more strictly parkland. When travelling to any of the four clubs, the A61 should be taken out of Leeds itself. Moortown is probably the most widely known course in southern Yorkshire (if one excludes Lindrick), however, many consider Alwoodley to be at least its equal. Play all four if you can! An outstanding place to stay in this area — just one mile from Moortown — is Weetwood Hall (0113) 2306000; less expensive but equally welcoming is the Harewood Arms Hotel (0113) 2886566 in Harewood. Other good courses to note around Leeds are **Howley Hall**, **Temple Newsham** a splendid new Karl Litton course at Cookridge Hall and the **Marriott Hollins Hall Hotel & Country Club** which has a fine hotel to complement the golf course.

Around Bradford

A second concentration of good golf courses is to be found to the north of Bradford, more particularly, **Northcliffe**, **Keighley** and **Shipley**. Northcliffe is probably the pick with some outstanding views of the nearby moors, but each is well worth a game. Between Bradford and Huddersfield at Brighouse, just off the M62, is **Willow Valley**, Jonathan Gaunt's essay in American design, and well worth stopping off for. Yet another trio encircles Huddersfield, with **Bradley Park** to the north, **Woodsome Hall** to the south and **Huddersfield** Golf Club to the west. It was on the latter course that Sandy Herd learnt his game. The Open Champion of 1902, Herd finished in the first five in the Championship on no fewer than twelve occasions. He would have doubtless won on several of those but for a fellow called Vardon from Ganton across the way.

Following the Wharfe

Following the Wharfe into the east of West Yorkshire one finds some superb countryside. This is the land of the Brontes. In Bramhope, a far cry from the romance of the Brontes but a particularly popular hotel for businessmen visiting Leeds, is Oulton Hall (0113) 2821000. Visiting golfers will find plenty of good but inexpensive accommodation in Leeds, the Aragon Hotel (0113) 2759306 being a fine example. The gem in this area however is Pool Court at 42 The Calls (0113) 2440099—a wonderful restaurant, it is also a throroughly engaging place to stay.

Two courses in this area demand to be visited—the first is **Ilkley** and the second is **Otley**. They are without question two of the county's most attractive courses. Our friend, the River Wharfe, winds its way through much of the Ilkley course and is a major hazard on several of the early holes. The equally charming course at Otley nestles majestically in the Wharfe valley.

Beyond the fairways, the river and the rough, the gourmet golfer is well catered for in this area. Here are some suggestions. In Ilkley, the Edwardian Breakfast at Rombalds (01943) 603201 is legendary but the hotel itself and the restaurant are both thoroughly recommended too. Elsewhere in Ilkley, a town where delightful antique shops clutter the streets, one finds the Craiglands Hotel (01943) 607676 which has a setting adjoining that famous moor and is most comfortable. Another good value establishment is the Cow and Calf (01943) 607335. A restaurant renowned for its fine cuisine is the Box Tree (01943) 608484—pricey but excellent.

In Otley, Chevin Lodge (01943) 467818 built in Finnish pine is an interesting option. Bradford, Bingley, Otley—all this area is riddled with enthusiastic cricket and rugby sides as well as golfers—popular pubs for one and all include the Fox at Menston, the Malt Shovel at Harden and in Ryburn, where there would seem to be a focal point, the Old Bridge and the Over the Bridge (both provide excellent lunches—perhaps in between rounds?)

Around Harrogate

Heading north, Harrogate probably offers most to both sightseer and golfer. **Pannal** and **Harrogate** are the pick of the courses in the area, the former being a fairly lengthy championship challenge. It is moorland in nature and heavily wooded. Harrogate is possibly the more attractive with its lovely setting at Starbeck near Knaresborough. **Rudding Park**, set in 18th century parkland, is an award-winning par 72 course offering a good test of golf together

with a fully equipped golf academy and driving range. Rudding Park House (01423) 871350 provides 4 star accommodation along with conference and banqueting facilities.

The town of Harrogate is renowned for its fine restaurants. They include the Drum and Monkey (01423) 502650 (superb seafood) and Cafe Fleur (01423) 503034. The restaurants in the town's hotels are generally particularly good, notably those at the Majestic (01423) 700300, the Old Swan (01423) 500055, the Studley (01423) 560425 and the Balmoral Hotel and Restaurant (01423) 508208. The Bistro (01423) 530708 is also most attractive.

North Yorkshire

To the south and west the Yorkshire Dales, to the north and east the Yorkshire Moors. North Yorkshire is England's largest county and quite possibly England's most beautiful.

The Dales and the Moors may not sound like great golfing country and indeed by far the greater number of Yorkshire's golf courses lie in the more populated and industrial regions of South and West Yorkshire. However, golfing visitors to North Yorkshire will not be disappointed; not only does the county boast the likes of Ganton and Fulford, two of England's greatest inland courses, but there are forty or so others, the majority of which are set in glorious surroundings.

Skipton is known as the 'Gateway to the Dales'. The ancient market town has a fine parkland course situated only a mile or so from the town centre. The views are magnificent and a mountain stream runs through the course adding to the many challenges. An appetite created, dinner is recommended at the Devonshire Arms (01756) 710441 in Bolton Abbey. If a good drink is simply all that's required then the Angel at Helton may be preferable.

Ripon is another very charming place. There are only nine holes of golf here (at **Ripon City**) though they offer great variety nonetheless. The surrounding countryside is quite stupendous. Jervaulx Abbey, founded in 1156 is well worth inspecting as is Fountains Abbey. For accommodation, Ripon has the Ripon Spa Hotel (01765) 602172 and in nearby Boroughbridge, the Crown (01423) 322328 is a comfortable old inn. Lovers of Theakstons should make a pilgrimage to the White Bear at Masham. One other hotel of distinction in the area is the charming Feversham Arms at Helmsley (01439) 770766 noted not just for its accommodation but also for its great lunches. The village is extremely pleasant and an ideal base for touring the Yorkshire moors and dales.

Two of North Yorkshire's most beautiful courses are situated fairly close to one another in the centre of the county: **Thirsk & Northallerton** and **Bedale**. The former lies very close to Thirsk racetrack. The views here are towards the Cleveland Hills on one side and the Hambleton Hills on another. Bedale Golf Club can be found off the A684 and is known for its beautiful spread of trees.

In the north of the county, **Richmond** Golf Club enjoys glorious surroundings. The town itself has a strange mixture of medieval, Georgian and Victorian architecture and is dominated of course by the famous castle. Fine restaurants once again abound: in nearby Moulton, the Black Bull Inn (01325) 377289 is excellent, as is the Bridge Inn (01325) 350106 at Stapleton. Firmly recommended also are the Millers House (01969) 622630 at Middleham and the Burgogne Hotel (01428) 884292 in Reeth. Just south of Richmond, **Catterick Garrison's** Golf Club is well worth a visit.

Cleveland

Due east at the top of the county, just south of the Tees in what was until recently Cleveland, the golf course at **Saltburn** isn't right by the sea, it's about a mile west of the town and is a well-wooded meadowland course. Further south along the coast, however, at Saltburn, **Hunley Hall** Golf Course provides wonderful cliff top views at this heritage coast. Around Teeside itself there are courses at Redcar (**Cleveland**), **Middlesborough** and **Billingham** but perhaps the best or most enjoyable in the area is found at **Eaglescliffe**, a hilly course where there are some marvellous views of the Cleveland Hills.

For a 19th hole, at Saltburn an excellent pub can be recommended, namely the Ship with its splendid sea views, while a little inland at Moorsholm the Jolly Sailor offers some very good food. Those playing at Eaglescliffe can enjoy midday sustenance (or evening celebration) at the Blue Bell.

South down the Coast

Yorkshire's coast contrasts greatly with that of Lancashire, with spectacular cliffs rather than dunes dominating the shoreline. Not surprisingly, there are no true links courses to be found here. However, visitors to the resort of **Filey** will find a pleasant parkland course and at Scarborough there are two clifftop courses **Scarborough North Cliff** and **Scarborough South Cliff**, the latter by Dr. Mackenzie. Near Flamborough Head there are testing layouts at **Bridlington** and **Bridlington Links**.

The Crown (01723) 373491 overlooking Scarborough's South Bay is a busy hotel to consider. East Ayton Lodge (01723) 864227 is also handy and very pleasant too. Slightly inland at Hackness, the Hackness Grange Country Hotel (01723) 882345 enjoys a beautiful setting and makes for a pleasant stay. There's also a pitch and putt course to sneak in some early morning practice. Meanwhile at Scalby, Wrea Head (01723) 378211 is a Victorian country house of character. Finally, situated between Scarborough and Whitby in Ravenscar, lies the **Raven Hall Country House Hotel and Golf Course** (01723) 870353, a historic house well worth a visit.

Inland, **Malton and Norton** shouldn't be overlooked. It is also particularly convenient for those heading towards **Ganton** on the A64. Ganton, thought by many to be the finest inland course in England, boasts a superb setting on the edge of the Vale of Pickering. It is explored fully on a later page. The White Swan (01751) 472288 in Pickering is welcoming place to stay and offers some excellent bar snacks. Our North Yorkshire tour complete we now drop into the East Riding.

The East Riding

The East Riding, like a phoenix, has risen from the ashes of Humberside and reappears in its former glory. Unfortunately try as I may, I cannot trot off a list of wonderful golf courses. There are enough of them about but there's no Ganton here, alas. The best in the county is arguably at **Hornsea**, famed, of course for its pottery. It is a beautiful heathland course with particularly outstanding greens. One tip—try not to kill the ducks on the 11th!

Beverley is no great distance from Hornsea and the Beverley Arms (01482) 869241 is a good place for a night's rest. Tickton offers the excellent Tickton Grange (01964) 543666 and for a pleasant drink visit the White Horse in Brandesburton. The Manor House (01482) 881645 is wonderfully peaceful and offers excellent accommodation and food to complete the picture.

If one has crossed all 1542 yards of the Humber Bridge to reach the county's largest town then the **Hull** Golf Club at Kirk Ella is probably the best choice for a game, although **Hessle** has developed into a very good course too. The Waterfront (01482) 227222 is the most attractive hotel in town. The seafood in Hull ought to be sampled, Ceruttis (01482) 28501 is one of the best places to do so.

En route to our final destination, York, it is worth noting **Selby** in the south of the county. Laid out over fairly sandy subsoil the course could be described as part links, part parkland. An enjoyable day's golf here might be followed by a visit to Monk Fryston and its fine hotel, Monk Fryston Hall (01977) 682369.

York

York, they say, is a city everyone should visit at least once. I recommend at least twice for there are two outstanding golf courses within three miles of York Minster: **Fulford** to the south and York Golf Club at **Strensall** to the north. Fulford (see feature page) is the better known, but York is also a championship course and has many admirers. It is a fine woodland type course, laid out on the edge of Strensall Common.

Staying in York is a delight: there is a wealth of attractions— Shambles has some marvellous shops, the Minster itself is sensational, there are museums galore and some first class hotels in and around the city. The star of the show is Middlethorpe Hall (01904) 641241, a beautiful mansion house with an exquisite restaurant. The Mount Royale (01904) 628856 is another excellently run hotel with good food and is less expensive, while closer to the centre of town the Judges Lodging (01904) 638733 is particularly elegant. The equally relaxing Grasmead House Hotel (01904) 629996 is excellent value.

The town centre has many tea shops and small restaurants as well as some pleasant pubs. Meltons (01904) 634341 is a particularly fine restaurant. A noted pub outside the city can be found in Wighill—the White Swan—good value bar snacks. In Fulford village two pubs very handy for the famous course are the Saddle and the Plough and convenient accommodation can be found in Hovingham at the Worsley Arms (01653) 628234, a delightfully elegant inn.

From north to south and across the breadth of the newly reunited county of Yorkshire the golfer can enjoy a wealth of outstanding courses and a fine array of hotels in a dramatically changing landscape. A visit is most heartily recommended.

RUDDING PARK *Photograph courtesy of:* **Rudding Park Hotel**

Ganton

They used to say at Ganton that when Harry Vardon played the course twice in the same day, in his afternoon round he'd often hit his tee shots into the very divots he'd created in the morning. The chances are that this was a little bit of Yorkshire bluff but then again the members at Ganton were fortunate to witness what were probably the very finest years of Britain's greatest ever golfer.

Vardon came to Ganton in 1896, just five years after the club's formation. Within a few weeks of his appointment he won his first Open Championship at Muirfield defeating the hat trick seeking John H Taylor in a play-off. In 1900 Vardon returned from America with the US Open trophy, by which time he'd added two more Open Championships and was half way towards his record number of six victories in that event. By the time that Vardon left the Club in 1903 the name of Ganton had been firmly put on the golfing map.

Located approximately nine miles from the sea, Ganton could hardly be called a golf links in the strict sense but it is often said that it has many of the features of links golf with crisp seaside turf and sandy subsoil. Indeed, whenever new bunkers are cut, sea-shells are often discovered lying beneath the surface—it appears that the whole of the surrounding area was once an arm of the sea.

Golfers wishing to play at Ganton must make prior arrangements with the club's **Secretary, Major R G Woolsey** who may be contacted via the **Ganton Golf Club, Ganton, Scarborough, North Yorkshire YO12 4PA tel: (01944) 710329** and **fax: (01944) 710922**. The club's **Professional, Gary Brown**, can be reached on **(01944) 710260**. Subject to proof of handicap and prior arrangement, visitors are made most welcome and it is possible to pre-book starting times. The green fees for 2000 are set at £52 for a day's golf during the week with £60 payable at the weekend or Bank Holidays.

Travelling to the course is made straightforward by the A64. This road links the village directly with Scarborough to the north east (12 miles) and to both York (30 miles) and Leeds (60 miles) to the south west. If approaching from the south a combination of the A164 to Great Driffield and the B1249 will take you to within two miles of the course. Travellers from further north can avoid the City of York by heading for Thirsk and thereafter heading for Malton by way of the A170 and the B1257. Malton lies on the A64 road and, like Scarborough, is approximately twelve miles from Ganton.

Ganton enjoys a beautifully peaceful setting nestling on the edge of the Vale of Pickering and the Yorkshire Moors. While the golf course is indeed beautiful, particularly when the gorse is in full bloom, it is very rarely peaceful and when the winds sweep across it can become fearsomely difficult. There are few inland courses with such cavernous bunkers—111 of them in all! In addition to the many bunkers and the great spread of gorse, there are numerous fir trees and pines which can come into play following a wayward shot—the dog-leg 18th being a notable example, and one that provides a very testing finishing hole.

The finest hole on the course is thought by many to be the 4th, where the second has to be played across a plunging valley towards a plateau green that is heavily bunkered to the right. Another outstanding hole on the front nine is the 7th, a marvellous swinging dog-leg, and on the back nine the 15th and 16th are both highly memorable two-shotters.

The 19th at Ganton has a welcoming atmosphere and offers an extensive range of catering. (Note the famous Ganton cake—the origins of which are unknown and the recipe a secret!) Dress is informal in the men's bar until 4pm Monday to Friday, although a jacket and tie should be worn in all other public rooms.

Inevitably Ganton's name will always be linked with Vardon's. But another great player also developed his talents on the Yorkshire course—Ted Ray, the famed long hitter who won the Open in 1912 and later found fortune in America winning their Open in 1920. In winning the latter he ironically held off the challenge of the then 50 year old Vardon. The greatest event in Ganton's distinguished history was undoubtedly the great Ryder Cup match of 1949 when the home team led by three matches to one at the end of the first day only to lose eventually by seven to five. Ben Hogan, convalescing from his near fatal accident, led the American side as non-playing captain.

Three times since the last war the Amateur Championship has been held at Ganton. The most recent staging was in 1991, the centenary year for the club. The Curtis Cup is scheduled for 24/25th June, 2000, the British Boys Championship, in August 2001 and the Walker Cup, in 2003.

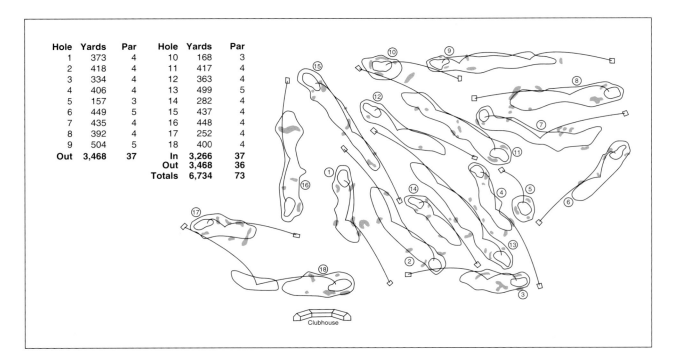

Hole	Yards	Par	Hole	Yards	Par
1	373	4	10	168	3
2	418	4	11	417	4
3	334	4	12	363	4
4	406	4	13	499	5
5	157	3	14	282	4
6	449	5	15	437	4
7	435	4	16	448	4
8	392	4	17	252	4
9	504	5	18	400	4
Out	**3,468**	**37**	**In**	**3,266**	**37**
			Out	**3,468**	**36**
			Totals	**6,734**	**73**

Clubhouse

Originally built in 1878 as a family home, Hollins Hall is a fine example of Elizabethan style architecture. The private house was converted to a hotel in 1991 and joined the world-wide Marriott hotel group in 1996.

Since then the hotel has undergone an extensive redevelopment programme at a cost of £11.4 million to become the Marriott Hollins Hall Hotel & Country Club, one of the region's finest hotel and country clubs. The final addition has been an 18-hole golf course set on 200 acres of land adjacent to the hotel. Described by Mark James, captain of Europe's Ryder Cup team, as: "the best new course I've seen for a long time."

The transformed hotel has 122 well-appointed bedrooms, two restaurants and Hollins bar. The Long Weekend Café Bar offers a varied menu, with everything from a light salad to a substantial steak on offer in relaxed surroundings. For a more formal occasion, the staff in Heathcliff's restaurant pride themselves on offering fine cuisine from around the world with impeccable service.

Designed by European Golf Design, the remarkable golf course, which is 6,682 yards long, par 71, offers classic golf for players of all levels.

The first nine holes take in the higher land to the north of the hotel and offer spectacular views over Baildon Moor. The last nine are more undulating in nature and include the the spectacular 14th which incorporates an existing railway viaduct as a backdrop. The club also has a superb locker room, putting green, and golf and leisure shop.

The hotel boasts an excellent leisure club, including two gyms - cardiovascular and resistance, an aerobic studio with various classes, as well as a sauna, steamroom, spa and solarium. There is an indoor heated swimming pool and new health spa facilities.

The extensive conferencing facilities, and the Marriott 'Golf Edge' services, make the hotel the perfect venue for corporate golf events. With the help of our staff, we are confident you'll strike the perfect balance between work and play.

Hollins Hall is close to many of Yorkshire's best attractions, including the Yorkshire Dales, and is within easy reach of both Harewood House and Haworth - home of the Brontë sisters. Also in the immediate area are Castle Howard, the city of Leeds with excellent shops and Emmerdale Country - with the original Woolpack pub only ten minutes walk away. For art lovers, there is David Hockney's 1853 Gallery at Salt's Mill which houses a permanent exhibition of over 300 of his works.

The hotel is on the A6038 between Shipley and Guiseley - close to junction 26 of the M62 motorway and to the commercial centres and tourist attractions of Leeds and Bradford. Leeds is on the main railway line to London, and for those with less time to spare the Airport is only a ten minute drive away.

Marriott Hollins Hall Hotel & Country Club
Hollins Hill
Baildon Shipley
West Yorkshire BD17 7QW
Tel: (01274) 530053
Fax: (01274) 534251

Moortown

Moortown enjoys an enviable situation. It lies within minutes of the town centre of Leeds, yet it also lies within minutes of the Pennines and the beauty of the Yorkshire Moors. The club was founded in the autumn of 1909 with the course being laid out by the great Alister Mackenzie. Less than twenty years after its formation Moortown was selected to host the first ever Ryder Cup to be played on British soil. It proved a momentous occasion.

The American side in 1929 was virtually identical to the one that crushed the British team 9-2 in the inaugural staging at Worcester, Massachusetts two years previously. It included Walter Hagen, the reigning British Open Champion, Gene Sarazen, Johnny Farrel the US Open Champion, Leo Diegel the US PGA Champion and A1 Watrous. To cut a long story short, the British side won by six matches to four. On the final day George Duncan defeated Walter Hagen by 10 and 8 and Archie Compston defeated Gene Sarazen 6 and 4. Whatever it may have done to American pride, and I note that Wall Street collapsed later that summer, it certainly secured Moortown's place in golfing lore.

With its great spread of heather and gorse Moortown is occasionally described as heathland, although the absence of sandy sub-soil more properly makes it a moorland type course. Either way, it has the fine combination of being sufficiently testing yet not too severe.

Measuring in excess of 7000 yards from the championship tees, the generally held view is that the front nine is much the easier of the two halves; this may have something to do with the fact that it begins with what golfers usually term a 'birdiable hole', being a short par five to a fairly open green. Perhaps Moortown's finest hole is the 10th, a par three measuring 176 yards, it calls for a shot to a plateau green built on a foundation of rock; it is called 'Gibraltar'—miss it and you're sunk. The 12th is an excellent par five, aptly titled 'The Long'

for it stretches to 554 yards; the aforementioned Archie Compston once holed out here in two strokes.

The difficult, dog-leg 18th at Moortown has an alarming effect on certain people. Countless numbers, including Severiano Ballesteros, have been known to overclub and fire the ball over the green into the clubhouse area. In the 1929 Ryder Cup during one of the foursomes matches, Joe Turnesa hooked his second behind the marquee adjoining the clubhouse whereupon his partner promptly sailed it back over the marquee to within a yard of the hole. In the 1974 English Amateur Strokeplay tournament one player actually put his second into the men's bar. Opening the clubhouse windows he played his third straight out onto the green. The clubhouse certainly has a welcoming atmosphere but this would seem to be taking things a little too far!

Moortown Golf Club, Harrogate Road, Alwoodley, Leeds, LS17 7DB
www.moortown-gc.co.uk

Sec/Manager	Chris Moore (0113) 268 6521
Professional	Bryon Hutchinson (0113) 268 3636
Green Fees	WD £45/round, £55/day
	WE £50/round, £60/day
Restrictions	Prior arrangement with Secretary or Professional

Directions
The A61 Leeds to Harrogate road takes you directly to Moortown.

Fulford

These days golf is not only played in every foreign field but it is also played in the most unlikely of places. In 1971 astronaut Captain Alan Sheppard struck two golf shots from the surface of the moon, becoming in the process the only man able to shank a ball 200 yards. Not to be outdone, as ever, Arnold Palmer in 1977 hit three golf balls off the second stage of the Eiffel Tower, while in 1981 at Fulford, Bernhard Langer decided to take golf into further alien territory by shinning up a rather large tree and playing his chip shot to the 17th green from amidst its spreading branches.

Fulford Golf Club was founded soon after the turn of the century, but it was only as recently as 1985 that the club celebrated 50 years of playing over the present course. Televised tournament golf has undoubtedly turned the North Yorkshire club into a 'golfing household name', but in golf's more discerning circles it has for a long time possessed the reputation of having one of the country's finest inland courses.

Measuring 6775 yards from the back tees (par 72) Fulford provides quite a stern test for the club golfer, but it is no more than a medium length course for the professionals. Much of the prodigiously low scoring achieved at Fulford during those European Tour events that it has staged has, however, had precious little to do with the length of the course. As the members will quickly tell you, it simply reflects the superb condition in which the fairways and the putting surfaces are maintained. Fulford is especially renowned for its fast and very true greens. Certainly, Ian Woosnam found them much to his liking as he holed putt after putt during an extraordinary sequence of eight successive birdies during his final round in the 1985 Benson and Hedges International Tournament. Woosnam's score of 62 that day set a new course record but unfortunately it wasn't quite good enough to prevent Sandy Lyle from joining a distinguished list of Fulford champions—a list which includes the likes of Tony Jacklin, Greg Norman and Lee Trevino.

The 'B&H' has since gone south to St Mellion, The Oxfordshire, and The Belfry, although in the early 1990s Fulford played host to a second European Tour event, the Murphy's Cup. In keeping with the tradition of eccentricity established by Bernhard Langer in 1981, the organisers announced before the inaugural 1990 event that the first player to hole in one at the 14th would receive 'one hour's output of Murphy's Irish Stout' (estimated to be 13,750 pints)!

Most golfers probably won't be leaving Fulford with a 62 under their belt—nor one presumes will they have been shinning up the trees or downing Murphy's by the bucketload—but they are sure to be heading home contented souls having spent a day on what is unquestionably one of the country's most pleasurable golf courses.

Fulford Golf Club, Heslington Lane, Fulford, York, YO1 5DY
www.fulfordgolfclub.co.uk

General Manager	Ron Bramley (01904) 413579
Professional	Bryan Hessay (01904) 412882
Green Fees	WD £35/round, £45/day
	WE £45
Restrictions	Prior arrangement with General Manager.

Directions
Fulford lies a mile south of York just off the A19.

Lindrick

There are two golf courses in England whose names will be forever linked with the Ryder Cup: one is The Belfry, the other is Lindrick—and they couldn't be more different. The Belfry (perhaps one should be precise and say the Brabazon Course) is a big strapping youngster, immature in some ways though agreeable in others. Lindrick is the seasoned campaigner. It's seen a lot in its lifetime (and in fact is old enough to have received a telegram in 1991). It is no giant but it is charming, subtle and full of challenge.

Before the Ryder Cup came to Lindrick in 1957, many golfing enthusiasts knew very little of this great course, indeed some knew nothing at all. By the end of that heady, windswept week in October, none present would ever forget it. It was the last time an exclusively British and Irish team would ever beat the mighty men from across the sea.

Lindrick lies close to the boundaries of Yorkshire, Nottinghamshire and Derbyshire. Although the golf course is entirely contained within the confines of South Yorkshire, the club's postal address is Lindrick, Notts—no doubt to the considerable annoyance of every Yorkshireman! The golf course occupies the best part of 200 acres of classic English common—Lindrick Common—and is essentially heathland in nature, lying on top of limestone rock. There is a mass of gorse which, when in bloom adds great colour (though it can be a devil if you land in it!) and a wealth of oak and silver birch—a delightful setting if ever there was one.

Visitors are very welcome to test their skills in this splendid environment, although prior arrangement with the club is required. The **Secretary** is **Lieutenant Commander R J M Jack RN, tel: (01909) 475282** or by **fax: (01909) 488685**. Written correspondence should be addressed to **Lindrick Golf Club, Lindrick Common, Worksop, Notts, S81 8BH**. All bookings should be made through the Secretary's office, but as a general guide, visitors are not permitted to play on Tuesday mornings and the first tee is normally reserved

for members for an hour around lunchtime, but again it's best to check.

The green fees at Lindrick vary according to the season. For 2000 they are set at £48 per day on weekdays and per round at weekends. Reductions of fifty per cent are available to junior golfers if accompanied by an adult. The club's **Professional** is **John King (01909) 475820**.

Although Lindrick Common may look a little isolated on the map, strangers shouldn't have too much difficulty in locating the course. Those coming from the south should find the M1 and the A1 of great assistance. The club is actually situated just off the A57 Worksop to Sheffield road, to the west of the former and is well signposted.

From the championship tees, the course measures 6606 yards, with the par a fairly tight 71. Quite refreshingly, it is not a long hitter's course—the fairway shots to the green being what Lindrick is all about—and there are some excellent par fours. The 2nd, with its slightly uphill approach, the 8th and the 17th are among the most subtle and cleverly designed holes, while the most demanding are the 7th, 12th and 13th. Perhaps the best known hole at Lindrick is the par five 4th. This requires a blind approach to a low lying green backed by trees and behind which the River Ryton flows. The green has a magnificent stage-like setting and it was here that the boundaries of Yorkshire, Derbyshire and Nottinghamshire once merged. In days of old, the stage was used for bare fist-fighting and cockfighting, contestants and spectators being able to step into a convenient county whenever unfriendly law authorities showed up.

The clubhouse at Lindrick provides golfers with a fine view of the 18th green and many a drama will have been witnessed. But I don't suppose there will ever be anything to equal the scenes of 1957 and the time when Dai Rees and his boys made the old campaigner smile.

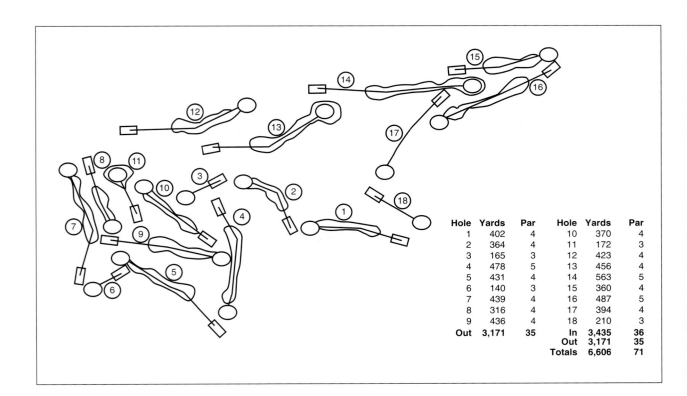

Hole	Yards	Par		Hole	Yards	Par
1	402	4		10	370	4
2	364	4		11	172	3
3	165	3		12	423	4
4	478	5		13	456	4
5	431	4		14	563	5
6	140	3		15	360	4
7	439	4		16	487	5
8	316	4		17	394	4
9	436	4		18	210	3
Out	**3,171**	**35**		**In**	**3,435**	**36**
				Out	**3,171**	**35**
				Totals	**6,606**	**71**

The hotel is the result of the tasteful blending of two beautiful William IV detached houses. The Mount Royale is owned and run by Richard and Christine Oxtoby and their son Stuart and daughter Sarah. Stuart has recently taken over as Managing Director. The Oxtoby's have spent a good deal of effort on restoring the former glory of these buildings and their efforts have been well rewarded.

Any traveller having an interest in English history must surely rate the fascinating city of York at least alongside London. The capital of the north and second city of the realm, it began its long and fascinating life around AD71 as a fortress to protect the Roman 9th legion. The marauding Vikings gave the city its name, derived from Jorvik or Yorvik. This period of history has been magnificently captured in the Jorvik Viking Centre, one of the most entertaining museums in the country.

The minster or cathedral is the largest medieval structure in Britain. There has been a minster on the site since the 7th century. The present one is the fourth and was started about 1220, taking 250 years to complete. The city is still protected by ancient city walls, guarded by defensive bastions, working portcullis and barbican at the Walmgate bar.

Wander around the Micklegate bar, where traitors' severed heads were displayed or visit the National Rail Museum.

Staying in York involves mixing with some of the most fascinating sights in the world. Relaxing afterwards in the intimate cocktail bar of the Mount Royale, or enjoying a delicious meal in the restaurant overlooking the delightful garden, enhances the whole experience. Enjoying the gracious beauty of the hotel, the style and antiquity of much of the furnishings, or slipping into the secluded heated swimming pool is the perfect way to pamper the body as well as the mind.

The hotel is ideal for the small conference or private party, and is only a short drive from the rolling Yorkshire Dales. The perfect base, offering peace and tranquillity in the heart of this wonderful city.

Mount Royale Hotel
The Mount
York, YO24 1GU
Tel: (01904) 628856
Fax: (01904) 611171
e mail: reservations@mountroyale.co.uk
web site: www.mountroyale.co.uk

Alwoodley

Whereas the best links golf in the North of England are to be found on the coast of Lancashire, it is Yorkshire that has the superior collection of inland courses. By general consensus the three finest golf courses in Yorkshire are Ganton in the north, Lindrick in the south and Alwoodley, which, situated just to the north of Leeds, lies somewhere in the middle. Collectively they comprise what writer Barry Ward calls 'The Great Triumvirate of Yorkshire Golf'.

All three golf courses could be described as heathland, although parts of Ganton resemble a seaside links and both Lindrick and Alwoodley provide more than a hint of moorland golf. Alwoodley, for instance, has far more trees - predominantly firs and silver birches - than a traditional heathland layout such as Walton Heath, and while the likes of Sunningdale and St Georges Hill have very little gorse to accompany the heather, the gorse at Alwoodley grows in abundance. The most distinctive feature of Alwoodley, however, owes more to the input of man than nature.

Alister Mackenzie, the creator of such golfing masterpieces as Augusta and Royal Melbourne, was the principal architect of Alwoodley. He designed several courses in Great Britain - and most of these in Yorkshire - before achieving international fame, but Alwoodley is widely acknowledged to be his premier British design. Amazingly, it was also his first. Harry Colt was originally approached (this was back in 1907) but after he had discussed the project with Mackenzie - then a medical practitioner with a keen interest in golf course architecture (and soon to be the club's first secretary) - it was Mackenzie who effectively assumed the role of course designer. The style and standard of the bunkering is the feature that particularly sets the course apart. It is very bold, almost 'flashy' in appearance, and it repeatedly turns strong holes into superb and extremely strategic ones. The other significant Mackenzie signature is the quality of the putting surfaces, which are generally quite large and always beautifully contoured.

Returning to our 'Great Yorkshire Triumvirate', despite Mackenzie's contribution Alwoodley is the least known of the trio. This is principally because, over the years, Ganton and Lindrick have regularly staged important championships - men's and women's, amateur and pro-

fessional - while Alwoodley on the other hand has preferred to maintain a much lower profile. A stubborn regard for privacy rather than any perceived 'stuffiness' has been the cause, although in recent years this resolve has eased and the club has hosted both the English and British Ladies Championships.

Provided arrangements are made in advance, visitors (who must have current handicaps) are welcome at Alwoodley. For 2000 the green fee rates are £50 during the week and £60 at weekends. The club's **Secretary, Mr C D Wilcher** can be contacted on **tel: (0113) 268 1680** and by **fax: (0113) 268 9458**. The **Professional, John Green** can be reached on **(0113) 268 9603**. Given its close proximity to Leeds, Alwoodley enjoys a surprisingly tranquil as well as attractive setting. Its precise location is five miles north of Leeds via the A61 Harrogate road. The Club's full address is **Alwoodley Golf Club, Wigton Lane, Alwoodley, Leeds LS17 8SA**. For further information visit **www.alwoodley.co.uk**

Measuring 6686 yards, par 72 from the back tees, Alwoodley's routing is unusual for an inland course (though similar to the West Course at Wentworth) in that it runs 'out and back' in classical links fashion. Not every hole follows this general trend, however, particularly on the outward nine, but the final six holes all confront the prevailing wind and invariably make for an exacting finish.

The outstanding holes on the front nine are the 3rd, a sweeping par five with its green set in a slight hollow, the 5th, a shortish par four but where the fairway has a pronounced left to right tilt, and the 8th, at 546 yards a big three-shotter with a chain of cross bunkers and a slightly raised green.

On the inward nine the two short holes, the tight uphill 11th and the 200 yards-plus 14th are both very challenging but arguably the two finest holes of the round must be tackled during the aforementioned tough 'finishing stretch'. The 15th has been described by Frank Pennick as 'the Pride of Alwoodley' and it features an undulating, curving fairway, some intelligent cross bunkering and an elusive plateaued green. Finally, an elevated tee at the 18th encourages the player to open his shoulders - although a legion of bunkers lie in wait, perfectly placed to thwart any hopes of a closing birdie.

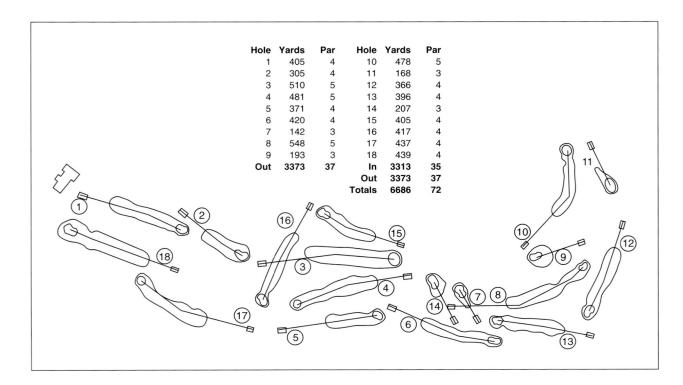

Hole	Yards	Par	Hole	Yards	Par
1	405	4	10	478	5
2	305	4	11	168	3
3	510	5	12	366	4
4	481	5	13	396	4
5	371	4	14	207	3
6	420	4	15	405	4
7	142	3	16	417	4
8	548	5	17	437	4
9	193	3	18	439	4
Out	**3373**	**37**	**In**	**3313**	**35**
			Out	**3373**	**37**
			Totals	**6686**	**72**

The Worsley Arms Hotel is an attractive stone built Georgian inn in the heart of Hovingham, near York, with a history stretching back to Roman times. The hotel was built in 1841 by Sir William Worsley, the first Baronet. Today the hotel still belongs to the Worsley family and is privately operated by Euan and Debbi Rodger. Hovingham Hall, the family house which stands on the edge of the village was designed around 1760 by Thomas Worsley, and is now the home of Sir Marcus Worsley, the fifth Baronet. His sister, Her Royal Highness the Duchess of Kent was born there.

This country inn of renown, named Yorkshire Life's Hotel of the Year for 1997/8, has the welcoming and restful atmosphere of a pleasant country house. The spacious sitting rooms are ideal havens for morning coffee, full afternoon tea, or an aperitif.

Food is undoubtedly a highlight. The chef, Andrew Jones, with a wealth of local produce on the doorstep, aims to combine the best of traditional and modern cooking with presentation that reflects an individual style. His food can be enjoyed in the Wyvern Restaurant or in the more informal Cricketers Bistro. In recognition of the quality of the food, the AA has, for the third year running, awarded the hotel two AA Rosettes.

The bedrooms, each with private bathroom, are individually and tastefully decorated, providing every comfort with extensive modern facilities.

The village is on the edge of a designated Area of Outstanding Natural Beauty; national parks are on the doorstep, the nearby Yorkshire Dales and the North York Moors. The area is rich in romantic and historic sites—the ruined abbeys of Rievaulx and Fountains, the castles of Helmsley and Pickering, the stately homes of Castle Howard, Duncombe Park and, of course, Hovingham Hall. Leisure pursuits abound as the hotel is ideally placed for quality racing, golfing (the championship courses of Ganton and Fulford are within half an hours drive), shooting and walking.

The Worsley Arms Hotel
Hovingham
York YO6 4LA
Tel: (01653) 628234
Fax: (01653) 628130

Key

*To avoid disappointment
it is advisable to telephone
in advance*

***Visitors welcome at most times
***Visitors usually allowed on
weekdays only*
**Visitors not normally permitted
(Mon, Wed) No visitors
on specified days*

Approximate Green Fees
A *£40 plus*
B *£25 to £40*
C *£20 to £30*
D *£15 to £25*
E *under £15*
F *Green fees on application*

Restrictions
G *Guests only*
H *Handicap certificate required*
H–*(24) Handicap of 24 or less*
L–*Letter of introduction required*
M–*Visitor must be a member of
another recognised club*

NORTH YORKSHIRE

Aldwark Manor G.C.
(01347) 838353
Aldwark, Alne, York
(18) 6171 yards/***/C

Ampleforth College G.C.
(01439) 770678
Helmsley, York
(10) 4018 yards/***/E

Bedale G.C.
(01677) 422451
Leyburn Road, Bedale
(18) 6565 yards/***/C

Bentham G.C.
(015242) 61018
Robin Lane, Bentham
(9) 5760 yards/***/D

Catterick G.C.
(01748) 833268
Leyburn Road, Catterick Garrison
(18) 6331 yards/***/C

Cleveland G.C.
(01642) 471798
Coatham, Redcar
(18) 6707 yards/**/C/H

Cocksford G.C.
(01937) 834253
Cocksford, Stutton
(18) 5518 yards/***/C

Crimple Valley G.C.
(01423) 883485
Hookstone Wood Road, Harrogate
(9) 2500 yards/***(pm only)/F

Drax G.C.
(01405) 860533
Drax, Selby
(9) 5510 yards/*/G

Easingwold G.C.
(01347) 821964
Stillngton Road, Easingwold
(18) 6262 yards/***/B/H

Filey G.C.
(01723) 513293
South Cliff, Filey
(18) 6104 yards/***/C/M

Forest of Galtres G.C.
(01904) 766198
Wideopen Farm, Skelton Lane
(18) 6312 yards/***/B

Forest Park G.C.
(01904) 400425
Stockton on Forest
(18) 6211 yards/***/C

Fulford G.C.
(01904) 413579
Heslington Lane, Heslington, York
(18) 6775 yards/**/A/H

Ganton G.C.
(01944) 710329
Ganton, Scarborough
(18) 6734 yards/**/A/H

Harrogate G. C.
(01423) 862999
Forest Lane Head, Starbeck
(18) 6241 yards/***/B/M

Heworth G.C.
(01904) 424618
Muncastergate, York
(11) 6141 yards/***/D

Hunley Hall G.C.
(01287) 676216
Brotton, Salrburn
(18) 6918 yards/***/C

Kilnwick Percy
(01759) 303090
Home Farm, Pocklington
(18) 6200 yards/***/D

Kirbymoorside G.C.
(01751) 431525
Manor Vale, Kirbymoorside
(18) 5958 yards/***/C

Knaresborough G.C.
(01423) 862690
Boroughbridge Road, Knaresborough
(18) 6232 yards/***/C/H

Malton and Norton G.C.
(01653) 697912
Welham Park, Malton
(18) 6456 yards/***/B/H
(18) 6267 yards/***/B/H

Masham G.C.
(01765) 689379
Swinton Road, Masham, Ripon
(9) 5244 yards/**/D

Middlesbrough G.C.
(01642) 311515
Brass Castle Lane, Marton
(18) 6106 yards/***/B

Middlesbrough Municipal G.C.
(01642) 315533
Ladgate Lane, Middlesbrough
(18) 6314 yards/***/E

Oakdale G.C.
(01423) 567162
Oakdale, Harrogate
(18) 6456 yards/***/B/M

The Oaks G.C.
(01757) 288577
(18) 6743 yards/**/B/H
Aughton, York

Pannal G.C.
(01423) 872628
Follifoot Road, Pannal, Harrogate
(18) 6659 yards/**/A/M/H

Pike Hills G.C.
(01904) 706566
Tadcaster Road, Copmanthorpe, York
(18) 6120 yards/**/D/M

Raven Hall Hotel & G.C.
(01723) 870353
Ravenscar
(9) 1938 yards/***/C

Richmond G.C.
(01748) 825319
Band Hagg, Richmond
(18) 5704 yards/***/D

Ripon City G.C.
(01765) 603640
Palace Road, Ripon
(9) 5750 yards/***/C

Romanby G.C.
(01609) 778855
Yafforth Road, Northallerton
(18) 6663 yards/***/D

Rudding Park G.C.
(01423) 844801
Rudding Park, Harrogate
(18) 6871 yards/***/C/4

Saltburn-by-the-Sea G.C.
(01287) 622812
Guisborough Road, Hobb Hill
(18) 5803 yards/***/C/H

Scarborough North Cliff G.C.
(01723) 360786
Burniston Road, Scarborough
(18) 6425 yards/***/B/M

Scarborough South Cliff G.C.
(01723) 374737
Deepdale Avenue, Scarborough
(18) 6085 yards/***/B/H

Scarthingwell G.C.
(01937) 557248
Scarthingwell, Tadcaster
(18) 6759 yards/**/C

Selby G.C.
(01757) 228622
Mill Lane, Brayton Barff, Selby
(18) 6246 yards/**/B/H/M

Settle G.C.
(01729) 825288
Buckhaw Brow, Settle
(9) 4600 yards/***(Sun)/D

Skipton G.C.
(01756) 795657
NW Bypass, Skipton
(18) 6191 yards/***(Mon)/B

Swallow Hall G.C.
(01904) 448219
Crockley Mill, York
(18) 3092 yards/***/E

Teesside G.C.
(01642) 616516
Acklam Road, Thornaby
(18) 6472 yards/***(pm only)/B

Thirsk & Northallerton G.C.
(01845) 522170
Thornton-le-Street, Thirsk
(9) 6257 yards/***/C/M

Whitby G.C.
(01947) 602768
Low Straggleton, Whitby
(18) 5706 yards/***/C/H

Wilton G.C.
(01642) 465265
Wilton Castle, Redcar
(18) 6104 yards/***(not Sat)/C

York G.C.
(01904) 491840
Lords Moor Lane, Strensall, York
(18) 6285 yards/***/B

SOUTH YORKSHIRE

Abbeydale G.C.
(0114) 236 0763
Twentywell Lane, Dore, Sheffield
(18) 6419 yards/***/B

Austerfield Park G.C.
(01302) 311977
Cross Lane, N Bawtry, Doncaster
(18) 6828 yards/***/C

Barnsley G.C.
(01226) 382856
Wakefield Road, Staincross
(18) 6048 yards/***/E

Beauchief G.C.
(0114) 236 7274
Abbey Lane, Sheffield
(18) 5423 yards/***/E

Birley Wood G.C.
(0114) 264 7262
Birley Lane, Sheffield
(18) 5483 yards/***/E

Bond Hay G.C.
(01909) 723608
Bond Hay Lane, Whitwell
(18) 6700 yards/***/D

Concord Park G.C.
(0114) 257 0111
Shiregreen Lane, Sheffield
(18) 4321 yards/***/E

Crookhill Park G.C.
(01709) 862974
Conisbrough, nr Doncaster
(18) 5846 yards/***/E

Doncaster G.C.
(01302) 868316
Bawtry Road, Bessacarr, Doncaster
(18) 6220 yards/**/B/M/H

Doncaster Town Moor G.C.
(01302) 535286
Belle Vue, Doncaster
(18) 6094 yards/***(Sun am)/D

Dore and Totley G.C.
(0114) 236 0492
Bradway Road, Sheffield
(18) 6265 yards/***/B/H

Grange Park G.C.
(01709) 558884
Upper Wortley Road, Rotherham
(18) 6461 yards/***/E

Hallamshire G.C.
(0114) 230 2153
Sandygate, Sheffield
(18) 6396 yards/***/B-A

Hallowes G.C.
(01246) 413734
Hallowes Lane, Dronfield, Sheffield
(18) 6342 yards/***/B/G/H

Hickleton G.C.
(01709) 896081
Hickleton, Doncaster
(18) 6361 yards/***/C/H/M

Hillsborough G.C.
(0114) 234 9151
Worral Road, Sheffield
(18) 6035 yards/**/B/H

Kings Wood G.C.
(01405) 741343
Thorne Road, Hatfield
(18) 6002 yards/***/E

Lees Hall G.C.
(0114) 255 2900
Hemsworth Road, Norton, Sheffield
(18) 6137 yards/***/C

Lindrick G.C.
(01909) 475282
Lindrick Common, Worksop
(18) 6606 yards/***(Tues am)/A/H

Owston Park G.C.
(01302) 330821
Owston Hall, nr Carcroft
(9) 6148 yards/***/E

Phoenix G.C.
(01709) 363864
Pavilion Lane, Brinsworth
(18) 6145 yards/***/C/M

Ponderosa G.C
(01302) 842057
Doncaster Road, Hatfield
(18) 6002 yards/***/E

Renishaw Park G.C.
(01246) 432044
Station Road, Renishaw, Sheffield
(18) 6253 yards/**/B-A/H/M

Rotherham G.C.
(01709) 850812
Thrybergh, Rotherham
(18) 6323 yards/**/B-A

Rother Valley G.C.
(0114) 247 3000
Wales Bar, Sheffield
(18) 6602 yards/***/D

Roundwood G.C.
(01709) 523471
Rawmarsh, Rotherham
(9) 5646 yards/**/D

Sandhill G.C.
(01226) 753444
Little Houghton, Barnsley
(18) 6214 yards/***/E

Sheffield Transport G.C.
(0114) 237 3216
Meadow Head, Sheffield
(18) 3966 yards/*/F/G

Sickleholme G.C.
(01433) 651306
Saltergate Lane, Bamford, Sheffield
(18) 6064 yards/***(Wed am)/B

Silkstone G.C.
(01226) 790328
Field Head, Silkstone, Barnsley
(18) 6045 yards/**/B-A/H

Sitwell Park G.C.
(01709) 541046
Shrogswood Road, Rotherham
(18) 6203 yards/***/B/M

Stocksbridge and District G.C.
(0114) 288 2003
Townend, Deepcar, Sheffield
(18) 5200 yards/***/C/H

Tankersley Park G.C.
(0114) 246 8247
High Green, Sheffield
(18) 6212 yards/**/C

Thorne G.C.
(01405) 812084
Kirton Lane, Thorne
(18) 5366 yards/***/E

Thornhurst Park G.C
(01302) 337799
Holme Land, Owsten
(18) 6085 yards/***/E

Thorpe Marsh G.C.
(01302) 886680
Bamby Down, Doncaster
(9) 4120 yards/***/E

Tinsley Park G.C.
(0114) 256 0237
High Hazel Park, Darnall, Sheffield
(18) 6064 yards/***/E

Wath G.C.
(01709) 582000
Abdy, Blackamoor, Rotherham
(18) 5857 yards/**/C

Wheatley G.C.
(01302) 831655
Armthorpe Road, Doncaster
(18) 6345 yards/***/C/H/M

Wombwell Hillies G.C.
(01226) 754433
Wentworth View, Wombwell
(9) 2095 yards/***/E

Wortley G.C.
(0114) 288 5294
Hermit Hill Lane, Sheffield
(18) 5983 yards/**/B/H/M

WEST YORKSHIRE

Alwoodley G.C.
(0113) 268 1680
Wigton Lane, Alwoodley, Leeds
(18) 6686 yards/**/A/H/M

Bagden Hall Hotel
(01484) 864839
Wakesfield Road, Scissett
(9) 3002 yards/***/E

Baildon G.C.
(01274) 582428
Moorgate, Baildon, Shipley
(18) 6225 yards/**/D

Ben Rhydding G.C.
(01943) 608759
High Wood, Ben Rhydding, Ilkley
(9) 4711 yards/**(Wed)/D

Bingley St Ives G.C.
(01274) 562436
St Ives Estate, Bingley
(18) 6480 yards/**/B

Bracken Ghyll G.C.
(01943) 831207
Skipton Road, Addingham
(9) 6560 yards/***/D

Bradford G.C.
(01943) 875570
Hawksworth Lane, Guiseley, Leeds
(18) 6259 yards/***(Sat/Sun am)/F

Bradford Moor G.C.
(01274) 638313
Scarr Hall, Pollard Lane, Bradford
(9) 5854 yards/***/D

Bradley Park G.C.
(01484) 539988
Bradley Road, Huddersfield
(18) 6202 yards/***/D

Brandon G.C.
(0113) 2737471
Holywell Lane, Shadwell
(18) 4000 yards/***/F

Branshaw G.C.
(01535) 643235
Branshaw Moor, Keighley
(18) 5858 yards/**/D/H

Calverley G.C.
(0113) 256 9244
Woodhall Lane, Pudsey
(18) 5516 yards/***(Sat/Sun am)/D

Castlefields G.C.
(01484) 712108
Rastrick Common, Brighouse
(6) 2406 yards/*/F/G

City of Wakefield G.C.
(01924) 367442
Howbury Road, Wakefield
(18) 6299 yards/***/E

Clayton G.C.
(01274) 880047
Thornton View Road, Bradford
(9) 5518 yards/***(Sun)/D

Cleckheaton and District G.C.
(01274) 851266
Bradford Road, Cleckheaton
(18) 5847 yards/***/B

Cookridge Hall G. & C.C.
(0113) 2300641
Cookrdige Lane, Leeds
(18) 6779 yards/***/D

Crosland Heath G.C.
(01484) 653216
Felk Site Road, Huddersfield
(18) 5962 yards/***/F

Crow Nest Park G.C.
(014842) 201216
Hove Edge, Brighouse
(9) 5910 yards/***/D

Dewsbury District G.C.
(01924) 492399
The Pinnacle, Sands Lane, Mirfield
(18) 6256 yards/**/C/H

East Bierley G.C.
(01274) 681023
South View Road, Bierley, Bradford
(9) 4692 yards/***(Sun)/D

Elland G.C.
(01422) 372505
Hammerstones, Leach Lane, Elland
(9) 5526 yards/***/D

Fardew G.C.
(01274) 561229
Carr Lane, East Morton
(9) 6212 yards/***/E

Ferrybridge 'C' G.C.
(01977) 674188
Stranglands Lane, Knottingly
(9) 5138 yards/*/E/G

Fulneck G.C.
(0113) 256 5191
Fulneck, Pudsey
(9) 5564 yards/**/D

Garforth G.C.
(0113) 286 3308
Long Lane, Garforth, Leeds
(18) 6296 yards/**/B/H/M

Gott's Park G.C.
(0113) 256 2994
Armley Ridge Road, Leeds
(18) 4960 yards/***/E

Halifax G.C.
(01422) 244171
Union Lane, Ogden, Halifax
(18) 6037 yards/***/B

Halifax Bradley Hall G.C.
(01422) 374108
Stainland Road, Holywell Green
(18) 6213 yards/***/B

Halifax West End G.C.
(01422) 363293
Highroad Well, Halifax
(18) 6003 yards/***/C/H

Hanging Heaton G.C.
(01924) 461606
White Cross Road, Bennett Lane, Dewsbury
(9) 5874 yards/**/D/M

Headingley G.C.
(0113) 267 9573
Back Church Lane, Adel, Leeds
(18) 6298 yards/***/B/H

Headley G.C.
(01274) 833481
Headley Lane, Thornton,Bradford
(9) 4914 yards/***/E

Hebden Bridge G.C.
(01422) 842732
Great Mount, Wadsworth
(9) 5064 yards/***/D

Horsforth G.C.
(0113) 258 6819
Layton Road, Horsforth, Leeds
(18) 6243 yards/***/B/H

Howley Hall G.C.
(01924) 478417
Scotchman Lane, Morley, Leeds
(18) 6029 yards/***(Sat)/B/H

Huddersfield G.C.
(01484) 426203
Fixby Hall, Fixby, Huddersfield
(18) 6424 yards/***/A

Ilkley G.C.
(01943) 600214
Middleton, Ilkley
(18) 6256 yards/***/A

Keighley G.C.
(01535) 604778
Howden Park, Utley, Keighley
(18) 6149 yards/**/B/H

Leeds G.C.
(0113) 265 8775
Elmete Lane, Leeds
(18) 6097 yards/**/C/M

Leeds Golf Centre
(0113) 288 6000
Wike Ridge Lane, Shadwell
(18) 6800 yards/***/D

Lightcliffe G.C.
(01422) 202459
Knowle Top Road, Lightcliffe
(9) 5388 yards/***(Wed/Sat)/D/M

Lofthouse Hill G.C.
(01924) 823703
Leeds Road, Wakefield
(9) 3167 yards/*/E/G

Longley Park G.C.
(01484) 426932
Maple Street, Huddersfield
(9) 5269 yards/**(Thurs)/D

Low Laithes G.C.
(01924) 261844
Parkmill Flushdyke, Ossett
(18) 6468 yards/**/C

Marsden G.C.
(01484) 844253
Mount Road, Hemplow, Marsden
(9) 5702 yards/**/E

Meltham G.C.
(01484) 850227
Thick Hollins, Meltham
(18) 6145 yards/***(Wed/Sat)/B

Middleton Park G.C.
(0113) 253 3993
Middleton Park, Leeds
(18) 5233 yards/***/E

Mid Yorkshire G.C.
(01977) 704522
Havercroft Lane, Darrington
(18) 6500 yards/***/C/H

Moor Allerton G.C.
(0113) 266 1154
Coal Road, Wike, Leeds
(27) 6045 yards/**/A/H
6222 yards/**/A/H
6930 yards/**/A/H

Moortown G.C.
(0113) 268 6521
Harrogate Road, Alwoodley, Leeds
(18) 7020 yards/***/A/H

Mount Skip G.C.
(01422) 892896
Hebden Bridge
(9) 5114 yards/***/F

Normanton G.C.
(01924) 892943
Syndale Road, Normanton,
(9) 5288 yards/***(Sun)/D

Northcliffe G.C.
(01274) 584805
High Bank Lane, Shipley
(18) 6104 yards/**(Sat/Tues)/B/H

Otley G.C.
(01943) 465329
West Busk Lane, Otley
(18) 6235 yards/***(Sat)/B

Oulton Park G.C.
(0113) 282 3152
Oulton, Leeds
(18) 6241 yards/***/E

Outlane G.C.
(01422) 374762
Slack Lane, Outlane, Huddersfield
(18) 6003 yards/***/C

Painthorpe House C.C.
(01924) 255083
Painthorpe Lane, Crigglestone
(9) 4520 yards/***(Sun)/E

Phoenix Park G.C.
(01274) 667573
Dick Lane, Thornbury
(9) 4774 yards/**/F

Pontefract & District G.C.
(01977) 792241
Park Lane, Pontefract
(18) 6227 yards/**/B-A

Queensbury G.C.
(01274) 882155
Brighouse Road, Queensbury
(9) 5102 yards/***/D/M

Rawdon G.C.
(0113) 250 6040
Buckstone Drive, Rawdon, Leeds
(9) 5960 yards/**/D/H

Riddlesden G.C.
(01535) 602148
Elam Wood Road, Riddlesden
(18) 4185 yards/***/D

Roundhay G.C.
(0113) 266 2695
Park Lane, Leeds
(9) 5166 yards/***/E

Ryburn G.C.
(01422) 831355
Norland, Sowerby Bridge, Halifax
(9) 5002 yards/***/D/H

Sand Moor G.C.
(0113) 268 5180
Alwoodley Lane, Leeds
(18) 6429 yards/**/B/M

Scarcroft G.C.
(0113) 289 2311
Syke Lane, Leeds
(18) 6426 yards/***/B/H

Shipley G.C.
(01274) 563212
Beckfoot Lane, Cottingley Bridge
(18) 6218 yards/***(Tues/Sat)/B

Silsden G.C.
(01535) 652998
High Brunthwaite, Silsden
(14) 4870 yards/***/D

South Bradford G.C.
(01274) 679195
Pearson Road, Odsal, Bradford
(9) 6004 yards/**/D

South Leeds G.C.
(0113) 270 0479
Gipsy Lane, Beeston Ring Road
(18) 5890 yards/**/C/M

Temple Newsam G.C.
(0113) 264 5624
Temple Newsam Road, Leeds
(18) 6448 yards/***/E
(18) 6029 yards/***/E

Todmorden G.C.
(01706) 812986
Rive Rocks, Cross Stone
(9) 5878 yards/***/C/H

Wakefield G.C.
(01924) 258778
Woodthorpe Lane, Sandal, Wakefield
(18) 6626 yards/**/B/H

Waterton Park G.C.
(01924) 259525
The Balk, Wakefield
(18) 6274 yards/C/G

West Bowling G.C.
(01274) 724449
Newall Hall, Rooley Lane, Bradford
(18) 5770 yards/**/B/H

West Bradford G.C.
(01274) 542767
Chellow Grange, Bradford
(18) 5752 yards/***/C

Wetherby G.C.
(01937) 583375
Linton Lane, Wetherby
(18) 6235 yards/***/B/H

Whitwood G.& C.C.
(01977) 558596
Altofts Lane, Castleford
(9) 6282 yards/***/F

Woodhall Hills G.C.
(0113) 255 4594
Woodhall Road, Calverley, Pudsey
(18) 6102 yards/***/B

Woodsome Hall G.C.
(01484) 602971
Fenay Bridge, Huddersfield
(18) 6080 yards/***(Tues)/B/H

Woolley Park G.C.
(01226) 380144
Woolley, Wakefield
(18) 5874 yards/***/D

EAST RIDING

Beverley & East Riding G.C.
(01482) 869519
The Westwood, Beverley
(18) 6164 yards/***/D

Bridlington G.C.
(01262) 606367
Belvedere Road, Bridlington
(18) 6491 yards/**(Sun pm)/D

Bridlington Links
(01262) 401584
Flanborough Road, Morton
(18) 6720 yards/***/D

Brough G.C.
(01482) 667374
Cave Road, Brough
(18) 6159 yards/**(Wed am)/B/H

Cave Castle Hotel & G.C.
(01430) 422245
South Cave, Brough
(18) 6409 yards/***/D

Cherry Burton G.C
(01964) 550924
Leconfield Road, Beverly
(9) 2278 yards/***/E

Cottingham G.C.
(01482) 842394
Spring Park Farm, Cottingham
(18) 6230 yards/**/D

Driffield G.C.
(01377) 253116
Sunderlandwick, Driffield
(18) 6199 yards/***/C

Flamborough Head G.C.
(01262) 850333
Lighthouse Road, Bridlington
(18) 5438 yards/***(Sun am)/D/M

Ganstead Park G.C.
(01482) 811280
Longdales Lane, Coniston, Hull
(18) 6801 yards/**/C/H

Grange Park G.C.
(01724) 762945
Butterwick Road,
(9) 2970 yards/***/E

Hainsworth Park G.C.
(01964) 542362
Brandesburton, Driffield
(18) 6003 yards/***/D

Hessle G.C.
(01482) 650171
Westfield Road, Cottingham, Hull
(18) 6638 yards/**(Tues am)/C/H

Hornsea G.C.
(01964) 532020
Rolston Road, Hornsea
(18) 6450 yards/***(Tues)/C

Hull G.C.
(01482) 658919
The Hall, Packman Lane, Kirk Ella
(18) 6242 yards/**/B/H

Springhead Park G.C.
(01482) 656309
Willerby Road, Hull
(18) 6439 yards/***/E

Sutton Park G.C.
(01482) 374242
Salthouse Road, Sutton, Hull
(18) 6251 yards/***/E

Withernsea G.C.
(01964) 612078
Chestnut Avenue, Withernsea
(9) 5112 yards/***/E

The map includes labels:

Berwick-upon-Tweed, *Berwick Upon Tweed (Goswick) GC*, Coldstream, *Holy Island*, *Bamburgh Castle GC*, *Seabouses GC*, *Dunstanburgh Castle GC*, Alnwick, *Alnmouth (Foxton) GC*, Amble, The Cheviot Hills, The Borders, Otterburn, *Linden Hall GC*, *Long Hirst Hall GC*, Ashington, Newbiggin-by-the-Sea, Morpeth, *Morbeth GC*, *Arcot Hall GC*, Bedlington, Blyth, *Bellingham GC*, NORTHUMBERLAND, Ponteland, Cramlington, *Whitley Bay GC*, *Ponteland GC*, *Matfen Hall GC*, Gosforth, *Northumberland GC*, NEWCASTLE UPON TYNE, South Shields, *Hexham GC*, Corbridge, Hexham, Gateshead, TYNE & WEAR, SUNDERLAND, *Slaley Hall GC*, *Whitburn GC*, CARLISLE, Brampton, *Brampton GC*, Consett, *Beamish Park GC*, Stanley, *Wearside GC*, Houghton le Spring, *Silloth-on-Solway GC*, Carlisle, *Carlisle GC*, Wigton, Chester-le-Street, *Ramside Hall GC*, Durham, Brandon, Peterlee, Alston, *Brancepeth Castle GC*, Maryport, *Maryport GC*, CUMBRIA, *Penrith GC*, Penrith, DURHAM, Spennymoor, Hartlepool, A1(M), *Seaton Carew GC*, *Saltburn-by-the-Sea GC*, Workington, *Keswick GC*, Keswick, *Appleby GC*, Appleby-in-Westmorland, Bishop Auckland GC, Newton Aycliffe, *Woodham GC*, Whitehaven, Brough, *Haughton Grange GC*, Darlington, *Darlington GC*, Egremont, Lake District, *Barnard Castle GC*, *Blackwell Grange GC*, Ambleside, *Windermere GC*, Windermere, Coniston, *Kendal GC*, Sedbergh, *Seascale GC*, Kendal, *Carus Green GC*, Kirkby Lonsdale, Millom, Ulverston, *Ulverston GC*, Grange-over-Sands, *Furness GC*, Barrow-in-Furness, *Isle of Walney*

_____ *Cumbria, Northumberland & Durham Choice Golf* _____

Just as Devon is often viewed by holidaymakers as a stepping stone to Cornwall (which as a Devonian pleases me greatly!) so the far north of England is often viewed by golfers as a mere pretty pathway to the delights of Scotland—Turnberry, Gleneagles etc. Indeed, some even believe that north of Lytham there's nothing much in the way of golfing challenges until the 'Bonnie Land' is reached. To those I simply say, 'shame on you!'

Our region covers Cumbria as well as the North East. Now admittedly, Cumbria is hardly perfect golfing territory. A Sunningdale in the middle of the Lake District is hard to imagine (although some spectacular holes are clearly possible!) But there are a number of golf courses in between the fells and the lakes, and furthermore Cumbria comprises more than just the Lake District. Before the counties were rearranged and renamed in the early seventies, Cumberland was the most northerly county in the West of England and home, not only to the famous sausage, but to the **Silloth-on-Solway** Golf Club which is, dare I say it, as good a links as you'll find anywhere in England.

As for the North East, **Seaton Carew** near Hartlepool offers championship golf of a very high calibre and **Slaley Hall** is full of Northumbrian promise, while even further north along the Northumberland coast lie a string of golfing pearls—**Alnmouth**, **Dunstanburgh**, **Bamburgh** and **Goswick**—good courses with breathtaking scenery.

Cumbria: The Lakes

Let us make a start in the Lake District with the hope that in addition to the picnic hamper and the climbing boots, we've left room in the back of the car for the golf clubs.

The Lake District is the land of poets, 'Where breezes are soft and skies are fair' (W C Bryant) and 'Where nature reveals herself in all her wildness, all her majesty' (S Roger). At Keswick the golfer meets the poet. **Keswick** Golf Club lies four miles east of the lakeland town via the A66. While the course now measures well over 6000 yards, it recently held a rather dubious claim to being the shortest course in Britain—in 1976 there was a splendid clubhouse but only five holes—no doubt some remarkable scores were returned! These days scoring is a little more difficult with several streams and some dense woodland to be avoided. As one might imagine the views are quite something and a visit will never disappoint.

Still in the Lakes we find **Kendal**, a fine parkland course, close to the town centre and only two miles from the M6 link road. Although a fair bit shorter than Keswick its first hole is often considered the toughest opener in Britain—231 yards, uphill all the way, out of bounds to the left and woods to the right! Should one make it to the 2nd the holes get much easier. However there is an infamous quarry on the right of the 15th fairway which has been known to receive more than golf balls. One frustrated chap after firing ball after ball into its murky depths decided to throw in his bag for good measure. Fortunately he didn't throw himself in as well but the word is he never played golf again. Who said it was only a game!

The Golf Club at **Windermere** should prove much more relaxing. The club recently celebrated its centenary and the course has improved considerably in the last few years. An ideal place for a game of golf while on holiday in the Lakes, we feature Windermere later page. Another first class course, still within the National Park boundary is at **Penrith**, close to the A6 but a lovely setting nonetheless with some beautiful views Ullswater and several very challenging holes. Talking of good views, the parkland course at **Ulverston** enjoys commanding views of Morecambe Bay and there is also a pleasant course at **Carus Green**.

Recommending both superior and reasonably priced establishments in the area is a difficult task, to put it mildly, simply because there are so many. But hopefully the following suggestions will be useful. Grasmere is a favourite and here Michael's Nook (015394) 35496 is an outstanding country hotel with an excellent restaurant. Antiques are dotted throughout the house and the gardens are a delight. The Wordsworth (015394) 35592 is also a grand hotel while at White Moss House (015394) 35295—the poet's former residence—another superb restaurant can be found. Another truly first class establishment in the area is the delightful Nanny Brow Hotel (015394) 32036 near Ambleside, more landscape gardens here with views to match. Nearer to Keswick, Armathwaite Hall (017687) 76551 in Bassenthwaite is charming, while for a really relaxing country inn, the Pheasant Inn (017687) 76234 in Bassenthwaite Lake can have few equals. In Keswick itself there is the Keswick Country House Hotel (01768) 772020 well suited for golf. The Brundholme (01768) 774495 is also good.

Penrith is a bustling town with numerous hotels. As an alternative to staying in town Ullswater naturally attracts and here the Sharrow Bay Hotel (017684) 86301 and its restaurant are particularly stylish. Cheaper accommodation is available nearby in one of the area's best pubs, the Queens Head at Askham, while the Old Church Hotel (017684) 86204 at Watermillock offers spectacular views and a lakeside settings. Also worth hunting out is the Brandelhow Guesthouse (01768) 864470.

Oh-so-popular Windermere offers a wealth of good hotels. Three meriting attention are the Miller Howe (015394) 42536 where breakfast is reputed to be among the best in the country, the Langdale Chase (015394) 32201 and the moderately priced Applegarth Hotel. Oregano (015394) 44954 in the High Street is another recommended restaurant. Among other first class establishments near Windermere Golf Club we can also recommend Gilpin Lodge Country House (015394) 88818 and Linthwaite House Hotel (015394) 88600, while the Burn How Garden House Hotel (015394) 46226 offers a luxurious and rather unique style of accommodation. Other ideas for a 19th hole in the Lake District must include the Old Vicarage (015395) 52381 at Witherslack, the Mortal Man (015394) 33193 at Troutbeck (wake up to a glorious setting), the Wild Boar in Crook (015394) 45225 and for a really popular pub try the Masons Arms in Cartmel Fell. Finally, consider Holbeck Ghyll (015394) 32375 a former hunting lodge and an excellent establishment.

Cumbria: The Coast

To the south of Cumbria the highly rated **Furness** Golf Club lays claim to being the oldest in the county. A true links and being quite exposed, scoring well is often more difficult than the card suggests. An after-golf thought here is the excellent Abbey House Hotel (01229) 838282, while Eccle Riggs Manor (01229) 716398 is also recommended. Also pleasant is Bridgefield House (01229) 885239 at Spark Bridge—excellent food here—and further inland the Uplands Country House Hotel (015395) 36248 is extremely good value and the restaurant is spectacular.

Further along Cumbria's coast, **Seascale** has a somewhat underrated links. One shouldn't be put off by the thought of being close to the Seascale nuclear installations (and jokes about balls glowing in the dark are uncalled for). It's an excellent test of golf—some tremendous views too towards the Wasdale Screes and the Scafell Range. North of Workington (en route to Silloth) there is a fair course at **Maryport**. There is doubtless some convenient accommodation nearby but I'll recommend a trip inland to another personal favourite, Buttermere, one of the more westerly lakes and where the Bridge Hotel (017687) 70252 is very comfortable.

Silloth-on-Solway has already been referred to and is featured separately on a later page. The course certainly deserves more than a fleeting visit and two handy hotels in the town are the Queen's Hotel (016973) 31373 and the Golf Hotel (016973) 31438. Both specialise in golf packages, as for that matter does the nearby Skinburness Hotel (016973) 32332.

Carlisle

Golfers in Carlisle are well catered for with two good courses in the area, **Carlisle** and **Brampton**—or Talkin' Tarn as it is sometimes called. (The Tarn End House (01697) 72340 is a magical place to eat!) Brampton, located to the east of Carlisle off the B6413, is a beautifully kept course, laid out four hundred feet above sea level with views towards the nearby hills. It is probably best described as moorland whereas Carlisle, equally well maintained, is more of a parkland type. For an overnight stop in Carlisle the Crown and Mitre (01228) 525491 is welcoming. Near Brampton, Farlam Hall (016977) 46234 is an excellent country house hotel with an outstanding restaurant and the Hare and Hounds (016977) 3456 is a comfortable inn. Fantails (01228) 560239 in Wetheral is a first class restaurant and for a pleasant waterside setting, the Crosby Lodge, an 18th century country mansion at Crosby-on-Eden (01228) 573618 is recommended.

Before leaving Cumbria, a quick mention for the somewhat isolated **Appleby** Golf Club. If you are in the vicinity it's well worth a visit. A splendid combination of moorland and heathland—very colourful. Remote, perhaps but in nearby Appleby-in-Westmorland the Appleby Manor (017683) 51571 awaits and for a nearby friendly inn note the Black Swan at Ravenstondale.

The North East

So to the North East—and what a mixture! Durham, Tyne & Wear and Northumberland. An area encompassing Tyneside, Teeside and Wearside, it also includes the Cleveland Hills, the Cheviots and the wild spectacular coast of ancient Northumbria. The area stretches from the far end of the Yorkshire Pennines and intrudes into the Scottish Borders, the greater part of Northumberland lying north of Hadrian's Wall.

The appeal of any golf course can be affected greatly by its surroundings and nowhere in Britain does the accompanying landscape seem to dictate the enjoyment of a game as much as in this part of the world. The contrast between the industrial and rural North East is dramatic. The golf courses in the former tend towards the uninspiring—Seaton Carew being one exception—whilst the likes of Bamburgh Castle and Hexham offer such magnificent scenery that the quality of the golf can often be relegated to a secondary consideration.

Durham

Beginning in the south of the region, **Seaton Carew** is far and away the best in the county. In fact, it is almost certainly the best links course on the East Coast of England, north of Norfolk. Seaton Carew is featured ahead.

The top hotel in this area for golfers is undoubtedly Hardwick Hall (01740) 620253 at Sedgefield, which is well placed for Seaton Carew and the courses in County Durham. There are a number of other good hotels in the county, although as everywhere some of them are very modern and unfortunately rather characterless. An exception to this is the Crathorne Hall Hotel (01642) 700398 at Yarm—a converted Edwardian mansion. Also handy for Seaton Carew is the Grand (01429) 266345 in Hartlepool.

Moving up to Durham itself, people often talk of Old Durham Town, but of course it's very much a city with a cathedral that has been adjudged the most beautiful building in the world. Without doubt the course to visit here is **Brancepeth Castle**, four miles south west of the city and set in very beautiful surroundings. Rather like St Pierre at Chepstow the course occupies land that was formerly a deer park, and a 13th century church and castle provide a magnificent backcloth. Perhaps the most convenient place to stay is at the Bridge Hotel (0191) 3780524 in Croxdale, a well run Toby House, but there are a number of good hotels in Durham itself including the Royal County (0191) 3866821. Just north of Durham is the historic Lumley Castle (0191) 3891111 which offers good food and accommodation overlooking the course at Chester-le-Street.

Further north, **Beamish Park** near Stanley is another laid out in a former deer park (belonging to Beamish Hall) and is worth a detour if heading along the A1. **Bishop Auckland** in the centre of the county is a pleasant parkland course. The land here belongs to the Church of England and one of the terms of the club's lease is that the course has to close on Good Friday and Christmas Day. Play then at your peril!

To the south west of Bishop Auckland, **Barnard Castle** enjoys yet another delightful setting. More of a moorland course than anything else, it has a stream that must be crossed seventeen times during

a round! There are some fine establishments nearby in which to celebrate (or perhaps even dry out?) In Barnard Castle the Jersey Farm Hotel (01833) 638223 is excellent value for a night's stay while those just looking for a bar snack and a drink might visit the nearby villages of Cotherstone (The Fox and Hounds) or Romaldkirk where you find The Rose and Crown (01833) 650213, a pleasant inn with some good food A slightly longer drive to Eggleston, also possible from Bishop Auckland, and one finds the Three Tuns—famed for its pub lunches. Midway between Bishop Auckland and Darlington at Newton Aycliffe is the **Woodham** Golf and Country Club which has a growing reputation.

Darlington is the largest town in the county. It may not have the appeal of Durham but for golfers there's a twin attraction: to the north, **Haughton Grange** with its great selection of MacKenzie greens and to the south, **Blackwell Grange** with its fine variety of trees. Both courses are parkland and always well maintained. For an ideal base one doesn't really have to look further than the 17th century Blackwell Grange Moat House (01325) 380888. A good restaurant to note in the town is Sardis (01325) 461222, an Italian inspired menu here, and for a drink and some accommodation try the Kings Head (01325) 380222. Outside the town try Headlam Hall (01325) 730238 or Hall Garth (01325) 300400 where there is a nine hole course. Further north still, one should not omit **Ramside Hall** (0191) 3865282 a pleasant hotel which now has a fine 27 hole layout by Jonathan Gaunt.

Tyne and Wear

Tyne and Wear is essentially a tale of two cities, Newcastle—the home of the Geordies and Sunderland where the welcome is second to none. There are plenty of golf courses in the area but the really

THE SLEEPING GIANT - THE NINTH HOLE AT DE VERE SLALEY HALL GOLF CLUB *Photograph courtesy of:* **De Vere Slaley Hall**

attractive golf lies further north along the coast. The **Northumberland** (Gosforth Park) Golf Club and **Ponteland** probably have the best two courses in Tyne & Wear. The former is situated alongside Gosforth Park Racecourse and like Seaton Carew has staged several national championships, it is renowned for its difficult finishing holes. The visitor may find it easier to arrange a game at Ponteland (at least during the week)—a particularly well-kept course this and very convenient if you happen to be flying to or from Newcastle Airport. **Whitley Bay** is another alternative. It is quite a long, windswept course with very large greens and a wide stream that can make scoring pretty difficult.

If there's one large town in England that could really do with a championship standard golf challenge it's Sunderland, a place of great character—golf architects please note! The best courses in the area are probably **Whitburn** and **Wearside**.

Staying in and around Newcastle some of the leading hotels are the Swallow Gosforth Park Hotel (0191) 2364111, the Holiday Inn (0191) 2365432 and the Marriott (0191) 493 2233, while the Copthorne on the Quayside (0191) 2220333 is fast developing a good name for itself. All offer all the mod. cons. and some first class leisure facilities. Jesmond offers a multitude of less expensive hotels and guesthouses—Chirton House Hotel (0191) 2730407 being but one example.

In Newcastle itself, the choice is tremendous. The city boasts a real 'Chinatown' along Stowell Street with a host of superb restaurants of which Ming Dynasty (0191) 261 5787 remains one of the best. For Indian (or Punjabi to be more accurate) cuisine of the highest order there can be only one selection and that is Sachins (0191) 2619035—do ring to reserve a table and get directions. An evening at 21 Queen Street (0191) 2220755 on the Quayside is always a culinary experience and there are now a number of other restaurants in the immediate vicinity to suit any palate or pocket. Finally, excellent cooking can always be found at either the Fisherman's Lodge (0191) 2813281 or Taylors Wharf (0191) 2321057. Outside the city and handy for Ponteland and the airport is Horton Grange (01661) 860686 offering an elegant restaurant in sumptuous surroundings.

Northumberland
Finally then, a look at Northumberland, a county with a splendid, almost mythical history. The first golf course on the way up, as it were, is Arcot Hall, six miles north of Newcastle and a most tranquil setting. A James Braid creation, **Arcot Hall** is a heathland course with a wealth of trees and a lake. The 9th here is a particularly good hole. The club has a sumptuous clubhouse but beware of the Grey Lady who ghosts in and out from time to time! If thoroughly frightened, many peaceful villages are at hand and some very good pubs. The Highlander at Belsay is one such place (and equally convenient incidentally after a day's golf at Ponteland).

Trekking northwards again, **Morpeth** is next on the agenda. Another pleasant course designed this time by one of James Braid's old rivals—Mr Vardon no less. One of England's finest Georgian country houses lies only a short distance away at Longhorsley—**Linden Hall** (01670) 516611. Its new championship length golf course is featured ahead. Also nearby is **Longhirst Hall** (01670) 791348 a 19th century stately home also with its own 18 hole parkland course.

Along the rugged coast some tremendous golf lies ahead. The course at Alnmouth (**Foxton**) is very pleasing and in the village is the comfortable Marine House Hotel (01665) 830349. Just a little beyond are the magnificent castle courses of **Dunstanburgh** (at Embleton) and **Bamburgh**. The golf is fun and the scenery superb. Dunstanburgh Castle, the ruins of which were immortalised in watercolour by Turner, occupies a wondrously remote setting. The course is a genuine links, hugging close to the shore and staring out across miles of deserted beach. Bamburgh Castle is perhaps even more special and is often referred to as England's most beautiful course. Not long by any

means—but the setting! Holy Island and Lindisfarne, the Cheviot Hills and a majestic castle. Furthermore, the fairways are bordered by a blaze of colour, with gorse, purple heather and numerous wild orchids. Bamburgh Castle is explored ahead. Not far from here is the fairly short but underrated course at **Seahouses**.

Having placated the golfing soul a few suggestions for the body include the Dunstanburgh Castle Hotel—as its name suggests, very handy for the golf course, the Lord Crewe Arms (01668) 214243 in Bamburgh—good for a drink with some accommodation also. Another good resting place is to be found in Belford, the Blue Bell Hotel (01668) 213543. Warren House (01668) 214581 is another hotel just outside Bamburgh but well worth seeking out. Among several good Northumbrian pubs are the Tankerville Arms in Wooler, the Olde Ship in Seahouses, the Jolly Fisherman in Craster and the Craster Arms in Beadnell.

For centuries the town of Berwick-upon-Tweed didn't know whether it was coming or going, passing between England and Scotland like the proverbial shuttlecock. However disorientated it has a fine links course at **Goswick**, three miles south of the town. Two thoughts for what may be one's last night in England—or maybe one's first?—are the Kings Arms Hotel (01289) 307454 and the excellent restaurant Funnywat'mekalivin' (01289) 308827. A little further afield try the Tillmouth Park Hotel (01890) 882255, a really pleasant place to stay.

The Tyne Valley
Having sent the golfer north of Newcastle I am aware of having neglected the lovely Tyne Valley and the historic Abbey town of Hexham.

Hexham Golf Club is only a short drive west of Newcastle, along either the A69 and is generally considered to be one of the best parkland courses in Northumberland and ejoys wonderful views of the Tyne valley. Just east of Hexham are the newly opened **Matfen Hall** and **Slaley Hall** which is featured ahead.

Slaley Hall International Resort and Spa (01434) 673350 is quite sumptuous with excellent restaurants and leisure facilities. The journey is well worth making as the course has a glorious setting. Nearby villages with their many inns include the Hadrian, at (would you believe) Wall. The Angel (01434) 632119 in Corbridge is good. Finally a restaurant of note is the Black House (01434) 604744 just south of the market town of Hexham. Less pricey, and within similarly easy reach of Slaley Hall, is the pleasantly informal Danielle's Bistro (01434) 601122 in Hexham itself, which offers imaginative food attentively served.

Finally, set high in Border Reever territory between Hadrian's Wall and the border, a rare treat, **Bellingham**, traditional moorland golf on a new 18 hole layout. A golfing holiday I believe is in order—and who needs Scotland!

LINDEN HALL GOLF CLUB Photograph courtesy of: Linden Hall

Matfen Hall is a magnificent Country House Hotel set in the heart of beautiful Northumberland countryside. It is easily accessible by road, rail and air. Sir Hugh Blackett has carefully restored his family's home into one of the North East's most prestigious venues for weddings, conferences, leisure breaks and of course golf.

In the short time it has been open the newly refurbished hall has already established a reputation for superb food and quality service. Built in 1830 and retaining most of its original character, Matfen Hall offers an idyllic setting for a relaxing weekend or golfing break.

The eighteen hole golf course was opened in 1994 and already displays maturity beyond its years. Measuring over 6500 yards from the back tees, the course is laid out on a classic parkland landscape with fairways and greens flanked by majestic trees. Away from the course Matfen Hall provides high quality accommodation for business and leisure guests, combining modern facilities with the traditional elegance you would expect from a country house.

After a long day you can enjoy a drink in the splendid Victorian conservatory overlooking the 18th green, or a pre dinner drink in the cocktail bar. The impressive library dining room, with its panoramic views over the course and beyond, offers fine table d'hote and à la carte dining.

Full conference and wedding facilities are available in the East Wing, or for the extra special event the magnificent Great Hall offers a truly unique setting to ensure a memorable day.

The local area offers the visitor a wealth of cultural and historic places to visit. There is easy access to the scenic coastal, rural and historic sites of Northumberland.

Within fifteen minutes lie: the city of Newcastle, the Metro Centre at Gateshead, one of Europe's premier shopping malls, and Newcastle International Airport. Whatever the reason for visiting Matfen Hall Country House Hotel you'll enjoy a luxurious break in scenic Northumberland.

Matfen Hall Country House Hotel
Matfen Hall
Matfen Northumberland
NE20 0RH
Tel: 01661 886500
Fax: 01661 886055
e mail: info@matfenhall.com
web site: www.matfenhall.com

Slaley Hall

Despite its close proximity to Scotland, the 'royal' and 'ancient' county of Northumberland has made little impact on the history of the royal and ancient game. In the future, however, this situation is likely to change. How come? The catalyst can be found deep in the countryside at Slaley Hall near Hexham.

Slaley Hall itself is today a hotel and leisure complex of the highest order and includes 36 holes of golf. The original championship golf course was designed by Dave Thomas and opened for play in July 1989. Let us at once say that Thomas has produced a masterpiece; he himself considers it his finest work. Immediately it opened, critics were describing it as 'The Woburn of the North' and with dense forest surrounding the course it doesn't need much imagination to see why. As for the luxury hotel, Greenalls acquired it in late 1998, adding it to their prestigious porfolio of 17 four and five star De Vere hotels around the UK. In summer 1999 the second championship course, the **Priestman**, designed by Neil Coles was opened and the original 18 was renamed the **Hunting** course.

Golfing visitors are welcome at Slaley Hall seven days a week. Whilst it is not a rule that you have to have to a handicap certificate, all players should have a good understanding of the etiquette of golf, which covers such points as safety, consideration for other players, pace of play, and care of the course.

Tee times may be booked in advance through **Golf Reservations tel: (01434) 673154**, while group booking enquiries should be directed to the **Sales Office (01434) 673350**, by **fax: (01434 673050** or by **e mail: slaley.hall@devere-hotels.com** The 2000 green fees are set at £55 per round on the Hunting course (standby £40) and £45 per round on the Priestman course (standby £30). Golf buggies are available for hire and can be reserved in advance.

Although it genuinely is situated in deepest, rural Northumberland, visitors shouldn't have too much difficulty finding Slaley Hall. Its precise location is 6 miles south of Hexham and 2 miles west of the A68 road, between Corbridge and Consett. The quickest route from Newcastle (and its airport) is to pick up the A69 towards Hexham. Thereafter take the A68 south and follow the signs. From Hexham, the road to take for Slaley is the B6306. Approaching from further afield, the A1/M1 is likely to be of most assistance for those motoring up from the South

and the Midlands, while to the north Hexham is linked to Scotland by the A68. The aforementioned Newcastle Airport is approximately 18 miles from the golf course.

In June 2000 the resort again plays host to the Compaq European Grand Prix which, with its £700,000 prize fund, is one of the most important events on the PGA European Tour. The Grand Prix will attract many of the big names in European golf and the quality of the course should be of such a standard to test all participants.

From its championship tees the Hunting course weighs in at a fairly formidable 7088 yards, par 72. Less daunting are the medal and 'social' tees which reduce the total length to 6530 yards. From the ladies' tees the course measures 5755 yards, par 75.

The 1st hole offers a chance to open the shoulders, for the fairway is fairly wide, but thereafter at least a little caution may be the order of the day. The 2nd and 3rd are excellent holes—the former being a swinging dog-leg where, if you're too greedy from the tee, the conifers will swallow your ball. Fir trees are ever present at Slaley Hall, lining just about every fairway and giving the course something of an alpine feel. The golfer must do battle with streams and small lakes at the 4th, 5th, 6th and 7th. The 8th is another of Slaley's swinging dog-legs and the 9th is a truly magnificent par four played over water and through a narrow avenue of towering pines and dense rhododendrons.

On the back nine, holes 11, 12 and 13 are highly memorable; laid out close to Slaley Hall, cherry trees abound and they are a spectacular sight when in bloom. Holes 14 to 17 have a distinctly moorland feel and the 18th is a classic, though very difficult, finishing hole.

Just a year after opening, the magazine Executive Golfer International featured Slaley Hall in its June 1990 edition, and had this to say: 'We feel confident in predicting that Slaley Hall will soon become a name synonymous with major golf events—in the same league as Wentworth, Gleneagles and Turnberry. But in addition, Slaley Hall will be the total resort for all reasons and all seasons—as they say, the ultimate dream.'

Ten years on (and now with 36 holes to savour) that dream has been fully realised.

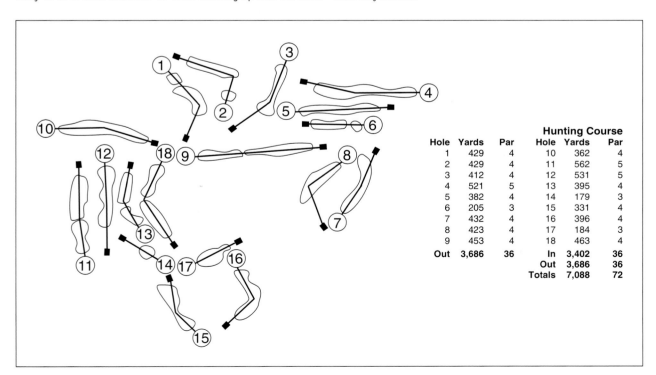

Hunting Course

Hole	Yards	Par	Hole	Yards	Par
1	429	4	10	362	4
2	429	4	11	562	5
3	412	4	12	531	5
4	521	5	13	395	4
5	382	4	14	179	3
6	205	3	15	331	4
7	432	4	16	396	4
8	423	4	17	184	3
9	453	4	18	463	4
Out	**3,686**	**36**	**In**	**3,402**	**36**
			Out	**3,686**	**36**
			Totals	**7,088**	**72**

Silloth-on-Solway

One of the greatest ever lady golfers, Miss Cecil Leitch once said, 'If you can play Silloth you can play anywhere'. The four times British Ladies Champion and the great rival of Joyce Wethered would have been able to judge better than most for she grew up in Silloth and it was on Silloth's championship links that she and her four golfing sisters learnt to play.

Today, Silloth is perhaps one of Britain's lesser known championship links, this doubtless a result of its somewhat remote situation 23 miles west of Carlisle. Hidden away it may be but it is a journey decidedly worth making, for not only is this one of Britain's greatest tests of golf but the Silloth Club is just about the most friendly one is likely to come across.

Measuring 6614 yards, par 72 from the championship tees (6357 yards from the medal and 5780 yards, par 75 from the ladies' tees), Silloth may not sound particularly frightening, and you may just be wondering what all the fuss is about. Standing on the 1st tee with the wind hammering into your face you'll know exactly what all the fuss is about! Two shots later (hopefully!) you'll also discover why the large greens at Silloth have acquired such a marvellous reputation.

The course meanders its way through and over some classic links terrain. There are occasional spectacular vantage points—the coastal views from the 4th and 6th tees being especially memorable—and the round calls for several demanding strokes, both going out and coming home. Of the many great holes however, perhaps the par five 13th stands out. Appropriately named 'Hogs Back' it has an exceptionally narrow fairway that is heather lined on either side and a plateau green. Hit a good drive and you'll be tempted to go for the green in two—miss it and you're in deep trouble.

The club is understandably proud of the fact that it has been selected to host the British Ladies Amateur Championship on three occasions since 1976. However, it can also be proud of the courage some of its members displayed back in 1912; for this information I am greatly indebted to the club's former Secretary, John Todd. On behalf of all the clubs in the British Isles Silloth appealed against the assessment to income tax on green fees. Unfortunately for the golf clubs the learned judge found in favour of the Inland Revenue, leaving Silloth with the task of finding £433 12s. 9d. for legal expenses. 81 clubs promised contributions to help towards the debt and they eventually raised £140 11s. between them, leaving Silloth with a deficiency of almost £300. One very famous club, I am told, subscribed one shilling—and I bet you'd like to know which!

Silloth on Solway Golf Club, Silloth on Solway, Carlisle, Cumbria CA5 4BL

Secretary	John Hill (01697) 331304
Professional	Jonathan Graham (01697) 332404
Green Fees	WD £25/day, WE £32/round
Restrictions	Must be a member of a recognised golf club

Directions
From the south—M6 junction 41, B5305 to Wigton, B5302 to Silloth. From the north/east—M6 junction 43, A69 to Carlisle, A595/596 to Wigton, B 5302 to Silloth.

Windermere

Whoever first coined that atrocious phrase, 'Golf is a good walk spoiled' was more than likely an idiot. One thing's for sure, he (or she) had never visited Windermere Golf Club in the Lake District. Golf not only 'takes us to such beautiful places', as Henry Longhurst used to say, but it also regularly guides us to some beautiful vantage points. Had the idiot who coined the former offering stood on the 8th tee at Windermere he would have assuredly been forced to revise his ill-informed comment. Golf, if nothing else, is a good walk with a good incentive. (Better not tell that idiot then that the 8th at Windermere is called 'Desolation'!)

Founded in 1891, Windermere has always been a popular course. It never had pretensions to becoming a champion-ship length course but has always offered an enjoyable challenge. With its outstanding views, its great swathes of heather, bracken and gorse, plus the marvellous condition in which the course is currently maintained, it is easy to understand why more and more people are calling it a 'mini Gleneagles.' Windermere is probably worthy of such flattery.

Measuring just 5132 yards and with a par of 67, there are, of course, many par three holes and, while none of the par fours is overly long, the naturally rugged landscape makes up for the lack of length. As on a links type course, awkward stances and blind shots are not uncommon at Windermere, and with the greens being fairly small a well-honed short game is often the key to a good round.

We have already singled out the short 8th as Windermere's 'signature hole': from the tee the green sits roughly at eye level but in between is a deep valley of gorse. The green is table-shaped and can be extremely difficult to hit. Distraction is the last thing a golfer needs here but over the player's shoulder is a marvellous view of Morecambe Bay while stretching ahead are the magnificent mountains of the Lake District.

Among other notable holes at Windermere one might include the 2nd, a very long par three; the 4th which is the stroke index one hole with its difficult drive to an acutely angled fairway and potentially even more difficult blind approach; the 6th and 7th where you play beside an attractive little reservoir and the three closing holes, which, according to the card run 5-4-3—scores that most players will be happy to settle for!

Having introduced Windermere with a regrettable quote, it seems only appropriate to conclude with one of the more noble philosophies on life and reputedly first uttered by the legendary golfer Walter Hagen: 'You're only here for a short while; don't hurry, don't worry, but be sure to smell the flowers along the way.' Of course at Windermere, they might even be found fluttering and dancing in the breeze.

Windermere Golf Club, Cleabarrow Windermere, Cumbria LA23 3NB

Secretary	Mr K Moffat (015394) 43123
Professional	Stephen Rook (015394) 43550
Green Fees	WD £24, WE £28
Restrictions	Players must be members of golf clubs and have official handicaps

Directions
From the M6, the best exit point is junction 36. The club is a mile and a half from Bowness on the B5284.

Seaton Carew

Seaton Carew near Hartlepool is a place of extraordinary contrasts. Here is where the industrial north east collides head on with a popular seaside resort. The North Sea washes a sweep of golden sand; beyond this strand are the dunes; beyond the dunes is the lively town (where in summer sedate guesthouses jostle for prominence with noisy arcades) and beyond the town is a backdrop of towering chimneys and their modern equivalents, which at night appear lit up like giant torches. Oh, we forgot to mention one thing: on the landward side of the dunes—though occasionally wandering in amongst them—is the Seaton Carew championship golf links, the finest 18 holes on the east coast of Britain between Hunstanton in Norfolk and Muirfield in East Lothian.

A golf club was formed here in 1874. Initially, there were just 9 holes and the club was named the Durham and Yorkshire Golf Club. There were 18 holes by 1891 but the course did not properly take shape until Alister MacKenzie made major revisions to the layout in the 1920s. Fifty years later, Frank Pennink constructed four new holes and today the club maintains all 22 holes.

Championship golf regularly visits Seaton Carew and in recent years it has hosted the English Strokeplay Championship and, on two occasions, the British Boys Championship.

The challenge commences with a hole called 'The Rocket'. The name has become particularly appropriate following the recent discovery (by the club's head greenkeeper) of two unexploded war time bombs on the adjacent practice area! There is plenty of variety in the 4-5-3 start but the two outstanding sequences at Seaton Carew occur around the turn and over the closing stretch, where sand dunes, undulating terrain, traditional seaside bunkers and a mass of buckthorn conspire to provide an exacting but enjoyable finish. The 371 yards, par four 9th, 'Lagoon' is possibly the best hole on the front nine. The Lagoon—essentially marshy ground—lies to the right of the fairway yet a tee shot directed to this side sets up a much easier second to a green with a steep fall-away on the right. The 10th heads directly towards the sea and, together with the rugged 12th is the pick of Frank Pennink's 'new' holes.

The imaginative (and prophetic) soul who thought up the names 'Rocket' and 'Lagoon' was presumably not consulted with regard to the 16th—it is called 'Dog Leg'! Still, it is a fine hole and leads to a truly great hole. The 17th at Seaton Carew features a bold drive over dunes and gorse and an approach to a raised green surrounded by subtle contours—Alister MacKenzie at his best. The 18th has plenty of character too, with an out of bounds to the right and a rippling fairway.

Seaton Carew Golf Club, Tees Road, Hartlepool TS25 1DE

Secretary	P R Wilson (01429) 261040
Professional	W Hector (01429) 890660
Green Fees	WD £29/day
	WE £40/day
Restrictions	Handicap certificates required.

Directions
2 miles south of Hartlepool off the A178.

Ramside

Michael Adamson, Ramside's owner, as a big man with big ideas; his beds are kingsize, his plates oversize and when he planned to build 27 holes around his hotel, his brief was for biggest is best. This was a challenge which was irresistible for Jonathan Gaunt who had already demonstrated at Callow Valley that he is not short of either imagination or the confidence to design memorable challenges to golfers of all levels.

Working closely with Roger Shaw, (ex Brancepath head greenkeeper), already appointed Course Manager, Gaunt has produced a stunning 27 hole layout in three loops named, appropriately in this county of the Prince Bishops, 'Princes', 'Bishops' and 'Cathedral'. The last named is also appropriate as there are panoramic views of England's greatest cathedral city, particularly from the fourth tee, (the hole is named 'Up A Hyght'), which, with its cathedral backdrop and foreground of twin lakes, contained fairways, thousands of new trees now beginning to define each hole, offers one of the best golf views in the country. It is a transformation made all the more remarkable when one considers the history of this area; a history recognised by the name given to the sixteenth hole: 'Back O The Shaft'.

Wide, well contoured fairways, well placed sand and water hazards (there are 14 lakes to negotiate) all provide either heroic or safe routes to golfers of all levels. Every hole has its own character and every USGA specification green is beautifully modelled. In our view, this Colt influenced course is destined to surpass its illustrious neighbour, Brancepath, designed by Colt and Macknaught and recently in Golf World's top 100.

Overall, the feeling at Brancepath is one of quality and attention to detail, from the Rams Head tee-box markers to the high specification of the driving range, (quite the best we know), and the A star system computerised indoor golf academy. The abiding memory however is of size; this is a big course as a development not short of big ideas; it isn't every course that can boast yardage markers hewn out of blocks of solid granite each weighing an average of eight tons!

Ramside Golf Club
Ramside Hall Hotel, Carrville, Durham DH1 1TD
www.ramsidehallhotel.com

Director	T I Flowers
Professional	Robert Lister (0191) 386 5282
Green Fees	WD £27/round £33/day
	WE £33/round £40/day
Restrictions	Soft spike course

Directions
Turn off the A1(M) at junction 62, head towards Sunderland on the A690 the club is located 200 yards on right.

Bamburgh Castle

Bamburgh Castle may be golf's ultimate 'hidden gem'. The setting is quite stunning. A number of Britain's golf courses fall within the gaze of nearby castles—Royal St. David's and Harlech Castle is perhaps the best known example, Cruden Bay and Dunstanburgh are others, but none is more dramatic than the situation at Bamburgh. Standing 150 feet high on a vast, rocky crag and covering over eight acres, Bamburgh is one of Britain's most spectacular castles. It towers over the village and is visible in all its majesty from the adjoining 18 hole links.

Apparently we have to thank the Normans for the splendid keep. It was they who built it, having acquired the original castle from Matilda, Countess of Northumberland, after threatening to take out the eyes of her captive husband—charming times!

Bamburgh has what might be described as an 'invigorating climate'. Situated on the north eastern coast of Northumberland, only Berwick-upon-Tweed lies further north in England and Bamburgh is a shade closer to the North Pole than either Prestwick, Turnberry or Troon. Despite its remoteness, the journey is a fairly straightforward one and is definitely worth making.

By any standards, Bamburgh Castle is a short course, measuring 5621 yards (par 68) from the men's tees and 5098 yards from the ladies' tees (par 70). Short it may be but it isn't without its tests; there are many whin bushes and several of the fairways are flanked with tangling heather. As with every seaside course, the moods of the wind must always be considered. In any event the golfer will not have come to Bamburgh to seek golf's toughest challenge—it is the splendour of the unique setting that is to be enjoyed. The castle isn't the only sight that demands attention: there are magnificent views across to nearby Holy Island and Lindisfarne and the Cheviot Hills provide a glorious backdrop. As for the course itself, in addition to the great spread of

purple heather, a number of fairways are lined with rare wild orchids. It is hardly surprising that Bamburgh is often described as Britain's most beautiful course. Especially memorable holes at Bamburgh include the short 8th with its tee shot over a valley, the 15th—from this tee the golfer can spy no fewer than four castles—and the 17th which is guaranteed to bring the dreaming golfer down to earth.

What about the 19th? In short, exceptionally friendly (as one comes to expect in this part of England). There are no formal dress requirements and lunches and dinners are offered daily in addition to light snacks.

There is a saying used in many sports that 'a good big'un' is always better than 'a good little'un'; the golf course at Bamburgh demonstrates that the phrase has no meaning whatsoever in the world of golf.

Bamburgh Castle Golf Club, The Club House, Bamburgh, Northumberland, NE69 7DE

Steward/Clubhouse	(01668) 214378
Secretary	Mr T C Osborne (01668) 214321
Green Fees	WD £30/day, Juniors £9
	WE £30/round, £35/day, Juniors £9/£12
	5 day weekday ticket £90, Juniors £20
Restrictions	Weekends busy
	Handicap certificates required.

Directions
Bamburgh is linked to the A1 (6 miles away) by the B1341 and the B1342.

Linden Hall

Linden Hall is an exceptionally beautiful country house, (not surprisingly the great architect, John Dobson has a hand in it),set in 300 acres of outstanding parkland. In 1981 the Callen brothers turned it into a four star country house hotel with all the usual health spa and swimming pool accompaniments and, being sports fanatics, planned a golf course which opened in 1997. Jonathan Gaunt's magnificent 18 hole golf course Roller-coasters through woodland, rolling border countryside and alongside and across established burns and lakes, all amidst a stunning backdrop of the Cheviot Hills and the Northumberland coastline.

The course fully lives up to its magnificent setting; very much a Gaunt trademark creation with its wide fairways and tight approaches to sculptured greens and surrounds, every hole lives in the memory long after the round is over. Perhaps most memorable are the four par 3's, all over water. The 15th which is reminiscent of Augusta's "Redwood", is perhaps the most striking, but even this can not compare with the beautiful 161 yard 4th which requires a well judged shot across an original estate pond (circa 1812) to a contoured green guarded by a majestic spruce.

Water into play (for the wayward golfer) on ten of Linden Hall's holes, but this is by no means an American style course, a little hybrid maybe, but much more James Braid's Gleneagles, Perthshire than Karl Litten's Gleneagles, Florida. Indeed, the short 8th, (only 290 yards from the medal tees), with its little pot bunkers its premium on accuracy and its gorse covered hillside setting epitomises the best of traditional Scottish inland golf.

The abiding memory of Linden Hall is of a great sense of serenity engendered by the spaciousness of the Northumbrian setting and the grace of the hotel. Followers of the fairways en route to Scotland are well advised to stop off at Linden Hall. Your editors happen to

know that the Duke of York is something of a fan of this course, an opinion that they share.

Linden Hall Golf Club
Longhorsley, Morpeth, Northumberland NE65 8XF
www.lindenhall.co.uk

Professional	David Curry (01670) 500011
Green Fees	WD £25/round £38/day
	WE £28/round £40/day
Restrictions	Telephone for tee times

Directions
A697 off the A1 to Coldstream, 5 miles through Longhorsley on right hand side.

CUMBRIA

Alston Moor G.C.
(01434) 381675
The Hermitage, Alston
(9) 5380 yards/***/E

Appleby G.C.
(017683) 51432
Brackenber Moor, Appleby-in-
Westmorland
(18) 5895 yards/***/D

Barrow G.C.
(01229) 825444
Rakesmoor Lane, Hawcoat
(18) 6209 yards/***/C

Brampton (Talkin Tarn) G.C.
(0169) 772255
Talkin Tarn,Brampton
(18) 6420 yards/***/C/H

Brayton Park G.C.
(016973) 20840
Lakeside Inn, Brayton Park
(9) 2521 yards/***/E

Carlisle G.C.
(01228) 513303
Aglionby, Carlisle
(18) 6278 yards/**/B/H

Carus Green G.C.
(01539) 721097
Burnside Road, Kendal
(18) 5642 yards/**/E

Casterton G.C.
(015242) 71592
Sedbergh Road, Casterton
(9) 3015 yards/***/E

Cockermouth G.C.
(017687) 76223
Embleton, Cockermouth
(18) 5496 yards/**/D

Dalston Hall G.C.
(01228) 710165
Dalston Hall, Dalston
(9) 2667 yards/***/E

Dunnerholme G.C.
(01229) 462675
Duddon Road, Askam-in-Furness
(10) 6181 yards/***(not Sun)/D

Eden G.C.
(01228) 573003
Crosby-on-Eden, Carlisle
(18) 6975 yards/***/D

Furness G.C.
(01229) 471232
Walney Island, Barrow-in-Furness
(18) 6363 yards/***/D

Grange Fell G.C.
(015395) 32536
Fell Road, Grange-over-Sands
(9) 4826 yards/***/D

Grange-over-Sands G.C.
(015395) 33180
Meathop Road, Grange-over-Sands
(18) 5938 yards/***/C/H

Kendal G.C.
(01539) 724079
The Heights, Kendal
(18) 5483 yards/***/C/H

Keswick G.C.
(017687) 79324
Threlkeld Hall, Keswick
(18) 6175 yards/***/C

Kirkby Lonsdale G.C.
(015242) 76365
Scaleber Lane, Barbon
(18) 6283 yards/***(Sun am)/D

Maryport G.C.
(01900) 812605
Bank End, Maryport
(18) 6272 yards/***/C

Penrith G.C.
(01768) 891919
Salkeld Road, Penrith
(18) 6026 yards/***/C/H

Seascale G.C.
(019467) 28202
The Banks, Seascale
(18) 6416 yards/***/C

Sedbergh G.C.
(015396) 21551
Catholes-Abbot Holme, Sedbergh
(9) 5504 yards/***/D

Silecroft G.C.
(01229) 774250
Silecroft, Millom
(9) 5712 yards/**/D

Silloth-on-Solway G.C.
(016973) 31304
Silloth-on-Solway
(18) 6614 yards/***/B-A/H

Silverdale G.C.
(01524) 701307
Red Bridge Lane, Silverdale
(12) 5417 yards/***/D

St Bees School G.C.
(01946) 824300
Rhoda Grove, Rheda, Frizington
(9) 5082 yards/***/E

Stonyholme Municipal G.C.
(01228) 34856
St Aidans Road, Carlisle
(18) 5783 yards/***/F

Ulverston G.C.
(01229) 582824
Bardsea Park, Ulverston
(18) 6142 yards/***/D-C/H

Windermere G.C.
(015394) 43123
Cleabarrow, Windermere
(18) 5006 yards/***/B/H

Workington G.C.
(01900) 603460
Branthwaite Road, Workington
(18) 6200 yards/***/C/M/H

CO DURHAM

Aycliffe G.C.
(01325) 312994
Aycliffe Lane, Newton Aycliffe
(18) 5430 yards/***/F

Barnard Castle G.C.
(01833) 638355
Harmire Road, Barnard Castle
(18) 5838 yards/***/D

Beamish Park G.C.
(0191) 370 1382
Beamish, Stanley
(18) 6205 yards/***(not Sun)/C/H

Billingham G.C.
(01642) 533816
Sandy Lane, Billingham
(18) 6460 yards/***/B/H

Bishop Auckland G.C.
(01388) 602198
Durham Road, Bishop Auckland
(18) 6420 yards/***/B

Blackwell Grange G.C.
(01325) 464458
Briar Close, Blackwell,
(18) 5587 yards/***(Wed)/C

Brancepeth Castle G.C.
(0191) 378 0075
Brancepeth, Durham
(18) 6300 yards/**/B/H

Castle Eden & Peterlee G.C.
(01429) 836220
Castle Eden, Hartlepool
(18) 6293 yards/***/C

Chester-le-Street G.C.
(0191) 388 3218
Lumley Park, Chester-le-Street
(18) 6054 yards/**/B/H/L

Consett and District G.C.
(01207) 502186
Elmfield Road, Consett
(18) 6001 yards/**/C/H

Crook G.C.
(01388) 762429
Low Jobs Hill, Crook
(18) 6016 yards/***/D

Darlington G.C.
(01325) 355324
Haughton Grange, Darlington
(18) 6032 yards/**/B/M

Dinsdale Spa G.C.
(01325) 332297
Middleton St George, Darlington
(18) 6078 yards/**/D

Durham City G.C.
(0191) 378 0069
Littleburn Farm, Langley Moor
(18) 6326 yards/***/C

Eaglescliffe G.C.
(01642) 780098
Yarm Road, Eaglescliffe
(18) 6275 yards/***/B

Hall Garth Hotel
(01325) 300400
Coatham, Mundeville, Darlington
(9) 6621 yards.***/F

Hartlepool G.& C.C.
(01429) 274398
Hart Warren, Hartlepool
(18) 6255 yards/**/C/H

Hobson Municipal G.C.
(01207) 271605
Hobson, nr Burnopfield,
(18) 6582 yards/***/E

Houghton-le-Spring G.C.
(0191) 584 1198
Copt Hill, Houghton-le-Spring
(18) 6450 yards/*/D/M

Knotty Hill G.C.
(01740) 620320
Sedgefield, Stockton-on-Tees
(18) 6668 yards/***/D

Mount Oswald G.C.
(0191) 386 7527
South Road, Durham
(18) 6101 yards/***/D

Norton G.C.
(01642) 676385
Junction Road, Norton
(18) 5870 yards/**/E

Oakleaf G.C.
(01325) 310820
School Aycliffe Lane, Newton Aycliffe
(18) 5430 yards/***/F

Ramside Hall
(0191) 386 9514
Ramside Hall Hotel, Carville
Princes (9) 3235/**/H/B
Cathedral (9) 2874/**/H/B
Bishops (9) 3285/**/H/B

Roseberry Grange G.C.
(0191) 370 0670
Grange Villa, Chester-le-Street
(18) 5628 yards***/E

Ryhope G.C.
(0191) 5217333
Leechmere Way, Ryhope
(9) 6000 yards/***/E

Seaham G.C.
(0191) 581 2354
Dawdon, Seaham
(18) 5972 yards/***/D

Seaton Carew G.C.
(01429) 261040
Tees Road, Hartlepool
(18) 6855 yards/***/B-A

South Moor G.C.
(01207) 232848
The Middles, Craghead, Stanley
(18) 6445 yards/**/D/H

Stressholme G.C.
(01325) 461002
Snipe Lane, Darlington
(18) 6511 yards/***/F

Woodham G. & C.C.
(01325) 320574
Burnhill Way, Newton Aycliffe
(18) 6770 yards/***/F

TYNE AND WEAR

Backworth G.C.
(0191) 268 1048
The Hall, Backworth
(9) 5930 yards/**/F

Birtley G.C.
(0191) 410 2207
Portobello Road, Birtley
(9) 5660 yards/**/D

Boldon G.C.
(0191) 536 4182
Dipe Lane, East Boldon
(18) 6348 yards/**/F

Elemore G.C.
0191 5536720
Elemore Lane, Hetton-le-Hole
(18) 5947 yards/***/F

City of Newcastle G.C.
(0191) 285 1775
Three Mile Bridge, Gosforth
(18) 6508 yards/***/C

Garesfield G.C.
(01207) 561309
Chopwell, Garesfield
(18) 6603 yards/**/C

George Washington G.C.
(0191) 417 2626
Nr Washington Moat House Hotel
(18) 6604 yards/***/D

Gosforth G.C.
(0191) 285 3495
Broadway East, Gosforth
(18) 6043 yards/**/C/H

Heworth G.C.
(0191) 469 9832
Gingling Gate, Heworth
(18) 6462 yards/**/D

Newcastle United G.C.
(0191) 286 4693
Ponteland Road, Cowgate
(18) 6498 yards/**/D/M

Northumberland G.C.
(0191) 236 2009
High Gosforth Park, Newcastle upon Tyne
(18) 6640 yards/**/A/L

Parklands G.C.
(0191) 2364480
High Gosforth Park, Newcastle upon Tyne
(18) 6060 yards/***/D

Ravensworth G.C.
(0191) 487 2843
Moss Heaps, Wrekenton
(18) 5872 yards/***/C/H

Ryton G.C.
(0191) 413 3253
Stanners Drive, Ryton
(18) 6034 yards/**/D

South Shields G.C.
(0191) 456 0475
Cleadon Hills, South Shields
(18) 6264 yards/***/B/L

Tynemouth G.C.
(0191) 257 4578
Spital Dene, Tynemouth
(18) 6403 yards/**/C/M

Tyneside G.C.
(0191) 413 2742
Westfield Lane, Ryton
(18) 6055 yards/**/C/H

Wallsend G.C.
(0191) 262 1973
Bigges Main, Wallsend
(18) 6608 yards/***/D

Washington Moat House G.C.
(0191) 417 8346
Stone Cellar Road, Usworth
(18) 6604 yards/***/C

Wearside G.C.
(0191) 534 2518
Coxgreen, Sunderland
(18) 6373 yards/***/B/M/H

Westerhope G.C.
(0191) 286 9125
Whorlton Grange, Westerhope
(18) 6407 yards/**/D

Whickham G.C.
(0191) 488 7309
Hollinside Park, Whickham
(18) 6129 yards/***/C

Whitburn G.C.
(0191) 529 2144
Lizard Lane, South Shields
(18) 5773 yards/***(Tues)/D

Whitley Bay G.C.
(0191) 252 0180
Claremont Road, Whitley Bay
(18) 6617 yards/**/C

NORTHUMBERLAND

Allendale G.C.
(01434) 683926
High Studdon, Allendale
(9) 5044 yards/***/E

Alnmouth G.C.
(01665) 830231
Foxton Hall, Alnmouth
(18) 6414 yards/**/B/H

Alnmouth Village G.C.
(01665) 830370
Marine Road, Alnmouth
(9) 6078 yards/***/D/H

Alnwick G.C.
(01665) 602632
Swansfield Park, Alnwick
(18) 6250 yards/***/D

Arcot Hall G.C.
(0191) 236 2794
Dudley, Cramlington
(18) 6389 yards/**/B/H

Bamburgh Castle G.C.
(01668) 214378
The Wynding, Bamburgh
(18) 5465 yards/**/B/H

Bedlingtonshire G.C.
(01670) 822457
Acorn Bank, Bedlington
(18) 6224 yards/***/D

Belford G.C.
(01668) 212433
South Road, Belford
(9) 6304 yards/***/E

Bellingham G.C.
(01434) 220530
Boggle Hole, Bellingham
(9) 5245 yards/***/D

Berwick-upon-Tweed G.C.
(01289) 387256
Goswick, Berwick-upon-Tweed
(18) 6425 yards/**/B

Blyth G.C.
(01670) 540110
New Delaval, Blyth
(18) 6300 yards/**/D

Burgham Park G.& C.C.
(01670) 787898
Felton, Morpeth
(18) 7139 yards/***/D

Close House G.C.
(01661) 852953
Heddon-on-the-Wall
(18) 5587 yards/**/D/G

Dunstanburgh Castle G.C.
(01665) 576562
Embleton, Alnwick
(18) 6038 yards/***/D

Haltwhistle G.C.
(016977) 47367
Greenhead, Haltwhistle
(18) 5968 yards/***/E

Hexham G.C.
(01434) 603072
Spital Park, Hexham
(18) 6272 yards/***/B/H

Magdalene Fields G.C.
(01289) 306384
Berwick-upon-Tweed
(18) 6551 yards/***/D

Matfen Hall G.C.
(01661) 886500
Matfen, Hexham
(18) 6732 yards/***/C

Morpeth G.C.
(01670) 515675
The Common, Morpeth
(18) 6215 yards/***/B/H

Newbiggin-by-the-Sea G.C.
(01670) 817344
Newbiggin-by-the-Sea
(18) 6452 yards/***/B

Ponteland G.C.
(01661) 822689
Bell Villas, Ponteland
(18) 6512 yards/**/B

Prudhoe G.C.
(01661) 832466
Eastwood Park, Prudhoe
(18) 5812 yards/**/C

Rothbury G.C.
(01669) 620718
Old Racecourse, Rothbury
(9) 5146 yards/***(not Sat)/D

Seahouses G.C.
(01665) 720794
Beadnell Road, Seahouses
(18) 5462 yards/***/D

De Vere Slaley Hall G. & C.C.
(01434) 673350
Slaley, Hexham
(18) 7073 yards/***/A/H

Stocksfield G.C.
(01661) 843041
New Ridley, Stocksfield
(18) 5594 yards/***/D/H

Swarland Hall G.C.
(01670) 787010
Coast View, Swarland
(9) 6517 yards/**/D

Tynedale G.C.
(01434) 608154
Tyne Green, Hexham
(9) 5706 yards/***/D

Warkworth G.C.
(01665) 711596
The Links ,Warkworth
(9) 5856 yards/***/D

Wooler G.C.
(01668) 281137
Dodd Law, Doddington, Wooler
(9) 6353 yards/***/D

Carmel
Head

Bull Bay GC

Amlwch

Holyhead

Holyhead GC

Holy Island

Anglesey
ISLE OF ANGLESEY

Llangefni

Menai
Bridge

Bangor

Caernarfon

Llanberis

Bethesda

*Caernarfon
Bay*

Nefyn & District GC

Lleyn Peninsula

Porthmadog

Criccieth

Pwllheli

Pwllheli GC **Royal St David's GC**

Abersoch

Abersoch

Bardsey
Island

North Wales GC **Llandudno GC** Prestatyn **Prestatyn GC**

Llandudno Colwyn Rhyl

Caernarfonshire GC Conwy Bay Abergele **Rhuddlan GC**

Llanfairfechan **Abergele & Pensarn GC** **Northop Park CGC**

Denbigh Flint **Mold GC**

FLINTSHIRE

Queensferry

CONWY

Llanrwst

Betws-
y-coed

Mold

Ruthin

DENBIGHSHIRE

Blaenau
Ffestiniog **Ffestiniog GC**
Ffestiniog

Ruabon **Wrexham GC**

Wrexham

Vale of Llangollen GC **Chirk G & CC**

Llangollen

Bala

GWYNEDD

Barmouth Dolgellau Llanfyllin

Mallwyd

Aberdovy GC Machynlleth Welshpool **Welshpool GC**

Tywyn

Aberdyfi Newtown **St Giles GC**

Borth & Ynyslas GC Montgomery

Aberystwyth Llanidloes **St Idloes GC**

Aberystwyth GC Llangurig

Penrbos GC Knighton

Rhayader Presteigne

*Cardigan
Bay*

Aberaeron Tregaron Llandrindod Wells **Llandrindod-Wells GC**

New Quay

CEREDIGION **Bullth Wells GC**

Lampeter Builth Wells

Strumble
Head Cardigan Hay-on-Wye

Newport GC Newcastle
Emlyn Llandovery **POWYS**

Fishguard

St Davids City GC **Cradoc GC** Brecon

Ramsey
Island St David's **PEMBROKESHIRE** **CARMARTHENSHIRE**

Carmarthen Llandeilo **Brecon
Beacons**

*St Brides
Bay* Narberth **Carmarthen GC** Crickhowell Abergavenny **Rolls of Monmouth GC**

Haverfordwest St Clears **Glynhir GC** Ebbw Brynmawr Monmouth

Skomer
Island Ammanford Vale Blaenavon **Monmouthshire GC**

Milford Haven GC Kidwelly Merthyr MONMOUTHSHIRE

Neyland Tydfil Rhymney

Milford Haven **Ashburnham GC** Llanelli Aberdare Pontypool Chepstow

Skokholm
Island Pembroke
Dock Tenby Aberdare GC Cwmbran **St Pierre G & CC**

Rembroke **Tenby GC** Neath Glyncorrwg **CAERPHILLY** Risca **Celtic Manor GC**

Pembroke Caldey
Island Swansea Maesteg RHONDDA Caerphilly Newport Caldicot

Clyne GC Mumbles CYNON **Mountain Lakes GC** **Newport GC**

St Govan's
Head **Fairwood Park GC** Talbot TAFF **St Mellons GC**

Pennard GC Pontypridd Bargoed **St Pierre G & CC**

Port Mumbles BRIDGEND Pont **St Mary's GC** **Cardiff GC**

Einon Head **Pyle & Kenfig GC** Talbot Wenvoe Castle GC

Royal Porthcawl GC Bridgend CARDIFF **CARDIFF**

Porthcawl VALE OF

Southerndown GC Cowbridge GLAMORGAN **Glamorganshire GC**

Barry

South Wales

Balls in South Wales are often large, oval-shaped and made of leather. However, those belonging to the much smaller dimpled breed—usually white, though these days sometimes shocking pink and yellow—are to be found in some particularly pleasant spots, and in a great variety of places between the Wye Valley and the Gower Peninsula. In addition to the Glamorgans and the Monmouth area our region takes in Mid Wales as well, that is the larger, less inhabited counties—'the real Wales', they'll tell you there.

Monmouth and Surrounds

For many travellers their first sample of golf in South Wales will be the impressive **St Pierre** Golf and Country Club at Chepstow (see feature page). Unfortunately, far too great a number make

St Pierre their one and only stop. Further up the Wye Valley both **Monmouthshire** and the **Rolls of Monmouth** offer an outstanding game in delightful surroundings. Bounded by the River Usk, the Monmouthshire Golf Club lies half a mile west of Abergavenny at Llanfoist. In 1992 the club celebrated its centenary—quite an achievement when one considers its unusual beginnings. Laid out on ground formerly used for polo and later for horseracing, golf was started here in 1892, as the club handbook tells you, 'the result of a bet as to whether such a venture could be run successfully at Abergavenny!' Clearly the golfers backed a winner. Golf at 'The Rolls' is explored on a later page.

The St Pierre Hotel (01291) 625261 is a 14th century mansion providing a whole range of facilities. However, those not wishing to wake up next to the famous 18th green, note the Castle View Hotel (01291) 620349, also in Chepstow and very comfortable. The Walnut Tree (01873) 852797 in Abergavenny is without doubt one of the finest restaurants in Wales and Llanwenarth House (01873) 830289 at Govilon to the west of Abergavenny makes an excellent base for golfing visitors. Monmouth provides the Riverside Hotel (01600) 715577 while the nearby Crown at Whitebrook (01600) 860254 offers award-winning cuisine and good accommodation.

Heading west of Chepstow, a very established course and one well worth a visit is **Newport** at Rogerstone. It is a very fine downland course and decidedly handy when travelling along the M4 (junction 27)—en route to Porthcawl perhaps? Undoubtedly the place to stay in Newport is the **Celtic Manor** Hotel Golf and Country Club Hotel (01633) 413000 which just happens to have two Robert Trent Jones designed golf courses and a Robert Trent Jones Jnr course right on its doorstep (see feature page).

The Glamorgans

Golfers in Cardiff (or Caerdydd) are quite fortunate having a number of well established courses close at hand. Not surprisingly they tend to be busier than the majority of Welsh courses and therefore before setting off it is especially important to contact the particular club in question. The **Cardiff** Golf Club is a superior parkland course situated some three miles from the city centre at Cyncoed. **St Mellons**, north east of the city, within easy access of the M4, is another popular parkland course—quite challenging, with several interesting holes. To the south west of Cardiff, **Wenvoe Castle**, one of the more hilly courses in South Glamorgan can be recommended as can the **Glamorganshire** course, located to the west of Penarth.

*LANGLAND BAY Photograph courtesy of: **Wales Tourist Board***

Perhaps the best hotels in Cardiff are the Marriott Hotel (029) 2039 9944 in the centre of the town, the Thistle Hotel (029) 2038 3471, the Angel Hotel (029) 2023 2633 and the Copthorne (029) 2059 9100. Among the better restaurants, are the ironically named Armless Dragon (029) 2038 2357 and the Blas-Ar Cymru (029) 2038 2132 which offers a delightful taste of Wales. Another good eating place is found in Penarth, Rabiotti's (029) 2070 2424, where excellent seafood accompanies fine views over the Bristol Channel. Also in Penarth, the Captain's Wife is recommended (a pub it should be added!). More pubs, and to the north and south of Cardiff are the Maenllwyd at Rudry and the beautifully thatched Bush at St Hilary. Still further south is the popular Blue Anchor at East Aberthan to the west of Penarth (superb lunches).

A short distance to the north of Cardiff, the town of Caerphilly is more famous for its castle and its cheese than for its golf; however, there is some good golf in the area, **Mountain Lakes** Golf and Country Club being particularly noteworthy and well worth a visit. Before heading off to the glorious coastal strip around Porthcawl a course certainly deserving a mention is **Aberdare**—an excellent woodland course, undoubtedly the finest in 'the Valleys. In Coychurch, the

Coed-y-Mwstwr Hotel (01656) 860621 is an extremely attractive hotel to consider.

One would have to travel many a mile to find a course the equal of **Royal Porthcawl** (also featured later this chapter) but its near neighbour to the east, **Southerndown** gets closer than most. Situated on high ground it is an outstandingly scenic downland type course measuring a little over 6600 yards (par 70). Even closer to Porthcawl is the fine links of **Pyle and Kenfig**, on more than one occasion the venue for the Welsh Amateur Stroke Play Championship. It is a very tough challenge, being open to the elements, and boasts some very large sand dunes. The **St Mary's** Golf Club offers 27 holes and numerous other attractions besides. Its close proximity to the M4 makes it very convenient. The hotel here (01656) 861100, converted from a 17th century farmhouse, is also one to note.

Additional ideas for a well earned night's rest in the area include in Porthcawl, the Atlantic Hotel (01656) 785011 and The Fairways (01656) 782085. In Nottage, the Rose and Crown (01656) 784850 is an excellent pub serving good food and with some accommodation, while another notable drinking establishment is the Prince of Wales in Kenfig. As a base for covering the whole region in style, the historic Great House at Laleston (01656) 657644 and the elegant Egerton Grey (01446) 711666 at Borth Kerry outside Barry are hard to beat.

Beyond Pyle and Kenfig the M4 heads into West Glamorgan passing through Port Talbot towards Swansea, and beyond Swansea is the beautifully secluded Gower Peninsula. If you are fortunate enough to be visiting these parts, three courses that can be strongly recommended are **Pennard** (featured ahead) **Fairwood Park**, and **Clyne**. Fairwood Park, situated close to Swansea Airport, is a second course over which racehorses once galloped. It is a much improved course and has several long par fours. Clyne offers a moorland challenge while from Pennard's clifftop course there are some splendid views out across the Bristol Channel.

A hotel for the night? Near to Swansea, the Langland Court Hotel (01792) 361545 is a comfortable clifftop inn of great character.and in nearby Mumbles, the Norton House Hotel (01792) 404891 is most relaxing. On the Gower, Fairyhill Country House (01792) 390139 is recommended, especially for its cuisine. As for a drink, there are numerous pubs. Here are two suggestions: the Joiners Arms in Bishopston and the Welcome to Town in Lanrhidian.

Carmarthen and Pembroke

The two championship courses in this region lie on the southern coast, some 30 miles apart. Both **Ashburnham** and **Tenby** (see ahead) were founded before the turn of the century and each has staged more than one Welsh Amateur Championship, Ashburnham in fact being a regular venue.

Located one mile west of Burry Port, Ashburnham's links is fairly close to industrial South Wales which, I suppose, extends as far as Llanelli, or at least to where the M4 from London fizzles out. The course measures 7000 yards from the championship tees and 6686 yards from the medal tees—certainly not a course for the inexperienced! Connoisseurs of the game, however, should find it an excellent challenge.

In Llanelli, the Diplomat (01554) 756156 is convenient for Ashburnham, but for a really relaxing 19th hole, golfers may prefer to stay in Tenby with its stylish Georgian harbour. Here Waterwynch House (01834) 842464 is recommended. The Tall Ships (01834) 842055 also enjoys a suitably convenient location. A local favourite is the St Brides Hotel (01834) 812304 which enjoys superb views of Carmarthen Bay and its restaurant makes the best use of locally captured lobster. Equally impressive in this respect is the excellent Penally Abbey (01834) 843033 in the quiet village of Penally and ideally situated for Tenby Golf Club. To the north, nestling in the foothills of the Black Mountains, is the town of Llandeilo and a stay at the delightful 18th century coaching inn of the Cawdor Arms Hotel (01558) 823500 is recommended. Another good hotel which also offers excellent seafood can be found in Broadhaven—the Druidstone Hotel (01437) 781221.

Moving westwards along the coast, the next 18 holes are to be found at **Milford Haven**, a medium-length parkland course to the west of the town. In days of old the former whaling town may well have been a haven but the present day 'landscape in oils' isn't everyone's cup of tea. More attractive is **St Davids** with its beautiful cathedral making it the smallest city in Britain. Unfortunately for golfing visitors there is only a modest 9 hole golf course 20 miles away at **Newport** there is a very fine golf course, and one which offers some tremendous sea views.

St Davids has many pleasing hotels, and Warpool Court (01437) 720300 is particularly good. St Non's Hotel (01437) 320239 is a good family hotel and offers special rates on St David's 9 hole course. Should one tire for some reason of the coast then the Wolfscastle Country Hotel (01437) 741225, in Wolfscastle is very welcoming (even though it may not sound like it). The 17th century Hotel Merineth (01437) 763353 in Haverford West is another comfortable hotel in this area. The Mariners (01437) 764523 is also well worth a visit. Perhaps the most appropriate place for golfers who have played somewhat waywardly is the village of Welsh Hook—Stone Hall (01348) 840212 is the establishment recommended—an excellent restaurant with rooms.. Good places for a drink include the contradictory Sailors Safety and the Ship Aground, both at Dinas and the Golden Lion in Newport. If you are still hungry then the best tip is to visit Cardigan and the Pantry (01239) 820420. Failing the Pantry, try the kitchen—the Castle Kitchen (01239) 615055, an informal but well run restaurant nearby.

GLIFFAES Photograph courtesy of: **Gliffaes**

Inland, there is precious little golf to speak of in southern Wales, though there is a fairly testing hilltop course at **Carmarthen**—one which is decidedly better in summer than in winter and an attractive parkland course, **Glynhir**, near the foothills of the Black Mountain Range. The latter is a particularly friendly club situated close to the Glynhir Mansion where the first news of Wellington's victory at Waterloo is reputed to have been received by carrier pigeon. (Must have been a pretty sharp pigeon!) One doesn't have to look far for a night's stay either: in Llandybie, the Mill at Glynhir (01269) 850672 overlooks the 14th green.

Mid Wales

For every person in New Zealand there are twenty sheep. Regrettably, I don't have the figures for mid Wales but I suspect they're fairly similar. The bad news is that the lack of human beings is unfortunately reflected by a low number of top class golf courses (unlike in New Zealand it should be said). However, the good news is that even during the summer months most of the courses remain relatively uncrowded, visitors are made very welcome and the green fees tend to be a lot cheaper than in most parts of Britain.

Ceredigion

The University town of **Aberystwyth** has an 18 hole course that looks out over Cardigan Bay. Try the Belle Vue Royal Hotel (01970) 617558 for a 19th hole here—a lovely hotel with seafront views over Cardigan Bay. A more impressive golf course though is **Borth and Ynyslas**, one of the oldest clubs in Wales. Borth is a superbly maintained seaside links. The B4353 road runs right alongside much of the course and is often peppered by golf balls. Taking out insurance before playing Borth is recommended.

Whether you've peppered the road or the flagsticks one of the many guesthouses in and around Borth may be the most convenient place for a good night's sleep. However, further north at Eglwysfach, 16th century Ynyshir Hall (01654) 781209 is well worth inspecting (note the nearby bird sanctuary) and in Machynlleth, the Wynnstay Arms (01654) 702941 is a cosy former coaching inn. Back in Borth, the Victoria Inn is a good pub and finally, a great example of friendly local hospitality in an elegant setting is the Conrah Country Hotel (01970) 61794 in Chancery near Aberystwyth, handy for the scenic **Penrhos** Golf and Country Club.

Powys

The golf courses in Powys are few and far between, but those there are tend to be set amidst some splendid scenery. There is an 18 hole course at **Welshpool** up in the hills near the English border (do try to visit Powys Castle and its superb gardens if you're in the area) and two interesting 9 hole courses at Newton (**St Giles**) and at Llanidloes (**St Idloes**) in the quiet of the Cambrian Mountains (note the very fine Glansevern Arms (01686) 440240 in Pant Mawr). Two of the region's best courses are situated right in the centre of Wales, **Llandrindod Wells** and **Builth Wells**. Both are attractive courses, but Llandrindod in particular offers spectacular views. For Builth Wells there can be no finer base to play from than the Lake Country House (015912) 202 while in the town itself is the Lion Hotel (01982) 553670, an historic inn and very pleasant too. In Llandrindod the large Metropole Hotel (01597) 823700 is very convenient, the Harp at Old Radnor is an ideal place for a drink and a snack after a round at Llandrindod, but for a real overnight treat a visit to either Llangoed Hall (01874) 754525 or to a Welsh Rarebits property (01686) 668030 is recommended.

One final course to mention in Powys, and one good enough to have held the Welsh Amateur Stroke Play Championship is **Cradoc** near Brecon. A lovely course this, and again, very scenic being within the Brecon Beacons National Park. Here's another tip: a drink at the White Swan in Llanfrynach followed by dinner and a relaxing stay at Gliffaes (01874) 730371 in Crickhowell, an ideal base from which to play many courses.

North Wales

One's first thoughts of North Wales are often of lakes, great castles and even greater mountains, or as a fine fellow by the name of Hywel ap Owain, 12th century Prince of Gwynedd, put it (I offer it in translation)

I love its sea-marsh and its mountains,
And its fortress by its forest and its bright lands,
And its meadows and its water and its valleys,
And its white seagulls and its lovely women.

A man who had obviously seen much of the world! Of course in the 12th century the Welsh didn't play golf, or at least if they did they kept it pretty quiet and in any case you can be pretty confident that Hywel ap Owain would have told us about it. Well, what about the golf in North Wales then? In a word, marvellous. Inland it tends to get hilly to put it mildly, and should you wish to venture up into 'them thar hills' as well as the climbing gear, don't forget to bring the waterproofs! But there again, leave room for the camera (hope you've got a large golf bag).

In the main though, it is to the coast that the travelling golfer will wish to head. Between Flint in the east and Aberdovey in southern Gwynedd are the impressive championship links of Prestatyn, Maesdu, North Wales, Conwy, Royal St Davids and of course Aberdovey itself. In addition, there are several with spectacular locations, Nefyn on the Lleyn Peninsula being an outstanding example.

Denbigh and Flint

Before journeying around the coast though, a brief mention for some of the inland courses in North Wales, with a few thoughts as to where one might stop off in order to eat, drink, be merry or simply rest the weary golf clubs. Away from the sea and sand probably the best two challenges are to be found at **Wrexham** and Llangollen. Wrexham, located just off the A53, is fairly close to the English border and indeed the views here are across the Cheshire plain. Two good holes to look out for are the 4th and 14th. Llangollen's splendid course, the **Vale of Llangollen**, is set out alongside the banks of the River Dee. There are some truly excellent holes, notably the 9th. Appropriately named the River Hole it is a really tough par four of 425 yards. The golfer who likes a spot of fishing (or perhaps even the golfing fisherman) would be in his element here and on a good day should see a few of the famous Dee salmon being landed—probably easier than netting a birdie. One name to watch in the future is the spectacular **Chirk Golf and Country Club**, south of Wrexham on the A483. Over 7000 yards of manicured fairways are complemented by a much less taxing par three course and driving range. North west of Wrexham on the road to Flint can be found the St Davids Park Hotel (01352) 840800 and **Northop Country Park** Golf Club complex. Excellent accommodation and a course now attracting PGA events make this well worth a visit.

As host to the famous International Eisteddfod Festival Llangollen has long been a popular tourist centre and there are a number of fine hotels in the town including the Hand (01978) 860303 and the Royal (01978) 860202. Also in Llangollen, Gales Wine Bar (01978) 860098 is well recommended and it also has rooms. The Bryn Howell (01978) 860331 is also good and the Cross Lanes (01978) 780555 is handy for visitors to Wrexham. Finally, visitors to Chirk should seek out the delightfully isolated Starlings Castle (01691) 718464—a charming restaurant with rooms.

In the unfortunately named town of **Mold** there is a pleasant parkland challenge, and the very worthy Beaufort Park Hotel. While still further north and getting nearer the coast is the **Rhuddlan** Golf Club. They say you should never rush a round at Rhuddlan. If you are heading for the tougher links courses on the coast then this is the ideal place to groove the swing. The course is laid out close to one of North Wales' famous massive fortresses in the grounds of Bodrhydden estate and overlooks the Vale of Clwyd. Just a couple of thoughts for golfers wishing to wet the whistle: the Dinorben Arms at Bodfari and the Salisbury Arms at Tremeirchion—two fine hostelries.

Exploring the countryside is a delight and there is a plentiful supply of country houses and inns to entice the traveller. A charming place to rest is the 16th century Hand Hotel (01691) 760666 at Llanarmon Dyffryn Ceiriog—all wooden beams and roaring fires—wonderful! Another thought is Soughton Hall (01352) 840811, an early 18th century mansion with good accommodation. Time to tear oneself away. The coast beckons and it's time to put that grooved swing into practice.

Conwy

Prestatyn warrants first attention. Close to Pontin's holiday camp it is a genuine links and when the prevailing westerly blows, can play very long (the championship tees stretch the course to 6714 yards). If a day at Pontin's isn't your cup of tea then the Traeth Ganol (01745) 853594 is worth a try. Thirsty golfers might also find the time to drive over the hill to the village of Gwaenysgor and the Eagle and Child pub—good food and good ale.

The A55 is the coastal road that should be followed to find our next port of call, the **Abergele and Pensarn** Golf Club, just west of Abergele. This course is a fairly new parkland layout lying beneath the walls of fairytale Gwrych Castle. Games are often won or lost on the last three holes at Abergele. The round is supposed to finish five, three, five—but not many scorecards seem to!

A trio of championship courses are to be found a little further along the coast and just over the county border in Gwynedd. Golfers in Llandudno are more fortunate than most, having two fine courses to choose from: **North Wales** and **Llandudno** (**Maesdu**). Both are of a high standard and each offers superb views across the Conwy estuary towards Anglesey.

The **Caernarvonshire** Golf Club lies the other side of the estuary at Conwy—yet another spectacular siting between the sea and mountains and another course where the wind can blow fiercely. A regular venue for the important Welsh Championships, it is a long course and is generally considered second only to Royal St Davids in terms of golfing challenges in North Wales. It possesses everything that makes links golf so difficult—gorse, rushes, sandhills and more gorse, rushes and sandhills—quite frightening!

The Llandudno-Conwy-Colwyn Bay area is riddled with places of interest and places to stay. Indeed it offers a veritable feast for the golfing gourmet. Here are a few thoughts. In Llandudno, famed for its Great Orme, are several excellent hotels, the Esplanade (01492) 860300 and the St Tudno Hotel (01492) 874411 (note the excellent restaurant here) are two first class examples, while slightly inland at Deganwy is the renowned 17th century Bodysgallen Hall (01492) 584466. Set amid quite idyllic grounds, the hotel offers great style as well as sumptuous cuisine. Less expensive accommodation of good quality can be found at the Bryn Cregin Garden Hotel (01492) 585266 also in Deganwy and highly recommended. Returning to Llandudno, a pair of pubs whose names you should have little difficulty in remembering are the Kings Head and the Queens Head, the latter a little to the south of the town at Llandudno Junction. Nearby in Conwy a liquid round can be enjoyed at the Liverpool Arms on the quay. There are many attractions in the area—the great castle and the town walls, Bodnant Gardens in the Conwy Valley and even the smallest house in Great Britain. Finally in Colwyn Bay among the many hotels two that merit attention are the Norfolk House (01492) 531757 and the Colwyn Bay Hotel (01492) 516555, a distinctive hotel high on a clifftop. Café Niçoise (01492) 531555 is a really good restaurant to try.

Gwynedd

Heading for the golf courses of the Lleyn Peninsular, many may wish to break their journey at Caernarfon. The castle is splendid and well worth inspecting. I suppose every golfer has at one time or another drawn up a mental listing of favourite golf courses. Anyone who has made the trip to **Nefyn** is almost certain to have the course high on such a list. A delight to play on (see feature page) Nefyn was a regular haunt of Lloyd-George, as was neighbouring Pwllheli, which was opened by him in 1909 when he was the Chancellor of the Exchequer. Not far from Pwllheli there is an interesting golf course at **Aberscoch**.

Handy hotels for Nefyn include the Linksway (01758) 720258, Woodland Hall (01758) 720425 and the Caeau Capel Hotel (01758) 720240. The Nanhoran Arms (01758) 720203 offers special golf packages and is worthy of consideration. There are numerous pubs, including the Ty Coch Inn (almost on the course itself), and the Sportsman. Close by, situated right on the cliffs is the provocatively named Dive Inn (01758) 877246 at Tudweiliog, which has an excellent restaurant. Another pleasant establishment is the lively Bryncyann Inn (01758) 720879 in Morfa Nefyn. In Pwllheli the Tower Hotel (01758) 612822, the Bel Air Restaurant (01758) 613198 and Porth Tocyn Hotel (01758) 7113303 are also recommended. A final thought is Plas Bodegroes (01758) 612363, a delightful restaurant with rooms.

Golfwise there is not a great deal more in the deeper realms of North Wales. **Ffestiniog**, famed for its mountain railway, has a short nine holes of the moorland variety but the scenery in these parts may prove a little too distracting. Ffestiniog nestles in the heart of Snowdonia and the encircling mountains are quite awe-inspiring.

Harlech and Aberdovey

A trip to the north west of Wales wouldn't be complete without a visit to Harlech, another great castle and certainly a great golf links, home of the **Royal St Davids** Golf Club (it too is explored on a later page). On the culinary side in Harlech there are two good restaurants, the Castle Cottage (01766) 780479 (some accommodation) and the Cemlyn (01766) 780425, while not far off in Talsarnau is the excellent Maes-y-Neuadd (01766) 780200 hotel and restaurant—extremely convenient for Royal St Davids, as is St Davids Hotel (01766) 780366. Finally in Harlech, Alexa House and Stable Cottages offer charming accommodation at a charming price. In Porthmadog is another good hotel, the Royal Sportsman (01766) 512015. Lastly, you cannot miss out on visiting Portmeirion, Clough Williams Ellis' attempt at creating the Italian Riviera on the coast of Wales. We recommend you stay at the Hotel Portmeirion (01766) 770228.

Heading further south and passing the splendid George III Hotel (01341) 422525 at Penmaenpool, **Aberdovey** is soon reached. The subject of favourite courses has been raised and Aberdovey was the choice of the celebrated golf writer Bernard Darwin, 'the course that my soul loves best of all the courses in the world.' It has an interesting layout, sandwiched between the sand dunes on the one side and a railway line on the other (the railway line in fact links Aberdovey to Harlech and is a pretty good service).

Golfers looking to play Aberdovey should consider the Corbett Arms (01654) 710264 and the Trefeddian Hotel (01654) 762213, which is exceptionally convenient for the course. Alternatives are the attractive Hotel Plas Penhelig (01654) 767676 which overlooks the Dovey estuary and the Penhelig Arms (01654) 767215, a delightful black and white inn with excellent food.

Isle of Anglesey

The Isle of Anglesey is linked by a road bridge to the mainland across the Menai Straits. There is a choice of six golf courses—perhaps the best two games to be found are at **Bull Bay**, near Amlwch, and at **Holyhead** (**Trearddur Bay**) on Holy Island. Both courses are very scenic and we have featured Holyhead separately. Bull Bay enjoys a fairly remote, and certainly spectacular setting on the island's northern coast. It is a hilly course with much gorse and several rocks to confront and when the wind blows it can be very tricky. The club handbook relates how in an exhibition match to mark the opening of the course, featuring John H Taylor and James Braid, the latter tangled with the gorse on the short third hole and finished up with an eight! There's hope for us all. Convenient resting places include the Bull Bay Hotel (01407) 830223 at Amlwch, the Lastra Farm Hotel (01407) 830906 (recommended by local golfers) and the impressive Trearddur Bay Hotel (01407) 860301 which lies adjacent to the Holyhead Golf Club. Ye Olde Bull's Head (01248) 810329 in Beaumaris is also recommended for its excellent restaurant and accommodation. In addition there are not surprisingly a vast number of reasonably priced guest houses on Anglesey—contact the Wales Tourist Board for details.

HARLECH ROYAL ST DAVIDS *Photograph courtesy of:* **Wales Tourist Board**

A thoroughly charming Victorian country house, Gliffaes boasts 33 acres of magnificent gardens and parkland with many rare trees and shrubs. Situated in the beautiful Usk Valley midway between the Brecon Beacons and Black Mountains yet only one mile off the main A40, it offers peace and tranquillity as well as being easily accessible.

Gliffaes' location makes it ideal for visiting golfers. The championship course of the Rolls of Monmouth is only 30 minutes away, while top courses such as Cradoc and Abergavenny lie within ten miles. St Pierre, Builth Wells and Llandrindod Wells are also reasonably close.

Other activities include fishing for wild brown trout and salmon on 2.5 private miles of the river Usk, tennis, putting, golf practice net, croquet and walking in the grounds. The Brecon Beacons and Black Mountains offer more challenging walking or, for those who prefer, there are nearby riding and pony trekking centres.

Built in 1885 as a private residence, Gliffaes faces due South and overlooks the Usk. Ideally adapted to provide spacious comfort in the country house tradition. There are 22 bedrooms, all individual in decor and furnishings and all with private bathrooms or showers.

The downstairs rooms include a large, panelled sitting room which leads into an elegant Regency style drawing room. From here, french windows lead to a large conservatory which opens onto the terrace. The dining room and comfortable bar also open onto the terrace, with glorious views of the surrounding hills and River Usk some 150 feet below.

A delicious breakfast is served from a buffet table and a wide variety of light lunches can be ordered in the bar. Dinner offers an outstanding choice of freshly cooked and beautifully presented dishes. Country house standards of the old order are maintained by the resident owners, the Brabner family, who have held sway here since 1948.

Gliffaes Country House Hotel
Crickhowell, Powys
Wales NP8 1RH
Tel: (01874) 730371 Fax: (01874) 730463
e mail: calls@gliffaeshotel.com
web site: www.gliffaeshotel.com

The Rolls of Monmouth

If this golf course didn't already have such a splendid name it would be necessary to invent one. 'Tranquillity Golf Club' might suffice. OK maybe that's a bit naff, but it wouldn't be in breach of the Trade Descriptions Act. The Rolls of Monmouth enjoys one of the most peaceful and secluded settings in Britain. The golf course is relatively young—it opened in 1982—but the accompanying countryside of gentle, circling hills and far off mountains cannot have altered greatly in hundreds of years.

The actual name is no mystery at all for the golf course lies within the grounds of the Rolls Estate, the former country home of Charles Stewart Rolls, who, together with Henry Royce, founded the famous Rolls Royce company. The imposing mansion that dominates the grounds and is visible from several parts of the course was largely built in the 18th century. Fortunately for we present day golfers the Rolls family were rather keen on landscaping and the grounds are blessed with a wonderful variety of trees and shrubs. Given such a setting and the fact that the Rolls course was laid out to championship specifications, incorporating several small lakes and streams, it isn't difficult to see why it has quickly established itself as one of the finest parkland tests in Britain.

The Rolls is very much a course of two halves, the two nines being laid out on opposite sides of the estate. The front nine opens fairly tamely (though prettily enough) with three gentle par fours all requiring slightly downhill approaches and the short 4th which has an attractive lake just behind the green and a semi-concealed bunker to the left. Then comes probably the most difficult series of holes in the round. The 5th has a deep ravine in front of the green and the only saving grace for the golfer is that it is a par five. The 6th is the stroke one hole and requires two very accurate shots across a severely contoured fairway and the 7th dramatically curls, tumbles and twists its way downhill for all of 500 yards until it meets a lake and a little

stream. As for the green it's still another thirty yards the other side of the stream. The 8th is an outstanding par three, and the 9th, a short par four played from a spectacular high tee.

Among the more memorable holes on the back nine are the 11th, a lovely sweeping downhill par four, the sharply dog-legging 15th at the far end of the course (some splendid mountain views here) and the two par threes, the 13th and the 18th. The former has been described as 'an absolute beauty' and the latter 'an absolute horror'. Water features on both holes, but while it merely helps to shape the 13th and make it a very picturesque one-shotter, it turns the 18th into a very intimidating closing hole. 'Tranquillity'? Tell that to the match waiting on the 18th tee with all bets in the balance!

The Rolls of Monmouth Golf Club, The Hendre, Monmouth NP25 5HG

Secretary	Mrs Sandra Orton (01600) 715353 Fax: (01600) 713115
Green Fees	WD £34, WE £38 Monday Special—coffee, 18 holes of golf and lunch, £28
Restrictions	Book to make a tee reservation

Directions
The club is four miles west of Monmouth off the B4233. Monmouth is linked to Chepstow by the A466 and to Ross-on-Wye and Hereford by the A40.

Royal St David's (Harlech)

With a St Andrews in Scotland and a St George's in England, it seems only right that there should be a St David's in Wales. Along with Royal Porthcawl in the South, the Royal St David's Golf Club at Harlech is one of the principality's two greatest Championship links.

The club was founded in 1894 by the Hon Harold Finch-Hatton together with Mr W H More who for twenty years acted as Hon Sec. The course itself was open for play at the end of 1894 and the opening competition was fittingly won by the greatest golfer of the day and the then reigning Amateur Champion, John Ball. St David's became Royal St David's early this century and in 1935 The Duke of Windsor (then Prince of Wales) became the club's captain.

Of its many attributes St David's is perhaps best known for its glorious setting. On the one side stretch the blue waters of Tremedog Bay, and on the other the imperious Snowdon and the other great mountains of Snowdonia National Park, while surveying all from its lofty perch is the almost forbidding presence of Harlech Castle. The massive fortress built by Edward I has known a particularly turbulent past. It played a prominent role in the War of the Roses when a great seige took place eventually ending in surrender. The seige is commemorated in the famous song 'Men of Harlech'.

The present 'Men of Harlech' are the **Secretary, Mr D L Morkill (01766) 780361** and the club's **Professional, John Barnett tel: (01766) 780857** or **fax: (01766) 781110.** The club's address is **Royal St David's Golf Club, Harlech, Gwynedd, LL46 2UB.**

St David's has a reputation for being one of Britain's friendliest clubs. Subject to being members of golf clubs, visitors and golfing societies are welcome at all times although those wishing to make party bookings must do so by written application to the Secretary. The cost of a day's golf in 2000 is set at £35 during the week with £40 payable at the weekend and on bank holidays.

Harlech alas isn't like the proverbial Rome and there is just one road that travellers must join, namely the A496. From the north this road approaches from Blaenau Ffestiniog via Maentwrog (east of Porthmadog) and from the south via Dolgellau and Barmouth. Those coming from further afield may find Bala (from the north) and Welshpool (from the south) useful towns to head for. Bala links with Maentwrog by way of the A4212 and the A487, while the A458 and A470 link Welshpool to Barmouth. Finally, for those not travelling by car, the train station at Harlech may prove of assistance.

Measuring less than 6600 yards from the championship tees, St David's may not at first glance seem overly testing. However the general consensus is that the course, to adopt golfers' terminology, 'plays long'. Par is a very tight 69 and there are only two par fives on the card. Furthermore the rough can be very punishing and it is very rare for there not to be a stiff westerly wind. Perhaps the most difficult holes on the course are the 10th, a long par four into the prevailing wind, and the classic 15th which requires a lengthy, angled drive followed by a precise approach. The round finishes with, to adopt another curious golfing expression, 'a nasty long short hole.' The nineteenth at St David's matches the high standards set by the previous eighteen. There is an excellent bar for celebration or recuperation and light snacks, lunches and dinners are all offered. With prior warning a full Anglo/Welsh breakfast can also be arranged.

As one might imagine, each of the major Welsh Championships is staged regularly at St David's; in addition the British Ladies Championship, (won for the fourth time by Cecil Leitch in 1926), the British Boys Championship and both Men's and Ladies' Home International Matches have also been played at Harlech.

Unfortunately there are still some English who consider the Welsh a little insular—a visit to Royal St David's makes one realise that Welsh golf clubs could teach many of their English counterparts a thing or two about hospitality . . . and on that controversial note, I wish you good golfing!

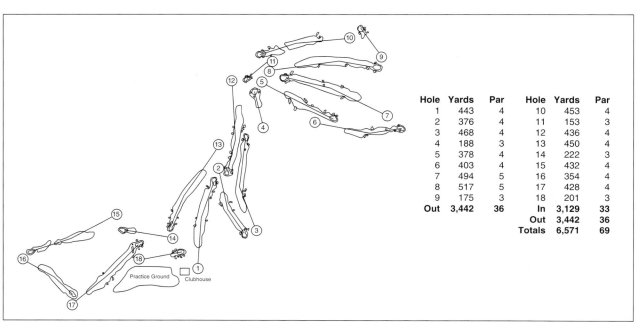

Hole	Yards	Par	Hole	Yards	Par
1	443	4	10	453	4
2	376	4	11	153	3
3	468	4	12	436	4
4	188	3	13	450	4
5	378	4	14	222	3
6	403	4	15	432	4
7	494	5	16	354	4
8	517	5	17	428	4
9	175	3	18	201	3
Out	3,442	36	In	3,129	33
			Out	3,442	36
			Totals	6,571	69

Royal Porthcawl

By common consent Royal Porthcawl is the finest course in Wales and one of the greatest championship links in the British Isles; yet like many famous clubs, Porthcawl's beginnings were rather humble. The club was founded in June 1891 and the following year a nine hole course was laid out on a patch of common land known as Lock's Common, consent having been given by the local parish vestry. Having to share the course with, amongst other things, cattle soon frustrated the members and a second nine holes were sought. These they found on the present site closer to the shore. By 1898 Lock's Common was abandoned altogether and the 'favoured' second nine holes were extended to a full eighteen. Once settled the club prospered and in 1909 patronage was bestowed. Royal Porthcawl had well and truly arrived.

The members were extremely fortunate in finding this new home for today Royal Porthcawl is not only considered to be one of Britain's finest golfing challenges but also one of the most beautifully situated. Every hole on the course provides a sight of the sea and from many points there are spectacular views across the Bristol Channel to the distant hills of Somerset and North Devon.

Presently presiding over the Royal domain is the club's helpful **Secretary, Mr Frank Prescott.** He may be contacted on **tel: (01656) 782251** and by **fax: (01656) 771687.** The **Professional, Peter Evans,** can be reached on **(01656) 773702.**

Golfers wishing to visit Royal Porthcawl can expect a warm welcome. Subject to possessing a golf club handicap there are no general restrictions; however, being an understandably popular club prior telephoning is advisable. Those wishing to organise golf society meetings should either telephone or address a written application to the **Secretary at The Royal Porthcawl Golf Club, Porthcawl, Mid Glamorgan, Wales, CF36 3UW.** Tuesdays and Thursdays are the usual society days.

The green fees at Royal Porthcawl for 2000 are set at £45 per round and £55 per day during the week (but note that visitors are not permitted on Wednesdays) with £60 per round and £70 per day at weekends. A rather novel and most encouraging policy is adopted towards junior golfers. Junior members of the club can introduce an outside junior for a green fee of just £1 during weekdays.

The course is situated approximately 15 miles east of Swansea and about 20 miles west of Cardiff. The M4 makes travelling to Porthcawl fairly straightforward. Approaching from either east or west the motorway should be left at junction 37, then following the A4229 into Porthcawl. The course's precise location is towards the northern end of the town.

In the opening paragraph Porthcawl was described as a 'links'. This isn't perhaps entirely accurate for although much of the course is certainly of a links nature, some parts are more strictly downland and heathland in character and there aren't the massive sandhills that feature so prominently on the great championship links of Lancashire, and which are indeed to be found at neighbouring Pyle and Kenfig. The absence of sandhills means there is no real protection from the elements on stormy days and when the winds blow fiercely Porthcawl can be as tough a challenge as one is likely to meet.

From its championship tees the course stretches to 6685 yards (par 72, SSS 74) and from the medal tees it measures 6406 yards (par 72) with the ladies playing over 5749 yards (par 75). Good scores at Porthcawl are likely to be fashioned on the first ten holes. The 2nd, 3rd, 5th and 9th are the best of the early challenges, while from the par three 11th some very difficult holes lie ahead. The second shot from the fairway on the dog-leg 13th is one not to be hurried, as the views out across the course are quite breathtaking. The 15th and 16th are two excellent and quite lengthy par fours and the round ends with a glorious downhill finishing hole.

As for its 19th, Porthcawl has a splendid clubhouse. There is an informal men's bar where spikes may be worn, a mixed lounge (jacket and tie after 7pm) and a dining room (jacket and tie at all times). Both lunches and dinners can be arranged with prior notice, and light snacks are offered at all times except on Sundays. Since 1995 the club has also offered very good value Dormy accommodation—telephone the secretary for details.

One final thought for those wishing to explore the delights of Royal Porthcawl; I beg you to consider carefully before deciding to visit late on a November's afternoon for as the light fades and a mist starts to descend upon the links, the ghost of the Maid of Sker walks the 17th fairway—don't say you haven't been warned!

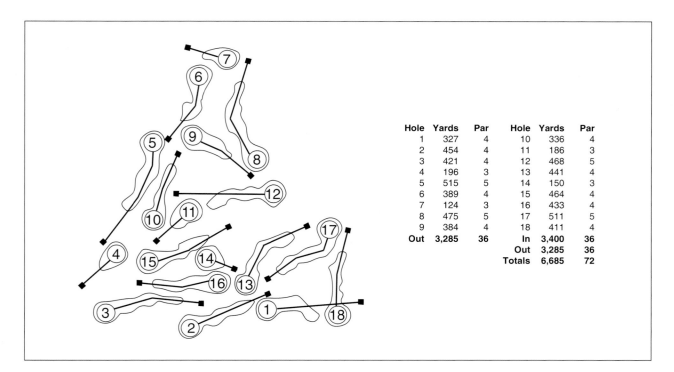

Hole	Yards	Par	Hole	Yards	Par
1	327	4	10	336	4
2	454	4	11	186	3
3	421	4	12	468	5
4	196	3	13	441	4
5	515	5	14	150	3
6	389	4	15	464	4
7	124	3	16	433	4
8	475	5	17	511	5
9	384	4	18	411	4
Out	**3,285**	**36**	**In**	**3,400**	**36**
			Out	**3,285**	**36**
			Totals	**6,685**	**72**

St Pierre

St Pierre was founded in 1961 and the Ken Cotton designed Old Course opened the following May. The first thing to strike you at St Pierre is the beautiful setting. The golf course land was originally a deer park and it has an abundance and great variety of mature trees. At the heart of the course there is also a lake covering eleven acres. Whilst the **Old** Course is understandably St Pierre's pride and joy, there are in fact 36 holes, as a second eighteen, the **Mathern** Course opened in 1975.

Visitors wishing to arrange a game at St Pierre must book starting times in advance. The club's **Professional, Craig Don** and his staff can be contacted on **tel: (01291) 625261** and by **fax: (01291) 629975.** All written correspondence should be addressed to **Stephen Follett, Golf Operations Manager, Marriott St Pierre Hotel and Country Club, St Pierre Park, Chepstow, Gwent NP6 6YA.**

There are no general restrictions on times of play. Officially visitors are not allowed at weekends but the rules can be bent if tee times are available. Societies are normally received only during the week unless they are resident at the hotel, in which case they may also play at weekends. Residential packages, inclusive of golf, are available on request.

The 2000 green fees are as follows: £50 for a round over the Old Course during the week and at weekends (when available), with £35 during the week and at weekends for a game on the Mathern Course. For junior golfers a single round on the Old Course is priced at £20 and the Mathern course at £15.

The golf club is located to the south of Chepstow off the A48. The M4 links Chepstow to Cardiff and Swansea in the west and to London and Bristol in the east. Leave the M4 at junction 21, then follow the M48 as far as junction 2 taking the A4666 into Chepstow where the A48 can be joined and followed to St Pierre. The best route for those approaching from Birmingham and the north of England is probably to travel south on the M5, leaving at exit 8, thereafter picking up the M50 to Ross-on-Wye. From Ross-on-Wye a combination of the A40 and A466 provides a pleasant drive through the Wye Valley to Chepstow.

The Old and the Mathern Course differ quite considerably in length. The Old is the championship course and from the back tees measures 6762 yards (par 71). The forward tees reduce the length to 6506 yards, while for the ladies it measures 5865 yards (par 75). The respective distances for the Mathern Course are 5732 yards (par 68), 5569 yards and 5212 yards (par 70).

Despite its relative youth, the Old Course has been the venue for a remarkable number of professional events. The Dunlop Masters and Silk Cut Masters were staged regularly here—illustrious winners including Tony Jacklin, Bernhard Langer and Greg Norman. The latter on his way to a seven stroke victory in 1982 drove the 362 yards 10th with a three wood. In more recent years the Epson Grand Prix tournament was also held at St Pierre and in 1989 Seve Ballesteros produced some remarkable golf to win his first title in Wales. In 1990 the tournament changed its format from matchplay to strokeplay which resulted in a popular home victory for Ian Woosnam, and a year later Jose Maria Olazabal strolled home nine shots ahead of the field.

In September 1996 St Pierre successfully hosted the 4th Solheim Cup, the premier team event in women's golf. For two days it looked as if Europe might repeat its famous victory at Dalmahoy in 1992, but the final day's singles were won emphatically by the United States.

Perhaps the most famous hole on the Old Course is the 18th, surely one of the most dramatic finishing holes in golf. A par three of 237 yards, it requires a brave tee shot across the edge of the lake with large trees lining the left hand side of the fairway.

Standing proudly behind the green is the ivy-clad St Pierre Hotel. The hotel is in fact a former 14th century country mansion and it serves the golfer as a particularly impressive 19th. In addition to two fine restaurants, there are three bars.

Celebrating at the end of a round is always to be recommended—particularly if the 18th hole has been tackled successfully. Spare a thought though for a person by the name of Arwyn Griffiths who came to the 18th needing a three for a gross 63. A few minutes later he walked off the green having taken eleven strokes—but even he found cause for celebration, for Arwyn still won the competition!

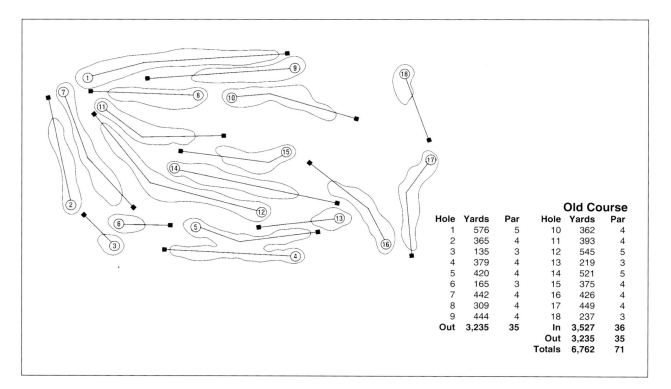

Old Course

Hole	Yards	Par	Hole	Yards	Par
1	576	5	10	362	4
2	365	4	11	393	4
3	135	3	12	545	5
4	379	4	13	219	3
5	420	4	14	521	5
6	165	3	15	375	4
7	442	4	16	426	4
8	309	4	17	449	4
9	444	4	18	237	3
Out	**3,235**	**35**	**In**	**3,527**	**36**
			Out	**3,235**	**35**
			Totals	**6,762**	**71**

Celtic Manor

If ten years ago someone had suggested to you that in the year 2000 the British Open would be held at St Andrews, the US Open at Pebble Beach, the Irish Open at Ballybunion and the Welsh Open at Celtic Manor, how would you have reacted?

I suspect my response would have been to have agreed with the first two predictions, to have said 'nice idea, but unlikely' to the third, and I would have been completely baffled by the final pronouncement. 'A Welsh Open? ... Where? ... How? ... Why?'

Well, ten years from now it seems there is every chance that we will be reading reviews of how Europe won (or lost) the 2009 Ryder Cup at Celtic Manor. Baffled? Visit Celtic Manor near Newport and you won't be for long. It is an extraordinary place: a golfing complex par excellence (to adopt a little known Welsh golfing term). In fact, its scale is such that it is more a golf resort than a golf complex. Celtic Manor boasts no fewer than three eighteen hole layouts – two of championship length and standard, a state-of-the-art golf academy, and a 400-room luxury hotel. If the Ryder Cup can be staged at The Belfry (in England) and The K Club (in Ireland), why shouldn't it be held at Celtic Manor in Wales?

Location, location, location' has been the mantra of those trying to justify the repeated selection of The Belfry to host golf's premier team event. If this is the key argument, then it should be mentioned that Celtic Manor is extremely accessible, being located very close to the M4 (junction 24), one of Britain's busiest motorways. Quality on-site accommodation is another plus, and in terms of having a wealthy individual to act as the driving force behind a bid for the Ryder Cup, then for Dr Michael Smurfit read Terry Matthews, Celtic Manor's entrepreneurial (even visionary) Welsh owner.

Of course the burning question is – or should be – is the golf good enough at Celtic Manor? We may have to wait until June 2000 and the Welsh Open for a definitive answer but, given that the names Robert Trent Jones and Robert Trent Jones Jnr are indelibly linked with the golf courses at Celtic Manor, there can be little doubt that they are. Robert Trent Jones is often referred to as the doyen of golf course architects and his son has become almost as famous. Their linkage with Celtic Manor is particularly appropriate since Trent Jones Snr was born in Aberystwyth.

The first two courses to be built at Celtic Manor were the Roman Road Course and the Coldra Woods Course, both designed in the mid

1990's by Trent Jones Snr. The Roman Road Course is the original championship layout. It runs along the ridge of Coldra Hill, straddling the ancient east to west Roman Road, Via Julia. The scenery is varied and spectacular, and characterised by deep ravines, steep ridges and stunning views. It was on this land that the Romans trained their gladiators. The course features many classic Trent Jones trademarks, including several water hazards, a multitude of large jigsaw-shaped bunkers and boldly undulating greens. It is a fine course, yet in the opinion of most golf course critics the Roman Road course has now been eclipsed by the dramatic new Robert Trent Jones Jnr design, the Wentwood Hills Course.

The Welsh Open will be played on the Wentwood Hill Course and, if the Ryder Cup bid is successful, 24 modern day gladiators will be doing battle on this prodigiously long and challenging layout. Wentwood Hills can be stretched to nigh on 7500 yards from the tips; the first two holes are a 471 yards par four, followed by a 613 yards par five! The second hole may sound like a monster (or a dragon?) of a hole but it journeys through some magnificent landscape – in fact the entire course has the beautiful countryside of both the Usk Valley and the Wentwood Hills as a backdrop – southern Wales in all its glory.

The 19th hole at Celtic Manor is, as you might imagine, a big and impressive affair – reputedly the largest clubhouse in Europe. As for the adjacent hotel, Golf World magazine recently likened it to 'Xanadu', the palatial home of Charles Foster Kane, the media mogul in the film Citizen Kane. Palatial it may be, but it's very welcoming and anything but exclusive.

Celtic Manor is located 100 minutes from Eros in Piccadilly Circus. For the clubhouse and courses leave the M4 at junction 24, take the A48 towards Newport for half a mile and Celtic Manor Clubhouse is on your right hand side. The full address is **Celtic Manor Hotel & Country Club, Coldra Woods, Newport, Gwent, NP6 2YA.**

Golfing visitors to Celtic Manor are advised to make arrangements in advance of intended play. For bookings **tel: (01633) 410311**, or visit the website on **www.celticmanor.com** The green fees in 2000 are £15 per round on the Coldra Woods Course, £35 for a game on the Roman Road Course and £45 to play the Wentwood Hills Course. The fees are slightly reduced for hotel residents. **Scott Patience** is the **Professional** and the **Director of Golf** is **Jim McKenzie**. Both can be contacted on the above number.

Coldra Woods Course

Hole	Yards	Par	Hole	Yards	Par
1	220	3	10	403	4
2	190	3	11	182	3
3	279	4	12	130	3
4	192	3	13	162	3
5	283	4	14	191	3
6	164	3	15	243	4
7	243	4	16	196	3
8	179	3	17	186	3
9	363	4	18	288	4
Out	2113	31	In	1981	30
			Out	2113	31
			Totals	4094	61

Roman Road Course

Hole	Yards	Par	Hole	Yards	Par
1	455	4	10	447	4
2	529	5	11	217	3
3	423	4	12	367	4
4	205	3	13	425	4
5	586	5	14	206	3
6	335	4	15a	395	4
7	218	3	16	380	4
8	439	4	17	182	3
9	461	4	18	449	4
Out	3651	36	In	3068	33
			Out	3651	36
			Totals	6719	69

Tenby

Where are the loveliest beaches in Britain? Since I grew up in Devon and my ancestors came from Pembrokeshire, someone will doubtless accuse me of being biased but in my opinion the two finest places to bring out the bucket and spade are on the North Devon coast at Saunton and at Tenby in South Wales. Both have wonderful long stretches of golden sand. What makes Saunton and Tenby even more appealing—and now I will admit to bias—is that their beaches are fringed by massive sand dunes, adjacent to which are wonderful natural links courses.

Beautiful beaches aside, the courses at Saunton and Tenby are actually like 'chalk and cheese'. Saunton's design is reminiscent of Royal Birkdale with its fairways running parallel to the dunes along relatively flat valleys, whereas the layout at Tenby follows the Royal St George's approach—it careers over the top of the dunes. Tenby is an unashamedly old fashioned links—awkward stances, the occasional blind shot, hidden pot bunkers and tricky greens that sit on natural plateaux. This is what golf at Tenby is all about. It has enormous character, and for links enthusiasts it is tremendous fun.

Founded in 1888, Tenby is the oldest golf club in Wales. It is also one of the most spectacularly situated with glorious views, not only down over those golden sands but across the sea to Caldey Island.

The 1st at Tenby measures 466 yards and the opening drive must be struck straight into the sandhills. The golfer then disappears into another world. The 3rd hole is named 'Dai Rees' and was a favourite of the great Welsh golfer. It is not long but precision is everything for it features a hog's back fairway, an approach across a plunging valley to a narrow table-like green with a pot bunker protecting the front entrance and steep banks on either side—a death or glory hole! The 4th is played from an elevated tee along a tumbling fairway bordered by huge dunes. The second shot is again downhill, this time to a blind green concealed beneath the dunes in a dell—shades of Lahinch and Prestwick! The 5th tee overlooks the beach as the course now heads off in a different direction.

Although some excellent two-shotters lie ahead, the most memorable holes from here on are the par threes—the short 6th, where the green is practically encircled by a sea of gorse, the 9th, the formidable 12th, with its crumpled fairway, and the exhilarating downhill 17th.

The closing hole is the intriguingly named 'Charlie's Whiskers' and, true to form, it bristles with character. You don't need to be biased—or a lover of golden sands—to fall in love with Tenby.

Tenby Golf Club, The Burrows, Tenby, Pembroke, SA70 7NP

Secretary	J A Pearson (01834) 842978
Professional	Mark Hawkey (01834) 844447
Green Fees	WD £25 WE £30
Restrictions	Handicap certificates required.

Directions
The club is located on the west side of Tenby off the A447, near the railway station.

Pennard

Just beyond the town of Swansea, and the wonderfully named resort of Mumbles, is the Gower Peninsula and a secret, immensely scenic kingdom. It was once claimed of the Gower that smuggling was not just a profitable exercise—it was a full scale industry. Here is a land of golden beaches and hidden coves. A miniature Cornwall perhaps? Not really. The Gower is much quieter, much more 'grockle' free. And you've probably heard of St Enodoc and Trevose, but are you familiar with Pennard?

Founded around the turn of the century, Pennard Golf Club is Wales' best kept secret. It is not exactly cut off from the outside world but is genuinely tucked away. It lies just beyond the tiny village of Pennard—a church a post office and not much else—and occupies high ground that looks set to slip into the sea at any moment. The views across Oxwich Bay and Three Cliffs Bay, particularly from the 16th fairway are arresting, and the golf is worthy of the setting.

Pennard is not entirely undiscovered. Tom Doak, a leading American golf course architect and controversial course critic wrote of Pennard in his book The Confidential Guide to Golf Courses, "This is one of my all-time favourites—the site is one of the most spectacular I've ever seen."

Pennard is essentially a links course, although, as at Royal Porthcawl, there is a slight moorland-cum-downland feel to some of the holes. At 6329 yards, par 71, it is not overly long but being routinely buffeted by strong winds that roar up the Bristol Channel it can provide a very stern challenge. Much of the rough consists of thick heather and dense, rust coloured bracken.

Like Tenby, there is a slightly eccentric, old-fashioned flavour to the links—the holes accommodate the land rather than vice versa.

It is capricious, wild terrain; there are a number of blind and semi-blind shots while some of the green sites border on the bizarre, but the golf is nothing if not adventurous.

The course is laid out in two distinct loops. The round starts and finishes with a strong par four but the greatest hole at Pennard is surely the 7th. Here you drive over a deep valley to find a fairway which runs alongside the ruins of a 12th century Norman castle and the site of a medieval church. Trying your best not to be distracted by the views, you must then play a deft pitch to a partially concealed, sunken green. It is a hole that personifies the character and charm of Pennard.

Pennard Golf Club, 2 Southgate Road, Swansea SA3 2BT

Secretary	Morley Howell (01792) 233131
	Fax (01792) 234797
Professional	M V Bennett (01792) 233451
Green Fees	WD £27, WE £35 and Bank Holidays
Restrictions	Proof of handicap required.
	Avoid Tuesday mornings.

Directions
The club is eight miles west of Swansea via the A 4067 and the B 4436.

Holyhead (Trearddur Bay)

Which do you reckon are the best holes at Holyhead? I asked a Mancunian friend who plays the course every summer without fail. 'They're all real crackers down there', he replied. 'In fact, it's a cracking course full stop'. And he's right. Trearddur Bay, as many people call it, is one of two superb golf courses on the Isle of Anglesey, the other being Bull Bay on the island's northerly tip at Amlwch.

A glance at the scorecard tells you that the course measures only just over 6000 yards in length from the back tees, moreover, from a distance, it looks relatively tame with only one serious hill to negotiate. Look a little closer, however, and you will soon realise that not only are the fairways extremely narrow and quite undulating but the rough comprises much gorse, heather, bracken and, as my friend puts it, 'all kinds of horror stories'—the words of one who has been thrilled too often—and then there is the wind which whips across from the Irish Sea.

So you had been licking your lips contemplating a very short, straightforward par four to open proceedings but you survey the scene ahead and suddenly there is the feeling you are looking down a gun barrel. The fearless big hitter will hope to fire one up the middle and perhaps even reach the green. Most golfers however, could only feel really comfortable playing this and the next few holes wearing blinkers.

The 2nd is a very tricky par three. Clammy hands is the sensation here—go left and you must visit the local farmer—stray right and you may tumble down the edge of a cliff on to an adjacent fairway from which the pitch to the green is less than inviting. The next is a tremendous hole—a par four from the front tees but the 3rd is a genuine five from the back markers. Here the drive is hit straight into the crest of a hill. Once over the hill, there is then a gentle climb

to the green; two good straight hits—usually into the wind—will be needed to set up any chance of a birdie. Then comes the shortest hole on the course, the 4th, played directly towards the sea. Very exposed to the elements, this hole can play anything from a long iron to a sand iron.

The challenge continues throughout the round with the 9th and 10th being two especially memorable holes. It also culminates with a glorious, if fiendish, finishing hole where to the right of the fairway the gorse and bracken have been permitted to run rampant. 'Can't remember the last time I hit the 18th green in two', my friend tells me. 'In fact, I can't remember the last time I parred it—it's far too tough for me' he says. Perhaps you should give Anglesey a miss this summer, I dare to suggest. Go to Spain perhaps? 'What! Five hours for a round under a blazing hot sun instead of playing golf here . . . you must be crackers. Absolutely crackers'.

Holyhead Golf Club, Trearddur Bay, Anglesey, LL65 2YL

Sec/Manager	John Williams (01407) 763279
Professional	Stephen Elliott (01407) 762022
Green Fees	WD £19/round, £25/day
	WE £25/round, £29/day
Restrictions	Telephoning advisable

Directions
Take the A5 from Bangor to Trearddur Bay.

Nefyn

We golfers in Britain are doubly fortunate—not only do we have an infinite variety of courses to play upon (contrast, for instance, the Surrey heathland with the Scottish links), but we also possess a wealth of outstandingly scenic courses. Perhaps one of our lesser known treasures is perched on the cliffs of North Wales' western tip. Nefyn, or more precisely Nefyn and District, was founded in 1907, although the course really came into its own in 1920 when an extension was opened by James Braid and John H Taylor (where was Harry Vardon you ask!)

I suppose Nefyn could be described as a classic holiday course: to begin with there is a very pleasant drive to the club and on arrival visitors are made very welcome; the course is always well maintained with particularly pleasing fairways; whilst the golf is by no means easy, it is never too severe or unfair (indeed, unless the wind blows fiercely, good scores should definitely appear on the cards); the views as mentioned are quite stupendous and, to cap it all, there is even a pub two thirds of the way round! Well, what more could a golfer ask for?

From the back markers Nefyn stretches to 6332 yards and has a par of 72. Ian Woosnam, the 1991 US Masters Champion, holds the professional course record of 67. I am reliably informed that another model of Welsh consistency, Lloyd-George, was a frequent visitor to Nefyn and that this trend was in turn followed by Clement Attlee—who doubtless found the golf here a welcome diversion from the pressures of No 10.

After a lengthy opener which certainly invites a hearty belt from the tee (sorry, controlled power) the course moves out along by the cliff edges for a number of spectacular holes. It then turns back on itself before heading in a different direction out on to a headland where arguably the best holes on the course, numbers 11 to 18 are found.

There is no real place on the course where you lose sight of the sea and you may just encounter the occasional sunbather who has lost his or her way. If the holiday mood really takes you, then down in a cove by the 12th green is the Ty Coch Inn. Yes, it is accessible from the course and on a really hot summer's day can doubtless be mistaken for a heavenly mirage. One cannot help wondering how many steady score cards have suddenly taken on erratic proportions from the 13th hole in!

Returning to the clubhouse you will find that full catering facilities are offered. There is a snooker room and a genuinely pleasant atmosphere in which to relax and reflect on your day. Well, if you have not enjoyed your golf at Nefyn then I must venture to suggest that you are an extremely difficult person to please!

The Nefyn & District Golf Club, Morfa Nefyn, Pwllheli, Gwynedd, LL53 6DA

Sec/Manager	J B Owens (01758) 720966
Professional	John Froom (01758) 720102
Green Fees	WD £25 (£30 per day)
	WE £30 (£35 per day)
Restrictions	Handicap certificates required.

Directions
From Colwyn Bay take the A55 towards Bangor then the A487 to Caernafon. From there the A499 and B4417 lead through Nefyn to Morfa Nefyn.

MONMOUTH & SURROUNDS

Alice Springs G.C.
(01873) 880914
Bettws Newydd, Usk
(18) 6041 yards/***/D
(18) 6400 yards/***/D

Blackwood G.C.
(01495) 223152
Cwmgelli, Blackwood
(9) 5300 yards/***/D/H/L

British Steel Port Talbot
(01639) 814182 or 871111
Sports & Social Club, Margam
(9) 4726 yards/**/F

Caerleon G.C.
(01633) 420342
Broadway, Caerleon
(9) 3092 yards/***/E

Celtic Manor G. & C.C.
(01633) 413000
Coldra Woods, Newport
(18) 7100 yards/***/A/H
(18) 4094 yards/***/F/H

Coed-Y-Mwstwr G.C.
(01656) 862121
The /clubhouse, Coychurch
(9) 5834 yards/H/D

Dewstow G.C.
(01291) 430444
Caerwent, Newport
(18) 6100 yards/***/D

Greenmeadow G.C.
(01633) 862626
Croesyceiliog, Cwmbran
(18) 5587 yards/***/F

Llanwern G.C.
(01633) 412029
Tennyson Avenue, Llanwern
(18) 6115 yards/**/B/H/L
(9) 5239 yards/**/B/H/L

Monmouth G.C.
(01600) 712212
Leasebrook Lane, Monmouth
(18) 5698 yards/***/D

Monmouthshire G.C.
(01873) 852606
Llanfoist, Abergavenny
(18) 6054 yards/***/B/H/G

Newport G.C.
(01633) 892643
Great Oak, Rogerstone, Newport
(18) 6431 yards/**/A/H/M

Oakdale G.C.
(01495) 220044
Llwynon Lane, Oakdale
(9) 1235 yards/***/E

Parc G.C.
(01633) 680933
Church Lane, Coedkernew
(18) 5136 yards/***/D

Pontnewydd G.C.
(016333) 482170
Maesgwyn Farm, West Pontnewydd
(10) 5353 yards/**/D/G

Pontypool G.C.
(01495) 763655
Lasgarn Lane, Trevethin
(18) 6046 yards/***/C/H/L

Raglan Park G.C.
(01291) 690077
Park Lodge, Raglan
(18) 6604 yards/***/D

The Rolls of Monmouth G.C.
(01600) 715353
The Hendre, Monmouth
(18) 6733 yards/***/A

St Pierre G.& C.C.
(01291) 625261
St Pierre Park, Chepstow
(18) 6762 yards/***/A/H
(18) 5732 yards/***/A/H

Shirenewton G.C.
(01291) 641642
Shirenewton, Chepstow
(18)6820/***/D

Tredegar Park G.C.
(01633) 894433
Bassaleg Road, Newport
(18) 5575 yards/***/B/H

Tredegar & Rhymney G.C.
(01685) 840743
Tredegar, Rhymney
(9) 5500 yards/***/D

Wernddu Golf Centre
(01873) 856223
Old Ross Road, Abergavenny
(18) 6600 yards/***/E

West Monmouthshire G.C.
(01495) 310233
Pond Road, Nantyglo
(18) 6118 yards/***(Sun)/D

Woodlake Park G.C.
(01291) 673933
Glascoed, Pontypool
(18) 6300 yards/***/C/H

THE GLAMORGANS

Aberdare G.C.
(01685) 872797
Abernant, Aberdare,
(18) 5874 yards/***(Sat)/D/H/L

Allt-y-Graben G.C.
(01792) 885757
Pontlliw, Swansea
(9) 2210 yards/***/E

Bargoed G.C.
(01443) 830608
Heolddu, Bargoed,
(18) 6000 yards/**/D

Bryn Meadows Golf Hotel
(01495) 225590
The Bryn, Hengoed,
(18) 6200 yards/***/C

Brynhill G.C.
(01446) 720277
Port Road, Barry,
(18) 6000 yards/***(Sun)/B/H

Caerphilly G.C.
(01222) 863441
Mountain Road, Caerphilly,
(14) 6000 yards/**/B/H

Cardiff G.C.
(01222) 753320
Sherborne Avenue, Cincoed,
(18) 6016 yards/**/B/H

Castell Heights G.C.
(01222) 886666
Blaengwynlais, Caerphilly,
(18) 7000 yards/***/E
(9) 2670 yards/***/E

Clyne G.C.
(01792) 401989
Owls Lodge Lane, Mayals,
(18) 6312 yards/***/B/H

Cottrell Park G.C.
(01446) 781781
Cottrell Park, St Nicholas, Cardiff
(18) 6176 yards/**/D/H

Creigiau G.C.
(01222) 890263
Creigiau, Cardiff,
(18) 5900 yards/**/B/G

Dinas Powis G.C.
(01222) 512727
Old Highwalls, Dinas Powis,
(18) 5377 yards/***/C/L

Earlswood G.C.
(01792) 812198
Jersey Marine, Neath
(18) 5174 yards/***/E

Fairwood Park G.C.
(01792) 297849
Upper Killay, Swansea,
(18) 6741 yards/***/B

Glamorganshire G.C.
(01222) 701185
Lavernock Road, Penarth,
(18) 6181 yards/***/B/H

Glyn Neath G.C.
(01639) 720452
Penycraig, Pontneathvaughan, t
(18) 5499 yards/**/D/H

Gower G.C.
(01792) 872480
Cefn Goleu, Three Crosses, Swansea
(18) 6400 yards/***/E

Grove G.C.
(01656) 788771
South Cornelly, Nr Porthcawl
(18) 6065 yards/***/D

I.N.C.O. G.C.
(01792) 843336
Clydach, Swansea,
(12) 6230 yards/***/F

Lakeside G.C.
(01639) 899959
Water Street, Margam, Port Talbot
(18) 4390 yards/***/E

Langland Bay G.C.
(01792) 361721
Llangland Bay, Swansea,
(18) 5830 yards/***/B

Llanishen G.C.
(01222) 755078
Cwm, Lisvane,
(18) 5296 yards/**/B/H

Llantrisant and Pontyclun G.C.
(01443) 224601
Llanelry Road, Talbot Green,
(12) 5712 yards/**/F/H/G

Maesteg G.C.
(01656) 734106
Neath Road, Maesteg,
(18) 5900 yards/***/C/H

Merthyr Tydfil G.C.
(01685) 723308
Cilsanws Mt, Cefn Coed,
(11) 5900 yards/***/F

Morlais Castle G.C.
(01685) 722822
Pant, Dowlais, Merthyr Tydfil,
(18) 6320 yards/**/D

Morriston G.C.
(01792) 796528
Clasemont Road, Morriston,
(18) 5800 yards/***/C/H

Mountain Ash G.C.
(01443) 479459
Cefnpennar, Mountain Ash,
(18) 5500 yards/**/D/H

Mountain Lakes G.C.
(01222) 861128
Blaengwynlais, Caerphilly,
(18) 5700 yards/***/C/H

Neath G.C.
(01639) 632579
Cadoxton, Neath,
(18) 6465 yards/**/C/G

Palleg G.C.
(01639) 842193
Lower Cwmtwrch, Swansea, t
(9) 3260 yards/**/D

Pennard G.C.
(01792) 233131
Southgate, Swansea,
(18) 6266 yards/***/C/H

Peterstone G.C.
(01633) 680009
Peterstone, Wentloog
(18) 6600 yards/***/C/H/M

Pontardawe G.C.
(01792) 863118
Cefn Llan, Pontardawe,
(18) 6061 yards/**/C/H

Pontypridd G.C.
(01443) 409904
Ty Gwyn Road, Pontypridd,
(18) 5650 yards/**/C/H/L

Pyle and Kenfig G.C.
(01656) 783093
Waun-y-Mer, Kenfig,
(18) 6640 yards/**/A/H

RAF St Athan G.C.
(01446) 751043
Barry, Cardiff,
(9) 5957 yards/***(Sun am)/D

Radyr G.C.
(01222) 842408
Radyr, Cardiff,
(18) 6031 yards/**/B/H/L

Rhondda G.C.
(01443) 441384
Penrhys, Rhondda,
(18)6428 yards/***/C/H

Royal Porthcawl G.C.
(01656) 782251
Porthcawl,
(18) 6600 yards/**/A/H/G

St Andrews Major G.C.
(01446) 722227
Cadoxton, Barry,
(9) 2931 yards/***/D

St Marys G. & C.C.
(01656) 860280
St Marys Hill, Pencoed,
(18) 5236 yards/***/D/H
(9) 2426 yards/***/E/H

St Mellons G.C.
(01633) 680408
St Mellons, Cardiff
(18) 6275 yards/**/C/H

Southerndown G.C.
(01656) 880476
Ewenny, Bridgend,
(18) 6613 yards/**/C-A/H

Swansea Bay G.C.
(01792) 816159
Jersey Marine, Neath,
(18) 6302 yards/***/C

Vale of Glamorgan G.C.
(01443) 222221
Hensol Park,near Bridgend
(18) 6507 yards/***/C

Virginia Park G.C.
(01222) 863919
Virginia Park, Caerphilly,
(9) 2566 yards/***/D

Wenvoe Castle G.C.
(01222) 593649
Wenvoe, Cardiff,
(18) 6411 yards/**/B/H/G

Whitchurch G.C.
(01222) 620985
Whitchurch, Cardiff,
(18) 6319 yards/**/B/H

Whitehall G.C.
(01443) 740245
Nelson, Treharris,
(9) 5750 yards/**/G

MID WALES

Aberdovey G.C.
(01654) 767602
Aberdovey
(18) 6445 yards/**/C

Aberystwyth G.C.
(01970) 615104
Bryn-y-Mor, Aberystywth
(18) 6100 yards/***/F

Ashburnham G.C.
(01554) 832269
Cliffe Terrace, Burry Port
(18) 6916 yards/***/B-A/H

Bala G.C.
(01678) 520359
Penlan, Bala
(10) 4962 yards/**/D

Bala Lake Hotel G.C.
(01678) 520344
Bala
(9) 4280 yards/***/F

Borth and Ynyslas G.C.
(01970) 871202
Borth, Aberystwyth
(18) 6000 yards/***/C/H

Brecon G.C.
(01874) 622004
Newton Park, Llanfaes, Brecon
(9) 5218 yards/***/D

Builth Wells G.C.
(01982) 553296
Golf Club Road, Builth Wells
(18) 5376 yards/***/D/H

Cardigan G.C.
(01293) 612035
Gwbert-on-Sea, Cardigan
(18) 6600 yards/***/C/H

Carmarthen G.C.
(01267) 281493
Blaen-y-Coed Road, Carmarthen
(18) 6212 yards/***/C

Chirk G. & C.C
(01691) 774407
Chirk, nr Wrexham
(18) 6800 yards/***/C

Cilgwyn G.C.
(01570) 45286
Llangybi, Lampeter
(9) 5318 yards/***/D

Cradoc G.C.
(01874) 623658
Penoyre Park, Cradoc, Brecon
(18) 6301 yards/***(Sun)/C

Dolgellau G.C.
(01341) 422603
Pencefn Road, Dolgellau
(9) 4512 yards/***/D

Ffestiniog G.C.
(01766) 831829
Y Cefn, Ffestiniog
(9) 5032 yards/***/F

Glyn Abbey G.C.
(01554) 810278
Pontnewydd, Trimsaren
(18) 6173 yards/***/E

Glynhir G.C.
(01269) 850472
Glynhir Road, Llandybie,
(18) 5900 yards/***(Sun)/D

Haverfordwest G.C.
(01437) 764523
Narberth Road, Haverfordwest
(18) 6005 yards/***/C

Knighton G.C.
(01547) 528646
Little Ffrydd Wood, Knighton
(9) 5320 yards/***/E

Llandrindod Wells G.C.
(01597) 823873
Llandrindod Wells
(18) 5749 yards/***/D

Llanstephan G.C.
(01267) 241526
Llanstephan
(9) 2165 yards/***/E

Llanymynech G.C.
(01691) 830983
Pant, Nr Oswestry
(18) 6114 yards/***/D

Machynlleth G.C.
(01597) 823873
Fford Drenewydd, Machynlleth
(9) 5726 yards/***/D

Maesmawr G.C.
(01686) 688303
Caersws, Newtown
(9) 2554 yards/***/E

Milford Haven G.C.
(01646) 692368
Hubberston, Milford Haven
(18) 6071 yards/***/D

Newport (Pembs) G.C.
(01239) 820244
Newport
(9) 5815 yards/***/D

Penrhos G.& C.C.
(01974) 202999
Llanrhystud, Aberystwyth
(18) 6641 yards/***/D

Old Rectory G.C.
(01873) 810373
Llangattock, Crickhowell
(9) 2878 yards/***/F

Rhosgoch G.C.
(01497) 851251
Rhosgoch, Builth Wells
(9) 4842 yards/***/E

St Giles Newtown G.C.
(01686) 625844
Pool Road, Newtown
(9) 5936 yards/**/D/H/L

St Idloes G.C.
(01686) 412559
Penrhallt, Llanidloes
(9) 5428 yards/**/D/H

St Davids City G.C.
(01437) 720312
Whitesands Bay, St Davids
(9) 5693 yards/***/D

South Pembrokeshire G.C.
(01646) 621453
Military Road, Pembroke Dock
(9) 5804 yards/***(evenings)/D

Tenby G.C.
(01834) 842978
The Burrows, Tenby
(18) 6232 yards/***/C/H

Trefloyne G.C.
(01834) 842165
Penally, Nr Tenby
(18) 6635 yards/***/D

Welsh Border Golf Complex
(01743) 884247
Bulthy, Middletown
(9) 3250 yards/***/E

Welshpool G.C.
(01938) 83249
Golfa Hill, Welshpool
(18) 5708 yards/***/D/H

NORTH WALES

Abergele & Pensarn G.C.
(01745) 824034
Tan-y-Goppa Road, Abergele
(18) 6520 yards/***/B

Abersoch G.C.
(01758) 712622
Abersoch
(18) 5910 yards/***/D/H

Betws-y-Coed G.C.
(01690) 710556
Betws-y-coed
(18) 4996 yards/***/D

Bryn Morfydd Hotel & G.C.
(01745) 890280
Llanrhaeadr, Denbigh
(18) 5601 yards/***/F
(9) 1190 yards/***/F

Caernarfon G.C.
(01286) 673783
Llanfaglan, Caernarfon
(9) 5860 yards/***/C

Caerwys G.C.
(01352) 720692
Caerwys, Mold
(9) 3080 yards/***/E

Clays Farm Golf Centre
(01978) 661406
Bryn Estyn Road, Wrexham
(18) 5600 yards/***/E

Conwy G.C.
(01492) 592423
Morfa, Conwy
(18) 6901 yards/**/B/H

Criccieth G.C.
(01766) 522154
Ednyfed Hill, Criccieth
(18) 5787 yards/***/D

Denbigh G.C.
(01745) 816669
Henllan Road, Denbigh
(18) 5650 yards/***/C

Flint G.C.
(01352) 732327
Cornist Park, Flint
(9) 5953 yards/**/D

Hawarden G.C.
(01244) 531447
Groomsdale Lane, Hawarden
(9) 5620 yards/**/C/G/H

Holywell G.C.
(01352) 713937
Brynford, Holywell
(9) 6484 yards/***/D

Kinmell Park G.C.
(01745) 833548
Bodelwyddan
(9) 1550 yards/***/E

Llandudno (Maesdu) G.C.
(01492) 876450
Hospital Road, Llandudno
(18) 6513 yards/***/B/H/M

Llandudno (North Wales) G.C.
(01492) 875325
Bryniau Road, West Shore
(18) 6247 yards/***/B/H

Llanfairfechan G.C.
(01248) 680144
Llannerch Road, Llanfairfechan
(9) 3119 yards/***/D

Mold G.C.
(01352) 741513
Clicain Road, Pant-y-Mwyn, Mold
(18) 5545 yards/***/C

Nefyn and District G.C.
(01758) 720966
Morfa Nefyn, Pwllheli
(18) 6332 yards/***/B/H

Northop Country Park
(01352) 840440
Northop, Chester
(18) 6735 yards/***/B-A

Old Colwyn G.C.
(01492) 515581
Woodland Avenue, Old Colwyn
(9) 5800 yards/**/D

Old Padeswood G.C.
(01244) 547401
Station Road, Padeswood, Mold
(18) 6639 yards/***/C

Padeswood and Buckley G.C.
(01244) 550537
Station Lane, Padeswood, Mold
(18) 5775 yards/***(Sun)/B

Penmaenmawr G.C.
(01492) 623330
Conwy Old Road, Penmaenmawr
(9) 5031 yards/***/C

Porthmadog G.C.
(01766) 514124
Morfa Bychan, Porthmadog
(18) 5838 yards/***/C/H

Prestatyn G.C.
(01745) 854320
Marine Road East, Prestatyn
(18) 6764 yards/***/C/H

Pwllheli G.C.
(01758) 612520
Golf Road, Pwllheli
(18) 6110 yards/***/C

Rhos-on-Sea G.C.
(01492) 549100
Penrhyn Bay, Llandudno
(18)

Rhuddlan G.C.
(01745) 590217
Meliden Road, Rhuddlan
(18) 6045 yards/***(Sun)/B/H

Rhyl G.C.
(01745) 353171
Coast Road, Rhyl
(9) 6185 yards/***/D

Royal St David's G.C.
(01766) 780857
Harlech
(18) 6427 yards/***/B/H

Ruthin-Pwllglas G.C.
(01824) 702296
Pwllglas, Ruthin
(10) 5418 yards/***/D

St Deniol G.C.
(01248) 353098
Penybryn, Bangor
(18) 5048 yards/***/D

St Melyd G.C.
(01745) 854405
Meliden Road, Prestatyn
(9) 5857 yards/***/C

Vale of Llangollen G.C.
(01978) 860906
Holyhead Road, Llangollen
(18) 6461 yards/***/C

Wrexham G.C.
(01978) 364268
Holt Road, Wrexham
(18) 6233 yards/***/F/H

ISLE OF ANGLESEY

Anglesey G.C.
(01407) 811202
Station Road, Rhosneigr
(18) 5713 yards/***/D

Baron Hill G.C.
(01248) 810231
Beaumaris
(9) 5564 yards/***/D

Bull Bay G.C.
(01407) 830960
Bull Bay Road, Amlwch
(18) 6160 yards/***/C/H

Holyhead G.C.
(01407) 763279
Trearddur Bay, Holyhead
(18) 6058 yards/***/D/H

Llangefni G.C.
(01248) 722193
Llangefni
(9) 1467 yards/***/F

Storwys Wen G.C.
(01248) 852673
Brynleg, Anglesey
(9) 2630 yards/**/D

PENMAENMAWR GOLF CLUB Photograph courtesy of: **Wales Tourist Board**

Dumfries, Galloway & Borders Choice Golf

The two modern counties of Dumfries & Galloway and Borders encompass most of the Scottish Lowlands. A beautiful area of Britain - as of course is most of Scotland - but surely not one terribly renowned for its golf? It may not be renowned but there is still certainly no shortage of exciting and challenging courses in the area. Indeed, the very fact that the great hordes head for the more famous venues further north means that Scotland's southerly golfing gems remain by and large marvellously uncrowded.

Dumfries & Galloway

The one true championship test in this region is found at **Southerness**. Of all Scotland's great links courses this is perhaps the least widely known. We have featured MacKenzie Ross's masterpiece on a separate page.

Powfoot is a fairly close neighbour of Southerness (at least as the crow flies) the course lying five miles west of Annan off the B724. A semi-links with plenty of heather and gorse, it offers a tremendous test of golf and is an admirable companion to Southerness. Adding to the enjoyment of a round at Powfoot is the setting- the course provides extensive views towards the Cumberland Hills to the south and the Galloway Hills to the west. The Isle of Man is also visible on a clear day.

Two convenient resting places after a game at Southerness are in Rockliffe, the Baron's Craig Hotel (01556) 630225 and a little closer in Colvend, the Clonyard House (01556) 630372. Good eating places include the Criffel Inn (01387) 850305 in New Abbey, and the Pheasant in Dalbeattie (01556) 610345. Powfoot has the Golf Hotel (01461) 700254 whilst a little further away is Canonbie and an exceptional restaurant at the Riverside Inn (01387) 371512. The rooms here are also very pleasant.

Nearby there are two good 18 hole courses at Dumfries, **Dumfries and County**, to the north of the town being the pick of the two, but golfers travelling north would do well to pay **Lochmaben** a visit as well. It is a very friendly club with an interesting course designed by James Braid. The setting around the Kirk Loch is most picturesque and the course is famed for its many beautiful old trees.

When inspecting any of the above courses, Dumfries, the county's largest town is a likely base and here the Cairndale Hotel (01387) 254111 is most pleasant. Other recommended establishments in the area include the Dryfesdale (01576) 202427 in Lockerbie, the Lockerbie Manor (01576) 202610 or the 14th century Comlongon Castle (01387) 870283.

Towards the western corner of Dumfries and Galloway there is more fine golf. Two 9 hole courses well worth playing are at Wigtown, **Wigtown and Bladnoch** and **Newton Stewart**.

Still further west, **Stranraer**, the ferry terminal for Lame, has a fine park- land course north of the town overlooking Loch Ryan. But the clifftop course at **Portpatrick** is surely the major golfing attraction in this area, indeed it is rated by many to be one of the most beautiful courses in Britain. Apparently for many years in the last century the town was Ireland's Gretna Green-couples sailing across the Irish Sea to get hitched in Portpatrick's tiny church. The golf course provides some breathtaking scenery-particularly outstanding is the view from the 13th fairway. It can often get quite breezy and although only 5644 yards in length, the course is certainly no pushover. There is one more treat in store back on the Wigtownshire peninsula, **St Medan's**, James Braid's magical 9 hole layout amongst the great dunes with views to Ireland and the Isle of Man. There is an honesty box if the little clubhouse is closed, and , just by, a lovely bronze statue of an otter in memory of Gavin Maxwell whose home was here.

Superb golf is accompanied by an exceptionally high number of first rate hotels in the area. In Castle Douglas, Milton Park (01644) 430286 is a recurring favourite while in Newton Stewart, the Kirroughtree Hotel (01671) 402141 is excellent. We would also recommend Creebridge House (01671) 402121-an extremely pleasant place to stay. Port William offers the very fine Corsemalzie House Hotel (01988) 600254. Cally Palace (01557) 814341 in Gatehouse of Fleet-a beautiful 18th century mansion-has its own golf course while a number of alternatives are found at Portpatrick. Pick of the bunch is the Knockinaam Lodge (01776) 810471 which has a glorious setting and a tremendous restaurant. Others to note are the Fernhill (01776) 810220, and the North West Castle (01776) 704413 in Portrodie.

Borders

Having sampled the delights of the coast of Southern Scotland one may head inland to the Border towns. En route one could slip 18 holes in at **Thornhill** or perhaps visit **Moffat**. The town has a very enjoyable moorland course with a marvellous setting in the valley of Annandale. The Black Bull is a welcoming hostelry after a round at Moffat and recommended places to spend an evening include the Beechwood Country House Hotel (01683) 220210 and Moffat House (01683) 220039.

The Border towns offer castles aplenty, some superb woollens and some excellent rugby. Golfwise, prior to the opening of The Roxburghe no course here could claim to be of championship proportions. However, the majority can boast spectacular settings, visitors are always encouraged and the green fees in these parts are just about the cheapest in Britain.

A cluster of courses are to be found in the centre of the county. The town of **Melrose** is famed for its ruined Abbey where the heart of Robert the Bruce is said to have been buried-gruesome stuff!) It has a fine 9 hole course and there are other equally pleasant courses at **Selkirk**, **Hawick**, **Lauder**, **St Boswells**, **Innerliethen** and **West Linton**. Kelso has an interesting layout being inside Kelso racecourse. Finally, well worth noting are **Peebles** and **Galashiels** - both are public courses, very well maintained and set amidst magnificent countryside.

Walter Scott's land really does deserve a lengthy inspection. Whether one is golfing in the Borders or simply breaking a journey, here are some ideas for places to stay. In Melrose, Burts Hotel (01896) 822285 lies in the very heart of Border country. It is a fine centre from which to explore the area and the hotel is comfortable and offers excellent food. In Peebles, there are two choice hotels: Cringletie House Hotel (01721) 730233 and the Peebles Hotel Hydro (01721) 720602. Good guest-houses are also plentiful, with Lindores (01721) 720441 and Whitestone House (01721) 720337 among the best.

Golfers who like a spot of fishing should also note the Tweed Valley Hotel (01896) 870636 in nearby Walkerburn. St Mary's Loch offers the Tibbie Shiels Inn (01750) 42231, Selkirk, Philipburn House (01750) 20747 and Tweedsmuir the cosy Crook Inn (01899) 880272. Ettrickshaws Hotel (01750) 52229 in Ettrickbridge is pleasant as is the Cross Keys Hotel (01573) 223303 in Kelso.

We end our trip, but we could equally well begin it, at the **Roxburghe** Hotel & Golf Course (01573) 450331 - one of the most delightfully relaxed country house hotels you will find anywhere. The Roxburghe course opened in 1997 and is a real treat; it is explored ahead.

THE 2ND ST BOSWELLS GOLF CLUB Photograph courtesy of: **David J Whyte, The Golf Photo Library**

The Roxburghe

The Roxburghe is the first championship course for the Borders and in time will become a place of pilgrimage for those travelling north to sample the more historic links of Fife or Ayrshire.

The course is set in 200 acres and makes exceptional use of the naturally contoured parkland. It also incorporates some stunning views of the River Teviot and the Borders countryside. The course was commissioned by the Duke of Roxburghe, an extremely keen golfer himself, and designed by Dave Thomas. It was created to appeal to all standards of golfer but make no mistake it is a tough course.

The clubhouse has been constructed to offer golfers every amenity, including a relaxing Spike Bar and restaurant, and enjoys views over the 1st and across the 12th and 13th. The hotel itself is magnificent, offering luxurious accommodation and first class food in a very special, intimate atmosphere. Hotel guests will have tee times arranged and can enjoy a host of other leisure facilities.

Back on the golf course, one would be hard pressed to find a more delightful hole than the par five 14th 'Viaduct' hole. Flanked by the river Teviot the hole is dominated by the Roxburghe Viaduct behind the green and is destined to become one of the most photographed holes in Scotland. As we played this hole we were distracted by the sight of a lone fisherman landing an 11lb salmon—a memorable sight indeed. A good tee shot will open up birdie opportunities for those who play a sensible shot to the front of the generous green.

Another water hole demanding nerve and commitment is the par four, 10th where careful club selection is crucial to avoid hitting the river behind the green whilst the long par four, 18th provides a testing finish to your round. Here, three deep bunkers guard the approach to the green. The course measures a giant total of 7111 yards from the championship tees and the last three holes seem extremely long (460, 398 and 437 yards respectively) and provide quite a challenge. It is at this point some may be glad of a buggy to carry them those extra final yards. Buggies and caddies can be hired from the clubhouse.

The greens are immaculate and Dave Thomas has made full use of the contours of the countryside to create rolling greens of generous proportions. The course record, set by Nick Faldo, is 67 and I can guarantee that anyone trying to better this will thoroughly enjoy the challenge.

The Roxburghe, Heiton, Kelso
Roxburghshire TD5 8JZ
www.roxburghe.net

Tel: (01573) 450333
Fax (01573) 450611

Professional   Gordon Niven

Green Fees   £40 per round/£60 per day
Restrictions   Handicap certificate

Directions
Travelling north on the A68 and follow signs to Kelso. The Roxburghe Hotel is just three miles south west of the border town and is clearly signpopsted.

THE ROXBURGHE, 14TH HOLE *Photograph courtesy of:* **The Roxburghe**

Southerness

Two of Britain's greatest (and least explored) links courses stare at one another across the Solway Firth—one is on the English side at Silloth and the other lies north of the border at Southerness. As close as they appear on the map, the only way of travelling from one to the other is by a fairly lengthy drive around the coast via Gretna Green. Before the war a bridge crossed the Solway, but before the war Southerness didn't have a golf course.

Situated 16 miles south of Dumfries, in an almost forgotten corner of southern Scotland, Southerness is the only true championship links in Great Britain to have been built since 1945. (Quite a contrast to Ireland where the likes of Tralee, The European, Connemara and the new links at Ballybunion and Ballyliffin have all been constructed within the last 20 years.)

So golf came to Southerness about 500 years after it came to St Andrews but one cannot help wondering why it took so long—after all, the much more remote golfing outposts of Dornoch and Machrihanish took root in the dim and distant past and a more natural and pleasanter site for the links it is hard to imagine. Sandy terrain, rampant heather, dense bracken and prickly golden gorse all present themselves in abundance here; as for that matter do firm, fast fairways and subtly contoured greens. If Mother Nature created the wonder of the setting then Mackenzie Ross (the architect of modern Turnberry) must be credited with the production of a genuine classic.

From the championship tees the links can be stretched to 7000 yards. Most mortal golfers will still find the 6566 yards, par 69 from the white tees (or 6105 yards from the yellow tees) an awesome challenge. The course's Standard Scratch is as high as 73; several of the par fours measure in excess of 400 yards (with prodigious carries to match) and two of the par threes are well over 200 yards long. A visit to Southerness is certainly recommended but pray that your long game is in fine fettle!

Before you set off, prior communication with the club's **Secretary, Mr I A Robin** is advisable. Visitors can book tee times beween 10.00—12.00 and 2.00—4.30 midweek and between 10.00—11.30 and 2.30—4.30 at weekends. Mr Robin can be contacted on **tel: (01387) 880677** or by **fax: (01387) 880644**. Written correspond-ence should be directed to **The Secretary, Southerness Golf Club, Southerness, Dumfries DG2 8AZ**. Golfing societies are equally welcome but organisers must contact the Secretary in advance. Southerness does not have a golf professional.

The green fees at Southerness compare favourably with those at many of Scotland's more celebrated championship courses. A full day's golf in 2000 costs £32 per day during the week and £45 at weekends. Junior visitors can play midweek for a green fee of just £10.

Southerness's situation is quiet rather than remote. Golfers from England, heading to or from Turnberry, Troon and Prestwick will likely drive through the town of Dumfries on the A75/A76 and Southerness is just half an hour's detour from Dumfries along the A710; a pretty drive via New Abbey. From the west the A710 approaches via Dalbeattie while Dumfries is linked to Glasgow by the A710 and the A74/M74, and to Edinburgh by the A702 and the A74.

Southerness opens with three dog-legged holes, the best of these being the 3rd, where there is a wonderfully natural green site in a wooded corner. After the short 4th with its impressively plateaued green the course doubles back on itself, then turns towards the sea. The views become more distracting but the challenge in no way diminishes. The 7th is the first of two long par threes and you aim your tee shot directly at the Solway but the best run of holes comes between the 10th, a par three surrounded by a sea of heather and the 13th, the longest par four on the card. The 12th is undoubtedly the best hole of all; here a well positioned drive (avoiding the deviously positioned fairway bunkers) is essential as the second shot must be fired towards a narrow green which sits on a plateau and looks down over a beautiful beach; deep bunkers guard the green front right and a pond will gleefully swallow any shot that strays left of centre.

The 15th is yet another outstanding par 3—expertly bunkered—while the toughest hole on the closing stretch is probably the 16th which is normally played into the teeth of the wind A four here may prove more elusive than at the par five 18th, where with the wind finally at our backs we have the chance of finding the green with two good blows.

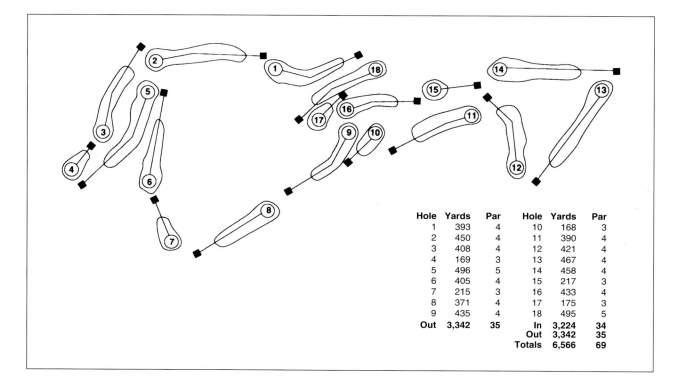

Hole	Yards	Par	Hole	Yards	Par
1	393	4	10	168	3
2	450	4	11	390	4
3	408	4	12	421	4
4	169	3	13	467	4
5	496	5	14	458	4
6	405	4	15	217	3
7	215	3	16	433	4
8	371	4	17	175	3
9	435	4	18	495	5
Out	**3,342**	**35**	**In**	**3,224**	**34**
			Out	3,342	35
			Totals	**6,566**	**69**

BORDERS

Duns G.C.
(01361) 882194
Hardens Road, Duns
(9) 5864 yards/***/D

Eyemouth G.C.
(018907) 50551
Gunsgreen House, Eyemouth
(9) 4608 yards/***/E

Galashiels G.C.
(01896) 753724
Ladhope Recreation Ground, Galashiels
(18) 5785 yards/***/D

Hawick G.C.
(01450) 372293
Vertish Hill, Hawick
(18) 5929 yards/**/E

Hirsel G.C.
(01890) 882678
Kelso Road, Coldstream
(18) 6092 yards/***/C

Innerleithen G.C.
(01896) 830951
Leithen Road, Innerleithen
(9) 5984 yards/***/D

Jedburgh G.C.
(01835) 863587
Dunion Road, Jedburgh
(9) 5522 yards/***/D

Kelso G.C.
(01573) 223009
Racecourse Road, Kelso
(18) 6066 yards/***/C

Lauder G.C.
(01578) 722526
Galashiels Road, Lauder
(9) 6002 yards/***/E

Melrose G.C.
(0189)6822855
Dingleton, Melrose
(9) 5579 yards/**/C

Minto G.C.
(01450) 870220
Minto Village, by Denholme, Hawick
(18) 5460 yards/**/D

Newcastleton G.C.
(013873) 75257
Holm Hill, Newcastleton
(9) 5748 yards/***/E

Peebles G.C.
(01721) 720197
Kirkland Street, Peebles
(18) 6160 yards/*/C/G/H

The Roxburghe G.C.
(01573) 450333
Kelso, Roxburghshire
(18) 7111 yards/***/F

St Boswells G.C.
(01835) 823527
St Boswells, Roxburghshire
(9) 2625 yards/***/D

Selkirk G.C.
(01750) 20621
The Hill, Selkirk
(9) 5620 yards/***/D

Torwoodlee G.C.
(01896) 752260
Edinburgh Road, Galashiels
(18) 6200 yards/***(Thurs)/D

West Linton G.C.
(01968) 660256
West Linton, Peebleshire
(18) 6132 yards/**/C

Woll G. C.
(01750) 32222
Woll House, Ashkirk, By Selkirk
(9) 6406 yards/***/F

DUMFRIES & GALLOWAY

Brighouse Bay
(01557) 870409
Borgue, Kirkcudbright
(9) 5426 yards/***/E

Castle Douglas G.C.
(01556) 502801
Abercromby Road, Castle Douglas
(9) 5408 yards/***(Thurs pm)/D

Colvend G.C.
(01556) 630398
Sandyhills, by Dalbeattie
(9) 2240 yards/***/D

Crichton Royal G.C.
(01387) 247894
Bankend Road, Dumfries
(9) 6168 yards/***/E

Dalbeattie G.C.
(01556) 611421
Dalbeattie
(9) 4200 yards/***/F

Dumfries & County G.C.
(01387) 253585
Edinburgh Road, Dumfries
(18) 5928 yards/**/B

Dumfries & Galloway G.C.
(01387) 253582
Laurieston Avenue, Dumfries
(18) 5803 yards/**/B

Gatehouse of Fleet G.C.
(01557) 814766
Gatehouse of Fleet
(9) 4796 yards/***/D

Gretna G.C.
(01461) 338464
Gretna
(9) 6430 yards/***/E

Hoddom Castle G.C.
(01576) 300251
Hoddom, Lockerbie
(9) 2274 yards/***/E

Kirkcudbright G.C.
(01557) 330314
Stirling Crescent, Kirkcudbright
(18) 5696 yards/***/D

Langholm G.C.
(013873) 381247
Langholm, Dumfriesshire
(9) 5744 yards/***/E

Lochmaben G.C.
(01387) 810552
Castlehillgate, Lochmaben
(18) 5357 yards/***/C

Lockerbie G.C.
(01576) 203363
Corrie Road, Lockerbie
(18) 5418 yards/***(Sat)/C

Moffat G.C.
(01683) 220020
Coatshill, Moffat
(18) 5218 yards/***(Wed pm)/C

New Galloway G.C.
(01644) 430455
Castle Douglas, Kircudbright
(9) 2503 yards/***/E

Newton Stewart G.C.
(01671) 402172
Kirroughtree Avenue, Minnigaff
(18) 5970 yards/***/C

Portpatrick (Dunskey) G.C.
(01776) 810273
Portpatrick, Stranraer
(18) 5644 yards/***/C/H

Powfoot G.C.
(01461) 700276
Cummertrees, Annan
(18) 6266 yards/**/CF

St Medan G.C.
(01988) 700358
Monreith, Port William
(9) 2277 yards/***/D

Sanquhar G.C.
(01659) 50577
Old Barr Road, Sanquhar
(9) 5594 yards/***/D

Southerness G.C.
(01387) 880677
Southerness, Dumfries
(18) 6566 yards/***/B

Stranraer G.C.
(01776) 703539
Crechmore, Stranraer
(18) 6300 yards/***/C

Thornhill G.C.
(01848) 331779
Blacknest, Thornhill
(18) 6011 yards/***/B

Wigtown and Bladnoch G.C.
(01988) 403354
Lightlands Avenue, Wigtown
(9) 2732 yards/***/E

Wigtownshire County G.C.
(01581) 300420
Mains of Park, Glenluce
(18) 5847 yards/***/C

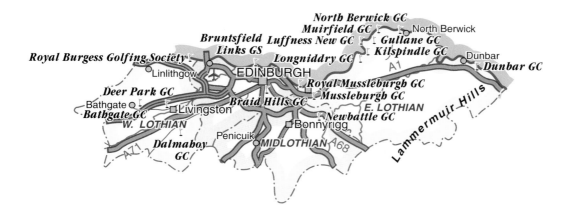

Edinburgh and the Lothians Choice Golf

'Hard by in the fields called the links, the citizens of Edinburgh divert themselves at a game called golf, in which they use a curious kind of bat tipt with horn and a small elastic ball of leather stuffed with feathers rather less than tennis balls, but out of a much harder consistency and this they strike with such force and dexterity that it will fly to an incredible distance.'

When Tobias Smollett wrote these words in 1771 golf had already been played in the 'fields' around Edinburgh for at least three hundred years. The seemingly harmless pastime wasn't always popular with the authorities. In 1593 the Town Council of Edinburgh deplored the fact that a great number of its inhabitants chose to spend the Sabbath in the town of Leith where 'in tyme of sermons' many were 'sene in the streets, drynking in taverns, or otherwise at Golf'. Shame on them! Today the east coast of Scotland is famous the world over, not only because it was here that it all began, but also because its many courses remain among the very finest the game has to offer. In a 30 mile coastal stretch between the courses of **Royal Burgess** and **Dunbar** lie the likes of **Muirfield**, **Gullane**, **North Berwick**, **Luffness New** and **Longniddry**—truly a magnificent seven—and there are many others.

Edinburgh

Visitors to the beautiful city of Edinburgh, the so called 'Athens of the North', should have little trouble getting a game. There are numerous first class courses in and around the capital; regrettably we only have space to mention a handful of the best. To the west of the city lie a particularly historic pair—**Bruntsfield Links** and **Royal Burgess**: between them they have witnessed nearly 500 years of golfing history. The latter club in fact claims to be the world's oldest. (A claim hotly disputed I might add by Muirfield's 'Honourable Company'!) These more prestigious courses are of course more difficult to play, but with advance preparation it is possible; restaurants in both clubhouses are of an extremely high standard. Another Edinburgh gem not to be missed is **Braid Hills**; in fact there are two fine public courses here, just south of the city. The **Dalmahoy** Hotel Golf and Country Club situated to the south west of the city nestles at the base of the Pentland Hills and has two excellent 18 hole courses. Dalmahoy, like Muirfield and Dunbar, is featured ahead. Towards the east side of Edinburgh is Musselburgh. The old Open championship links is not what it was, alas, although you can still play the nine holes adjacent to Musselburgh racecourse for history's sake. However, perhaps the best place for a game

THE 14TH WEST LINKS, NORTH BERWICK *Photograph courtesy of:* **David J. Whyte**

is at **Royal Musselburgh**, a beautiful parkland course and a little further out of the city the course at **Newbattle** can also be highly recommended.

Spending a few days in Edinburgh is a real treat whether one is a golfer or not. The city's leading hotels include the magnificent Balmoral Hotel (0131) 556 2414, and the Caledonian Hotel (0131) 459 9988. The latter's Pompadour Restaurant is quite superb. Among the many other hotels, the Sheraton Grand (0131) 229 9131 is almost on a par with the city's best while the George (0131) 225 1251 is a most impressive edifice and is a great favourite for post-rugby celebrations. Johnstounburn House (01875) 833696 at nearby Humbie offers an out of town alternative as does the Dalmahoy Hotel (0131) 333 1845 at Kirknewton—golfcourse, restaurants and very much more besides.

Edinburgh is as well blessed with restaurants as it is with hotels. These are some of the many worth considering: The Atrium (0131) 228 8882 and L'Auberge (0131) 556 5888 will delight, whilst the Kalpna (0131) 667 9890 is a first class Indian restaurant. In Leith a noted restaurant is Skippers (0131) 554 1018. Finally, Channings (0131) 315 2226 is a sophisticated and elegant hotel with excellent facilities and a country house feel.

The courses of West Lothian are not as well known as their eastern counterparts. However, two are particularly worth considering, **Bathgate**, a fine moorland course and the **Deer Park** Golf and Country Club at Livingston, both lie within easy access of Edinburgh.

East of Edinburgh: Links Golf

Travellers wishing to explore the delights of the East Coast should aim to pick up the A198 at Prestonpans near Musselburgh. Before it reaches Longniddry the road passes through Seton, where Mary Queen of Scots is known to have sharpened up her golf swing more than 400 years ago. At 13 miles east of Edinburgh, **Longniddry** ought not to be considered as merely a stopping place en route to **Muirfield**. It is a superb course, part links part parkland, with every hole having a view

of the sea. **Kilspindie** Golf Club is also worth a little detour while **Luffness New** and the three neighbouring courses of **Gullane** lie only a short distance further along the coast. Each is outstanding in its way, though if you only have time to play two then Luffness New and Gullane Number One are probably the pick—although the former can be difficult to get on! The panoramic view from the top of Gullane Hill on the latter's 7th hole is one of the most famous in golf. The West Links at **North Berwick** has a wealth of charm and tradition; it is one of the most natural courses one is likely to come across and several blind shots must be encountered. Two of its holes, the 14th 'Perfection' and the 15th 'Redan' have been imitated by golf architects all over the world. As at **Dunbar**, there are some splendid views across to Bass Rock.

Time for a 19th hole. Hotels are numerous, as indeed are good restaurants. In Gullane, Greywalls (01620) 842144 has gained an enviable reputation and is literally on the doorstep of Muirfield and the three links of Gullane. La Potiniere (01620) 843214 is a restaurant to savour when in these parts—eating on a par with the outstanding golf. Gullane is also resplendent with guest houses; the Golf Tavern (01620) 843259 is but one recommended illustration. In Aberlady the Kilspindie House Hotel (01875) 870682 is welcoming, as is clearly the Open Arms (01620) 850241 in the pretty village of Dirleton, an excellent restaurant with rooms. The Marine Hotel (01620) 892406 is convenient for North Berwick while other well priced alternatives include the Mallard (01620) 843228 and the Golf Hotel (01620) 892202. Towards Dunbar, in the town itself the Bayswell (01368) 862225 is a comfortable hotel, while the Courtyard (01368) 864169 at Woodush Brae offers award-winning cuisine. South of Dunbar, the Craw Inn (018907) 61253 at Auchencraw is recommended for its fish. Many super establishments are to be found a little inland. Note especially the Tweedale Arms (01620) 810240 at Gifford. Travelling back westwards, 15th century Borthwick Castle (01875) 820514 at Gorebridge is another first class establishment. For the touring golfer in Scotland, a country cottage can serve as an ideal base and both Blakes Country Cottages (01603) 783227 and Mackays (0131) 225 3539 offer a range of self-catering accommodation.

MUIRFIELD Photograph courtesy of: **Scottish Tourist Board**

Muirfield

Muirfield is of course much more than one of the world's greatest golf links, it is also the home of the world's oldest golf club. The Honourable Company of Edinburgh Golfers are the direct descendants of the Gentlemen Golfers who played at Leith Links from at least as early as the 15th century. On 7th March 1744 several 'Gentlemen of Honour, skilful in the ancient and healthful exercise of Golf', petitioned the city fathers of Edinburgh to provide a silver club to be played for annually on the links at Leith. The winner of this competition became Captain of Golf and the club was paraded through the city. In 1744 the Edinburgh Golfers formulated the game's first code of rules—The Thirteen Articles—which were adopted almost word for word ten years later by the Royal and Ancient Club at St Andrews.

The company played over the five holes at Leith for almost a hundred years before overcrowding forced the decision to move to the nine hole course at Musselburgh, to the east of the city. Long before they had left Leith the members had begun to dine and play in the famous red uniform; failure to wear this usually resulted in a fine. A minute from the 1830s records how one member was fined two tappit hens for playing golf without his red coat! The Open Championship first came to Musselburgh in 1874 and was held there every third year until 1889. Meanwhile Musselburgh, like Leith, had become terribly crowded and the company decided that the time had come for a second move. Again, they looked to the east and almost twenty miles from Edinburgh, under the lee of Gullane Hill, they discovered Muirfield.

The course was initially designed by 'Old' Tom Morris and opened for play on 3rd May 1891. In its early years the course received much criticism. One professional described it as 'nothing but an auld watter meddie' but it appears that this had more to do with jealousy, because when the Honourable Company left Musselburgh it took the Open Championship with it. It was held at Muirfield in 1892 and never again returned to Musselburgh. Following the success of the 1892 Championship, Muirfield's reputation grew rapidly. In the 1920s Harry Colt and Tom Simpson made substantial revisions to the links and today Muirfield is widely considered to be the fairest, if not the finest test in golf.

Visitors wishing to play at Muirfield must make prior arrangements with the **Secretary, Group Captain J A Prideaux**, who may be contacted on **tel: (01620) 842123** and by **fax: (01620) 842977.**

For gentlemen golfers there is a requirement that they belong to a recognised golf club and carry a handicap of 18 or less, while for lady golfers (who may only play if accompanied by a gentleman player) the handicap limit is 24. The days on which visitors are welcome are Tuesdays and Thursdays. It should also be noted that by tradition foursome matches are strongly favoured at Muirfield and fourball games will only be permitted in the mornings. All written correspondence should be addressed to **The Secretary, The Honourable Company of Edinburgh Golfers, Muirfield, Gullane, East Lothian, EH31 2EG**. The green fees for 2000 are set at £80 for a single round, with £105 entitling the visitor to a full day's golf.

Travelling to Muirfield (or Gullane) will often be by way of Edinburgh. Gullane is connected to the capital city by the A198. Northbound travellers can avoid Edinburgh by approaching on the A1 which runs to Dunbar to the east of Gullane. From Dunbar the A198 can be picked up. Those coming from the north and west of Scotland will need to travel via Edinburgh. The M8 links Glasgow to Edinburgh, while the M9 should be taken from Stirling and the M90 from Perth.

One of the unique features of Muirfield (or at least unique in terms of a Scottish championship links) is its layout of two separate loops, an outer and an inner. This ensures that the golfer will not have to play several successive holes into or against the same wind direction. Although occasionally quite undulating, the course has only one blind shot (the drive at the 11th) and this contributes much to Muirfield's fairness tag. From the championship tees the links stretch to 6941 yards, and with the often prodigiously thick rough and deep, cavernous bunkers, it can be a very severe test of golf. From the medal tees Muirfield still measures a fairly lengthy 6601 yards, par 70.

Since 1892 the Open Championship has been played at Muirfield on 14 occasions. Before the last war winners included Harry Vardon, James Braid and Walter Hagen. The first Open to be held at Muirfield after the war was in 1948, when Henry Cotton won his third title. Gary Player won in 1959 and Jack Nicklaus in 1966. Perhaps the most dramatic Open in Muirfield's history came in 1972 when Lee Trevino holed his famous chip shot from the edge of the 17th green and in the process stole the title from Tony Jacklin. In recent times British fortunes have revived dramatically, however, with Nick Faldo winning in 1987 and again in 1992, when he so memorably produced 'the best four holes of my life' to deny the unfortunate John Cook. One wonders what the 21st century has in store. The Open is to return to Muirfield in 2002.

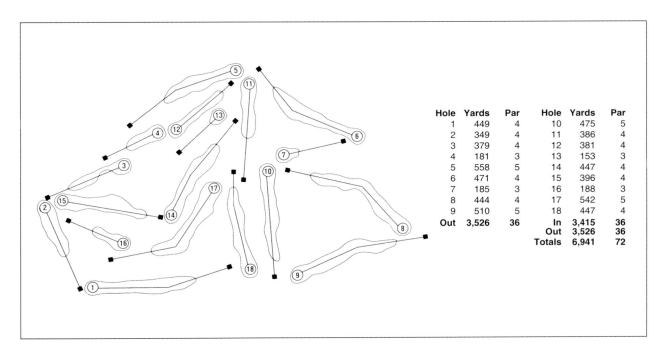

Hole	Yards	Par		Hole	Yards	Par
1	449	4		10	475	5
2	349	4		11	386	4
3	379	4		12	381	4
4	181	3		13	153	3
5	558	5		14	447	4
6	471	4		15	396	4
7	185	3		16	188	3
8	444	4		17	542	5
9	510	5		18	447	4
Out	**3,526**	**36**		**In**	**3,415**	**36**
				Out	**3,526**	**36**
				Totals	**6,941**	**72**

North Berwick

The golfer who journeys to Ayrshire essentially to inspect the links at Turnberry and Troon, but discovers that he actually prefers Prestwick, is the same player who visits Muirfield (and, yes, enjoys the challenge) but falls in love with nearby North Berwick.

Prestwick charms. North Berwick charms. Both bristle with character. If the Open Championship had begun on the East instead of the West coast of Scotland in the middle of the last century, Musselburgh would doubtless have been the birthplace (it was the then home of the Honourable Company) but the West Links at North Berwick would have made a much better venue.

With the exception of a few staunch traditionalists—Ben Crenshaw immediately springs to mind—today's champion golfers would regard North Berwick as too unpredictable: they abhor any degree of blindness on a golf course and expect a good shot always to be rewarded with a perfect level lie. The fact of the matter is that courses like North Berwick and Prestwick are too intricate for their tastes and many top players simply do not possess the varied armoury of shot-making skills necessary to tame a classic 'old fashioned' links. Besides, where is their spirit of adventure?!

North Berwick Golf Club was founded in 1832 although golf had already been played over the site of the present links for centuries. Like the Old Course at St Andrews, the West Links starts and finishes in town—and, like St Andrews, North Berwick is an attractive seaside town that lives and breathes golf. It is claimed that the ghost of Old Tom Morris stalks the fairways of the Old Course. At North Berwick it is the spirit of Ben Sayers, and not even he can master the contours of the legendary 16th green.

North Berwick's setting is one of the most captivating in golf. The first three holes run adjacent to the shore, as, broadly speaking, do the 10th to the 14th on the inward nine—the course being laid out in the shape of a figure of eight. The Forth Estuary is on the golfer's right side as he plays the opening holes. Bass Rock, a miniature Ailsa Craig, and a host of rocky islets command attention, as does a great sweep of sandy beach.

Visitors have always been made extremely welcome at North Berwick. Bookings can be made in advance by phoning the **Golf**

Office on **tel: (01620) 892135** or by **fax: 01620 893274**. The club's full address is **North Berwick Golf Club, New Clubhouse, Beach Road, North Berwick EH39 4BB**. The **Course Manager** is **David Huish**, a former Captain of the British PGA who has been attached to the club since 1967. His son **Martyn Huish** is the resident **Teaching Professional**. Finally, it is worth noting that the Starter may require visitors to produce proof of a current handicap.

Green fees in 2000 are £36 per round, £54 per day during the week, £54 per round, £72 per day at weekends.

The character and eccentricities of North Berwick are apparent from the outset. The opening tee shot is invariably played with a fairway wood or long iron in order to lay up short of a deep gully. This is followed by a short but semi-blind second to a green that occupies a craggy hilltop and slopes sharply towards the sea. The drive at the 2nd must flirt with the shore—a spectacular hole this is—and at the 3rd the approach is hit over an ancient stone wall that traverses the fairway. And so it continues. Along with the 2nd, the finest holes on the outward nine are probably the two par threes, the 4th and 6th, and the par five 9th.

Turning for home, a marvellous vista unfolds from the elevated back tee at the short 10th. Next is a curving par five that hugs the base of some formidable dunes. The 12th is a teasing, bite-off-as-much-as-you-dare dog-leg, and then comes a truly classic sequence of holes. The 13th features another approach over a stone wall but a far more precise second (not to mention an intelligently positioned drive) is required on this occasion to find a green squashed between the wall and the dunes. The 14th is called 'Perfection'—a somewhat controversial name for a blind hole! The real perfection, however, relates to the setting of the green which is perched right on the edge of the links, seemingly on the verge of slipping into the sea. And then you confront the par three 'Redan' and a green complex that is surely the most imitated in golf. Here at North Berwick is the original prototype. If the 'Redan' doesn't defeat you, the incredible slopes of the 16th green probably will. A very difficult 17th and a benign 18th bring you back to reality.

So enjoy North Berwick. Remember to bring that armoury of shot-making skills with you—and leave your lob wedge behind!

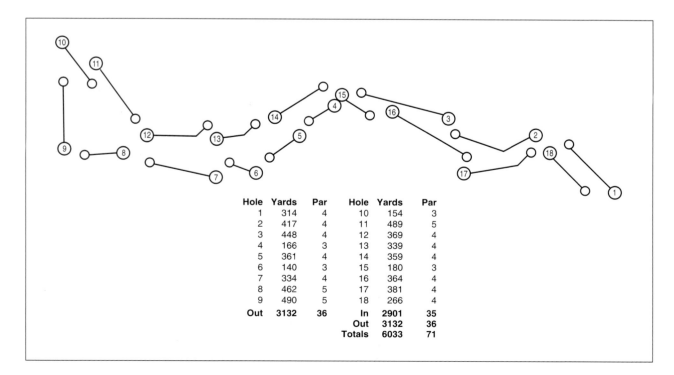

Hole	Yards	Par	Hole	Yards	Par
1	314	4	10	154	3
2	417	4	11	489	5
3	448	4	12	369	4
4	166	3	13	339	4
5	361	4	14	359	4
6	140	3	15	180	3
7	334	4	16	364	4
8	462	5	17	381	4
9	490	5	18	266	4
Out	**3132**	**36**	**In**	**2901**	**35**
			Out	**3132**	**36**
			Totals	**6033**	**71**

Dalmahoy

Dalmahoy, near Edinburgh has a lot in common with Moor Park, near London. Apart from being an easy drive from its country's capital (although it is much easier to escape from central Edinburgh than central London) both have two parkland courses—the one being much more testing than the other; both have staged televised professional tournaments over their championship course and most immediately striking of all is that the courses of Dalmahoy and Moor Park are each overlooked by magnificent mansion houses which act as extraordinarily elegant 19th holes.

Dalmahoy's mansion is a three storey Georgian building, originally designed for the Earl of Morton in 1735. To wander around its interior is an experience itself; many magnificent paintings adorn the walls and a wonderful sense of wellbeing pervades the building. The mansion has in fact been the focal point of a considerable amount of activity in recent times. The Georgian building has been sympathetically restored and is now the centrepiece of a 215 bedroomed luxury hotel and country club. The whole development plan comprised an investment of some £14 million. Lord knows what the Earl of Morton would have thought of it all!

Golf has been played at Dalmahoy since the 1920s, five times Open Champion James Braid designing both courses, the championship East and the West, in 1927. From the day the very first ball was struck they have been held in extremely high esteem. The courses exemplify all that is best in parkland golf and offer a very real contrast to the nearby challenges of Muirfield, North Berwick and Dunbar. Again, like Moor Park, Dalmahoy's fairways are quite undulating and provide some far-reaching views; Edinburgh Castle sits proudly on the horizon.

Measuring 6677 yards, par 72, the East Course is considerably longer than the West at 5185 yards, par 68. Both however are maintained in the same superb condition all year round. The course

record was set in the final round of the 1981 Tournament Players Championships when Brian Barnes, cheered on by a partisan crowd stormed around the course in an unbelievable 62 strokes and eventually went on to win in a play off against Brian Waites. In 1992 Dalmahoy played host to the Solheim Cup and is now indelibly linked with that memorable week in October when Catrin Nilsmark holed a momentous putt on the 16th hole to give the European Ladies team their only victory to date over the USA.

In more recent times the Championship East Course has hosted four Scottish Region PGA Championships, two ladies Scottish Opens and in 1998 the PGA Scottish Seniors Open Championship, confirming Dalmahoy as a superb tournament venue and well worth a visit.

Marriott Dalmahoy Hotel, Golf and Country Club, Kirknewton, Midlothian, EH27 8EB
www.marriotthotels.com

Director of Golf	Brian Anderson (0131) 335 8010
Green Fees	East WD £60, WE £75/round
	West WD £35, WE £45/round
Restrictions	10 day advance bookings (0131) 333 1845; weekend golf limited.

Directions
The club is 7 miles south west of Edinburgh off the A71 Kilmarnock road. Travelling from Glasgow leave the M8 at junction 3, using the A599 to link with the A71.

Dunbar

In common with much of eastern Scotland it isn't entirely clear when golf was first played at Dunbar. Whilst the Dunbar Golf Club was founded in 1856 following a meeting in the Town Hall, the Dunbar Golfing Society had been instituted in 1794. Furthermore, records suggest that some cruder form of golf had been played in the area at least as early as the beginning of the 17th century. In 1616 two men of the parish of Tyninghame were censured by the Kirk Session for 'playing at ye nyne holis' on the Lord's Day and in 1640 an Assistant Minister of Dunbar was disgraced 'for playing at gouff'. Times, as they say, change and 350 years later 'gouff' is still played at Dunbar, although no one is likely to be censured or disgraced for doing so and there are now 18 splendid holes.

Dunbar is very much a natural links, laid out on a fairly narrow tract of land closely following the contours of the shoreline. It is bounded by a stone wall which runs the full length of the course. While Dunbar is by no means the longest of Scottish links, when the winds blow it can prove to be one of the most difficult—this may have something to do with the fact that there is an 'out of bounds' on the 3rd, 4th, 5th, 6th, 7th, 8th, 9th, 16th, 17th and 18th holes, and the beach can come in to play on the 4th, 5th, 6th, 7th, 12th, 14th, 15th, 16th and 17th—straight hitting would appear to be called for!

Dunbar is without doubt one of the east coast's most attractive links with some splendid views out across the sea towards Bass Rock. The first three holes are played fairly close to the clubhouse, the opening two being relatively tame par fives and the 3rd a spectacular short hole played from an elevated tee. The 4th then takes you alongside the beach as the course begins to move away from the clubhouse. Perhaps the most testing holes occur around the turn, the 9th to the 12th, and there is no let-up either on the closing stretch with the beach readily receiving the mildest of slices. The 18th can also be a card-wrecker with the stone wall out of bounds running the

entire length of the fairway to the right.

All the major Scottish Championships have been played at Dunbar, including the Scottish Amateur, Scottish Boys and Scottish Professional Championships. The club has also staged the British Boys Championship and in 2002 Dunbar will be an Open Qualifying Course when the championship returns to Muirfield.

Dunbar's 19th is a comfortable and informal building with views of the Firth of Forth and across much of the course. And just one final thought as you relax in the clubhouse—one of the regulations of the Dunbar Golfing Society dated 1794 reads as follows: 'When the expense of each member for dinner amounts to two shillings and sixpence, the club shall be dissolved'. Times, as they say, most certainly change!

The Dunbar Golf Club, East Links, Dunbar, East Lothian, EH42 1LL

Sec/Manager	Liz Thom (01368) 862317
Professional	Jacky Montgomery (01368) 862086
Caterer	(01368) 862317
Green Fees	WD £28/round; £35/day
	WE £35/round; £45/day
Restrictions	No visitors on Thursdays

Directions
Dunbar is on the A1 between Berwick-upon-Tweed and Edinburgh. From the Borders take a combination of the A68 and A6137 to Haddington, there picking up the A1.

Aberlady G.C.
(01875) 870374
Aberlady, East Lothian
(18) 5410 yards/***/F

Baberton G.C.
(0131) 453 4911
Baberton Avenue, Edinburgh
(18) 6098 yards/***/C/H

Balbardie Park G.C.
(01506) 634561
Balbardie Park, Bathgate
(9) 1237 yards/***/E

Bass Rock G.C.
(01620) 822082
Harperdean, Haddington
(18) 6420 yards/***/B-A

Bathgate G.C.
(01506) 630505
Edinburgh Road, Bathgate
(18) 6362 yards/***/D

Braid Hills G.C.
(0131) 447 6666
Braid Hill Road,Edinburgh
(18) 5239 yards/***/E
(18) 4832 yards/***/E

Braids United G.C.
(0131) 452 9408
Braid Hills Approach, Edinburgh
(18) 5239 yards/***/E
(18) 4832 yards/***/E

Broomieknowe G.C.
(0131) 663 9317
Golf Course Road, Bonnyrigg, Midlothian
(18) 6046 yards/**/C

Bruntsfield Links G.C.
(0131) 336 1479
Barton Avenue, Davidsons Mains
(18) 6407 yards/**/F/H

Carrick Knowe G.C.
(0131) 337 1096
Glendevon Park, Edinburgh
(18) 6299 yards/***/E

Carrickvale G.C.
(0131) 337 1096
Glendevon Park, Edinburgh
(18) 6299 yards/***/F/H

Castle Park G.C.
(01620) 810733
Gifford, Haddington
(9) 5810 yards/***/D

Craigentinny G.C.
(0131) 554 7501
Craigentinny Avenue, Edinburgh
(18) 5418 yards/***/E

Craigmillar Park G.C.
(0131) 667 0047
Observatory Road, Edinburgh
(18) 5851 yards/**/B/H or L

Marriott Dalmahoy Hotel G. & C.C.
(0131) 333 1845
Dalmahoy, Kirknewton, Midlothian
(18) 6667 yards/**/B-A/G
(18) 5185 yards/**/B-A/G

Deer Park G.C.
(01506) 438843
Carmondean, Livingston
(18) 6636 yards/***/D

Dirleton Castle G.C.
(01620) 843496
Gullane, East Lothian
(18) 6466 yards/**/F
(18) 6244 yards/***/F
(18) 5166 yards/***/F

Duddingston G.C.
(0131) 661 7688
Duddingston Road, Edinburgh
(18) 6420 yards/**/B/H

Dunbar G.C.
(01368)1416
East Links, Dunbar
(18) 6426 yards/***/B

Dundas Park G.C.
(0131) 331 1416
Loch Road, South Queensferry
(9) 6800 yards/***/E/M/H

Gifford G.C.
(01620) 810591
Edinburgh Road, Gifford
(9) 6243 yards/**/E

Glen G.C.
(01620) 892221
Tantallon Terrace, North Berwick
(18) 6098 yards/***/D

Glencorse G.C.
(01968) 677177
Milton Bridge, Penicuik, Midlothian
(18) 5217 yards/***/C-B

Greenburn G.C.
(01501) 770292
Fauldhouse, West Lothian
(18) 6210 yards/**/E/H

Gullane G.C.
(01620) 842255
Gullane, East Lothian
(18) 6466 yards/**/F
(18) 6244 yards/***/F
(18) 5166 yards/***/F

Haddington G.C.
(01620) 8233627
Amisfield Park, Haddington,
(18) 6280 yards/**(pm)/D

Harburn G.C.
(01506) 871256
West Calder, West Lothian
(18) 5843 yards/***/D

Muirfield G.C.
(01620) 842123
Muirfield, Gullane, East Lothian
(18) 6601 yards/(Tues, Thurs only)/
A/H (18)/M/L

Kilspindie G.C.
(018751) 870358
Aberlady, East Lothian
(18) 5410 yards/***/F

Kingsknowe G.C.
(0131) 441 1145
Lanark Road, Edinburgh
(18) 5979 yards/***/C

Liberton G.C.
(0131) 664 3009
Gilmerton Road, Edinburgh
(18) 4882 yards/**/C

Linlithgow G.C.
(01506) 842585
Braehead, Linlithgow, West Lothian
(18) 5858 yards/***(Wed/Sat)/D

Longniddry G.C.
(01875) 852141
Links Road, Longniddry, East Lothian
(18) 6210 yards/**/B-A/H

Lothianburn G.C.
(0131) 445 2206
Biggar Road, Fairmilehead
(18) 5750 yards/**/D

Luffness New G.C.
(01620) 843336
Aberlady, East Lothian
(18) 6122 yards/**/B

Merchants of Edinburgh G.C.
(0131) 447 1219
Craighill Gardens, Edinburgh
(18) 4889 yards/**/C

Mortonhall G.C.
(0131) 447 6974
Braid Road, Edinburgh
(18) 6557 yards/***/B/H

Murrayfield G.C.
(0131) 337 3478
Murrayfield Road, Edinburgh
(18) 5725 yards/**/B/H

Musselburgh G.C.
(0131) 665 2005
Monktonhall, Musselburgh
(18) 6623 yards/***/D

Musselburgh Links G.C.
(0131) 665 5483
Balcarres Road, Musselburgh
(9) 2700 yards/***/E

Musselburgh Old Course G.C.
(0131) 665 6981
Millhill, Musselburgh
(9) 5380 yards/***/F

Newbattle G.C.
(0131) 663 2123
Abbey Road, Dalkeith, Midlothian
(18) 6025 yards/**/D

Niddry Castle & G.C.
(01506) 891097
Castle Road, Winchurch
(9) 5476 yards/***/E

North Berwick G.C.
(01620) 892135
Beach Road, North Berwick
(18) 6420 yards/***/B-A

Polkemmet G.C.
(01501) 743905
Whitburn, Bathgate
(9) 2967 yards/***/E

Portobello G.C.
(0131) 669 4361
Stanley Road, Portobello, Edinburgh
(9) 2419 yards/**/C

Prestonfield G.C.
(0131) 667 1273
6 Prestonfield Road North, Edinburgh
(18) 6178 yards/**(Sat, Sun pm)/B-A

Pumpherston G.C.
(01506) 432869
Drumshoreland Road, Livingston
(9) 5434 yards/*/E/G

Ratho Park G.C.
(0131) 333 2566
Ratho, Newbridge, Midlothian
(18) 5900 yards/***/B-A

Ravelston G.C.
(0131) 315 2486
24 Ravelston Dykes Road, Edinburgh
(9) 5200 yards/*/C/G

Royal Burgess G.S.
(0131) 339 2075
Whitehouse Road, Edinburgh
(18) 6494 yards/**/F/L/H

Royal Musselburgh G.C.
(01875) 810276
Prestongrange House, Prestonpans,
(18) 6237 yards/**/B/H

Silverknowes G.C.
(0131) 336 3843
Silverknowes, Parkway, Edinburgh
(18) 6210 yards/***/E

Swanston G.C.
(0131) 445 2239
Swanston Road, Edinburgh
(18) 5024 yards/**/D/H

Tantallom G.C.
(01620) 892114
Westgate, North Berwick
(18) 6420 yards/***/B-A

Torphin Hill G.C.
(0131) 441 1100
Torphin Road, Colinton, Edinburgh
(18) 5024 yards/***/D

Turnhouse G.C.
(0131) 339 1014
Turnhouse Road, Edinburgh
(18) 6171 yards/**/F/G

Uphall G.C.
(01506) 856404
Uphall, West Lothian
(18) 5600 yards/***/D

West Lothian G.C.
(01506) 826030
Airngarth Hill, Linlithgow, West Lothian
(18) 6578 yards/**/D

Whitekirk G.C.
(01620) 870300
Whitekirk Mains, Dunbar
(18) 6420 yards/***/D

Winterfield G.C.
(01368)862280
St Margarets, North Road, Dunbar
(18) 5155 yards/***/F

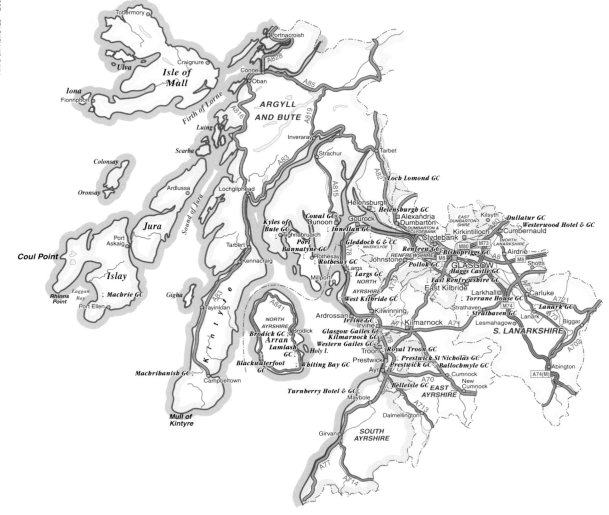

Western Scotland Choice Golf

Ayrshire

An ancient golfing rhyme from the land of Burns runs:
'Troon and Prestwick, old and classy,
Bogside, Dundonald, Glasgow Gailes, Barassie,
Prestwick St Nicholas, Western Gailes,
St Cuthbert, Portland—memory fails,
Troon Municipal (three links there)
Prestwick Municipal, Irvine, Ayr,
They faced the list with delighted smiles -
Sixteen courses within ten miles'.

Even without Turnberry, that 'little corner of heaven on earth', some 15 miles south of Ayr, an extraordinarily impressive list, and little wonder that this small region of Scotland's coast has become nothing short of a Mecca for golfers the world over.

Prestwick, **Troon** and **Turnberry** have of course each staged the Open Championship. Prestwick was the birthplace of the event back in 1860 and is probably the most classic test of traditional links golf—'penal' the American architects would describe it, on account of the many blind shots. The Open is no longer held at Prestwick but the history of the place is overwhelming and quite magnetic. Troon and Turnberry are both firmly on the 'Open' rota. It was last played over the latter's Ailsa course in 1994 (Nick Price's great victory) and was last held at Troon in 1997, when it was won by Justin Leonard. Understandably the golfer making a pilgrimage to the Ayrshire coast will be drawn towards this famous trio. However, if time isn't of the essence, it would be bordering on a disgrace not to sample as many of the nearby delights as possible. As the old rhyme relates, within short distance of one another lie a number of outstanding courses, at any of which it may be easier to arrange a game.

While not all roads lead to Ayr, as the largest town on the coast, it's probably as good a starting point as any. Here we find a belle—**Belleisle** to be precise and a most attractive parkland course. Considered by many to be the finest public course outside of St Andrews and Carnoustie and, being somewhat sheltered, it's an admirable retreat from the more windswept links nearby. Furthermore as a municipal course the green fees are relatively cheap.

Just north of Ayr lie a series of outstanding links courses, all within a mile or two of one another. **Western Gailes**, Prestwick and Troon are featured on later pages (as is Turnberry) but also in this area one finds first class courses at **Prestwick St Nicholas**, **Barassie**, **Glasgow** (**Gailes**) and **Irvine** (also known somewhat unfortunately as **Bogside**). Each warmly welcomes visitors and, although they are less busy than the more famous courses, prior telephoning is strongly recommended, especially during the peak summer months. Weekdays are inevitably the best times for a visit.

Just as there is a proliferation of golf courses on the Ayrshire coast, so the region is inundated with all manner of hotels, guesthouses, pubs and restaurants. A few thoughts follow. To start at a pinnacle, undoubtedly one of the best hotels in Britain is the Turnberry Hotel (01655) 331000, the first ever purpose-built hotel and golf course. Both hotel and restaurant are truly outstanding. For beautiful views over the Isle of Arran, we also recommend nearby Malin Court (01655) 331457. If staying in this area, Culzean Castle (open between April and October) is well worth a visit and in nearby **Girvan** where there is an underrated municipal course, an excellent place for liquid refreshment is the King's Arms (01465) 713322. Golfers may also find the nearby Bardrochat country house hotel (01465) 881232 ideal accommodation—it is particularly good for small groups. If you've food on your mind we suggest you forget about calories and go for a slap-up meal in Splinters! (01465) 713481.

Returning northwards, perhaps the most popular, and certainly the most convenient hotel for Royal Troon is the Marine Highland (01292) 314444. It proudly overlooks the Old Course Championship links and boasts excellent leisure facilities. Two other hotels in Troon are Piersland House (01292) 314747 and the Ardneil (01292) 311611, a less stylish but thoroughly welcoming establishment. Highgrove House (01292) 312511 in nearby Loans provides excellent cuisine and agreeable accommodation. A similar commendation is given to Lochgreen House (01292) 313343 in Southwood two miles south of Troon. Two hotels in Ayr to note are Fairfield House (01292) 267461 and the Pickwick (01292) 260111 while close by in Alloway is the excellent Northpark House (01292) 442336 and in Maybole, the Ladyburn Hotel (01655) 740585 is good value. On to Prestwick, which if you've arrived by plane may well be your first port of call. Here, the Carlton Toby (01292) 476811 and the Parkstone (01292) 477286 stand out from the crowd and there are numerous B&Bs and small hotels. The Fairways Hotel (01292) 470396 and North Beach Hotel (01292) 479069 are always popular retreats. Kilmarnock is now a busy industrial centre yet it was here that Robbie Burns' first collection of poems was published. Just to the north of the town at Irvine is the Thistle Irvine (01294) 274272 which, in keeping with its name, is most welcoming. If an escape to the countryside is sought then a trip to Stewarton is highly recommended. Kilwinning is a final recommendation for this area, the Montgreenan Mansion House

(01294) 557733 is superbly situated with excellent facilities including some practice holes to warm up on before sallying forth.

To the north of the famous golfing stretch there is plenty of less testing golf to be found. This may well be necessary in order to restore battered pride! **West Kilbride** (another links type) and **Largs** (a well wooded parkland course) should suit admirably. Both also offer some magnificent views across to Argyll and the Isle of Arran where there are no fewer than seven golf courses, and an ideal base to play them from is the Auchrannie Country House Hotel (01770) 302234 and the excellent Kilmichael Country House (01770) 302219. Also roughly due east of Ayr, close to the A76 there is a very good course at **Ballochmyle**.

Lanarkshire

Before heading for Glasgow a quick mention for three courses lying due south of the city: **Torrance House, Lanark** and **Strathaven**. All are very easily reached by way of the A7, although Strathaven is quite a bit of a way from the city and by the time you arrive at the course you'll have climbed 700 feet above sea level. But a lovely setting and a most convenient hotel, the Strathaven (01357) 521778 await.

Glasgow

Glasgow is Britain's third largest city after London and Birmingham and, being Scottish to boot, not surprisingly has a huge number of golf courses. Indeed some wag once said of Glasgow that there was a pub in every street with a golf club around each corner. One interesting statistic is that between 1880 and 1910 more than

TURNBERRY *Photograph courtesy of:* **The Turnberry Hotel**

THE 10TH GLENCRUITTEN GOLF CLUB *Photograph courtesy of:* **David J Whyte, The Golf Photo Library**

80 golf courses were built in the Greater Glasgow area—so much for today's golf boom! Unfortunately the problem for the golfing stranger to Glasgow is that many of the city's leading clubs permit visitors to play only if accompanied by a member. Among the city's more traditional courses—and where arranging a game can be difficult—are **Haggs Castle** and **Pollok**. Other suggestions include **Renfrew** and **East Renfrewshire**, to the north west and south west respectively, and **Bishopriggs and Cawder** to the north of Glasgow. There are a number of public courses in Glasgow so the visiting golfer confined to Glasgow need not get too depressed.

Forgetting the golf for a moment, it came as something of a surprise for many south of the border when Glasgow was chosen as European City of Culture for 1990, in succession to Athens and Paris, among others. Of course those familiar with the city will know that it has changed out of all recognition in the past decade or so. Good hotels are not as thick on the ground as golf courses but a list of the best would include the Glynhill Leisure Hotel (0141) 886 5555 which caters equally well for individuals and groups and offers various golfing packages.

Others to note are the Glasgow Hilton (0141) 204 5555, the Glasgow Marriott (0141) 226 5577, the Glasgow Thistle (0141) 332 3311 and the less modern (and with a much more attractive exterior) Stakis Grosvenor (0141) 339 8811. One Devonshire Gardens (0141) 339 2001 also combines old-fashioned elegance and service. For more contemporary surroundings Malmasion (0141) 572 1000 is a real gem. As for restaurants, Glasgow is pretty well endowed. Fish lovers will enjoy Rogano (0141) 248 4055 in Exchange Square while those seeking first class French cuisine should head for the Buttery (0141) 221 8188 on Argyle Street. High quality Chinese and Indian restaurants also abound, with the Amber (0141) 339 6121 and Balbir's Ashoka West End (0141) 339 0936 both well worth seeking out. For a sample of Glasgow's culture the Theatre

Royal (0141) 332 9000 offers distinguished ballet, opera and drama and the Burrell Collection in Pollok Park is Scotland's leading art gallery.

Further Afield

Time for a spot more golf, and the **Gleddoch House** Hotel Golf and Country Club (01475) 540711 provides the solution. Located at Langbank it is close to the Clyde Estuary and offers views of the Kilpatrick Hills. It is easily accessible from Glasgow by way of the M8 and in a nutshell could be described as a darn good hotel with a darn good restaurant and a darn good golf course!

From Glasgow, the great challenges of Troon, Turnberry and Prestwick lie to the south west (the A77 is incidentally the most convenient route), and, of course, to the north west on the shores (or 'bonnie banks') of **Loch Lomond** is the outstanding Loch Lomond Golf Course (featured ahead). Good golf can also be found to the north and east of Glasgow where two courses lie in the vicinity of Cumbernauld. Firstly, the **Westerwood Hotel** (01236) 457171 and its golf course offer a fine combination of golf, leisure and accommodation. The golf course is very challenging and calls for many daring shots, which is not altogether surprising since Seve Ballesteros had a hand in its design in association with Dave Thomas. Secondly, **Dullatur** is another fine parkland course also designed by Dave Thomas. For Dullatur a hotel to note is Crow Wood House (0141) 779 3861 and an excellent restaurant, La Campagnola (0141) 779 3405—both are in Muirhead.

There are more fantastic panorama to be seen at **Kyles of Bute** and at **Port Bannantyne** but best of all the hill course at **Rothesay**. Designed by James Braid and Ben Sayers it provides a good test of golf and the views from every hole are to die for. The countryside is quite glorious and there are some extremely fine hotels and country houses nestling in and around the hills, all making splendid bases for exploring the magnificent scenery of these parts. North of Loch Lomond one finds Stonefield Castle (01880) 820836 at Tarbert alongside Loch Fyne. If inspecting the delights of Oban a detour to Kilchrenan is highly recommended—Ardanaiseig (01866) 833333 is the place—outstandingly relaxing and in a beautiful setting overlooking Loch Awe. Still nearer to Oban at Kilninver, the Knipoch Hotel (01852) 316251 offers great comfort together with all manner of country pursuits.

Into the West

Heading west along the north bank of the Clyde a stop is recommeded for **Helensburgh** a sporting moorland course which enjoys superb views over the Clyde and also **Innellan** and **Cowal**, either side of Dunoon, (a mere 10 miles as the crow flies but nearly 60 by road). This area of Argyle and Bute is stunningly beautiful, with typical highland hills and deep lochs (hence the tortuous detours).

Two great courses still remain to be charted—those magical 'M's—**Machrie** and **Machrihanish**. Each enjoys a kind of splendid isolation and is a superb test of traditional links golf. Machrie is to be found on the distant Isle of Islay at Port Ellen. As it can now be reached by plane from Glasgow there can be no excuse for not making the trip—besides, right on the course is the Machrie Hotel (01496) 302310. Many have already made the pilgrimage to Machrihanish and as it too is reachable by air a large number are certain to follow. Following The Fairways has also succumbed to its charms and Machrihanish is explored on a later page.

There are a number of hotels and guesthouses nearby, both in Machrihanish itself and in Campbeltown, and it's well worth spending a few days here. The Putechan Lodge (01583) 421323 can be highly recommended and, like several local hotels, offers special golfing breaks. Balegreggan Country House (01586) 552062 is renowned

for its food, and Ardell House (01586) 810235 offers some good accommodation.

Before you leave the area a mellow tune may come to mind—Mull of Kintyre by one Paul McCartney. The music inspired millions: the golf course and its surrounds will almost certainly give equal satisfaction.

THE 1ST LAMLASH GOLF CLUB
Photograph courtesy of: **David J Whyte, The Golf Photo Library**

Loch Lomond

There may be a handful of inland courses that are as challenging, as well designed and even one or two that are as perfectly maintained as Loch Lomond, but does any golf course in the world enjoy a more beautiful setting ? Surely not, Loch Lomond is in a class of its own.

The golf course is laid out alongside the legendary "bonnie banks" of Loch Lomond. It is practically encircled by mountains and hills—the start of the Scottish Highlands—and occupies the heart of an historic 800 year old estate, the ancestral home of the Clan Colquhoun who fought with Robert the Bruce. The estate is blessed with an extraordinary wealth of trees including many giant pines and several ancient oaks. Rhododendrons and azaleas provide seasonal splashes of colour while the ruins of a 15th century castle watch over the 18th green. For good measure the clubhouse at Loch Lomond is the palatial Rossdhu House, built in 1773.

Designed by Tom Weiskopf and Jay Morrish, Loch Lomond has established itself as a favourite among the world's golfing elite. September 1996 saw the inaugural staging of the World Invitation Tournament, won by Denmark's rising star, Thomas Bjorn. During the event Nick Faldo described the course as "absolutely fabulous—as good as any I've seen". In 1997 the tournament was moved to the week before the Open Championship and it produced another fine champion in Tom Lehman. The 1998 World Invitational was won by one of Europe's top golfers, Lee Westwood and the 1999 event, sponsored by Standard Life, was won in superb style by Scotland's Colin Montgomerie.

The design of the course takes good advantage of the lochside setting. Either the tee or green is adjacent to the Loch on eight of the holes, and a stream or burn affects another four. In addition to the many varied water hazards, Loch Lomond's defences include some distinctive marshes and an array of dazzling jigsaw shaped bunkers.

The most memorable holes on the front nine are the par five 3rd, the extremely photogenic short 5th where the tee shot must be aimed directly at the Loch, and the 6th and 7th—a gorgeous par five and a swinging left to right dog-leg.

On the back nine the par four 15th heralds the start of an extraordinary finish. From an elevated tee the fairway flows down towards a shallow, sloping green beautifully framed by dark woods. The sweeping par five 16th dares you to attempt to carry the burn in front of the green with your second shot. The 17th is a superbly challenging par three with a tee shot across marshes to a tightly bunkered green and the 18th curves spectacularly around Rossdhu Bay to a huge green elegantly perched on the edge of the of the Loch–a marvellous ending to a marvellous course.

**Loch Lomond Golf Club, Rossdhu House,
Luss By Alexandria, Dumbartonshire G83 8NT**

Sec/Manager	K Williams(01436) 655555
Professional	C Campbell
Green Fees	Members and their guests only
Restrictions	As above

Directions
From Glasgow Airport take the M898-A82 North.

Turnberry

Not so many years ago it was said that the golfing visitor to Scotland journeyed to St Andrews for the history and to Turnberry for the beauty. Incomparable is a word often used to describe Turnberry's setting—magnificent and majestic are two others. Quite what causes Ailsa Craig to be so mesmerising is a mysery, but mesmerising it is and the views towards the distant Isle of Arran and the Mull of Kintyre can be equally captivating and enchanting. Since 1977, Turnberry has possessed history as well as beauty.

The Open Championship of 1977, Turnberry's first, is generally considered to have been the greatest of all championships. Nicklaus and Watson, the two finest golfers of the day, turned the tournament into a titanic, head-to-head confrontation—the 'Duel in the Sun' as it came to be known. On the final day, both having pulled along way clear of the field, Nicklaus held a two stroke advantage as they left the 12th green. "Who in the world can give Jack Nicklaus two shots over six holes and beat him?" asked Peter Alliss—the rest, as they say, is history.

There are two championship courses at Turnberry: the better known **Ailsa** Course, to which the Open returned for a third time in 1994, and the **Arran** Course. *Turnberry Hotel owns and runs both courses and tee times are reserved for hotel residents.* Arrangements can be made prior to arrival at the hotel by contacting the **Director of Golf, Brian Gunson**. Mr Gunson and his staff can be contacted on **tel: (01655) 331000** and by **fax: (01655) 331706**. Letters should be addressed to **The Turnberry Hotel, Turnberry, Ayrshire KA26 9LT**.

In 2000 the green fee for hotel residents is £95 for one round over the Ailsa Course, for non residents fees are £120 weekdays, £150 weekends. The Arran Course is presently being upgraded and is closed at the time of writing.

The hotel and golf courses lie approximately 17 miles south of the town of Ayr off the A77. For those travelling from the Glasgow region, the A77 runs direct from Glasgow to Turnberry and is dual carriageway for much of the journey. Motoring from Edinburgh the A71 is the best route, picking up the A77 at Kilmarnock. Approaching from England, Carlisle is likely to be a starting point (M6 to Carlisle). The distance from Carlisle to Turnberry is one of just under 120 miles, and although there are two choices, the quickest route is to head north on the A74 leaving (in what appears to be no man's land) and

joining the A70 towards Ayr. Finally, Prestwick Airport is situated just to the north of Ayr.

From its elevated perch, the red-roofed Turnberry Hotel enjoys a commanding view over both courses. It will have witnessed much of Turnberry's rather turbulent past. During the War the rolling expanse of links had been used as an air base and a vast runway had been constructed. Much levelling of the ground had also taken place and in 1945 the last thing Turnberry must have looked was the setting for two Championship courses. Mackenzie Ross is the architect we all have to thank for the restoration and trans-formation of the links.

From its medal tees, the Ailsa Course isn't a great deal longer than the Arran, their respective distances being 6440 yards, par 69, and 6014 yards, par 68. The same from the ladies tees are 5757 yards, par 75 and 5501 yards par 72. When Turnberry's second Open was staged in 1986 the Ailsa course weighed in at 6950 yards, par 70 and the fairways had been narrowed to alarming proportions. Greg Norman's second round 63, achieved in far from perfect weather conditions, was a remarkable feat.

After three holes 'inland' as it were, the Ailsa course hugs the shore tightly for a series of dramatic holes between the 4th and the 11th. The 6th, named Tappie Toorie, is possibly the most difficult par three on the course; the lengthy tee shot is to a heavily guarded green across a valley (play it into the wind and you may be short with a driver).

The 9th and the 10th, though, are the holes most likely to be remembered. The 9th 'Bruce's Castle', is played alongside the famous Turnberry lighthouse, built over the remains of Turnberry Castle, birthplace of Robert the Bruce. The championship tee is perched on a pinnacle of rock with the sea crashing below. Play this hole and the wonderfully curving 10th and you can appreciate why parallels have often been drawn between Turnberry and Pebble Beach. Following the par three 11th, the holes turn inland and if the scenery is a little less spectacular the challenge in no way diminishes.

The closing holes in fact produced a marvellous climax to the 1994 Open when Jesper Parnevik birdied five of his final eight holes yet was still overtaken by Nick Price. The popular Zimbabwian birdied the 16th and then eagled the 17th with a putt of fully 60 feet. Watson, Norman and Price—Turnberry's great triumvirate.

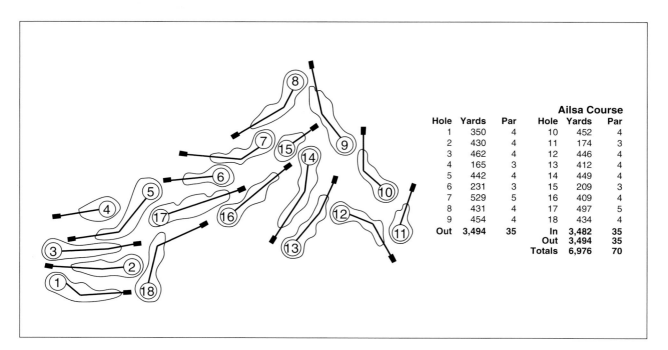

Hole	Yards	Par	Hole	Yards	Par
			Ailsa Course		
1	350	4	10	452	4
2	430	4	11	174	3
3	462	4	12	446	4
4	165	3	13	412	4
5	442	4	14	449	4
6	231	3	15	209	3
7	529	5	16	409	4
8	431	4	17	497	5
9	454	4	18	434	4
Out	**3,494**	**35**	**In**	**3,482**	**35**
			Out	**3,494**	**35**
			Totals	**6,976**	**70**

Royal Troon

O'a the links where I hae golfed
Frae Ayr to Aberdeen,
On Prestwick or Carnoustie and mony mair I ween
What tho' the bents are rough and bunkers yawn aroun'
I dearly lo'e the breezy links, the breezy links o' Troon. (Gilmour)

When the golfing mind focuses on Troon it invariably thinks of the Postage Stamp, the par three 8th on the Old Course, unquestionably the world's most celebrated short hole. During the 1973 Open Championship, Gene Sarazen, then at the mature age of 71, holed out with his punched five iron shot in front of the watching television cameras. Sarazen declared that he would take with him to heaven a copy of the film to show to Walter Hagen and Co. Legend has it that on hearing of Sarazen's feat an American flew to Britain and travelled to Troon. He strode to the 8th tee and proceeded to strike 500 balls in succession towards the green. Not surprisingly he failed to equal Sarazen's achievement, whereupon he left the course and duly flew home to America. Who said it was only mad dogs and Englishmen?

Anyone contemplating the above ought at least to consult the **Secretary/Manager** first, **Mr J W Chandler** being the gentleman in question. He can be contacted at the **Royal Troon Golf Club, Craigend Road, Troon, Ayrshire KA10 6EP tel: (01292) 311555** or by **fax: (01292) 318204**.

The Royal Troon Club Golf possesses two 18 hole courses, The **Old** and The **Portland**. Gentleman visitors are welcome to play both courses on Mondays, Tuesdays and Thursdays provided prior arrangement is made with the Secretary. Lady golfers are also welcome, although they are limited to playing on the Portland Course. All visitors must be members of a recognised club and be able to produce a certificate of handicap (maximum 30 for ladies, 20 for men).

In 2000 a green fee of £125 entitles the visitor to a round on each course, while a fee of £85 secures a full day's golf on the Portland Course; both fees are inclusive of lunch. There are no concessionary rates for junior golfers who, in any event, must have attained the age of eighteen before they will be permitted to play over the Old Course. Sets of clubs and trolleys may be hired from the club's **Professional, Brian Anderson (01292) 313281**. A caddy can also usually be organised.

Troon lies just to the north of Prestwick and Ayr. The town can be reached from Glasgow and the north via the A77, which also runs from near Stranraer in the south. The A78 is the coastal road, running from Largs through Irvine to Loans just east of Troon. Travelling from Edinburgh, the A71 should be taken, while from the North of England the best route is probably via the A74 and the A71. Finally, Prestwick Airport is no more than two miles away. Bordering the Firth of Clyde, the wind often blows very fiercely across the links and Troon is hardly a place for the faint-hearted golfer.

The Old Course at Troon has both the longest hole of any Open Championship course—the 6th at 577 yards—and the shortest—the Postage Stamp—which measures a mere 126 yards. In the 11th it also possesses one of the toughest, with its railway out-of-bounds, thick gorse and painfully narrow fairway. Along with the fabled 8th, the best holes at Troon are probably the 7th, which is played from an elevated tee to a stage-like green surrounded by tall dunes and deep pot bunkers, and the 13th, which features a wonderful, naturally undulating fairway.

At 6274 yards the Portland Course represents a more modest test but it is nonetheless a very fine course and although in parts it closely resembles a moorland-type course, it has all the challenges of traditional links golf.

The club is naturally proud of its great history. When it was founded in 1878 by twenty-four local enthusiasts there were originally only five holes. By 1923 it had staged its first Open Championship. Since then the club has held a further six Opens: in 1950, 1962 (when a rampant Palmer stormed to a six stroke victory) 1973, 1982 (Tom Watson's fourth victory) 1989 (where a dramatic playoff concluded an unforgettable final day's play) and most recently in 1997, when Justin Leonard shot a final round 66 to eclipse the unfortunate Jesper Parnevik.

If you have played all 36 holes at Troon and waged a successful war against the elements you will have earned your drink at the 19th. The clubhouse provides all the usual facilities and the catering has a very good reputation. When you leave you will probably not have a video to take to heaven, but you will at least know that you have visited one of the earth's greatest golfing shrines.

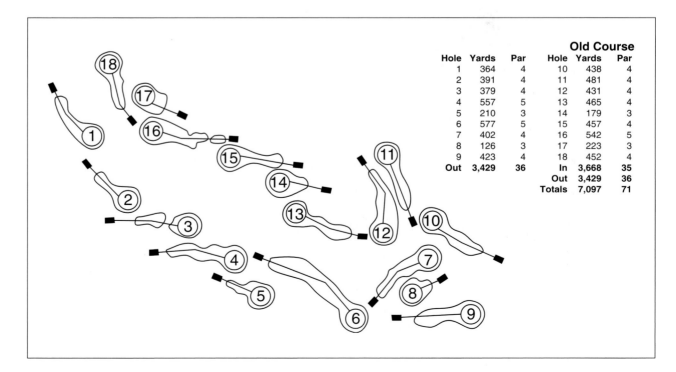

Old Course

Hole	Yards	Par	Hole	Yards	Par
1	364	4	10	438	4
2	391	4	11	481	4
3	379	4	12	431	4
4	557	5	13	465	4
5	210	3	14	179	3
6	577	5	15	457	4
7	402	4	16	542	5
8	126	3	17	223	3
9	423	4	18	452	4
Out	**3,429**	**36**	**In**	**3,668**	**35**
			Out	**3,429**	**36**
			Totals	**7,097**	**71**

Prestwick

One could be forgiven for thinking that they take their golf a little too seriously at Prestwick—especially when one hears of such stories as the one about the monk from a nearby monastery who played a match against the Lord of Culzean to settle a deadly feud: at stake was the monk's nose!

The truth more likely is that Prestwick folk are a competitive breed. Only nine years after the formation of their club in 1851 the members got together and decided to stage an annual Open competition. The winner of the event was to receive an elegant red belt subscribed for by the members. Whilst there may have been only eight entrants, the 1860 Open marks the birth of the world's most prestigious championship.

Willie Park of Musselburgh (a 'foreigner from the east coast') won the 1860 Open and it was decided that if anyone should win the event three years in succession they would win the belt outright. 'Young' Tom Morris was the greatest player of his day and fittingly enough in 1870 won his third title in as many years. Whereas Tom may have kept the belt, Prestwick didn't keep the Open, or at least not the sole rights, as St Andrews and Musselburgh now joined Prestwick in the dawning of a new era.

In those days the combatants played over a twelve hole course. Today there are eighteen holes, though the distinctive flavour remains (seven of the original greens are in the same place). The modern day golfer must still play over the humps and hillocks, face blind shots and tackle the deep sleeper-faced bunkers and eccentrically contoured greens that are so much the charm of Prestwick.

Visitors wishing to play the historic course are advised to approach **Mr Ian Bunch**, the club's **Secretary**, to book a starting time. Mr Bunch can be contacted at **The Prestwick Golf Club, 2 Links Road, Prestwick, Ayrshire, KA9 1QG tel: (01292) 477404** or by **fax: (01292) 477255**. Visitors should note that they are not permitted to play at weekends or after 11.34am on Thursdays, and that the first tee is reserved for members between the hours of 9am-10am and 12.36pm and 2.52pm. Furthermore, three-ball and four-ball matches are not allowed prior to 9.00am.

In 2000 the green fees are £100 per day. However, on Thursdays and for the mornings or afternoons on Mondays, Tuesdays, Wednesdays and Fridays the green fee is £75 for a single round. Sets of golf clubs can be hired through the **Professional, Frank Rennie, (01292) 479483**. Caddies can be hired through the **Caddiemaster on (01292) 671019**.

I suppose, like most things at Prestwick, the clubhouse could be described as having a traditional but friendly atmosphere. Ladies are not permitted in the dining and smoking rooms where jackets and ties must be worn at all times, but all may enter the Cardinal Room where some fine light lunches are offered.

At one time Prestwick was a fairly remote place. Improved roads and the opening of an international airport has made the area much more accessible from all directions. By road, the A77 runs directly from Glasgow in the north and along the coast from Stranraer in the south. Those travelling from Edinburgh should use the A71, before joining the A77 at Kilmarnock.

From the back markers Prestwick measures 6544 yards and has a par of 71. Perhaps not overly long by modern championship standards, it is nonetheless extremely challenging and local knowledge (not to mention rub of the green) can make a considerable difference. At 346 yards the opening hole is small beer in comparison to the first on the original twelve hole layout—that one measured a lengthy 578 yards and in an age of hickory shafts and gutty balls no doubt proved a stiff bogey six. One can only wonder as to how in the 1870 Open, en route to his aforementioned hat trick, 'Young' Tom Morris managed to hole out in three strokes! Another of Tom's notable achievements at Prestwick occurred in the 1868 Open when he scored the first ever recorded hole in one.

The 3rd hole at Prestwick is probably the most famous. Here the golfer must carry the vast Cardinal bunker which stretches the entire width of the fairway right at the point of the dog-leg. The infamous Pow Burn shapes the difficult 4th and then comes the fabled 'Himalayas'—a blind par three played over a massive dune. Almost every hole at Prestwick bristles with character and curiosity. The 10th 'Arran' and the 13th 'Sea Headrig' are regarded as two of the greatest two-shot holes in golf; the fairway at the 15th is surely one of the narrowest and the bunker at the 17th the most magnetic? As for the 18th, at only 284 yards it must be a straightforward hole? Tell that to the golfer who stands one down to the Lord of Culzean.

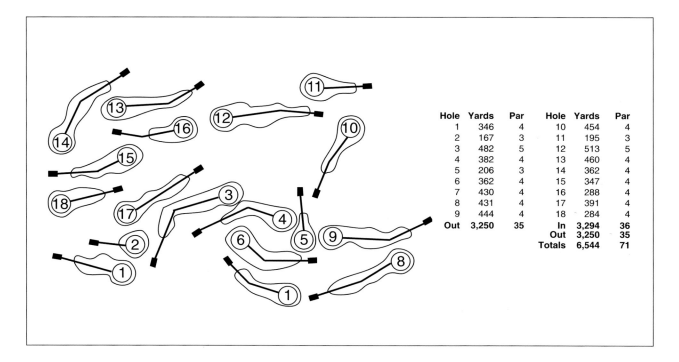

Hole	Yards	Par	Hole	Yards	Par
1	346	4	10	454	4
2	167	3	11	195	3
3	482	5	12	513	5
4	382	4	13	460	4
5	206	3	14	362	4
6	362	4	15	347	4
7	430	4	16	288	4
8	431	4	17	391	4
9	444	4	18	284	4
Out	**3,250**	**35**	**In**	**3,294**	**36**
			Out	**3,250**	**35**
			Totals	**6,544**	**71**

Western Gailes

Sam McKinlay once wrote, 'Western Gailes represents to the true golfer, to the connoisseur of the game, something approaching the ideal in golf.' Squeezed onto a narrow tract of land between the Atlantic Ocean and the Ayrshire coast's ubiquitous railway line, Western Gailes is indeed a marvellous links. It may not have the history of Prestwick (though the club celebrated its centenary in 1987) and the setting may not be as mouth-wateringly beautiful as Turnberry, nor does the links provide quite the stern, uncompromising challenge that is the hallmark of Royal Troon, but if a player wishes to experience a fine blend of all three then Western Gailes is the place to head for.

The 1st hole, with its humpy, hillocky fairway, and its green heavily contoured and partially concealed in a dell could have been plucked from Prestwick. The long par four 2nd is bordered by the railway line—now you could be playing the 11th at Troon. And when you stand on the tee at the par three 7th and gaze out to sea at Ailsa Craig and the Isle of Arran or along the coast which the course hugs for a series of holes you could believe you were at Turnberry. It is classic links golf—deep revetted pot bunkers and meandering burns, thick marram grass topping the dunes, and heather and gorse fringing the fairways.

While Troon and the Ailsa Course are essentially 'out and back' layouts, at Western Gailes the clubhouse sits in the middle of the links. And yet, rather than having two loops of nine—as at Muirfield—the golfer at Western Gailes is lured away from the clubhouse for four holes and invited to play nine close to the sea before being reeled in from the 14th hole onwards. At 6714 yards, par 71, it is long enough and testing enough to have staged many significant championships—it is a regular qualifying venue for the Open Championship and in 1972 hosted the Curtis Cup.

The sequence between the 4th and 7th at Western Gailes is considered one of the finest in golf, and it certainly reveals the course's great variety. The 4th is a medium length two-shotter with a raised and superbly angled Redan style green. The 5th is a big par four that features a minefield of pot bunkers and a fairly narrow entrance to the green—not surprisingly it is the Stroke Index One hole. The 6th is a really characterful par five, its fairway twisting and tumbling towards a green mischievously hidden behind tall dunes. And then comes a famous and much photographed par three. The 7th tee is raised and overlooks the sea From there you play down to a bulb-shaped green backed by dunes and fiercely defended by an assortment of grassy swales and pot bunkers—some revetted and some with wooden sleepered faces. Yes, shades of Turnberry, Troon and Prestwick all in one hole!

Western Gailes Golf Club,
Gailes, By Irvine, Ayrshire KA11 5AE

Secretary	Mr Andrew McBean (01294) 311649
	Fax (01294) 312312
Green Fees	WD £70/round; £95/day including lunch
Restrictions	No visitors Thurs, Sat or Tues.
	Ring to book tee times.

Directions
The club is on the west coast between Troon and Irvine, two minutes south of Irvine on the A78 Irvine-Greenock road.

Machrihanish

The chief purpose of Following the Fairways is to guide the golfer around the counties of Great Britain and Ireland seeking out the finest golfing challenges (and some of the most welcoming 19th hole establishments). Let us imagine, for once, that we are only allowed to play 18 holes but that we may assemble these 18 from any course in Great Britain and Ireland—a dream round if you like.

If there is any romance in our souls we will conclude this round on the 18th green of the Mahony's Point Course at Killarney, no doubt lining up a twenty footer for a two in the lengthening shadows of the encircling pines, and with the gentle lapping of Lough Leane in the background. And if we are bold we will step on to the 18th tee after tackling the Road Hole 17th at St Andrews. But what do we choose for our opening hole? Well, if we are both romantic and bold we will select the 1st at Machrihanish. Let us hope that we have picked a mild day and that any wind is at our backs.

Machrihanish—the very name borders on the mystical—was founded in 1876 (although it was in fact originally named the Kintyre Golf Club). Situated on the south western tip of the Mull of Kintyre, it is perhaps the most geographically remote of all the great courses in the British Isles.

If the situation is exhilarating and invigorating in itself, the golf course will in no way disappoint—certainly for the lover of traditional links golf, Machrihanish has everything. The layout has altered quite a bit since the late 19th century when it was designed by 'Old' Tom Morris, but the natural character of the course remains. Not only are the fairways among the most naturally undulating in the British Isles, but the greens are some of the most amazingly contoured—awkward stances and blind shots are very much a feature of Machrihanish.

There is nothing blind, however, about the 1st hole—from the tee the challenge ahead is very visible. It is a long par four of 423 yards and the only way of ensuring that the green can be reached in two shots is by hitting a full-blooded drive across the waters of Machrihanish Bay. From the back tees a 200 yard carry is called for. 'Intimidating' is the description: 'Death or Glory' is the result.

After the 1st the rest must be easy? Not a chance! If the opening hole tests the drive, several of the following holes will test the approach shot, particularly perhaps the 2nd, 7th and 14th. Machrihanish has its own 'Postage Stamp' hole, the 4th—just 123 yards—and there are successive short holes at the 15th and 16th. The course starts to wind down at the 17th and pars here are frequently followed by birdies at the 18th and, of course, considerable celebration at the 19th.

The Machrihanish Golf Club,
Machrihanish, by Campbeltown, Argyll PA28 6PT

Secretary	Mrs Anderson (01586) 810213
Professional	Ken Campbell (01586) 810277
Green Fees	Sun - Fri £28/round; £45/day
	Saturday £35/round; £55/day
Restrictions	Book starting times with the
	Professional.

Directions
The course is on the south-west tip of the Mull of Kintyre. Fly from Glasgow with Loganair, or take a

Airdrie G.C.
(01236) 762195
Rochsoles, Airdrie
(18) 6004 yards/**/D/L

Alexandra Park G.C.
(0141) 556 1294
Sannox Gardens, Glasgow
(9) 4016 yards/***/E

Annanhill G.C.
(01563) 521512
Irvine Road, Kilmarnock
(18) 6270 yards/***(Sat)/E

Ardeer G.C.
(01294) 464542
Greenhead, Stevenston
(18) 6630 yards/***(Sat)/D

Auchenharvie G.C.
(01292) 603103
Moor Park Road, Saltcoats
(9) 2456 yards/***/D

Ayr Seafield G.C.
(01292) 441258
Belleisle Park, Doonfoot Road
(18) 5498 yards/***/D/H

Ballochmyle G.C.
(01290) 550469
Ballochmyle, Mauchline
(18) 5952 yards/**/D

Balmore G.C.
(0141) 332 0392
Golf Course Road, Balmore
(18) 5516 yards/***/F

Barshaw G.C.
(0141)889 2908
Glasgow Road, Paisley
(18) 5073 yards/***/E

Bearsden G.C.
(0141) 942 2351
Thorn Road, Bearsden, Glasgow
(9) 6014 yards/***/E

Beith G.C.
(01505) 503166
Threepwood Road, Beith
(18) 5600 yards/***/C

Belleisle G.C.
(01292) 441258
Doonfoot Road, Ayr
(18) 6477 yards/***/C/H

Bellshill G.C.
(01698) 745124
Motherwell Road, Orbiston
(18) 5900 yards/***/C

Biggar G.C.
(01899) 220319
Broughton Road, Biggar
(18) 5229 yards/***/E

Bishopbriggs G.C.
(0141) 762 4883
Brackanbrae Road, Glasgow
(18) 6041 yards/*/F/H/L

Blairbeth G.C.
(0141) 634 3355
Burnside, Rutherglen, Glasgow
(18) 5518 yards/***/C

Blairmore & Strone G.C.
(01369) 840676
High Road, Strone, by Dunoon
(9) 2112 yards/***/E

Bonnyton G.C.
(01355) 302781
Eaglesham, Glasgow
(18) 6255 yards/**/B

Bothwell Castle G.C.
(01698) 852052
Blantyre Road, Bothwell
(18) 6243 yards/**/B/H

Brodick G.C.
(01770) 302349
Brodick, Isle of Arran
(18) 4404 yards/***/D

Brunston Castle G.C.
(01465) 811471
Dailly, Girvan
(18) 6858 yards/***/B

Buchanan Castle G.C.
(01360) 660307
Drymen, Glasgow
(18) 6086 yards/**/B

Bute G.C.
(01700) 83648
Kingarth, Bute
(9) 2497 yards/***(Sat pm)/E

Calderbraes G.C.
(01698) 813425
Roundknowe Road, Uddingston
(9) 5046 yards/*/D

Caldwell G.C.
(01505) 850329
Uplawmoor, Renfrewshire
(18) 6228 yards/**/B

Cambuslang G.C.
(0141) 641 3130
Westburn Drive, Cambuslang
(9) 6072 yards/*/G/F/L

Campsie G.C.
(01360) 310244
Crow Road, Lennoxtown
(18) 5517 yards/***/F

Caprington G.C.
(01563) 521915
Ayr Road, Kilmarnock
(18) 5718 yards/***/E

Cardross G.C.
(01389) 841213
Main Road, Cardross
(18) 6466 yards/**/F

Carluke G.C.
(01555) 771070
Mauldslie Road, Hallcraig
(18) 5805 yards/**/C

Carnwath G.C.
(01555) 840251
Main Street, Carnwath
(18) 5955 yards/**/C

Carradale G.C.
(01583) 431643
Carradale, Campbeltown, Argyll
(9) 2387 yards/***/E

Cathcart Castle G.C.
(0141) 638 9449
Mearns Road, Clarkston
(18) 5832 yards/*/F/H/L

Cathkin Braes G.C.
(0141) 634 4007
Cathkin Road, Rutherglen, Glasgow
(18) 6266 yards/**/C/H/L

Cawder G.C.
(0141) 772 7101
Cadder Road, Bishopbriggs
(18) 6295 yards/**/B/H
(18) 5877 yards/**/B/H

Clober G.C.
(0141) 955 0382
Craigton Road, Milngavie
(18) 4763 yards/*/E

Clydebank Municipal G.C.
(01389) 873289
Glasgow Road, Hardgate
(18) 5612 yards/**/D/H

Clydebank Overtoun G.C.
(0141) 952 8698
Overtoun Road, Dalmur
(18) 5033 yards/***/E

Coatbridge G.C.
(01236) 421492
Townhead Road, Coatbridge
(18) 6026 yards/***/E

Cochrane Castle G.C.
(01505) 320146
Scott Avenue, Craigston
(18) 6226 yards/**/B/H

Colonsay G.C.
(01951) 200316
Scalasaig, Isle of Colonsay
(18) 4775 yards/***/E

Colville Park G.C.
(01698) 265378
Jerviston Estate, Motherwell
(18) 6265 yards/*/G/C

Corrie G.C.
(01770) 810223
Sannox, Isle of Arran
(9) 1948 yards/***/E

Cowal G.C.
(01369) 702216
Ardenslate Road, Kirn, Dunoon
(18) 6251 yards/**/C

Cowglen G.C.
(0141) 632 0556
Barrhead Road, Glasgow
(18) 6098 yards/***/C-D

Craignure G.C.
(01680) 812370
Scallastle, Isle of Mull
(9) 5072 yards/***/E

Crow Wood G.C.
(0141) 779 2011
Garnkirk Estate, Muirhead
(18) 6261 yards/**/C

Cumbernauld G.C.
(01236() 734969
Palacerigg Country Park
(18) 6412 yards/***/E

Dalmally G.C.
(01838) 200370
Orchy Bank, Dalmally
(9) 4514 yards/*/E

Deaconsbank G.C.
(0141) 638 7044
Stewarton Road, Eastwood
(18) 4800 yards/***/F

Dalmilling G.C.
(01292) 263893
Westwood Avenue, Ayr
(18) 5752 yards/*/E

Doon Valley G.C.
(01292) 531607
Hillside, Patna
(9) 5654 yards/***/E

Dougalston G.C.
(0141) 956 5750
Strathblane Road, Milngavie
(18) 5946 yards/**/D

Douglas Park G.C.
(0141) 942 2220
Hillfoot, Bearsden
(18) 5957 yards/*

Douglas Water G.C.
(01555) 880361
Ayr Road, Rigside, Lanark
(9) 2947 yards/**/E

Drumpellier G.C.
(01236) 472 4139
Drumpellier Avenue, Coatbridge
(18) 6227 yards/**/B

Dullatur G.C.
(01236) 723230
Dullatur, Glasgow
(18) 6195 yards/**/F

Dumbarton G.C.
(01389) 732830
Broadmeadows, Dumbarton
(18) 6017 yards/**/D

Dunavert G.C.
(01586) 830677
Southend, Campbeltown, Argyll
(18) 4799 yards/***/E

Easter Moffat G.C.
(01236) 842289
Mansion House, Plains
(18) 6221 yards/**/C

East Kilbride G.C.
(013552) 47728
Chapelside, Nerston
(18) 6419 yards/***/C-B/H

East Renfrewshire G.C.
(01355) 500206
Loganswell, Pilmuir
(18)6100 yards/*/F

Eastwood G.C.
(01355) 500280
Muirshield, Loganswell
(18) 5844 yards/**/B

Elderslie G.C.
(01505) 322835
Main Road, Elderslie
(18) 6175 yards/**/C/H

Erskine G.C.
(01505) 862302
Bishopston, Renfrewshire
(18) 6298 yards/**/B

Ferenze G.C.
(0141) 880 7058
Ferenze Avenue, Barrhead
(18) 5962 yards/**/C/G

Gigha G.C.
(01583) 506287
Isle of Gigha, Kintyre
(9) 5042 yards/***/E

Girvan G.C.
(01465) 714346
Girvan
(18) 5095 yards/***/D

Glasgow (Gailes) G.C.
(01294) 311347
Gailes, by Irvine
(18) 6510 yards/***/A

Glasgow (Killermont) G.C.
(0141) 942 1713
Killermont, Bearsden
(18) 5968 yards/***/A

Gleddoch G.& C.C.
(01475) 540704
Langbank, Renfrewshire
(18) 6375 yards/***/A

Glencruitten G.C.
(01631) 562868
Glencruitten Road, Oban
(18) 4250 yards/***/D

Gourock G.C.
(01475) 631001
Cowal View, Gourock
(18) 6494 yards/**/C/H

Greenock G.C.
(01475) 720793
Forsyth Street, Greenock
(18) 5838 yards/***(Sat)/F/L

Greenock Whinhill
(01475) 724694
Beith Road, Greenock
(18) 5504 yards/F

Haggs Castle G.C.
(0141) 427 3355
Dumbreck Road, Glasgow
(18) 6464 yards/*/B-A

Hamilton G.C.
(01698) 282324
Riccarton, Firniegair, Hamilton
(18) 6264 yards/*/F/G

Hayston G.C.
(0141) 775 0882
Campsie Road, Kirkintilloch
(18) 6042 yards/**/B

Helensburgh G.C.
(01436) 674173
East Abercromby Street, Helensburgh
(18) 5773 yards/**/C

Hilton Park G.C.
(0141) 956 5125
Auldmarroch Estate, Milnagavie
(18) 6707 yards/**/B
(18) 5374 yards/**/B

Hollandbush G.C.
(01555) 893646
Acretophead, Lesmahagow
(18) 5791 yards/***/D

Innellan G.C.
(01369) 830242
Knockmillie Road, Innellan
(9) 2343 yards/***/E

Inveraray G.C.
(01499) 302508
Dalmally Road, Inverary
(9) 5600 yards/***/E

Irvine G.C.
(01294) 275979
Bogside, Irvine
(18) 6408 yards/**/B/H

Irvine Ravenspark G.C.
(01294) 276467
Kidsneuk, Irvine
(18) 6429 yards/***/D

Isle of Eriska G.C.
(01631) 720371
Isle of Eriska
(6) 1588 yards/

Kilbirnie Place G.C.
(01505) 683398
Largs Road, Kilbirnie
(18) 5517 yards/**A-C

Kilmacolm G.C.
(01505) 872139
Portafield Road, Kilmacolm
(18) 5964 yards/**/B/G/H

Kilmarnock (Barassie) G.C.
(01292) 313920
Hillhouse Road, Barassie,Troon
(18) 6473 yards/*(Wed)/A

Kilsyth Lennox G.C.
(01236) 824115
Tak-Ma-Doon Road, Kilsyth, Glasgow
(9) 5944 yards/***(W/E am)/E/H

Kingarth G.C.
(01700) 831648
Kilchattan Bay, Isle of Bute
(9) 2497 yards/**/E

Kings Park G.C.
(0141) 630 1597
Carmunock Road, Glasgow
(9) 4142 yards/***/E

Kirkhill G.C.
(0141) 641 7972
Greenless Road, Cambuslang
(18) 5862 yards/***/F

Kirkintilloch G.C.
(0141) 775 2387
Campsie Road, Kirkintilloch
(18) 5269 yards/*/G/D/H/L

Knightswood G.C.
(0141) 959 6358
Lincoln Avenue, Knightswood
(9) 5726 yards/***/E

Kyles of Bute G.C.
(01700) 811601
Tighnabruaich, Argyll
(9) 4778 yards/***(Sun am)/F

Lamlash G.C.
(01770) 600296
Lamlash, Brodick, Isle of Arran
(18) 4640 yards/***/D

Lanark G.C.
(01555) 663219
Whitelees Road, Lanark
(18) 6423 yards/**/B

Langlands G.C.
(013552) 24685
Auldhouse Road, East Kilbride
(18) 6202 yards/***/C

Largs G.C.
(01475) 673594
Irvine Road, Largs
(18) 6220 yards/**/F/H

Larkhall G.C.
(01698) 881113
Burnhead Road, Larkhall
(9) 6700 yards/**/F

Leadhills G.C.
(01659) 74222
Leadhills, Biggar
(9) 4354 yards/***/E

Lenzie G.C.
(0141) 776 1535
Crosshill Road, Lenzie
(18) 5982 yards/**/C/H

Lethamhill G.C.
(0141) 770 6220
Cumbernauld Road, Millerston
(18) 5836 yards/***/E

Linn Park G.C.
(0141) 637 5871
Simshill Road, Glasgow
(18) 5005 yards/***/E

Littlehill G.C.
(0141) 772 1916
Auchinairn Road, Bishopbriggs
(18) 6240 yards/***/E

Lochgilphead G.C.
(01546) 602340
Blarbuie Road, Lochgilphead
(9) 4484 yards/***/E

Loch Lomond G.C.
(01436) 860223
Luss, Alexandria
(18) 7053 yards/*/G

THE 5TH ISLE OF ERISKA GOLF CLUB *Photograph courtesy of:* **David J Whyte, The Golf Photo Library**

Lochranza G.C.
(01770) 830273
Lochranza, Isle of Arran
(9) 5454 yards/***/E

Lochwinnoch G.C.
(01505) 842153
Burnfoot Road, Lochwinnoch
(18) 6243 yards/**/B/H

Loudoun G.C.
(01563) 820551
Galston, Ayrshire
(18) 5600 yards/**/F

Machrie G.C.
(01496) 302310
Machrie Hotel, Port Ellen, Isle of Islay
(18) 6226 yards/***/B/H

Machrie Bay G.C.
(01770) 850232
Machrie, Isle of Arran
(9) 2143 yards/***/E

Machrihanish G.C.
(01586) 810213
Machrihanish, Campbeltown
(18) 6228 yards/***/C/H

Maybole G.C.
(01292) 612000
Memorial Park, Ayrshire
(9) 2635 yards/***/E

Millport G.C.
(01475) 530306
Millport, Isle of Cumbrae
(18) 5828 yards/***/D

Milngavie G.C.
(0141) 956 1619
Laighpark, Milngavie, Glasgow
(18) 5818 yards/*/G/F

Mount Ellen G.C.
(01236) 872277
Johnston Road, Gartcosh
(18) 5526 yards/**/D/G

Muirkirk G.C.
(01290) 661257
Furnace Road, Muirkirk
(9) 5380 yards/***/E

New Cumnock G.C.
(01290) 423659
Lochmill, New Cumnock
(9) 5176 yards/***/E

Old Ranfurly G.C.
(01505) 613612
Ranfurly Place, Bridge of Weir
(18) 6089 yards/**/F/L/H

Paisley G.C.
(0141) 884 3903
Braehead, Paisley
(18) 6466 yards/*/B/H/L

Palacerigg G.C.
(01236) 734969
Country Park, Cumbernauld
(18) 6444 yards/***/E

Pollok G.C.
(0141) 632 4351
Barrhead Road, Glasgow
(18) 6257 yards/**/B/H/L

Port Bannatyne G.C.
(01700) 502009
Mains Road, Port Bannatyne, Bute
(13) 4730 yards/***/E

Port Glasgow G.C.
(01475) 704181
Devol Road, Port Glasgow
(18) 5592 yards/**/D

Prestwick G.C.
(01292) 477404
Links Road, Prestwick
(18) 6544 yards/**/A/L

Prestwick St Cuthbert G.C.
(01292) 477101
East Road, Prestwick
(18) 6470 yards/**/C

Prestwick St Nicholas G.C.
(01292) 477608
Grangemuir Road, Prestwick
(18) 5952 yards/**/B/H

Ralston G.C.
(0141) 882 1349
Strathmore Avenue, Ralston
(18) 6100 yards/*/G/F

Ranfurly Castle G.C.
(01505) 612609
Golf Road, Bridge of Weir
(18) 6284 yards/**/B/L/H

Renfrew G.C.
(0141) 886 6692
Inchinnan Road, Renfrew
(18) 6818 yards/**/G/F/H/L

Rothesay G.C.
(01700) 502244
Canada Hill, Rothesay, Bute
(18) 5370 yards/***/D/H

Rouken Glen G.C.
(0141) 620 0826
Stewarton Road, Glasgow
(18) 4800 yards/***/E

Routenburn G.C.
(01475) 673230
Greenock Road, Largs, Ayrshire
(18) 5650 yards/**/E/H

Royal Troon G.C.
(01292) 311555
Craigend Road, Troon
(18) 7097 yards/**/A/H/L
(18) 6386 yards/**/B/H/L

Ruchill G.C.
(0141) 946 8793
Brassey Street, Glasgow
(9) 4434 yards/***/E

Sandyhills G.C.
(0141) 778 1179
Sandyhills Road, Glasgow
(18) 6253 yards/***/D/H

Shiskine G.C.
(01770) 860226
Blackwaterfoot, Isle of Arran
(12) 2990 yards/***/D

Shotts G.C.
(01501) 820431
Blairhead, Shotts
(18) 6205 yards/**/C

Skelmorlie G.C.
(01475) 520152
Skelmorlie, Ayrshire
(13) 5056 yards/***(Sat)/C

Strathaven G.C.
(01357) 520421
Overton Avenue, Glasgow Road
(18) 6226 yards/**/B

Strathclyde Park G.C.
(01698) 429350
Motehill, Hamilton
(9) 3147 yards/***/E

Tarbert G.C.
(01880) 820565
Kilberry Road, Tarbert
(9) 4460 yards/***/E

Tobermory G.C.
(01688) 302020
Tobermory, Isle of Mull
(9) 4890 yards/***/E

Torrance House G.C.
(013352) 48638
Strathaven Road, East Kilbride
(18) 6437 yards/***/C

Troon Municipal G.C.
(01292) 312464
Harling Drive, Troon
(18) 6785 yards/***/C
(18) 6501 yards/***/C
(18) 4822 yards/***/C

Turnberry Hotel G.C.
(01655) 331000
Turnberry, Ayrshire
(18) 6976 yards/***/A/H
(18) 6014 yards/***/A/H

Vale of Leven G.C.
(01389) 752351
Northfield Road, Alexandria
(18) 5167 yards/**/D/H

Vaul G.C.
(01879) 2203399
Scarinish, Isle of Tiree
(9) 2911 yards/***/E

Westerwood Hotel & G.C.
(01236) 457171
St Andrews Drive, Cumbernauld
(18) 6601 yards/***/B

Western Gailes G.C.
(01294) 311649
Gailes, by Irvine
(18) 6639 yards/**/A/H

West Kilbride G.C.
(01294) 823911
Fullerton Drive, Seamill
(18) 6542 yards/**/A/L/H

Whinhill G.C.
(01475) 721064
Beith Road, Greenock
(18) 5504 yards/***/E

Whitecraigs G.C.
(0141) 639 4530
Ayr Road, Newton Mearns
(18) 6230 yards/**/B/H

Whiting Bay G.C.
(01770) 700487
Whiting Bay, Arran
(18)4405 yards/***/E/H

Williamwood G.C.
(0141) 637 1783
Clarkston Road, Netherlee
(18) 5878 yards/*/C/G

Windyhill G.C.
(0141) 942 2349
Bal Jaffray Road, Bearsden
(18) 6254 yards/**/B

Wishaw G.C.
(01698) 372869
Cleland Road, Wishaw
(18) 6051 yards/***/C

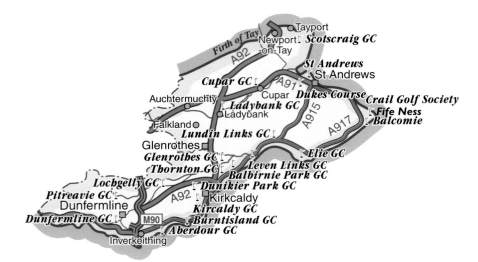

Fife Choice Golf

Many years ago, watching an England versus Scotland soccer game at Wembley, I remember being amused by one of the banners carried by a group of Scottish supporters which boldly declared, 'Remember Bannockburn'. Being a pigheaded Englishman I thought to myself, they ought to remember it—it was just about the only battle they won in centuries. Of course, all is now abundantly clear—the Scots were far too busy priming their golfing skills to bother themselves fighting the Sassenachs.

As long ago as 1457 the Scottish Parliament, unimpressed by the performance of its sharpshooters, felt that too much golf and football were to blame for the lack-lustre performances on the battlefields. An act was passed stating that because of their interference with the practice of archery, the 'fute-ball and golf be utterly cryit down and nocht usit'. History would seem to suggest that the Scots didn't take a blind bit of notice, and golf steadily grew in popularity. Juggle the figures that make up 1457 and we have 1754, perhaps the most significant date in golf's history—the year the Society of St Andrews golfers drew up its written rules of golf.

Today **St Andrews**, deep in the Kingdom of Fife, is the place every golfer in the world wants to visit. Even if you have only swung a club at the local municipal you'll be itching to do the same at St Andrews. However, for those contemplating a pilgrimage to the centre of the golfing world it should be said that St Andrews has several near neighbours that warrant the most discerning attention. Between Dunfermline, to the west of Fife, and St Andrews lie what are undoubtedly some of the finest courses in Scotland.

Travelling Around the Coast

For six hundred years Dunfermline was the country's capital and the body of its most famous king, Robert the Bruce, lies buried in Dunfermline Abbey (minus his heart, apparently, which is in Melrose Abbey). The town has two courses, **Dunfermline** and **Pitreavie**. Both are parkland courses at which visitors are welcome provided some prior arrangement is made. Neither is unduly hard on the pocket. For those wishing to spend a day or two in the old royal town, the appropriately named King Malcolm Thistle Hotel (01383) 722611 provides convenient comfort. Alternatively, the Keavil House (01383) 736258 at Crossford has excellent accommodation and good food.

East of Dunfermline there is a testing links at **Burntisland** with fine views over the Firth of Forth and there are again two courses in Kirkcaldy, the **Dunnikier Park** and **Kirkcaldy** golf clubs, (and make

sure you pronounce it Ker-coddy!) Dunnikier Park is a public course. One other good golf club to note in the area is **Aberdour**. A peaceful night's sleep and good fare is abundantly available at the Old Rectory Inn (01592) 651211 in Dysart. In Burntisland, Kingswood (01592) 872329 is most convenient. Beyond Kirkcaldy, out along a glorious stretch of spectacular coast are Fife's famous five—**Leven Links**, **Lundin Links**, **Elie**, **Balcomie** and of course **St Andrews**. This outstanding quintet has now been joined by the magnificent new course at **Kingsbarns**.

Leven and Lundin are often considered as a pair, probably on account of there being very little land in between (an old stone wall serves as the boundary). Two proud clubs share the 6433 yards links at Leven, the Leven Golfing Society and Leven Thistle, however, the visitor is always made to feel welcome—as indeed he or she is at the more hilly Lundin—an excellent course, which although very much a links has an abundance of trees on the back nine.

Elie, or the Golf House Club, lies a short distance from the two across Largo Bay, the A917 linking the town with Leven. Elie is famed for its unique periscope by the first tee and for the fact that it was here that James Braid fashioned many of the skills that won him five Open Championships. A charming and very natural links—you won't see trees anywhere here—and not too demanding in length, several of the holes are laid out right alongside a rocky shoreline. A ballot system operates at Elie during the summer but otherwise there are no general restrictions on times visitors can play.

Following the aforementioned A917 eastwards from Elie, the town of Crail is soon reached. Just beyond the town at Fifeness is the magnificent Balcomie links, home of the two hundred year old **Crail Golfing Society**. Together with St Andrews and Kingsbarns it is featured a few pages on. Incidentally, when visiting St Andrews, or if just passing by, try to visit the British Golf Museum (01334) 478880— right next to the 1st tee on the **Old Course** it provides a memorable insight into the glorious game.

In addition to the numerous hotels in St Andrews, there is plenty of accommodation near to the other great links courses of Fife and it is generally inexpensive. A great number are geared almost solely towards the interests of the golfing community and are situated within pitching distance of the nearest fairway. Here are a few thoughts. In Lundin Links, the Old Manor Hotel (01333) 320368 is highly thought of with a particularly good restaurant while less grand accommodation can be enjoyed at the Lundin Links Hotel (01333) 320207, an especially popular retreat for golfers. The Golf Hotel (01333) 330209 in Elie is self explanatory and extremely popular. On a fine day, before the season reaches its height, Elie is a particularly charming place to be. Just a short distance away in Anstruther, is the popular Craws Nest Hotel (01333) 310691—located midway between Elie and Crail it's an excellent base. In Anstruther one might also visit the Smugglers Inn (01333) 310506, a cosy 300 year old tavern. The Cellar (01333) 310378 is a really pleasant restaurant specialising in seafood. Crail is a delightful fishing village and here the Golf Hotel (01333) 450206 is another obvious choice. It's a place of great character and is one of Scotland's oldest licensed inns. Still in Crail, the Caiplie Guest House (01333) 450564 is good value and the Balcomie Links Hotel (01333) 450237 is very convenient as its name suggests. Two other restaurants that can be strongly recommended for the area are found a little inland, namely, Ostlers Close (01334) 655574 at Cupar and the exceptional Peat Inn (01334) 840206 on the road to Cupar. For people who consider themselves golfing gourmets, this establishment should be very high on their list. A number of pleasant bedrooms complete the picture. Further north, at the interestingly named Wormit, you will find Sandford House (01382) 541802, a country house hotel which comes highly recommended.

Drumoig Golf Hotel

Drumoig, Leochars,
St Andrews KY16 0BE
Tel: (01382) 541800 Fax: (01382) 541122
e mail: drumoig@sol.co.uk
www.drumoigleisure.com

A privately owned hotel set amongst 330 acres, it comprises 24 bedrooms located in unique lodges, a further four executive rooms and a honeymoon suite are found on the upper level of the main building. All the bedrooms are tastefully decorated and many over look the 18th fairway.

Drumoig's well stocked bar has views of the 18th fairway and green, the restaurant offers a wide range of tempting cuisine and also has excellent views over the 9th fairway nestled between Drumoig's own two lochs. The 18 hole Championship golf course boasts some 7000 yards of challenging golf. Drumoig is home to the Scottish Golf Union and the recently completed Scottish National Golf Centre which has the most modern facilities for practising both indoor and outdoor golf. Drumoig Hotel and Golf Course is an ideal choice for the golfer looking to play and stay at one of Scotland's finest and newest golf developments.

It isn't an overstatement to say that St Andrews is the centre of the golfing world. As early as 1691 it was described as the 'Metropolis of Golfing'. With pilgrims today making the trip from all corners of the globe the number of hotels and guesthouses is understandably considerable. The St Andrews Old Course Hotel (01334) 474371, sumptuously refurbished, is unquestionably one of Scotland's leading hotels and, overlooking the most famous hole in golf, the Road Hole 17th on the Old Course, couldn't be better positioned. More aesthetically pleasing than prior to its restoration, it now oozes class both within and without. The hotel's own golf course, the highly acclaimed Peter Thomson-designed **Duke's Course** is featured on a later page. Rufflets Hotel (01334) 472594 just outside the town is also an excellent base with award-winning gardens while another room with a view can be booked at the Rusacks Hotel (01334) 474321, formerly the Golf Inn, which oozes golfing history (the restaurant is also good and rather appropriately named the Niblick). The other hotels which might just hint at a round of the good old game include the St Andrews Golf Hotel (01334) 472611 and the Scores Hotel (01334) 472451—both are good value and pleasant.

There is also any number of comfortable guesthouses and B&Bs in town; noteworthy examples include the Albany (01334) 477737, Arran House (01334) 474724 and the Amberside (01334) 474644. While golf clearly takes centre stage one should not forget the pleasant coastline nearby (scenes from Chariots of Fire were filmed on St Andrews' vast sands), nor the 12th century cathedral and Scotland's oldest university.

Inland Golf

Just as the leading courses of Surrey aren't all heathland and gorse, neither are those of Fife all seaviews and sandhills. **Ladybank** is actually only a few miles north of Leven but is completely different in character with heathland fairways and much pine and heather—a very beautiful course and well worth a visit. North of Ladybank lies **Cupar**, one of the oldest 9 hole golf courses in Scotland and a clubhouse that has to be approached through a cemetery (slightly older even than the golf course!)

In an area steeped in history, **Glenrothes** is a relative newcomer to the scene. Young, perhaps, but an excellent course nonetheless. Situated to the west of the town it is a fairly hilly parkland type, offering many superb views. A friendly welcome awaits but the names of two of the holes worry me a little—the 11th, titled 'Satan's Gateway' and the 18th 'Hells End'!

A restful 19th is clearly in order and fortunately in Glenrothes quality places abound. The Balgeddie House (01592) 742511 is secluded and most relaxing, while the charming Rescobie Hotel (01592) 742143 at Leslie and the Rothes Arms (01592) 753701 should also placate the soul. Letham is only a short distance from Ladybank and here Fernie Castle (01337) 810381 is recommended. Equally convenient and comfortable is the Lomond Hills Hotel at Freuchie (01337) 857329. Not to be forgotten either is the classical mansion Balbirnie House (01592) 610066 at Markinch, a luxury hotel set in over 400 acres of landscaped woodland and situated adjacent to **Balbirnie Park** Golf Club. The restaurant here is also first class.

Two other courses that are well worth visiting if journeying inland in Fife are at **Thornton**, where the River Ore makes for some challenging holes, and at **Lochgelly**—convenient if travelling between Dunfermline and Kirkcaldy. The final mention though goes to **Scotscraig**, an Open Championship qualifying course at Tayport. Although close to the sea it is actually a downland type course rather than a true links, but is an admirable test of golf. Following that testing game at Scotscraig one is likely to be left with a difficult decision: to the north, Carnoustie and many other great challenges await—but then no golfer who has experienced the pleasures of the Kingdom of Fife ever left easily.

Crail Golfing Society - Balcomie Links

On 23rd February 1986 the seventh oldest golf club in the world celebrated its bicentenary. Some three years before the Bastille was stormed a group of eleven gentlemen met at the Golf Inn in Crail and together formed the Crail Golfing Society. The records of that historic day are still preserved; indeed remarkably the Society possesses a complete set of minutes from the date of its inception. In those early days the Society members wore scarlet jackets with yellow buttons and dined at the Golf Inn after a day on the links. The local punch flowed and a good time was doubtless had by all—now those were the days!

Since 1895 the club has played over the Balcomie Links which is located approximately two miles north east of Crail at Fifeness. Earlier the Society had used a narrow strip of land at Sauchope, slightly closer to Crail (and of course to the Golf Inn).

The atmosphere is still jovial and visitors are made most welcome. With the exception of a few competition days there are no general restrictions on times of play. However, individual visitors are advised to telephone the **Professional, Graeme Lennie** the day before playing. He can be contacted on **(01333) 450967** or **(01333) 450960**. Societies, or golfing parties, are equally welcome and advance bookings can be made at all times apart from during the peak summer period. Written enquiries should be addressed to **The Manager, Crail Golfing Society, Balcomie Clubhouse, Crail, Fife KY10 3XN**. The **Manager, Jim Horsfield**, can be reached on **tel: (01333) 450686** and by **fax: (01333) 450416**.

The green fees for 2000 are pitched at £25 per round, £35 per day during weekdays or £30 per round and £45 per day at weekends. Juniors can play for £12.50 during the week and £15 at weekends but only if accompanied by a full fee paying adult—otherwise the adult fee is applicable.

The Balcomie Links is ideal for 'holiday golf'. Without being overly long (5922 yards, par 69)—though the wind can affect distances greatly—it offers some exceptionally spectacular scenery and, similar to Cruden Bay further north, a nearby castle casts a watchful eye. Balcomie Castle, where Mary of Guise, mother-to-be of Mary Queen of Scots, spent her first few days in Scotland, comes complete with ghost.

The course is always well maintained and the greens especially have acquired an enviable reputation. The holes have been laid out so that each provides a view of the sea. There is an unusual balance to the round with the front nine containing six par fours and the back nine only three; as for the par threes, the second nine boasts four short holes including the 18th. There are some rather interesting names too: 'Fluke Dub' (4th) 'Hell's Hole' (5th) and 'Lang Whang' (11th). The aforementioned 'Hell's Hole' really lives up to its name. You stand on the tee of the fearsome 5th at Crail and decide whether to 'go for it' or not—ie whether to go for a brave carry over rocks, sea and sand or to play safe.

The temptation for many on crossing the Forth Road Bridge is of course to head straight for the Royal and Ancient. Although St Andrews may be the undisputed sovereign in the so-called Kingdom of Fife, there are also a number of handsome princes. The Balcomie links stands comparison with the best and is a course of which the two hundred year old society can justifiably be proud.

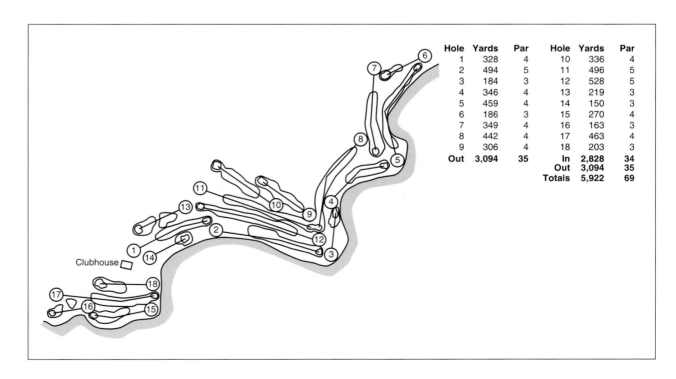

Hole	Yards	Par		Hole	Yards	Par
1	328	4		10	336	4
2	494	5		11	496	5
3	184	3		12	528	5
4	346	4		13	219	3
5	459	4		14	150	3
6	186	3		15	270	4
7	349	4		16	163	3
8	442	4		17	463	4
9	306	4		18	203	3
Out	**3,094**	**35**		**In**	**2,828**	**34**
				Out	**3,094**	**35**
				Totals	**5,922**	**69**

Clubhouse

Crail has just added a second links course to complement their renowned Balcomie Links layout, and the new Craighead links looks set to join Balcomie as one of the "must play" courses in Scotland.

American designer Gil Hanse studies, plays and is a mine of information about the Scottish courses and classic links. He has a philosophy on golf course design, "Keep it simple. Keep it natural". These words serve to describe this fine course he has created using the natural undulations of the ground. It has a natural panoramic seascape as well as country views and is perfectly located just South of the present clubhouse.

The new course was routed so as to afford constant change of direction in battling the wind, constant variety in length and challenge of the holes and to visit the sea at various points during the round. The terrain of the greens is such that the contouring is always interesting and relies on subtle breaks, inter connected undulations and character, as opposed to the multi levels and sharp turns. The bunkering on the course is the most striking feature of all. The appearance is as natural as possible with motion, depth and vegetation that mimics the original bunkers carved by the wind from natural dunes.

The end result is a course that reaches a level of character, charm and elegance that matches those from early days of course architecture. With this in mind the Craighead Links compliments the older traditional Balcomie Links.

With a radius of almost 100 miles the views from the course are even more spectacular than from Balcomie - past Carnoustie and the Bell Rock to the north, St Abbs Head, North Berwick and May Island to the south, Muirfield and Edinburgh to the west. Indeed whilst construction of the course took place, some of the oldest human occupation remains in Scotland were discovered, and with the views found you can understand why they chose such a site.

For a club of such long and excellent standing, Crail has remained forward looking, friendly and hospitable, a pleasure to play and visit. Obviously the eleven original members who dined together "for happy evenings with accustomed hilarity and good-fellowship" have cast a long shadow over those who followed.

For further information on playing Craighead Links the **Manager, Jim Horsfield** can be contacted on **(01333) 450686**, and the **Professional, Graeme Lennie** on **(01333) 450960**.

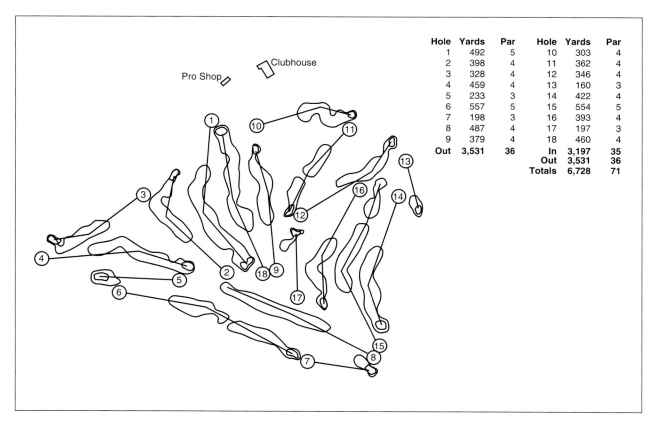

Hole	Yards	Par		Hole	Yards	Par
1	492	5		10	303	4
2	398	4		11	362	4
3	328	4		12	346	4
4	459	4		13	160	3
5	233	3		14	422	4
6	557	5		15	554	5
7	198	3		16	393	4
8	487	4		17	197	3
9	379	4		18	460	4
Out	3,531	36		In	3,197	35
				Out	3,531	36
				Totals	6,728	71

Clubhouse

Pro Shop

It is the talk of golf. Or at least, whenever the merits of Scottish links courses are being discussed, someone will mention Kingsbarns, the remarkable new layout situated just a few miles down the road from St Andrews.

For some time now Scotland has been craving for an outstanding new links course. Soon after the last war Southerness took its bow and Turnberry was restored in magnificent style, but since then all major golf development in Scotland has occurred either inland or on non-links coastal sites. Meanwhile, just across the sea, Ireland has unveiled at least a dozen excellent links challenges in the past 25 years or so: Waterville, Tralee, the new courses at Ballybunion, Portmarnock and Ballyliffin, The European Club, Carne, Murvagh, Connemara ... And as the Irish Tourist Board will gleefully confirm, ever more holidaying golfers (notably Americans in search of links golf) are visiting the Emerald Isle – in preference to Scotland.

Kingsbarns, which officially opens for play during the week of the 2000 St Andrews Open, may be about to stem the Irish tide. This is possible because the golf course (unlike Loch Lomond) is not the centrepiece of a private club. In fact there are no members at all at Kingsbarns, and no hotel residents for whom tee times are reserved.

Moreover, if some of the informed comments one reads and hears are accurate, the Kingdom of Fife may one day have a second Open Championship venue: In America especially, Kingsbarns is receiving rave reviews. LINKS Magazine, North America's leading golf course oriented publication featured Kingsbarns on the front cover of its March 2000 issue. In a lengthy article inside, Editor Jo Passov described the course in glowing terms: "Honestly, they (the development team) got everything right. Every hole provides views of the sea, and seven holes play over it or adjacent. There are modern touches of the spectacular – witness the Pebble Beach-like, left curving, 590 yards par five 12th, and the all-carry, have-your-camera-ready, 215 yards par three 15th. Needless to say, the aesthetics at Kingsbarns are sensational. What makes it truly great, however, is the design itself, which is varied, fun, challenging and sophisticated all at the same time."

But talk of one day staging the Open Championship at Kingsbarns – surely that's a little fantastic (never mind premature)? It may be; however, this is what Sir Michael Bonallack, the former secretary of the R&A, has said about Kingsbarns: "Mere words cannot convey just how extraordinary the place is. It must be seen to be believed. And once seen it will never be forgotten."

Better put that Irish trip on hold!

Kingsbarns Golf Links, Kingsbarns, Fife KY16 8QD
www.kingsbarns.com

General Manager	Stuart McEwen (01334) 880222
Director of Golf	David Scott
Green Fees	£85/round, £130 per day
Restrictions	Ring to book tee times.

Directions
Directions 6 miles south of St Andrews on the A917 to Crail, the clubhouse is signposted.

Elie (Golf House Club)

Nobody really knows who was the original architect of this splendid old links, but there's no doubting who made it famous. James Braid, Scotland's greatest ever player, learnt his golf at Elie, and he was never shy to sing its praises. The five-time Open champion once declared that the par four 13th at Elie was, 'the finest hole in all the country.' Braid's comments shouldn't be dismissed lightly since he was also Scotland's most prolific golf course architect.

Braid is not the only golfer to have fallen in love with Elie. Located 10 miles south of St Andrews, it enjoys a glorious setting beside West Bay. In fact, at times the golf course almost descends on to the beach.

Of short to medium length, Elie is not an especially demanding links, except of course when the elements are stirred, but it has plenty of character, and one rather eccentric touch. By the 1st tee there is an old submarine periscope: golfers (or more likely the Starter) must peer into it to ensure that the fairway ahead is clear – it being largely concealed behind a high mound.

The layout of the course is also unconventional in that it includes no fewer than 16 par fours! The other two holes are par threes. The terrain comprises classic seaside turf – crisp and playable all year round. There are no trees on the links (and thus little shelter), nor is there any heather. What Elie does possess is some of the finest and truest putting surfaces in the whole of Scotland.

The most memorable holes on the front nine at Elie include, of course, the 1st (beware an out of bounds to the right and beyond the green), the short 3rd, the 6th (beware an old quarry!) and the difficult 9th. The finest sequence, however, occurs at the beginning of the back nine, between the 10th and 13th, all of which run close to the sea. As for Braid's favourite hole, the 13th features a superbly angled green which is slightly raised above the level of the fairway and slopes from right to left – towards the sea. Adding to the challenge is the fact that the hole is often played into a mischievous crosswind.

The 18th is a good finishing hole. There is an out of bounds to the right, bunkers aplenty and, just in front of the green, a large depression: it is Elie's version of the Valley of Sin.

Golf House Club, Elie, Fife KY9 1AS

Professional	Robin Wilson (01333) 330301
Green Fees	WD £40 per day, WE £55 per day
Restrictions	Advisable to book in advance.

Directions
Travelling through Leven, head for St Andrews and Elie is signposted along the road

If there is such a thing as a truly global sport then it has to be golf. From parochial beginnings on the east coast of Scotland it is now played on every continent, in every conceivable corner. Not only are there golf courses on the exotic islands of Tahiti and Bali but there is one in the Himalayas and even in the Arctic. Golf has even been played on the Moon. For all this there remains but one home—St Andrews.

Whilst we will never be able to put an exact date on the time golf was first played on the famous links, several documents refer to a crude form of the game being played as early as the mid 1400s.

As for the right to play at St Andrews, which, of course, the whole world enjoys, the origins are confirmed in a licence dated 1552 drawn up by the Archbishop of St Andrews. It permitted the Archbishop to breed rabbits on the links and confirmed the right of the citizens of St Andrews to 'play at golf, futeball, schueting, at all gamis with all uther, as ever they pleis and in ony time'. Furthermore the proprietor was bound 'not to plough up any part of the said golf links in all time coming.' Organised golf came to St Andrews in 1754 when twenty two Noblemen and Gentlemen formed the St Andrews Society of Golfers. In 1834 the Society became the Royal and Ancient Golf Club.

Not only can all the world play at St Andrews, but all the world wants to and arranging a game on the **Old** Course takes planning. The St Andrews Links Trust handles all matters relating to times of play and they should be contacted well in advance. The summer months are naturally the busiest period and it is best to write to the Trust twelve months prior to intended play, offering if possible a number of alternative dates. The address to write to is **The St Andrews Links Trust, Pilmour Cottage, St Andrews, Fife, KY16 9SF.**

The **General Manager, Mr Alan McGregor** and his staff can be contacted on **tel: (01334) 466666**, by **fax: (01334) 477036** and via the Internet. The handicap limits to play on the Old Course are 28 for men and 36 for ladies, (the men's limit came down to 24 from 1 April 2000) and a handicap certificate is required. It should also be noted that there is no Sunday golf on the Old Course. In 2000 the green fee for a round in summer is priced at £80.

St Andrews is situated 57 miles north east of Edinburgh. For northbound travellers the most direct route to take is the M90 after crossing the Forth Road Bridge. The A91 should be joined at junction 8. This road can be followed to St Andrews. Southbound travellers should head for Perth which is linked in turn to Dundee by the A85 and to the north of Scotland by the A9. From Perth a combination of the A90 and the A913 takes one to Cupar where the A91 can be picked up.

In addition to the Old Course there are four other eighteen hole links at St Andrews: the **New Course**, which dates from 1895, the **Jubilee** (1897)—recently lengthened and improved by Donald Steel—the **Eden** (1914) and the new **Strathtyrum** Course. No handicap certificate is required to play over any of these courses although changes are imminent. The New Course, for instance now has a handicap restriction at 24 for men and 36 for ladies.

The green fees for 2000 on each of the above are £40, £35, £25 and £17 respectively. A nine hole course, the Balgove, is also available (green fee of £7 for 18 holes), together with a driving range and practice facilities.

It was nature that fashioned St Andrews and over the centuries the Old Course has seen little change. Its myriad tiny pot bunkers remain both a fascination and a frustration—providing just enough room, as Bernard Darwin put it, 'for an angry man and his niblick'. Laid out on a narrow strip of land ranging from 50 to 100 yards in width, the Old Course is famed for its enormous double greens. There are seven in all and some are more than an acre in size. With little definition between the fairways there tends to be no standard way of playing a particular hole and as a rule the wind direction will determine the preferred line. Individual holes are not likely to be easily remembered the first time of playing, especially as one will probably be walking the course in a semi-trance.

History is everywhere, and on the first hole as you cross the bridge over the Swilcan Burn a voice from somewhere says, 'they've all walked this bridge'—and of course they have, just as they've all passed through the Elysian Fields, tackled Hell Bunker, the Beardies and the Principal's Nose. And then of course they've all faced the Road Hole with its desperate drive and even more desperate approach and then finally strolled over the great expanse of the 18th fairway towards the Valley of Sin with the famous R & A clubhouse beyond.

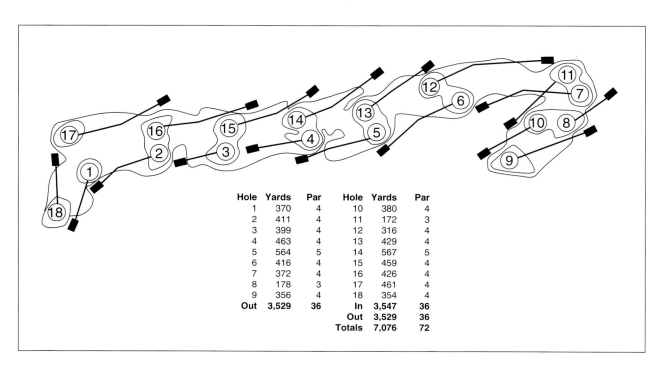

Hole	Yards	Par	Hole	Yards	Par
1	370	4	10	380	4
2	411	4	11	172	3
3	399	4	12	316	4
4	463	4	13	429	4
5	564	5	14	567	5
6	416	4	15	459	4
7	372	4	16	426	4
8	178	3	17	461	4
9	356	4	18	354	4
Out	**3,529**	**36**	**In**	**3,547**	**36**
			Out	**3,529**	**36**
			Totals	**7,076**	**72**

"Tee it high and let it fly"
at the 'Golf International' 1998 Hotel of the Year

Balbirnie is a quite unique multi-award winning hotel which combines understated luxury with superb service and outstanding value. It is a delightful old Georgian house, Grade 'A' listed circa 1777, and sits as the centrepiece of a beautiful 400 acre country estate. Privately owned and managed, this small luxury hotel has a warmth of welcome which is more than a match for the distinctive grace and serenity of the interiors. Individually designed guest bedrooms and suites, elegantly comfortable public rooms and private areas for special events all reflect the splendour inherited from the historic origins of the house.

The hotel offers a varied range of potential dining experiences. The menus incorporate a traditional and classical approach with a light and inventive touch. Balbirnie has the accolade of four AA red stars as well as the RAC Blue Ribbon and was also recently awarded Hotel of the Year by Taste of Scotland.

Views from the house extend over well-manicured lawns and picturesque gardens to the beautifully landscaped Balbirnie Park golf course, a satisfying par 71 challenge which was a prime consideration in the winning of the Golf International 'Hotel of the Year' award. Locally, the championship courses of Leven Links, Lundin Links and Ladybank offer the opportunity to sample Scottish golf at its very best. The Mecca of St Andrews (5 courses) is only half an hour by car and possibly the hardest test of all, Carnoustie is 45 minutes away. All in all there are over a hundred golf courses within one hour of Balbirnie, many being well renowned and justly so.

Balbirnie House's location in the centre of the Kingdom of Fife makes it an ideal base for exploring the historic sights and attractions of the region, with St Andrews, Perth, Dundee and Edinburgh all only a short drive away.

Why not visit and try "The Golfing Enthusiasts Stay" giving the opportunity to enjoy 'golf on the doorstep'. The price includes one round of golf on Balbirnie Park with shared superior accommodation, a feature four course dinner and full Scottish breakfast. £115.00 per person per night sharing double/twin room. (Reserved tee times are generally available) Small to medium size groups can be accommodated in midweek or weekend subject to availability.

Balbirnie House
Balbirnie Park
Markinch, Fife KY7 6NE
Tel: (01592) 610066 Fax: (01592) 610529
e mail : balbirnie@btinternet.com
web site: http://www.balbirnie.co.uk

The Duke's Course (St Andrews)

As our 'British Golf Venue of the Year' feature (see page 14) makes clear no hotel in the world enjoys a better golfing situation than the five star Old Course Hotel at St Andrews. With views over much of the historic links, it literally overlooks the 17th fairway of the Old Course, the most famous—and most infamous—hole in golf.

However, guests of the sumptuous hotel have no special playing privileges on the Old Course—a round cannot be guaranteed. This fact was the major spur behind the hotel owner's decision to construct a new 18 hole championship course within St Andrews. Good links land simply wasn't available so the new course had to be built on an inland site. A few traditionalists were aghast at the notion, although the quality of the end-product has converted all but the diehards. Moreover, perhaps two things should be immediately emphasised. Firstly, the Duke's Course, as it is called, is not the exclusive preserve of hotel residents—it is open to the golfing public—and secondly, sound choices were made with regard to selection of both site and architect.

The Duke's Course was built over a 330 acre site at Craigtoun, just two miles (or a five minute drive) from the Old Course Hotel. It occupies high ground with commanding views over the town of St Andrews, the Eden Estuary and north along the coast to Arbroath and Carnoustie. A mixture of undulating farmland and parkland prior to construction, it included many mature trees, notably silver birch and larch, plus a fair smattering of sentinel pines.

Most traditionalists were persuaded of the wisdom of creating the new course as soon as it was announced that Peter Thomson had been appointed as course architect. A five-time winner of the Open, including the 1955 Championship at St Andrews, the Australian's reputation as a leading course designer has been built around his appreciation of traditional—even classical—principles of golf architecture. To these values he adds a very distinctive personal style and plenty of imagination. Work on the new course began in 1993 and the Duke's was officially opened during the 1995 St Andrews Open.

The design of the Duke's Course encapsulates its architect's philosophies. According to Thomson, 'golf is a game of strategy. It should be played on the ground not in the air . . . the challenge is getting the ball to the green not merely landing on it'. Notwithstanding the nature of the terrain, there is a genuine links feel to many of the holes. Subtle contours have been incorporated into the fairway landing areas and around many of the greens, several of which are plateaued. Pitch and run shots are also encouraged.

The bunkering is particularly impressive. Many are of a links pot-bunker style, not just around the greens but also on the edges, and occasionally in the centre of the fairway! In this respect, and with its isolated stands of trees and burns affecting four of the holes, the Duke's Course resembles Carnoustie. For strategic as well as visual enhancement, gorse and broom have been introduced to the site with the result that on the higher parts of the course there is a distinct heathland-cum-moorland flavour to the holes—a hint of Ganton perhaps?

The round commences with two strong holes. The 1st is a meandering par five and at the 2nd you drive over a marshy area then play an approach to a narrow bunkerless green. Next comes a scenic short hole—the 3rd—enclosed by birch woods with a plateaued green defended by a burn and a deep central bunker. The 4th and 5th are two of the best par fours on the Duke's Course. The wide fairway of the 6th is a welcoming sight whilst a cluster of traps await you to the right of the 7th fairway and one very large bunker protects the entrance to the green on the formidable par three 8th. You return to the clubhouse by way of a curving fairway and a demanding second to a cleverly angled green.

The second nine also begins with a strong hole. The 10th sweeps dramatically downhill from the tee; then dog-legs to the left and is crossed by a burn as it climbs towards the green. The 11th is a huge par five and is followed by a tough par three where the green is perched on a plateau. The 13th charges downhill and features some impressive fairway bunkering. Now comes one of the best and most strategic two-shotters of the round. The drive on the 14th is to a fairway bisected (vertically and diagonally) by a burn. The brave drive is to the right half of the fairway and it sets up a much easier second. The par five 15th looks a birdie opportunity on the card but the approach is severely uphill and the green is guarded by no fewer than eight bunkers. The 16th green is also fiercely defended and the round concludes with an attractive par three and a testing uphill par four with a big, two-tiered stage-like green.

Green fees to play the Duke's in 2000 were £45 per round for hotel residents. Non residents pay £50 per round Mondays to Fridays and £55 per round at weekends. The **Golf Professional** is **John Kelly**. He and his staff can be contacted on **tel: (01334) 474371** and by **fax: (01334) 479456.**

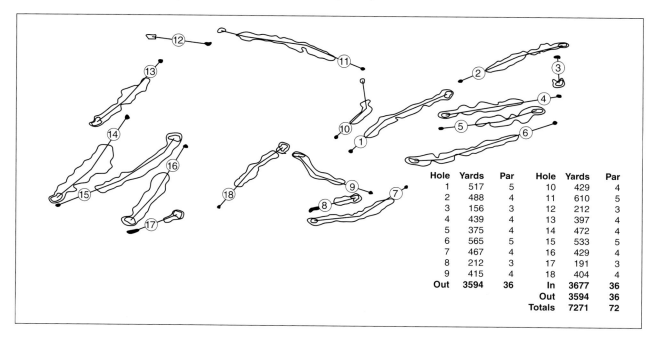

Hole	Yards	Par	Hole	Yards	Par
1	517	5	10	429	4
2	488	4	11	610	5
3	156	3	12	212	3
4	439	4	13	397	4
5	375	4	14	472	4
6	565	5	15	533	5
7	467	4	16	429	4
8	212	3	17	191	3
9	415	4	18	404	4
Out	**3594**	**36**	**In**	**3677**	**36**
			Out	**3594**	**36**
			Totals	**7271**	**72**

St Andrews Golf Hotel is a tastefully modernised Victorian House situated on the cliffs above St Andrews Bay, some 200 yards from the 18th tee of the 'Old Course'.

There are 22 stylish bedrooms all with private bath/shower, furnished individually to a high degree of comfort, with telephone, radio, satellite TV, trouser press, hair dryer and tea/coffee making facilities. A nice touch is the fresh flowers and welcoming fruit basket.

There is a quiet front lounge for residents and a most interesting golfers' cocktail bar featuring pictures and photographs of Open champions past and present. This leads out onto a small south facing patio garden.

With a separate entrance is 'Ma Bells' bar and restaurant—popular with students and visitors alike—serving tasty food all day till 9pm.

Relaxed with a great atmosphere the bar offers an impressive range of beers, spirits, wines and cocktails.

The central feature of the hotel is the award winning 2 AA Rosette Restaurant, candlelit, oak panelled with a magnificent sea view. The à la carte menu features the best of local produce - fish, shellfish, beef, lamb, game and vegetable—conjured into delightful dishes by Chef Colin Masson and served with a warm welcome by restaurant manager Ann and her team. The food is well complemented by an interesting and comprehensive list of wines selected by owner Brain Hughes.

Golf of course, is the speciality of the hotel, and you can find either prepared golf packages and golf weeks or have something tailored to you particular requirements, using any of the 30 or so courses within 45 minutes of St Andrews.

St Andrews Golf Hotel
40 The Scores
St Andrews
Fife KY16 9AS
Tel: (01334) 472611
Fax: (01334) 472188
e mail: thegolfhotel@standrews.co.uk

Aberdour G.C.
(01383) 860080
Seaside Place, Aberdour
(18) 5460 yards/***(Sat)/C

Anstruther G.C.
(01333) 310956
Shore Road, Anstruther
(9) 4537 yards/***/D

Auchterderran G.C.
(01592) 721579
Woodend Road, Cardenden
(9) 2525 yards/***/D

Balbirnie Park G.C.
(01592) 752006
Markinch, Glenrothes
(18) 6210 yards/***/B-A

Ballingry G.C.
(01592) 860086
Crosshill, Lochgelly
(9) 6482 yards/***/E

Burntisland Golf House Club
(01592) 873247
Dodhead, Burntisland
(18) 5908 yards/***/C-B

Canmore G.C.
(01383) 724969
Venturefair Avenue, Dunfermline
(18) 5474 yards/***/C

Cowdenbeath G.C.
(01383) 511918
Cowdenbeath
(9) 6552 yards/***/E

Crail G.S.
(01333) 450686
Fifeness, Crail
(18) 5720 yards/***/C-B

Cupar G.C.
(01334) 653549
Hilltarvit, Cupar
(9) 5300 yards/***/D

Dunfermline G.C.
(01383) 723534
Pitfirrane, Crossford, Dunfermline
(18) 6244 yards/**/B

Dunnikier Park G.C.
(01592) 261599
Dunnikier Way, Kirkcaldy
(18) 6601 yards/***/D

Earlsferry Thistle G.C.
(01333) 330301
Golf Club House, Elie, Leven
(18) 6261 yards/**/B-A
(9) 2277 yards/**/B-A

Elie Golf House Club
(01333) 330301
Elie, Leven
(18) 6261 yards/**/B-A
(9) 2277 yards/**/B-A

Falkland G.C.
(01337) 857404
The Myre, Falkland
(9) 2622 yards/***/F

Glenrothes G.C.
(01592) 758686
Golf Course Road, Glenrothes
(18) 6444 yards/***/D

Kinghorn G.C.
(01592) 890345
McDuff Crescent, Kinghorn
(18) 5629 yards/***/E

Kirkcaldy G.C.
(01592) 260370
Balwearie Road, Kirkcaldy
(18) 6004 yards/***(Sat)/C

Ladybank G.C.
(01337) 830814
Annesmuir, Ladybank
(18) 6641 yards/***/B

Leslie G.C.
(01592) 620040
Balsillie, Leslie
(9) 4940 yards/***/E

Leven Links G.C.
(01333) 421390
The Promenade, Leven
(18) 6434 yards/***/B

Lochgelly G.C.
(01592) 780174
Cartmore Road, Lochgelly
(18) 5491 yards/***/D

Lochore Meadows G.C.
(01592) 414300
Crosshill, Lochgelly
(9) 5554 yards/***/E

Lundin Links
(01333) 320202
Golf Road, Lundin Links
(18) 6377 yards/**(Sun)/C/H

Lundin Ladies
(01333) 320832
Woodie Lea Road, Lundin Links
(9) 4730 yards/***/F

Methil G.C.
(01333) 425535
Links Road, Leven
(18) 6434 yards/***/C

Pitreavie (Dunfermline) G.C.
(01383) 722591
Queensferry Road, Dunfermline
(18) 6032 yards/***/C

St Andrews (01334) 475757
(18) 7076 yards/**(Sun)/A/H/L(Old)
(18) 6604 yards/***/F(New)
(18) 5094 yards/***/F(Strathtyrum)
(18) 6805 yards/***/F(Jubilee)
(18) 6112 yards/***/F(Eden)
(9) 1520 yards/***/F(Balgove)
(18) 7271 yards/***/A(Dukes)

St Michaels G.C.
(01334) 839365
Leuchars, St Andrews
(9) 5510 yards/***(Sun am)/D

Saline G.C.
(01383) 852591
Kinneddar Hill, Saline
(9) 5302 yards/***(Sat)/E

Scoonie G.C.
(01333) 427057
North Links, Leven
(18) 5500 yards/***/F

Scotscraig G.C.
(01382) 552515
Golf Road, Tayport
(18) 6496 yards/**/B/M

Thornton G.C.
(01592) 771111
Station Road, Thornton Village
(18) 6177 yards/***/C-B

Tulliallan G.C.
(01259) 730396
Alloa Road, Tullliallan, Kincardine
(18) 5982 yards/**/F

THE DUKES COURSE, ST ANDREWS
Photograph courtesy of: **Scottish Tourist Board**

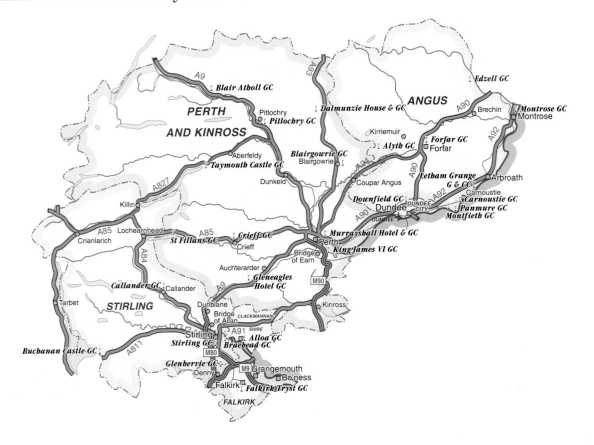

_____ *Tayside & Central Scotland Choice Golf*_____

Inland Gems

If, as the song says, the streams of the mountains please you more than the sea then it is to the likes of **Gleneagles**, **Pitlochry** and **Murrayshall** you will head. If you are one of the diehards who think there is but one form of golf then you will probably set course for **Carnoustie**, **Monifieth** and **Montrose**. Then again, if it is felt that variety is the spice of golf a choice combination of the two can be devised. The heart of Scotland has much to offer of everything.

While there is an inevitable temptation to head for the 'bigger clubs', the Gleneagles and the Carnousties, the region boasts a staggering number of smaller clubs where golf can be equally enjoyable. **Taymouth Castle** and **Callander** are perhaps two of Scotland's lesser known courses, at least to many south of the border, yet they are two of the most scenic courses one is likely to find anywhere. At Callander in early spring the deer come down from the Perthshire hills to forage, a glorious sight, while the course at Taymouth Castle is situated in a conservation area surrounded by beautiful woods.

For golfers travelling northwards, before Gleneagles is reached some excellent golf is to be found at **Falkirk Tryst**, **Glenbervie (Larbert)**, **Braehead** and **Alloa**, while over to the west of the Central region and somewhat isolated is picturesque **Buchanan Castle**. The town of **Stirling** is known as the 'Gateway to the Highlands' and Stirling's golf course has a beautiful setting beneath the Ochil Hills and in the shadow of Stirling Castle.

The world renowned **Gleneagles Hotel** (01764) 662231 near Auchterarder is a superb base, not only to secure a game on one or more of its own magnificent courses (see feature) but also for exploring the many fine golf courses nearby. However, there is certainly no shortage of very good alternatives for a night's stay.

Three miles away the Auchterarder House Hotel (01764) 663646 is excellent and is set amid beautiful gardens. Duchally House (01764) 663071 also has great charm. In Cleish, Nivingston House (01577) 850216 is a small, very pleasant family-run hotel—ideal for the M90 (exit 5), while at Dunblane set in its own 3000 acre estate is the celebrated Cromlix House (01786) 822125 (note especially the marvellous restaurant). Stirling, with its splendid castle offers the Park Lodge (01786) 474862, Fintry the outstanding Culcreuch Castle (01360) 860228, Callander the Roman Camp Hotel (01877) 330003 with its first rate accommodation and restaurant, and Drymen the Buchanan Arms (01360) 860588 a former coaching inn, now modernised with a leisure centre.

After Gleneagles, **Blairgowrie** is probably the best known inland course and it too is featured on a later page. However, the golfer should undoubtedly pay a visit to the 'fair city of Perth'. The **King James VI** Golf Club on Moncrieffe Island is steeped in history while nearby at Scone—former crowning place of kings—is the **Murrayshall** Country House Hotel and its attractive golf course (see ahead). A round here is strongly recommended and the hotel (01738) 551171 offers some of Scotland's best accommodation and cuisine. To the south of Perth at Glenfarg lies the welcoming Glenfarg Hotel and Restaurant (01577) 830241, a true golfing haven set in beautiful surroundings and ideal for St Andrews, Gleneagles and Carnoustie. Visitors tackling Blairgowrie have a choice of two excellent hotels. Dupplin Castle (01738) 623224 is a magnificent country house well situated for all the area's attractions and Altamount House Hotel (01250) 873512 provides stunning Scottish cuisine in a delightful atmosphere.

Those wishing to stay in Blairgowrie itself should consider the Rosemount Golf Hotel (01250) 872604 or the Moorfield House Hotel

(01828) 627303. Another really first class hotel is Kinloch House (01250) 884237, a delightful example of a Scottish country house.

A little distance to the west of Perth there is more fine golf at **Crieff** where there are 27 holes (note the Crieff Hydro (01764) 655555 and a very pretty 9 hole course even further west at **St Fillans** where the Four Seasons (0176485) 333 is a charming place to stay. To the north of our region and tucked away amid some breathtaking scenery **Dalmunzie House** (01250) 885224 should not be forgotten; situated at Spittal O'Glenshee, the hotel has its own spectacular 9 hole golf course where drives are said to travel further in the rarified atmosphere! The Ardeonaig Hotel (01567) 820400 near Killin combines splendid views with comfortable accommodation, and in this respect Kinnaird (01796) 482440 can also never be too highly praised. This is a superb hotel where fishermen as well as golfers will be content.

Dalmunzie House Hotel
Spittal O'Glenshee, Blairgowrie,
Perthshire PH10 7QG
Tel: (01250) 885224 Fax: (01250) 885225

Dalmunzie House enjoys a glorious position in the mountains of the Scottish Highlands. The hotels stands in its own 6000 acre mountain estate. It is owned and run by the Winton family who have been in the glen for a number of decades and have many years experience in looking after guests.

The hotel itself is cosy, the atmosphere is cosy and welcoming, with the emphasis on friendliness. All the bedrooms are en suite, each with its own individual character with charming decor and restful tranquility relfecting the ambience found all around at Dalmunzie.

Many activities can be pursued here, the hotel has its own private golf course, tennis court and games room. Patrons can fish, shoot and stalk, and even ski at the nearby Glenshee Ski Centre. The perfect stay awaits you at Dalmunzie.

13th TEE, GLENS COURSE, LETHAM Photograph courtesy of: **Letham Golf Club**

Returning to Blairgowrie, if a game cannot be arranged on either of the club's outstanding courses, then the heathland course at **Alyth** is very close and certainly won't disappoint. The Lands Of Loyal (01828) 633151 is a comfortable hotel close to the course and the nearby Losset Inn (01828) 632393 is more modest but equally accommodating. Drumnacree House (01828) 632194 is another winner—excellent food and good value accommodation. Perth's delights as mentioned are at hand to the south, while to the west is **Taymouth Castle** and

to the north along the A9 stands **Pitlochry**. The latter is another course many will choose to play, for this is one of the most attractive in Britain—a veritable 'theatre in the hills'. Green fees at all these courses are relatively inexpensive and certainly very good value. Still further north the scenic 9 holer at **Blair Atholl** is also worth a visit. In Strathtay, near Pitlochry a recommended 19th hole is the Grantully Hotel (01887) 840207, while Westlands of Pitlochry (01796) 472266 is another to offer good quality and value.

More ideas for a relaxing stay include the Kenmore Hotel (01887) 830205 in Kenmore, ideal for Taymouth Castle. Scotland's oldest inn is the Killiecrankie Hotel (01796) 473220 in Killiecrankie (north of Pitlochry). Other ideas include the sporty Ballathie House (01250) 883268 at Kinclaven by Stanley, and the Log Cabin (01250) 881288 at Kirkmichael. Indeed, the list is almost endless, such is the popularity of this magnificent area.

East of Dundee
Some of Scotland's greatest links courses are to be found between Dundee and Montrose on the Tayside coast. However, just to the north west of Dundee lies **Downfield** one of the country's finest inland courses. Indeed, five times Open Champion Peter Thomson rates this heavily wooded parkland course as one of the best inland courses in the world. It is said that Downfield is very popular with American visitors because it reminds them of some of their better courses 'back home'.

East of Dundee, the Medal Course at **Monifieth** has staged the Scottish Amateur Championship, while **Panmure** at Barry has in the past hosted the Seniors' Championship. Both are classic links courses and fairly inexpensive to play over. **Carnoustie** is, of course, one of Scotland's greatest golfing shrines and along with Montrose, Gleneagles, Letham Grange, Murrayshall and Blairgowrie is featured ahead. **Montrose**, like Monifeith, is a public links (two courses at each in fact) and when the winds blow can be extremely difficult. As earlier noted, green fees along this great coastal stretch are relatively cheap and provided some forward planning is done a game is possible at most times.

A brief word on staying in the area. In Carnoustie, the Carnoustie Golf Hotel (01241) 411999 is obviously very convenient for the Carnoustie Links, as are the Park Hotel (01674) 673415 and Links Hotel (01674) 671000 in Montrose which both offer golfing packages. The Castleton House (01307) 840340 by Glamis is another establishment few will find fault with, and for those seeking excellent value, the Kingsley Guesthouse (01241) 873933 in Arbroath provides exactly that. Moorfield House (01828) 627303 in Cupar Angus is also well worth trying. Back in Carnoustie, one restaurant worth trying is 11 Park Avenue (01241) 853336.

Finally, two inland courses to the north east of Tayside which strongly merit attention are **Edzell** and **Letham Grange**. The former, just north of Brechin, and in a charming village is a beautiful heathland course where some marvellous mountain views can be enjoyed. The Glenesk Hotel (01356) 648319 is but a par four away. Letham Grange is a hotel and country club (01241) 890373 and is situated at Colliston

near Arbroath. The hotel is a splendidly restored Victorian mansion with 36 holes of golf now on offer, is well worth a visit.

13th HOLE, QUEEN'S COURSE, GLENEAGLES
Photograph courtesy of: David J. Whyte

CARNOUSTIE *Photograph courtesy of:* **Scottish Tourist Board**

Gleneagles

There is a vast oil painting that hangs in the Tate Gallery in London; the artist is John Martin and the painting is titled 'The Plains Of Heaven'. Some may know it well, others will wonder what on earth I'm gibbering on about—suffice to say that it depicts in the most vivid colours imaginable the artist's impression of Paradise. I suspect that John Martin wasn't a golfer. Blasphemy isn't intended but for many of us who stalk the fairways of the world, Gleneagles is just about our best idea of how heaven might look—give or take a couple of angels.

The Gleneagles Hotel and its golf courses are set in the heart of some of the most glorious Perthshire countryside. Surrounded by the foothills of the Grampian Mountain range, everywhere one turns there is a shock of colour. The mountains themselves often appear wrapped in purples and blues. Heather, silver birch and rowan cover the crisp moorland turf. With so much around one could be forgiven for losing a little concentration, yet the golf too is glorious and for those wishing to enjoy their golf in leisurely five star surroundings there really is nothing quite like Gleneagles.

The land was first surveyed with a view to designing one or more golf courses before the first World War and James Braid was called in to direct affairs. By 1919 the **King's** and **Queen's** courses were both open for play. Braid's work met with instant acclaim and in 1921 the forerunner of the Ryder Cup was staged at Gleneagles, when a team of British professionals played a team from America.

Until quite recently The Gleneagles Hotel managed and maintained four 18 hole golf courses, the Prince's and Glendevon courses being opened in 1974 and 1980 respectively. However, the Prince's and Glendevon courses no longer exist for a very good reason: in May 1993 a Jack Nicklaus-designed championship course opened for play. It is Nicklaus' first course in Scotland and, like his first ventures in England (St Mellion) and Ireland (Mount Juliet), it has generated an enormous amount of interest. Laid out on land previously utilised by the Prince's and Glendevon courses, plus adjacent acquired land, the **Monarch's** Course measures in excess of 7000 yards from the championship tees.

Things are certainly happening apace at Gleneagles and a sparkling new clubhouse has also been constructed. Its architectural style is in keeping with the Edwardian hotel. In 2000 the green fee for hotel residents is £85 per round (on any of the three courses) from May to October, reducing to £60 from November to April. **Greg Schofield**, the Gleneagles' golf **Professional** can be reached on **tel: (01764) 662231** or by **fax: (01764) 662134.**

Located approximately midway between Perth and Stirling and half a mile west of Auchterarder, Gleneagles is easily reached by road. The A9, which in fact links Perth to Stirling is likely to prove of most assistance. Travelling from the Glasgow region a combination of the A80 and the M80 should be taken to Stirling. Those approaching from further south can avoid Glasgow by following the A74 and the M74/M73 joining the A80 below Stirling. Motoring from Edinburgh the best route is to cross the Forth Road Bridge via the A90 heading for Dunfermline and thereafter taking the A823 road to Auchterarder. Southbound travellers will find the A9 helpful if coming from the Highlands via Blair Atholl and Pitlochry, while from the north east of Scotland, the A92 links Aberdeen to Dundee and Dundee is in turn linked to Perth by the A85. The Gleneagles Hotel can also be reached by rail, with a bus meeting trains from Gleneagles station.

Measuring 6471 yards, par 70, the King's course is some 500 yards longer that the Queen's at 5965 yards, par 68. Perhaps the best known hole at Gleneagles is Braid's Brawest, the 13th on the King's Course—a tough par four requiring a long straight drive to carry a ridge and a second to a raised and heavily guarded sloping green. Other fine holes include the highly characterful 3rd, the par three 5th, the cavalier 9th and the extremely picturesque 14th.

Many will have first viewed the glories of Gleneagles through the medium of television. The BBC Pro-Celebrity series was staged on several occasions during the 1970s and in the mid 1980s the European Tour brought the Scottish Open to Gleneagles. It was played over the King's Course for 6 years, before 'moving east' to Carnoustie—and then disappearing altogether . . . Paradise Lost?!

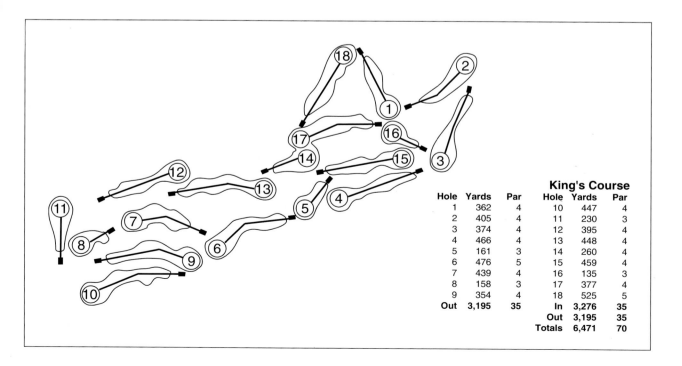

Hole	Yards	Par	Hole	Yards	Par
1	362	4	10	447	4
2	405	4	11	230	3
3	374	4	12	395	4
4	466	4	13	448	4
5	161	3	14	260	4
6	476	5	15	459	4
7	439	4	16	135	3
8	158	3	17	377	4
9	354	4	18	525	5
Out	**3,195**	**35**	**In**	**3,276**	**35**
			Out	**3,195**	**35**
			Totals	**6,471**	**70**

King's Course

Blairgowrie

With so many outstanding courses to choose from, all within fairly close proximity of one another, even the most blinkered of diehard Englishmen would be forced to concede that Scotland is just about the finest place on earth for a week's golfing holiday. Given seven precious days a large number of would-be travellers on opening their maps of Scotland are likely to plan a trip thus: three days on the west coast playing Prestwick, Turnberry and Troon; a day in the middle visiting Gleneagles, finishing with three on the east coast taking in Carnoustie, St Andrews and Muirfield. Marvellous stuff of course, but many of the golfing sages hold the opinion that such an itinerary misses out the finest gem of all—the Rosemount Course at Blairgowrie.

There are in fact two 18 hole courses at Blairgowrie, the older and more celebrated **Rosemount**, designed by James Braid and the **Lansdowne** Course, a fairly recent addition, the work of Peter Alliss and Dave Thomas. On each, golf is played over beautiful moorland fairways, lined by great forests of pine, larch and silver birch. A liberal sprinkling of purple heather and gorse add considerable colour to an already majestic setting—as one obviously bewitched observer put it, 'somebody seems to have gone mad with a paintbrush!'

Measuring 6590 yards, par 72 from the medal tees (6239 yards, par 70 from the forward tees) the Rosemount Course may not be the toughest challenge one is likely to face but it must rank among the most enchanting. The course and surrounding landscape abound with wildlife, from pheasants and partridge to deer and winter geese, but the golfer who lifts his head too much is likely to suffer over the closing stretch—the 16th, 17th and 18th are all difficult holes, especially the 16th where the golfer must twice confront the infamous Black Loch.

The official course record at Rosemount stands at 64, though in 1973, during a practice round for the Sumrie Better-Ball tournament, professional Lionel Platts achieved an amazing ten consecutive birdies between the 8th and 17th—quite obscene don't you think?! The Lansdowne course is slightly longer than its older brother, and many would say a much sterner test—either way a game on each is strongly recommended.

It need hardly be added that Blairgowrie with its two courses—three if one includes the aptly named Wee Course, a short nine-holer—has a more than adequate 19th. Lunches, high teas, dinners and light snacks are all offered. There are also two bars—comfortable places where many will choose to go and celebrate a magnificent day's golfing in one of the most glorious settings the game has to offer. Planning a week's golf?

**Blairgowrie Golf Club, Golf Course Road,
Blairgowrie, Perthshire, PH10 6LG
www.blairgowrie-golf.co.uk**

The Starter	(01250) 872594 (tee reservations)
Sec/Manager	J N Simpson (01250) 872622
Professional	Charles Dernie (01250) 873116
Green Fees	WD £50 (£60 per day)
	WE £55 (£75 per day)
Restrictions	Handicaps required

Directions
Two miles south of Blairgowrie off the A93

Letham Grange

There are 'dreamers' and there are 'doers'. Once in every blue moon—thank heavens—the two combine.

Soon after the late Sir Henry Cotton officially opened Letham Grange in 1987, Malcolm Campbell, the then editor of Golf Monthly bravely announced, 'We now have the "Augusta of Scotland". In a generally critical article a second leading UK golf magazine later lambasted this judgement saying it was, 'a bit like trying to sell blended whisky as a twelve year old malt.' But then we are a nation of 'knockers' aren't we? Of course Letham Grange isn't the equal of Augusta, where the azaleas and dogwoods run riot, but it is a wonderfully enjoyable place to play golf nonetheless and there is at least one parallel in the manner of its creation. Like Augusta, Letham Grange is the result of one man's dream. Down in Georgia the guiding force was a man named Jones; up in Angus it was a man called Smith. Letham Grange was Ken Smith's dream and aside from the quality of the end product I wouldn't be quick to criticise Letham Grange for the very fact that Ken Smith had the guts, vision and determination to do something about his dream.

It is an extraordinary place. Letham Grange is where a typical and, until recently, 'oh so timeless' Scottish country estate confronts a 20th century 'hotel and country club golf' head on. In fact, the Victorian mansion which presides over the heavily wooded and rolling estate had become derelict by the mid 1970s, before the golfing dream was conceived. This same mansion is now one of Scotland's most luxurious 19th hole retreats. Moreover, time no longer stands still at Letham Grange for since 1991 the estate has boasted two 18 hole courses—the slightly revised 1987 layout now being called the Old Course(!)

At 5528 yards, par 68, the Glen's Course is more than 1000 yards shorter than its older sister (6614 yards, par 73) and there are none of the water hazards that make the Old Course at once potentially treacherous and positively spectacular.

The finest run of holes at Letham Grange occurs between the 8th and 10th on the Old Course—a stunning sequence and one which has been compared with the celebrated 10th, 11th and 12th at St Mellion. The pick of these is probably the two-shot 10th where the player drives from an elevated tee (usually with an iron), threading it along an ever-narrowing fairway and then fires an approach across the corner of an encroaching lake to a stage-like green. Another superb hole is the par three 16th: here the green is once again the 'wrong side' of water and is set at such an angle that only the very bold, precisely struck tee shot will be rewarded. Not a hole for the nit-picking 'knockers'.

**Letham Grange Hotel and Golf Courses, Colliston,
by Arbroath, Angus, DD11 4RL
www.lethamgrange.co.uk**

Golf Professional	Steven Moir (01241) 890377
Golf Administrator	Ewan Wilson (01241) 890377
	Fax (01241) 890725
Green Fees	Old WD £35/WE £40
	Glen's WD £18/WE £22.50
	Above prices per round
Restrictions	Tuesday, Friday and weekend mornings

Directions
The club is 4 miles north of Arbroath off the A933.

Letham Grange Mansion House Hotel and Golf Courses

At the heart of 'Carnoustie country' lies the superb Letham Grange Hotel and Golf Courses. The magnificent Victorian mansion house hotel overlooks this stunning Donald Steel course.

The mansion has been restored to its former glory as a top quality, four star hotel with 20 bedrooms, offering a style and standard of living which is both traditional and sumptuous. In addition 22 modern bedrooms are available in the Letham Grange Golf Estate accommodation.

36 holes of magnificent golf! Widely acclaimed as 'the Augusta of Scotland', the Old Course provides a blend of tree-lined parkland and open rolling fairways. With water playing a major role, the course is both scenic and dramatic and will host the Scottish Amateur Strokeplay in June.

The Glens Course, although slightly shorter—and without the water hazards—offers golfers a more relaxed and less arduous round. However, it is deceptively tricky!

Letham Grange Hotel
Colliston by Arbroath
DD11 4RL
Tel: (01241) 890373
Fax: (01241) 890725
e mail: lethamgrange@sol.co.uk
web site: www.lethamgrange.co.uk

Montrose

Perhaps there are two things that strike you most when you arrive at one of the famous golfing links on the east coast of Scotland:. The first will almost certainly be the thought, 'So this is where it all started'—which can often leave one slightly numb. The second, and equally numbing, is likely to be the thought, 'Will this wretched wind ever die down?' The famous links at Montrose is just such a place.

Golf has been played on Montrose links since the 16th century and according to the best records it is the fifth oldest course in the world. By course is meant the **Medal** Course, for there are two 18 hole links at Montrose, the Medal and the shorter **Broomfield** Course, the former having altered surprisingly little through the ages. One interesting fact is that in the 1800s, at a time when one or two more famous clubs had only 5 holes, the Medal Course at Montrose boasted 25! All of which were played in a unique tournament in 1866 won by a Mr T Doleman from Glasgow who played the 25 holes in 112 strokes. Willie Park, winner of the first Open Championship in 1860, finished second scoring a 115.

In common with St Andrews and Carnoustie, Montrose is a public links and although three golf clubs play over the two courses—the Royal Montrose, Caledonia and Mercantile Clubs—both courses are managed by the Montrose Links Trust who handle all administrative matters.

Apart from their length—the Medal Course measures 6470 yards (par 71) and the Broomfield 4865 yards (par 66)—the two courses differ in other respects. The Broomfield is laid out on the landward side of the Medal and is considerably flatter. With its many subtle—and many not-so-subtle—undulations the Medal is by far the more testing so it is not surprising that major championships are held here. These have included the Scottish Professional Championship, the Scottish Amateur Championship, and the British Boys Championship and Internationals.

For twelve of its eighteen holes, the Medal Course follows the line of the dunes, with the par three 3rd, the 4th and the 9th being especially memorable. However, some of the best holes appear at the end of the round—the 16th (Gully) being a particularly long par three with a wildly contoured green and the 17th (Rashes) with its raised shelf-like green, one of those par fours requiring, as a caddy once put it, three damned good shots to get up in two! For a 19th hole, visitors are more than adequately catered for by the golf clubs, each of which has a clubhouse adjacent to the links.

There are no airs and graces about Montrose—it is what might be described as a good honest links. But if you've come to Scotland to admire the golf, then Montrose is clearly one that shouldn't be missed.

Montrose Links Trust, Traill Drive, Montrose Angus, DD10 8SW	
Sec/Manager	Mrs Margaret Stewart (01674) 672932
Professional	Kevin Stables (01674) 672634
Green Fees	Medal WD £28/round, WD £38/day
	Medal WE £32/round, WE £48/day
	Broomfield WD £12 per day
Restrictions	Medal: No visitors Saturdays before 2.30 pm or Sundays before 10 am. Handicap certificates required.
	Broomfield: No restrictions.
Directions	
North of Montrose, signposted off the A92.	

Murrayshall

Perth is a legendary place, a city steeped in history and one surrounded by stunning natural beauty. Perthshire the county evokes thoughts of everything Scottish. To North Americans, mention of the very word 'Perthshire' is enough to send them drooling. It is arguably one of the most romantic places in the world and for golfers, whether from the New World or the Old, the contemplation of a game of golf in the heart of Scotland is enough to make us forget a tweaked three footer (well almost).

It is often said that a person's golfing education is incomplete until he or she has swung a club in Scotland. And how can you visit Scotland without visiting Perth, the ancient crowning place of kings? To the south west of Perth, and half an hour's drive away is Gleneagles which, along with St Andrews and Augusta, is surely one of the three best known golfing centres in the world. Almost due north of Perth and again about 30 minutes by road is Blairgowrie and the delights of the Rosemount and Lansdowne courses. A little further, but still no more than an hour, are St Andrews and Carnoustie. Perth cannot be a bad place sitting amidst all this finery! But there is more. Right on the city's doorstep, not four miles from the town centre, is a comparatively modern golfing jewel—the Murrayshall Country House Hotel and Golf Course.

Murrayshall is where the peacocks strut, the pheasants call and the deer run freely in the woods. Designed by J Hamilton Stutt and opened in 1981, the golf course is set in 300 acres of truly rolling parkland The holes weave their way in and out of the copses and alongside ponds. In fact, there is quite a lot of water at Murrayshall—little lakes, ponds and streams—but the golfer is guided over and around them via quaint stone bridges. Some 200,000 tulips adorn the hotel grounds and golf course. Yes, Murrayshall makes folks drool and perhaps at least smile after that missed three foot putt.

From the back markers, Murrayshall measures 6441 yards, par 73. The forward tees reduce the course to around the 6000 yards mark. It isn't a long course by any means but is both attractive and challenging and certainly full of interest. Many of the fairways are bordered by magnificent oaks, copper beeches and chestnuts—not to mention those marvellous tulips. There are also some wonderful views from the higher parts of the course.

Notable holes include the 3rd, one of those par four and a half holes; the short 4th, where if you mishit you will land in the pond; the severely dog-legged 7th—so severe that it is known as the 'dog's grave'—and most people's favourite, the short par four 10th where the approach is played over water to a raised green.

Murrayshall Country House Hotel and Golf Course, Murrayshall, Scone, Perthshire, PH2 7PH	
Golf Manager	Alan Reid (01738) 552784
	Fax (01738) 552595
Professional	Book through the Golf Manager
Green Fees	WD £25/round, £40/day
	WE £27/round, £40/day
	Reduced rates for hotel residents.
Directions	
Perth is easily reached from all directions, being linked to Edinburgh by the M90, the Highlands by the A9 and	

Set on a hillside overlooking the Vale of Strathmore to the Sidlaw Hills beyond, lies the Lands of Loyal. This impressive Victorian mansion was built in the 1830s, commissioned by Sir William Ogilvy, who on his return from Waterloo chose Loyal Hill as the site for this magnificent home. The Lands of Loyal was subsequently owned by a succession of families until it was converted into an hotel in 1945.

Since then it has been very prominent in the area, holding fond memories for the oldest generations. It is also highly regarded as a second home to country sportsmen who have remained loyal for many years. More recently extensive refurbishment of the public rooms has further enhanced the unique atmosphere of this much respected country house hotel.

The restaurant is highly acclaimed in its own right, with a style of cuisine that is both traditional and imaginative, making full use of local fish and game. An extensive wine list, is available to complement your meal.

The Lands of Loyal makes an ideal base for the ambitious golfer. Perthshire has 30 golf courses in total with remarkable variety. All courses are within an hour's drive of the hotel with some of the most famous and desirable spots only a few minutes away.

As fundamentally a sportsman's hotel, The Lands of Loyal appreciates the needs of the golfer. Very early breakfasts and unusually flexible dining arrangements, quality packed lunches etc, are offered courteously. Private rooms for parties can can also be requested in advance.

The hotel management are delighted to arrange a complete itinerary for the golfer, whether an individual or a group. Tee times can be arranged and any correspondence with golf clubs will gladly be undertaken..

The Lands of Loyal provides a complete and competitive golfing package. A full colour brochure and tariff is available on request.

Karl-Peter & Patricia Howell
The Lands of Loyal Hotel
Alyth
Perthshire
Scotland PH11 8JQ
Tel: (01828) 633151
Fax: (01828) 633313
e mail: info@landsofloyal.co.uk
web site: www.landsofloyal.com

Carnoustie

Walter Hagen—a shrewd judge you might think—once described Carnoustie as the greatest course in the British Isles. There are many who would agree with the great man, though doubtless the disciples of St Andrews and several honourable gentlemen at Muirfield would beg to differ. Greatest or not, very few would dispute that when the winds blow—as they invariably do in these parts—Carnoustie is the toughest of all our championship links.

In the days when the Campbells and the MacDonalds were busy slaughtering each other up in the Highlands, down at Carnoustie more civilised pursuits were taking place. Records suggest that golf was being played on the adjoining Barry Links as early as the 16th century. The first official club at Carnoustie—today there are six—was founded in 1842 and golf was played over a ten hole course laid out by Allan Robertson. Later, 'Old' Tom Morris came on the scene and extended the links to a full 18 holes, but the present championship course didn't really take shape until James Braid made several alterations in 1926. By 1931 Carnoustie was ready to stage its first Open Championship.

As previously mentioned there are presently six clubs at Carnoustie and play is now over three 18 hole courses: the **Championship**, the **Burnside** and the **Buddon**. Administrative matters are in the hands of the Carnoustie Golf Links Management Committee and those wishing to visit Carnoustie should direct correspondence to the committee's **Secretary, John Martin.** Their full address is **The Carnoustie Golf Links Management Committee, Links Parade, Carnoustie, Tayside, DD7 7JE tel: (01241) 853789 and fax: (01241) 852720.** Handicap certificates are required for the Championship course and starting times must be booked in advance.

In 2000, the green fees to play at Carnoustie are £70 for a single round on the Championship course with £85 securing a round over both the Championship and Burnside courses and £85 for a round over the Championship course and Buddon Links. Fees to play just the Burnside course (£25 per round or £50 per day) or Buddon Links(£20 per round or £40 per day) are good value. Details of these tickets can be obtained by phoning the above number. Caddies can also be arranged.

The cluster of clubs that go to make up Carnoustie's permanent golfing village have traditionally provided all the ususal amenities

for the visiting golfer—golf shops for clothing, equipment and club hire and of course a more than adequate 19th hole; to this we can now add the fine facilities offered by the Carnoustie Golf Hotel which overlooks the 18th green on the Championship Links.

Travelling to Carnoustie shouldn't present too many problems. The Forth Road Bridge and the M90 link the Edinburgh region with Perth. Perth in turn is linked to Dundee by the A85 (dual carriageway all the way) and Dundee to Carnoustie by the A390. Those on golfing tours will quite likely be coming via St Andrews. The A91 (A919) runs from St Andrews towards Dundee. It picks up the A92 just before the Tay Road Bridge and on crossing the bridge the A930 should immediately be joined. Approaching from northerly directions, the A92 runs from Aberdeen (and beyond) to within a couple of miles of Carnoustie at Muirdrum, while the A958 links the town with Forfar. Carnoustie can also be reached by train with connections from Perth, Dundee and Aberdeen.

It isn't only the wind that makes Carnoustie such a difficult and daunting test. When the championship tees are in use the course stretches close to 7000 yards. From the club medal tees, 6941 yards is still a formidable proposition. The bunkering at Carnoustie is extremely impressive. A few courses may have more bunkers but nowhere are they quite so cavernous or as consistently well positioned.

Scotland is the land of Burns. It is also the land of burns—streams or creeks anywhere else in the English-speaking world—and Carnoustie is famous for them (just ask John van der Velde). The ubiquitous Barry Burn and its wee brother Jockie's Burn traverse the fairways in the most unfriendly and awkward of places, often in front of greens and across the spot you'd ideally like to drive to.

More than anything else though, Carnoustie is renowned for its incredibly tough finishing stretch. The 16th is an exceptionally long short hole, the 17th has the Barry Burn meandering across its fairway, making it a particularly difficult driving hole and at the 18th the Burn crosses in front of the green, necessitating one of the most exciting (or nerve-racking) closing shots in golf.

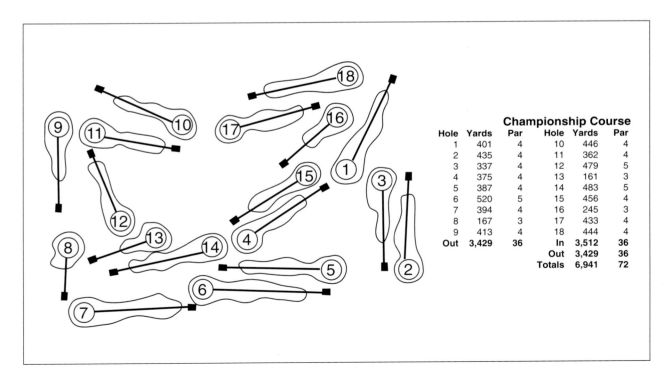

Championship Course

Hole	Yards	Par	Hole	Yards	Par
1	401	4	10	446	4
2	435	4	11	362	4
3	337	4	12	479	5
4	375	4	13	161	3
5	387	4	14	483	5
6	520	5	15	456	4
7	394	4	16	245	3
8	167	3	17	433	4
9	413	4	18	444	4
Out	3,429	36	In	3,512	36
			Out	3,429	36
			Totals	6,941	72

Aberfeldy G.C.
(01887) 820535
Taybridge Road, Aberfeldy
(18) 5972 yards/**/D

Aberfoyle G.C.
(01877) 382493
Braeval, Aberfoyle
(18) 5218 yards/***/C

Alloa G.C.
(01259) 722745
Schawpark, Sauchie
(18) 6240 yards/**/D

Alva G.C.
(01259) 760431
Beauclerc Street, Alva
(9) 2423 yards/**/D/H

Alyth G.C.
(01828) 632268
Pitcrocknie, Alyth
(18) 6226 yards/***/F

Arbroath G.C.
(01241) 875837
Elliot, Arbroath, Angus
(18) 6090 yards/**/C

Arbroath Artisans G.C.
(01241) 875872
Elliot. Arbroath
(18) 6185 yards/*/F

Auchterarder G.C.
(01764) 662804
Ochil Road, Auchterarder
(18) 5778 yards/***/C/H

Bishopshire G.C.
(01592) 780203
Kinneswood, Kinross
(10) 4700 metres/***/E

Blair Atholl G.C.
(01796) 481274
Blair Atholl, Perthshire
(9) 5620 yards/***/D

Blairgowrie G.C.
(01250) 872622
Rosemount, Blairgowrie
(18) 6588 yards/***(Wed)/B-A/H
(18) 6895 yards/***(Wed)/B-A/H
(9) 4654 yards/***(Wed)/F/H

Bonnybridge G.C.
(01324) 812822
Larbert Road, Bonnybridge
(9) 6060 yards/***/F

Braehead G.C.
(01259) 725766
Cambus, by Alloa
(18) 6041 yards/***/D/H

Brechin G.C.
(01356) 622383
Trinity, by Brechin, Angus
(18) 6200 yards/***/C-B/H

Bridge of Allan G.C.
(01786) 832332
Sunlaw, Bridge of Allan, Stirling
(9) 4932 yards/***(Sat)/E

Buchanan Castle G.C.
(01360) 660307
Drymen
(18) 6015 yards/***/F

Caird Park G.C.
(01382) 434706
Mains Loan, Dundee
(18) 6303 yards/***/C

Callander G.C.
(01877) 330090
Aveland Road, Callander
(18) 5125 yards/***/C/H

Camperdown G.C.
(01382) 434706
Camperdown Park, Dundee
(18) 6561 yards/***/E

Campsie G.C.
(01360) 310920
Crow Road, Lennoxtown
(18) 5517 yards/**/D

Carnoustie
(01241) 853789
Links Parade, Carnoustie, Angus
(18) 6941 yards/***/A/H (Championship)
(18) 6020 yards/***/B/H (Burnside)
(18) 5420 yards/***/C/H (Buddon)

Comrie G.C.
(01764) 670055
Cowden Way, Comrie
(9) 4040 yards/***/D

Craigie Hill G.C.
(01738) 622644
Cherrybank, Perth
(18) 5386 yards/**/D

Crieff G.C.
(01764) 652909
Perth Road, Crieff
(18) 6402 yards/***/C
(9) 4772 yards/***/D

Crieff Hydro G.C.
Crieff, Perth
(01764) 651615
(9) 2137 yards/***/D

Dalmunzie Hotel & G.C.
(01250) 885224
Spittal of Glenshee, Blairgowrie
(9) 2035/***/E

Dollar G.C.
(01259) 742400
Brewlands House, Dollar
(18) 5242 yards/***/D

Downfield G.C.
(01382) 825595
Turnberry Avenue, Dundee
(18) 6822 yards/***/C-B/H

Dunblane New G.C
(01786) 823771
Perth Road, Dunblane
(18) 5957 yards/**/C

Dunkeld and Birnam G.C.
(01350) 727524
Fungarth, Dunkeld
(9) 5240 yards/***/D

Dunning G.C.
(01764) 684747
Rollo Park, Dunning, Perth
(9) 4836 yards/***/D/G

Edzell G.C.
(01356) 647283
High Street, Edzell, by Brechin
(18) 6348 yards/***/F/H

Falkirk G.C.
(01324) 611061
Stirling Road, Cumlins, Falkirk
(18) 6230 yards/**/D

Falkirk Tryst G.C.
(01324) 562415
Burnhead Road, Larbert
(18) 6053 yards/**/C/H

Forfar G.C.
(01307) 462120
Arbroath Road, Forfar, Angus
(18) 6052 yards/***/B-A/H

Glenalmond G.C.
(01738) 880275
Trinity College, Glenalmond
(9) 5812 yards/*/G

Glenbervie G.C.
(01324) 562605
Stirling Road, Larbert
(18) 6469 yards/**/B-A/L

Gleneagles Hotel & G.C.
(01764) 663543
Auchterarder
(18) 7081 yards/*/A/G
(18) 6471 yards/*/A/G
(18) 5965 yards/*/A/G

Grangemouth Municipal G.C
(01324) 711500
Polmont Hill, Polmont, Falkirk
(18) 6314 yards/***/E

Green Hotel G.C.
(01577) 863407
Beeches Park, Kinross
(18) 6257 yards/***/D
(18) 6456 yards/***/D

Kenmore G.C.
(01887) 830226
Kenmore, Aberfeldy
(9) 6052 yards/***(Thurs pm)/D

Killin G.C.
(01567) 820312
Killin
(9) 5200 yards/***/D

King James VI G.C.
(01738) 445132
Moncreiffe Island, Perth
(18) 5664 yards/**/D

Kirriemuir Players G.C.
(01575) 573317
Kirriemuir, Angus
(18) 5510 yards/**/C/H

Leitie Links G.C.
(01828) 633322
Alyth, Blairgowrie
(9) 1719 yards/***/E

Letham Grange G.C.
(01241) 890373
Letham Grange, Colliston
(18) 6614 yards/**/B
(18) 5528 yards/**/C

Milnathort G.C.
(01577) 864069
South Street, Milnathort
(9) 5969 yards/***/D

Monifieth Links G.C.
(01382) 532767
Dundee, Angus
(18) 6657 yards/***(Sat)/B/H
(18) 5123 yards/***(Sat)/B

Montrose Links Trust
(01674) 672932
Traill Drive, Montrose, Angus
(18) 6470 yards/**/C
(18) 4865 yards/**/E

Muckhart G.C.
(01259) 781423
Drumburn Road, Muckhart, Dollar
(18) 6034 yards/***/C/H

Murrayshall Hotel & G.C.
(01738) 552784
Murrayshall, Scone, Perth
(18) 6446 yards/***/B

Muthill G.C.
(01764) 681523
Peat Road, Muthill, Crieff
(9) 4700 yards/***/D

North Inch G.C.
(01738) 636481
Hay Street, Perth
(18) 5178 yards/***/E

Panmure G.C.
(01241) 855120
Barry, Angus
(18) 6317 yards/***(Sat)/B-A

Pitlochry G.C.
(01796) 472792
Golf Course Road, Pitlochry
(18) 5811 yards/***/C/H

Polmont G.C.
(01324) 711277
Maddiston, by Falkirk
(9) 3033 yards/**/E/H

St Fillans G.C.
(01764) 685312
St Fillans, Perthshire
(9) 5268 yards/***/D

Stirling G.C.
(01786) 473801
Queens Road, Stirling
(18) 6438 yards/**/C/H

Strathtay G.C.
(01350) 727797
Dalguise, Dunkeld
(9)4980 yards/**/E

Taymouth Castle G.C.
(01887) 830228
Kenmore, by Aberfeldy
(18) 6066 yards/***/C/H

Tillicoultry G.C.
(01259) 750124
Alva Road, Tillicoultry
(9) 2528 yards/***/E

Whitemoss G.C.
(01738) 730300
Dunning, Perthshire
(18) 6000/**/D

© MAPS IN MINUTES ™2000

Caledonia & Highlands Choice Golf

Mist-covered mountains and bottomless lochs, bagpipes, whisky and haggis. I doubt whether there is a more romantic place in the world than the Highlands of Scotland. I doubt also that there is a place quite so shatteringly beautiful. The area extends from the Cairngorms northwards, encompassing the Great Glen and the Western Isles, across the entire north east corner of Scotland. This part of the country was at one time covered by a dense forest of pine broken only by the soaring granite peaks of the Grampian mountain range. This was the home of the savage Caledonian tribe, a land where wolves hunted in packs. Nowadays very little of the forest remains. As for the wolves, most of them were killed by the Caledonians, but then unfortunately most of the Caledonians were killed by the Romans. No wonder they called life 'nasty, brutish and short'!

Aberdeen and Moray

Let us make a start in the north east. Forgetting the wolves, the savages and the Romans, what we need is a good 18 holes—and, of course, a suitable 19th. Aberdeen is a fine place to begin. Balgownie and Murcar lie right on the town's doorstep and are unquestionably two of the finest courses in Scotland. Balgownie links is the home of the **Royal Aberdeen** Golf Club and is featured ahead but **Murcar** is certainly not overshadowed and is a true championship test. It is a classic Scottish links with plenty of sandhills and a meandering burn and is quite a bit more undulating than Balgownie.

If the above are the best two courses around Aberdeen, (there are dozens in the area) and they are to the north of the city then perhaps the most spectacular is to the south at **Stonehaven**, laid out right alongside the lashing North Sea. And in total contrast to

Stonehaven—and indeed to Aberdeen's great links layouts is the new Dave Thomas 'American-style' course at **Newmachar**, north west of the city.

There are even more hotels in Aberdeen than golf courses but a large number are modern and somewhat unattractive and many may prefer to stay outside the town where establishments such as the excellent Ardoe House (01224) 867355 can be found. One other hotel strongly recommended by the golfing fraternity is the Atholl (01224) 323505 in Kings Gate. Many of the city's innumerable guesthouses provide a friendly ambience with Cedars Private Hotel (01224) 583225 a prominent example. An excellent seafood restaurant to visit is Atlantis (01224) 591403 while Gerard's (01224) 639500 and the Silver Darling (01224) 576229 are highly thought of. Our final thought is the excellent Marcliffe at Pitfodels (01224) 861000 on the western outskirts of the city.

North of Aberdeen, the popular Udny Arms (01358) 789444 at Newburgh enjoys a peaceful situation overlooking the Ythan Estuary and is a total contrast to the modern hotels of Aberdeen. Due west of the city another striking location is found at Kildrummy by Alford. Here the Kildrummy Castle (019755) 71288 is a first class establishment. To the north west, the Pittodrie House Hotel (01467) 681444 at Pitcaple enjoys glorious surroundings and in Old Meldrum one finds the similarly splendid **Meldrum House Hotel** (01651) 872294. The golf course here has received warm praise, it is not overly used and from the back tees represents a truly challenging test of golf. It is peaceful and spectcular with large undulating greens - a Championship Golf course of the future without question.

Looking to play outside the Aberdeen area, the golfer is faced with two equally appealing choices—one can either head north along the coast towards Cruden Bay, or alternatively head inland along the A93. The latter choice broadly involves following the path of the River Dee and will take the traveller through some truly magnificent scenery. The 18 hole courses at **Banchory**, **Aboyne**, **Ballater** and **Braemar** all lie along this road and not surprisingly boast spectacular settings. There are several superb places in which to stay as you golf your way along the Dee. Near Banchory, Raemoir House (01330) 824884 is outstanding and the Tor-na-Coille (01330) 822242 has excellent facilities, as does the Banchory Lodge Hotel (01330) 822625. The especially attractive town of Ballater boasts a number of fine establishments. Tullich Lodge (01463) 701400 is one of the leading mansion houses in Scotland with delightful bedrooms and excellent food, but also note the Craigendarroch Hotel (013397) 55858 with its fine restaurant and first class leisure facilities. Darroch Learg (013397) 55443 and Balgonie Country House (013397) 55482 are also of a very good standard. Should you time it right then Braemar boasts that magnificent spectacle, the Highland Games.

Banchory Lodge Hotel
Banchory, Banchory on Royal Deeside,
Aberdeen AB31 5HS
Tel: (01330) 822625 Fax: (01330) 825019

The Banchory Lodge Hotel combines Georgian charm with the distinctive leisured atmosphere of a country house.

The public rooms, including the dining room, where cuisine of a very high standard is served, offer superb views of the River Dee. All 22 bedrooms are individually furnished and have private bathrooms, colour television and tea-making facilities.

There is ample opportunity for sport and relaxation, with local golf courses, tennis courts, putting and bowling, forest walks and nature trails nearby. Salmon fishing on the River Dee can also be arranged.

Journeying due northwards from Aberdeen, **Cruden Bay** is clearly the first stopping point. A truly splendid golf links this, situated some 23 miles north of Aberdeen on Scotland's Buchan Coast. It is detailed on a later page. The old fishing and whaling town of **Peterhead** has an interesting seaside course where fierce sea winds can make scoring tricky. The Red House Hotel (01779) 812215 in Cruden Bay is recommended as a good place to take shelter.

Morayshire
From fishing port to Georgian elegance—the **Duff House Royal** Golf Club at Banff is overlooked by an impressive baroque-style mansion. The course too has a touch of class having been designed by

CRUDEN BAY GOLF COURSE *Photograph courtesy of:* **Scottish Tourist Board**

Alister Mackenzie immediately prior to his constructing the legendary Augusta National course in America—note the many two-tiered greens. Although not far from the sea, Duff House is very much a parkland type challenge. Nearby **Royal Tarlair** at Macduff is well worth a visit and like Duff House is always beautifully maintained. To the south of Banff along the A947 **Turriff** can also be recommended, while even further inland (but a marvellous drive anyway) from the Banff/ Macduff area on the A97, is the charming course at **Huntly** and the very relaxing Castle Hotel (01466) 792696. West of Huntly lies the well run and excellent Craigellachie Hotel (01340) 881204. In Banff's High Street, the Country Hotel (01261) 815353 is another to note. Also to be found in Banff is the charming Carmelite House Hotel (01261) 812152. Nearby, Cullen Bay has the welcoming Cullen Bay Hotel (01542) 840432.

Crossing the salmon-filled River Spey at Fochabers the City of **Elgin** is soon reached. Of the few cathedrals in this part of the world Elgin, the capital of Morayshire, has a beautiful one that dates from the 13th century. It also has one of the finest inland golf courses in the north of Scotland. A mile or so south of the city and some distance away from the often fierce coastal winds, the course is sheltered by many pines and silver birch. Inevitably, it occupies a glorious setting with distant purple hills forming a spectacular horizon.

Inland from Elgin, a drive through the Glen of Rothes will lead the golfer to **Dufftown** where there is a pleasant and not too difficult course, but if a coastal challenge is sought then Lossiemouth is the place to head for. Here, the **Moray** Golf Club has two links courses, the championship 'Old Course', which is more than a hundred years old and the 'New Course', a little over ten years old. Whilst the fighter aircraft from nearby RAF Lossiemouth may occasionally irritate, it would be difficult to find a finer combination of superb natural golf and scenic splendour.

In Elgin, two hotels; the Mansion House (01343) 548811 and Mansefield House (01343) 540883 are recommended and in Rothes, the Rothes Glen (01340) 831254 is superbly relaxing. In Forres, the Knockomie Hotel (01309) 673146 is very accommodating. Finally in Lossiemouth, ideal for golf at Moray, is the adjacent Stotfield Hotel (01343) 812011.

The Cairngorms
Further south, the area around Aviemore has become an increasingly popular holiday retreat, particularly for winter sports enthusiasts. However, whilst the skis must go on the roof, the golf clubs can fit in the boot, and there are five or six courses at hand each of which possesses a truly glorious setting. Picking two of the best, the **Kingussie** and **Boat of Garten** golf clubs lie either side of Aviemore close to the A9. Both have spectacular courses at which visitors are always made welcome. Neither is particularly long, though the hills at Kingussie and the narrow fairways and small greens at Boat of Garten can make scoring extremely difficult and you are more likely to see eagles than score one! At Boat of Garten you may also catch

a glimpse of one of the famous ospreys which nest in the area. Boat of Garten is featured ahead.

Some thoughts for the 19th include in the Newtonmore-Kingussie area, the Highlander (01540) 673341 and the Osprey (01540) 661510, both pleasant hotels, and the Cross (01540) 661166 is an outstanding restaurant in Kingussie with charming rooms. In Boat of Garten, the Boat (01479) 831258 is convenient overlooking the golf course (note the special 'golf weeks'). The Dalrachney Lodge (01479) 841252 at Carrbridge caters exceptionally well for golfing and fishing guests. Both Seafield Lodge (01479) 872152 and the Grant Arms Hotel (01479) 872526 in Grantown-on-Spey are comfortable and good value, whilst nearer the coast at Advie is the gracious Tulchan Lodge (01807) 510200. We also recommend Muckrach Lodge (01479) 851257 and Auchendean Lodge (01479) 851347 at Dulnain Bridge. Both make a fine base for touring the region.

The Highlands

In Scotland, where there is land there is golf and although the Highland region may be a wild and remote part of the country it nonetheless has its share of golfing gems—and more than that, in the minds of many, it has in **Royal Dornoch** the finest of them all.

As well as its gems, the region has a number of golf's genuine outposts, none more so than the **Gairloch** Golf Club situated in the far west of Scotland with views across to the Isle of Skye. There are 9 holes at Gairloch, each wonderfully named. The 6th, however, baffles me—'Westward Ho!' is its title?! The 9th has more of a Celtic ring to it—'Mo Dhachaidh'. There is no Sunday golf at Gairloch, though visitors can play at all other times. Others in the 'lonely' category include **Fort Augustus** on the edge of Loch Ness and **Fort William**, a moorland course laid out in the shadows of Ben Nevis. In addition, the intrepid golfer will find a number of courses to play in the Western Isles and the Hebrides, although the scenery may cause many to lift their heads too quickly.

Near Fort William one finds Inverlochy Castle (01397) 702177, one of the country's finest hotels and restaurants, while two other gems are the remote Arisaig House (01687) 450622 on the western coast and in Ballachulish, the Ballachulish Hotel (01855) 811606.

Inverness and Nairn

Inverness, as the 'Capital of the Highlands', is where many may choose to spend a day or two—the Loch Ness monster lives nearby and the famous fields of destruction at Culloden Moor are only a few miles to the east. Golfers may wish to note the **Inverness** 18 hole course just south of the town centre. However, many are drawn towards **Nairn** (16 miles away) where in addition to the magnificent championship links—see feature—there is an excellent second course, **Nairn Dunbar**.

Both Inverness and Nairn have a number of good hotels. Near the former, Dunain Park (01463) 230512 is outstanding and the 18th century Kingsmills (01463) 237166 is also ideal. Near to the famous battlefield is the impressive Culloden House Hotel (01463) 790461 where a portrait of the Bonnie Prince will welcome you. Relaxation and comfort can also be found at Glenruidh House (01463) 226499 and Ballifeary House Hotel (01463) 235572. In Nairn, the Golf View Hotel (01667) 452301 is situated right alongside the famous championship course but there are strong recommendations also for the Claymore House Hotel (01667) 453731, the Newton Hotel (01667) 453144, the charming Lochloy House (01667) 455355 and the Clifton Hotel (01667) 453119 (good restaurant here), all in Nairn.

North of Inverness

On the Chanonry Peninsula, linked to Inverness by way of the Kessock Bridge, the A9 and the A832, is the flattish links course of **Fortrose and Rosemarkie**—surrounded by sea and well worth a visit. **Strathpeffer Spa**, a moorland course, is one of the prettiest stepping stones for those heading north of Inverness along the A9, and Craigdarroch Lodge Hotel (01997) 421265 will provide comfort. Alternatively, the Royal Hotel (01381) 600217, Cromarty, is pleasant. This road passes through **Tain**, home of the famous Glenmorangie whisky, and where there is another outstanding 18 holes—but by now most will be itching to reach Dornoch. If you do decide to sample the whisky, the appropriately named Morangie House (01862) 892281 should oblige.

Royal Dornoch is regularly ranked among the top ten golf courses in Britain. For those wishing to reflect on their day's golf, the Dornoch Castle (01862) 810216 the Royal Golf Hotel (01862) 810283, Burghfield House (01862) 810212 and the Mallin House Hotel (01862) 810335 can all be recommended. Having played Royal Dornoch, many will surely wish to inspect the nearby golf course at **Skibo Castle**. Both are explored separately ahead.

There are two fine courses a short distance to the north at Dornoch—**Golspie** and **Brora**. Both are testing links courses set in the most majestic surroundings with views to distant hills and along what is a truly spectacular coast. Brora (where the greens are reputed to be the equal of those at Royal Dornoch and are ringed by electric fences to keep the sheep out!) stretches out right alongside three miles of deserted sandy beach. Being so far north, golf can be played at absurdly late hours during the summer months and at both the green fees are very inexpensive. In Brora, the excellent Royal Marine (01408) 621252 and the Links (01408) 621225 hotels are both strategically placed on the aptly named Golf Road, while another well titled hotel can be found at Golspie, the Golf Links Hotel (01408) 633408.

Beyond Brora we really are getting remote! However, the A9 makes it all the way to John O'Groats. There are 18 hole courses at **Wick** and **Reay**, but the furthest north is **Thurso**, not too far from the Dounreay Power Station, and if you do make it there accommodation in true country house style is available at the Melvich Hotel (01641) 531206. I should imagine it gets pretty cold in these parts but if you are still looking for fresh challenges then there is always the golf club in the Arctic—fittingly called the 'Polar Bear Club'—and which, I suppose it goes without saying, was founded by Scotsmen!

THE CARNIEGE CLUB *Photograph courtesy of:* **The Carniege Club**

Meldrum House dates from the 13th century and originally took the form of a Z plan tower house, built on an outcrop of rock.

This part of the house has formed the nucleus for later additions in the 17th and 19th centuries. The most significant additions are the 17th stone staircase, completed in 1625 by William Seton and built over the original entrance, and the stable block with its own impressive gatehouse.

Set in 15 acres of landscaped parklands and gardens, the house lies beside a small lake stocked with a variety of trout which may be fished by residents. River fishing, clay pigeon shooting and horse-riding can be arranged on request. Meldrum House enjoys an atmosphere closer to that of a private country home rather than a hotel, with a fine collection of antiques, objets d'art and ancestral portraits.

Personally run by Douglas and Eileen Pearson, the house offers every comfort. Meldrum House boasts nine luxury en-suite bedrooms, all individually furnished and full of unique Scottish character.

Renowned for its culinary excellence the restaurant offers high quality Scottish cuisine combined with an international flavour. Its menu features the very best of local produce and is complemented by an extensive wine list and large selection of malt whiskys. After feasting guests can relax and enjoy the warm ambience of the drawing room or the private bar.

Meldrum House now has its own exclusive golf course, Paul Lawrie British Open Champion is touring professional, its par is 70 and the course measures 6425 yards. The course is surrounded by mature woodland and has an abundance of attractive water features. In fact, water will come into play at twelve of the holes - it is as scenic as it is challenging. Many approach shots will require a good deal of nerve with decisions having to be made as to whether an attempt should be made to carry the water guarding greens.

The creation of the course has been a labour of love for designer Graeme Webster, a local man who still lives in the village of Oldmeldrum. He has also been involved in the construction of quality golf courses all over Scotland and in England, Spain and Germany. Meldrum House incorporates the best features of all the work he has done.

The Practice Academy, so important in a modern golf complex, include a long-game range, target greens, greens for practice chipping, a very large, contoured putting green and practice There is also PGA tuition for those who want learn or brush up on their game. The clubhouse overlooks the spectacular 18th hole and provides a comfortable and elegant environment for relaxing after a round. It also features business meeting facilities and a well stocked pro shop.

The hotel is also ideally situated for golfing parties with a great number of golf courses in the vicinity, including the top class courses of Royal Aberdeen and Cruden Bay to the east, Newmachar to the west and Duff House Royal and Royal Tarclair to the north.

Meldrum House & Golf Club forms an ideal venue for the discerning golfer wishing to take a relaxing break in wonderful surroudings. It will also provide the perfect location for corporate events or on a more personal note, a delightful romantic break.

Meldrum House & Golf Club
Oldmeldrum
Aberdeenshire
AB51 OAE
Tel: (01651) 872294
Fax: (01651) 872464
email: DPMELDRUM@aol.com
web site: www.medlrumhouse.com

Royal Aberdeen

Founded in 1780, Royal Aberdeen is the sixth oldest golf club in the world. For the first thirty five years of its existence the club was known as The Society of Golfers at Aberdeen, with membership of the society being determined by ballot. They were clearly a meticulous group of gentlemen for in 1783 they became the first to introduce the five minute limit on searching for golf balls. A sensible idea, you may think, but one that has caused the modern day Aberdeen golfer much distress—a subject to which I shall return in due course.

In 1815, on the eve of the Battle of Waterloo, the Society changed its name to the Aberdeen Golf Club and in 1903 the Royal prefix was bestowed on the club.. Originally the members played over a strip of common land between the Rivers Don and Dee but in the second half of the 19th century the club acquired its own course at Balgownie on the northern side of the River Don. Today Balgownie Links is regarded as one of Scotland's greatest championship courses.

Ronnie MacAskill is the **Director of Golf** and **Head Professional** at Royal Aberdeen Golf Club and **Sandra Nicolson** is the **Administration Secretary**. They may be contacted for tee reservations Monday to Friday on **tel: (01224) 702571** while the **Pro shop** can be contacted all week on **tel: (01224) 702221**. All correspondence should be addressed to: **The Royal Aberdeen Golf Club, Links Road, Bridge of Don, Aberdeen, AB23 8AT.**

Visitors are made extremely welcome at Royal Aberdeen and they may play at Balgownie on any day subject to making a tee reservation. The green fees for 2000 are set at £55 per round or £75 per day during the week (the tee being available between 10.00—11.30 and 2.00-3.30) with a £65 fee for a single round at the weekend (available after 3.30pm).

Travelling to Aberdeen is made fairly straightforward by the A92. From the south this road passes along the coast from Dundee via Arbroath, Montrose and Stonehaven to Aberdeen. It also connects the town to Fraserburgh in the north. Those approaching from the north west should find the A96 helpful (it in fact runs directly from Inverness.) Other roads which may prove of assistance are the A947 from Oldmeldrum and the A93 which links Aberdeen to Perth and passes through Blairgowrie. The links itself is situated two miles north of Aberdeen and can be sighted immediately to the right after crossing the River Don.

From its medal tees, Balgownie measures 6372 yards, par 70 (SSS 71) with the forward tees reducing the length to 6104 yards, par 69. Although perhaps not overly long, the course is very exposed to the elements and the wind can often make a mockery of some of the distances. There is also a considerable spread of gorse and the rough can be very punishing. It should be added that there are no fewer than ninety-two bunkers—ten of which appear on the short par three 8th! Balgownie has the traditional 'out and back' links layout, the front nine hugging the shore and the back nine returning on the landward side towards the clubhouse.

The outward nine is definitely the more interesting of the two halves—the eminent golf writer Sam McKinlay was moved to say: 'There are few courses in these islands with a better, more testing, more picturesque outward nine than Balgownie'. However, the most difficult hole on the course is possibly the last hole—a lengthy par four, well bunkered and usually played into the teeth of the prevailing wind.

Golfers may also wish to investigate the club's second course, the shorter Silverburn Course which measures 4066 yards, par 60.

Royal Aberdeen has played host to a number of major events including the British Youth's Championship, the Scottish Amateur Championship and the Northern Open Championship. In 1993, the British Seniors Championship was played over the Balgownie links. Numerous exhibition matches have also taken place; participants have included Tom Morris Junior, Harry Vardon, James Braid, John H Taylor, Walter Hagen and Henry Cotton.

I now return to the matter of the five minute rule. In the opening paragraph, I mentioned how in 1783 the Aberdeen Golfers had introduced the five minute limit on searching for lost balls. Well, somebody somewhere, it seems, didn't approve and 200 years later a plague of crows was sent to deliver retribution. Throughout the long summers of 1983 and 1984 the crows determined that no one should search for his ball. They descended on the links stealing Titleists and Top-Flites, Pinnacles and Penfolds. Several members had more than one ball stolen in a round. Numerous suggestions were put forward as to how to rid the links of this turbulent pest but alas to no avail. Even a crow trap was built but still they plundered. Then, just as suddenly as they came, they left, never it is presumed to return. Sanity restored, Balgownie became once more one of Britain's friendliest links.

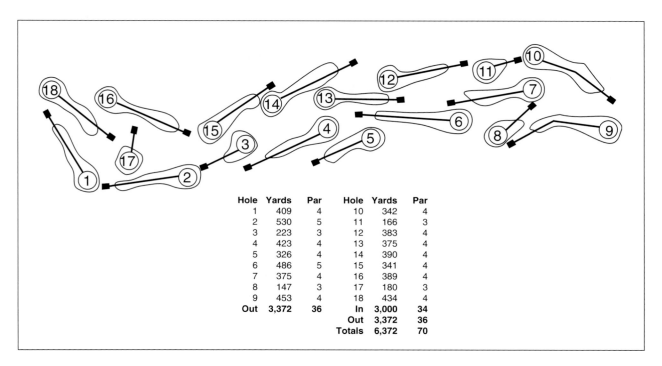

Hole	Yards	Par	Hole	Yards	Par
1	409	4	10	342	4
2	530	5	11	166	3
3	223	3	12	383	4
4	423	4	13	375	4
5	326	4	14	390	4
6	486	5	15	341	4
7	375	4	16	389	4
8	147	3	17	180	3
9	453	4	18	434	4
Out	3,372	36	In	3,000	34
			Out	3,372	36
			Totals	6,372	70

Cruden Bay

One often reads of famous golf clubs having been founded in local hotels and hostelries: Deal (The Black Horse), Crail (The Golf Inn) and Hoylake (The Royal) to name but three. Well, the birth of Cruden Bay apparently took place during a meeting in the North of Scotland Bank—one presumes this was a much more sober affair! The precise date of the meeting was 16th June 1898 and in March of the following year the Cruden Bay Hotel and Golf Course was opened.

The hotel (long since demolished) and the 18 hole golf course were originally both owned by the Great North of Scotland Railway Company. Within a month of their opening the company staged a professional tournament which attracted many of the day's leading players, including Harry Vardon (then Open Champion), James Braid and Ben Sayers. The event proved an outstanding success with Vardon taking the first prize of £30.

The club's full address is the **Cruden Bay Golf Club, Aulton Road, Cruden Bay, Peterhead, Aberdeen-shire AB42 ONN**. In addition to the 18 hole **Championship Course** there is also a 9 hole short course, the **St Olaf**.

The present **Secretary** is **Mrs Rosemary Pittendrigh**. She may be contacted via the above address or **tel: (01779) 812285**, and **fax: (01779) 812945**. The club's **Professional, Robbie Stewart**, can be reached on **tel: (01779) 812414**.

Casual visitors are welcome at Cruden Bay, although not surprisingly certain restrictions apply during Saturdays and Sundays. It is generally advisable to telephone the club to make an advance reservation, particularly as a starting sheet is in operation daily from April to September. Visitors should also note that they are not permitted to play the 18 hole course between 4.30 pm and 6.30 pm on Wednesdays and that at weekends, unless accompanied by a member, handicap certificates must be provided. No specific restrictions relate to the St Olaf course.

In 2000 the green fee to play on the Championship course is £45 for a round and £60 per day with £55 payable at weekends Under 18s pay £25 and £30 respectively. A day's golf on the St Olaf course can be obtained for £15 during the week and £25 at weekends. (Half price for juniors)

Cruden Bay is situated on Scotland's Buchan Coast, some 23 miles north of Aberdeen and seven miles south of the old whaling port of Peterhead. The course itself has a dramatic setting with Slains Castle providing a rather eerie backdrop. Bram Stoker, who spent several summers in Cruden Bay is reputed to have been inspired by the castle when writing his Dracula stories. Fortunately the surrounding countryside bears little resemblance to Transylvania and strangers should find travelling in the area a pleasant experience. The best route from the south is probably the A90 coastal road which runs from Dundee via Montrose and through Aberdeen. Leave the A90 near Newburgh and follow the A975 direct to Cruden Bay. The A90 approaches from the north via Fraserburgh and Peterhead.

Originally laid out by Old Tom Morris but substantially revised by Tom Simpson, Cruden Bay is very much a traditional links and there are a number of blind and semi-blind shots. Measuring 6395 yards from the back tees, par is a fairly tight 70 (SSS 71). From the ladies' tees the course measures 5761 yards (par 74). A good old Scottish burn is a prominent feature of the course affecting several of the holes. There are a number of vast sand dunes and hills to be negotiated while the beach too, can come into play around the 14th and 15th. The finest sequence of holes, however, comes between the 4th, one of the finest par threes in golf, and the 7th.

The views over the Bay of Cruden naturally add to the pleasure of the round, and it isn't difficult to comprehend why Golf World magazine ranks Cruden Bay amongst its top 40 courses in the British Isles—and why in September 1999 Golf Magazine (an American publication) rated it as high as 52nd best course in the world.

The magnificently appointed clubhouse has the kind of atmosphere one comes to expect in this part of the world—very friendly—and casual dress may be worn at all times. Meals are served throughout the day with lunches, high teas, dinners and some delightful steak suppers being offered in addition to bar snacks.

South of Hadrian's Wall, Cruden Bay is probably not as well known as it ought to be. The legions who arrange their golfing trips around the more traditional favourites often miss out on some of Scotland's finest courses. Cruden Bay should be included in anyone's itinerary—it is a genuinely spectacular course and perhaps of equal importance, a place where the warmest of welcomes can be guaranteed.

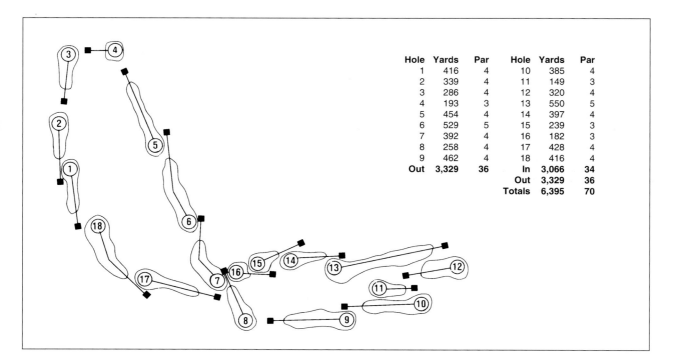

Hole	Yards	Par	Hole	Yards	Par
1	416	4	10	385	4
2	339	4	11	149	3
3	286	4	12	320	4
4	193	3	13	550	5
5	454	4	14	397	4
6	529	5	15	239	3
7	392	4	16	182	3
8	258	4	17	428	4
9	462	4	18	416	4
Out	**3,329**	**36**	**In**	**3,066**	**34**
			Out	**3,329**	**36**
			Totals	**6,395**	**70**

Located just off the main A9, one hour's drive north of Inverness, this privately-owned Edwardian hotel is superbly situated overlooking James Braid's famous 18-hole links golf course, and boasts unobstructed views across the Dornoch Firth and heather-carpeted Highlands.

There are 22 individually appointed en-suite bedrooms with sea or mountain views. The chef in the hotel's Seaforth Restaurant uses only the very best of local produce and seafood to create memorable dishes. For a spot of relaxation guests might like to sample one of the many local malt whiskies that are on offer in the lounge bar or watch the sun setting from the garden terrace

Golfers are spoilt for choice with the challenging Brora links course just steps away, and neighbouring Royal Dornoch, Golspie and Tain courses are all within easy travelling distance and provide interesting and varied alternatives.

Guests at The Links have full use of all facilities at The Royal Marine Hotel (see below), which is just 200 metres away. Also available are self-catering luxury Links View Apartments.

The Links Hotel
Golf Road
Brora
Sutherland KW9 6QS
Tel: (01408) 621225
Fax: (01408) 621181
e mail: highlandescape@btinternet.com
web site: www.highlandescape.com

The Royal Marine Hotel
Golf Road
Brora
Sutherland KW9 6QS
Tel: (01408) 621252
Fax: (01408) 621181
e mail: highlandescape@btinternet.com
web site: www.highlandescape.com

In the midst of wild, yet stunning, scenery, a warm Scottish welcome awaits you at The Royal Marine Hotel.

Originally designed in 1910 as a private Country House by the renowned Scottish Architect Sir Robert Lorimer, the Royal Marine is a family-run hotel offering traditional Highland hospitality. Combining the charm of a bygone era with all the amenities expected of a quality hotel, the Royal Marine is a veritable oasis in the Highlands.

Overlooking the mouth of the river Brora and adjacent to James Braid's 18-hole links golf course the hotel has 22 individually appointed en-suite bedrooms. A fully equipped leisure centre includes heated indoor pool, jacuzzi, sauna and steam rooms, gym, solarium, and curling rink. After dining on delicious Scottish fare in the AA Rosette-awarded restaurant, guests can relax in front of roaring log fires with a dram of the local malt whisky, Clynelish.

The hotel offers a wide range of activities: golf can be arranged at Brora, or on neighbouring courses at Golspie, Royal Dornoch, and Tain; salmon fishing from the hotel's boats on Loch Brora; snooker; and croquet.

Royal Dornoch

Usually when a person describes his first visit to a golf course as 'the most fun I've had playing golf in my whole life,' very little is thought of it. However, when that person happens to be Tom Watson, five times Open Champion, one tends to sit up and take notice. Like Ben Crenshaw, Nick Faldo and Greg Norman who have also made the pilgrimage, Watson was enchanted by the 'Star of the North'.

There are two words that are normally associated with Royal Dornoch; one is 'greatness' and the other is 'remoteness'. Situated fifty miles north of Inverness, Dornoch enjoys a kind of splendid isolation. It is often described as the course every golfer wants to play but the one that very few actually do.

So what is the charm of Dornoch? Firstly, there's the setting. Bordered by the Dornoch Firth and a glorious stretch of sand, distant hills with their ever-changing moods fill the horizon creating a feeling that one is playing on a stage. And then of course, there's the history: Royal Dornoch Golf Club dates from 1877 but mention is made of golf being played on the links at least as early as 1616. Writing in the 17th century Sir Robert Gordon wrote of Dornoch: 'About this town are the fairest and largest links on any part of Scotland, fit for Archery, Golfing, Ryding and all other exercises; they doe surpasse the fields of Montrose and St Andrews.' Finally, there's the very links itself—described on more than one occasion as the most natural golf course in the world; to quote Tom Watson again, 'One of the great courses of the five continents.'

Mr John Duncan is the **Secretary/Manager** and he may be contacted on **tel: (01862) 811220**. All written correspondence should be addressed to the **Secretary/Manager, Royal Dornoch Golf Club, Golf Road, Dornoch, IV25 3LW**. Reservations and enquiries may be made on **tel: (01862) 810219**, by **fax: (01862) 810792** or at **www.royaldornoch.com** Andrew Skinner is the club's **Professional**; he may be reached on **tel: (01862) 810902**.

Visitors are welcome at Royal Dornoch Sundy to Friday, with some access late Saturday. It is wise to telephone the club prior to setting off to make a tee reservation as an ever-growing number of people are now making the trip and during the months of June to August the links can get busy. The cost of a single round on the **Championship** Course in 2000 is set at £57 between Monday and Friday and £67 at the weekend. A three day ticket is available priced at £144 in 2000. There is a second eighteen hole course at Dornoch, the **Struie** Course measuring 5438 yards, par 69. A day ticket, enabling a round over both courses is available (between Monday and Friday only) at a cost

of £62. A day ticket for the Struie Course alone can be purchased for £24 (£17 per round) with £95 securing a full week's golf. A £10 discount on green fees for the Championship Course is given to those staying in the Dornoch area in hotels, B&B's, rented accommodation and caravan sites which are members of HOST. Details are available from the premises or the Scottish Tourist Office.

Travelling to Dornoch gets ever easier. The A9 runs from Perth to John O'Groats, Perth being linked to Edinburgh by the M90. There are regular flights from London and other parts of the country to Inverness Airport and the links itself has an adjacent landing strip for light aircraft and a helipad beside the Clubhouse; moreover, there is now a road bridge over the Dornoch Firth and this reduces the motoring time from Inverness.

By today's standards Dornoch could probably be described as being of only medium length, the links measuring 6514 yards, par 70 (SSS 73). However, the last thing in the world that Dornoch is, is an easy course. It has been said that the prevailing wind at Dornoch comes from every direction but even when the winds don't thunder in from across the Firth or down from the hills, the links can be the proverbial 'smiler with the knife'.

Although the club was founded in 1877, ten years later when 'Old' Tom Morris was brought from St Andrews to survey the links there was still only a nine hole layout. The master craftsman not only completely redesigned the nine but extended the course to a full eighteen holes. By using the natural contours of the terrain many magnificent plateau greens were created and despite major alterations made to the links by John Sutherland and John H Taylor thirty years later, it is the plateau greens that remain the hallmark of Dornoch. Among the most classic holes are the 4th, 5th (Watson's favourite), 10th, 14th and 17th.

Donald Ross, considered by many to be the greatest of all golf architects was born in Dornoch and between 1895 and 1899 was the professional and head green keeper. Several of the great American courses he designed incorporate many of Dornoch's features.

There are signs that Dornoch is at last shedding its remoteness tag. In 1985 the club staged the Amateur Championship for the first time in its history—this being in the minds of many alarmingly overdue—and in 2000 Dornoch will host the Scottish Amateur. It may be to indulge in pure fantasy but one cannot help wondering what it would be like if the hallowed links were ever visited by the greatest of all compliments.

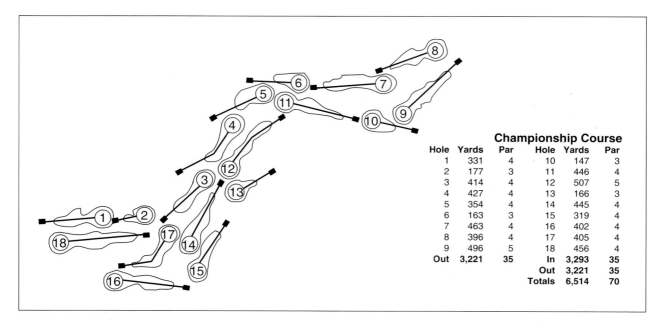

Championship Course

Hole	Yards	Par	Hole	Yards	Par
1	331	4	10	147	3
2	177	3	11	446	4
3	414	4	12	507	5
4	427	4	13	166	3
5	354	4	14	445	4
6	163	3	15	319	4
7	463	4	16	402	4
8	396	4	17	405	4
9	496	5	18	456	4
Out	3,221	35	In	3,293	35
			Out	3,221	35
			Totals	6,514	70

The Carnegie Links

Golfers embarking on a grand tour of Scotland used to have one world class excuse for venturing north beyond Inverness - they simply had to visit Royal Dornoch. Now they have a second justification, and it is located only four miles from the famous links.

Skibo Castle is an extraordinary place. According to legend, it was a Viking by the name of Sigurd who built the first castle at Skibo. Towards the end of the last century Andrew Carnegie, a Scot who emigrated to America after borrowing £20 to pay for his passage, returned to his homeland one of the richest men in the world. He settled in Sutherland and for his private residence created the palace that is the modern day Skibo Castle.

Like all good Scotsmen, Carnegie was a golfer, although his talent in this field didn't remotely match his talent for making millions. In fact, he was rather wary of displaying his golfing prowess at Dornoch and so decided to construct a nine hole course within the grounds of his immense estate. In 1898 he invited the Secretary at Dornoch, John Sutherland (an accomplished architect) to lay out the links and took lessons from the five-times Open Champion, John H Taylor - Carnegie never did anything by halves. He died in 1919 and while his golf course continued to be played until the Second World War its spirit never really survived him.

In 1990 the Skibo estate was acquired by Peter de Savary - another ambitious and colourful character - who determined not merely to re-establish golf at Skibo but to create one of the world's most exclusive leisure retreats. De Savary conceived the idea of the Carnegie Club and commissioned British golf architect Donald Steel to assess the potential for building an outstanding links (the one aspect of the development that wouldn't be totally private).

Donald Steel has created many fine courses around the world but he has never worked on a finer site than this. The land he had to shape was essentially dune land - not of the rugged Ballybunion type perhaps but certainly rolling, gorse-studded linksland. Occupying a peninsula, it is bordered by water on three sides and enjoys an incomparable backdrop. At nearby Royal Dornoch the hill and mountain scenery is striking but it appears on the horizon - at Skibo you feel as if you are playing right amidst the Scottish Highlands.

Steel is a golfing purist, a great advocate of 'natural golf'. Like Peter Thomson, he believes the game should be played 'on the ground' rather than 'in the air'; a golf course should not impose itself on the land, rather it should blend harmoniously with it. He has definitely achieved this at Skibo.

Although the course only opened in 1995 it looks a century old. It is not hard to envisage Andrew Carnegie - elegantly clad in plus twos - slashing his way around with a set of hickory shafted clubs. The Carnegie Links, as the new course is called, certainly invokes the mood of a bygone age, and yet Steel has also created an extremely challenging test of golf. It plays just like a links should play - firm and fast - and the rough is encouraged to grow. How good is it? In November 1996 Golf World magazine rated it 'Best New Course in the British Isles' and declared, "The thing about a visit to Skibo is that there are so many breath-taking experiences it is a wonder that you ever managed to catch a breath at all".

The course can play anything from 5436 yards from the most forward tees to 6671 yards (par 71) from the back markers. Par threes are often the most memorable holes on a golf course and Skibo has no fewer than five of them. The pick of these may be the 3rd, which is played slightly uphill over a deep bunker to an undulating plateaued green, and the picturesque 15th - its green overlooking the waters of Pollna Caorach. Variety is a constant factor throughout the round. Steel has managed to include a number of genuine par fives (employing cross bunkers - an almost forgotten yet highly strategic as well as penal hazard) and a selection of two-shot holes ranging from the drivable (yet heavily pot-bunkered) 267 yards 17th to the mighty 468 yards 16th. Among the best of the par fours are the 5th with its ever-narrowing fairway which is bordered to the left by a protective area of lichen heathland (incidentally the site abounds with precious habitats) and by the Dornoch Firth to the right: the 8th which curves gracefully around the edge of Loch Evelix, and the aforementioned 17th, a skilfully designed risk-reward hole.

Golfers wishing to play the Carnegie Links can book tee times by contacting the **Head Professional, John Black** on tel: **(01862) 894600**. Visitors (with handicaps) are restricted to teeing off between 11.00 and 12.00 Monday through Friday.

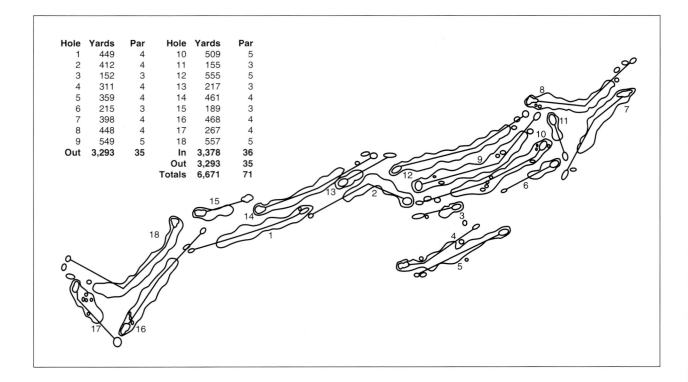

Hole	Yards	Par	Hole	Yards	Par
1	449	4	10	509	5
2	412	4	11	155	3
3	152	3	12	555	5
4	311	4	13	217	3
5	359	4	14	461	4
6	215	3	15	189	3
7	398	4	16	468	4
8	448	4	17	267	4
9	549	5	18	557	5
Out	3,293	35	In	3,378	36
			Out	3,293	35
			Totals	6,671	71

"Driving up the approach to the Dornoch Bridge we could see in the distance a spectacular double rainbow arching over the Firth towards Skibo Castle."

It was perhaps the only clue to the where-abouts of this enchanted and secluded estate, for Skibo is virtually invisible from the public roads that happily signpost you to Dornoch, Clashmore and Meikle Ferry North (no ferry). This last gnomic sign encapsulates the overwhelming feeling you have on arriving at Skibo, that it is not really of this world, but a place that exists somewhere over the rainbow.

As we swept round the corner of the single track road that leads up to the castle along the beech-lined avenue, it's difficult to argue with Andrew Carnegie's description of Skibo as "Heaven on Earth". But just as the end of a rainbow shifts the moment you get close, any attempt to define or describe Skibo moves the reality further from one's grasp. The experience is akin to sipping an exotic potion. Peter de Savary, the Carnegie Club's founder, or custodian, as he likes to call himself, says; "Even a short stay at Skibo is something that never leaves you. The place really gets into your system, and like a fine claret, it has a marvellous aftertaste. Once you leave you can be in New York, Chicago or Munich and find that at certain moments you hark back to what you love and enjoy about Skibo."

And for the members of the exclusive Carnegie Club that have access to the castle and surrounding estate, there are unlimited pleasures in which to indulge. Most members, however, are golf fanatics who come to play on what has to be one of the most scenic courses in the world, the eighteen-hole Carnegie Championship Links. Donald Steel, the internationally-renowned links architect has effected a reconstruction of Carnegie's original links course, to provide an outstanding eighteen-hole championship challenge. Located on a peninsula, it is straddled by Loch Evelix and the Dornoch Firth and overlooked by the heather-clad Struie Hill in the distance. Great care has been taken to ensure that the experience of playing the Carnegie Links (which are within four miles of the world famous Royal Dornoch Golf Club) is authentic to the era of Andrew Carnegie. The course offers the golfer a rare opportunity to play a links course which remains firm and fast. Requiring a broad repertoire of shots, rather than the modern style of aerial bombardment, the course demands that the golfer plays

an imaginative and thoughtful game. At 6,671 yards from the back tees, the course is not long by modern standards, but in a wind, it will test even the mightiest. Its varied layout takes the golfer past exceptionally rare wildlife habitats which have been carefully retained and protected and are now managed to ensure their future. Birdlife abounds and with the sea on three sides and the hills of Sutherland and Ross-shire all around, this course must have one of the finest settings in the world. For a different challenge there is the nine-hole Monks' Walk Parkland course. Also designed by Donald Steel, this enchanting course wends its way through ponds, copses and marshes amidst the glorious scenery of northern Scotland. Intended to be enjoyed by all standards of player, with two options on the par, played as a sporty par 3 or a par 35 from the back tees, the Monks' Walk is adjacent to the castle allowing members and guests to build up an appetite before breakfast or perhaps walk off dinner during the summer months. The other attraction of Skibo is the genteel and luxurious lifestyle that has more in common with 1898 than 1998. De Savary has wisely altered little of Carnegie's Highland paradise.

When Carnegie more or less rebuilt Skibo in 1898, he introduced facilities that were way ahead of their time, for instance the glass-covered marble swimming pool on the shores of Loch Ospisdale. Originally, the pool was filled by salt water from the estuary and heated by a boiler, along with the adjacent greenhouses. In the castle Carnegie installed hot and cold running water, central heating and the most up-to-date plumbing services which even Buckingham Palace lacked at the time. When Edward VII visited he was so taken with Carnegie's novel up-lighting in Mrs Carnegie's drawing room he did something similar at Windsor Castle. Fear of fire destroying his beloved books led Carnegie to install massive steel fire-doors behind wooden panelling in the main downstairs rooms. As an added precaution he also left beautiful blue glass bottles containing water throughout the house to be broken in case of fire.

The Carnegie Club at Skibo Castle welcomes guests for an initial visit, during which time Membership can be considered and if accepted, will allow for future enjoyment of the Club.

Enjoy the very best of the Scottish Highlands, outstanding private golf, and the grandeur of a castle and its many acres or, in the words of Andrew Carnegie, 'Heaven on Earth'.

The Carnegie Club at Skibo Castle
Dornoch, Sutherland IV25 3RQ
Tel: (01862) 894600 Fax: (01862) 894601
e mail: skibo@carnegieclubs.com
web site: www.carnegieclub.co.uk

Nairn

A glorious setting, a superb championship course and a warm welcome to visiting golfers—that, in the proverbial nutshell, is Nairn. In 1987 the club celebrated its centenary and played host to both men's and ladies' Scottish Amateur Championships. In 1994 the club staged the British Amateur Championship and in September 1999 the Walker Cup was played at Nairn - Great Britain and Ireland achieving a spectacular victory.

Originally laid out by Archie Simpson and modified two years later by 'Old' Tom Morris, the present layout owes much to the work of James Braid, arguably the greatest of all Scottish golf architects. Nairn is very much a traditional links with the opening holes stretching out along the shoreline. At the 10th comes the inevitable about-turn, and the head for home. It is a fine test of golf and with the abundant heather, the great sea of gorse and the distant mountains providing a spectacular backdrop, this is a veritable heaven.

Being so far north Nairn has probably not received the recognition it must surely deserve—at least in terms of attracting professional tournaments. Yet with an airport (Inverness) a mere 8 miles away and an adequate road and rail network, Nairn ought not to be considered too remote in the way that Royal Dornoch traditionally is.

From the medal tees the course measures 6472 yards, par 71. Nairn is certainly no monster and accuracy rather than length should determine the quality of scoring. The front nine is the shorter of the two although the prevailing south-westerly may well cause this to be the tougher half. Anyone suffering a bout of the dreaded sliced tee-shot is likely to find himself doing battle with the Moray Firth—the early holes really do run very close to the sea.

Perhaps the best series of holes, however, are found on the back nine, namely holes 12, 13 and 14. Anyone who can manage three pars here can call himself a golfer. Staying out of the gorse and avoiding the numerous well-positioned bunkers is undoubtedly the key to a good round, for with the magnificent, and not overly large greens, there is no excuse for poor putting at Nairn.

And so, as they say, to the 19th and at Nairn that means entering one of the most relaxing clubhouses in Britain. Built in 1990, it was extended in 1997 with the addition of the "Gordon Bulmer Wing" and a newly fitted pro shop. During summer the club hosts a number of open competitions and these are invariably well supported. It isn't difficult to imagine why. For those of us who enjoy our golf in pleasant and dramatic surroundings and who occasionally feel the urge to get away from it all, there can surely be no finer place to visit than Nairn.

Nairn Golf Club, Seabank Road
Nairn, Highland IV12 4HB

Secretary	Jim Somerville (01667) 453208
	Fax (01667) 456328
Professional	Robin Fyfe (01667) 452787
Green Fees	WD £60
	WE £65
Restrictions	No fourballs before 9..30 am

Directions
Eight miles from Inverness airport, situated on the town's western shore.

Boat of Garten

A sk a golfer who has never been to the Highlands of Scotland which are the country's three most scenic inland courses and he'll probably say Loch Lomond, Gleneagles Kings and Gleneagles Queens. Ask the same question of a golfer who has savoured the delights of Boat of Garten and he'll probably give you a different answer. Boat of Garten's scenery is nothing short of awesome.

At Loch Lomond you play much of the round alongside the 'Bonnie Banks', at or near water level. At Gleneagles you climb the foothills and gaze at the distant peaks. When you play golf at Boat of Garten there is a sense of being right in amongst the mountains. Nowhere else does the air seem as crisp or as invigorating. The accompanying views are utterly enchanting as the golf course wanders—and frequently plunges—through avenues of birch and rowan liberally sprinkled with heather and broom.

Like the Kings and Queens at Gleneagles, Boat of Garten was designed by James Braid. Measuring a shade under 6000 yards from the back tees it is not the longest of challenges, yet it is anything but easy! The fairways are generally quite narrow and they really do undulate significantly. Moreover, several of them ripple in a links-like manner thus awkward stances are not uncommon. There are occasional blind shots too, making Boat of Garten something of an inland Cruden Bay—an old fashioned, thoroughly bewitching test of golf.

The only plain hole at Boat of Garten is the 1st, a modest par three played over flat terrain. But then the excitement begins. At the 2nd you drive downhill to one of those rippling fairways that changes gear midway, climbing to a green sitting roughly at eye level. The 3rd is another short hole, this time played over a valley of heather, while the 4th is a dramatic par five where the fairway cascades in tiers before once again rising in front of the green. The 5th hole is more 'up' than 'down' but is equally spectacular. And so it continues.

The 6th and 8th are both very strong two-shotters and the front nine concludes with a par three at which sand, heather and broom all conspire to ensure that the only place to be is on the green.

The highlights of the back nine are the views from the 12th tee—a glorious panorama—the complexities of the 13th (an unusual green site here), the eccentricities of the 15th (where both the drive and approach are blind!) and the all-round star quality of the 18th, a wonderful finishing hole that features an exciting downhill tee shot, a gently curving fairway and a green perched precariously on a hilltop. A thrilling conclusion to an exhilarating round.

Boat of Garten Golf Club
PH24 3BQ

Gen Manager	Paddy Smyth (01479) 831282
Professional	J R Ingram (01479) 831282
Green Fees	WD £23/round; £28/day
	WE £28/round; £33/day
Restrictions	Handicap certificates required

Directions
Situated east of the A9, 5 miles north of Aviemore.

Culloden House is a handsome Georgian mansion with a tradition of lavish hospitality stretching back hundreds of years. Among its famous visitors was Bonnie Prince Charlie who fought his last battle by the park walls. The house stands in 40 acres of elegant lawns and parkland, enhanced by stately oaks and beech trees.

The long term Scottish resident staff, dedicated to your comfort and service, are on-hand at all times to extend a warm welcome to all visitors to their hotel. Culloden House is decorated to the highest standard, particularly the comfortable drawing room which is decorated with magnificent Adam-style plasterwork.

Dining is a memorable experience at Culloden House. The emphasis in the Adam style dining room is on friendly and unobtrusive service matched by the highest standards of cuisine. The wine cellars hold a superb range of wines from the great vineyards of the world and there is a wide selection of aged malt whiskies.

Every bedroom is individually decorated and has direct dial telephone, television, trouser press, bath and shower. Guests can choose from four poster rooms, standard rooms or a room with a jacuzzi. The Garden Pavilion, situated by the ancient listed walled garden, and the newly refurbished west wing Pavilion on the main house, offer the discerning non-smoking guest luxurious suite and junior suite accommodation.

Leisure facilities include a hard tennis court, sauna, free weights and exercise bicycle with future plans for spa development. There is so much to visit in the area—golf, fishing and shooting can be arranged and the Highlands, Loch Ness and Inverness are just waiting to be explored. Also nearby are Cawdor Castle, the Clava Cairns and Culloden Battlefield.

Situated three miles from the centre of Inverness, off the A96 Inverness-Nairn Road, Culloden House extends the best of Scottish hospitality to all its guests.

Culloden House
Inverness IV1 2NZ
Tel: (01463) 790461
Fax: (01463) 792181
Toll Free Fax: (USA) 1800 3737987
e mial: resv@cullodenhouse.co.uk
web site: www.cullodenhouse.co.uk

uilt in 1878 by a local manufacturer for his wife, the majestic, turreted Ardoe House is designed in the Scottish Baronial style favoured by Queen Victoria for Balmoral Castle.

Situated within its own beautifully landscaped grounds with magnificent views over the River Dee and open countryside. Ardoe House has the style of an elegant country mansion with all modern comforts. Rich oak panelling, ornate ceilings and stained glass windows abound. The Great hall reception area is truly spectacular, the richly furnished public rooms are relaxing and there are various small secluded areas where guests can privately enjoy a glass of malt whisky.

Each bedroom has a pleasant and comfortable atmosphere and whatever your taste in cuisine, the fare available in the hotel's two AA Rosette award-wining restaurant will more than match expectations. Ardoe House is only ten minutes from Aberdeen City Centre yet is an ideal gateway to tour Royal Deeside.

A new fully equipped leisure centre opened in January 2000 comprising of an 18 x 8 metres swimming pool, sauna, steam room, state of the art techno gym and trimnasium, aerobics studio, blitz room and four health and beauty treatment rooms. The use of the leisure club is complimentary to all guests of the hotel during their stay.

Golf packages, which include accommodation in a deluxe room with a full Scottish breakfast, four course dinner and packed lunch are available all year round. Details are available on request from reservations.

MACDONALD   *Ardoe house*
★ ★ ★ ★

enjoy the difference

Ardoe House Hotel and Restaurant
South Deeside Road,
Blair, Aberdeen,
AB12 5YP
Tel: (01224) 860600
Fax: (01224) 861283
e-mail: info@ardoe.macdonald-hotels.co.uk

ABERDEEN & MORAY

Aboyne G.C.
(01339) 886328
Formaston Park, Aboyne
(18) 5975 yards/***/C

Alford G.C.
(01975) 562178
Montgarry Road, Alford
(18) 5290 yards/***/D

Auchenblae G.C.
(01561) 320308
Auchenblae, Laurencekirk
(9) 2174 yards/***/E

Auchmill G.C.
(01224) 715214
Auchmill, Aberdeen
(18) 5439 metres/***/F

Ballater G.C.
(01339) 755567
Ballater, Aberdeenshire
(18) 6127 yards/***/C/H

Banchory G.C.
(01330) 822365
Kinneskie, Banchory
(18) 5245 yards/***/C/H

Balnagask G.C.
(01224) 871286
St Fitticks Road, Aberdeen
(18) 5468 yards/***/F

Bon Accord G.C.
(01224) 633464
Golf Road, Aberdeen
(18) 6384 yards/***/F

Braemar G.C.
(01339) 741618
Cluniebank, Braemar
(18) 4916 yards/***/C

Buckpool G.C.
(01542) 832236
Barhill Road, Buckie
(18) 6259 yards/***/C

Caledonian G.C.
(01224) 632443
Golf Road, Aberdeen
(18) 6384 yards/**/F

Cheyne G.C.
(01569) 762702
Fetteressoe, Stanehaven
(18) 6685 yards/***/E

Cruden Bay G.C.
(01779) 812285
Aulton Road, Cruden Bay
(9) 4710 yards/**/B-A/H
(18) 6395 yards/**/B-A/H

Cullen G.C.
(01542) 840685
The Links, Cullen, Buckie
(18) 4610 yards/***/D

Deeside G.C.
(01224) 867697
Bieldside, Aberdeen
(18) 5972 yards/**/B/H
(9) 6632 yards/**/B/H

Duff House Royal G.C.
(01261) 812062
Barnyards, Banff
(18) 6161 yards/***/C/H

Dufftown G.C.
(01340) 820325
Tomintoul Road, Dufftown
(18) 5308 yards/***/D

Dunecht House G.C.
(01330) 860404
Dunecht, Skene
(9) 3135 yards/***/F/G

Elgin G.C.
(01343) 542338
Hardhillock, Elgin
(18) 6401 yards/***/D-C

Forres G.C.
(01309) 672250
Muiryshade, Forres
(18) 6236 yards/***/D

Fraserburgh G.C.
(01346) 516616
Philorth, Fraserburgh
(18) 6278 yards/***/C

Garmouth and Kingston G.C.
(01343) 870388
Garmouth, Fochabers, Moray
(18) 5616 yards/***/D/H

Grantown-on-Spey G.C.
(01479) 872079
Grantown-on-Spey, Moray
(18) 5672 yards/**.*/D

Hazlehead G.C.
(01224) 315747
Hazlehead Park, Aberdeen
(18) 5303 metres/***/F
(18) 5673 metres/***/F
(9) 2531 metres/***/F

Hopeman G.C.
(01343) 830687
Hopeman, Moray
(18) 5531 yards/***/C

Huntly G.C.
(01466) 792643
Cooper Park, Huntly
(18) 5399 yards/***/F

Insch G.C.
(01464) 820363
Golf Terrace, Insch
(9) 5488 yards/***/D

Inverallochy G.C.
(01346) 582000
Inverallochy, Nr Fraserburgh
(18) 5137 yards/***/E

Inverurie G.C.
(01467) 624080
Blackhall Road, Inverurie
(18) 5711 yards/***/D

Keith G.C.
(01542) 882469
Fife Park, Keith
(18) 5791 yards/***/C

Kemnay G.C.
(01467) 642225
Monymusk Road, Kemnay
(9) 5502 yards/***(Mon/Tues/Thurs pm)/E

Kings Links G.C.
(01224) 641577
Golf Road, Kings Links, Aberdeen
(18) 5838 metres/***/D

Kintore G.C.
(01467) 632631
Balbithan Road, Kintore, Inverurie
(18) 5997 yards/***/D

Longside G.C.
(01779) 821558
Longside, Peterhead
(18) 5201 yards/***/D/H

Macdonald G.C.
(01358) 720576
Hospital Road, Ellon
(18) 5986 yards/***/F

Moray G.C.
(01434) 812018
Stotfield Road, Lossiemouth
(18) 6667 yards/***/B/H
(18) 6005 yards/***/C/H

Murcar G.C.
(01224) 704370
Bridge of Don, Aberdeen
(18) 6241 yards/***/F/H

Newburgh-on-Ythan G.C.
(01358) 789058
Newburgh, Aberdeenshire
(18) 6162 yards/***/D
(9) 6438 yards/***/D

Newmachar G.C.
(01651) 863002
Swailend, Newmachar
(18) 6605 yards/**/B/H

Nigg Bay G.C.
(01224) 871286
Balnagask, Aberdeen
(18) 5984 yards/***/F/G

NAIRN GOLF CLUB, INVERNESS-SHIRE Photograph courtesy of: Scottish Tourist Board

Old Meldrum G.C.
(01651) 872648
Kirkbrae, Old Meldrum
(18) 5442 yards/***/C

Peterculter G.C.
(01244) 734994
Burnside Road, Aberdeen
(18) 5947 yards/***/D

Peterhead G.C.
(01779) 472149
Craigewan Links, Peterhead
(18) 6173 yards/***/F/H
(9) 4322 yards/***/F/H

Portlethen G.C.
(01224) 781090
Badentoy Road, Portlethen
(18) 6707 yards/***(Sat am)/C/H

Rosehearty G.C.
(01346) 571645
Rosehearty, Fraserburgh
(9) 1684 yards/***/E

Rothes G.C.
(01340) 831277
Blackhall, Rothes
(9) 4956 yards/***/E

Royal Aberdeen G.C.
(01224) 702571
Balgownie, Bridge of Don
(18) 6372 yards/**/A/H
(18) 4033 yards/**/B/H

Royal Tarlair G.C.
(01261) 832897
Buchan Street, Macduff
(18) 5866 yards/***/D

Spey Bay G.C.
(01343) 820424
Spey Bay, Fochabers, Moray
(18) 6092 yards/***/D

Stonehaven G.C.
(01569) 762124
Cowie, Stonehaven
(18) 5103 yards/**/C

Strathlene G.C.
(01542) 831798
Portessie, Buckie
(18) 5957 yards/***/D

Tarland G.C.
(01339) 881413
Tarland, Aboyne
(9) 5812 yards/***/D

Torphins G.C.
(01339) 882115
Golf Road, Torphins, Banchory
(9) 2342 yards/***/D

Turriff G.C.
(01888) 562982
Rosehall, Turriff
(18) 6105 yards/***/C/H

Westhill G.C.
(01224) 742567
Westhill Heights, Westhill, Skene
(18) 5291 yards/*/C/G

THE HIGHLANDS

Abernethy G.C.
(01479) 821305
Nethybridge
(9) 4986 yards/***/E

Aigas G.C.
(01463) 782942
By Beauly, Invernesshire
(9) 2439 yards/***/D

Alness G.C.
(01349) 883877
Ardross Road, Alness
(9) 5160 yards/***/E

Askernish G.C.
(01878) 700541
Askernish, Lochboisdale, South Uist
(9) 5042 yards/***/E

Boat of Garten G.C.
(01479) 831282
Boat of Garten
(18) 5837 yards/***/C/H

Bonar Bridge G.C.
(01549) 421248
Bonar Bridge, Ardgay
(9) 2313 yards/***/E

Brora G.C.
(01408) 621417
Golf Road, Brora, Sutherland
(18) 6110 yards/***/C

Carnegie Club
(01862) 894600
Skibo Castle, Dornoch
(18) 6671 yards/***/A/H

Carrbridge G.C.
(01479) 841623
Carrbridge
(9) 2623 yards/***/C

Cawdor Castle G.C.
(01667) 404615
Nairn, Invernesshire
(9) 1161 yards/***/E

Colonsay G.C.
The Hotel, Colonsay, Argyll
(01951) 200316
(18) 4774 yards/***/E

Craignure G.C.
(01680) 812370
Craignure, Isle of Mull
(9) 5072 yards/***/E

Durness G.C.
(01971) 511364
Balnakeil, Durness
(9) 5545 yards/***(Sun am)/E

Fort Augustus G.C.
(01320) 366660
Markethill, Fort Augustus
(9) 5454 yards/***(Sat pm)/E

Fortrose and Rosemarkie G.C.
(01381) 620529
Ness Road East, Fortrose
(18) 5858 yards/***/C

Fort William G.C.
(01397) 704464
Turlundy, Fort William
(18) 6217 yards/***/F

DURNESS GOLF COURSE *Photograph courtesy of:* **Scottish Tourist Board**

Gairloch G.C.
(01445) 712407
Gairloch
(9) 2046 yards/***(Sun)/D

Golspie G.C.
(01408) 633266
Ferry Road, Golspie, Sutherland
(18) 5836 yards/***/E

Helmsdale G.C.
(01431) 821240
Helmsdale, Sutherland
(9) 1860 yards/***/E

Invergordon G.C.
(01349) 852715
Cromlet Drive, Invergordon
(9) 6028 yards/***/E

Isle of Coll G.C.
(01879) 230334
Isle of Coll, Argyll
(9) 2053 yards/***/E

Inverness G.C.
(01463) 239882
Culcabock Road, Inverness
(18) 6226 yards/**/F

Kingussie G.C.
(01540) 661600
Gynack Road, Kingussie
(18) 5504 yards/***/C

Lochcarron G.C.
(01520) 722252
Lochcarron, Strathcarron
(9) 3578 yards/***/E

Loch Ness G.C.
(01463) 713335
Castle Heather, Inverness
(18) 6772 yards/***/C

Lybster G.C.
(01593) 721215
Main Street, Lybster, Caithness
(9) 1898 yards/***/E

Muir of Ord G.C.
(01463) 870825
Great Northern Road, Muir of Ord
(18) 5202 yards/***/C/H

Nairn G.C.
(01667) 453208
Seabank Road, Nairn
(18) 6745 yards/***/A/H

Nairn Dunbar G.C.
(01667) 452741
Lochloy Road, Nairn
(18) 6712 yards/***/A/H

Newtonmore G.C.
(015403) 673328
Golf Course Road, Newtonmore
(18) 6029 yards/***/D

Reay G.C.
(01847) 811288
By Thurso, Caithness
(18) 5884 yards/***/D

Royal Dornoch G.C.
(01862) 810219
Golf Road, Dornoch, Sutherland
(18) 6514 yards/***/A/H
(18) 5438 yards/***/D/

Sconser G.C.
(01478) 613059
Sconser, Isle of Skye
(9) 4798 yards/***/E

Skeabost G.C.
(01470) 532202
Skeabost Bridge, Isle of Skye
(9) 1528 yards/***/E

Spean Bridge G.C.
(01397) 704954
Spean Bridge, Fort William
(9) 2203 yards/***/E

Stornoway G.C.
(01851) 702240
Stornoway, Isle of Lewis
(18) 5178 yards/***(Sun)/D

Strathpeffer Spa G.C.
(01997) 421219
Strathpeffer
(18) 4792 yards/***/D

Tain G.C.
(01862) 892314
Tain, Ross-shire
(18) 5082 yards/***/E

Tarbat G.C.
(01862) 871236
Portmahomack
(9) 2368 yards***(Sun)/E/H

Thurso G.C.
(01847) 893807
Newlands of Geise, Thurso
(18) 5818 yards/***/E

Tobermory G.C.
(01688) 302020
Erray Road, Tobermary
(9) 4890 yards/***/E

Torvean G.C.
(01463) 711434
Glenurquhart Road, Inverness
(18) 5784 yards/***/D

Traigh G.C.
(01687) 450377
Back of Kewppoch, Arisaig
(9) 2405 yards/***/E

Wick G.C.
(01955) 602726
Wick, Caithness
(18) 5976 yards/***/C

ORKNEY AND SHETLAND ISLES

Asta G.C.
(01598) 880231
Scalloway, Shetland
(9) 2023 yards/***/E

Orkney G.C.
(01856) 872457
St Ola, by Kirkwall, Orkney
(18) 5411 yards/***/E

Shetland G.C.
(01595) 840369
PO Box 18, Lerwick
(18) 5776 yards/***/E/H

Stromness G.C.
(01856) 850772
Ness, Stromness, Orkney
(18) 4762 yards/***/D

Whalsay G.C.
(01806) 566481
Skantaig, Shetland
(18) 6009 yards/***/E

STONEHAVEN GOLF CLUB Photograph courtesy of: **Scottish Tourist Board**

Golf in Ireland

WATERVILLE HOUSE & GOLF LINKS Photograph courtesy of: Waterville House & Golf Links

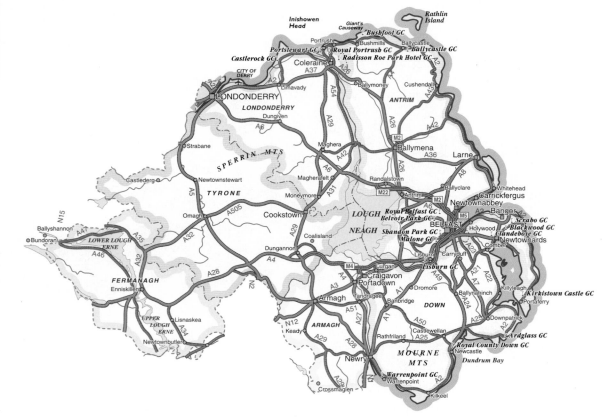

© MAPS IN MINUTES ™ 2000

Northern Ireland Choice Golf

It is no secret that Northern Ireland has experienced a turbulent history—what is less widely known, however, is that it is a stunningly beautiful place. It is a land of forests and lakes, of mountains and glens. It boasts some of the most spectacular coastal scenery in the British Isles and where else can you view the handiwork of a giant? So much in a country no larger than Yorkshire.

The quality of golf is equally outstanding. There are approximately seventy courses in all, a large number of which are to be found close to the coast enjoying some quite splendid isolation. Belfast, which is about the size of Bristol, has no shortage of good courses, and not just parkland types either, and then, of course, there are the two jewels in the crown—Portrush and Newcastle, or if you prefer, Royal Portrush and Royal County Down.

Belfast and County Down

Belfast is a likely starting point and getting there should be fairly straightforward. Approaching from Dublin it is a case of following the N1 and the A1, while from Britain car ferries run regularly from Stranraer. And travelling by air is even simpler should you be thinking of hiring a car when you arrive.

Having declared nothing but your urge to break 80, resist at all costs the temptation to zoom off northwards to Portrush or southwards to Newcastle—Belfast offers much more than you probably imagine. The best known golf course immediately at hand is the appropriately named **Royal Belfast**. It is situated just outside the city on the north coast alongside Belfast Lough and is a classic example of well manicured parkland golf. A number of holes here are very scenic, particularly around the turn and there is considerable challenge to combine with the charm. Royal Belfast, together with **Ardglass**, **Portstewart**, **Portrush** and **County Down**, is featured on a later page.

Remaining in Belfast, **Malone** Golf Club at Dunmurry is one of the leading inland courses in all Ireland—a visit is therefore strongly recommended—and two 'Parks' are also decidedly worth inspecting. The first is Belvoir (pronounce it, 'Beever') and the second is Shandon. **Belvoir Park** lies five miles south of the city centre, **Shandon Park** just to the north: both are championship courses. The former is definitely the pick of the two with its magnificent tree-lined fairways, however Shandon has the advantage of offering some interesting views over historical Stormont.

Clandeboye Golf Club, situated not too far from Royal Belfast along the Bangor Road offers a different challenge. Clandeboye is more wooded and 'heathy' with a considerable splash of gorse. There are two courses, the more difficult Dufferin and the Ava. Very close by golfers should also note the **Blackwood** Golf Centre.

To the south of Newtownards, **Scrabo** Golf Club is worth an inspection—its opening hole is reckoned to be the toughest in Ireland—and circling back towards Belfast, **Lisburn** is almost in the same league as Malone and Belvoir Park.

A good base is required from which to visit these courses. In Belfast itself, the Wellington Park Hotel (028) 9038 1111 offers comfortable rooms and a thriving nightlife, particularly at weekends. Alternatively, the Europa Hotel (028) 9032 7000 is both modern and very comfortable but the most popular choice for golfers will probably be the Culloden Hotel (028) 9042 5223 at Holywood (very convenient for Royal Belfast). The Culloden is an impressive building, a baronial styled Victorian mansion. Its restaurant is particularly recommended. Another good eating place in Holywood is Sullivans (028) 9042 1000 and on the subject of sumptuous fare, Belfast offers Speranza (028) 9023 0213 and Nick's Warehouse (028) 9043 9690. Belfast in fact is becoming renowned for its eating places and Cayenne (028) 9033 1532 and Manor House (028) 9023 8755 are two further places that offer particularly appealing fare. The former is particularly excellent. Whatever you do though don't forget to sample one or two of the local pubs—in most the atmosphere is tremendous. The Marine Court Hotel (028) 9145 1100 is recommended for those wishing to stay in Bangor, but for a cosy inn the best bet is to head towards Crawfordsburn where the Old Inn (028) 9185 3255 is a superb hostelry—full of character, its food is first class and there are some delightful bedrooms. Finally, adjacent to the new Blackwood Golf Centre (and obviously convenient for Clandeboye Golf Club as well) is the elegant Clandeboye Lodge Hotel (028) 9185 2500. Incidentally, the restaurant at Blackwood, the intriguingly named Shanks (028) 9185 3313 is very well thought of.

Relaxed, well fed, well lubricated and swing nicely grooved, the next golf course to play is **Kirkistown Castle**. It lies near the foot of the Ards Peninsula (once described somewhat alarmingly as the proboscis of Ulster!) Kirkistown is a real old-fashioned gem. James Braid assisted in the design of the course and is reputed to have commented wistfully 'If only I had this within 50 miles of London'. The town of Portaferry is no great distance away and the Portaferry Hotel (028) 4272 8231 is a marvellous place to spend the night. It is another of those cosy inns (note the splendid seafood here).

If you're not in a rush it is worth spending some time on the Ards Peninsula. It is a remote and beautiful corner of Ireland and Lough Strangford is one giant bird sanctuary and wildlife reserve. From Portaferry, take a ferry to Strangford and from here a short drive will take you to **Ardglass** on the coast. Perched on craggy rocks, the layout is reminiscent of some of the better seaside courses in Cornwall. A true 'hidden gem', Ardglass may be Northern Ireland's best kept golfing secret.

Beyond St John's Point and around Dundrum Bay, a journey of approximately twelve miles, lies Newcastle, an attractive seaside town and where, as the famous song tells you, 'the mountains of Mourne sweep down to the sea'. For golfers it is a paradise. Royal County Down Golf Club is quite simply one of the greatest courses in the world. For those lucky people who can enjoy a few days here, the Burrendale Hotel (028) 4372 2599 on Castlewellan Road is very popular with golfers (and only about a five minute drive from the course). Equally recommended is the Slieve Donard Hotel (028) 4372 3681 which practically adjoins the famous links—in fact you'll be aiming a couple of drives at its spires. There are, alas, fewer and fewer hotels nowadays able to combine old-fashioned elegance with modern comforts but the Slieve Donard is a memorable example. Newcastle is a holiday town and good quality guesthouses and bed and breakfasts abound. If one is staying in the area some sightseeing is strongly advised.

ROYAL COUNTY DOWN GOLF CLUB
Photograph courtesy of: **Royal County Down Golf Club**

To the south and west the mountain scenery is quite magnificent while the southern coastal road takes in some very different but beautiful views. Smuggling was once notorious here and, before reaching the border, we recommend that you smuggle in a quick 18 holes at **Warrenpoint**, where Ronan Rafferty learnt to play. Also try to make an excuse to visit Annalong and more specifically Glassdrumman Lodge (028) 4476 8451. This is a really delightful place to stay and dine—just ask Nick Faldo!

The Causeway Coast

Our journey now takes us back northwards, past Belfast to the Antrim coast. Here there is perhaps the most spectacular scenery of all and, equally important, yet more glorious golf.

Now, what kind of being can pick thorns out of his heels whilst running and can rip up a vast chunk of rock and hurl it fifty miles into the sea? Who on earth could perform such staggering feats? The answer is Finn McCool (who, alas, is not eligible for Ryder Cup selection). Finn was the great warrior giant who commanded the armies of the King of all Ireland. He inhabited an Antrim headland, probably not far from Portrush in fact. Having fallen madly in love with a lady giant who lived on the Hebridian Island of Staffa, Finn began building a giant bridge to bring her across the water. Either Finn grew fickle or the lady blew him out but the bridge was never completed Still, the Giants Causeway remains a great monument to one Finn McCool.

Royal Portrush is a monument to the Royal and Ancient game. However, don't limit your golf to Portrush—there are three other superb 18 hole courses nearby. To the east of Portrush, **Ballycastle** has an attractive situation overlooking an inviting stretch of sand and, if it didn't look so cold, the sea would be equally inviting. It is nothing like as tough as Portrush, more of a holiday course really, but tremendously enjoyable all the same.

Midway between Ballycastle and Portrush there is a pleasant nine holes at **Bushfoot** in Portballintrae. One should visit the famous Bushmills Distillery nearby—the oldest distillery in the world where whiskey has been produced since 1608. Just think what Finn might have done after a magnum of Black Bush. An equally popular place to stay is the excellent Bushmills Inn (028) 2073 2339—ideal for those who wish to avoid both kinds of drinking and driving! Portrush's most celebrated eating place is Ramore on the quay, where there is a top class restaurant (028) 7082 5098 and a casual wine bar (028) 7082 3444. Those who have overindulged in Portrush and are seeking a comforting bed for the night should look (or stumble) no further than the excellent Magherabuoy House (028) 7082 3507. Alternatively we can recommend the Royal Court Hotel (028) 7082 2236, whose location high above the famous links is the envy of every hotel in Ireland and the Causeway Coast Hotel (028) 7082 2435.

Four miles west of Portrush and further along the coast is the fishing town of Portstewart. The Edgewater Hotel (028) 7083 3314 in town is near the golf club and there are numerous small hotels and B&Bs. Also convenient for both Portrush and Portstewart is Maddybenny Farm (028) 7082 3394, one of the finest guesthouses in the country. Further west again lies the course at **Roe Park** set in the grounds of the Radisson Roe Park Hotel (028) 7772 2222, a fine hotel with course to match.

Further inland close to Ballymena you will find Galmgom Manor (028) 2588 1001 which is situated close to the golf course at the nearby castle. Another fine stopover is the Adair Arms Hotel (028) 2565 3674 set in the centre of Ballymena.

One final course remains to be played on the splendid Causeway coast. **Castlerock** lies a few miles across the River Bann from Portstewart. Again a classic links set amid towering sand dunes, a game here will test every aspect of your game! There are many golfing delights in Northern Ireland that we have not explored, however, should Castlerock be your last port of call you'll have no excuse for not leaving Ireland a contented soul.

The magnificent Slieve Donard Hotel is located in Newcastle, County Down, just 45 minutes south of Belfast. Situated "Where the Mountains of Mourne sweep down to the sea", the Slieve Donard Hotel stands in six acres of private grounds which extend to an extensive golden strand.

Originally a luxurious railway hotel, the Slieve Donard offers 4 star accommodation and excellent facilities. It is the most popular hotel in the Province for a conference, holiday or golf break. All of its 126 luxury bedrooms are beautifully appointed with all the modern facilities you would expect from a top international hotel.

The Slieve Donard Hotel is the first choice for golfers who play at the world famous Royal County Down Golf Club. It is only two minutes through a beautiful hedged, arched walk to the course. Other courses close at hand are Kilkeel, Ardglass and Warrenpoint.

The hotel warmly welcomes all golfers and can arrange starting times with local courses, including Royal County Down. A hospitality car can be provided by the hotel for residents.

Within the hotel, the Elysium Health and Leisure Club is a must for all visitors, with tennis, swimming in the luxurious indoor pool, putting on the lawn, or a relaxing sauna or jacuzzi.

Other popular venues are Chaplin's Bar and the Percy French, an informal pub/restaurant in the grounds of the hotel, named after the writer of "The Mountains of Mourne".

The Slieve Donard is truly one of Ireland's great holiday hotels - renowned for its warm welcome, the efficiency and courtesy of its service, and, of course, for the gourmet food and fine wines served in the Oak Restaurant.

Newcastle town is the gateway to the magnificent Mourne Mountains and Tollymore Forest Park where guests can enjoy excellent fishing, hiking on clearly marked trails, and pony-trekking.

The Slieve Donard is a member of Hastings Hotels, the leading group of hotels in Northern Ireland—a further guarantee of its excellence.

Slieve Donard Hotel
Downs Road, Newcastle
Co Down
Tel: (028) 4372 3681
Fax: (028) 4372 4830
e mail: res@sdh.hastingshotels.com
web site: http://www.hastingshotels.com

Royal County Down

Approximately thirty miles to the south of Belfast and beneath the spectacular gaze of the Mountains of Mourne there lies the most beautiful golf course in the world. A daring statement perhaps, but will anyone who has visited disagree?

Royal County Down is situated in Newcastle and the course stretches out along the shores of Dundrum Bay. It was originally laid out in 1889 by 'Old' Tom Morris from St Andrews, who for his labours, we are told, was paid the princely sum of four guineas. In a way though, there was little that Old Tom had to do, for Royal County Down is also one of the world's most natural golfing links.

Within four years of the first ball being struck the course was considered good enough to stage the Irish Open Amateur Championship which was duly won by the greatest amateur of the day, John Ball. Before the 20th century had dawned, County Down was already being considered the finest course in all Ireland and some were even extending the accolade further.

Beautiful and natural, what next? Degree of difficulty. 'It was, in fact, the sternest examination in golf I had ever taken', the words of the very knowledgeable and well travelled golf writer Herbert Warren Wind. From its championship tees, Royal County Down measures 7037 yards, par 71. The fairways are often desperately narrow, the greens small, slick and not at all easy to hold; there are a number of blind tee shots amid the dunes and the rough comprises heather and thick gorse. Imagine what it's like in a fierce wind! Royal County Down is one of the toughest courses in the world.

Those wishing to pay homage should telephone the club well in advance of intended play. Visitors are certainly welcome, but the course can naturally only accommodate so many. Weekends are best avoided as indeed are Wednesdays, but Mondays, Tuesdays, Thursdays and Fridays are relatively easy for visitors; a letter of introduction from the golfer's home club is helpful. The **Secretary, Mr Peter Rolph** can be approached by **tel: (028) 4372 3314** and by **fax: (028) 4372 6281.** The address to write to is **Royal County Down Golf Club, Golf Links Road, Newcastle, Co. Down BT33 0AN.** For further information visit **www.royalcountydown.org** The club's **Professional, Kevan Whitson,** can be contacted on **tel: (028) 4372 2419.** In summer 2000 the green fees are £70 per round during the week with £80 payable at the weekend.

Visitors looking for a more sedate (but equally beautiful) challenge should take note of the Annesley Links at Royal County Down.

Recently upgraded under the direction of Donald Steel, this course now measures 4681 yards, par 66 (par 68 for ladies). It is open to visiting golfers all week, with green fees currently set at £16 during the week and £23 at weekends.

The thirty mile journey from Belfast is via Ballynahinch along the A24 and the A2. The road is a good one and it should take less than an hour. From Dublin to the south the distance is about ninety miles and here the route to follow is the N1 to Newry and then again the A24, this time approaching Newcastle from the west.

Unlike many of the great natural links courses, Royal County Down doesn't have the traditional 'out and back' type of layout; rather there are two distinct loops of nine. The outward loop, or half, is closer to the sea and hence is more sandy in nature and the dunes are consistently larger. You can hear the breaking of the waves as you play down the 1st fairway and your first blind tee shot comes as early as the par four 2nd. It is said that you can always spot the first time visitor to Newcastle for he walks up the 1st fairway backwards, so enchanting is the view behind!

Among the finest holes on the front nine are the 3rd with its extraordinary split-level fairway, the par three 4th, the dog-legged 5th, the 8th and the 9th, where an uphill drive must be targeted at the red spire of the Slieve Donard Hotel and followed (assuming the drive has successfully flown the hill and descended into the valley below) by a long second shot to a well guarded plateau green—a particularly memorable hole to conclude what many people consider to be the finest nine holes in golf.

The back nine may not have so many great sandhills, but there is still a plentiful supply of heather and gorse. Of the better holes perhaps the 13th, where the fairway curves its way through a beautiful heather-lined valley and the very difficult 15th stand out.

Given its remote situation and the lack of facilities or space to cope with a vast crowd of spectators the Open Championship could sadly never be staged at Royal County Down. The Amateur Championship has been played here though, most recently in 1999, when it was won by Graham Storm. The Irish Amateur Championship visits Newcastle regularly and there have been some truly memorable finals. In 1933, Eric Fiddian playing against Jack McLean, holed in one at the 7th in the morning round and then again at the 14th in the afternoon. A magical moment in a magical setting—and I don't suppose Fiddian felt too sore when McLean eventually won the match.

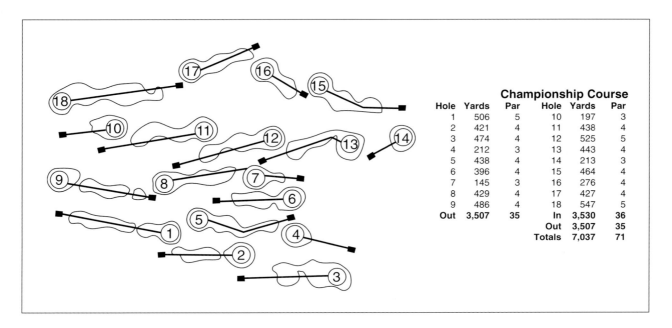

Hole	Yards	Par	Hole	Yards	Par
1	506	5	10	197	3
2	421	4	11	438	4
3	474	4	12	525	5
4	212	3	13	443	4
5	438	4	14	213	3
6	396	4	15	464	4
7	145	3	16	276	4
8	429	4	17	427	4
9	486	4	18	547	5
Out	**3,507**	**35**	**In**	**3,530**	**36**
			Out	**3,507**	**35**
			Totals	**7,037**	**71**

Championship Course

Royal Portrush

In May 1988, Royal Portrush celebrated its one hundredth birthday. One could say that this famous club was born with a golfing silver spoon in its mouth. Within four years of its foundation patronage was bestowed, and there could never be a finer natural setting for a championship links. The course is laid out amid huge sand dunes which occupy slightly elevated ground providing commanding views over the Atlantic. And what views! The Antrim coast is at its most spectacular between the Giant's Causeway and Portrush and overlooking the links are the proud ruins of a magnificent castle, Dunluce, from which the championship course takes its name. The first professional the club employed was Sandy Herd, who went on to win the Open Championship in 1902, and as if by way of a final blessing, in 1951 Portrush became the first (and to this day the only) club in Ireland to stage the Open Championship

There are in fact two championship courses at Portrush. When people talk of 'the championship links' they are invariably referring to the **Dunluce** Course—this is where the Open and the 1993 Amateur Championship were staged—but there is also the **Valley** Course which can stretch to 6278 yards and is used for many important events. Somewhat surprisingly it has only twenty bunkers. Visitors are made very welcome at Portrush and can play either course on any day of the week except Wednesday and Friday afternoons. The Valley course is also closed to visitors on Sunday mornings. It is always wise to telephone the club in advance as the tees may have been reserved and Portrush is popular in the summer.

In 2000 the green fees to play over the Dunluce Course are set at £70 per round between Monday and Friday and £80 for a single round at weekends and bank holidays (when available). Visitors may play a second round for an additional charge of £35. Fees for the Valley Course are £25 per round during the week and £32 at weekends, with an extra round costing a further £15. Golfing societies are equally welcome, subject of course to prior arrangement with the **Secretary, Wilma Erskine**. She may be contacted by writing to the **Royal Portrush Golf Club, Dunluce Road, Portrush, Co. Antrim BT56 8JQ tel: (028) 7082 2311 or fax: (028) 7082 3139**; the club's **Professional, Gary McNeill**, can be reached on **tel: (028) 7082 3335.**

The golf club lies about half a mile from Portrush town. Portrush itself is easily accessible as it is linked by coastal road to Portstewart and Ballycastle, and to Belfast by major road—a distance of approximately sixty miles. Londonderry is about thirty five miles to the west. The club is located immediately off Bushmills Road and don't forget to visit the famous distillery when you're in the area—it's less than 10 minutes from the links and is guaranteed to do wonders for your golf!

Although golf has been played at Portrush for more than a hundred years, the Dunluce Course bears little resemblance to the original championship course. Harry Colt is responsible for the present layout and we all owe him a great debt. Work was carried out between 1929 and 1932 and he is said to have considered it his masterpiece—and Harry Colt built many a great course. Bernard Darwin wrote in The Times after viewing the links during the 1951 Open: 'It is truly magnificent and Mr H S Colt, who designed it in its present form, has thereby built himself a monument more enduring than brass'.

Portrush's most celebrated holes are the 5th and the 14th. The 5th, 'White Rocks', is one of the most exhilarating two-shot holes in golf. From the tee, there is a splendid view of the Antrim Coast towards the White Rocks and the Giant's Causeway beyond. However spellbound you may be, considerable care is required with both the drive and the approach. The hole is properly a dog-leg and although a brave drive can cut the angle, failure will result in a trip into the deep, deep rough—over-hit your second and you're in the Atlantic! The green here nearly fell into the sea some years ago but a retaining wall was built and it has been saved. The 14th is titled 'Calamity', and not without good reason—a par three of over 200 yards in length, the direct line to the pin requires a very precise shot to carry an enormous ravine—mishit this one and you can be playing your next shot from at least fifty feet below the hole.

The course poses a considerable challenge but it's a fair one nonetheless. In the 1951 Open only twice during the entire tournament did a player break 70. Silver spoon or not, you can be sure my good friend Finn McCool would have been mightily impressed.

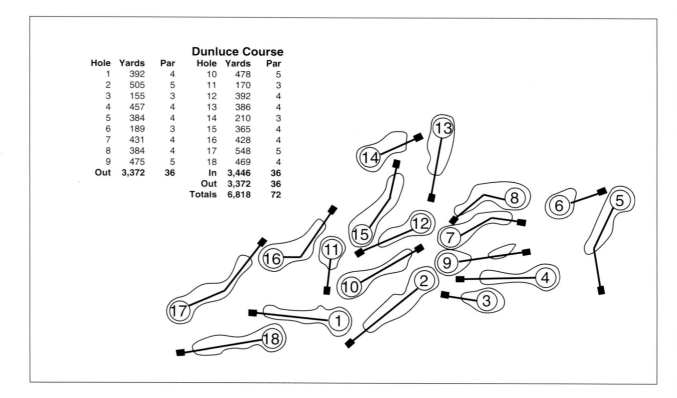

Dunluce Course

Hole	Yards	Par	Hole	Yards	Par
1	392	4	10	478	5
2	505	5	11	170	3
3	155	3	12	392	4
4	457	4	13	386	4
5	384	4	14	210	3
6	189	3	15	365	4
7	431	4	16	428	4
8	384	4	17	548	5
9	475	5	18	469	4
Out	3,372	36	In	3,446	36
			Out	3,372	36
			Totals	6,818	72

Portstewart

The Causeway Coast of Northern Ireland—essentially the coast of Antrim with a bit of County Londonderry stuck on—has long been regarded as a fine place for a golfing break with three very good courses and one outstanding championship links to play. The last-mentioned is, of course, Royal Portrush, the only golf links in Ireland to have staged the Open Championship, the three supporting courses being Ballycastle, Portstewart and Castlerock. In the last few years all this has changed. It is not the opening of a new course (although some might describe it as such) but rather the extraordinary transformation of one of the supporting cast. Portstewart now ranks among the greatest courses in Ireland. How come? Two words will suffice, Thistly Hollow.

Visitors to Portstewart have always marvelled at the magnificent 425 yard, par four lst hole. 'The best opening hole in Ireland' is the proud boast, and only the members at Portrush seem to grumble loudly. Of course the difficulty of having such a spectacular starter is that the main course has got a lot to live up to. Although the following seventeen holes at Portstewart were considered well above average, they were not able to sustain the sensation of wonder—that is until now. After playing the glorious lst, golfers used to gaze up into the nearby range of sandhills, known as Thistly Hollow, and ruminate on how fantastic it would be if only they could build some golf holes amidst those towering dunes. Well now they have—and that is why Portstewart is such a fantastic golf course.

One of the people best able to tell you how this came about—for he presided over much of it—is the club's enthusiastic **Secretary, Michael Moss.** Visitors wishing to explore the awesome sandhills and the rest of the links are advised to contact the club a little in advance. The full address is **Portstewart Golf Club, 117 Strand Road, Portstewart, Co Londonderry, BT55 7PG.** Mr Moss can also be contacted on **tel: (028) 7083 2015** and by **fax: (028) 7083 4097,** while Portstewart's **Professional, Alan Hunter** can be reached on **(028) 7083 2601.**

Although it is easy to get carried away with the major reshaping of the **Championship** Course it should be pointed out that there are 45 holes of golf to enjoy at Portstewart. The short 18 hole **Old** Course has been around for a little while but a new nine hole course, the **Riverside 9** has evolved following the aforementioned reshaping

of the championship links. Broadly speaking, what has happened is that much of the former back nine at Portstewart has become the Riverside 9 and the new holes have been 'inserted' to immediately follow the famous lst. This is only roughly what has happened for the 'new' 18th is still more or less the 'old' 18th—confused? The best bet is to pay a visit!

Portstewart welcomes visitors, although a round on the championship course is not normally possible on Saturdays and only limited times are available on Sundays. The summer green fee in 2000 for the championship course is £50 during the week and £70 at the weekend. A full eighteen holes on the Riverside 9 is priced at £12 midweek and £17 at weekends, while at similar times the green fee for the Old Course is £10 and £14 respectively.

Portstewart is situated right on the coast, some 4 miles from Coleraine and no greater a distance from Portrush which is to the east of Portstewart. The road that links each to the other is the A2. Belfast is approximately 65 miles away, though its airport is a little nearer. From there one doesn't have to journey through the capital to get to the Causeway Coast—the A26 is a very direct route. Londonderry is about 30 miles to the west and there is a second airport there.

So having played the splendid dog-leg lst with its superbly elevated tee (every bit as exhilarating as the 5th at Portrush) and amphitheatre-like green, instead of gazing up into the sandhills the golfer playing the championship links must now get in amongst them. The 'new' front nine holes at Portstewart are being compared favourably with the back nine holes at Tralee Golf Club in County Kerry—and anyone who has played that exceptional links, designed by Arnold Palmer, will know that this is a mighty compliment. The views that these holes afford are also quite breathtaking and at times quite terrifying! The sight from the back tee at the 2nd, a stunning par four, provides an early example of both sensations. There are two tremendous short holes, the 3rd and the 6th, but perhaps even better are the long dune-fringed, sweeping par five 4th, and the classic stroke index one 5th.

The golfer may feel in a world of his own as he plays these holes but then that's Portstewart—a quite extraordinary golf course.

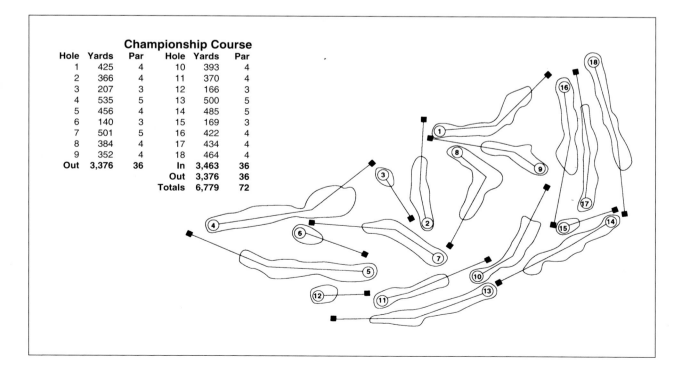

Championship Course

Hole	Yards	Par	Hole	Yards	Par
1	425	4	10	393	4
2	366	4	11	370	4
3	207	3	12	166	3
4	535	5	13	500	5
5	456	4	14	485	5
6	140	3	15	169	3
7	501	5	16	422	4
8	384	4	17	434	4
9	352	4	18	464	4
Out	**3,376**	**36**	**In**	**3,463**	**36**
			Out	**3,376**	**36**
			Totals	**6,779**	**72**

Royal Belfast

Just as London is famed for the quality of its heathland courses, so Belfast is renowned for the quality of its parkland challenges. Within a short distance of the city centre are the likes of Belvoir Park, Shandon Park, Malone, Lisburn and, perhaps most famous of all, Royal Belfast.

Founded in 1881, Royal Belfast is the oldest golf club in Ireland. Its golf course is situated at Craigavad to the east of the city on the southern shores of Belfast Lough. The club's home has not always been here—there were two previous sites—but since 1925 it has enjoyed this genuinely spectacular location. The course was designed by Harry Colt, the same architect who transformed the links courses at Royal Portrush and Royal Dublin and who created a splendid layout at nearby Belvoir Park.

The land at Craigavad tilts consistently towards the Lough (something to remember when lining up putts!). This slope was used to dramatic effect in Colt's routing which includes no fewer than 13 distinct changes of direction. There is a good mix of uphill and downhill holes as well as left and right angled dog-legs. On the higher parts of the course golf is played along mature tree-lined avenues with occasional glimpses of the Lough. Down on the waterfront there is a very open, almost links feel to some of the holes. Colt's talent for cunning placement and elegant shaping of bunkers is also very evident, although in recent years Donald Steel has added and removed a few hazards to compensate for the effects of modern equipment.

The round begins with a strong two-shotter, a slightly uphill, curving dog-leg to the left, and is immediately followed by the first of several exhilarating downhill tee shots. After touring the fringes of the property, the course turns towards the Lough at the 5th and 6th. The 7th, an outstanding par three, swings back uphill but the 8th charges back down again to a green situated close to the shore.

A few loughside joggers may pass comment on your drive at the 9th, and then come two of the best and most characterful holes on the course.

The 10th is a short par four that dog-legs to the left. The tee shot must be precisely placed for the green nestles in a tight, pocket-like corner, its entrance protected by an assortment of over-hanging trees and a bunker that eats into the front right side. The 11th is an intimidating par three played slightly uphill over rocky terrain that is covered in gorse bushes and scrub. The tempo momentarily relaxes at the next hole then builds to a strong finish with the 18th, a beautifully landscaped par five, providing a fitting finale to a most pleasurable round.

**Royal Belfast Golf Club, Station Road
Craigavad, Co Down BT18 0BP
e mail: royalbelfastgc@btclick.com**

Sec/Manager	Susanna Morrison (028) 9042 8165
	Fax (028) 9042 1404
Professional	Chris Spence (028) 9042 8586
Green Fees	WD £35/round
	WE £45/round
Restrictions	Proof of handicap required. Ring beforehand
	for bookings.

Directions
The Club is 7 miles north east of Belfast on the A2 Bangor road, about a mile outside Holywood.

Ardglass

The golfer in a hurry—or the golfer without a soul—will travel to Portrush from Belfast by journeying inland, by driving through the heart of Northern Ireland after picking up the A26 at Ballymena, bypassing the Causeway coast. That same person will head speedily for Newcastle, travelling due south via Ballynahinch. A bally idiot you might think.

The route to Newcastle we recommend is a very leisurely trip round the Ards Peninsula. Such a route will please the birdwatcher, for the road runs alongside Strangford Lough—one of the finest bird sanctuaries in Europe—fascinate the country house enthusiast and historian, as the road passes several magnificent houses as well as numerous castles, abbeys and monuments, and delight the golfer, for a game could be sneaked in at Kirkistown Castle. On reaching Portaferry the traveller takes a quick ferry ride and then heads for Ardglass, just seven scenic miles away along the coast of Co Down. The Mountains of Mourne loom on the horizon and Newcastle is just 12 miles beyond Ardglass. Now we suggest that all and sundry make a decent length pit stop.

Ardglass is an historic little town. It has a great seafaring tradition and was once, though it's hard to believe now, the busiest port in Ulster. It is particularly famous for its collection of 14th to 16th century castles (there are about half a dozen of them in various states of ruin) and is apparently celebrated for its herrings, though I cannot recall ever having sampled any. Perhaps they are a speciality at the 19th hole of Ardglass Golf Club? 18 holes of golf here will certainly create an appetite, though my guess is that the first-time visitor will be even more keen on getting back out and playing a second round on what is unquestionably one of the most spectacular and sporting courses in Ireland. What makes Ardglass so enjoyable is its dramatic layout with several tees and greens overlooking the ocean. Measuring little more than 6000 yards it is not particularly long, although it has

a really rugged feel and is part links, part clifftop in nature. Much of the course is overrun with vast swathes of purple heather.

The front nine holes are the more memorable, especially the first five which all run right alongside the sea. The par three second is many people's favourite—and many people's undoing—with its tee shot needing to be fired across a rocky inlet. It is a real death-or-glory hole and somewhat reminiscent of the 3rd at Tralee. By contrast the 18th offers a good chance of a closing birdie. Then, of course, it is off to the 19th, which being Ardglass is a converted ancient castle, and time to relax with a drink or two—unless, that is, you are a golfer in a hurry, or a golfer without a soul.

**Ardglass Golf Club, Castle Place
Ardglass, Co Down BT30 7TP**

Club Manager	Debbie Polly (028) 4484 1219
	Fax (028) 4484 1841
Professional	Philip Farrell (028) 4484 1022
Green Fees	WD £18
	WE £24

Directions
The club is seven miles south of Downpatrick on the

CO ANTRIM

Ballycastle G.C.
(028) 2076 3319
Cushendall Road, Ballycastle
(18) 5882 yards/***/D-C

Ballyclare G.C.
(028) 9332 2696
Springvale Road, Ballyclare
(18) 6282 yards/**/D/H

Ballymena G.C.
(028) 2586 1487
Raceview Road, Broughshane
(18) 5245 metres/***(Sat)/D/H

Bushfoot G.C.
(028) 2073 1317
Portballintrae, Bushmills
(9) 5572 yards/***/D/H

Cairndhu G.C.
(028) 2858 3324
Coast Road, Ballygally, Larne
(18) 6112 yards/***(Sat)/D

Carrickfergus G.C.
(028) 9336 3713
North Road, Carrickfergus
(18) 5765 yards/**/D

Cushendall G.C.
(028) 2177 1318
Shore Road, Cushendall, Ballymena
(9) 2193 metres/***/E

Down Royal Park G.C.
(028) 9262 1339
Dunygarton Road, Maze
(18) 6824 yards
(9) 2500 yards/***/D/E

Galgorm Castle G. & C.C
(028) 2564 6161
Galgorm Road, Ballymena
(18) 6724 metres/***/D

Gracehill G.C.
(028) 2565 1209
141 Ballinlea Road, Stranocum
(9) 5377 metres/***/E

Greenacres G.C.
(028) 9335 4111
153 Ballyrobert Road, Ballyclare
(18) 5820 yards/***/E

Greenisland G.C.
(028) 9086 2236
Upper Road, Greenisland
(9) 5887 yards/***(Sat)/D

Lambeg G.C.
(028) 9266 2738
Bells Lane, Lambeg, Lisburn
(9) 4583 yards/***/E

Larne G.C.
(028) 9338 2228
Ferris Bay Road, Islandmagee, Larne
(9) 6082 yards/***/E

Lisburn G.C.
(028) 9267 7216
Eglantine Road, Lisburn
(18) 6647 yards/**(am)/B

Massereene G.C.
(028) 9442 8096
Lough Road, Antrim
(18) 6559 yards/***(Fri)/C/H

Royal Portrush G.C.
(028) 7082 2311
Bushmills Road, Portrush
(18) 6818 yards/**(am)/A/H(24)
(18) 6278 yards/**(am)/C/H(24)

Whitehead G.C.
(028) 9335 3631
McCraes Brae, Whitehead
(18) 6362 yards/**(Sat)/D/G

CO ARMAGH

Ashfield G.C.
(028) 3086 8180
Freeduff, Cullyhana
(18) 5616 yards/***/E

County Armagh G.C.
(028) 3752 5861
Newry Road, Armagh
(18) 5649 metres/**/D

Craigavon Golf & Ski Centre
(028) 3832 6606
Silverwood, Lurgan
(18) 6496 yards/***/E

Edenmore G.C.
(028) 9261 1310
Drumnabreeze Road, Craigavan
(9) 6152 yards/***/E

Lurgan G.C.
(028) 3832 2087
The Demesne, Lurgan
(18) 5836 metres/***(Sat)/C

Mallusk G.C.
(028) 9084 3799
Newtonabbey
(9) 4444 metres/***/F

Portadown G.C.
(028) 3835 5356
Gilford Road, Portadown
(18) 5649 yards/**/C

Silverwood G.C.
(028) 3832 6606
Turmoyra Lane, Lurgan
(18) 6459 yards/**(am)/E/M

Trandragee G.C.
(028) 3884 1272
Trandragee, Craigavon
(18) 5446 metres/***(Thurs/Sat)/D

BELFAST

Ballyearl G.C.
(028) 9084 8287
Doagh Road, Newtonabbey
(9) 2362 yards/***/E

Balmoral G.C.
(028) 9038 1514
Lisburn Road, Belfast
(18) 5488 metres/**/C

Belvoir Park G.C.
(028) 9049 1693
Newtownbreda, Belfast
(18) 6516 yards/***(Wed)/B/H

Cliftonville G.C.
(028) 9074 6595
Westland Road, Belfast
(9) 2853 yards/**/D

Dunmurry G.C.
(028) 9061 0834
Dunmurry Lane, Belfast
(18) 5348 metres/**(Fri/Sat)/C/H

Fortwilliam G.C.
(028) 9037 0770
Downview Avenue, Belfast
(18) 5642 yards/***(Sat)/C

Gilnahirk G.C.
(028) 9044 8477
Manns Corner, Upper Brawiel Road
(9) 5398 yards/***/F

Knock G.C.
(028) 9048 3251
Summerfield, Dundonald
(18) 6435 yards/**/B/H

Malone G.C.
(028) 9061 2758
Upper Malone Road, Dunmurry
(18) 6476 yards/***(Sat/Wed)/A

Mount Ober G.& C.C.
(028) 9040 1811
Ballymaconaghy Road, Knockbracken
(18) 5391 yards/**/E

Ormeau G.C.
(028) 9064 0700
Park Road, Belfast
(9) 5306 yards/***/D

Shandon Park G.C.
(028) 9040 1856
Shandon Park, Belfast
(18) 6252 yards/***/C

CO DOWN

Ardglass G.C.
(028) 4484 1219
Castle Place, Ardglass
(18) 6048 yards/**/C

Ardminnan G.C.
(028) 4277 1321
15 Ardminnan Road, Portaferry
(9) 2766 metres/***/E

Banbridge G.C.
(028) 4066 2211
Huntly Road, Banbridge
(18) 5000 metres/***/D

Bangor G.C.
(028) 9127 0922
Broadway, Bangor
(18) 6424 yards/**/C

Blackwood G.C.
(028) 9185 2706
Clandeboye
(36)/***/F

Bright Castle G.C.
(028) 4484 1319
Bright, Downpatrick
(18) 7143 yards/***/D/H

Carnalea G.C.
(028) 9127 0368
Station Road, Bangor
(18) 5584 yards/***/D

Clandeboye G.C.
(028) 9127 1767
Conlig, Newtownards
(18) 6648 yards/**/C/G
(18) 5755 yards/**/C/G

Crossgar G.C.
(028) 4483 1523
Derryboye Road, Crossgan
(9) 4139 metres/***/E

Donaghadee G.C.
(028) 9188 3624
Warren Road, Donaghadee
(18) 5760 yards/***(Sat)/D

Downpatrick G.C.
(028) 4461 5947
Saul Road, Downpatrick
(18) 5615 metres/***/D

Helens Bay G.C.
(028) 9185 2815
Helens Bay, Bangor
(9) 5176 metres/***(Sat)/F

Holywood G.C.
(028) 9042 3135
Nuns Walk, Demesne Road
(18) 5153 metres/***/C

Kilkeel G.C.
(028) 4176 5095
Mourne Park, Ballyardle
(9) 6625 yards/***(Sat)/C

Kirkistown Castle G.C.
(028) 4277 1233
Cloughey, Newtownards
(18) 5596 metres/**/D-C

Mahee Island G.C.
(028) 9154 1234
Comber, Mahee Island
(9) 5580 yards/***/D

Newry G.C.
(028) 3026 3871
11 Forkhill Road, Newry
(18) 3000 metres/***/E

Ringdufferin G.C.
(028) 4482 8812
Toye, Killyleagh
(18) 4698 yards/***/E

Rockmount G.C.
(028) 9081 2279
28 Drumalig Road, Carryduff
(18) 6373 yards/(Sat)/D

Royal Belfast G.C.
(028) 9042 8165
Holywood, Craigavad
(18) 5963 yards/***/B/H/M

Royal County Down G.C.
(028) 4172 3314
Newcastle
(18) 7037 yards/**/A/H
(18) 4681 yards/**/D/H

Scrabo G.C.
(028) 9181 2355
Scrabo Road, Newtownards
(18) 5699 metres/***/D/H

Spa G.C.
(028) 9756 2365
Grove Road, Ballynahinch
(18) 6003 metres/**/D

Temple G.C
(028) 9263 9213
60 Church Road, Boardmills.
(9) 5451 yards/***/E

Warrenpoint G.C.
(028) 4175 3695
Lower Dromore Road, Warrenpoint
(18) 6215 yards/***(Wed)/D/H

CO FERMANAGH

Ashwoods Golf Centre
(028) 6632 5321
Sligo Road, Enniskillen
(14) 1930 yards/***/F

Castlehume G.C.
(028) 6632 7077
Castle Hume, Eniskillen
(18) 6139 metres/***/D

Enniskillen G.C.
(028) 6632 5250
Enniskillen
(18) 5588 metres/***/D/H

CO LONDONDERRY

Benone G.C.
(028) 7775 0555
53 Benone Avenue, Limavady
(9) 1458 yards/***/E

Brown Trout G.& C.C.
(028) 7086 8209
Agivey Road, Aghadovey, Coleraine
(9) 2800 yards/***/E

Castlerock G.C.
(028) 7084 8314
Circular Road, Castlerock
(18) 6687 yards/***/C/M
(9) 2457 metres/***/C/M

City of Derry G.C.
(028) 7134 6369
Prehan, Londonderry
(18) 6487 yards/***/D/H
(9) 2354 yards/***/D/H

Foyle G.C
(028) 7135 2222
Alder Road, Londonderry
(18) 6678 metres/***/

Kilrea G.C.
(028) 2582 1048
Drumagarner Road, Kilrea
(9) 4326 yards/*(Tues/Wed/Sat)/E

Moyola Park G.C.
(028) 7946 8468
Shanemullagh, Castledawson
(18) 6522 yards/**/D

Portstewart G.C.
(028) 7083 2015
Strand Road, Portstewart
(18) 6779 yards/**/A/H
(18) 4733 yards/***/E
(9) 2662 yards/***/E

Roe Park G.C.
(028) 7776 0105
Limavady
(18) 6318 yards/***/C
CO TYRONE

Aughnacloy G.C.
(028) 8555 7050
99 Tullyvar Road, Aughnacloy
(9) 3017 metres/***/E

Dungannon G.C.
(028) 8772 2098
Mullaghmore, Dungannon
(18) 5433 metres/***/D

Fintona G.C.
(028) 8784 1480
Fintona
(9) 6250 yards/***/F

Killymoon G.C.
(028) 8676 3762
Killymoon, Cookstown
(18) 6013 yards/***/D/H

Newtownstewart G.C.
(028) 8166 1466
Golf Course Road,
Newtownstewart
(18) 6100 yards/***/E

Omagh G.C.
(028) 8724 1442
Dublin Road, Omagh
(18) 5633 metres/***/D
(18) 5429 metres/***/D

Strabane G.C.
(028) 7138 2007
Ballycolman, Strabane
(18) 5552 metres/***/D/H/M

HOLE 13, ROYAL COUNTY DOWN GOLF CLUB *Photograph courtesy of:* **Royal County Down Golf Club**

Dublin & North East Ireland Choice Golf

From the time you arrive in Ireland and crack your first drive straight down the middle, to the time you leave, having holed that tricky putt on the final green (and then drained your last drop of Guinness at the 19th), you cannot fail to be impressed by the natural charm and helpfulness of the Irish people. Nowhere is it more immediately apparent than in Dublin—what a contrast to many of the world's capital cities! Nothing seems rushed and nothing seems too much trouble. You see, the Irish welcome is quite simply second to none. As the century comes to a close we would recommend as warmly as ever a visit to this delightful island.

Dublin

Within ten miles of the city centre there are four great links and at least twenty other courses, most of which are of a very high standard. Two of the links are at Portmarnock—world-famous **Portmarnock Golf Club** and the impressive **Portmarnock Hotel and Golf Links**. The other two—and what a contrasting pair they make—are **Royal Dublin** to the south of Portmarnock, and **The Island** to the north near Malahide. All four links courses are explored later in this chapter. Not too far from Malahide (and close to Dublin Airport) is the championship parkland layout of the **St Margaret's Golf & Country Club**. Again, we investigate the course later in this chapter.

In Malahide the Grand Hotel (00 353) 1 845 0000 provides a perfect place to base oneself when playing the North Dublin courses. It is particularly handy for The Island and is less expensive (and certainly more attractive) than the majority of the capital's more

THE ALEXANDER HOTEL *Photograph courtesy of:* **Alexander Hotel**

LUTTRELLSTOWN CASTLE GOLF AND COUNTRY CLUB
Photograph courtesy of: **Irish Tourist Board (Brian Lynch)**

centrally located hotels. The Portmarnock Hotel and Golf Links (00 353) 1 846 0611 has 108 luxury bedrooms and is the first choice of many golfers visiting Portmarnock. However, if one does wish to be more in the middle of things then among the better hotels in Dublin are the Shelbourne (00 353) 1 676 6471, the Berkeley Court (00 353) 1 660 1711 (which is possibly the best), the Burlington (00 353) 1 660 5222, Davenport (00 353) 1 607 3500, Alexander Hotel (00 353) 1 607 3700, Mont Clare (00 353) 1 661 6799 and Jury's (00 353) 1 660 5000. A recommended hotel for St Margaret's is the Forte Posthouse (00 353) 1 844 4211. Also well worth noting is the Royal Marine in Dun Laoghaire (00 353) 1 280 1911. In Howth, the King Sitric (00 353) 1 832 5235 is a well known seafood restaurant, and again particularly convenient for the courses to the north of Dublin. Good restaurants abound in the centre of Dublin and suggestions could include La Stampa (00 353) 1 677 8611, Patrick Guilbaud (00 353) 1 676 4192, Dobbins (00 353) 1 676 4679, Le Coq Hardi (00 353) 1 668 9070 and Locks (00 353) 1 454 3391. Visiting a Dublin bar is an experience in itself and ought not to be missed. One final thought for those of you visiting Dublin, try the Unicorn (00 353) 1 676 2182 - some good value but beautifully furnished apartments here and a restaurant to make you smile whatever the standard of your golf!

South of Dublin

If most of the celebrated links golf courses are found to the north of Dublin, there are many more parkland challenges to the south and west of the capital, indeed, the city is practically encircled by golf courses. Without question the most talked about inland course in the south Dublin area is the Tom Craddock/Pat Ruddy designed **Druids Glen** golf course at Kilcoole in Co Wicklow, just south of Bray. Druids Glen, the Arnold Palmer designed course at the Kildare Country Club, **The K Club** (00 353) 1 627 3333 and **Luttrellstown Castle** (00 353) 1 808 9900 at Clonsilla are all explored ahead. The hotels at these establishments are also outstanding.

In pre-Druids Glen days the leading club to the south of Dublin was **Woodbrook**. It too has played host to the Irish Open, in addition to many other important tournaments. Woodbrook offers a mixture of semi-links and parkland golf and has recently been extensively renovated.

A few miles further down the coast is the pleasant course at **Greystones**, from the back nine of which there are some marvellous views of the Wicklow Mountains, and a nearby 18 hole golf and hotel complex, the attractively priced **Charlesland** Golf and Country Club Hotel (00 353) 1 287 6764—more great views. Near the town of Wicklow, **Blainroe** Golf Club has a much improved—and pretty demanding—championship length layout, and there is a very scenic course at **Woodenbridge**. It's a bit of a drive from Dublin, but well worth it. Just south of Wicklow at Brittas Bay is **The European Club**, which is explored in our South East Ireland section.

Following a round in South Dublin, Roly's restaurant (00 353) 1 668 2611 in Ballsbridge is recommended. The Stillorgin Park Hotel (00

Glenview Hotel

Glen O'The Downs, Delgany,
Co. Wicklow, Ireland
Tel: (00 353 1) 287 3399 Fax: (00 353 1) 287 7511
e mail: glenview@iol.ie
web site: www.glenviewhotel.ie

The Glenview Hotel is situated in beautiful countryside just 30 minutes south of Dublin's city centre. With 74 deluxe bedrooms, 5 conference and meeting rooms, an 18 metre pool, five star leisure club and a dedicated Business Centre this is the ideal venue for business or pleasure.

The Woodlands restaurant with breathtaking views of the famed Glen O'The Downs provides award-winning cuisine in elegant and comfortable surroundings.

The hotel is an ideal base for a golfing break with a fine selection of championship standard courses in close proximity to the hotel including Druid's Glen, Powerscourt, The European Club and Charlesland to name a few.

A warm welcome awaits you whatever the reason for your visit.

ST MARGARETS GOLF CLUB, CO DUBLIN *Photograph courtesy of:* **Irish Tourist Board (Brian Lynch)**

353) 1 288 1681 is very lively, while in Bray, not far from Greystones an evening spent at the Tree of Idleness (00 353) 1 286 3498 should be extremely relaxing. The Wicklow area is well served by Fitzpatricks Castle Hotel (00 353) 1 284 0700 and the Glenview Hotel (00 353) 1 287 3399, which is close to Druids Glen. Finally, a really attractive pair of Co Wicklow courses are **Powerscourt** and **Rathsallagh**. Both are featured ahead. For truly superb accommodation there is Rathsallagh House (00 353) 4 540 3112 and in Rathnew, the outstanding Tinakilly House (00 353) 404 69274 and Hunter's Hotel (00 353) 404 40106. It is well worth emphasising that the above

SEAPOINT GOLF CLUB, CO. LOUTH
Photograph courtesy of: **Irish Tourist Board (Brian Lynch)**

are just a rich part of Irelands many golf courses - there are many more who welcome visitors and offer good value green fees with clubhouses of excellence.

North of Dublin

Thirty miles north of Dublin in the charming village of Baltray near Drogheda is the **County Louth** Golf Club. Baltray, as the course is known, enjoys a wonderfully remote setting, but while it may be a peaceful place the course will test your game to the full. Baltray is featured ahead. One needn't look far for a bed as the club offers its own accommodation and meals are available. (Telephone (00 353) 41 22329 for details.) However, if there's no room at the 19th the best bet is either the Boyne Valley Hotel (00 353) 41 983 7737 in Drogheda, or the Neptune (00 353) 41 982 7107 in nearby Bettystown.

This latter hotel is very close to the **Laytown and Bettystown** links which, while not in the same class as Baltray, certainly poses enough problems. It is the home club of the former Ryder Cup player Des Smyth. Just north of Baltray (in fact visible just beyond the 14th tee at Co Louth) is the **Seapoint** Golf Club at Termonfeckin (00 353) 41 9822329.

Further north the course at **Dundalk** deserves inspection. Again it's not in the same league as Baltray, but then very few are. Still, it's definitely worth visiting if only for the tremendous scenery it offers. Although very much a parkland type challenge, the course is set out alongside the shores of Dundalk Bay with the Mountains of Mourne and the Cooley Mountains providing a spectacular backdrop. The Ballymascanlon House (00 353) 42 937 1124 in Dundalk is very good value if a night's stopover is required, while for an outstanding restaurant try Quaglinos (00 353) 42 933 8567.

Dundalk provides a fine base for playing our final recommendation in the north east, the course at **Greenore** where a more dramatic location couldn't be wished for. Alongside Carlingford Lough, Greenore have recently built three new holes which are destined to be the envy of every golf course in Ireland. You don't believe it? Then go and visit—you'll be made most welcome!

Travelling Inland

For those who enjoy horseracing as well as golf (this must include near enough every Irishman), a good route to take out of Dublin is the N7. Given a clear road the Curragh is little more than half an hour's drive away. This is the Newmarket of Ireland. Golf has been played on the great stretch of heathland since the 1850s and the **Curragh** Golf Club was founded in 1883 making it the oldest golf club in the Republic. Rather like England's senior links, Westward Ho!, the fairways are shared with the local farmer's sheep. There's also a nearby army range—one presumes golf is rarely uneventful at the Curragh! It's actually a very good course and the green fees are typically modest. Barberstown Castle (00 353) 1628 8157 at Celbridge is an excellent place to head for after a day on the heath, especially if a game of golf has been combined with a day at the races. Others to note include Moyglare Manor (00 353) 1628 6351 at Maynooth, a delightful Georgian country house and the Hotel Keadeen (00 353) 4543 1666 in Ballymany.

Venturing further inland, **Mullingar** in County Westmeath, **Headfort** near Kells and **Royal Tara** at Navan (both in County Meath) and **Tullamore** in County Offaly are four of Ireland's best 'established' parkland layouts. Mullingar is probably the pick of the bunch, but all enjoy delightful locations and welcome visitors at most times. Those planning to stay in the area might consider the Hodson Bay Hotel (00 353) 902 92444 in Athlone or the Greville Arms (00 353) 444 8563 in Mullingar. Alternatively, Dunderry Lodge (00 353) 463 1671 is a restaurant to delight.

Finally, two hotel golf courses that are not exactly close to Dublin, but decidedly worth inspecting, are the picturesque parkland course at the **Nuremore Hotel** (00 353) 42 966 1438, near Carrickmacross in Co Monaghan and the spectacular course at the **Slieve Russell Hotel Golf & Country Club** (00 353) 49 9526 4444 at Ballyconnell in Co Cavan (featured in our North West section). Both offer comfortable accommodation and a myriad other facilities.

DRUIDS GLEN *Photograph courtesy of:* **Druids Glen Golf Club**

PORTMARNOCK GOLF CLUB *Photograph courtesy of: Irish Tourist Board (Brian Lynch)*

Royal Dublin

The links at Royal Dublin may be the closest thing in Ireland to the Old Course at St Andrews. Laid out over a narrow tract of land, it is the only one of Ireland's great links that stretches out and back in traditional 'Scottish' style. Harry Colt is credited as the architect rather than Mother Nature but it is a very minimalist design. Like St Andrews the land is essentially flat with subtle undulations (although Royal Dublin's fairways do not possess the Old Course's myriad little humps and hillocks). Wind and pin position dictate a player's strategy, the greens are kept firm and fast, and bump and run is king.

The golf club dates from 1885. Initially 'home' was a confined area in Phoenix Park, but in 1889 the club moved to its present site at Bull Island, still within the city limits. Bull Island is accessed by a wooden bridge and the duneland terrain is shared by golfers, bird watchers and botanists. It is an extraordinary domain—the backdrop is industrial and not particularly pretty but the island itself is a haven, a true sanctuary.

The **Manager** at Royal Dublin is **John Lambe** he can be contacted on **tel: (01) 833 6346 fax: (01) 833 6504**. Written correspondence should be directed to **Royal Dublin Golf Club, Bull Island, Dollymount, Dublin 3**. The Professional is **Leonard Owens tel: (01) 833 6477**. Green fees for 2000 are set at £65 weekdays (no visitors on Wednesdays or any day between 12.30 and 2pm, weekends (Friday, Saturday, Sunday) £80. The club is 15-20 minutes out of Dublin city centre on the road to Clontarf through Fairview.

A combination of greater length and the prevailing wind ensures that the inward nine is invariably the tougher half. However, the outward nine includes arguably the two best holes, namely the par four 5th and the par five 8th. The former is called 'Valley', an apt description since the hole funnels along a narrow corridor of dunes; and the fairway has more undulations than any other. There is an out of bounds to the right of the hole and the left side of the green is guarded by a very deep pot bunker. The 8th curves from left to right, its green sitting on a plateau with a sharp fall-away to the left and a truly cavernous trap eating into the front right.

The inward nine starts to bare its teeth at the 11th, a tough par five that features another out of bounds all along the right edge of the fairway and a severely contoured two-tier green. The 12th is a long par three to a bowl-shaped green and the 13th is a formidable two-shotter where the entrance to the green is cambered and very narrow—again rather appropriately, the hole is called 'Dardanelles'.

The most famous hole at Royal Dublin is the 18th, 'Garden', a right-angled par four. The approach must be fired directly over an out of bounds field (the eponymous garden) to reach the green in two. Royal Dublin has staged many important championships over the years and the closing hole has provided many dramatic finishes. Christy O'Connor once finished 2-3-3 to win a tournament. Between 1983 and 1985 the club hosted the Irish Open Championship and the winners were Ballesteros, Langer and, in centenary year, Ballesteros again—the Spaniard defeating the German in a thrilling sudden death play-off.

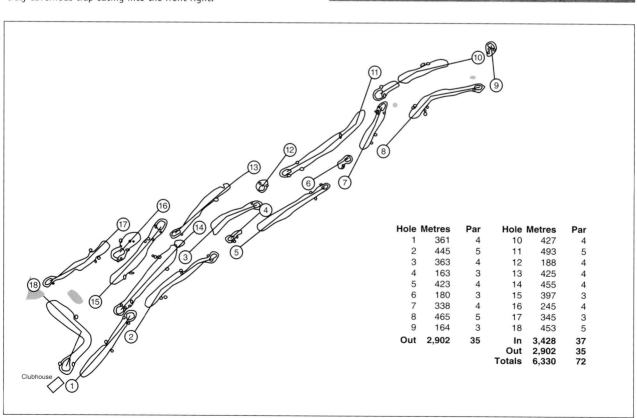

Hole	Metres	Par	Hole	Metres	Par
1	361	4	10	427	4
2	445	5	11	493	5
3	363	4	12	188	4
4	163	3	13	425	4
5	423	4	14	455	4
6	180	3	15	397	3
7	338	4	16	245	4
8	465	5	17	345	3
9	164	3	18	453	5
Out	**2,902**	**35**	**In**	**3,428**	**37**
			Out	**2,902**	**35**
			Totals	**6,330**	**72**

The K Club (Straffan)

In timeless fashion, and without a care in the world the River Liffey meanders its way through the ancient Straffan Estate in Co Kildare en route to Dublin and the Irish Sea. In 1988 the estate was acquired by Ireland's largest, and possibly most ambitious company, Jefferson Smurfit—undoubtedly the great attraction being the vast 19th century Straffan House, one of the most striking country houses in Ireland. For some time it had been the dream of company chairman Dr Michael Smurfit to develop a 'world class country club'. At Straffan he saw the potential for an extremely grand, even palatial 5 star hotel (the restored and extended Straffan House) and sufficient land to build a challenging championship length golf course, one good enough to host national and international tournaments. Thus the Kildare Country Club, or The K Club as everyone calls it, was born.

When it came to the design of the golf course the word 'challenging' was clearly given special emphasis, for though four leading golf architects submitted proposals for the 18 hole layout, it seems there was not much of a contest once Arnold Palmer and his team had presented their ideas. Palmer had already created one course in Ireland, the ultra-spectacular links at Tralee on the west coast. Now was the opportunity to demonstrate his swashbuckling design theories on an inland site, just 25 miles south west of Dublin.

The golf course (which measures 7178 yards from its championship tees) was officially opened in 1991. To suggest that Palmer has succeeded in creating a challenging layout would be a gross understatement. With holes weaving their way through an extraordinary landscape, the unsuspecting golfer is likely to be awestruck and amazed by some of the shots he is asked to take on . . . Straffan is no ordinary golf course.

Notwithstanding its youth, The K Club has become the home of the European Open, one of the most prestigious events on the PGA European Tour, and in 2005 it will host the Ryder Cup - the first ever staging on Irish soil.

The golf course immediately lays down the gauntlet: the par five 1st offers possibly the first realistic birdie opportunity! Next comes an excellent par four with a thrilling downhill second shot to a stage-like green. A pair of par threes top and tail the dog-legging 4th, a front to back sloping green is the key feature of the 5th.

The 7th is often rated as the best par five in Ireland. From tee to green it is one long voyage of discovery as the hole double dog-legs its way over sand, rough and water and in amongst a variety of colourful trees and shrubs. The green occupies its own little island and is sandwiched between two arms of the River Liffey. A quaint old iron bridge transports players to and from the island. The Liffey is a constant companion at the left-to-right curving 8th (a hooker's nightmare), and you return to the clubhouse by way of another demanding par four.

The first two holes of the back nine are strong par fours and the 12th may be the most intimidating (and best) par three on the course; the tee shot must be struck over a small lake to a superbly angled green – between the lake and the green is a deep 'beach style' bunker where the sand literally runs into the water's edge. The 13th, 'Arnie's Pick', is an exhilarating downhill par five and it is followed by a tough uphill par four. You charge downhill again at the 15th, then play a heroic two-shotter where water threatens both the drive and the approach. The short 17th is framed by the River Liffey and a good drive at the par five 18th begs one final question: dare you risk a watery grave and go for the green in two – a real grandstand finish in front of the magnificent clubhouse? Well, what would Arnie do?

The **Director of Golf** at The K Club is **Paul Crowe** and the **Professional** is **Ernie Jones**. Visitors can make tee reservations on **tel: (01) 601 7300**, by **fax: (01) 601 7399** or via **email: golf@kclub.ie.** All players must be golf club members and have a handicap. The green fee in 2000 is £140 with a reduced rate of £95 per person for groups of 16 and more.

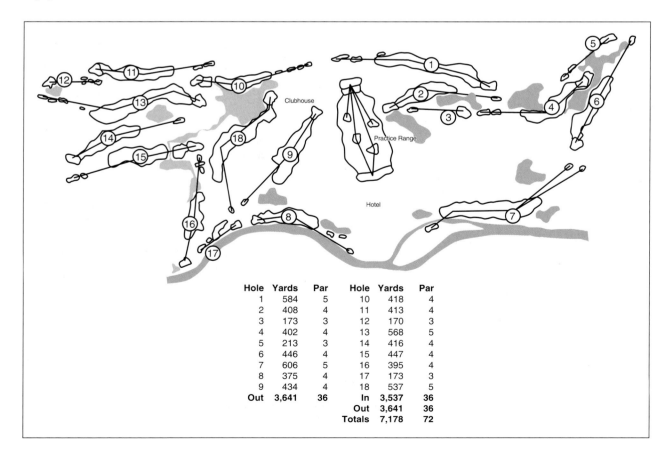

Hole	Yards	Par	Hole	Yards	Par
1	584	5	10	418	4
2	408	4	11	413	4
3	173	3	12	170	3
4	402	4	13	568	5
5	213	3	14	416	4
6	446	4	15	447	4
7	606	5	16	395	4
8	375	4	17	173	3
9	434	4	18	537	5
Out	**3,641**	**36**	**In**	**3,537**	**36**
			Out	**3,641**	**36**
			Totals	**7,178**	**72**

The 15th of July 1991 saw the official opening of the Kildare Hotel and Country Club, widely acclaimed as Ireland's premier resort development and a five star complex to rival the very best that Europe can offer.

The Kildare Hotel and Country Club has been developed at a cost of £27.5 million by Jefferson Smurfit Group plc. Ireland's world class hotel and sporting facility encompasses an 18 hole golf course designed by the legendary Arnold Palmer, salmon and trout fishing, indoor and outdoor tennis, exercise, swimming and croquet.

The entire project was created in less than three years and involved the complete renovation of the existing Straffan House. A new wing was added in the style of the existing house, establishing in the process a 45 bedroom hotel, whose exacting standards have few equals.

The bedrooms and suites are complemented by exquisitely appointed self-contained apartments and a magnificent three bedroom lodge in the grounds. Meetings and private dining take place in the Tower and River rooms, where work can happily be combined with play by taking advantage of the wide range of leisure and recreational activities. The

Kildare Country Club, simply known as The K Club, is a multi-facility sporting paradise. Members, hotel guests and visitors alike can enjoy the championship golf course, river and lake fishing, indoor and outdoor tennis, squash, gym, swimming pool, beauty treatment rooms, sauna and solarium.

The Arnold Palmer designed golf course has received many accolades and is home to the Smurfit European Open one of the richest tournaments on the European Tour. In January 1999 it was announced that The K Club would be the host for the Ryder Cup 2005, its first visit to Ireland. The course covers some 177 acres of former stud farm land and has a total length of 7,179 yards, par 72

Among eighteen exquisitely and imaginatively sculpted holes, particularly outstanding memories could stem from the huge par five 16th, the water-clad 17th or the spectacular par three 8th. Every hole, however, has its own challenge and beauty.

In the words of Arnold Palmer himself, reflecting proudly on his creation whilst standing on the terrace of the elevated clubhouse sited behind the eighteenth green; "We could draw for 100 years and not come up with as good a vision as we have here."

The K Club
Straffan
Co Kildare
Ireland
Tel: (00 353 1) 601 7200 (Hotel) 601 7300 (Clubhouse)
Fax: (00 353 1) 601 7299 (Hotel) 601 7399 (Clubhouse)
e mail: golf@kclub.ie

Portmarnock

One day in 1893, a Scot named W L Pickeman domiciled in Dublin was riding his bicycle along the road from Baldoyle to Portmarnock when, so the story goes, looking across the estuary it occurred to him that he was looking at magnificent golfing terrain. . . .

Portmarnock is located to the North of Dublin and lying on a peninsula is surrounded by water on three sides. It can be as tough a challenge as any in the world—more than 7000 yards from the back tees with the rough often mercilessly punishing (knee-high in parts!) But Portmarnock, rather like Muirfield, offers a genuinely fair challenge. There is only one blind shot, there are no hidden traps and the greens are among the finest in the world. As for that rough, well, as an obviously straight-hitter once remarked, you've no business being there in the first place and you cannot really argue with that! Portmarnock has its beauty too. . . to the south, the Hill of Howth and the great sweep of Dublin Bay and to the north west, Drogheda and the distant Mountains of Mourne. On a fine day the links provides the player with a spectacular 360 degree vista; all in all it is a truly wonderful place to pursue the Royal and Ancient game.

The **Secretary** at Portmarnock is the very helpful **Mr John J Quigley.** He may be contacted by writing to **Portmarnock Golf Club, Portmarnock, Co Dublin**, by **tel: (01) 846 2968** and by **fax: (01) 846 2601** (the code is (00 353) 1 from the UK) The club's **Professional** is **Joey Purcell**, who can be reached on **tel: (01) 846 2634.**

Providing visitors possess a handicap of 24 or less they are very welcome to play the famous links, although ladies cannot play at weekends or on bank holidays. It seems that half of Dublin wants to play Portmarnock (not to mention you and me) and the course can be extremely popular. The wisest move is to telephone the club before you set off. The green fees as set in 2000 are £75 from Monday to Friday (although there are no visitors on Wednesdays) and £95 at the weekend (subject to availability). Golfing societies are equally welcome subject to prior arrangement with the Secretary.

It is far easier to travel to Portmarnock than to many of the country's other great golfing attractions. The capital is very well served by international flights and Dublin's airport is only six miles from the links. From Britain, it is also worth noting that both B&I and Sealink sail regularly to Dublin. As mentioned, Portmarnock lies to the north of the capital, a distance of about eight miles. By road it's essentially a case of heading for Portmarnock village and then looking out for signs—from Dublin the course should be signposted off to the right, and from Malahide, look to your left.

The casual visitor will not have to attempt the full 7000 yards plus, but he's still likely to be facing a good 6800 yards so he'd better have his game in fine fettle! Happily there is a relatively gentle break-in with three holes measuring less than 400 yards. The course then changes direction and the 4th, the stroke one hole confronts you. Normally, the wind will be with you, but don't bank on it! A number of second shots will be played to plateau greens which can be very difficult to hold and a good Irish pitch-and-run may be needed frequently. Two outstanding holes to note on the front nine are the par five 6th and the 8th. The most celebrated holes on the back nine are undoubtedly the 14th and the 15th. The former has been described by Henry Cotton as one of the greatest par fours in golf and it's easy to see why. The hole is played towards the sea along a gently curving, tumbling fairway; the narrow green sits on a plateau and is protected by two bunkers set into a natural rise just short of the green, with many humps and hillocks surrounding the putting surface—nothing but a precise second shot will do. As for the 15th, Ben Crenshaw has called it, 'one of the greatest short holes on earth'. Out of bounds in the form of the beach lurks the length of the hole to the right. Even then there is no let up and the five-four-four finish is one of the toughest around.

The gentle wind down of course begins at the 19th. Portmarnock has a splendid clubhouse, though not the original, which unfortunately burned down. The atmosphere is tremendous and some very good value snacks are offered daily with dinner also possible during the week.

The club has staged many great championships in the past including, somewhat surprisingly, the (British) Amateur Championship which was won—it goes without saying—by an Irishman. The World Cup was played at Portmarnock in 1960, Palmer and Snead winning for the United States, while winners of the Irish Open on this links have included Americans Crenshaw and Hubert Green and an illustrious quartet of European stars: Ballesteros, Langer, Woosnam and Olazabal—proving the old adage that a great course will always produce a great champion.

In 1991 Portmarnock successfully hosted the Walker Cup and there are many who consider it a travesty that the Ryder Cup matches did not come here in 1993.

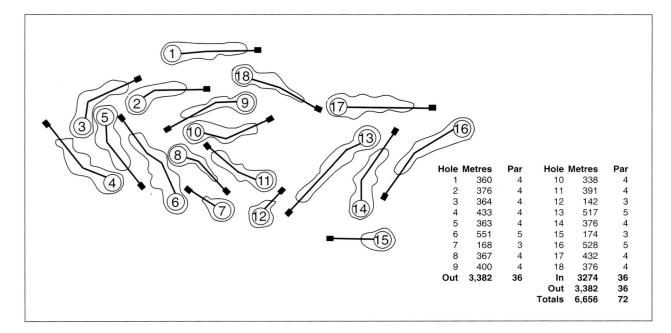

Hole	Metres	Par	Hole	Metres	Par
1	360	4	10	338	4
2	376	4	11	391	4
3	364	4	12	142	3
4	433	4	13	517	5
5	363	4	14	376	4
6	551	5	15	174	3
7	168	3	16	528	5
8	367	4	17	432	4
9	400	4	18	376	4
Out	**3,382**	**36**	**In**	**3274**	**36**
			Out	**3,382**	**36**
			Totals	**6,656**	**72**

The Davenport Hotel heralds a new era of splendour in Dublin. Located at Merrion Square in the heart of Georgian Dublin, the hotel is situated within walking distance of Dublin's finest shopping district, Grafton Street and St Stephen's Green. This area offers an eclectic mix of shopping, pubs, coffee houses, restaurants and galleries with something for everyone. Adjacent to the hotel you will find Trinity College, the National Gallery, Natural History Museum and the Irish Parliament-a collection of the finest buildings in Dublin.

The facade of the hotel, originally that of Merrion Hall, dates from 1863 and has been restored to its original beauty. Indeed, excellence is the Davenport Hotel's motto - in everything from architecture to the service provided for the guests.

The hotel boasts 120 fully air conditioned, well appointed rooms, comprising 2 suites, 10 junior suites, 48 king size double rooms, 33 double rooms and 27 twin rooms. With the business traveller in mind, junior suites contain an executive desk with direct fax line and laser printer. ISDN lines are provided in all guestrooms.

Offering exquisite food, The Davenport prides itself on offering the finest international cuisine. This is served at Layton's Restaurant where guests can relax in the comfort of the traditional Georgian interiors. There is also the Gandon Suite which can accommodate from 100 to 500 people. Whether for a conference, gala, ball or banquet the Gandon Suite is the perfect venue.

The new fitness suite is also available for use by guests. It is equipped with the most up to date cardio-vascular machines and free weights. The Fitness Suite is open 24 hours.

For the golfer, the Davenport is the ideal venue for several of the finest courses in Ireland. Within easy reach you will find Portmarnock, Royal Dublin, The Island, St Margaret's, Druids Glen, The K Club, The European Club, Powerscourt and Rathsallagh to name but a few. Golf can be arranged through the hotel and an impressive day's golf will be found without much trouble.

The Davenport is owned by O'Callaghan Hotels and situated in Dublin you will find their other properties, The Alexander Hotel and Mont Clare Hotel, in close proximity and the recently opened Stephen's Green Hotel a short walk across St Stephen's Green. All the hotels are of an excellent standard and can be contacted through the head office (00 353) 1 607 3900.

The Davenport Hotel

The Davenport Hotel
Merrion Square Dublin 2
Ireland
Tel: 00 353 1 607 3500
Fax: 00 353 1 661 5663
e mail: davenportres@ocallaghanhotels.ie
web site: www.ocallaghanhotels.ie

O'Callaghan
Hotels

Portmarnock Hotel & Golf Links

From Co Kerry to Co Wicklow and from Co Donegal to Co Dublin, more links courses have been built in Ireland since the mid 1970s than have appeared in Britain this century.

It was Eddie Hackett who first set the ball rolling. The genial Irishman roamed the western shores of Ireland and left his mark at such wonderful places as Connemara, Enniscrone, Murvagh and, most famously, Waterville.

Then in the 1980s two of the greatest names in golf, Robert Trent Jones and Arnold Palmer, crossed the Atlantic and headed for the dunes at Ballybunion and Tralee. By the time they departed, Co Kerry had two more precious gems and the south west of Ireland was fast establishing itself as the greatest golfing region in the world.

Now enter Pat Ruddy. Never one to miss out on things, he summoned a helicopter and proceeded to scour the entire coast of Ireland before concluding that Brittas Bay in Co Wicklow was the perfect place to put down some roots. The dunes, the marram grass—everything else was in place. He created the European Club there, and then teamed up with Tom Craddock to build a second links course for Ballyliffin Golf Club in Co Donegal.

The Glashedy Links at Ballyliffin opened in August 1995. It is the country's most northerly situated course and is destined to become one of its greatest. But it wasn't the only outstanding links that was preparing to take its bow that summer. For the majority of the Irish—particularly those living in Dublin—there was one much closer to home.

The Portmarnock Hotel & Golf Links lies adjacent to Portmarnock Golf Club. The hotel, once the home of the Jameson (whiskey) family, became fully operational in June 1996. The new links was designed by Bernhard Langer, a three-time winner of the Irish Open, and the architect was Stan Eby. Together they have produced a masterpiece.

Perhaps the most immediately striking aspect of the links is how natural it appears. There is nothing flamboyant about the design and it is refreshing to see that no fewer than five of the par fours measure less than 380 yards. The course flows, almost gracefully, from green to tee to green. As at St Andrews and Ballybunion Old Course there are no lengthy walks in between holes.

The other very obvious feature is the quality and extent of the bunkering. There are almost 100 bunkers in total and each has been painstakingly and skilfully constructed with steep revetted faces, similar to Carnoustie and Muirfield. In fact, the Portmarnock Hotel links bears more of a resemblance generally to those two great Scottish courses than to neighbouring Portmarnock. More specifically, the front nine is reminiscent of Carnoustie and the back nine of Muirfield, although it could be argued that the final four holes are more thrilling than those at either of the Scottish links.

In true Carnoustie style then, the opening few holes demand a 'keep your head down' approach. The views are hardly distracting but the challenge is very evident. The landscape becomes more appealing from the 8th hole onwards. Aside from the climactic finish, the 8th is possibly the finest hole on the course. The fairway dog-legs sharply to the left before tumbling in classic links fashion towards a severely sloping green perched amid some very wild-looking dunes. The par three 9th calls for an extremely precise shot to a table-shaped green, the 12th surely rivals the 14th at Baltray as the best short par four in Ireland and the 13th is an all-or-nothing par three.

The great finish begins at the 15th, where the approach must somehow be threaded past (or over) a sea of deep traps. The 16th is played from a superbly elevated tee. The 17th is yet another formidable short hole—beware the very cavernous greenside bunker—and the 18th descends from a lofty tee to an amphitheatre green surrounded by towering sand dunes and devilish pot bunkers. The perfect stage for a winning birdie!

Visitors are able to play the course on any day of the week but should make advance arrangements. The **Golf Director, Moira Cassidy** can be reached on **tel: (01) 846 1800** and by **fax: (01) 846 2442.** For hotel residents the green fees in 2000 are £38 per round. For non residents, they are £60 per round throughout the week.

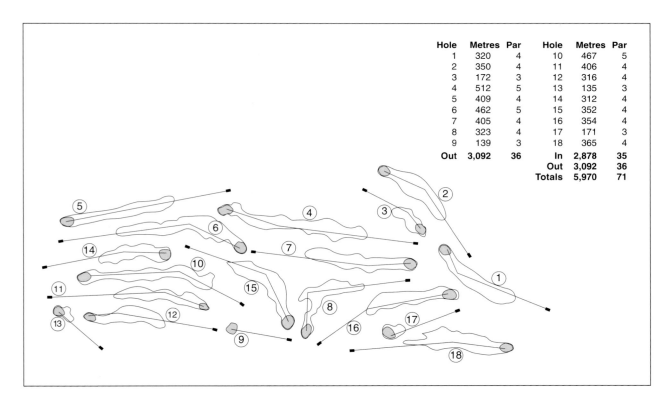

Hole	Metres	Par	Hole	Metres	Par
1	320	4	10	467	5
2	350	4	11	406	4
3	172	3	12	316	4
4	512	5	13	135	3
5	409	4	14	312	4
6	462	5	15	352	4
7	405	4	16	354	4
8	323	4	17	171	3
9	139	3	18	365	4
Out	**3,092**	**36**	**In**	**2,878**	**35**
			Out	**3,092**	**36**
			Totals	**5,970**	**71**

Portmarnock Hotel & Golf Links is the venue for a truly outstanding Irish golfing break. You will enjoy the formidable challenge of a Bernhard Langer designed championship links and a deluxe hotel (Golf Hotel of the Year 1999) offering great comfort and the best of traditional Irish hospitality. The hotel incorporates the 19th century home of the Jameson whiskey family, which complete with many original features, provides a measure of old style character and charm. Course and hotel lie side by side against the dunes of Ireland's East Coast, just 11 miles from the entertainment and bustling shops of Dublin and 6 miles from Dublin International Airport.

Portmarnock Links makes full use of the dunes and natural terrain to provide a layout that will please most ardent of links purists.The use of natural features combined with elevated tees and greens, blind approaches and acute doglegs - not to mention typical links sea breezes, will keep you thinking through every round. Gently undulating luxuriously sprung fairways leading to large fast greens must be negotiated through 98 strategically placed bunkers, whilst hillocks, wild grasses and gorse await any wayward shots. Measuring 6195 metres, par 71, the 1st tee and 18th green are conveniently situated just a wedge shot from the hotel and clubhouse.

"It is a great honour to represent Portmarnock Hotel & Golf Links, which in my opinion is one of the best courses in Europe. Bernhard Langer's design provides a challenge for golfers of all abilities, but low handicap players will need precision driving, a sharp short game, and good course management to achieve a good score". Darren Clarke - Touring Professional - Portmarnock Hotel & Golf Links.

Many other championship golf courses are within easy reach of the hotel so as a base you would be hard pushed to find any finer. The 103 bedrooms are cleverly designed to ensure that you are either looking over the sea or the splendour of the golf course. A choice of elegantly appointed accommodation is yours, ranging from historic four posters, to executive suites and deluxe bedrooms. Every modern convenience has been included so that you feel cosseted at all times. The personal service will ensure that you enjoy all the luxuries of an international hotel alongside the personal touch of a country home.

Portmarnock Hotel & Golf Links
Portmarnock
Co Dublin
Ireland
Tel: (00 353 1) 846 1800
Fax: (00 353 1) 846 1077
web site: http://www.portmarnock.com

I wonder what Old Tom Morris would have made of the recently opened St Margaret's Golf and Country Club. Not a lot probably. I'm not suggesting that he would necessarily disapprove of it but he probably wouldn't understand it. In fact, it would probably be as much a mystery to him as the jumbo jet aircraft at nearby Dublin Airport. Old Tom inhabited a very different world. It was Old Tom who designed the original golf links at Lahinch in Co Clare and Lahinch is about as different from St Margaret's as it is possible for a golf course to be. In many ways (historically, geographically and technically for a start) Dublin's lavish new parkland layout is the antithesis of the famous west coast links, the so called 'St Andrews of Ireland'. One of the advantages of being a present day golfer, however, is that it is possible to play both courses and discover that such contrasting challenges can be equally enjoyable.

There is a favourite saying among purveyors of real estate that the two most important aspects of a property are its location . . . and its location! Situated close to the international airport and not far from the centre of Dublin, no club in Ireland is better placed to capture the attention of an ever increasing golf hungry public. Aesthetically speaking, the St Margaret's site was a fairly unremarkable piece of farmland before the bulldozers and the architects appeared on the scene. Now no one could ever describe St Margaret's as unremarkable—unrecognisable, yes. It is undoubtedly a very fine golf course and one without any obvious weaknesses.

St Margaret's has a very welcoming atmosphere and can be contacted on **tel: (01) 864 0400**. There are no specific restrictions as to the time when visitors can play although advance booking is recommended. The individual green fees in 2000 are £40 per round—Monday through Wednesday, £45 on Thursday and Sunday and on Friday and Saturday a round costs £50.

From its championship tees, St Margaret's measures a shade under 7000 yards, or in other words, when the elements are stirred it can be a brute! Most players of course will not have to confront the many challenges from the back markers but playing from the forward tees in no way diminishes the character of the holes. This is because the real strength and flavour of St Margaret's lies in the great range of approach shots that the player is invited to take on. Perhaps the best example of this is provided by the 7th, where following a downhill drive the approach shot to the green invokes memories of the celebrated par three 12th at Augusta—with water and a bunker in front of what is a raised and narrow putting surface and twin bunkers posing menacingly behind the flag at the back of the green.

As one might expect on a modern championship styled course, water not only features prominently, but shapes a number of fairways and greens at St Margaret's. The hole immediately following the 'slice of Augusta,' the dramatic par five 8th, illustrates the point perfectly. Here the golfer must avoid a lake to the left of the tee, another to the right of the fairway and a third which bisects the fairway immediately in front of the green—it all adds up to one of the most perilous journeys in Ireland!

On the back nine, the 12th is an absolute beauty but the 'piece de resistance' has to be the glorious finishing hole. The long, twisting par four 18th at St Margaret's features a dramatically positioned green which nervously overlooks a lake and which is in turn imperiously overlooked by the large clubhouse. It makes for a spectacular climax to the round, although golfers might feel more comfortable playing this hole wearing a blindfold. Blind shots at St Margaret's? Come back Old Tom.

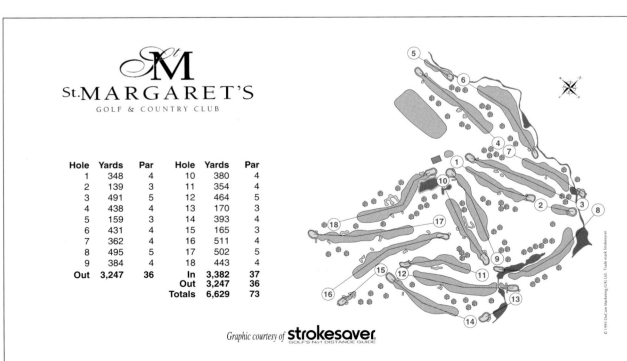

St. MARGARET'S
GOLF & COUNTRY CLUB

Hole	Yards	Par	Hole	Yards	Par
1	348	4	10	380	4
2	139	3	11	354	4
3	491	5	12	464	5
4	438	4	13	170	3
5	159	3	14	393	4
6	431	4	15	165	3
7	362	4	16	511	4
8	495	5	17	502	5
9	384	4	18	443	4
Out	**3,247**	**36**	**In**	**3,382**	**37**
			Out	**3,247**	**36**
			Totals	**6,629**	**73**

Graphic courtesy of **strokesaver** GOLF'S No1 DISTANCE GUIDE

© 1995 DuCam Marketing (UK) Ltd. Trade mark Strokesaver

With its location just ten minutes from Dublin airport and only 20 minutes from the city centre, for any golfer visiting Dublin a round of golf at St Margaret's is a must. The course designers, Tom Craddock and Pat Ruddy, have created at St Margaret's Golf and Country Club a course which, within two years of opening, has been accoladed as one of Ireland's premier golfing venues.

The designers have turned a couple of hundred acres of flat farmland into a magnificent expanse of sculpted parkland. The modern design approach makes use of water hazards and each of the 18 holes is framed by manmade hills and huge undulating greens.

Challenging in terms of length the course has five par fives and four par threes—the rest being par fours. Flexible teeing allows the middle and high handicap golfer a fairer challenge on this course.

The par five 8th measures 525 yards and is set to become one of the most notorious holes in Europe. It features a lake to the left of the tee, a second lake to the right on the second shot and a third lake in front of the green. The 12th is perhaps the most picturesque of all the holes and features a generous rollercoaster fairway that crosses a brook below the majestic elevated green.

The 18th hole is one of the finest in golf today and not for the faint hearted. The overall design of the course, the obvious attention to every small detail and the sheer beauty of the features all combine to inspire an excellent round of golf.

The clubhouse is designed with luxury in mind. It has a spacious bar ideal for relaxing after a challenging round of golf. The clubhouse also boasts a spike grill, luxury golf shop, an elegant restaurant and purpose-built conference suite. The overall effect is a welcoming building suitable for relaxing or for conducting business. Corporate days and society outings are also welcomed and expertly catered for under the guidance of Denis Kane and his experienced and friendly staff.

St Margaret's is designed as a place where golf is to be played recreationally and competitively. The club played host to the 1994/95 Ladies Irish Open and in 1997 to the Irish Seniors.

For intending visitors bookings are simple—phone Angela Comerton, Reservations Manager, to reserve a tee time (pre booking is recommended).

St Margaret's Golf & Country Club
St Margaret's
County Dublin Ireland
Tel: (00 353 1) 8640400
Fax: (00 353 1) 8640289
E mail: stmarggc@indigo.ie
web site: www.st-margarets.net

Luttrellstown Castle

'I love it over here', said the great Seve Ballesteros to his Irish host. 'You have a wonderfully relaxed way of doing things. Surely there's an Irish word for our "Mañana"?' 'Good heavens, no', replied the stunned host, nothing quite so urgent'.'

An apocryphal story perhaps, but you understand the point. Go to Luttrellstown Castle and you'll experience the feeling. Luttrellstown is situated at Castleknock near Phoenix Park, just seven miles from the centre of Dublin yet it seems a world apart. It is not as if the spectacular castle and its splendid grounds are caught in a time warp—a great deal has happened here of late—but there is an air of timelessness about the place and, yes, it is wonderfully relaxing. Moreover, for golfers it has a special appeal since the opening in July 1993 of the Luttrellstown Castle Golf and Country Club.

As far as I am aware, 'the great Seve' has never been to Luttrellstown but an equally legendary figure has, namely the late American, Gene Sarazen. At a sprightly 91 years of age, golf's 'Oldest Member' visited Luttrellstown Castle and took a buggy ride out to view the pristinely new golf course. He didn't play, but as he journeyed around the layout he was heard to declare, "This is one of the finest parkland courses I have ever seen." A spellbound Sarazen had no doubt been charmed by the majesty of the surroundings but as one who has played golf all over the world for some 80 odd years, he must know a really good course when he sees one. Despite his Italian ancestry, Sarazen is an American through-and-through and he lives in Florida where fine golf courses are two a penny. What I suspect he liked about Luttrellstown is that it is a thoroughly Irish parkland course in a thoroughly Irish setting. Had he been given a guided tour around the nearby K Club he might have imagined he was back in Florida, with all its vast manmade mounds, its beach like bunkers and plethora of do-or-die shots across water.

Luttrellstown is very different. There is no shortage of water. Mind you, indeed there are several dramatic water carries to be confronted during the 18 holes, but this is what the purists would describe as a very natural parkland course. The beautifully landscaped ponds and lakes exist primarily for the benefit of wildlife not golfers. There is no overt mounding but with gently undulating terrain and a glorious assortment of trees (ancient oaks, limes, beeches and a sprinkling of cedar and pine) there is plenty of definition to the holes and no

need to frame the fairways with huge hills. And who in any event would wish to hide away the many delightful vistas—the serenity of the Dublin Mountains, the glimpses of an adjoining wooded glen with its waterfalls and cascades, an ancient bridge, a Doric Temple and an ivy-clad castle?

Under the skilful direction of architect Dr Nicholas Bielenberg, the golf course accommodates and takes advantage of its natural inheritance. From the championship markers it measures over 7000 metres (par 72) although from the forward and ladies' tees the challenge is less daunting. There are several highly memorable holes, with a particularly strong sequence between the 7th and 12th and none that could be described as dull. The putting surfaces are among the best conditioned in Ireland and the clubhouse—built in Finnish pine—is one of the country's most stylish, Luttrellstown has charmed this writer as well! But I am sure no visitor will be disappointed by a trip to Luttrellstown Castle. With 2000 green fees: Monday/Friday 18 holes £50, 36 holes £75 and Saturday/Sunday £55 and £82.50 respectively. There can be few more enjoyable places to while away the hours.

Tee reservations can be made by contacting the club's **Professional, Edward Doyle** and his staff on **tel: (01) 808 9988**, or **fax: (01) 808 9989**, or by **e mail: golf@luttrellstown.ie**

Hole	Metres	Par	Hole	Metres	Par
1	419	4	10	187	3
2	517	5	11	347	4
3	423	4	12	579	5
4	388	4	13	440	4
5	396	4	14	436	4
6	224	3	15	462	4
7	393	4	16	171	3
8	138	3	17	533	5
9	556	5	18	412	4
Out	**3,454**	**36**	**In**	**3,567**	**36**
			Out	**3,454**	**36**
			Totals	**7,021**	**72**

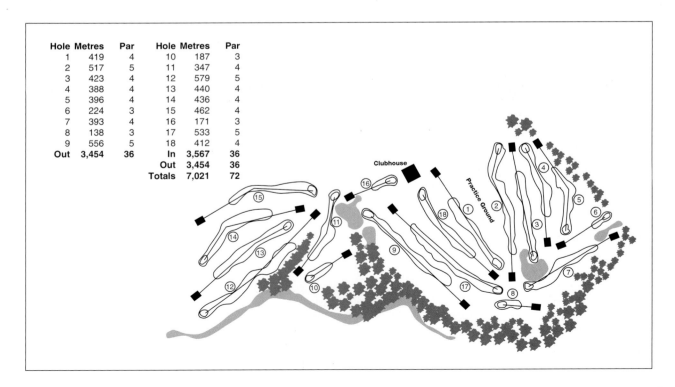

Set in the grounds of the magnificent 560 acre Luttrellstown Castle estate this superbly well maintained course is being hailed as one of Ireland's finest.

Dublin City and International airport, although a mere 15 minutes away, never intrudes as you savour the peace and beauty of the estate. Though cleverly exploiting the natural contours, the course has retained the integrity of a mature and ancient parkland. This championship facility offers many excellent features and is particularly renowned for the quality if its greens.

The clubhouse provides superb facilities for individuals and groups alike. A first class bar and restaurant, private meeting rooms and a well stocked pro shop all contribute to making this the ultimate destination for the discerning visitor.

The Castle is internationally renowned as a venue for exclusive private and corporate entertaining. There are 14 bedrooms and 5 reception rooms. The Castle is fully staffed and serviced to the highest standard, offering a variety of sporting activities within the estate.

Alternative accommodation is also available on the estate in self catering courtyard apartments.

Enquiries for additional information and bookings should be addressed to Adrienne Clarke at Luttrellstown Castle.

Luttrellstown Castle Golf & Country Club
Castleknock Dublin 15
Republic of Ireland
Tel: (00 353 1) 808 9900 (Castle) 808 9988 (Golf)
Fax: (00 353 1) 808 9901 (Castle) 808 9989 (Golf)
e mail Castle: enquiries@luttrellstown.ie
e mail Golf: golf@luttrellstown.ie

Druids Glen

The brief was straightforward enough: 'Go and build the best inland course in Ireland . . . and then send us the bill.' Straightforward (and generous) but not simple. Better than Killarney? Better than The K Club and Mount Juliet? Before it was finished the hype began. There was no point in being modest: 'Druids Glen, Co Wicklow The Garden of Eden in the Garden of Ireland'. The burning question then, does it live up to its billing?

Druids Glen opened in 1995 and was immediately selected to host the 1996 Irish Open. This was such a success that the course was chosen as the Open venue for the next three years as well. Colin Montgomerie won in 1996 and 1997 and narrowly missed out on a hat trick in 1998.

Druids Glen is indeed a special and stunning place. The chosen site near Newtownmountkennedy, the Woodstock estate at Kilcoole , was beautiful to begin with—not to mention historic. It was also perfect for building a golf course—undulating, well wooded and well watered. Today, the landscape is not so much beautiful, as shatteringly beautiful. And yes, the golf course is quite possibly the finest inland course in Ireland. It is certainly the most imaginatively conceived and the most visually striking.

Tom Craddock and Pat Ruddy are the architects of Druids Glen. It was they who relished and boldy rose to the challenge. Their design is an inspirational one—in both senses of the word. It is impossible to visit Druids Glen and not be reminded of Augusta. It was by no means the only influence but Druids Glen resembles Augusta National more than any other course on this side of the Atlantic—Jack O'Connor has seen to that.

Landscape gardener and nurseryman extraordinaire, O'Connor was commissioned to 'add background colour'. In fact, he went brilliantly berserk. At any time of the year, Druids Glen is a riot of colour. When I asked the club if he might be able to provide me with the names of a few of the more unusual flowers and shrubs, together with a list of some of the amazing trees that adorn the course, I was promptly sent a seven page fax! It makes incredible reading. The variety and the commitment (again in more senses than one) is staggering. Moreover, I have now become an authority on gold lonicera baggesoros or, if you prefer, hebe buxafolia. I also know that the large Celtic cross that has so magically sprouted on the face of the 12th tee was planted with dark green dwarf hebes and yellow spirea. The fax concluded with the words, 'Planting and landscaping continues'!

The famous American course architect, Charles Blair Macdonald once suggested, 'Putting greens are to golf courses what faces are to portraits'. The greens at Druids Glen are remarkable in terms of both contouring and condition. One could even go so far as to describe them as pioneering. In this regard, the designers were able to call upon the expert services of the renowned agronomist, James Lynch. He advised on the introduction of a new strain of creeping bent grass. The result is that Druids Glen can boast some of the best putting surfaces in Ireland.

Some golf courses begin benignly (in relative terms) then build to a dramatic climax; the new course at Adare is a good example, as is The K Club. The design of Druids Glen adopts a different approach. It starts strongly—the beautifully sweeping par four 1st where the green, according to the fertile imagination of Pat Ruddy 'lurks like a dangerous woman in the sunlit trees' (!) and the short 2nd (which was inspired, believe it or not, by the 17th at St Andrews) are two of the best holes on the course—and it finishes in a blaze of glory. In between, there are two purple patches. One on the front nine from the 7th to the 9th and another on the back nine, from the cathedral-like 12th (it is here that the druids built their altar) to the 14th—the Amen Corner of Ireland. As for the finishing blaze of glory, the 17th at Druids Glen is a potentially terrifying par three played across water to an island green—the first of its kind in Ireland. Water again threatens at the 18th, this time in the form of three lakes close to the green which, according to my friend Jack O'Connor, have been planted with 600 water lilies, and cascade over weirs one into the other.

The 19th hole facilities at Druids Glen are as impressive as one might expect, the clubhouse being the restored and extended 18th century Woodstock House.

Visitors are very welcome at Druids Glen. Subject to making a tee reservation they can play on any day of the week (in 2000) for a green fee of £85 (£70 for groups of 16 or more) with slightly lower rates between mid-October and mid-April. The **Golf Director, Donal Flynn**, can be contacted on **tel: (01) 287 3600** and by **fax: (01) 287 3699**.

So then, 'Druids Glen, Co Wicklow—the Garden of Eden in the Garden of Ireland'? Why not. But then again, would the druids have sanctioned such biblical links? We'll

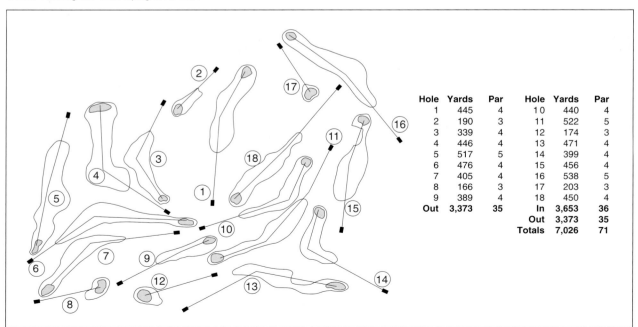

Hole	Yards	Par	Hole	Yards	Par
1	445	4	10	440	4
2	190	3	11	522	5
3	339	4	12	174	3
4	446	4	13	471	4
5	517	5	14	399	4
6	476	4	15	456	4
7	405	4	16	538	5
8	166	3	17	203	3
9	389	4	18	450	4
Out	**3,373**	**35**	**In**	**3,653**	**36**
			Out	**3,373**	**35**
			Totals	**7,026**	**71**

Hunter's Hotel, one of Ireland's oldest coaching inns, has been established for over 250 years from the days of post horses and carriages. Indeed some of the earliest written recommendations date back over 150 years and bear testimony to the hospitality of the Hunter family who have run the hotel for five generations. The owners today, the Gelletlie Family are proud to carry on the traditions of their great great grandfather, John Hunter, who back in 1840 was considered to have the best inn in the county.

This area is the ideal centre for a golfing holiday. There are 16 18-hole golf courses within a half hour's drive of the hotel - the nearest a mere 5 minutes drive. Druids Glen - venue for 1996-1999 Murphy's Irish Open - is 10 minutes drive. The European Club a new links course voted 7th best course in Ireland - 25 minutes drive. From mature parkland to links courses, there is golf to suit beginners to single figure handicap golfers. All arrangements, tee-off times, club hire, tuition, transport etc. can be made directly through the hotel.

Hunter's Hotel is also an excellent base for riding, hunting, tennis, swimming and hiking. The 'garden of Ireland' is at the guests' doorstep with well known beauty spots such as Mount Usher Gardens, Powerscourt, Russborough House, Avondale House, Glendalough, The Devil's Glen and Roundwood all within easy reach. And for those keen to savour the atmosphere of another great Irish tradition, there is always the racing at Leopardstown, while the Curragh and Punchestown are about an hour or so away.

The character of this hotel lies in the charm and elegance retained from bygone days with antique furniture, open fires, fresh flowers, polished brass and wonderful gardens.

Hunter's Hotel
Newrath Bridge
Rathnew
Co Wicklow
Ireland
Tel: (00 353) 404 40106
Fax: (00 353) 404 40338
email: hunters@indigo.ie

County Louth (Baltray)

Golfing visitors to the east coast of Ireland can almost be forgiven if having arrived in Dublin they fail to travel any real distance beyond the fair city. Dotted around the fringes of Ireland's capital are numerous first rate challenges, something like 20 courses within 10 miles (or half an hour's drive) of O'Connell Street. (How many within thirty minutes of Piccadilly Circus?)

There is great variety too with classic links courses to the north, including world famous Portmarnock and Royal Dublin and some very pleasant, well manicured parkland courses to the south and west of the city. The quality of golf isn't the only reason why so many decide not to venture away from Dublin—the city and its people have much to offer. But I did say at the beginning, 'can almost be forgiven', because one of the greatest courses in Ireland lies no more than 40 miles north of Dublin (and about an hour's drive) just beyond Drogheda in the small fishing village of Baltray. This is where County Louth Golf Club is situated, and a truly magnificent and totally natural golf links.

Baltray, as everyone calls it, is one of the least widely known of Ireland's great championship links. Give the Club a major professional tournament and all this would probably change, but for the moment Baltray retains a fairly low profile, which doubtless suits many of the members! Not that they won't welcome you, mind you, for this must be one of the most friendly and informal clubs around. A genuinely relaxed Saturday afternoon atmosphere prevails throughout the week.

One gentleman who helps maintain the marvellous mood is the **Secretary, Michael Delany.** Visitors wishing to arrange a game at Baltray should contact him in advance of intended play either by writing to him at **County Louth Golf Club, Baltray, Co Louth, tel: (041) 982 2329 fax: (041) 982 2969,** (00 353) 41 from Great Britain. The green fees in 2000 are £50 during the week and £60 at the weekend with reduced rates for juniors. Club competitions may make it difficult to arrange a game for the weekend but usually the only other day to try to avoid is Tuesday. Golf societies normally visit Baltray on Mondays and Thursdays. One other person you may wish to consult before striding out on to the links is the club's affable **Professional, Paddy McGuirk, tel: (041) 982 2444.**

As already mentioned, Baltray is about an hour's drive from Dublin—less from the city's airport which is located 8 miles north of the capital. The road to pick up, both from Dublin and the airport is the N1. It links the city with Drogheda (and indeed carries on towards

Belfast) and is well signposted—if you follow the course of the River Boyne towards the sea you cannot go far wrong, but make sure you journey north of the river.

We were about to stride out onto the links, and tackle all 6567 yards, par 73 from the medal tees (6783 yards, par 73 from the back markers). The first two holes tempt us to open the shoulders (after all, the rough doesn't look too menacing) but on both holes a wayward drive can easily find a bunker, and this is the story all the way around. Architect Tom Simpson may have been presented with a wonderful piece of golfing terrain to work with when he designed the course in the 1930s, but he clearly put an enormous amount of thought into the positioning of bunkers and other hazards. The good shot at Baltray, however, is always rewarded, no more so than at the par five 3rd where the second must be played blind over a rise in the fairway to a narrow green. The 4th is only a drive and a pitch but it is a classic links hole with a tumbling, folding, dune-lined fairway. The 5th green is actually perched high in these dunes. It is a splendid short hole and one of Baltray's 'four little gems'.

For many the most exciting holes appear between the 12th and 16th at the far end of the links, the part closest to the sea and where nature presents the dunes at their wildest. The entire 12th fairway appears to have been carved out of the surrounding towering sandhills. The shot to the green has to be targeted through a gap in the dunes and only a perfect long iron will suffice—spray it to the left or right and disaster awaits. The 13th is almost as difficult but the far reaching views from the elevated 14th tee will placate the most wounded souls. This is a beautiful and historic part of the world and as you drive at the 14th (a hole which is arguably the finest short par four in Ireland) the broad estuary of the River Boyne, famed for its 17th century battle, stretches out ahead. Over your shoulder are the far off romantic Mountains of Mourne. Another fine par four comes at the 16th where the angled approach is played into an amphitheatre green. It is a superb dog-leg hole, and again one of several at Baltray. A new championship tee has added considerable teeth to the par five 18th, however from the forward tees it still offers a real chance of a finishing birdie.

The way to celebrate such a feat at Baltray is with a drop of the famous black and white stuff—almost, but not quite obligatory. Good food and overnight accommodation in the clubhouse can also be arranged. Like every good Irish golf club, Baltray has 19 splendid holes.

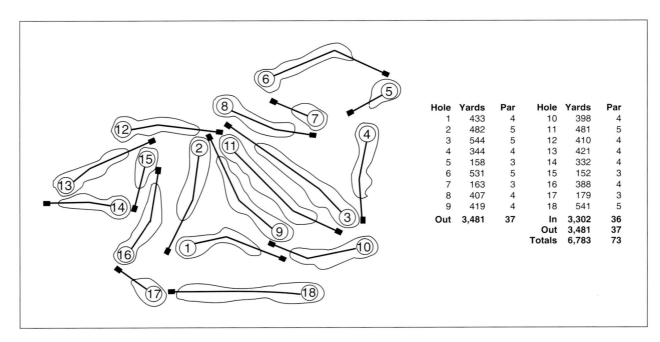

Hole	Yards	Par	Hole	Yards	Par
1	433	4	10	398	4
2	482	5	11	481	5
3	544	5	12	410	4
4	344	4	13	421	4
5	158	3	14	332	4
6	531	5	15	152	3
7	163	3	16	388	4
8	407	4	17	179	3
9	419	4	18	541	5
Out	**3,481**	**37**	**In**	**3,302**	**36**
			Out	**3,481**	**37**
			Totals	**6,783**	**73**

Bettystown in Co. Meath is attracting much interest these days with the development of the new deluxe Neptune Beach Hotel and Leisure Club. The hotel has the most spectacular setting on the beautiful sandy beach at Bettystown.

All 38 spacious and luxurious en-suite bedrooms, most of which will command breathtaking views of the sea, are complete with trouser press, ironing facilities, hair dryer, satellite television and direct dial telephone.

The large comfortable foyer with its glowing log fire and relaxing leather furniture provides a warm and welcoming atmosphere for all guests. Morning and afternoon tea is served in the foyer and a relaxing drink can be enjoyed in the Victorian style Neptune Bar.

The elegant restaurant 'Le Pressage', is the ideal setting for a business luncheon or an intimate dinner. The cuisine is always of the highest standard with fine food and superb wines to suit all tastes.

After dinner guests can also enjoy a cocktail in the stylish Seaview Lounge.

The Neptune Beach is the perfect venue for conferences and banquets of any size from small business meetings to exhibitions or seminars for up to 200 people. The main conference/banqueting room boasts spectacular sea views and is equipped with the most up to date audio visual equipment.

The leisure club provides the very best in health and fitness equipment, with a spectacular 20 metre swimming pool, jacuzzi, steam room and a hi-tech fitness suite.

The Hotel is ideally located just 30 minutes north of Dublin Airport and 5 miles from Drogheda. The Neptune Beach is a golfer's delight with three championship courses in the surrounding area, while the racing fraternity will be perfectly placed for the courses at Fairyhouse, Bellewstown, Dundalk, Laytown and Navan.

Neptune Beach Hotel & Leisure Club
Bettystown
Co. Meath
Tel: 00 353 41 982 7107
Fax: 00 353 41 982 7412
e mail: info@neptunebeach.ie
web site: www.neptunebeach.ie

Powerscourt

There was a time when golfing visitors to Ireland took a quick look around Dublin—sneaking in a round, perhaps, at Portmarnock—then raced off to the magical west. Now there has been some serious reappraisal. During the 1990s three outstanding courses (plus a handful of above average layouts) have opened in County Wicklow, directly south of Dublin. The first was Rathsallagh, the second Druids Glen and the most recent is Powerscourt—the closest to Dublin, situated just 12 miles south of the city at Enniskerry.

All three courses provide classic parkland golf, which is not surprising since each was laid out in the grounds of a well wooded estate. Indeed, Powerscourt is probably the most famous estate in all Ireland. Its name dates back to 1300 when the land was acquired by the Norman Le Poer family. In the 17th, 18th and 19th centuries the estate was owned by the Wingfields, who built Powerscourt House and gradually developed the gardens. Today those gardens cover 45 acres and are stunningly beautiful—a dash of Italy and a hint of Japan in the heart of Ireland.

The course is approached via an avenue of towering beech trees. You then turn into the golf club and are confronted by a handsome Georgian style clubhouse. Powerscourt House is close to the 1st tee and you are surrounded by rolling countryside. But there is still one more striking feature—Sugarloaf Mountain. Along with Croagh Patrick in Co Mayo this is Ireland's most famous peak and it dominates the horizon at Powerscourt.

Golf Manager at Powerscourt is **Bernard Gibbons**, **Paul Thompson** is the **Professional** they can both be contacted on **tel: (01) 204 6033**. Send written correspondence to **Powerscourt Golf Club, Powerscourt Estate, Enniskerry, Co Wicklow**. Green fees in 2000 are £60 per round, bookings are preferred.

Powerscourt is located 12 miles south of Dublin off the N11, just south of Bray and adjacent to the village of Enniskerry.

The design is refreshing. The architect, Peter McEvoy, has placed an emphasis on subtlety and harmony and has not attempted to force or manufacture the spectacular. The course flows with the land and there are only two water hazards in the entire layout. And yet there is enormous variety. The first five holes, for instance, comprise a medium par four dog-legging mildly to the right, a par five that swings to the left, a short hole, a teasingly short par four where the tee shot must flirt with an out of bounds, and a big par three that plunges dramatically downhill. As for the quality of the greens, Golf Monthly described them in March 1996 as "18 of the best shaped putting surfaces since God had a hand in shaping Prestwick".

The variety continues. At the 8th McEvoy has employed old-fashioned crossbunkers while at the 11th, a tough two-shotter, there are no bunkers. The par three 16th occupies a 'secret corner' of the course and here is where you confront water—but you must also avoid three pot bunkers. Finally a huge par five and a sweeping par four guide you back to that most elegant of 19th holes.

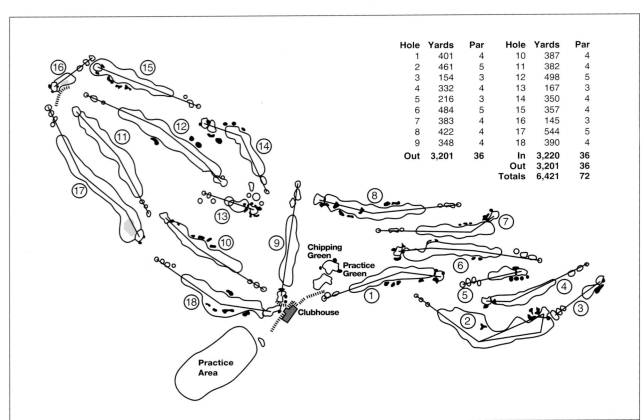

Hole	Yards	Par	Hole	Yards	Par
1	401	4	10	387	4
2	461	5	11	382	4
3	154	3	12	498	5
4	332	4	13	167	3
5	216	3	14	350	4
6	484	5	15	357	4
7	383	4	16	145	3
8	422	4	17	544	5
9	348	4	18	390	4
Out	**3,201**	**36**	**In**	**3,220**	**36**
			Out	**3,201**	**36**
			Totals	**6,421**	**72**

Situated some 12 miles south of Dublin, Powerscourt Estate provides a beautiful setting for its recently constructed parkland course, Powerscourt Golf Club. The clubhouse itself has been constructed in keeping with the Georgian style of Powerscourt House. It provides an extensive pro shop on the ground floor together with superb changing facilities, while upstairs a beautiful function and dining room can seat up to 120 guests. An imaginative bar menu and a full a la carte menu is available, in addition the fully licensed bar leads out onto a balcony overlooking the 9th and 18th holes.

Studio apartments are now available on the estate which were converted from the outbuildings adjacent to the main house. They can be rented by the night or for longer periods at reduced rates including special green fees. The apartments are within strolling distance of the course and clubhouse. All have fully equipped kitchens, a twin bedroom and en suite bathroom.

Powerscourt also boasts a golf academy with some of the finest practice facilities in Ireland. With the guidance of the PGA Professionals, a variety of instruction programmes are available to beginners through to seasoned veterans. Individual lessons, video lessons, academy sessions and residential programmes are some of the options available.

The golf course which has been built to championship standard has an abundance of mature trees and natural features, with stunning views to the sea and the most striking feature, Sugar Loaf Mountain, which dominates the skyline. Powerscourt can also cater for group golf, with the ability to organise corporate and competition days for groups of 20 to 120. Further information can be provided by calling the golf society secretary.

Whatever golfing ideas you have planned, Powerscourt will be able to cater for them all.

POWERSCOURT
GOLF CLUB

Powerscourt Estate
Enniskerry
Co Wicklow
Tel: (00 353) 1 204 6033
Fax: (00 353) 1 276 1303

When an American golfer travels to Scotland he feels compelled to visit the great Open Championship links—St Andrews, Muirfield, Carnoustie, Turnberry and Troon. That same person visiting Ireland will want to play at one or more of its famous five—Portmarnock, Ballybunion, Lahinch, Portrush and County Down. But what if he is an informed adventurer—a devotee of classic links golf who has already paid homage to those hallowed shrines? Well, when in Scotland he must decide whether to travel north to Dornoch and Cruden Bay or south to Machrihanish. And when he visits the Emerald Isle? Of course there is an array of glittering links courses to explore, but if he is 'in the know' and is a genuine connoisseur of traditional, old-fashioned links golf, he will not wish to roam far from Dublin. He will head straight for The Island Golf Club near Malahide.

Although founded over a century ago, The Island is Ireland's greatest golfing secret. There are several reasons for this, chief of which is the links' close proximity to Royal Dublin and Portmarnock, two very well established championship venues. Another is that until quite recently the principal mode of transport to The Island was by ferry.

In fact it isn't literally an island—the course occupies a peninsula and the club's founders chose to build their clubhouse on the tip of that peninsula, directly across the estuary from Malahide. The rather eccentric voyage discouraged many but for those with a spirit of adventure it merely added to the allure and charm of the links.

The Island enjoys some of the most naturally rugged terrain on the east coast. It has been called 'the Lahinch of the east', and the sandhills dwarf those at Portmarnock. When the course was originally laid out (it is not clear by whom), little attempt was made to tame the landscape and the links was built right in amongst the dunes.

Although changes have occurred over the years (the ferry was discontinued in 1973 when a newly sited clubhouse opened), the course has kept its essential character. In 1990, the club's centenary year, a revised layout was unveiled. It included several new holes but also retained the best of the old layout, including the wonderful sequence between the 12th and the 15th, which tour the tip of the peninsula.

American writer Jim Finegan eloquently summarised the attractions of The Island in his book *Emerald Fairways and Foam Flecked Seas*: "The Island is a great course, compelling our respect for the testing quality of its holes, winning our admiration for its naturalness, endowing us from start to finish with the unique joy of seaside golf at its best. The world should be beating a path to its door".

The Island Golf Club, Corballis, Donabate, Co Dublin	
Sec/Manager	John Finn (01) 843 6104
	Fax (01) 843 6860
Professional	Kevin Kelliher (01) 843 5002
Green Fees	WD £60/round; WE £70/round
Restrictions	Booking essential. Very limited availability Wed, Thur, Sat, Sun.
Directions	

From the airport, take the Dublin-Belfast road (N1). Two miles past Swords make a right turn towards Donabate

---

It must be wonderful to own a property right on the edge of a golf course; to be able to rise early and sneak out for a few holes before breakfast. A less expensive alternative is to spend a few days at Rathsallagh House in CoWicklow. It is a luxurious home-from-home and, importantly, it has a splendid 18 hole championship golf course at the bottom of its garden.

Nestling beneath the Wicklow Mountains near Dunlavin, Rathsallagh is a large estate with centuries of history. The golf course is a mere youngster, although you would never know. It was designed by Peter McEvoy and Christy O'Connor Jr (the architects of Fota Island) and opened for play in 1994. Gently rising and falling, the course meanders its way through more than 250 acres of mature parkland and woodland. Giant beech trees, oaks and limes adorn the grounds and some of the holes are played amid great avenues of trees, while others are attractively routed alongside winding streams and ponds.

The Irish press have been quick to lavish praise on the course. John Redmond described it as, 'Augusta without the azalea' and added, 'I would have no hesitation in declaring that it is as good a layout and challenge as you will find anywhere in Irish golf'. Comparisons with Augusta may be stretching the imagination a little but Rathsallagh is undoubtedly a fine course and on a glorious spring or summer's day there can be few more pleasant places to play golf. And imagine how colourful it becomes in autumn when those giant trees turn crimson and gold.

The most distinguishing feature of Rathsallagh is the quality of the putting surfaces—their design, construction and condition. Each of the greens is beautifully shaped and as they were built to USGA specification, they are extremely quick.

Among many strong holes on the front nine one might single out the par four 2nd, a beautifully conceived hole with a broad, sweeping fairway bordered by towering trees and a heavily guarded green. But the most celebrated sequence begins at the 6th, a zig-zagging minefield of a par five. The 7th is a very picturesque short hole and the 8th, an almost L-shaped par four where the approach must be fired across sand and water.

The finest holes on the back nine are possibly the 10th, which sweeps dramatically downhill, the par three 13th and the 15th which features a vast greenside bunker. As for the most difficult hole at Rathsallagh, how about the 18th— from the back tee it measures 450 yards and runs uphill towards a huge and severely contoured green. Anyone achieving a birdie at this hole deserves to be granted the freedom of Rathsallagh.

Rathsallagh Golf Club, Dunlavin, Co Wicklow, Ireland www.rathsallagh.com	
Secretary	Susan Chadwick (045) 403316
Green Fees	£30 (Mon), £40 (Tues-Thurs), £50 (Fri-Sun)
Restrictions	Telephone in advance to reserve tee times. Members only weekends before 11.00 am.
Directions	

Rathsallagh lies 1 mile south of Dunlavin and 30 miles from the centre of Dublin. From south Dublin travel via Tallacht and Blessington and from north Dublin

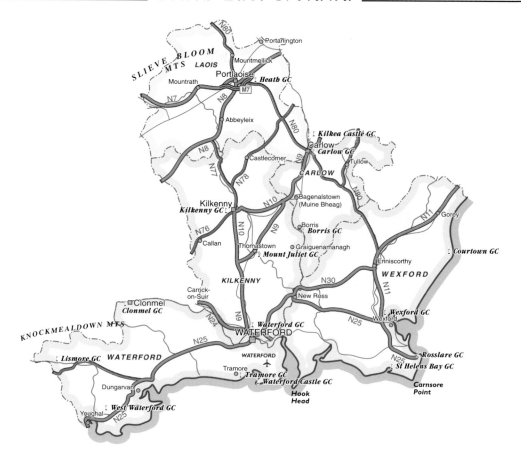

South East Ireland Choice Golf

Continuing to wander down through the counties of Ireland, County Laois is the next we come across. There's only one 18 hole course, the **Heath** and no guesses as to the type of golf offered. The course is laid out on common land and rather like the Curragh, there's a fair chance that you'll spot more sheep than golfers. Also like the Curragh it is a most historic course and has special apeal to those interested in the game's heritage.

Carlow

Stumbling into County Carlow we find the best inland course (aside from Mount Juliet) in south east Ireland. **Carlow** is a superb course: well bunkered and well wooded, it presents a considerable test of golf but a very fair one nonetheless. Carlow is highlighted later in this chapter. There are a number of convenient hotels in Carlow itself but for a real treat stay in Castledermot at **Kilkea Castle** (00 353) 503 45156, a splendidly converted 12th century castle. Kilkea has its own turf nursery and has opened an 18 hole golf course in the grounds. The Seven Oak Hotel (00 353) 503 31308 in Carlow also offers good food; plain by comparison with the stately hotels of the area, but excellent value. A very popular restaurant is also found in Castledermot, the Doyles School House (00 353) 503 44282.

Kilkenny

Kilkenny is one of those places that has to be visited. It's a town steeped in Irish history. In medieval times it housed the Irish Parliament, then there's the famous Kilkenny Castle, an impressive collection of churches and Kytelers Inn. The city's golf course is a bit of a youngster in comparison, but it's a fine parkland course, very typical of Ireland's better inland courses. The Newpark Hotel (00 353) 562 2122 is one of several comfortable establishments in the town.

Nearby, Thomastown is the setting for the magnificent **Mount Juliet** complex (00 353) 562 4455, featuring 18 spectacular holes designed by Jack Nicklaus (see ahead) and a luxurious country house hotel and excellent restaurant. Less formal but thoroughly gracious accommodation can be found at Hunters Yard at Mount Juliet (00 353) 56 24725. It is an 18th century converted stable block packed with character. For non residents, the Loft Restaurant is good value with a good atmosphere and excellent food. One mile from Thomastown and adjacent to Jerpoint Abbey is the Abbey House (00 353) 562 4192—a highly recommended guesthouse.

From Kilkenny it's a pleasant drive to **Borris** where there is an excellent 9 holer and it's certainly not a long way to Tipperary either. Visitors to the county with the famous name should slip a game in at **Clonmel**. This is a fairly isolated part of Ireland and you may just have the course to yourself on a quiet weekday. However, it is but a short trip to Waterford, of which, more later.

A good place to put the feet up after a game is the Hotel Minella (00 353) 52 22388, considered by many the best in this area, or alternatively, the Clonmel Arms Hotel (00 353) 522 1233. Not too far away in Cashel, (and be sure to visit the magnificent Rock) the Cashel Palace Hotel (00 353) 626 2707 and its restaurant, the Four Seasons are quite outstanding. The former Archbishop's Palace also has some magnificent gardens in which to reflect on one's swing.

An alternative route down to Waterford from Dublin is by the east coast, starting with a quick recommendation for the 18 hole course at **Courtown**, close to the north Wexford coast which boasts some fabulous beaches—in fact the golden sands stretch practically all the

*MOUNT JULIET Photograph courtesy of: **Mount Juliet Golf Club***

Waterford

First the city of Waterford. The world famous Waterford crystal factory is reason enough for stopping a while in the Waterford area, but there are other sound reasons too. The first is **Waterford Castle**, the kind of place you dream about: an ivy-clad 12th century castle dominating a small island which can only be reached by ferry. Today, the castle is one of Ireland's finest hotels (00 353) 51 878203. Moreover, the island isn't quite so small that space could not be found for an 18 hole golf and country club! The course, designed by Ryder Cup golfer Des Smyth, opened in the summer of 1992. The second is the **West Waterford** Golf Club at Dungarvon, a new Eddie Hackett course, and well worth a visit.

way south to Wexford town, where the **Wexford** golf club provides panoramic views of the Wexford coastline and mountains. A charming place to stay when playing Courtown is Marlfield House (00 353) 55 21124 at Gorey, one of the finest country houses in Ireland.

Whilst at the south east corner of Ireland, **St Helen's Bay** is well worth inspecting from a base such as the Ferrycarrig Hotel (00 353) 53 22999 in Wexford. Alternatively try the cosy cottages beside St Helens Bay (00 353) 53 33234. The restaurant here is held in particularly high regard.

For those whose irish sojourn ends with the Rosslare ferry crossing back to the UK, where better to finish than **Rosslare**, which may not have the glamour of a Portmarnock or a Royal Dublin but for lovers of the traditional game—rolling sand dunes and a hammering wind—it will do perfectly.

Those of you seeking immediate sustenance, or possibly a place to shelter after your ferry crossing should certainly consider Kelly's Strand Hotel (00 353) 53 32114. There are good facilities here, making it a fine base from which to commence or conclude a journey in this truly delightful land. One final thought before we move on, golfers might care to visit the splendidly named Ballyhack. A restaurant to mention here is the Neptune (00 353) 51 389284 on the harbour—excellent seafood and an ideal place in which to reflect upon your day's golf.

Two other good reasons for visiting Waterford are **Tramore** Golf Club and **Waterford** Golf Club—both offer very good parkland golf. The former, just 15 minutes from the town of Waterford, is a real test for all standards of golfer with fairways lined by evergreen trees, calling for accurate shot placement, and was good enough to have staged the Irish Amateur Championship in 1987. The latter, however, is possibly the more enjoyable of the two, having the greater variety, especially on the back nine which features a magnificent downhill finishing hole.

Places to stay include Jurys (00 353) 51 832111, a focal point for the town, whilst those visiting the Dungarvon area should certainly try to visit Lawlors Hotel (00 353) 58 41122, another hotel with a reputation for entertaining.

*MOUNT JULIET Photograph courtesy of: **Irish Tourist Board (Brian Lynch)***

Mount Juliet

Joseph II of Austria (1741-1790) was an enlightened despot and a thoroughly miserable soul to boot. He wrote his own epitaph: 'Here lies a man who never succeeded in anything he attempted.' When, and let's hope it's a long, long way off, people begin to consider a fitting epitaph for Jack William Nicklaus someone should suggest, 'Here lies a man who succeeded in almost everything he attempted'.

Not content to go down in history as merely the greatest golfer who ever lived, the 'Golden Bear' is determined to establish himself as one of the finest golf architects the world has known. Jack's original career goal was to better Bobby Jones' record of 13 major championship victories: by 1986 he had totalled 20. Many believe that he would have won even more major titles had he not devoted so much of his energy to designing championship golf courses. But then again, had he not done so there would of course be no Muirfield Village, no St Mellion, no Glen Abbey—and no Mount Juliet.

Nicklaus once said, 'Building a golf course is my total expression. My golf game can only go on so long. But what I have learned can be put into a piece of ground to last beyond me'. Mount Juliet estate is a heavenly piece of ground, in fact 1500 acres of sublimely beautiful Irish countryside through which the River Nore flows and on which Jack Nicklaus has built a masterly 18 hole golf course.

Situated approximately 75 miles south of Dublin (via the N7/N9) on the outskirts of Thomastown in Co Kilkenny, Mount Juliet may just be the ultimate golfing oasis. The Mount Juliet Hotel, a splendidly refurbished 18th century mansion house, and the golf course have only recently opened yet the reputation of both is already immense. Some people are predicting that Mount Juliet will become the Turnberry or Gleneagles of Ireland, yet there appears to be none of their overt 'flashiness' or commercial brashness. Everything about Mount Juliet seems very understated and the ambience is at once graceful and peaceful. In front of the great house, somewhere between the hotel reception and the 11th tee, is a veritable Garden of Eden. Amid the ancient oaks, beeches and lime trees a hundred colours dazzle the eye and Mount Juliet's famous parading pheasants can simply vanish into the floral background. It is the perfect place for an early morning 'get your mind together' stroll before going out and tackling Jack's formidable but spectacular parkland layout.

Golf at Mount Juliet is not restricted to residents and golf club members, although hotel guests do pay reduced green fees. Advance bookings can be made for any day of the week by telephoning the club on **tel: (056) 73064**. The **Director of Golf, Jill O'Hare**, can be contacted on **tel: (056) 73082** and the **Professional, Ted Higgins**, is available on **tel: (056) 73063**. Handicap certificates are required and the non-resident green fees for 18 holes in summer 2000 are £75 midweek and £85 at weekends. Special group rates are available and there are reductions for those teeing off after 5.30pm.

The course officially opened on 14th July 1991 and a vast crowd was present to watch Nicklaus play a friendly match against Christy O'Connor Sr. Even bigger crowds assembled in June 1993 to watch Mount Juliet's first Irish Open, which was won by Nick Faldo—his third successive victory in the event—and again in 1994 and 1995 as Bernhard Langer and Sam Torrance also claimed victories in the Irish Open.

Although the course is certainly a mighty challenge from the back markers (all 7101 yards of it) each hole has four sets of tees so one needn't get too despondent! From the medal tees the course measures 6641 yards and from the ladies' tees, 5472 yards, par 73.

When writing the piece on East Sussex National I fantasised about a 'dream nine holes' made up entirely from some of the finest holes on East Sussex National's West Course. To that nine I'm now going to add the 2nd, 3rd, 5th, 8th, 10th, 11th, 13th, 14th and 18th from the Mount Juliet course. This collection will provide three exceptional short holes: the 3rd (which has a serious water carry), the 11th (over a plunging valley occupied by a cascading stream and rockery) and the 14th (with its marvellous backdrop of trees); three par fours: the 2nd (a beautifully shaped dog-leg), the 13th (a hint of Augusta's back nine) and the 18th (a classic Nicklaus closing hole) as well as three outstanding par fives, namely the double dog-legging 5th, the 8th (a fabulous elevated tee here) and the 10th (where, like the 5th, a real sea of traps must be negotiated en route to a superbly angled green). A dream round for sure, but sweet dreams? Potential nightmares, I reckon!

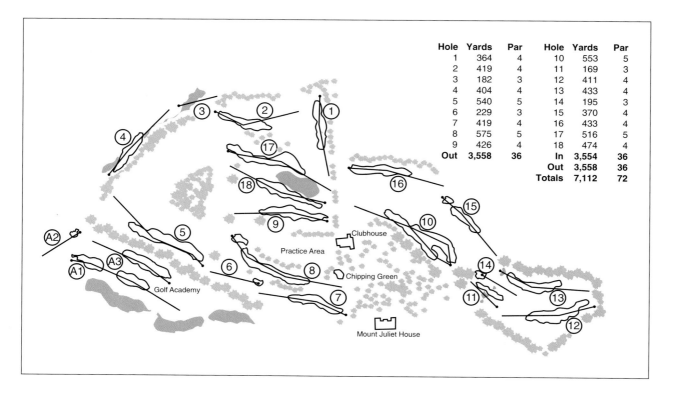

Hole	Yards	Par	Hole	Yards	Par
1	364	4	10	553	5
2	419	4	11	169	3
3	182	3	12	411	4
4	404	4	13	433	4
5	540	5	14	195	3
6	229	3	15	370	4
7	419	4	16	433	4
8	575	5	17	516	5
9	426	4	18	474	4
Out	3,558	36	In	3,554	36
			Out	3,558	36
			Totals	7,112	72

Clubhouse

Practice Area

Chipping Green

Golf Academy

Mount Juliet House

The European Club

'Rugged dunes, deep bunkers and sea breezes; fast running fairways, large undulating greens that invite the pitch-and-run approach and acres of tall waving marram grass. This is the very essence of golf—as it was at the beginning and was always meant to be'.
(Pat Ruddy)

Legend has it that when W L Pickeman pedalled along the estuary from Baldoyle and saw the great stretch of linksland at Portmarnock he almost fell off his bicycle. Almost a century later, Robert Trent Jones was led deep into the sandhills at Ballybunion and has never been the same man since. Imagine then how Pat Ruddy must have felt when he first saw the vast expanse of 'rugged dunes' and 'tall waving marram grass' just south of Brittas Bay in Co Wicklow. What effect on a man with golf in his soul?

Another legend is developing, for it is being claimed that Ruddy drove a JCB on to the same stretch of land in 1987 and didn't venture out the other side until 1993, and they believe it everywhere in Ireland, except at St Margaret's.

It is the proud boast of golfers at Mount Juliet that they play 'the course that Jack built'. In Co Wicklow we can now experience the links that Pat built, and whatever else Pat Ruddy achieves in his life the European Club will stand as his monument to golf.

The word 'great' should be used very sparingly in relation to golf courses but the links at Brittas Bay is undoubtedly a great links. It has many great qualities. The sandhills are not quite of Ballybunion-like proportion but they dwarf those at Portmarnock and Baltray. Better still, the golf course never leaves the dunes. There is balance and consistency and no feeling of mild disappointment, as is sometimes expressed in relation to the final few holes at Lahinch and Newcastle—and indeed with regard to the first few at Portmarnock and Ballybunion. The Irish Sea is the golfer's constant companion. You see it as you leave the 1st green, you hear it as you approach the 3rd and smell it as you stroll down the 7th—and you can almost touch it as you play along the 12th and 13th.

There are at least six genuinely great holes: the beautifully flowing downhill 3rd, the 7th with its fairway bordered by haunting marshland,

the 8th, the 11th, the 12th and the fabulous 17th which plunges through a secluded dune–lined valley. These could all be described as great holes, and one final treat—or is it shock—awaits at the 18th, but who are we to spoil the surprise?

Ruddy's dream is that the European Club will one day be spoken of in the same breath as Ireland's 'Big Four' of Portmarnock, Portrush, Ballybunion and Newcastle. Most who have seen the course believe he has an evens chance of succeeding, and people who know Pat Ruddy will tell you that he eats such odds for breakfast.

The European Club, now in mature condition, can be properly compared with the aforementioned 'Big Four'—which is quite an achievement since the course was only fully opened for play in May 1993. What is certain is that you are made to feel very relaxed at Brittas Bay. A unique 'welcome to the family' atmosphere is developing. Ruddy says he wants to encourage a 'spirit of simplicity' and to recreate the mood of a time when golf was enjoyed in less hurried, less crowded and less pretentious circumstances. 'I've been to clubs where you see guys dressed like undertakers. Golf is meant to be fun', he says.

The course and club facilities are open to visitors seven days a week. The only restriction as such is that the number of players is carefully controlled. Priority is naturally given to those who have made advance arrangements, so booking a tee time is recommended. For written correspondence contact The European Club, Brittas Bay, Wicklow, Co Wicklow. The club's **Secretary** is **Mr Pat Ruddy tel: (0404) 47415 fax: (0404) 47449**. The green fees in 2000 are set at £60 per round weekdays and weekends.

Brittas Bay is approximately 40 minutes south of Dublin and the European Club is slightly closer to the capital than Baltray (Co Louth) is to the north. It is often claimed that a golfer hasn't experienced the full flavour of Irish links golf until he or she has made a pilgrimage to Ballybunion. One day the same might be said about Brittas Bay. The golf course is genuinely amazing and when a club is very personally run by a man whose motto in life is 'Grab some sticks and let's go golfing', how can you possibly resist?

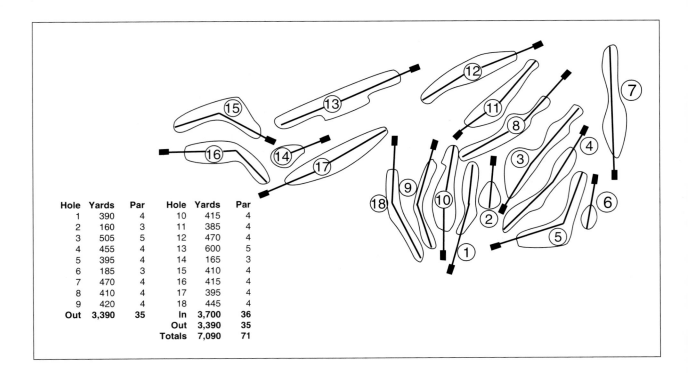

Hole	Yards	Par	Hole	Yards	Par
1	390	4	10	415	4
2	160	3	11	385	4
3	505	5	12	470	4
4	455	4	13	600	5
5	395	4	14	165	3
6	185	3	15	410	4
7	470	4	16	415	4
8	410	4	17	395	4
9	420	4	18	445	4
Out	**3,390**	**35**	**In**	**3,700**	**36**
			Out	**3,390**	**35**
			Totals	**7,090**	**71**

Waterford Castle dates as far back as the 11th century and is the former home of the Fitzgerald family. It is two miles from Waterford City and is uniquely situated on its own 310 acre island surrounded by woodlands and its own championship 18-hole golf course in the estuary of the River Suir.

The island's car ferry waits to take you across a channel of centuries, for here is both retreat and refuge, sanctuary and seclusion. A stone arched doorway leads to the castle's main entrance hall where the crackling log fire welcomes all its guests.

Dinner is served each evening in the award winning Elizabethan oak-panelled dining room using fresh local produce where possible prepared by the castle's head chef.

The castle offers accommodation of a high standard. It includes superb four-poster suites and deluxe twin and double bedrooms. All rooms are individually decorated to reflect the quality throughout.

Completing the picture are the leisure facilities available to guests at Waterford Castle Golf Club located only 300 metres from the Castle. These include an indoor heated swimming pool and tennis courts. Discounted green fees are also extended to all hotel residents and enquiries may be made directly with the Golf Club on (00 353) 51 871633.

For tranquillity and luxury inherited from the island's past, there is nothing quite like An Island Dream at Waterford Castle.

Waterford Castle Hotel, Golf and Country Club
The Island
Ballinakill
Waterford
Ireland
Tel: (00 353 51) 878203
Fax: (00 353 51) 878342
e mail: info@waterfordcastle.com
web site: www.waterfordcastle.com

Carlow

While it may be little known internationally, Carlow Golf Club has a proud reputation in Ireland. In 1978 it hosted the Irish Close Championship—normally the preserve of links courses—and in its annual poll of Ireland's 'Top 30 Golf Courses', the Irish Golf Institute rate Carlow among the country's top three inland courses built before 1990. In August 2001 Carlow will be hosts of the Irish Ladies Golf Union Home International.

Strictly speaking, Carlow is a parkland type course and it certainly boasts a wealth of wonderfully mature trees. However, in places it has much more of a moorland, even heathland feel and the subsoil is quite sandy. In fact Carlow is something of a cross between Yorkshire's Moortown and Fulford—and it's just as good. The course was designed by Cecil Barcroft, a native of Portrush. It opened in 1922 and was remodelled in 1937 by Thomas Simpson, assisted by Molly Gourlay.

Visitors have always been made very welcome. The **Secretary** at Carlow is **Margaret Meaney** and she can be contacted on **tel: (0503) 31695** or **fax: (0503) 40065**. Advance bookings are recommended and although it is naturally much easier to arrange a game during the week, weekend golf is always a possibility. The 2000 green fees are set at £28 on weekdays (groups of 20 plus pay £25) and £34 at weekends (groups of 20 plus pay £30). Weekly tickets can also be purchased and reduced rates are available for parties of 20 and over. Carlow's **Professional** is **Andrew Gilbert** and he can be reached on **tel: (0503) 41745**.

The county town of Carlow is located approximately 50 miles south of Dublin and the road linking each to the other is the N9. The same road joins Carlow with Thomastown (Mount Juliet), Kilkenny and Waterford to the south. The golf club is situated just to the north of the town, immediately off the Dublin Road.

From the championship tees Carlow is certainly no monster, measuring just over 6500 yards, (5974 metres) but it has a fairly tight par of 70 and is never 'torn apart'. The round begins with a pair of very contrasting par fours. The 1st is one of Carlow's toughest, a lengthy dog-leg left to a heavily guarded green: only a long straight drive up the right hand side of the fairway will suffice. At the 2nd, though, the sensible shot is to lay up with an iron off the tee, still leaving only a pitch to the green: a big smash with a driver might get you close to the green but it might also cause you to take a drop out of the water hazard. Probably the best two holes on the front nine are the stroke one 7th where the fairway meanders around to the left yet tries to throw your ball off to the right—a marvellously sited green here—and the spectacular downhill 8th where if you were prudent and held back on the 2nd tee no one could begrudge you now winding up and letting fly from this superbly elevated tee.

The real fun, however, is still to come. Carlow's back nine is exceptionally good and precision becomes the name of the game. A deft pitch is required over an attractive pond at the 10th and disaster can befall the shot that misses the green at the 12th: Carlow's rough is nothing if not punishing! A trio of par fours, the 14th, 15th and 16th guide you into deepest Co Carlow—each is a really fine hole. The 16th, which is played through a tunnel-like valley, is perhaps the most demanding two-shotter of the entire round, and is followed immediately by the most celebrated par three hole. I mentioned 'precision' earlier, well, tackling the 17th at Carlow has been likened to threading a needle. How's your eyesight! The par five 18th offers the chance of a closing birdie and a grandstand finish as it tumbles downhill all the way back to the clubhouse. A good ending to a memorable round.

Carlow is less than 25 miles from Mount Juliet. It offers a very different type of challenge from the new Nicklaus designed course, but if you happen to be in this delightful part of 'Middle Ireland' why not play the pair? You won't regret it, that's for certain.

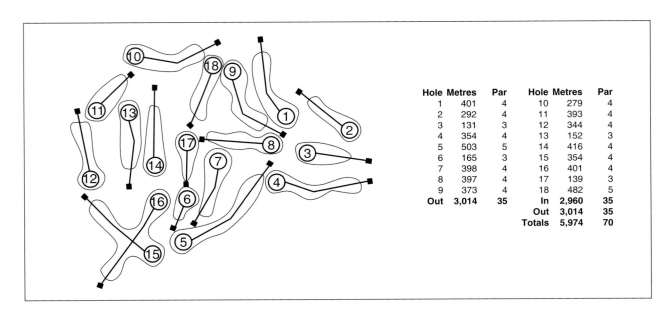

Hole	Metres	Par		Hole	Metres	Par
1	401	4		10	279	4
2	292	4		11	393	4
3	131	3		12	344	4
4	354	4		13	152	3
5	503	5		14	416	4
6	165	3		15	354	4
7	398	4		16	401	4
8	397	4		17	139	3
9	373	4		18	482	5
Out	**3,014**	**35**		**In**	**2,960**	**35**
				Out	**3,014**	**35**
				Totals	**5,974**	**70**

South West Ireland Choice Golf

County Clare and County Limerick

We begin our brief tour of south west Ireland in County Clare where **Lahinch** is found. The famous links is featured ahead but ideas for staying in the area must include the excellent Aberdeen Arms Hotel (00 353) 65 7081100—good food here. In Ennis, Auburn

LAHINCH GOLF CLUB, CO. CLARE
*Photograph courtesy of: **The Irish Tourist Board (A Pat Odea)***

Lodge (00 353) 65 6821247 offers first rate accommodation. Slightly nearer Limerick in Newmarket-on-Fergus, Hunter's Lodge (00 353) 61 368577 is inexpensive and very welcoming while **Dromoland Castle** (00 353) 61 368144 is for the true connoisseur—the person who stayed at Ashford Castle will probably be staying here. Again the hotel has a golf course, although Dromoland's course has 18 holes and has recently been upgraded. The Clare Inn Hotel (00 353) 61 368161 is very convenient for Dromoland golfers who wish to save some punts. Not far from Dromoland, **Shannon** Golf Club is also well worth a visit—friendly and a very good parkland golf course. It is handy for the airport, as is the Great Southern Hotel (00 353) 61 471122.

Around Limerick, the most exciting development is the new Robert Trent Jones designed course at Adare Manor (00 353) 61 396566, one of the finest hotels in Ireland. **Adare** Golf Club is featured ahead. Close by, the Dunraven Arms (00 353) 61 396633 offers pleasant accommodation and the Mustard Seed (00 353) 61 396451 is a restaurant of excellence. Another course with accommodation (in the shape of twelve holiday cottages) and worth a visit is the **Limerick Country Club** (00 353) 61 351881, while golf is just one of a number of sporting pursuits to be enjoyed from the Clonlara Hotel (00 353) 61 354141.

Kerry's Gold

If we have crossed the Shannon via the Tarbert Ferry or have headed west from Limerick along the N69 **Ballybunion** is the first great club we come across in County Kerry. Like **Killarney**, **Waterville** and **Tralee** it is explored later in this chapter. Killarney, which, apart from the golf and fishing club, also has a fine new parkland course at **Beaufort**, which also provides the most central base and as an enormously popular tourist destination has numerous hotels and guesthouses.

little longer than you expect but no golfer in the world should be disappointed when he reaches this course. Perhaps the best hotel for golfers in Tralee itself is the Mount Brandon Hotel (00 353) 66 7123333 but more adjacent in Barrow is the popular Barrow House (00 353) 66 7136437 guesthouse. One hotel to match the quality of the golf at Ballybunion is undoubtedly Glin Castle (00 353) 68 34173 at Glin, near Limerick while two hotels to note in Ballybunion are the Marine (00 353) 68 27522—a good seafood restaurant here—and the Ballybunion Golf Hotel (00 353) 68 27111.

TRALEE GOLF CLUB, CO. KERRY *Photograph courtesy of:* **Irish Tourist Board (A Pat Odea)**

Undoubtedly one of the best places to base oneself is the Killarney Country Club (00 353) 64 44655, four miles from Killarney Golf Club at Faha—superb accommodation and a friendly welcome await. Other fine establishments in Killarney are the Aghadoe Heights (00 353) 64 31766 (stunning views and an outstanding restaurant here), the Muckross Park Hotel (00 353) 64 31938, the Great Southern (00 353) 64 31262, the very attractive Cahernane (00 353) 64 31895, the International (00 353) 64 31816 and the Castlerosse (00 353) 64 31144. Eating establishments are equally plentiful. The panoramic restaurants of the Hotel Europe (00 353) 6431900 provide a feast for the eyes as well as the palate while Gabys (00 353) 64 32519 comes highly recommended. To the south of Killarney, the Park Hotel Kenmare (00 353) 64 41200 is where our friends from Dromoland Castle will now be heading. Also in Kenmare, Sheen Falls Lodge (00 353) 64 41600 is welcoming and rapidly establishing itself as one of the finest hotels in the country. It is set within woodland on the banks of the River Sheen—delightful. For an intimate and inexpensive stopover in Killarney, Kathleen's Country House Hotel is highly recommended (00 353) 64 32810, as is the 19th Green guesthouse (00 353) 64 32868, almost adjacent to the famous golf club.

Tralee is about 20 miles north west of Killarney. The links is actually some eight miles from the town itself; the journey takes a

There are very reasonable 18 hole courses at **Dingle** (Ballyferiter) and **Dooks** but **Waterville** is the other great course in County Kerry. Waterville is one of the longest courses in Europe when played from the back tees. It has its charm as well though and has been described as 'the beautiful monster'. Suggestions for a 19th hole in Waterville include the elegant Waterville House (00 353) 66 9474102, recently upgraded and extended, and the Butler Arms Hotel (00 353) 66 9474144. Two restaurants to savour here are the Huntsman and the Smugglers Inn (00 353) 66 9474330.

Cork and Tipperary

Coming down from rather dizzy heights, County Cork deserves an inspection. In the city itself, **Cork** Golf Club at Little Island is decidedly worth a visit. About five miles east of the town centre the course overlooks Cork Harbour and is one of the top ten inland courses in Ireland. It was at Little Island that one of Ireland's legendary golfers Jimmy Bruen learnt to play. Other golfing challenges near to Ireland's second city include **Muskerry** (a spectacular challenge) **Monkstown**, **Harbour Point** and **Douglas**, plus two very fine new 18 hole courses, the much acclaimed **Fota Island** (see feature page) and **Lee Valley**.

A delightful place to stay in Cork—and particularly convenient for Fota Island is Midleton Park (00 353) 21 631767. Other options include the Arbutus Lodge (00 353) 21 501237 while less expensive, but equally welcoming, is the popular Rochestown Hotel (00 353) 21 892233. Just outside Cork in Shanagarry is Ballymaloe House (00 353) 21 652531, where the restaurant is particularly outstanding. Cork also boasts the Silver Springs Hotel (00 353) 21 507533, which has numerous leisure facilities including its own 9 hole golf course.

Down on the coast at the Old Head of Kinsale there is a spectacular new course, the **Old Head**, which is featured ahead. Kinsale itself is packed with superb restaurants, while further east, but still on the coast lies the historic town of **Youghal** with a very pleasant

FOTA ISALND GOLF CLUB Photograph courtesy of: **Fota Island Golf Club**

18 holes. Here the Walter Raleigh Hotel (00 353) 24 92011 and Ahernes (00 353) 24 92424 offer pleasant and friendly accommodation. Further inland at **Mallow** the order of the day is an enjoyable round of golf followed by a relaxing stay at Longueville House (00 353) 22 47156—sheer bliss!

We complete this all too brief introduction to golf in the south west of Ireland in Co Tipperary—not strictly 'south west', but then not a great distance from the delights of County Kerry either. Between Tipperary and Cashel stands Dundrum House (00 353) 62 71116: a splendid hotel and an 18 hole golf course, **County Tipperary** Golf & Country Club designed by Philip Walton await.

18TH GREEN AT KILLARNEY GOLF CLUB (MAHONYS POINT) *Photograph courtesy of:* **Irish Tourist Board (Brian Lynch)**

You look at the brochure, you read the reviews and still you wonder whether it's half as good as they say. The Old Head Golf Links near Kinsale—what was Joe Carr calling it "the eighth wonder of the golfing world"? Well, as co-designer he would say that, wouldn't he! But why should Christy O'Connor Sr be telling everyone he meets that he has just seen "six of the best holes in all of golf" ? And then there was the article by leading Irish golf writer Charlie Mulqueen declaring Old Head to be "a golfing location that will never be rivalled in terms of drama and beauty". Strong stuff.

One evening in March 1997 this editor found himself in Kinsale exploring 'the nicest small town in Ireland' (not to mention the nation's culinary capital) and eagerly looking forward to a morning visit to Old Head. Since the course was not due to be opened until the summer this was something of a sneak preview.

Anticipation turned to frustration when the curtains were drawn back to reveal a foggy, chilly day. It was no less fogbound as I reached the narrow neck of land that joins Old Head to the rest of Co Cork. Driving past the ghostly castle ruins I could just make out the ocean, crashing against the rocks some 200 feet below. Fortunately the fog lifted a little as I approached the 2nd tee and I knew this was the first of the acclaimed clifftop holes . . . The moment of truth. Was this really the Cypress Point or Pebble Beach of Ireland? In a word, yes! It was—it is—an astonishing sight. The entire fairway runs along the edge of the cliffs while the green appears all set to fall into the sea. The 3rd is a par three, again its green overlooks the abyss, while the 4th is a longer and if anything more spectacular version of the 2nd.

While Old Head seems destined to be compared with the celebrated courses of the Monterey Peninsula, a flavour of two other great courses is experienced on the back nine. The fairway on the par four 15th is not only bordered to the right by the ocean but it cascades in terrace-like fashion from a high tee. In this respect it is very reminiscent of the fabled 11th on the Old Course at Ballybunion. A magnificent par three and a huge par five lead you to the 18th tee which is overlooked by the 19th century Old Head lighthouse. The drive that follows is pure Turnberry.

The **Professional** at Old Head is **David Murray** he can be contacted on **tel: (00 353) 21 778 444** or write to **Old Head Golf Links, Kinsale, Co Cork, Ireland**. The Green Fees for 200 are set at £120 per round. The club is located 20 miles south of Cork City via Kinsale; follow signs to the 'Old Head.'

Old Head is undoubtedly a great golf course. Exactly how great it is too early to say. At the time of my visit many of the bunkers were still being shaped and the fairways seemed a trifle raw—the subtleties have still to be developed. But I'll say this—Charlie Mulqueen did not exaggerate. Even on a foggy day in March the Old Head Golf Links appeared visually incomparable, stunning, magical . . .

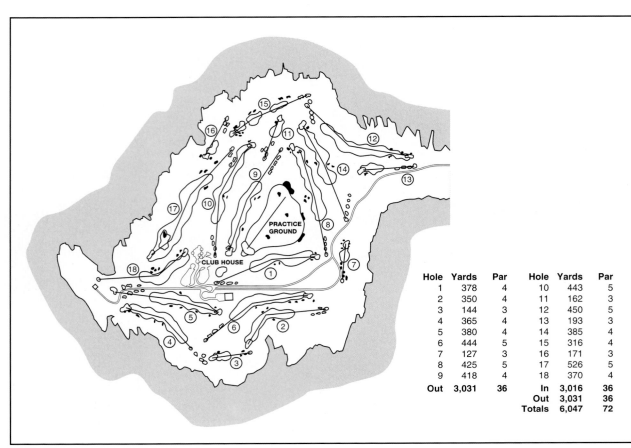

Hole	Yards	Par	Hole	Yards	Par
1	378	4	10	443	5
2	350	4	11	162	3
3	144	3	12	450	5
4	365	4	13	193	3
5	380	4	14	385	4
6	444	5	15	316	4
7	127	3	16	171	3
8	425	5	17	526	5
9	418	4	18	370	4
Out	**3,031**	**36**	**In**	**3,016**	**36**
			Out	**3,031**	**36**
			Totals	**6,047**	**72**

The Old Head of Kinsale is one of the most remarkable developments ever conceived in the history of golf—one of the most spectacular and scenic golf courses you are likely to find anywhere in the world. Set on an Atlantic promontory that will never be rivalled in terms of drama and beauty, nine holes run along the coastline, unique amongst the world's great links courses.

The Old Head is ideally located on the South Coast of Ireland, 30 minutes drive from Cork International Airport. It is easily accessible from the other great links courses of south west Ireland such as Ballybunion, Waterville and Lahinch.

The course is set on a rugged, roughly heart shaped and historic peninsula rising hundreds of feet above dramatic cliffs, surrounded by ocean on all sides and commanding spectacular views. The Old Head peninsula comprises around 220 acres, with the golf course situated on the flat area of the headland, allowing composition of a 7100 yard, par 72 golf course, configured as two returning loops of nine holes plus a practice ground facility.

A number of the most famous names in Irish golf are associated with the project; the course was designed by a combination of Ireland's greatest past golfing heroes and recognised contemporary design experts led by Joe Carr, Ron Kirby, Paddy Merrigan and Eddie Hackett. Carr said of the course "The Old Head of Kinsale as a golf links, will in my estimation rate with the great courses in the world. Its location,

scenic reality and spectacular terrain remind me of Cypress Point and Pebble Beach, two of America's most famous courses. To be associated with the design of this course is to me the thrill of a lifetime. I see Old Head as a golfers' paradise with the potential of being the eighth wonder of the world in golfing terms."

The Old Head of Kinsale is a national monument and an ancient Roman site, fortified by a castle at the narrowest part of the headland. Other landmarks include the lighthouse which was built in 1853 and the small stone circles which are thought to be the remains of Iron Age dwellings.

The ancient harbour town of Kinsale is about seven miles north of Old Head—one of the most attractive towns in Ireland, it is today considered the gourmet capital of the country. A cosmopolitan seaside town, it boasts three busy yacht marinas and many excellent restaurants and bars. The golfer is assured of being very well catered for here.

The course has taken over ten years to develop, mainly due to environmental objections, but now the clubhouse and course are completed and the result is beyond any expectations—a unique golfing experience. The magnificent location and the quality of the course will make this a truly memorable experience for golfers of all standards, with the vagaries of the Atlantic winds providing a fresh challenge each day.

Old Head Golf Links
Kinsale
Co Cork Ireland
Tel: (00 353) 21 778444
Fax : (00 353) 21 778022
e mail: info@oldheadgolf.ie
web site: www.oldheadgolflinks.com

Tralee

Like the Beatles, there will never be another Arnold Palmer. In his prime he attacked golf courses the way Errol Flynn attacked pirates. He led golf away from its stuffy, gin and tonic, plus fours image and took a vast army of hero-worshipping fans with him. When he stopped winning golf tournaments around the world, Palmer became involved in golf course design. Now let's face it, a man whose middle name is 'Charge' is unlikely to construct humdrum golf courses. Hardly! He designs courses that any golfer with high blood pressure ought to steer well clear of. Tralee's golf course, perched on the edge of the incomparably dramatic coast of County Kerry, is one that should carry such a health warning.

Tralee (the golf course is actually eight miles north west of the town at Barrow) understandably prides itself on being the first golf course that Arnold Palmer designed in Europe. Apparently, he had been looking to build across the water for some time but until the mid 1980s when he was approached by some remarkably astute Irish gentlemen he hadn't found a venue that suited. Doubtless the Irish chatted him up good and proper as only they can, but Palmer didn't need the Ancient Mariner's treatment. One look at the proposed site convinced him. 'I have never come across a piece of land so ideally suited for the building of a golf course', he declared.

For decades Tralee golfers had played on a rather ordinary 'town course.' When they discovered the tract of links land at Barrow they sensed they had discovered something very special—hence the bold approach to Palmer and the decision to 'quit town' and head for the coast.

The drive from Tralee to Barrow doesn't remotely hint at the pot of gold that awaits at the end of the long, winding road. The situation is sensational in the extreme and Palmer was the perfect choice to lay out a daring and heroic course alongside such a beautifully rugged coastal stretch: a seascape described by Peter Dobereiner as being 'in a different class even to California's Monterey Peninsula.'

The **Club Manager** at Tralee is **Mr Patrick Nugent** who can be contacted by on **tel: (066) 713 6379** or by **fax: (066) 713 6008** (00 353 66 from the UK). The club's full address is **Tralee Golf Club, West Barrow, Ardfert, County Kerry**. Visitors wishing to test their skills at Tralee must be in possession of a current handicap and advance booking with the club is required. The best days to arrange a game at Tralee are Mondays, Tuesdays, Thursdays and Fridays when there are no general restrictions. No visitors are allowed on Sundays and there are no Wednesday green fees during June, July and August but in other months the tee is available from 7.30-10.30. Visitors can also book to play on Saturdays from 11.00-1.20. The green fees in 2000 are set at £60 per round.

Measuring 6252 metres (about 6900 yards) from the championship tees, Tralee has the appearance of being two courses rather than one. The gentler outward half opens with an exacting par four where the second shot immediately guides you to the edge of the precipice—one of several greens overlooking the ocean and in this case, down over a vast, desolate beach that featured prominently in the film Ryan's Daughter. The 2nd is a banana-shaped par five that follows the cliff edges—invigorating stuff! Then comes the classic short 3rd across the rocks, a hole that often reminds American visitors of Pebble Beach. The view of the hole from the championship tee is enough to make a brave man tremble. The 6th, 7th and 8th ('Palmer's Loop') offer more exhilarating golf and provide views of a ruined 12th century castle and an old smugglers' haunt, but it is the back nine holes that leave most first-timers gasping.

After passing in front of the clubhouse and playing the 10th the golfer then disappears into another world, a world of extraordinarily wild and massive dunes. This is where Palmer (and Mother Nature) really went to town. In true Arnie fashion, desperately daring carries are the order of the day. The par four 12th is surely one of the most examining two-shot holes in golf. Although slightly downhill it is invariably played into the teeth of the wind—and my, how it can blow in these parts! The second must be fired over a huge ravine which continues around the left side of what is a painfully narrow table green. Barely do you have time to regain your breath when you must confront the par three 13th—there the tee shot must carry an even deeper chasm! As you play these holes, all around are magnificent vistas of the Atlantic Ocean, the Dingle Peninsula and the great sweep of Kerryhead. The drama doesn't let up and the downhill, par three 16th (reminiscent of the 15th at Ballybunion Old), and the dog-legged 17th (which is called 'Ryan's Daughter') are two more outstanding holes. On reaching the magnificently appointed clubhouse you will probably feel that you've tackled more than just an extraordinary golf course—you may even feel you have challenged Palmer head to head. But then that's Tralee—a unique golfing experience.

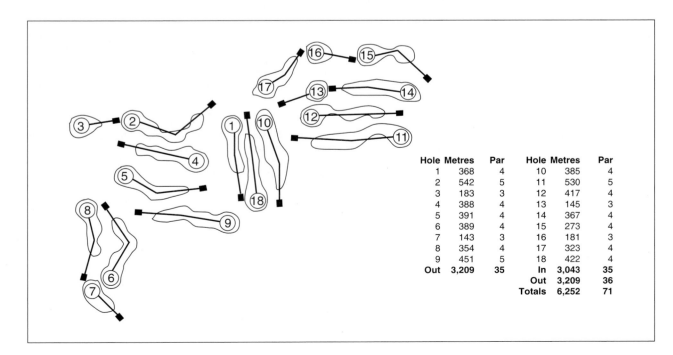

Hole	Metres	Par	Hole	Metres	Par
1	368	4	10	385	4
2	542	5	11	530	5
3	183	3	12	417	4
4	388	4	13	145	3
5	391	4	14	367	4
6	389	4	15	273	4
7	143	3	16	181	3
8	354	4	17	323	4
9	451	5	18	422	4
Out	**3,209**	**35**	**In**	**3,043**	**35**
			Out	**3,209**	**36**
			Totals	**6,252**	**71**

On entering the warmth and elegance of Midleton Park Hotel, you will receive the luxury and personal service you deserve. The hotel is situated only ten miles from Cork Airport and car ferry terminal and the business capital of the south, yet in a location very removed from city living and the interruptions of everyday life. Of all the counties in Ireland, Cork is the largest. In the path of the Mid Gulf Stream the climate is temperate, the scenery intoxicating and the choice of pursuits almost endless.

Golf is, of course, one of the specialities of the hotel and there is a selection of packages tailored to suit your requirements for that well deserved getaway.

For the golf fanatic, the hotel is situated only four miles from the picturesque but challenging par 72 championship, Fota Island Golf Course which would satisfy the most discerning of golfers.

For non golfers, it is just seven miles to the seaside village of Ballycotton with its unspoilt sandy beaches and relaxing mountain walks and at Fota Island Wildlife Park you can see the rarest species of wildlife from all five continents. No other county in Ireland offers such a fine tapestry of beauty, historical riches and sporting and leisure possibilities.

To round off the perfect day, Midleton Park offers you the ideal place to relax with its luxurious guest rooms and award-winning restaurant where you can sample local cuisine and catches from the local waters. For a less formal atmosphere, there is the option of the comprehensive lounge menu which is available throughout the day. In the hotel bar you can indulge and sample the 'spirit of Ireland' the local distilled and world famous Irish whiskeys. . . Jameson and Midleton Rare to name just two. You can also visit the 18th century distillery which has been restored.

The hotel also offers excellent business and conference facilities with three superior conference suites and four syndicate rooms catering for anything from 2 to 400 delegates. Daily delegate and 24 hour delegate rates are available on request.

The Midleton Park Hotel is a hotel where you can combine business and pleasure and discover a welcome as warm as the memories you will take back.

Midleton Park Hotel
Midleton
Co Cork Ireland
Tel: (00 353 21) 631767
Fax: (00 353 21) 631605

Fota Island

For many years overseas golfers have tended to view Co Cork as a mere gateway to the delights of Co Kerry. Arriving by boat or plane, most have simply passed through Ireland's second city before descending upon Killarney, then on to Ballybunion, Waterville and Tralee. But things are beginning to change. Cork Golf Club with its fine layout at Little Island (designed in the 1920s by master architect Alister MacKenzie) has at last been discovered, while no great distance away on historic Fota Island is a course of sufficient quality that it has hosted not only the **Irish PGA Championship** but no fewer than three **Irish Amateur Opens**.

Fota Island lies to the east of the city in Cork Harbour. Despite its rather mystical, Norse sounding name, it was a Norman family who first developed the island and it remained in family ownership from 1228 until 1975. Today the 780 acre estate is listed in the **Inventory of Outstanding Landscapes of Ireland**. It is beautifully wooded, has a handsome Regency house, wildlife park, striking arboretum and gardens, and since 1993, one of the country's finest parkland golf courses.

In an article assessing new developments in Ireland **Golf World** magazine described Fota Island as the *'pick of the bunch'*. **Golf Monthly** has also been very generous in its praise: *'It's a mark of imaginative design when a new course appears old before the paint has dried . . . some of the innovations evoke other times and other values'*. The latter coment is a reference to the course's very natural, almost old fashioned look.

Although water hazards feature quite prominently in the design, the inspiration is more St Andrews than Sawgrass. The greens at Fota are generally large and undulating and are defended by grassy swailes and deep pot bunkers. Measuring 6927 yards, par 71, the course is sufficently long to test the top professionals but invariably rewards 'brain rather than brawn'.

The clubhouse is the perfect place to relax. Being built from medieval stone and with the Niblick restaurant overlooking the 18th you will be well catered for in all departments.

General Manager at Fota Island is **Kevin Mulcahy tel: (00 353) 21 4883700**, to make reservations or contact the **Professional, Kevin Morris tel: (00 353) 214 883710** you can also write to: **Fota Island Golf Club, Fota Island, Carrogtwohill, Co Cork, Ireland** or **e mail: reservations@fotaisland.ie**. Green fees in 200 are set at £45 per round weekdays, £55 per round weekends.

It has recently been announced that Fota Island will be home to the **Murphy's Irish Open** in 2001 and 2002. Joining the ranks of such pretigious past venues as Portmarnock, Ballybunion, Druid's Glen and Mount Juliet.

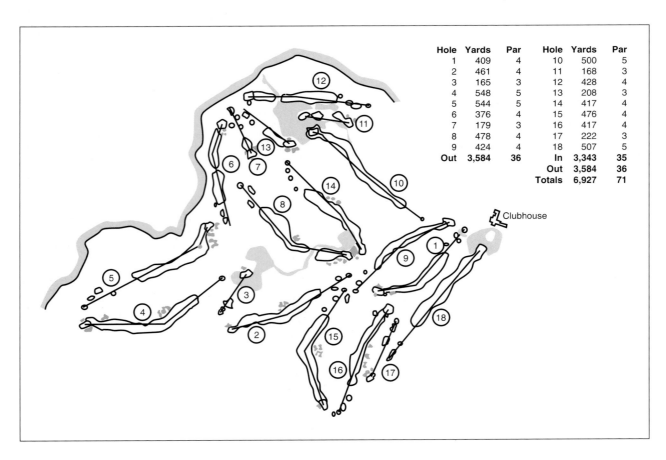

Hole	Yards	Par	Hole	Yards	Par
1	409	4	10	500	5
2	461	4	11	168	3
3	165	3	12	428	4
4	548	5	13	208	3
5	544	5	14	417	4
6	376	4	15	476	4
7	179	3	16	417	4
8	478	4	17	222	3
9	424	4	18	507	5
Out	**3,584**	**36**	**In**	**3,343**	**35**
			Out	**3,584**	**36**
			Totals	**6,927**	**71**

Fota Island Golf Club, situated a few minutes drive east of Cork City, lies in the heart of a 780 acre estate which is listed in the **Inventory of Outstanding Landscapes of Ireland**. With Fota's internationally renowned arboretum and gardens nearby, the splendid woodlands are woven into a challenging par 71 championship course.

The terrain is gently undulating parkland, offering glimpses of Cork Harbour from various points around the course. While Fota is a new development, it is very much traditional in design and its location, amid the mature woodlands gives the impression that the course has been there for generations.

It is difficult to attribute the design of the new Fota Island golf course to a single architect, since several were involved in its original conception and its current evolution. The course opened in 1993, reflecting the design of Irish Ryder Cup hero, Christy O'Connor Jnr., and British Walker Cup Captain, Peter McEvoy. Further work was undertaken in 1999 by Jeff Howes, who worked with Jack Nicklaus on the Mount Juliet course. Each development has added to the golfing challenge on which the course's reputation is built.

Describing his design philosophy, Peter McEvoy wrote, "*Fota island is not a piece of land, it is a place. It deserves the best. It is mature and should not have a shiny modern course imposed upon it*".

The American publication **Golf Digest**, couldn't agree more. "*For a breath of true golfing air, Fota Island, just outside Cork in Ireland, is the very place. Here the run up shot is given due regard. Almost every green invites more than one approach. Depending upon how you 'see' the shot in your mind, you could be playing any one of three different clubs. In other words it makes you think. It's real golf.*"

Golf Digest continues, "*Fota eschews Schwarzenegger-like brutality in favour of guile and subtlety*". This was achieved by the use of slopes and the positioning of hazards to dissuade the golfer from trying to overpower the course. Peter McEvoy explains. "*All too often nowadays golfers missing a green will end up in water or a bunker. At Fota, we have created many grassy hollows, dips and mounds to try to keep or even bring back pitching and chipping. A good course should test all these skills.*"

Fota's traditional approach means a ball can be played through the air and along the ground. The links-style "bump and run" is often called for. Holes like the 2nd, 4th, 9th & 15th use slopes and hazards to discourage golfers trying to overpower the course through the air. "Not that it's easy", say **Golf Digest**, "*You can still compile a sizeable score, it. just happens more gradually*".

The signature hole at Fota is undoubtedly the 18th - a par 5 which barely measures 500 yards. The tee shot must be threaded between a belt of woodland on the right and a copse of beech trees on the left. A long straight drive leaves the green exposed but not defenceless. The second shot provides ample food for thought with a cluster of pot bunkers and a green surrounded by water. It is a hole where bold play can produce a 3 or a 7.

The 10th hole, "Fuchsia Hill", is another par 5 that winds its way down a hill to a green defended by water. It is a thinking man's hole. An iron off the tee and another off the fairway should normally produce regulation figures. Those wishing to challenge the hole can ruin a scorecard here.

Water also comes into play on three of the par threes, while the four pars are all strong holes - with the short 6th being the most memorable. It is small wonder, then, that Fota hosted no fewer than three **Irish Amateur Opens** plus the 1997 **Irish PGA Championship**. Fota Island will also be home to the 2001 and 2002 **Muphy's Irish Open**.

Fota Island Golf Club
Fota Island, Carrigtwohill,
County Cork, Ireland
Tel: (00 353 21) 4883700 Fax: (00 353 21) 4532047
e mail: reservations@fotaisland.ie
web site: www.fotaisland.com

Lahinch

On the rugged coast of County Clare, two miles from the spectacular Cliffs of Moher lies the 'St Andrews of Ireland'.

In 1892, officers of the famous Black Watch Regiment stationed in Limerick discovered a vast wilderness of duneland. Being good Scotsmen, they knew at once that this was the perfect terrain for a golf links. On Good Friday 1893, Lahinch was duly founded. The obvious choice of person to design the course was 'Old' Tom Morris of St Andrews. Tom accepted but then other than laying out the tees and greens, he felt there was little he could do. He said: 'I consider the links is as fine a natural course as it has ever been my good fortune to play over'. More praise was to follow. During 1928, Dr. Alister Mackenzie was invited to make a number of adjustments to the links. On completion he suggested that 'Lahinch will make the finest and most popular course that I, or I believe anyone else, ever constructed'. Not perhaps the most modest statement ever made but coming from a man who would very shortly design Cypress Point and later help to to create the legendary Augusta, it can hardly be taken lightly.

Visitors wishing to play at Lahinch will find the Club extremely welcoming. The only restrictions are as follows: Monday to Friday between 9.00am and 10.00am and 12.00 to 1.30pm and at weekends between 8.00am and 11.00am and 12.30pm to 2.00pm. The **Secretary** is **Mr Alan Reardon**, who can be contacted on **tel: (065) 708 1003** or by **fax: on (065) 708 1592**. The **Professional, Robert McCavery**, can be reached on **tel: (065) 708 1408**.

Since Dr Mackenzie's alterations, there have been two 18 hole courses: the championship **Old Course** and the shorter **Castle Course**, the latter having been extended from nine holes to eighteen in 1975. Green fees in 2000 to play on the **Old** Course are set at £60 per round, £70 per day between April and September, with a reduced rate of £45 per round for midweek golf between January and March and in November and December. Green fees on the **Castle** Course were £30 per round, £40 per day during summer and £20 per round in winter. Golfing societies are equally welcome and bookings can be made for any day other than Sunday.

Travellers coming from Britain (or indeed Europe and America) should find Lahinch more accessible than any of the great links of Co Kerry. International flights to Shannon are frequent and Lahinch is located approximately thirty miles to the north west of the airport. On leaving Shannon, Ennis is the town to head for, and thereafter, Ennistimon, just two miles from Lahinch. The road passes through some marvellous countryside, and incidentally, do try to visit the Cliffs of Moher—in places they rise to a sheer drop of over six hundred feet, the highest in Europe. Golfers on a west of Ireland pilgrimage approaching from Ballybunion should cross the Shannon via the Tarbert Ferry. It leaves every 30 minutes—on the hour and at half past.

The Old Course at Lahinch is not as tough as the courses at Portmarnock or a Waterville. It doesn't have the length for a start, but then again it's anything but straightforward. The golfer who enjoys the challenge of Ballybunion will fall in love with Lahinch. The seascapes are just as dramatic and the fairways twist and tumble in a similar fashion. A premium is placed on accurate tee shots and the slightest straying will put you amongst the dunes. Many greens sit on natural plateaux and can be tricky to hold. It isn't easy to select the best holes, for so many are memorable, but perhaps the finest sequence is found between the 7th and 10th—four really tremendous par fours.

The most famous holes, however, are undoubtedly the 5th and 6th, both of which Mackenzie was forbidden to touch. Having won four Open Championships at Prestwick, 'Old Tom' clearly relished the blind shot and this is what is called for at both the 5th (Klondyke) and the 6th (Dell). Not too many quibble with the 5th—it is a par five, although the blind second shot is over a prodigious sandhill and the green is a further two hundred yards on. The 6th however, is a par three! The green nestles between two steep sand dunes and all the player sees from the tee is a white marker-stone placed on the fronting hill to indicate the current pin position—'hit and hope' perhaps, but charming all the same.

The par 70 Castle Course is literally over the road from the Old and occupies much more level ground. The fairways wind their way around the remains of O'Brien's Castle. It presents an attractive, if slightly less demanding challenge, and some £300,000 has recently been spent on upgrading the course.

The clubhouse at Lahinch is marvellously intimate and certainly an excellent place to adjourn should the heavens open. And you'll have ample warning of the impending doom for legend has it that the goats that graze on the dunes will always make an early retreat towards the shelter of the 19th. A bit of Irish mist? Try telling that to the members!

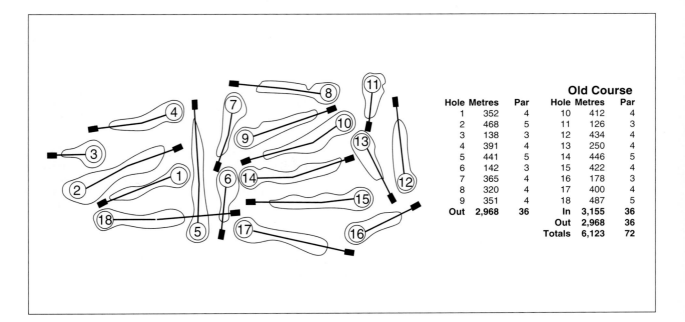

Old Course

Hole	Metres	Par	Hole	Metres	Par
1	352	4	10	412	4
2	468	5	11	126	3
3	138	3	12	434	4
4	391	4	13	250	4
5	441	5	14	446	5
6	142	3	15	422	4
7	365	4	16	178	3
8	320	4	17	400	4
9	351	4	18	487	5
Out	2,968	36	In	3,155	36
			Out	2,968	36
			Totals	6,123	72

Carleton Resort is Located in Youghal, East Cork, only 35 minutes drive form Cork airport, 1 hour and 45 minutes from Rosslare Ferry Port and three and a half hours from Dublin.

Carleton Wharf is situated immediately adjacent to Youghal 18 hole golf course and is also in close proximity to over 20 of the finest championship golf courses in the South of Ireland and is the ideal accommodation destination for the golf enthusiast. It introduces an entirely new experience in Luxury self catering accommodation with the golfer particularly in mind.

Should you wish to book tee times, the staff are very familiar with all the golf clubs in the area and are very willing to arrange special golf packages for all guests. The range of golf courses in the area include, Fota Island, Old Head of Kinsale, Mount Juliet, West Waterford, Cork Golf Club, Harbour Point, East Cork, Lismore and Fermoy all of which are within one hours drive of the Carleton Resort.

Carleton Village is a spectacular 20 acre site with historic walled garden, overlooking Youghal Bay, with spectacular ocean views. The village has a range of four star villas and apartments to rent, on a weekly, weekend or mid week basis. All the main bathrooms have a Jacuzzi and all guests have direct access to ISDN lines.

Located on the sea front and a short distance from Carleton Village is Carleton Wharf which comprises 54 four star apartments ranging from a choice of two or three bedroomed apartments sleeping from four to six people. All have fully fitted kitchen, satellite TV, direct dial telephone and all have either a private balcony or patio.

Carleton Resort have numerous facilities available including the following, reception, Laundry facilities, the Famous Moll Goggins Bar and recently opened "The Dinning Room" restaurant. There is also a wine bar and a late night club bar on site.

Carleton Resort has a state of the art conference room which has a seating capacity of 100 people available. Special rates available to include accommodation and dinning facilities. By early 2001 Carleton Resort will also boast the opening of a state of the art leisure Centre with fully equipped gym and health studio, an indoor heated swimming pool and tennis courts.

Carleton Resort
Youghal
Co Cork
Ireland
Tel: 00 353 24 90044
Fax: 00 353 24 90045
e maiL: Bookings@carletonyoughal.com
web site: http://www.carletonyoughal.com

Ballybunion

Ballybunion is a place of true pilgrimage. To golfers this is where gold has been struck, not once, but twice with two of the greatest golf courses in the world lying side by side. The Old Course at Ballybunion has long been regarded as the ultimate test in links golf. It lies in a remote corner of County Kerry close to the Shannon estuary amid the largest sandhills in the British Isles. It has a very wild beauty—no course could be closer to the sea and a number of the holes run right along the cliff edges. It's incredibly spectacular stuff and when the wind lashes in from the Atlantic, it is not a place for faint hearts.

The **Old** Course was begun in 1896, although a full eighteen holes were not completed until thirty years later. The renowned American writer Herbert Warren Wind said of the creation: 'It is the finest seaside course I have ever seen'. When Tom Watson first visited in 1981 (and he has returned many times since), he instantly supported Wind's contention and went on to tell the members as much in a personal letter of thanks to the club. What then of the New Course (now known as the **Cashen** Course) constructed in the mid 1980s? Architect Robert Trent Jones had this to say: 'When I first saw the piece of land chosen for the new course at Ballybunion, I was thrilled beyond words. I said it was the finest piece of links land I had ever seen. I feel totally confident that everyone who comes to play at Ballybunion will be as thrilled as I was by the unique majesty of this truly unforgettable course'.

Happily, Ballybunion isn't jealous of its treasures and visitors are always made to feel welcome. The **Golf Manager** at Ballybunion is **Jim McKenna**. He can be contacted on **tel: (068) 27146** or by **fax: (068) 27387**. The code from the UK is (00 353 68). The **Professional** at Ballybunion, **Brian O'Callaghan**, can also be reached on the above number. A full day's green fee in 2000 is priced at £80. This entitles the visitor to a round over both the Old and the Cashen—not of course compulsory, but if the body can take it (and it's likely to receive a fair battering en route) it would be a tragedy not to play the pair. A single round over the Old Course is priced at £60 in 2000 with £35 payable for 18 holes on the Cashen.

Helped by the lavish praise of Messrs Watson and Co, Ballybunion has become a lot busier in recent years and visitors should book some time in advance of intended play. Weekdays are naturally the easiest times for a visit and Sundays should be avoided if a game on the Old Course is sought.

The nearest airports to Ballybunion are at Shannon, a distance of approximately sixty miles to the north east, and the new Kerry Airport at Farranfore, some thirty miles due south. Cork's airport is about eighty miles to the south east. From either Cork or Shannon the journey can take about an hour and a half but there cannot be a soul on earth who wouldn't enjoy a trek through the south west of Ireland. From Shannon, travel via Limerick and from Cork via Mallow and Listowel. From Ballybunion town the course is about a mile's drive along the coast.

There is certainly no shortage of land at Ballybunion and, if necessary, both courses could be stretched to 7000 yards—an alarming prospect! From the medal tees the two are of fairly similar length, the Old measuring 6503 yards, par 71, the Cashen 6477 yards, par 72. But don't be fooled by the scorecard—each is a monster when the mood takes it.

The truly great holes on the Old Course begin at the 6th which has a frighteningly narrow entrance to a plateau green. The 7th fairway runs its entire length along the shore—one of the most spectacular par fours one is likely to play. The 8th is a shortish downhill par three, but if you miss the green you can be in serious trouble. And so it continues with the 11th being perhaps the most famous hole on the course. The sight from the tee is intimidating to put it mildly—the Atlantic waves are beneath you to the right, with some enormous sand dunes to the left. The fairway drops in tiers until it finally culminates on a windswept plateau green overlooking the ocean. It is unquestionably one of the greatest two-shot holes anywhere in the world.

The Cashen Course is arguably more dramatic! The sand hills are even more massive, and some of the carries required from the tee are prodigious. Some people rate the course on a par with the Old. Most critics don't agree, although it certainly includes some magnificent holes.

The 19th at Ballybunion, a brand new clubhouse opened by Tom Watson in 1993, is a grand place for recuperation. It is conveniently situated midway between nature's two masterpieces. Nowhere are stories swapped so enthusiastically and perhaps nowhere will you hear so often the phrase, 'Just wait until next time!' Gold diggers them all.

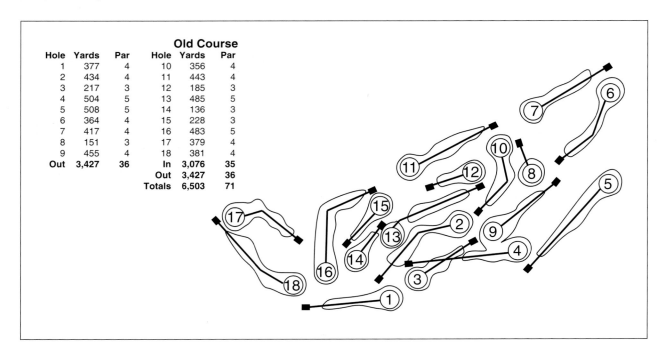

Old Course

Hole	Yards	Par	Hole	Yards	Par
1	377	4	10	356	4
2	434	4	11	443	4
3	217	3	12	185	3
4	504	5	13	485	5
5	508	5	14	136	3
6	364	4	15	228	3
7	417	4	16	483	5
8	151	3	17	379	4
9	455	4	18	381	4
Out	**3,427**	**36**	**In**	**3,076**	**35**
			Out	**3,427**	**36**
			Totals	**6,503**	**71**

Some of the best golf in the world is to be found in south west Ireland and golfers looking for accommodation to match are cordially invited to sample the hospitality and service provided Glin Castle. Ideal for the celebrated links at Ballybunion and the great courses of Killarney, Tralee and Lahinch. Glin castle stands proudly in its wooden demesne on the banks of the River Shannon. Golfers taking advantage of the special tailormade breaks of three days can expect nothing less than a warm welcome in the finest of Irish traditions as house guests in the home of the 29th Knight of Glin and Madam Fitzgerald.

The present Castle, which succeeds the medieval ruin in the village of Glin, was built in the late 18th century with entertaining in mind. Its toy fortress like quality is echoed by three sets of battlemented Gothic folly lodges, one of which is a restaurant–the Glin Castle Gate Shop. The entrance hall with its Corinthian pillars has a superb neo-classical ceiling. A series of reception rooms are filled with a unique collection of Irish 18th century furniture. Family portraits and Irish pictures line the walls and the library bookcase has a secret door leading to the hall and a very rare flying staircase.

The dining room windows catch the setting sun reflected in the river whilst inside, the room is filled with baronial oak furniture. Across the

hall in the drawing room there is an Adam style ceiling and a matching inlaid Bossi chimney piece. Here frequently after-dinner coffee and conversation takes place.

After a stroll in the well kept grounds, the sitting room with its crackling fire makes a cosy gathering place for drinks. The cuisine is good country house cooking with fresh fruit, vegetables and fresh meat from the local butcher.

There are a variety of rooms available within Glin Castle, each with its own special appeal, including a four poster. The rooms are scattered with rugs and chaises longues and the walls are hung with interesting paintings and plates.

The Castle makes an ideal base for exploring the surrounding countryside and there is a hard tennis court in the walled garden.

Also close by is Foynes sailing club, whilst it is possible to hunt with the Limerick hounds at Adare. The countryside is breathtaking making it ideal for touring and there are important historical sights such as Lough Gur, Adare and many fascinating ruined castles and country houses.

Glin Castle
Glin
Great Limerick
Ireland
Tel: (00 353 68) 34173/34112
Fax: (00 353 68) 34364
e mial: knight@iol.ie

Waterville

How often have you read, or heard it said that 'Waterville is for the Big Man?' Given that Waterville is very much in the land of the Little People this sounds terribly exclusive. Wot, no Irishmen? Unlike Ballybunion, the name of the place sounds rather Anglo-French but the major influence has undoubtedly been American. In fact, modern Waterville is very much the result of an American dream.

Oddly it was an Anglo-American fisherman who first 'discovered' Waterville. Not your average fisherman, but one Charles Chaplin who regularly came here after the war to escape the clutches of stardom. In Waterville he found total peace (as well as some marvellous fishing).

The man we have to thank for creating the golfing majesty that is Waterville Links is an Irish-American, John A Mulcahy. Like all the others who had explored this part of the world he fell in love with the area, and like Castlerosse of Killarney fame he was both wealthy and loved the game of golf. In the early seventies Mulcahy talked to leading Irish course designer Eddie Hackett—and the rest is history.

Immediately Mulcahy's Waterville opened for play, it was showered with the highest praise. People like Henry Cotton, Sam Snead, Gary Player, Tom Watson and Ray Floyd have since been and marvelled at the creation, the last named in particular who thought it, 'the finest links I have ever played'.

Today, more and more people are 'discovering' Waterville, although at most times the links is still relatively and wonderfully uncrowded. The reason for this is its remoteness. Waterville is 50 miles from Killarney and the nearest airport is at Farranfore—by car a journey time of approximately one and a half hours. The international airports at Cork and Shannon are 100 and 115 miles away respectively. But what a journey it is! The direct route from all points is via Killarney, and Killarney is the starting point for the Ring of Kerry, one of the most scenic roads in the world. Whether the approach to Waterville is 'along the top' via Killorglin and Cahiraveen (this is the quicker but less dramatic route) or 'along the bottom' via Kenmare and Parknasilla, much of the Ring of Kerry will be taken in. Nobody in their right minds could arrive at Waterville uninspired and surely nobody will leave on anything less than a high.

In 2000 the green fee at Waterville is set at £75 per round, seven days per week, but with a special rate of £40 for those teeing off before 8.00 am from Monday to Thursday. Second rounds are available on request. Tee times can be guaranteed by making an advance booking with the office. In this instance a 25 per cent deposit is payable one month in advance of the date of playing. The **Secretary/Manager** at Waterville is **Noel Cronin**. He can be contacted by on tel: **(066) 9474102** and by fax: **(066) 9474482**. From the UK the code is (00 353) 66. The club's **Professional, Liam Higgins** can be reached on tel: **(066) 9474102**.

The danger of encouraging the description of a golf course as being 'for the big man' is that it risks putting off anyone who cannot thump a ball 300 yards. Naturally it is an advantage to be able to hit the ball like Liam Higgins, who once holed in one at the 16th—all 350 yards of it—but if you've got a twitchy short game, you are still going to be struggling, and besides, how often are you going to be asked to play Waterville from the championship tees? From the forward tees Waterville is no more or less frightening than the other great links courses of Ireland, and Waterville is certainly as enjoyable.

Although there are many good holes on the front nine, that quickly introduces the player to the complexity and beauty of links golf, it is the back nine at Waterville that everyone raves about. In golfing terms, this is life in the fast lane. The dunes are high and the fairways tumble. There are some spectacular carries and magnificent vantage points and three holes that are widely regarded as being world class—I refer to the 11th, 12th and 17th.

The 12th and 17th are both longish, short holes. On both the tee shot must be carried over a sea of dunes and at the 12th, the 'Mass Hole', over a gaping gully as well. If the 12th tee is elevated then the 17th must be on a mini-mountain. In fact it is on 'Mulcahy's Peak', a purpose-built tower of a tee from which there is a superb view, not just down to the elusive green but across the entire links.

The 11th, 'Tranquillity' is rated by many to be one of the greatest par fives in the world. The fairway winds its entire length beneath sand dunes that are reminiscent of Ballybunion or Birkdale. It is possible to reach the green in two, for much of the last eighty yards or so is downhill, but only if the drive has been perfectly positioned.

Great champions continue to find their way to Waterville–Els, Furyk, O'Meara, Stewart and Woods to prepare for the 1998 British Open which was then won by Mark O'Meara. Prior to the 1999 Open O'Meara, Stewart and Woods were joined by Appleby, Duval and Jansen, all of whom became members of Waterville. Later that year at a ceremony during the now famous Ryder Cup in Brookline Massachuttes, United States team member Payne Stewart accepted Honorary Captaincy of Waterville for the year 2000–the last golf honour he would receive before his tragic death. The Waterville Golf Club applauds his life and his friendship with a life sized bronze statue, dedicated by his family and friends, overlooks all of Waterville. Truly a mystical links in the Kingdom of Kerry.

Venue for the World Invitational Father & Son Golf Tournament (1990 - 2000)

Hole	Yards	Par	Hole	Yards	Par
1	430	4	10	475	4
2	469	4	11	506	5
3	417	4	12	200	3
4	179	3	13	518	5
5	595	5	14	456	4
6	387	4	15	407	4
7	178	3	16	350	4
8	435	4	17	196	3
9	445	4	18	582	5
Out	3,535	35	In	3,690	37
			Out	3,535	35
			Totals	7,225	72

Geographically speaking, Waterville is something of an Irish Dornoch. No-one could pretend that it is anything but remote, but then who would really want it to be anything else? With remoteness comes the peace of a lost world; with remoteness comes charm.

Waterville sits at the far end of the Ring of Kerry. West of Waterville there is nothing for 2000 miles, save the Atlantic Ocean, while completing the circle to the North, South and East are brooding mountains, majestic lakes, soft hills and babbling streams.

It may surprise some to learn that golf has been played at Waterville from at least the early 1880s. Initially it was by those gallant and indomitable men who laid the trans-Atlantic cable, so bringing the New World close to the old. The land that these pioneering golfers played over was classic, sandy links terrain—greatly exposed to the elements, but neatly maintained by the local sheep.

Until the late 1960s Waterville was largely its own best-kept secret. About this time a second team of golfing pioneers led by the visionary Irish-American Jack Mulcahy, architect Eddie Hackett, and Master Champion Claude Harmon determined that Waterville links should realise its full potential. 'Determined' is the word for in a few short years they, to adopt the words of leading Irish golf writer Pat Ruddy, 'transformed Waterville from a cosy localised scale to the pinnacles of world class'.

In the 25 years since 'modern' Waterville Links opened for play it has been showered with praise—but there is more to Waterville than spectacular golf. For one thing the 19th hole is one of the most comfortable clubhouses in Ireland and for lovers of golfing art and memorabilia it is a genuine treasure trove. And then there is Waterville House, the Irish residence of the owners of Waterville Links and a temporary home to guests who enjoy an intimate and timeless country house ambience.

Built in the late 18th century and recently refurbished, Waterville House presides serenely on the shores of Ballinskelligs Bay. It has ten bedrooms all overlooking the pure waters of Butler's Pool (a favourite old fishing haunt of Charlie Chaplin) the wider seascapes and landscapes of the Atlantic and the magnificent, untouched countryside. In addition to the warm hospitality and fine cuisine (note the hearty Irish breakfast!) Waterville House offers its guests a heated pool, sauna, steam room, snooker and billiard room and golf practice facilities including a putting green.

Great champions have always played Waterville: Els, Furyk, O'Meara, Stewart and Woods visited to prepare for the 1998 British Open. Could it be mere coincidence that three of the top four finishers were in this group? Waterville - a mystical links in the Kingdom of Kerry.

Waterville House & Golf Links
Waterville
Co. Kerry Ireland
Tel: (00 353 66) 9474102
Fax: (00 353 66) 9474482
E mail: wvgolf@iol.ie
web site: www.watervillegolf.com

Killarney

Killarney is often described as 'paradise on earth', and not merely by we blasphemous golfers. This is Ireland's most famous beauty spot; somehow the lakes here seem a deeper and clearer blue and the mountains a more delicate shade of purple. It is a place where even the most miserable of wretches would be forced to smile.

The three golf courses of the Killarney Golf and Fishing Club take full advantage of the majestic surroundings. A Gleneagles afloat perhaps? Not really. The golf at Killarney is parkland rather than heathland or moorland, but it can generate a similar degree of pleasure and, like Gleneagles, can be a welcome retreat from the tremendously testing links courses nearby. A place to soothe one's damaged pride.

Killarney has lived through a somewhat chequered history. Golf has been played here since the late 19th century. The first course was nothing grand, laid out in an old deer park owned by the Earl of Kenmare. However, in 1936 the Earl's very keen golfing heir, and a great character of his time, Lord Castlerosse, decided that Killarney deserved a course that would reflect the glorious setting. Eighteen holes were laid out by Sir Guy Campbell and the new course opened in 1939. Castlerosse, who had played a very active role in the design, was pleased with the creation but continued to suggest imaginative improvements, unfortunately, not all of which were carried through following his untimely death in 1943. In the 1970s a second eighteen holes were built and the two present courses, **Mahony's Point** and **Killeen** are each a combination of the old holes and the new. Basking beside the shores of Lough Leane and encircled by the splendour of the Macgillicuddy Reeks and the Carrauntoohill Mountains, Killarney really is a golfer's dream.

This dream was further enhanced in 1999 when the club opens its third championship course. Designed by Donald Steel, the new Lackabane Course will measure 6450 metres from the championship tees.

The present **Secretary** at Killarney is the affable **Tom Prendergast**, who may be contacted on **tel: (064) 31034 fax: (064) 33065** (from the UK 00 353 64) 31034). Any written correspondence should be addressed to **The Secretary, Killarney Golf and Fishing Club, O'Mahony's Point, Killarney, Co. Kerry, Ireland**. The club's **Professional, Tony Coveney** can be reached on **tel: (064) 31615**. As seems to be the case with all of Ireland's great courses, visitors are warmly greeted—and they come from every foreseeable golfing

country! There are no specific restrictions on playing during the week, although some do exist at the weekend, so it's always a good idea to telephone the club before making any firm arrangements. The green fees in 2000 at Killarney are £43 per round - on either course - seven days per week. Handicap certificates are required for both courses.

Killarney is the most accessible of Kerry's golfing delights, the town being linked to both Limerick (70 miles) and Cork (60 miles) by major road. The nearest airport is at Farranfore (Kerry Airport). The golf club lies about three miles west of the town off the N72 Killorglin Road and is well signposted. Those staying in the area might note that Killarney is the starting point of the famous one hundred mile Ring of Kerry road, which takes in surely some of the most marvellous scenery to be enjoyed anywhere in the world.

In such a setting, inspired golf is clearly on the cards (or so one hopes!) Mahony's Point is still probably the better known of the two courses, largely on account of its spectacular finishing holes, although in 1991 and 1992 it was the Killeen Course that hosted the Carrolls Irish Open, and on both occasions victory went to Nick Faldo. The Killeen also staged the 1996 Curtis Cup match, won by Great Britain and Ireland. It is in fact the longer of the two courses, measuring 6474 metres, par 72, compared with Mahony's Point, which measures 6164 metres, par 72.

Among the better holes on the Killeen Course are the dog-legged 1st, which follows the curve of Lough Leane's shore, the stunning par three 3rd, also alongside the water's edge and the exacting 13th—one of Castlerosse's favourites from the Campbell layout—a long par four which has a stream crossing the fairway to catch the mishit second.

On the Mahony's Point Course the celebrated finish begins at the par five 16th where the course returns toward Lough Leane. The 18th is the hole everyone remembers. It's a par three, which is fairly unusual at the end of a round, and the tee shot is played directly across the edge of the lake, practically all carry. Rhododendron bushes and pine trees frame the green: very beautiful, yet potentially very treacherous. 'The best short hole in the world', enthused Henry Longhurst. He also suggested that it might be a fitting place to end one's days. I can think of many worse places than the 18th green on Mahony's Point, but to pass over the club's magnificently appointed 19th hole would be at best

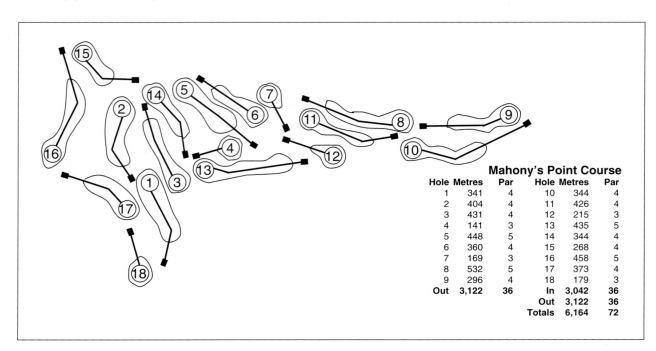

Mahony's Point Course

Hole	Metres	Par	Hole	Metres	Par
1	341	4	10	344	4
2	404	4	11	426	4
3	431	4	12	215	3
4	141	3	13	435	5
5	448	5	14	344	4
6	360	4	15	268	4
7	169	3	16	458	5
8	532	5	17	373	4
9	296	4	18	179	3
Out	**3,122**	**36**	**In**	**3,042**	**36**
			Out	**3,122**	**36**
			Totals	**6,164**	**72**

A warm friendly welcome awaits you at the International Hotel. Established almost 100 years ago, this beautiful hotel has been brought into the 21st century with a carefully planned refurbishment programme over the past few years, yet it still retains all the charm and elegance of those bygone days. The International Hotel is one of Killarney's most prominent and centrally situated hotels, it provides the perfect base for touring, shopping, and entertainment.

All bedrooms are en-suite and have all the comforts and features you would expect from a three star hotel. The restaurant and grill bar offer very good food, using only the freshest local produce, superbly cooked and served in a truly relaxing atmosphere.

Killarney is the perfect place for a golfing break. It offers visitors the finest facilities for golf with the renowned Killarney Golf & Fishing Club only five minutes from the hotel. Other courses in this golfing haven include Ballybunnion, Waterville and Tralee, indeed five of Kerry's golf courses are featured in the list of 'Ireland's 30 Greatest Golf Courses'. In fact there are seven championship courses to choose from within 50 miles. Tee times can be arranged through the hotel at various courses in the area with both large and small groups catered for.

Killarney also has a fine fishing reputation in the lakes and rivers around the area, you can also enjoy all sorts of other activities that take place in the 25,000 acre National Park at Muckross.

There is so much to see and do in Killarney, and what better place to base yourself than the charming International Hotel, for a warm welcome and truly relaxing stay.

International Hotel
Killarney
Co Kerry
Ireland
Tel: (00 353) 64 31816
Fax: (00 353) 64 31837
e mail: inter@iol.ie
website: www.killarney-inter.com

Adare

If you are the world's most famous golf course architect you can afford to be choosy. If there is one place in Ireland (perhaps on earth) where you would seek to build a links course, it is amidst the sandhills of Ballybunion. And if there is one place in Ireland (above all others) where you might wish to design a parkland course, where else than in the grounds of Adare Manor? The incomparable Robert Trent Jones and the incomparable Adare Manor—a golf match made in heaven.

Just as the great man was mesmerised when he first saw the linksland at Ballybunion, so he couldn't help but be charmed when he first set eyes on Adare Manor. Only Ashford Castle has an equal capacity to bewitch the first time visitor. Adare Manor has both beauty and history. For a century and a half it was the ancestral home of the Earls of Dunraven, one of the great families of Ireland. In recent times it has established a reputation as one of the world's finest hotels. Today it has a Robert Trent Jones designed championship golf course.

Actually, it didn't need a genius to spot the golfing potential of Adare Manor. (Merely one to bring it to fruition!) The site has many natural advantages. The River Maigue flows, and occasionally meanders, through the heart of the estate. From giant oaks, beech trees and ash to glorious cedars and towering pines, few estates in Ireland have such a wealth and mix of splendid mature trees. Then there are the romantic ruins of an Augustinian abbey (built in 1313) and a Franciscan friary (1464). The Earls of Dunraven left a wonderful legacy—and it is one that all golfers (hotel residents and non-residents alike) can now experience.

The course opened for play in August 1995. The 2000 green fees are £45 per round, £65 per day for residents and £50 per round, £75 per day for non-residents. All golf enquiries should be directed to the **Director of Golf, Brian Shaw** on **tel: (061) 395044** and by **fax: (061) 396987**. From outside Ireland the code is (00 353) 61.

A theme that distinguishes many of the best golf courses in the world is the way the level of drama increases as the round progresses. The challenge doesn't necessarily become any greater but subtley gradually surrenders to drama. When you walk from the 10th green on the Old Links at Ballybunion your heart begins to pound—especially when you peer down the 11th fairway!

The inland equivalent to this sensation occurs when you stand on the tee of the par three 11th at Adare. Already several very good holes have been played. The par five 7th, where the fairway curves tantalisingly around the edge of a lake, couldn't be described as anything less than spectacular, but equally strong are some of the more subtle par four holes, notably the 2nd, 5th, 8th and 10th. Also by this time the famous Trent Jones jigsaw-shaped bunkers and the magnificently contoured greens may have exacted their toll.

. . . So you are standing on the 11th tee at Adare—heart pounding. Only a perfectly struck iron will find the putting surface, which is surrounded by traps and set at an angle on the 'wrong side' of the River Maigue. Assuming you survive this watery duel, the fairway at the 12th charges uphill then sweeps down to the left towards a sea of sand and a green backed by beautiful trees. The 13th carves a path through an extraordinary avenue of woodland, the 14th heads out towards the ruined abbey and the 15th turns back in the direction of the manor. Accompanying the 15th for its entire length is the River Maigue—a slicer's nightmare. The 16th is a stunning par three played directly beside the manor across a lake. It is modelled on the famous 4th at Baltusrol and in terms of fear-inducement is somewhat reminiscent of the 17th at Kiawah Island. Adare's 17th journeys back through the woods and then comes the classic and yes, dramatic, par five 18th. Trent Jones regards it as possibly the greatest finishing hole in golf. Perhaps he is a little biased, but for sheer panache it is hard to beat.

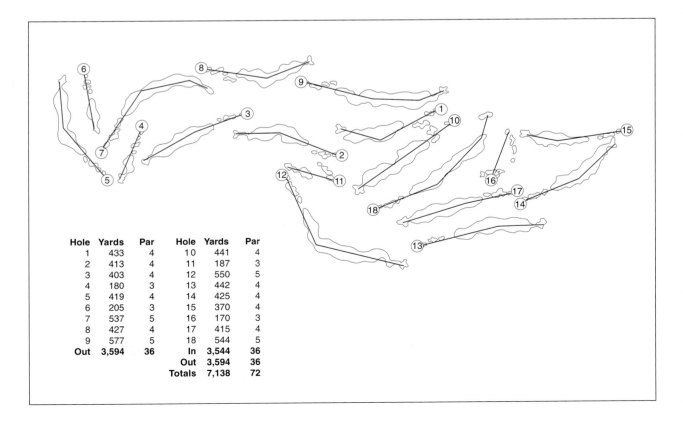

Hole	Yards	Par	Hole	Yards	Par
1	433	4	10	441	4
2	413	4	11	187	3
3	403	4	12	550	5
4	180	3	13	442	4
5	419	4	14	425	4
6	205	3	15	370	4
7	537	5	16	170	3
8	427	4	17	415	4
9	577	5	18	544	5
Out	**3,594**	**36**	**In**	**3,544**	**36**
			Out	**3,594**	**36**
			Totals	**7,138**	**72**

Adare Manor, an RAC five star hotel, is located 22 miles from Shannon airport in the picturesque village of Adare, Co. Limerick. Home for the past two centuries to the Earls of Dunraven, Adare Manor has been lovingly transformed into a world class hotel with 63 luxury bedrooms.

Adare Manor Hotel is an architectural masterpiece of towers, turrets and stonework, with full leisure facilities including an indoor heated swimming pool, fitness centre, sauna, horse riding, fishing and clay pigeon shooting.

The restaurant is famed for its wonderful European food with an Irish influence. From its windows one can view the parterre gardens and the golf course. The famous long gallery is modelled on the Hall of Versailles and will seat over 200 for gala dinners.

The 18 hole championship course was designed by one of the most respected and best known golf course architects in the world, Robert Trent Jones, Sr.

The course, constructed to world class championship standards, stretches over 230 acres of the 840 acre Adare estate. A 14 acre lake, one of three around the course, dominate the front nine hole, whilst the River Maigue meandering through the back nine creates a sense of beauty and challenge, particularly on the 18th hole, which Mr Jones foresees as one of the finest finishing par 5 holes in the world.

Each hole has four tees, built to greens specification, with a championship yardage of 7138. The Adare Golf Club has an exquisite parkland atmosphere with a magnificent variety of trees.

Adare Manor Hotel & Golf Club
Adare
Co Limerick
Ireland
Tel: (00 353 61) 396566 Golf 395044
Fax: (00 353 61) 396124 Golf 396987
USA toll free reservations: 800 462 3273 (800-Go Adare)

Originally built in 1838 as Archdeacon Nathaniel P. Forester's rectory, Killeen House was entirely renovated in 1990-91 and in 1992 Michael and Geraldine Rosney purchased this fine property. With extensive experience in the hospitality industry, they had no doubts about the attractions the property had to offer. "A charming little hotel" describes the style and character of this unique facility set in 1.5 acres of beautifully manicured gardens. It now enjoys the charm and elegance of the early 19th century hand-in-hand with the comfort and convenience at the 21st Century.

The hotel has recently undergone a major renovation programme and now comprises 23 en suite bedrooms (8 of which are 'deluxe' Championship Rooms), an award winning restaurant and a small Pub which, for some weird reason, has around 8000 golf balls stuck on its walls!

With golf in mind, Killeen House Hotel is just 10 minutes drive from the centre of Killarney and only 5 minutes from Killeen and Mahoney's Point golf courses. History is unclear as to whether Conrad Hilton had Aghadoe in mind when he declared the three most important criteria for any hotel - Location, Location, Location!

The Southwestern coast of Ireland has been blessed with some of the finest Links and Parkland Courses that are to be found anywhere in the World. When you get the likes of Tiger Woods, Ernie Els, Mark O'Meara, and even Bill Clinton coming over to play our courses you know some of the best courses are right on the hotel's doorstep. Simply put, if there were no such thing as golf, there would be no such place as the Killeen House Hotel. They eat it, sleep it, drink it. So for the travelling golfer a more welcoming retreat you would be hard pushed to find.

Killeen House
Aghadoe
Killarney
Co. Kerry
Tel: (00 353) 64 31711
Fax: (00 353) 64 31811
e mail: charming@indigo.ie
web site: www.killeenhousehotel.com

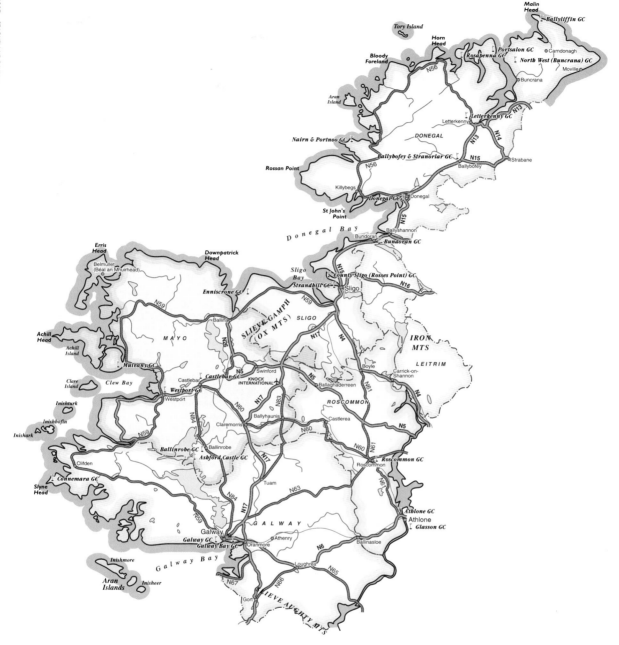

Without any shadow of doubt some of the greatest golf courses in the world are to be found in the south west of Ireland. But as any Irishman worth his Guinness will tell you, great golf in the west of Ireland certainly isn't confined to the south western corner—it starts from County Donegal downwards. Apart from its magnificent golf, the south west is renowned for its beautiful scenery: majestic Killarney, the glorious Ring of Kerry and the Dingle Peninsula—stunning for sure but further north can be equally spectacular. This is what W M Thackeray had to say of the area around Westport: 'It forms an event in one's life to have seen the place, so beautiful is it, and so unlike all other beauties that I know of'. Clearly inspired, he continued: 'But the Bay—and the Reek which sweeps down to the sea—and a hundred islands in it, were dressed up in gold and purple and crimson, with the whole cloudy West in a flame'. Marvellous! And have you ever been to Connemara?

Donegal

And have you ever been to Donegal! I don't suppose many golfers are likely to begin a tour in the very far north and head all the way downwards but we shall have a go all the same. (It is possible I suppose if one were approaching from the Causeway Coast?) Let us start at **Ballyliffin** on the very northern tip of Donegal, not far from Malin Head. Now Ballyliffin is a club we overlooked in the early editions of Following The Fairways. This has now been rectified (see feature ahead). Suffice to say at this juncture that we believe it has the potential to become the 'Dornoch of Ireland'—or even, perhaps, the 'Ballybunion of the North'. Two recommended hotels in Ballyliffin are the Strand Hotel (00 353) 77 76107 and the Ballyliffin Hotel (00 353) 77 76118, while Rossaor House (00 353) 77 76498—with its amazing views—is one of several fine guesthouses.

Rosapenna is our next port of call. Like Ballyliffin it is somewhat isolated, but a fine course nonetheless. It was laid out in 1893 by Old Tom Morris and is part links, part inland in nature. The place has a bleak beauty and the coast is very dramatic—note the spectacular nearby Atlantic Drive. Rosapenna is explored further ahead. The Rosapenna Golf Hotel (00 353) 74 55301 provides a very comfortable and convenient base while those looking for really deluxe accommodation might consider Rathmullan House (00 353) 74 58188 in Rathmullan, a Georgian building with splendid gardens. Not far from Rosapenna there is a magnificently situated course at **Portsalon** and three other Donegal links courses to recommend are Dunfanaghy, **North West (Buncrana)** and **Narin and Portnoo**. Further inland, 18 holes can be played at **Letterkenny** and again at **Ballybofey & Stranorlar** where the Kee's Hotel (00 353) 74 31018 provides a perfect base for exploring the mountains and hills of Donegal.

Donegal town, famed for its tweeds and woollens, has one of the longest courses in Ireland measuring 7200 yards (try playing it in a fierce wind!) The course is actually outside of the county town at Murvagh. A truly great course this and again we explore it on a later page. There are a number of hotels and guesthouses in Donegal and for golfers looking for a lively night there is the Schooner Inn (00 353) 73 21671 on Upper Main Street. More sedate accommodation is to be found at Rossnowlagh, here the splendid Sand House Hotel (00 353) 72 51777 enjoys superb views over Donegal Bay and there is a short 9 hole golf course within the hotel grounds. Other possibilities in Donegal town include the Abbey Hotel (00 353) 73 21014 and the Hyland Central (00 353) 73 22107 while outside the town one finds two really pleasing establishments, St Ernan's House (00 353) 73 21065, which enjoys a delightful wooded setting with views of Donegal Bay or alternatively, Harvey's Point (00 353) 73 22208 with its loughside setting and excellent restaurant. A little south of Rossnowlagh is Bundoran, another tough, though fairly open links. Right in the middle of the course is the Great Northern Hotel (00 353) 72 41204 which has 150 rooms.

The West

Our next visit is a more established favourite. **County Sligo**, or **Rosses Point** as it is commonly known, is rated among the top ten courses in Ireland and is the home of the prestigious West of Ireland Amateur Championship. Laid out right alongside the Atlantic coast, it is a true links and can be greatly affected by the elements. This great course is tackled ahead. County Sligo and surrounds is another charming area of Ireland. It is the country of W B Yeats and the landscape is dominated by the formidable Ben Bulben mountain. An outstanding seafood restaurant is located in Rosses Point—the Moorings (00 353) 71 77112. The Sligo Park Hotel (00 353) 71 60291,

GALWAY BAY GOLF CLUB *Photograph courtesy of:* **Irish Tourist Board (Brian Lynch)**

Ballincar House Hotel (00 353) 71 45361 and the Yeats Country Ryan Hotel (00 353) 71 77211 are all very convenient for the course. To the south of Sligo at Riverstown, Coopershill (00 353) 71 65108 is another fine and extremely welcoming hotel and at Colloney, Markree Castle (00 353) 71 67800 is superb. Rosses Point is marketed alongside **Enniscrone**, **Donegal** and the new **Carne** Golf Club at Belmullet as one of the 'West Coast Links' but there are many other fine golfing challenges in this part of Ireland and a neighbour of Rosses Point is the links at **Strandhill**, adjacent to Sligo airport.

Perhaps the most underrated of the West Coast links is Enniscrone. Laid out on the shores of Killala Bay it is, to quote Peter Dobereiner, 'an undiscovered gem of a links, and it has also recently been upgraded with seven new holes built deep in the dunes.' The best place to stay nearby is the Downhill Hotel (00 353) 96 21033 in Ballina . This hotel is really welcoming and is also convenient for the links at Belmullet. Note also a superb inn on the quay at Ballina, the lively River Boat (00 353) 96 22183.

A short drive from Ballina and we reach **Westport**, Thackeray's paradise. The town nestles in the shadows of the massive Croagh Patrick mountain. It was on its peak that St Patrick is said to have fasted and prayed for 40 days. The golf course (from which there are many marvellous views of Croagh Patrick) is another on the grand scale—7000 yards when fully stretched. It's a relatively new course having been designed by Fred Hawtree in 1973. Although some holes run spectacularly along the shoreline (note particularly the superb par five 15th which curves around Clew Bay) Westport is most definitely a parkland type course and is a very friendly club. The Irish Amateur Championship has been played here twice in recent years.

There is no shortage of good accommodation in Westport and many hotels offer golfing packages. One of the most comfortable hotels in town is the Hotel Westport (00 353) 98 25122 near Westport House, although the Castlecourt Hotel (00 353) 98 25444 is also popular with travel-weary golfers and in nearby Newport, Newport House (00 353) 984 1222 is first class. Also highly commended for those seeking a homely atmosphere in one of Ireland's top inns, Healy's Hotel (00 353) 94 56443. Approximately twenty miles away at Cong stands the redoubtable **Ashford Castle** (00 353) 92 46003 a place fit for a king and possibly the finest hotel in Ireland. Its setting on the edge of Lough Corrib is quite breathtaking; it also boasts a 9 hole golf course within the grounds of the hotel .

Connemara Golf Club (see feature page) is located about 30 miles south of Westport amid very rugged

ROSSES POINT GOLF CLUB *Photograph courtesy of:* **Irish Tourist Board (Brian Lynch)**

CONNEMARA GOLF CLUB *Photograph courtesy of:* **Irish Tourist Board (Brian Lynch)**

On to Galway—a fascinating and lively city. Golfwise, there is the established **Galway** Golf Club at Salthill, and the new **Galway Bay** Golf and Country Club near Oranmore, the creation of Christy O'Connor Jr. This is an idyllic location for a good break - some excellent holiday homes here as well (00 353) 9179 0500. Galway has a number of centrally located hotels including the Great Southern Hotel (00 353) 9156 4041 and Ardilaun House (00 353) 9152 1433. In Spiddal, the Bridge House (00 353) 918 3118 is a cosy inn, and at Oranmore, very convenient for Galway Bay, is the Oranmore Lodge Hotel (00 353) 91 94400. Also convenient is the Glenlo Abbey (00 353) 91 26666, a restored 18th century house and church .

Finally to a part of Ireland perhaps more renowned for its fishing than golf. The Roscommon-Athlone area doesn't have many courses but both **Athlone** Golf Club and **Roscommon** Golf Club are worth exploring and there is also the outstanding **Glasson** Golf & Country Club which is featured ahead, along with Slieve Russell. Among a number of pleasant places to stay we can recommend the Hodson Bay Hotel (00 353) 902 92444 which is surrounded by Athlone golf course itself, the Prince of Wales Hotel (00353) 902 72626, also in Athlone, and the Abbey Hotel (00 353) 903 26240 in Roscommon.

country. It is a wild, remote and incredibly beautiful part of the world. The links course at Ballyconneely must be one of the toughest one is ever likely to meet. Despite the remoteness there are several first class establishments at hand. The best places for a night's stay are the Rock Glen Country House Hotel (00 353) 95 21035, the Ardagh Hotel and Restaurant (00 353) 95 21384 and the Abbeyglen Castle Hotel (00 353) 95 21201. All three are in Clifden and all are good. They need to be—you'll need a medicinal whiskey or two and a good night's sleep before (or after) tackling Connemara. Another superb establishment is found close by in Cashel Bay, the Cashel House Hotel (00 353) 95 31001—a delightful country house with marvellous gardens.

Slieve Russell

The unsuspecting traveller's first impression of the Slieve Russell Hotel is that it must be an incredible mirage. The knowledgeable golfer's lasting impression of Slieve Russell is that it is an extraordinary oasis.

Deep in the countryside of Co Cavan a remarkable new hotel and championship golf course has seemingly 'sprung from nowhere' and now demands to be discovered. Ballyconnell is the place—a small town in a quiet, sleepy part of the world, one much more renowned as a fisherman's paradise than a golfer's—although this would appear set to change. The landscape of this part of Ireland is dominated by numerous lakes, hence all the fishing, and one other rather more unusual feature, drumlins. (Remember them from your geography studies of glacial drift?) These are curvaceous little hills or mounds and they are dotted all over the valleys of west Cavan. So a land of lakes and curvaceous mounds? Clearly Mother Nature intended. . .

Mother Nature aside, the founder and guiding force behind the development of Slieve Russell has been successful local entrepreneur, Sean Quinn. His original concept was for the 18 hole golf course to complement the extensive leisure facilities of a luxury 150 bedroomed hotel. The Slieve Russell Hotel opened its doors in 1990 but sometime before the projected opening date for the golf course (summer 1992) it became apparent that this was to be no typical hotel resort type course. It would not have been hyperbole to suggest that the Slieve Russell construction team, lead by architect Paddy Merrigan, were busy creating a masterpiece.

Slieve Russell is most definitely a parkland golf course although occasionally the extreme contouring—both natural and strategically introduced—produces an almost links type feel. Two large lakes, connected by a wandering stream are the dominant features of the design and are responsible for creating several outstanding and

dramatic holes. Water in fact must be confronted as early as the 2nd, a truly marvellous swinging dog-leg hole where, after trying to avoid the lake to the left of the fairway with the drive, the approach must then be played over the stream to a raised and two tiered green. The severity of the undulations (including some of the putting surfaces!) will be understood by the time the rollercoasting 3rd has been played. Both the 2nd and 3rd are superb par four holes but the quartet of par threes will probably create an even greater impression on the mind of the first time visitor—especially perhaps the 16th, an absolute gem of a short hole, and the amazing par five 13th, where for its entire length the fairway follows the curving edge of the second lake. You stand on the tee at the 13th and the green is straight ahead—the direct route to the flag however requires a water carry of some 400 yards!

Slieve Russell Hotel Golf & Country Club,
Ballyconnell, Co Cavan, Ireland
www.quinn-group.com

Director of Golf	P J Creamer (00 353 49) 952 6444
	Fax (00 353 49) 952 6640
Green Fees	Resident Sun-Fri £22; Sat £28
	Non resident Sun-Fri £32; Sat £40
	Above prices per round.
Restrictions	Bookings preferred.

Directions
Take the N3 from Dublin, leaving on the R200 for

Ballyliffin

Picture this—365 acres of spectacular duneland surrounded by curvaceous hills and mountains. The only other boundary is the sometimes stormy, sometimes sparkling Atlantic Ocean.

Ballyliffin enjoys such a setting. Ireland's most northerly golf club is situated close to Malin Head on Donegal's Inishowen Peninsula. The links hugs the shore beside Pollan Bay and overlooks a vast stretch of sand. The massive bulk of Binion Hill slips into the sea at one end of the bay and at the other are the ancient ruins of Carrickabraghy Castle. Just off the coast, surveying everything, is Glashedy Rock, Ballyliffin's own Ailsa Craig.

But it isn't just the hidden beauty of the location that captivates and casts a spell over all who travel to Ballyliffin. Nick Faldo made a surprise visit in June 1993 and went away describing **The Old Links** as the most natural golf course he had ever played.

Stories began to circulate of an undiscovered links that possessed the most amazing rippling fairways. Overseas commentators started to call Ballyliffin 'the Dornoch of Ireland.' Then, in the summer of 1995, the club unveiled a second 18 hole course, the appropriately named **Glashedy Links**, designed by Pat Ruddy and Tom Craddock.

The new course is, quite simply, a diamond of a links. Laid out on predominantly higher ground above and beyond The Old Links, it revels in the majesty of the setting. The sandhills are generally larger and the terrain more sweepingly undulating. If The Old Links is guaranteed to charm, so Glashedy Links is certain to thrill.

Visitors can make tee reservations by telephoning the **Secretary/ Manager, Cecil Doherty** on **tel: (077) 76119** or by **fax: (077) 76672** or visit **www.ballyliffingolfclub.com** Green fees in 2000 for The Old Links are £21 per round midweek, £24 at weekends and for the Glashedy Links, £30 per round midweek and £35 at weekends. The club has recently constructed a new clubhouse at a cost of £1.3 million.

Glashedy Links has been designed in heroic fashion with vast greens and deep revetted bunkers. With its championship tees stretching the course to 7102 yards (par 72) it is much longer than The Old Links (6612 yards, par 71) but there are fewer awkward stances to contend with—provided, that is, you keep to the fairways.

There is no gentle break-in on the Glashedy Links. It opens with three formidable par fours, each measuring over 420 yards from the back tees. The green at the 1st is perched, rather enticingly, between two large sandhills; the threat of hitting out of bounds looms at the 2nd—as does an alarmingly cavernous bunker in front of the green—and the landing area appears painfully narrow from the elevated tee at the 3rd. The dunes increase in size as you approach the dog-leg at the 4th and just as the fairway swings to the right and a cross bunker reveals itself, so Glashedy Rock comes fully into view directly behind the green. It is a magical moment.

Glashedy becomes an almost constant companion for the remainder of the round. It dominates the backdrop to the par three 5th, the first of the short holes. Stand on the tee of this hole on a lovely summer's evening with the sun reflecting off the sea and you may think Ballyliffin the most heavenly place on earth. The 6th is perhaps the most gentle of the par fours and after a vertigo-inducing tee shot at the 7th, where you play from the top of an enormous sandhill down to a green sited almost 100 feet below, the course flows gracefully back to the clubhouse.

The second nine is longer and tougher! Holes 10-12 weave a path through The Old Links and lead the golfer back out towards the higher, wilder duneland behind the great sandhill. Then begins a superb sequence of holes. The 13th is a massive par five—uphill and breathtaking in both senses of the word. Its rollercoasting fairway shadowed by towering sandhills is reminiscent of Ballybunion. The view over the shoulder, however, (back to Glashedy) is pure Turnberry. The 14th is arguably the best and most seductive of the short holes, and the 15th with its exhilarating downhill drive and fairway, which this time dog-legs to the left, is another excellent two-shotter.

From the 16th tee the course returns towards the clubhouse. It is a testing and potentially perilous journey home—an arrow-straight par four into the prevailing wind, a second par five that seems to stretch forever and a day, and finally, a classic finishing hole. The 18th is a sweeping dog-leg where the approach has to be targeted between tall dunes to find a heavily guarded green.

While some may think it a little premature to judge the quality of the new course no one could deny that it is both beautiful and dramatic. There seems every possibility that it will one day take its place alongside Portrush and Newcastle as one of the three great courses in the north of Ireland. Add the unique character of The Old Links to the equation and you have a fine golfing destination. The Ballybunion of the North, perhaps?

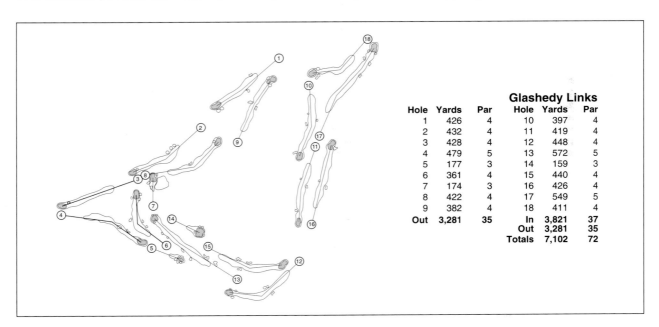

Glashedy Links

Hole	Yards	Par	Hole	Yards	Par
1	426	4	10	397	4
2	432	4	11	419	4
3	428	4	12	448	4
4	479	5	13	572	5
5	177	3	14	159	3
6	361	4	15	440	4
7	174	3	16	426	4
8	422	4	17	549	5
9	382	4	18	411	4
Out	**3,281**	**35**	**In**	**3,821**	**37**
			Out	**3,281**	**35**
			Totals	**7,102**	**72**

Donegal

The Irish have an inborn wanderlust that is perhaps rivalled only by Australians and New Zealanders. This partly explains how, wherever you go in the world, you bump into an Irishman, sooner rather than later. And why sooner rather than later, you'll hear the phrase 'to be sure' or 'tis grand'. It also partly explains why the names of numerous relatively small towns in Ireland are famous the world over—places like Limerick, Blarney and Tipperary for example. Another place that just about everybody has heard of is Donegal—not for its rhymes, kisses or songs of course but for its tweed. Yet like Limerick, Blarney and Tipperary not all that many people born outside Ireland have visited Donegal. Every golfer however, given the chance, should visit the country's most north westerly county. There are many wonderful courses here and they are all wonderfully uncrowded. And every brave golfer should visit Donegal, the county town itself, and play its majestic links at nearby Murvagh.

Why only every brave golfer? This is because to get the most out of Murvagh you must enjoy a mighty challenge. It is the longest golf course in Ireland. A local joke is that if you are a short hitter you can spend a full day at Murvagh and not complete 18 holes. Donegal really is a tiger of a links: from the Championship tees it measures over 7100 yards (or 6547 metres as the card will tell you.) In reality, most of us are never going to tackle the links from the tiger tees and while it is still a very long course from the tees of the day, real challenge becomes entwined with real pleasure.

Murvagh enjoys considerable seclusion. It is not exactly off the beaten track—Donegal is only six miles away—but quite a bit of the course is bordered by some fairly thick woodland, and being situated on a peninsula, there is an added feeling of isolation. The other border, of course, is the great Atlantic Ocean.

Few golf clubs are as keen for visitors to come and experience the charms of their course as Donegal (the club is understandably proud of the fact that Nick Faldo visited the course in 1993). The green fees in 2000 are £25 per day, Monday to Thursday with £30 payable on Fridays, weekends and on bank holidays. The club operates a timesheet system from May 1st to September 30th. Also restrictions apply on Mondays, which is ladies' day. Donegal's **Secretary, John McBride** can be contacted on **tel: (073) 34054** (00 353 73) from the UK, and by **fax: (073) 34377** or **e-mail: info@donegalgolfclub.ie** There is no professional at the club but the **Steward, Eugene**

McLoughlin is very helpful. Meals and snacks are available in the clubhouse throughout the day although players are requested to place an order for meals before teeing off.

As already mentioned, Murvagh is approximately six miles from the centre of Donegal. The linking road is the N15 and the route off to the golf course is signposted. The town itself is about an hour's drive from the nearest airport which is at Sligo and again the route is the N15. Knock Airport is 80 miles away and Belfast 110 miles. Sligo Airport is obviously the most convenient and anyone playing golf at Donegal should try to include a game at County Sligo (or vice versa). Rosses Point and Murvagh—what a double for links enthusiasts!

Rather like at Rosses Point, the course opens with a fairly gentle hole. This time it is a par five and like every par five at Murvagh (there are four others) it is a dog-leg, but the approach to the green is not too demanding and the putting surface is fairly large. Things start to hot up at the 2nd. This is a very tough par four that plays every bit of its 416 yards. Thick, tangling rough lines the left hand side of the fairway on this hole and there is an out of bounds on the right. As for the green, it sits on a natural shelf.

Neither the 3rd or 4th is an easy hole and the 5th can be a horror. This is one of two really tremendous par threes at Donegal; the tee shot must be struck perfectly to carry a ravine—mishit it slightly and you can be playing your second from sand 30 feet below the green. Beyond the green is the beach. A brilliant sequence of holes comes after the 5th. This is where the course runs close to Donegal Bay and the views (if you care to clamber up the sandhills) are tremendous.

Perhaps the most memorable holes on the back nine at Murvagh are the 10th, 11th and 15th, while the most demanding are the 12th and 16th. The former is once again a huge par five; from the back tees it is (as some wag once suggested) a reasonable train journey and, as on most three-shot holes, the key is the second. If we are talking train distances then as par threes go the 16th must be the equivalent of the Trans-Siberian Express! One could sit behind this green all day and not see anyone reach the green with their tee shot. When the elements are stirred this is the kind of hole where, in days gone by, Jack Nicklaus would have peeled off his sweater and teed up with his driver. But then, Donegal is a place where another of those lovely Irish expressions 'good crack' takes on a new meaning.

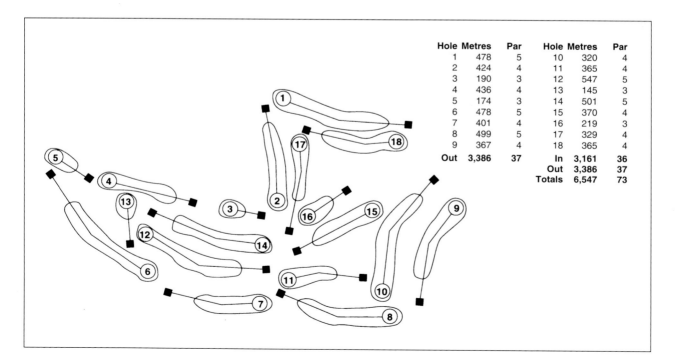

Hole	Metres	Par	Hole	Metres	Par
1	478	5	10	320	4
2	424	4	11	365	4
3	190	3	12	547	5
4	436	4	13	145	3
5	174	3	14	501	5
6	478	5	15	370	4
7	401	4	16	219	3
8	499	5	17	329	4
9	367	4	18	365	4
Out	**3,386**	**37**	**In**	**3,161**	**36**
			Out	**3,386**	**37**
			Totals	**6,547**	**73**

Glasson

It is becoming known as the 'Glasson experience': you don't just go and play Glasson you experience it. Clever marketing? Maybe. But it is true. Glasson has the capacity to overwhelm in at least four different ways. Firstly, there is the setting—it is simply sublime. Secondly, the welcome is one of the warmest you are ever likely to receive. Thirdly, there is the course itself—one of the most interesting you are ever likely to play. And finally, perhaps no golf club in the world offers the opportunity to roll up at its gates in quite so stylish a manner.

The setting: Glasson is the Killarney of the Irish Midlands. Positioned 75 miles from Dublin via the N6 and 6 miles north east of Athlone on the N55 Cavan/Longford road, there is not much in the way of mountain scenery but Lough Ree is every bit as enchanting as Lough Leane. Moreover, the golf course at Glasson makes better use of its lakeside setting than either of the courses at Killarney. The site is quite elevated in places, allowing Lough Ree to be seen from almost every hole. From the highest parts of the course there are breathtaking 360 degree views.

The welcome: Glasson Golf and Country Club is the realisation of a dream—Tom and Breda Reid's dream. A charming and modest couple, together with their daughter **Fidelma** who is the **Director of Golf tel: (0902) 85120 fax: (0902) 85444** if you are ringing from outside Ireland on't forget to dial (00 353), they provide a very personal, 'family' welcome. Considerable care and attention to detail has gone into the design of their course as well as the accompanying off-course facilities. In fact, the 19th is one of the best of many great holes at Glasson. For futher details write to **Glasson Golf & Country Club, Glasson, Athlone, Co Westmeath, Ireland** or visit **www.glassongolf.ie**

The green fees for 2000 are set at Monday–Thursday £30, Friday/Sunday £32 and Saturday £35.

The golf course: Christy O'Connor Jr has designed several courses in Ireland but probably none is destined to be as famous (or as photographed) as his work at Glasson. And Christy knows it: "it is one of the most scenic pieces of land I have ever seen". There are tantalising glimpses of Lough Ree as you play down the fairways of the 1st and 2nd and you confront it head on at the par three 3rd. The 6th hole sweeps down to the most attractive area on the front nine, a point where the 6th and 8th greens and 7th tee converge, and where each is separated from the other by an attractive water hazard. The dramatic approach to the 8th is one no golfer will quickly forget. Nor could anyone tire of playing the skilfully designed par four 13th, the stunning par five 14th and the extraordinary par three 15th where both the tee and green protrude into the waters of Lough Ree.

The stylish arrival: Glasson has its own lakeside jetty, enabling golfers to arrive by cruiser after journeying from the west of Ireland along the River Shannon. Did you ever hear of a better way of getting one up on your opponent even before you hit a ball?

An exciting new development is underway at Glasson, a 30 bedroom hotel will be up and running by April 2001 'play and stay'.

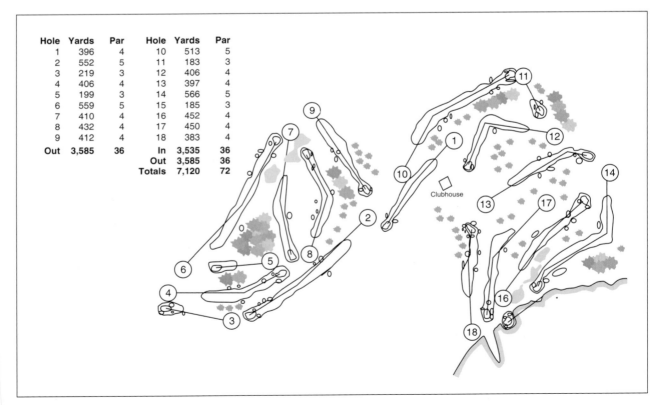

Hole	Yards	Par		Hole	Yards	Par
1	396	4		10	513	5
2	552	5		11	183	3
3	219	3		12	406	4
4	406	4		13	397	4
5	199	3		14	566	5
6	559	5		15	185	3
7	410	4		16	452	4
8	432	4		17	450	4
9	412	4		18	383	4
Out	**3,585**	**36**		**In**	**3,535**	**36**
				Out	**3,585**	**36**
				Totals	**7,120**	**72**

Clubhouse

Rosapenna

There is perhaps no more romantic adventure in all the golf world than a journey to Rosapenna and Portsalon, the obscure, almost forgotten links on the rugged Donegal coast'—*Links of Heaven*, Richard Phinney and Scott Whitley.

Imagine the scene about a hundred years ago: Old Tom Morris, his legendary beard now a whiter shade of grey, surveys his work. Rosapenna he concludes, must be the most natural links he was ever invited to lay out. "I'll accept a few guineas for my efforts but perhaps Mother Nature should take most of the credit." He retires to the elegant hotel, fraternises with the holidaying English gentry over dinner then takes an evening stroll along one of the most beautiful stretches of coast he has ever seen.

After Tom Morris came Harry Vardon and James Braid—not only in respect of their impact on the world of golf, but both made the trip to Rosapenna. And, being celebrated course architects as well as players, neither could resist tinkering with Old Tom's design.

Then times became hard. Long before the outbreak of World War Two the numbers of holidaying English gentry began to dwindle. The hotel lost its way and as a consequence, Rosapenna became almost forgotten—that is, until Frank Casey came along. Here isn't the place to discuss the life and times of Frank Casey—besides he is a modest man—suffice to say he presides over a marvellous 'new' Rosapenna Golf Hotel. The condition of the links (which is managed by the hotel) would bring a twinkle to Old Tom's eye and it is rapidly shedding its 'forgotten' tag. Furthermore, 18 additional holes, designed by Pat Ruddy in a vast stretch of adjoining duneland, will soon be completed and ready for play. Rosapenna is going places.

Frank Casey, Owner/Manager of **Rosapenna Hotel & Golf Course, Downings, Co Donegal, Ireland** can be contacted on **tel: (00 353) 74 55301, fax: (00 353) 74 55128** or visit **www.rosapenna.ie** Green Fees for 2000 are weekdays £22, weekends £27. Visitors are welcome but bookings are preferred. The course is located 25 miles north west of Letterkenny via the R245 from Milford.

The present links appears very much as Vardon and Braid left it. True, it now measures 6271 yards (par 70) but there is an unmistakably old-fashioned flavour about Rosapenna. It is also a course of two halves, or rather two distinct loops. The first 10 holes occupy fairly level ground beside Sheephaven Bay while the remaining eight holes wind their way around—and eventually career over the top of a vast hill that overlooks Mulroy Bay on one side and Sheephaven Bay on the other. Throughout the round there are glimpses of the Donegal Hills and the imperious (and splendidly named) Muckish Mountain.

Among the most memorable holes within the first loop are the 4th, with its incredibly contoured green, and the par three 6th, where the tee shot must be fired across a chasm of dunes to find an elusive table shaped green. On the back nine a cattle grid and country road have to be negotiated at the quaint old 12th, but the outstanding hole is undoubtedly the 13th, a brilliantly designed dog-leg that charges downhill towards Mulroy Bay.

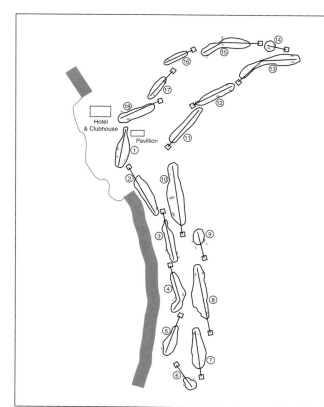

Hole	Yards	Par	Hole	Yards	Par
1	298	4	10	543	5
2	428	4	11	427	4
3	446	4	12	342	4
4	386	4	13	455	4
5	255	4	14	128	3
6	167	3	15	418	4
7	367	4	16	216	3
8	485	5	17	358	4
9	185	3	18	367	4
Out	**3,017**	**35**	**In**	**3,254**	**35**
			Out	**3,017**	**35**
			Totals	**6,271**	**70**

Connemara

Not many people reading this book will have visited the moon and, unless NASA is keeping an extraordinary secret under wraps, only one man has ever played golf there—our friend from La Moye and Fulford, Admiral Alan Sheppard. I suspect the closest most of us are ever likely to get to experiencing golf in a lunar-like landscape is if we visit Connemara on the west coast of Ireland.

While much of County Kerry basks in picture-postcard prettiness, the countryside of Connemara boasts a truly rugged kind of splendour. Some of Connemara appears almost prehistoric. Great grey rocks are strewn all over a hilly, green landscape. Connemara National Park is surely where Finn McCool and his giant buddies staged an all-night rock throwing party but forgot to clear up afterwards. The village of Ballyconneely is about as far west as you can go in Connemara without slipping into the Atlantic and Ballyconneely is where Connemara Golf Club is found.

Before 1973 it used to be reckoned that the only people who ventured this far west were lost. This of course was in the days before golf came to Ballyconneely. Connemara's championship golf links is worth discovering. It may not be in quite the same league as Rosses Point to the north or Ballybunion to the south but it is a wonderful golfing experience.

Connemara hosted its first professional tournament, the Carroll's Irish Matchplay Championship, in 1980, and the AIB Connemara pro-am, held in September, is now recognised as one of the major fixtures on the Irish PGA calendar.

Ballyconneely is 9 miles south of Clifden (where transatlantic aviators Alcock and Brown fell to earth) some 15 to 20 minutes along a fairly deserted road. Clifden is joined to Galway by the N59, a distance of approximately 50 miles and a journey that no one should rush. According to Thackeray this is 'one of the most beautiful districts that is ever the fortune of the traveller to examine.' Thackeray was biased, but a thousand watercolours cannot lie. The N59 also links Clifden with Westport to the north east and the route via Leenane (where 'The Field', which starred Richard Harris was filmed) is at least as dramatic.

Golfing visitors to Connemara are always made extremely welcome. Greatly responsible for the hospitable atmosphere at the club is the **Secretary/ Manager John McLoughlin**. It is advisable to contact Mr McLoughlin in advance for tee reservations. The club's address is

Connemara Golf Club, Ballyconneely, Clifden, Co Galway, tel: **(095) 23502** or **fax: (095) 23662** (from the UK the code is 00 353 95). During the summer months and at holiday weekends a starting sheet system is operated. Subject to the above, and being able to provide proof of handicap, there are no general restrictions on the times when visitors may play. Green fees for 2000 are May—September £35, April and Ocotber £30, January—March and November—December £22. For society outings of at least 20 people the fees are July—August £30, June £28, May and September £22, January—April and October—December £18. The club's **Professional** is **Hugh O'Neill**.

Few clubhouses enjoy a better vantage point than the one at Connemara. Perched on high ground, there are not only some magnificent views over the ocean (particularly splendid when the western sun dips into the sea on a summer's evening) but also across much of the course. It is a wonderful place in which to relax. But first we must tackle the course.

The first seven holes at Connemara occupy the flattest part of the links. They are by no means easy holes—very testing ones, in fact—but in the opinion of many they serve as mere appetisers for the feast that follows. Some of the holes between the 8th and 18th are as good as any one is likely to play: 'So good they are nearly ridiculous' reckoned Irish golf writer Pat Ruddy. The 8th is the stroke index one hole and the approach is a very testing one to a broad but plateau green. As for the 9th, it is a real gem of a hole. Again a two-shotter, the player drives downhill from a magnificently placed high tee;. Over the player's shoulder as he drives is a mountainous backdrop, the famous Twelve Bens, and stretching out ahead is the sea, the Atlantic Ocean—the next terra firma being Long Island.

If the 9th is a memorable hole, the par three 13th is out of this world. This is where landscape is replaced by moonscape. As at the 9th, an exhilarating downhill tee shot is called for. From the back tees a long-iron shot will be needed as the carry is all of 200 yards. The 14th, a par five where you can really open the shoulders, and the 15th, which is a little reminiscent of the 14th at Portmarnock with its uphill second to a shelf-like green, are two more marvellous holes. Water can play the devil at the 16th while the 17th and 18th are a pair of par fives that seem to stretch for ever and a day.

If you've played Connemara from the back tees (well over 7000 yards) the chances are you'll be breathless by the finish. Breathless at Connemara—like being on the moon.

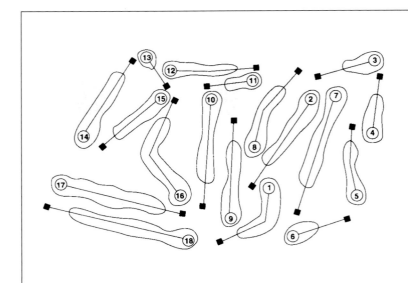

Hole	Metres	Par		Hole	Metres	Par
1	331	4		10	383	4
2	366	4		11	151	3
3	145	3		12	399	4
4	335	4		13	180	3
5	342	4		14	460	5
6	175	3		15	349	4
7	482	5		16	370	4
8	418	4		17	468	5
9	344	4		18	475	5
Out	**2,938**	**35**		**In**	**3,235**	**37**
				Out	**2,938**	**35**
				Totals	**6,173**	**72**

Portsalon

Where in the world can you play golf alongside a beach as pure and as perfect as the one at Portsalon? The official answer is nowhere. A few years ago an international panel of travel writers adjudged Portsalon Strand 'The Second Most Beautiful Beach in the World'. Apparently there is a more beautiful one in the Seychelles but it has no golf course. And the beach really does come into play at Portsalon!

The 'romantic journey' referred to in *Links of Heaven* (see Rosapenna feature) can never adequately prepare first time visitors for the drama of Portsalon's setting. Tucked away on the tip of the Fanad Peninsula on the northern shores of Lough Swilley, the Knockalla Mountains provide a stunning backdrop. Linking with heather-clad hills, they shield and semi-circle the links, creating a stage-like effect. Add the glistening waters of Lough Swilley, those glorious golden sands and 18 spectacular holes to the equation and for we blasphemous golfers, *this* is the links of heaven.

Local enthusiasts have played golf amid such natural splendour for more than a century. The club was established in 1891 and became one of the founding members of the Golfing Union of Ireland. Again, like Rosapenna, the links benefitted in its early years from the close proximity of a stylish hotel and when the hotel faded, so did the fame of Portsalon—although not before it twice hosted the Irish Ladies Championship. The great May Hezlet triumphed at Portsalon in 1905 and Mabel Harrison won when the event returned in 1912.

By modern standards the course is quite short, weighing in at 5880 yards, par 69. In terms of character and charm, however, it has very few peers. A journalist from Fore magazine inspected the links in 1995 and it seems was no less captivated than Phinney and Whitley. When he put pen to paper he declared, 'If I could play only one golf course for the rest of my life I would choose Portsalon. No contest'. Presumably he avoided hooking his opening drive into the sea, remained similarly dry at the par three 2nd ('the best short hole in the British Isles') and survived the vertigo-inducing tee shot at the 3rd, before successfully threading his approach between the twin rocky outcrops that guard the entrance to that green.

Portsalon is an extraordinary golf course. At the 6th players must occasionally wade across water to drive from an island tee, and on the 13th, they have to climb (or scale) a tee known as 'The Matterhorn'. There are blind holes, fairways that rollercoast and greens so heavily contoured that they resemble crumpled duvets. Extraordinary? Better make that eccentric. Yes, Portsalon is an eccentric, turn of the century masterpiece. Long may it remain so.

Portsalon Golf Club, Portsalon Fanad, Co Donegal, Ireland	
Secretary	Peter Doherty, tel & fax: (00 353) 74 59459
Green Fees	WD £18 WE £22
Restrictions	None, but it is best to ring ahead for bookings
Directions	
20 miles north of Letterkenny via Ramelton, Milford. and Kerrykeel.	

PORTSALON - VIEW FROM 1ST FAIRWAY *Courtesy of:* **Portsalon Golf Club**

County Sligo (Rosses Point)

Which is the best golf course in Ireland? Is it the Old Course at Ballybunion? Or perhaps Portmarnock near Dublin? Or what about the two 'Royal' courses north of the border, Portrush and County Down? These four courses invariably receive the most nominations in the age-old favourite 19th hole debate. But there is another golf course that many people believe deserves to be spoken of in the same breath and that is County Sligo, more commonly known as Rosses Point.

Of this magnificent five, Royal County Down at Newcastle has perhaps the strongest claim to possessing the finest front nine holes and Ballybunion the greatest back nine. But taking each of the eighteens as a balanced whole, Rosses Point must have a creditable claim—indeed Peter Alliss has been quoted as saying 'Rosses Point stands right at the very top of the list of Irish golf courses.' Another famous supporter is the great Tom Watson. If he were asked to name his three favourite links courses in Great Britain and Ireland (excluding those at which he won an Open Championship!) he would probably rattle off the names Ballybunion, Royal Dornoch and Rosses Point.

As well as having a glorious golf course, County Sligo Golf Club enjoys a glorious situation. The golf links (and the surrounding countryside) is dominated by the extraordinary mountain, Benbulben, which is a dead ringer for Cape Town's Table Mountain. Immediately adjacent to the links is a wonderfully sweeping bay with three beautiful beaches: little wonder that the scenery so intoxicated Ireland's greatest poet, W B Yeats.

Visiting golfers who wish to become similarly intoxicated by the golfing challenge are advised to contact the club in advance. The **Manager, Jim Ironside** at Rosses Point can be contacted on **tel: (071) 77134** (from the UK the code is 00 353 71) and by **fax: (071) 77460**. There is no firm requirement that visitors produce handicap certificates but they must, however, be players of a 'reasonable standard'. The club's **Professional, Leslie Robinson** can be reached on **tel: (071) 77171**. The green fees for summer 2000 are IR£35 Monday—Thursday and IR£45 Friday—Sunday. IR£55 for 36 holes midweek and IR£65 for 36 holes at weekends. Recently opended at County Sligo is the **Bomore** Course which has 9 holes, and on which the green fees are IR£15 Monday—Thursday and IR£25 Friday—Sunday.

Rosses Point is often tagged 'remote', not as remote as Waterville but more so than most of Ireland's finest golfing attractions. Naturally, it depends where one is coming from but there is an airport (County Sligo) just 20 minutes drive away at Strandhill. The town of Sligo is no more than 10 minutes away from the links (via the R291 road); Donegal is about one hour's drive north (N15) and Westport approximately an hour and a half to the south west (N17/N5/N60).

The 1st at Rosses Point is a medium length par four, fairly straight and gently uphill all the way to a well protected green. The 2nd is much more severely uphill and the approach shot, although likely to be no more than a short iron, can be very difficult to judge. On reaching the green at the 2nd one can feel on top of the world, almost literally, for the panoramic view from here is as vast as it is sensational. Benbulben is genuinely awe-inspiring, a geological freak which, if located in a more widely known part of the world, would be universally acclaimed. From such dizzy heights the Atlantic looks positively inviting—so does the downhill drive at the 3rd! This hole can be reached with two well struck shots but a series of fiendishly positioned bunkers await to punish the less accurate.

The 4th is a fine par three where the green sits on a natural plateau and this is followed by another vertigo-inducing tee shot at the 5th. The 6th is perhaps the weakest hole on the course and the 7th looks fairly straightforward for a stroke index one hole—that is until your second shot plummets into the brook in front of the green. The brook reappears on the 8th, which is a magnificent and much photographed dog-leg. The front nine concludes with the excellent par three 9th where the green is surrounded by bunkers.

The 10th and 11th offer the closest views of Benbulben and they are a very good pair of par fours. A fairly blind par five is followed by the difficult one-shot 13th, where the tee looks down over the sea and sands. Then comes Tom Watson's favourite. The 14th is a superb and extremely testing par four and when the wind is blowing can make even the 8th seem tame. If the wind is against on the 14th then it will be so again on the 15th, which is bad news because the drive needs to be carried far over some very wild dunes close to the shore. The 16th is the longest par three at Rosses Point and the 17th calls for a long uphill second to an amphitheatre green. Then at long last, comes a fairly gentle hole! It is the last and if you play it on a fine summer's evening you may be lucky enough to see the sun setting behind the 18th green: now wouldn't that be the perfect end to a perfect round!

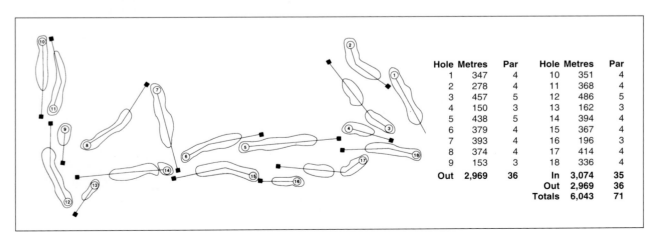

Hole	Metres	Par	Hole	Metres	Par
1	347	4	10	351	4
2	278	4	11	368	4
3	457	5	12	486	5
4	150	3	13	162	3
5	438	5	14	394	4
6	379	4	15	367	4
7	393	4	16	196	3
8	374	4	17	414	4
9	153	3	18	336	4
Out	**2,969**	**36**	**In**	**3,074**	**35**
			Out	**2,969**	**36**
			Totals	**6,043**	**71**

CARLOW GOLF CLUB *Photograph courtesy of:* **Irish Tourist Board (Brian Lynch)**

CO CARLOW

Borris G.C.
(01503) 73143
Deerpark, Borris
(9) 6026 yards/***/D

Carlow G.C.
(0503) 31695
Deerpark, Dublin Road, Carlow
(18) 6428 yards/***/D

CO CAVAN

Belturbet G.C.
(049) 22287
Erne Hill, Belturbet
(9) 5347 metres/***/E

Blacklion G.C.
(072) 53024
Toam, Blacklion
(9) 6098 yards/***/E

Cabra Castle G.C.
(042) 67904
Kingscourt
(9) 5839 yards/***/F

County Cavan G.C.
(049) 32183
Arnmore House, Drumellis, Cavan
(18) 5519 metres/***/D

Slieve Russell G.C.
(049) 26444
Slieve Russell Hotel, Ballyconnell
(18) 6580 yards/***/B/H/M

Virginia G.C.
(049) 47235
Virginia
(9) 4900 metres/***/E

COUNTY CLARE

Clonlara G.C.
(061) 354141
Clonlara
(9) 5289 metres/***/E

Dromoland Castle G.C.
(061) 368144
Newmarket on Fergus
(18) 6098 metres/***/B/H

East Clare G.C.
(061) 921322
Bodyke
(9) 5675 metres/***/E

Ennis G.C.
(065) 24074
Drumbiggle, Ennis
(18) 5316 metres/**(Sun)/C/M

Kilkee G.C.
(065) 56048
East End, Kilkee
(9) 5900 metres/***/D

Kilrush G.C.
(065) 51138
Parknamoney, Kilrush
(9) 2739 yards/***/F

Lahinch G.C.
(065) 81003
Lahinch
(18) 6123 metres/***/A/H/M
(18) 5138 metres/***/C/H/M

Shannon G.C.
(061) 471849
Shannon Airport, Shannon
(18) 6874 yards/**/B/H/M

Spanish Point G.C.
(065) 84198
Spanish Point, Miltown Malbay
(9) 1787 yards/***/D

Woodstock G.C.
(065) 29463
Shanaway Road, Ennis
(18) 5879 metres/***/C

CO CORK

Bandon G.C.
(023) 41111
Castlebernard, Bandon
(18)5879 metres/***/C

Bantry Park G.C.
(027) 50579
Donemark, Bantry
(9) 2973 yards/***/D

Berehaven Park G.C.
(027) 70700
Millcove, Castletownbere
(9) 4763 metres/***/E/H/M

Charleville G.C.
(063) 81257
Ardmore, Charleville
(18) 6430 yards/**/D

Cobh G.C.
(021) 812399
Ballywilliam, Cobh
(9) 2518 yards/**(W/E am)/E

Coosheen G.C.
(028) 28182
Schull
(9) 3362 metres/***/E

Cork G.C.
(021) 353451
Little Island, Cork
(18) 6115 metres/**(Thurs)/B/H

Doneraile G.C.
(022) 24137
Doneraile, Cork
(9) 5528 metres/**(W/E am)/F

Douglas G.C.
(021) 891086
Douglas, Cork
(18) 5644 metres/**(Tues)/C

Dunmore G.C.
(023) 33352
Muckross, Clonakilty
(9) 4464 metres/***(Sun)/D

East Cork G.C.
(021) 631687
Gortacrue, Midleton
(18) 5207 metres/**/D/H

Fermoy G.C.
(025) 31472
Carrin Cross, Fermoy
(18) 5550 metres/***(Mon/Wed)/F

Fernhill G.C.
(021) 373103
Carrigaline
(18) 5000 metres/***/F

Fota Island G.C.
(021) 883710
Carrigtwohill, Cork
(18) 6891 yards/***/B

Frankfield G.C.
(021) 361199
Douglas, Cork
(9) 5191 yards/***/E

Glengarriff G.C.
(027) 63150
Glengarriff
(9) 2047 metres/***/E

Harbour Point G.C.
(021) 353094
Clash Road, Little Island, Cork
(18) 5773 metres/***/B

Kanturk G.C.
(029) 50534
Fairy Hill, Kanturk
(9) 5527 metres/***/E

Kinsale G.C.
(021) 772197
Ringenane, Belgooly
(9) 2666 metres/**/D/M
(18) 6500 yards/**/D/M

Lee Valley G.& C.C.
(021) 331721
Clashanure, Ovens
(18) 6705 yards/**/B/H

Macroom G.C.
(026) 41072
Lackaduve, Macroom
(9) 5439 metres/***/D/H

Mahon G.C.
(021) 362480
Cloverhill, Blackrock
(18) 4818 metres/***/E

Mallow G.C.
(022) 21145
Ballyellis, Mallow
(18) 6559 yards/**(Tues)/D

Mitchelstown G.C.
(025) 24072
Mitchelstown
(15) 5057 metres/***/D

Monkstown G.C.
(021) 841376
Parkgarriffe, Monkstown
(18) 5669 metres***/B/H(20)/M

Muskerry G.C.
(021) 385297
Carrigrohane, Blarney
(18) 5426 metres/**(Mon/Tues)/D

Old Head Golf Links
(021) 778444
Kinsale
(18) 6400 yards/***/A

Raffeen Creek G.C.
(021) 378430
Ringaskiddy
(9) 5800 yards/***/D

Skibbereen G.C.
(028) 21227
Licknavar, Skibbereen
(18) 5774 yards/***/D

Youghal G.C.
(024) 92787
Knockaverry, Youghal
(18) 5664 metres/***(Wed)/D/H/M

CO DONEGAL

Ballybofey & Stranorlar G.C.
(074) 31093
Stranorlar, Ballybofey
(18) 5913 yards/*(not am)/D/H

Ballyliffin G.C.
(077) 76119
Ballyliffin, Cardonagh
(18) 6384 yards/***/D/M

Buncrana G.C.
(077) 62279
Buncrana
(9) 2020 yards/***/F

Bundoran G.C.
(072) 41302
Great Northern Hotel, Bundoran
(18) 6159 yards/***/D/H

Cruit Island G.C.
(075) 43296
Kincasslagh, Dungloe
(9) 5297 yards/***/E

Donegal G.C.
(073) 34054
Murvagh, Donegal
(18) 6863 yards/***/D/H/M

Dunfanaghy G.C.
(074) 36335
Dunfanaghy, Letterkenny
(18) 5006 yards/***/D

Greencastle G.C.
(077) 81013
Moville, Greencastle
(18) 5386 yards/**/D

Gweedore G.C.
(075) 31140
Derrybeg, Gweedore
(18) 6201 yards/***/E

Letterkenny G.C.
(074) 21150
Barnhill, Letterkenny
(18) 6239 yards/***/D

Narin and Portnoo G.C.
(073) 45107
Narin, Portnoo
(18) 5322 metres/**(Sun)/F/H

North West G.C.
(077) 61027
Lisfannon, Fahon, Lifford
(18) 5968 yards/**/D/H/M

Otway G.C.
(074) 58319
Saltpans, Rathmullen
(9) 4134 yards/***/E

Portsalon G.C.
(074) 59459
Portsalon, Letterkenny
(18) 5878 yards/***/D

Redcastle G.C.
(077) 82073
Redcastle, Moville
(9) 5528 yards/***/D

Rosapenna G.C.
(074) 55301
Downings, Rosapenna
(18) 6271 yards/***/C

CO DUBLIN

Balbriggan G.C.
(01) 841 2229
Blackhall, Balbriggan
(18) 5881 metres/***/D

Balcarrick G.C.
(01) 843 6228
Corballis, Donabate
(18)6912 yards/***/D

Ballinascorney G.C.
(01) 512516
Ballinascorney
(18) 5464 yards/***/D

Beaverstown G.C.
(01) 843 6439
Beaverstown, Donabate
(18) 5551 metres/**/D/H

Beech Park G.C.
(01) 458 0100
Johnstown, Rathcoole
(18)5730 metres/**/C

Castle G.C.
(01) 490 4207
Woodside Drive, Rathfarnham
(18)5653 metres/**/B

Carrickmines G.C.
(01) 295 5972
Carrickmines, Dublin
(9) 6103 yards/***/C/G

City West G.C.
(01) 458 8566
Saggart
(18) 6822 yards/***/B

Clontarf G.C.
(01) 833 1892
Malahide Road
(18) 5459 metres/**/B

Coldwaters G.C.
(01) 864 0324
Newton House, St Margarets
(18) 5973/***/E

Corballis G.C.
(01) 8436583
Donabate
(18) 4971 metres/***/F

Corrstown G.C.
(01) 864 0553
Corrstown, Killsallaghan
(18) 5584 yards/*/G

Deer Park Hotel & G.C.
(01) 832 2624
Howth Castle, Howth
(18) 6503 yards/***/D
(18) 6778 yards/***/D

Donabate G.C.
(01) 843 6059
Donabate
(18) 6187 yards/**/F

Dublin Mountain G.C.
(01) 458 2662
Gortlum, Brittas
(18) 5433 metres/***/A/H

Dun Laoghaire G.C.
(01) 280 1055
Eglinton Park, Dun Laoghaire
(18) 5712 yards/***/B

Edmondstown G.C.
(01) 493 1082
Edmondstown, Rathfarnham
(18) 5663 metres/***/B/H

Elm Park G.C.
(011) 269 3438
Nutley House, Donnybrook
(18) 5422 metres/***/A/H/M

Finnstown Fairways G.C.
(01) 628 0644
Newcastle Road, Lucan
(9) 2695 yards/***/D

Forrest Little G.C.
(01) 840 1183
Forrest Little, Cloghran
(18) 6451 yards/**/F/H/M

Foxrock G.C.
(01) 289 5668
Torquay Rd, Foxrock
(9) 6234 yards/**/C

Grange G.C.
(01) 932832
Grange Road, Rathfarnham
(18) 5517 metres/***/A/M

Hazel Grove G.C.
(01) 452 0911
Mount Seskin Road, Jobstown, Tallaght
(9) 5225 yards/**/D

Hermitage G.C.
(01) 626 5396
Lucan
(18) 5814 metres/***/B/H(24)/M

Hollywood G.C.
(01) 8207 3406
Hollywood, Ballyboughal
(18) 5674 yards/***/D

Howth G.C.
(01) 832 3055
Carriackbrack Road, Sutton
(18) 5618 metres/***/C/H/

Island G.C.
(01) 84366104
Corballis, Donabate
(18) 6658 yards/***/A

Killiney G.C.
(01) 285 1983
Ballinclea Road, Killiney
(9) 5626 metres/***/C/M

Kilternan Hotel G.C.
(01) 295 5559
Enniskerry Road, Kilternan
(18) 4952 metres/***/C/H(24)

Lucan G.C.
(01) 6280264
Celbridge Road, Lucan
(18) 5650 metres /***/C

Luttrellstown Castle G.C.
(01) 820 8210
Clonsilla, Dublin 15
(18) 6032 metres/**/A/M

Malahide G.C.
(01) 846 1611
Beechwood, The Grange, Malahide
(18) 6619 yards/**/B-A/H/M
(9) 6257 yards/**/B-A/H/M

Milltown G.C.
(01) 497 6090
Lower Churchtown Road
(18) 5638 metres/***/A/H/M

Newlands G.C.
(01) 45932903
Clondalkin
(18) 5714 metres/**/B

Open Golf Centre
(01) 8764 0324
Newton House, St Margaret's
(18) 5973 yards
(9) 2370 yards/***/E

Portmarnock G.C.
(01) 846 2968
Portmarnock
(18) 6497 metres/**/A/L/M
(9) 3478 yards/**/A/L/M

Portmarnock Hotel G.C.
(01) 846 0611
Strand Road, Portmarnock
(18) 6195 metres/***/A/H

Rathfarnham G.C.
(01) 493 1201
Newtown, Rathfarnham, Dublin 16
(9) 5787 yards/**(Tues)/C

Royal Dublin G.C.
(01) 833 6346
Bull Island, Dollymount, Dublin 3
(18) 6076 metres/**/A
(18) 5755 metres/**/A

Rush G.C.
(01) 843 7548
Rush
(9) 6850 yards/**/D/H

St Annes G.C.
(01) 833 6471
Bull Island, Dollymount, Dublin 5
(18) 5797 metres/***/C

St Margaret's G.& C.C.
(01) 864 0400
St Margaret's, Dublin
(18) 6900 yards/***/B-A

Skerries G.C.
(01) 8491204
Hackestown, Skerries
(18) 6113 metres/**/C/H(20)

Slade Valley G.C.
(01) 458 2739
Lynch Park, Brittas
(18) 5337 metres/**/C/H

Stackstown G.C.
(01) 494 2338
Kellystown Road, Rathfarnham
(18) 5952 metres/***/D-C

Sutton G.C.
(01) 832 3013
Cush Point, Barrow Road, Sutton
(9) 2859 yards/***(Tues/Sat)/C

Westmanstown G.C.
(01) 820 5817
Clonsilla, Dublin
(18) 6400 yards/***/C

CO GALWAY

Athenry G.C.
(091) 794466
Palmerstown, Oranmore
(18) 5552 metres/***(Sun)/D

Ballinasloe G.C.
(0905) 42904
Ballinasloe, Rosgloss
(18) 5868 metres/***/D/M

Connemara G.C.
(095) 23502
Ballyconneelly, Clifton
(18) 6611 metres/***/C/H

Connemara Isles G.C.
(091) 572498
Lettermore, Connemara
(9) 5720 yards/***/E

Galway G.C.
(091) 522033
Blackrock, Salthill, Galway
(18) 6376 yards/**(Tues)/C

Galway Bay G.& C.C.
(091) 790500
Renville Oranmore
(18) 6453 metres/***/E

Gort G.C.
(091) 31336
Laughtyshaughnessy, Gort
(9) 4976 metres/***(Sun am)/E

Loughrea G.C.
(091) 41049
Bullaun Road, Loughrea
(18) 5613 yards/***/D

Mountbellew G.C.
(0905) 79259
Shankhill, Mountbellew
(9) 5564 yards/***/F

Oughterard G.C.
(091) 82131
Gortreevagh, Oughterard
(18) 6141 yards/***/D/H

Portumna G.C.
(0509) 41059
Ennis Road,Portumna
(18) 5776 yards/***/D

Tuam G.C.
(093) 28993
Barnacurragh, Tuam
(18) 6321 yards/**/D

CO KERRY

Ballybunion G.C.
(068) 27146
Sandhill Road, Ballybunion
(18) 6241 yards/***/A/H(24)/L
(18) 5941 yards/***/A/H(24)/L

Beaufort G.C.
(064) 44440
Churchtown, Beaufort
(18) 6792 yards/***/B

Castlegregory G.C.
(066) 39444
Stradbally, Castlegregory
(9) 5488 yards/***/D

Ceann Sibeal G.C.
(066) 56255
Ballyferriter, Tralee
(18) 6650 yards/***/C

Dooks G.C.
(066) 68205
Dooks, Killorglin
(18) 6010 yards/**/C/H/M

Kenmare G.C.
(064) 41291
Kenmare, Killarney
(9) 5950 yards/***/D

Killarney G.& C.C.
(064) 31034
O'Mahony's Point, Killarney
(18) 6867 yards/***/B/H
(18) 7126 yards/***/B/H

Killorglin G.C.
(066) 61979
Steelroe, Killorglin
(18) 6464 yards/***/B

Parknasilla G.C.
(0644) 5122
Parknasilla, Sneem
(9) 4834 yards/***/D

Tralee G.C.
(066) 36379
West Barrow, Ardfert
(18) 6252 metres/**(Weds)/B/H/M

Waterville G.C.
(066) 74545
Ring of Kerry, Waterville
(18)7184 yards/***/A/H/M

CO KILDARE

Athy G.C.
(0507) 31729
Geraldine, Athy
(18) 6308 yards/**/D

Bodenstown G.C.
(045) 87096
Bodenstown, Sallins
(18) 5788 metres/**/D
(18) 5428 metres/**/D

Castlewarden G.& C.C.
(01) 458 9254
Castlewarden, Straffan
(18) 6008 metres/**/D

Cill Dara G.C.
(045) 21433
Kildare Town
(9) 6426 yards/***/D

Craddockstown G.C.
(045) 97610
Naas
(18) 6134 metres/***/D

Curragh G.C.
(045) 341714
Curragh
(18) 6603 yards/***/D

Highfield G.C.
(0405) 31021
Highfield House, Carbury
(18) 6278 yards/***/E

Kilcock G.C.
(01) 6284074
Kilcock
(9)/***/E

Kildare Country Club ('K' Club)
(01) 6273111
Straffan
(18) 6368 metres/**/A/H

Kilkea Castle
(0503) 45156
Castledermat
(18) 6200 metres/***/B

Killeen G.C.
(045) 866003
Killenbeg, Kill
(18) 5452 yards/***/D

Knockanally G.& C.C.
(045) 869322
Donadea, N. Kildare
(18) 6424 yards/***/B

Leixlip G.C.
(01) 624 6185
Leixlip
(18) 5550 metres/***/D

Naas G.C.
(045) 97509
Kerdiffstown, Salins, Naas
(18) 5660 metres/***/D

CO KILKENNY

Callan G.C.
(052) 25136
Geraldine, Callan
(9) 5844 metres/***/E

Castlecomer G.C.
(056) 41139
Dromgoole, Castlecomer
(9) 6515 yards/***/C

Kilkenny G.C.
(056) 65400
Glendine, Kilkenny
(18) 6450 yards/***/C/M

Mount Juliet G.C.
(056) 4455
Thomastown
(18) 7101 yards/***/A/H

CO LAOIS

Abbey Leix G.C.
(0502) 31450
Abbey Leix, Portlaoise
(9) 5680 yards/***/E

Heath G.C.
(0502) 21074
The Heath, Portlaoise
(18) 5736 metres/***/D/H/M

Mountrath G.C.
(0502) 32558
Knockanina, Mountrath
(9) 5300 yards/***/E

Portarlington G.C.
(0502) 23115
Garryhinch, Portarlington
(18) 6206 yards/***/D/L

MOUNT JULIET GOLF CLUB
Photograph courtesy of: **Irish Tourist Board (Brian Lynch)**

Rathdowney G.C.
(0505) 46170
Coulnaboul West, Rathdowney
(9) 6086 yards/***/F

CO LEITRIM

Ballinamore G.C.
(078) 44346
Crevy, Ballinamore
(9) 5680 yards/***/F

Carrick on Shannon G.C.
(079) 67015
Woodbrook, Carrick on Shannon
(9) 5584 metres/***/D

CO LIMERICK

Adare Manor G.C.
(061) 396204
Adare
(18) 5800 yards/***/D/H

Castletroy G.C.
(061) 335261
Castletroy, Limerick
(18) 6335 yards/**/B

Killeline G.C.
(069) 61600
Newcastle West
(18) 5924metres/***/D

Limerick G.C.
(061) 414083
Ballyclough, Limerick
(18) 5938 metres/**(Tues)/B/H/M

Limerick County G.& C.C.
(061) 351881
Ballyneery
(18) 6137 metres/***/C

Newcastle West G.C.
(069) 76500
Ardagh, Newcastle West
(18) 5482 yards/***(Sun)/D

CO LONGFORD

County Longford G.C.
(043) 46310
Dublin Road, Longford
(18) 6008 yards/***/D/H(24)

CO LOUTH

Ardee G.C.
(041) 53227
Townparks, Ardee
(18) 6200 yards/***/D/H

County Louth G.C.
(041) 22329
Baltray, Drogheda
(18) 6728 yards/***/B/H/M

Dundalk G.C.
(042) 21731
Blackrock, Dundalk
(18) 6776 yards/***(Tues/Sun)/C

Greenore G.C.
(042) 73212
Greenore, Dundalk
(18) 6506 yards/***/D/H(20)

Killinbeg G.C.
(042) 39303
Killin Park, Dundalk
(12) 3322 yards/***/E

CO MAYO

Achill Island G.C.
(098) 43456
Keel, Achill
(9) 2723 yards/***/E

Ashford Castle G.C.
(092) 46003
Cong
(9) 2896 yards/***/D

Ballina G.C.
(096) 21050
Mossgrove, Shanaghy, Ballina
(9) 5702 yards/***/D

Ballinrobe G.C.
(092) 41659
Claremorris Road, Ballinrobe
(18) 6234 metres/***/D

Ballyhaunis G.C.
(0907) 30014
Coolnaha, Ballyhaunis
(9) 5393 yards/***/E

Belmullet G.C.
(097) 82292
Carn, Belmullet
(18) 6058 metres/***/D

Castlebar G.C.
(094) 21649
Rocklands, Castlebar
(18) 5698 metres/***(Sun)/D

Claremorris G.C.
(094) 71527
Rushbrook, Castlemaggaret
(9) 6454 yards/***/F

Mulrany G.C.
(098) 36262
Mulrany, Westport
(9) 6380 yards/***/E/M

Swinford G.C.
(094) 51378
Brabazon Park, Swinford
(9) 5230 yards/***/E

Westport G.C.
(098) 25113
Carrowholly, Westport
(18) 6950 yards/***(Sun)/C

CO MEATH

Ashbourne G.C.
(01) 835 2005
Anderstown, Ashbourne
(18) 5778 metres/**/C

Black Bush G.C.
(01) 825 0021
Thomastown, Dunshaughlin
(18) 6930 yards /***/D
(9) 2800 yards/***/E

Gormanston College G.C.
(01) 841 2203
Franciscan College, Gormanston
(9) 2170 yards/*/F

Headfort G.C.
(046) 40857
Kells
(18) 6480 yards/***(am)/D/H

Laytown and Bettystown G.C.
(041) 27170
Bettystown, Drogheda
(18) 5668 metres/***/C/H

Moor Park G.C.
(046) 27661
Mooretown, Navan
(18) 5600 metres/***/F

Royal Tara G.C.
(046) 25244
Bellinter, Navan
(18) 5757 metres/***(Tues)/D
(9) 3184 metres/***/D

Trim G.C.
(046) 31438
Newtownmoynagh, Trim
(18) 6870 yards/***/D

CO MONAGHAN

Castleblayney G.C.
(042) 40197
Muckno Park, Castleblayney
(9) 2678 yards/***/E

Clones G.C.
(049) 56017
Hilton Park, Scotshouse, Clones
(9) 5790 yards/***/E

Mannan Castle G.C.
(042) 63308
Donaghmoyne, Carrickmacross
(9) 5804 metres/***/E

Nuremore G.C.
(042) 61438
Carrickmacross
(9) 5906 metres/***/C

Rossmore G.C.
(047) 81316
Rossmore Park, Monaghan
(18) 6082 yards/***/E-D

CO OFFALY

Birr G.C.
(0509) 20082
The Glenns, Birr
(18) 5748 metres/***/D/H(26)

Castleharnagh G.C.
(0506) 53384
Daingean
(18) 5595 metres/***/E

Edenderry G.C.
(0405) 31072
Boherberry, Edenderry
(9) 5791 yards/**/E

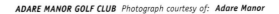

ADARE MANOR GOLF CLUB *Photograph courtesy of:* **Adare Manor**

Tullamore G.C.
(0506) 21439
Brookfield, Tullamore
(18) 6314 yards/***/D/H/M

CO ROSCOMMON

Athlone G.C.
(0902) 92073
Hodson Bay, Athlone
(18) 5922 metres/***/D/H(22)

Ballaghadereen
(0907) 60295
Ballaghadereen, Roscommon
(9) 5663 yards/**/E

Boyle G.C.
(079) 62594
Roscommon Road, Boyle
(9) 4957 metres/***/E

Castlerea G.C.
(0907) 20068
Clonalis, Castlerea
(9) 5466 yards/***(Sun)/E

Roscommon G.C.
(0903) 26382
Moate Park, Roscommon
(18) 6162 metres/**/D

Strokestown G.C.
(078) 33303
Cloonfinlough, Strokestown
(9)5230 metres/***/E

CO SLIGO

Ballymote G.C.
(071) 83460
Carrigans, Ballymote
(9) 5152 yards/***/E

County Sligo G.C.
(0171) 77186
Rosses Point
(18) 6565 yards/**/C-B/M

Enniscrone G.C.
(096) 36297
Ballina Road, Enniscrone
(18) 6720 yards/**/D

Strandhill G.C.
(071) 68188
Strandhill
(18) 6032 yards/***/D/M

Tubbercurry G.C.
(071) 85849
Ballymote Road, Tubbercurry
(9) 5490 metres/***/E

CO TIPPERARY

Ballykisteen G.&.C.C.
(062) 85849
Ballykisteen, Monard
(18) 6765 yards/***/C/M

Cahir Park G.C.
(052) 41474
Kilcommon, Cahir
(9) 5690 yards/***/E

Carrick on Suir G.C.
(051) 40047
Garravoone, Carrick on Suir
(9) 5948 yards/***(Sun)/E

Clonmel G.C.
(052) 21138
Mountain Road, Clonmel
(18) 5768 metres/***/D

County Tipperary G.& C.C.
(062) 71116
Dundrum House,Dundrum, Cashel
(18) 6709 yards/***/C

Nenagh G.C.
(067) 31476
Beechwood, Nenagh
(18) 5491 metres/***/D/H/M

Rockwell College G.C.
(062) 61444
Rockwell College, Cashel
(9) 4136 yards/*/F

Roscrea G.C.
(0505) 21130
Derryvale, Dublin Road, Roscrea
(18) 5750 metres/***/D

Templemore G.C.
(0504) 31400
Manna South, Templemore
(9) 5442 yards/***/E

Thurles G.C.
(0504) 21983
Turtulla, Thurles
(18) 6494 yards/**(Tues)/C

Tipperary G.C.
(062) 51119
Rathanny, Tipperary
(18) 6385 yards/***/D

CO WATERFORD

Dungarvan G.C.
(058) 41605
Knocknagranagh, Dungarvan
(18) 6134 yards/***/D

Dunmore East G.C.
(051) 383151
Dunmore East
(9) 2408 yards /***/E

Faithlegg G.C.
(051) 82241
Faithlegg House, Faithlegg
(18) 6057 metres/***/C/H

Goldcoast G.C.
(058) 42249
Ballinacourty, Dungarven
(9) 5786 metres/***/D

Lismore G.C.
(058) 54026
Ballyin, Lismore
(9) 5715 yards/***/D/H

Tramore G.C.
(051) 386170
Newtown Hill, Tramore
(18) 6622 yards/***/C/H/M

Waterford G.C.
(051) 76748
Newrath, Waterford
(18) 6237 yards/***/C/M

Waterford Castle G.C.
(051) 71633
The Island, Waterford
(18) 6209 metres/***/B

West Waterford G.C.
(058) 43216
Coolcormack, Dungarvan
(18) 6771 yards/***/D

CO WESTMEATH

Delvin Castle G.C.
(044) 64315
Delvin
(18) 6300 yards/***/D/H

Glasson G.C.
(0902) 85120
Athlone
(18) 7083 yards/***/B

Moate G.C.
(0902) 81271
Ballinagarby, Moate
(9) 5348 yards/***/E

Mount Temple G.C.
(0902) 81841
(18) 6500 yards/***/D/H

Mullingar G.C.
(044) 48366
Belvedere, Mullingar
(18) 6200 yards/**/C

CO WEXFORD

Courtown G.C.
(055) 25166
Kiltennel, Gorey
(18) 5898 metres/***/C

Enniscorthy G.C.
(054) 33191
Knockmarshal, Enniscorthy
(18) 6266 yards/***/D/H/M

New Ross G.C.
(051) 21433
Tinneranny, New Ross
(9) 6133 yards/***(Tues/Sun)/D

Rosslare G.C.
(053) 32203
Rosslare Strand, Rosslare
(18) 6554 yards/***/C/H/M
(9) 3153 yards/***/D/H/M

St Helens Bay G.& C.C.
(053) 33234
St Helens, Kilrane
(18) 6163 yards/***/C

Wexford G.C.
(053) 42238
Mulgannon, Wexford
(18)6120 yards/***/D/H/M

CO WICKLOW

Arklow G.C.
(0402) 32492
Abbeylands, Arklow
(18) 404 metres/***/D/H/M

Baltinglass G.C.
(0508) 81350
Baltinglass
(9) 5554 yards/***/E

Blainroe G.C.
(0404) 68168
Blainroe
(18) 6788 yards/***/C/H

Bray G.C.
(01) 286 2484
Ravenswell Road, Bray
(9) 5761 metres/**/C

Charlesland G.& C.C.
(01) 287 6764
Greystones
(18) 6739 yards/***/B

Coollattin G.C.
(055) 29125
Coollattin, Shillelagh
(9)6203 yards/***/D

Delgany G.C.
(01) 2874645
Delgany
(18) 5290 metres/***/C/M

The European Club
(0404) 47415
Brittas Bay
(18) 6729 yards/***/B

Glenmalure G.C.
(0404) 46679
Greenane, Rathdrum
(18) 5237 metres/***/C

Greystones G.C.
(01) 287 6624
Greystones
(18) 5401 metres/***/B

Kilcoole G.C.
(01) 287 2066
Kilcoole
(9) 5506 metres/**/D

Old Conna G.C.
(01) 282 6055
Ferndale Road, Bray
(18) 6551 yards/**/B/H

Rathsallagh G.C.
(045) 53112
Nr Dunlavin
(18) 6956 yards.***/A

Tulfarris Hotel & C.C.
(045) 864574
Blessington
(9)2806 yards/***/F

Wicklow G.C.
(0404) 67379
Dunbar Road, Wicklow
(9) 6260 yards/**/D

Woodbrook G.C.
(01) 2824799
Dublin Road, Bray
(18) 5966 metres/**(Tues)/B-A

Woodenbridge G.C.
(0402) 35202
Woodenbridge, Arklow
(9) 6318 yards/***(Sat)/B

Royal Lytham & St Annes, England

The Belfry, 10th Hole, England

The Belfry, 18th Hole, England

Royal St George's, England

Wentworth, England

Sunningdale, England

*Royal St George's, England

*Royal Birkdale, England

Carnoustie, Scotland

Royal Dornoch, Scotland

*Turnberry, 10th Hole, Scotland

*Turnberry, 18th Hole, Scotland

*Muirfield, 4th Hole, Scotland

Royal Troon, Scotland

Ailsa Course, Turnberry, Scotland

Prestwick, Scotland

St Andrews, Swilcan Bridge, Scotland

St Andrews, Swilcan Burn, Scotland

St Andrews, Snow Scene, Scotland

St Andrews, R & A, Scotland

*St Andrews, 17th Hole, Scotland

*St Andrews, Old Course, Scotland

Portmarnock, Ireland

Lahinch, Ireland

Killarney Killean Course, Ireland

Ballybunion, Ireland

Royal County Down, Ireland

Order Form

Edition	Edition	Price (£)	Qty.	Cost
Golf in England - Page 324				
Royal Lytham & St Annes, England	N/A	29.50		
The Belfry, 10th Hole, England	N/A	29.50		
The Belfry, 18th Hole England	N/A	29.50		
Royal St George's, England	N/A	29.50		
Wentworth England	N/A	29.50		
Sunningdale England	N/A	29.50		
*Royal St Geroge's, England	850	110.00		
*Royal Birkdale, England	850	110.00		
Golf in Scotland - Page 325				
Carnoustie, Scotland	N/A	29.50		
Royal Dornoch, Scotland	N/A	29.50		
*Turnberry, 10th Hole, Scotland	850	110.00		
*Turnberry, 18th Hole, Scotland	850	110.00		
*Muirfield, 4th Hole, Scotland	850	110.00		
Royal Troon, Scotland	N/A	29.50		
Ailsa Course, Turnberry, Scotland	N/A	29.50		
Prestwick, Scotland	N/A	29.50		
The Home of Golf - Page 326				
St Andrews, Swilcan Bridge, Scotland	N/A	29.50		
St Andrews, Swilcan Burn, Scotland	N/A	29.50		
St Andrews, Snow Scene, Scotland	N/A	29.50		
St Andrews, R&A, Scotland	N/A	29.50		
*St Andrews, 17th Hole, Scotland	850	110.00		
*St Andrews, Old Course, Scotland	850	110.00		
Golf in Ireland - Page 327				
Portmarnock, Ireland	N/A	29.50		
Lahinch, Ireland	N/A	29.50		
Killarney, Killean Course, Ireland	N/A	29.50		
Ballybunion, Ireland	N/A	29.50		
Royal County Down, Ireland	N/A	29.50		
Postage and Packing				£5.00
All prices include VAT			Total	

* Limited edition prints are numbered, individually signed and embossed - overall size 54 x 64.8 cm, image size 43.8cm x 55.2cm

Open edition prints are individually signed - overall size 30.48cm x 40.6cm, image size 25.4cm x 35.4cm

I enclose a cheque for the sum of £_____ payable to Kensington West Productions Ltd

Please debit my: Access/Visa/Amex card by the sum of £_____

Card no _____   Expiry Date _____

Name _____   Address _____

_____   Tel. No. _____

**All orders should be sent to: Kensington West Productions Ltd.
5 Cattle Market, Hexham, Northumberland NE46 INJ Tel: 01434 609933 Fax: 01434 600066**

*There are a wide range of other Baxter open and limited edition prints available from
Kensington West Productions please call (01434) 609933 or visit www.golfcourseguide.com for further details*